*Physically Handicapped Children:
A Medical Atlas for Teachers*

Physically Handicapped Children: A Medical Atlas for Teachers

Second Edition

Edited by

EUGENE E. BLECK, M.D.

Chief, Orthopaedic and Rehabilitation Services
Children's Hospital at Stanford
Palo Alto, California, and
Professor of Clinical Surgery (Orthopaedic)
Stanford University School of Medicine
Stanford, California

DONALD A. NAGEL, M.D.

Professor and Head
Orthopaedic Division
Department of Surgery
Stanford University School of Medicine
Stanford, California

Bleck

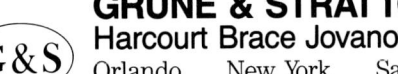

GRUNE & STRATTON, INC.
Harcourt Brace Jovanovich, Publishers
Orlando   New York   San Diego   London
San Francisco   Tokyo   Sydney   Toronto

Library of Congress Cataloging in Publication Data
Main entry under title:

Physically handicapped children.

Includes bibliographies and index.
1. Physically handicapped children. 2. Children—Diseases. 3. Physically handicapped children—Education.
I. Bleck, E. E. (Eugene Edmund), 1923– . II. Nagel, Donald A. [DNLM: 1. Handicapped—Education. 2. Pediatrics. WS 200 P578]
RJ138.P45   1981   618.92′7   81-6804
ISBN 0-8089-1391-3   AACR2

© 1982 by Grune & Stratton, Inc.

All rights reserved. No part of this publication may be reproduced or transmitted in any form or by any means, electronic or mechanical, including photocopy, recording, or any information storage and retrieval system, without permission in writing from the publisher.

Grune & Stratton, Inc.
Orlando, Florida 32887

Distributed in the United Kingdom by
Grune & Stratton, Ltd.
24/28 Oval Road, London NW 1

Library of Congress Catalog Number 81-6804
International Standard Book Number 0-8089-1391-3
Printed in the United States of America

86 87 88 89   10 9 8 7 6 5 4 3

*Dedicated to handicapped children everywhere
in this,
the International Year of the Disabled Person
(United Nations, 1981).*

Contents

Acknowledgments   xi

Foreword   xiii

Preface from First Edition   xv

Preface   xvii

Contributors   xix

1. *Anatomy: Basic Parts and Terms of the Nervous and Musculoskeletal Systems*   1
   EUGENE E. BLECK, M.D.

2. *Amputations in Children*   17
   YOSHIO SETOGUCHI, M.D.

3. *Arthrogryposis—Multiple Congenital Contractures*   27
   EUGENE E. BLECK, M.D.

4. *Asthma*   31
   BIRT HARVEY, M.D.

5. *Cancer in Childhood*   43
   MICHAEL P. LINK, M.D.

6. *Cerebral Palsy*   59
   EUGENE E. BLECK, M.D.

7. *Communication Disorders: Speech and Hearing*   133
   KATHRYN R. BEADLE, Ph.D.

8.	*Nonoral Communication*	**145**
	Augmentative Communication System: Blissymbolics SHIRLEY McNAUGHTON	**146**
	Sign Language: Examples of Classroom Survival Signs	**155**
	Systems and Devices for Nonoral Communication MAURICE LeBLANC, C.P., M.S.	**159**
9.	*Convulsive Disorders* BRUCE O. BERG, M.D.	**171**
10.	*Counseling: Perspectives and Resources*	**181**
	Counseling: A Developmental Approach JUDY HOWARD, M.D.	**182**
	Take It Easy When Evaluating the Mentally Retarded Child GUNNAR B. STICKLER, M.D.	**193**
	Counseling Parents JOYCE KELLNER, M.S.W., L.C.S.W.	**194**
	Understanding the Atypical Child: How I Learned to Live with My Handicapped Daughter PATRICIA CRAVEN	**202**
	Another Parent's Experience: Letting Handicapped Children Do Things for Themselves	**211**
	Society Versus the Wheelchair: The Experiences of a Handicapped Child ROSE MARIE MacELMAN, CHARLES E. BURDEN, M.D.	**212**
	Literature for Parents and Professionals	**217**
	Community, State, National, and International Resources for Recreation and Leisure	**229**
11.	*Cystic Fibrosis* BIRT HARVEY, M.D.	**255**
12.	*Dermatomyositis* JOHN J. MILLER, III, M.D., Ph.D.	**265**
13.	*Juvenile Diabetes Mellitus* ROBERT O. CHRISTIANSEN, M.D., RAYMOND L. HINTZ, M.D.	**269**
14.	*Down's Syndrome* LIEBE S. DIAMOND, M.D.	**279**
15.	*Physically Disabled Driver*	**293**
16.	*Emergencies* EUGENE E. BLECK, M.D.	**301**

17.	*Friedreich's Ataxia* JUDITH KOEHLER, M.D.	309
18.	*Heart Disease in Children* DAVID BAUM, M.D.	313
19.	*Hemophilia* F. RALPH BERBERICH, M.D.	325
20.	*Normal Infant Motor Development* FRAN FORD, R.P.T.	333
21.	*Myelomeningocele, Meningocele, and Spina Bifida* EUGENE E. BLECK, M.D.	345
22.	*Multiply Handicapped Child: Severe Physical and Mental Disability* JEAN G. KOHN, M.D.	363
23.	*Muscular Dystrophy—Duchenne Type* EUGENE E. BLECK, M.D.	385
24.	*Temporary Orthopedic Disabilities in Children* DONALD A. NAGEL, M.D.	395
25.	*Osteogenesis Imperfecta* EUGENE E. BLECK, M.D.	405
26.	*Traumatic Paraplegia and Quadriplegia* DONALD A. NAGEL, M.D.	413
27.	*Poliomyelitis* EUGENE E. BLECK, M.D.	419
28.	*Juvenile Rheumatoid Arthritis* JOHN J. MILLER, III, M.D., Ph.D.	423
29.	*Rubella Syndrome* EUGENE E. BLECK, M.D.	431
30.	*Scoliosis* LAWRENCE A. RINSKY, M.D.	433
31.	*Sexual Development in Handicapped Children and Adolescents* IRIS F. LITT, M.D.	445
32.	*Short Stature and Growth* WILLIAM A. HORTON, M.D., DAVID L. RIMOIN, M.D., Ph.D.	451
33.	*Sickle Cell Disease* F. RALPH BERBERICH, M.D.	469
34.	*Spinal Muscular Atrophy of Childhood* JUDITH KOEHLER, M.D.	477
35.	*Visual Disorders* A. RALPH ROSENTHAL, M.D.	483
	Glossary	497
	Index	513

Acknowledgments

As usual the Division of Instructional Media, under the guidance of Charlene Levering, Director, Stanford University School of Medicine, came through with outstanding graphics. We thank them for their competence, creativity, and courtesy and for always being a pleasure to work with.

Foreword

This is a handbook of medical information for teachers of physically handicapped children and for college educators responsible for preparation of those teachers. The fundamental medical facts are presented and are accompanied by practical suggestions for those who teach disabled children in special schools and in the regular classroom.

The field of special education has lacked information dealing with orthopedic problems, special health conditions, and some sensory deficits of disabled students. The materials and references currently available are primarily from the field of medicine and are directed primarily to medical personnel. This has posed difficulties for teachers who use and interpret the data.

Dr. Bleck, through his lectures and work with the students and staff of the Special Education Department of San Francisco State University, became aware of this lack of educationally oriented medical information. This book is his response to this need and his contribution to the field of education.

This medical atlas describes disabling conditions with thoroughness and in a language comprehensible to school personnel. It includes line-drawn illustrations and plates that can be prepared and projected for group viewing or duplicated for distribution. It includes graphic suggestions for adaptive aids and equipment. Indeed, the format of this book charts a course for easy location of needed information for the teacher.

Readers, however, will find here more than just a well organized and pertinent medical overview. Background is provided in the chapters on normal motor development and anatomy. Psychological implications of exceptionality and related impact on parents and students are also discussed. The chapter on emergency procedure is particularly helpful to teachers in any setting. In short, the overall content is thorough and most exciting.

We commend Dr. Bleck and his associates for their pioneer effort in writing this atlas of understanding for teachers.

June Bigge, Ed. D.　　　　　　*Christina Kusaba*
Professor of Special Education　*Assistant Professor of Special Education*
San Francisco State University　*San Francisco State University*

Preface from First Edition

This book is an outgrowth of a need perceived just a few years ago when the San Francisco State University Department of Special Education asked our help in designing and teaching prospective special education teachers in a medically oriented course about physically handicapped children. All too often teachers have had little or no formal exposure to the types of conditions in the children whom they would be expected to educate. The course was intended to meet this need. This book attempts to present in concise lay language the essentials of medical diagnosis, treatment, and prognosis of the major physically handicapping conditions originating in childhood. It will not supersede a formal course and should be used only as a guide and an introduction. The illustrations are drawn and arranged so that they may be shown by an overhead projector in the classroom or copied as 35-mm slides for projection.

Not all of these conditions will be found in a handicapped children's school program. Some that are not really very serious have been included in Chapter 24 on Temporary Orthopedic Disabilities in Childhood. We hope this chapter will help teachers of physical education when they encounter P.E. excuses for what might seem to be esoteric conditions.

Our special thanks go to the Stanford University School of Medicine for their clear and creative drawings; to the Grune & Stratton staff, who have been so patient and courteous in the production of the book; and finally to our colleagues for their assiduity and promptness in preparing their excellent manuscripts.

Eugene E. Bleck, M.D.
Donald A. Nagel, M.D.

Stanford University

Preface

"When change is not necessary, it is not necessary to change."
Lord Melbourne, Prime Minister of England, during the reign of Queen Victoria

In considering a revision of a textbook, this admonition seems sensible. Some chapters have been changed very little while others have been expanded upon to reflect new knowledge and perspectives. Chapters on new subjects have been written to meet the perceived needs of teachers of the physically handicapped; for example, "Cancer in Childhood," "Short Stature and Growth," "Down's Syndrome," "Nonoral Communication," and the sections in Chapter 10 dealing with counseling.

Regrettably there have been no cures for the chronic handicapping conditions since the first edition in 1975, nor are there likely to be any if there is to be another edition five years hence. What we will see, however, is continued advancement in prevention of some of the serious physical defects. We've already witnessed the disappearance of poliomyelitis in the United States and the astounding prevention of severe cerebral palsy due to the Rh factor disease in newborns (erythroblastosis fetalis, kernicterus) as a result of immunizing pregnant Rh negative mothers. Some other advances over the past years have been the progressive eradication of both types of measles, encephalitis, and severe brain damage through immunization of children and vastly improved obstetrical care and anesthesia, a reduction in the number of children with severe cerebral palsy, and a progressive minimization in the effects of prematurity on the brain.

Antibiotics and antibacterial chemicals have made the serious consequences of infections rare, and they have made tuberculosis of the musculoskeletal system almost unknown in this country. Since 1975 the widespread availability of the missing blood factor in hemophilia (Factor 8) has drastically reduced the crippling effects in growing children of bleeding into joints.

We have seen a vastly improved management of disabled children. It has gradually dawned on most professionals that children are not subjects to be dealt with as patients, pupils, or clients but as *persons*. "Look to the person behind the handicap," as a 20-year-old person with cerebral palsy told me about 10 years ago. We are trying, therefore, to give up the disease-oriented approach (that is, trying to cure cerebral palsy, spina bifida, and osteogenesis imperfecta) and adopt the functional-oriented approach directed toward optimum independence in adult life. We do not want permanent "patients," "medicalized subjects," "clients," or "pupils."

Despite this philosophy, we continue to encounter educators and professionals who do not appreciate the severe limits of remedial treatments and therapies that are always focused on promised cure.

The impact of Public Law 94-142 continues to be experienced everywhere. Unquestionably the intent of the law is good—to desegregate the handicapped child and give him or her the maximal opportunity for integration into the life of the community. We have heard and witnessed a good deal of turmoil among medical and paramedical professionals, parents, and educators in trying to do what they think the law says. In most instances much of the turmoil is due to a lack of understanding of what a particular disease is all about, its natural history, and the limits of cure versus management directed toward function. We hope this text deepens understanding for teachers and will lead to reason, prudence, and wisdom in helping handicapped children and their parents deal with disability and cope with it, not as objects of pity but as human beings whom we cherish and welcome as partners in our lives.

Eugene E. Bleck, M.D.

Stanford University

Contributors

David Baum, M.D.
 Professor of Pediatrics
 Department of Pediatrics
 Stanford University School of Medicine
 Stanford, California

Kathryn R. Beadle, Ph.D.
 Executive Director
 Mid-Peninsula Speech and Language Clinic
 Redwood City, California

F. Ralph Berberich, M.D.
 Children's Hospital at Stanford
 Palo Alto, California

Bruce O. Berg, M.D.
 Professor of Neurology and Pediatrics
 Director, Child Neurology Division
 University of California School of Medicine
 San Francisco, California

Eugene E. Bleck, M.D.
    Chief, Orthopaedic and Rehabilitation Services
    Children's Hospital at Stanford
    Palo Alto, California, and
    Professor of Clinical Surgery (Orthopaedic)
    Stanford University School of Medicine
    Stanford, California

Charles E. Burden, M.D.
    Costal Pediatrics
    Brunswick, Maine

Robert O. Christiansen, M.D.
    Professor of Pediatrics
    Charles R. Drew Postgraduate Medical School
    Los Angeles, California

Patricia Craven
    Menlo Park, California

Liebe S. Diamond, M.D.
    Director of Clinical Research
    The James Lawrence Kernan Hospital, Inc.
    Baltimore, Maryland

Fran Ford, R.P.T.
    Pediatric Physical Therapy Consultant
    Jackson, Mississippi

Birt Harvey, M.D.
    Clinical Professor of Pediatrics
    Stanford University School of Medicine
    Palo Alto, California

Raymond L. Hintz, M.D.
    Associate Professor of Pediatrics
    Chief, Pediatric Endocrinology and Metabolism
    Department of Pediatrics
    Stanford University School of Medicine
    Stanford, California

William A. Horton, M.D.
    Assistant Professor of Medicine
    Department of Medicine
    University of Kansas Medical Center
    Kansas City, Kansas

Judy Howard, M.D.
    Assistant Professor of Pediatrics
    UCLA School of Medicine
    UCLA Rehabilitation Center
    Los Angeles, California

Joyce Kellner, M.S.W., L.C.S.W.
Children's Hospital at Stanford
Palo Alto, California

Judith Koehler, M.D.
Palo Alto, California

Jean G. Kohn, M.D., M.P.H.
Clinical Evaluation Coordinator
Rehabilitation Engineering Center
Children's Hospital at Stanford
Palo Alto, California

Maurice LeBlanc, C.P., M.S.
Director of Research
Rehabilitation Engineering Center
Children's Hospital at Stanford
Palo Alto, California

Michael P. Link, M.D.
Assistant Professor of Pediatrics
Department of Oncology
Children's Hospital at Stanford
Palo Alto, California

Iris F. Litt, M.D.
Associate Professor of Pediatrics
Director of Adolescent Medicine
Stanford University School of Medicine
Stanford, California

Rose Marie MacElman
Brunswick, Maine

Shirley McNaughton
Director, Blissymbolics Communication Service
Ontario Crippled Children's Center
Toronto, Ontario

John J. Miller III, M.D., Ph.D.
Associate Professor of Pediatrics
Children's Hospital at Stanford
Palo Alto, California

Donald A. Nagel, M.D.
Professor and Head
Orthopaedic Division
Department of Surgery
Stanford University School of Medicine
Stanford, California

David L. Rimoin, M.D., Ph.D.
    Professor of Pediatrics and Medicine
    Chief, Division of Medical Genetics
    Harbor UCLA Medical Center
    Torrance, California

Lawrence A. Rinsky, M.D.
    Assistant Professor of Orthopaedic Surgery
    Stanford University School of Medicine, and
    Associate Chief of Orthopaedic Rehabilitation Services
    Children's Hospital at Stanford
    Palo Alto, California

A. Ralph Rosenthal, M.D.
    Professor of Ophthalmology
    Department of Ophthalmology
    Leicester, Royal Infirmary
    Leicester, England

Yoshio Setoguchi, M.D.
    Medical Director
    Child Amputee Prosthetics Project
    UCLA Rehabilitation Center
    Los Angeles, California

Gunnar B. Stickler, M.D.
    Mayo Clinic
    Rochester, Minnesota

Physically Handicapped Children:
A Medical Atlas for Teachers

1

Anatomy: Basic Parts and Terms of the Nervous and Musculoskeletal Systems

EUGENE E. BLECK, M.D.

TERMINOLOGY

The anatomical position is face forward with the palms of the hands facing forward (Fig. 1-1).

    Anterior (ventral): front of body
    Posterior (dorsal): back of body
    Medial: nearest midline of body
    Lateral: farthest from midline
    Proximal: nearest to trunk (e.g., shoulder is proximal to elbow)
    Distal: farthest from trunk (e.g., hand is distal to elbow)
    Superior (cephalad): nearer head (e.g., lungs are superior to stomach)
    Inferior (caudad): farthest from head (e.g., anus is at the caudad portion of intestines)

Body Planes

    Coronal: bisects body and is parallel to face
    Sagittal: bisects body parallel to side of head
    Transverse: bisects body parallel to floor

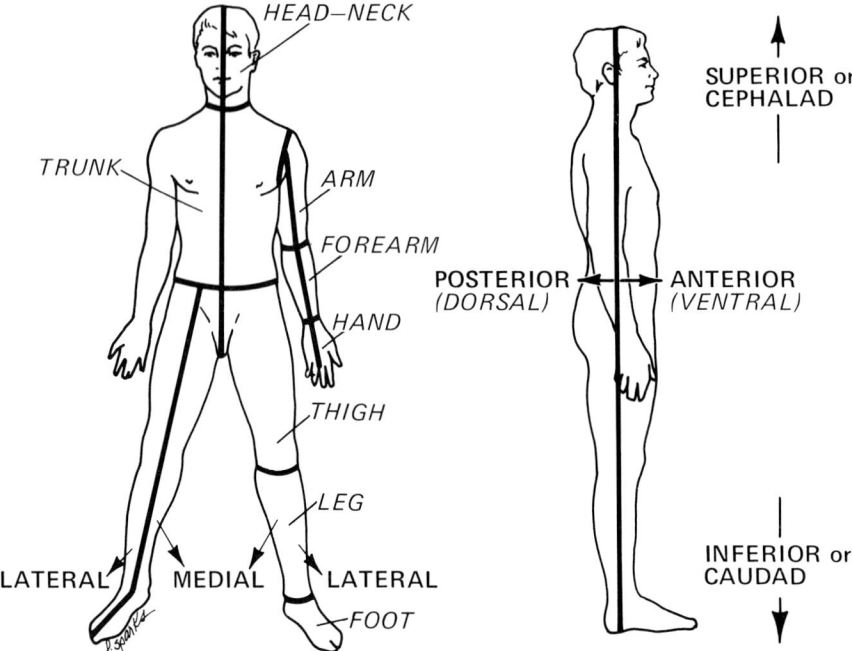

Fig. 1-1. View of the body from the front, in the anatomical position with palms facing forward. The appropriate terms are shown on the diagram. The side view indicates the terminology for the front and back portions of the body as well as the head and lower portions.

NERVOUS SYSTEM

Brain Structure

Gross Structure.

The brain consists of:

1. Two halves identical in structure—the cerebral hemispheres; together they make up the cerebrum (Fig. 1-2).
2. A small, lobulated brain attached in the back and below the hemispheres—the cerebellum.
3. Four fluid filled cavities (ventricles) inside the brain: a lateral ventricle in each hemisphere and a third and fourth ventricle common to both (Fig. 1-3).
4. A centrally located collection of nerve cells (neurons)—the basal ganglia and thalamus.
5. The surface of the brain—the cerebral cortex—contains nerve cells or gray matter (neurons) and supporting cells or white matter (glial cells). These are thrown into folds and grooves (gyri) on the brain surface.
6. Nerve fibers (axons) from the nerve cells descend through the brain to connect with other cells in the brain and the spinal cord.
7. The brainstem is the part of brain that remains after the cerebral hemispheres and the cerebellum are removed. It is continuous with the spinal cord. It consists of four parts: the medulla, the pons, the midbrain, and the thalamus. These areas contain the centers (nuclei) for function of the cranial nerves (e.g., taste, eye movement, tongue movement, facial expression and sensation, swallowing), for respiration control, for nerve cells that inhibit or facilitate spinal cord nerve cells, and for cells that function in the appreciation of pain and temperature.

Anatomy: Basic Parts and Terms

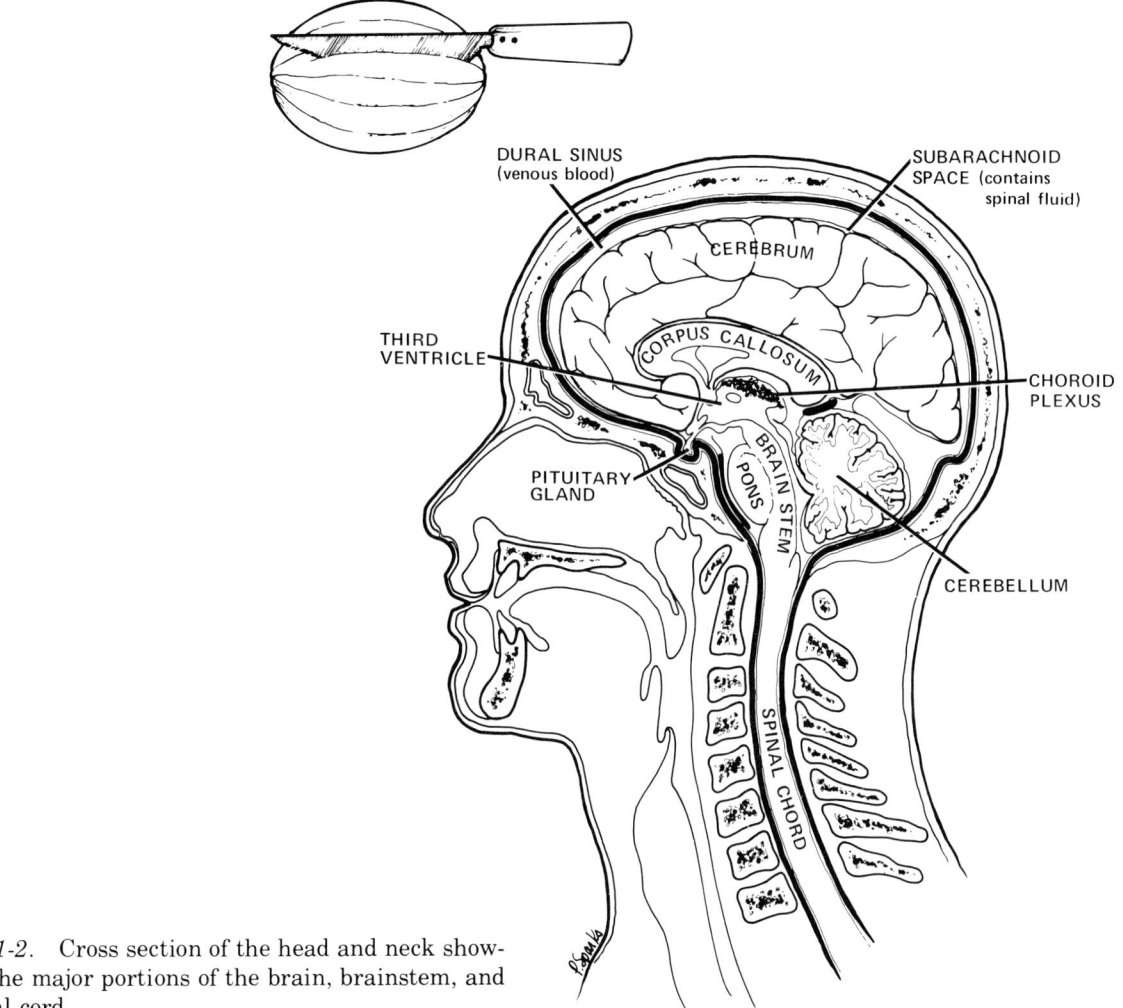

Fig. 1-2. Cross section of the head and neck showing the major portions of the brain, brainstem, and spinal cord.

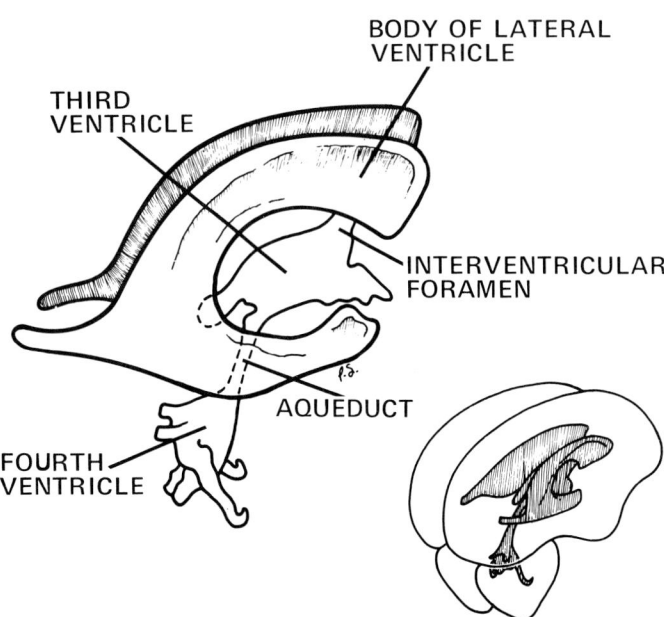

Fig. 1-3. The fluid cavities of the brain (ventricles). The smaller figure on the right depicts the location of the ventricles within the brain.

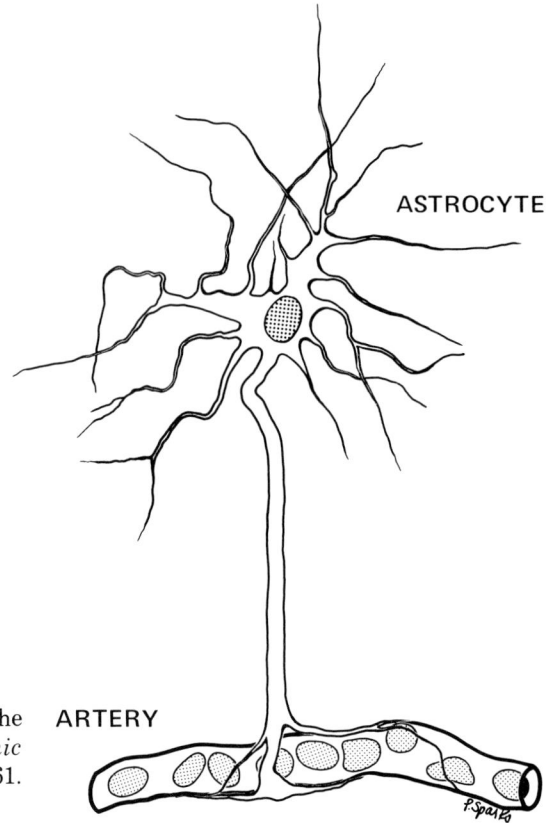

Fig. 1-4. One of the main supporting cells of the brain—the astrocyte. (Redrawn from Peele, T., *The Neuroanatomic Basis for Clinical Neurology,* New York, McGraw-Hill, 1961. With permission.)

Microscopic Structure

All brain cells derive from the primitive embryonic cell, the neuroblast. The primitve neuroblast has several possible paths of development. First, it can become a neuron—one of the most highly specialized and most important cells in the body. For this grandeur, however, there is a price to pay—it must remain stationary and can never divide and thereby replace itself. Second, it can become a glial, or supporting, cell—either an astrocyte or an oligodendroglial cell. Because it is not a specialized cell, the glial cell is free to move about and can replace itself. The astrocyte is star-shaped and is like a spider monkey, with its tail on a blood vessel (Fig. 1-4). The oligodendroglial cells are small and round and form a supporting meshwork.

The neuron has a long tail (axon); it sits in its place supported by the glial cells like a fat Buddha in a cage. Now and then it belches, sending a stream of protoplasm down its tail (the axon) (Fig. 1-5). The electrical activity of the brain is due to the "belching" of neurons and the movement of the glial cells. This electrical activity is recorded by the electroencephalograph (EEG).

Brain Development, Organization, and Function

The brain is enormously complex. The schematic diagram of the cerebral hemisphere (Fig. 1-6) indicates the general areas of cerebral cortex responsible for various functions. The cerebellum is concerned with integration of movement and posture.

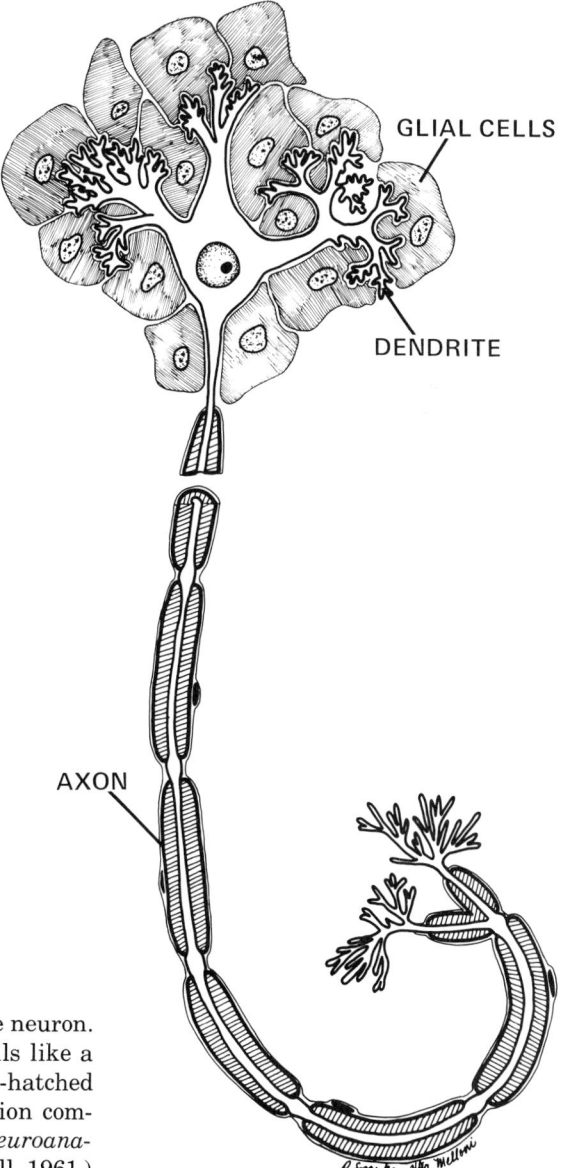

Fig. 1-5. The main cell of the brain and spinal cord—the neuron. The neoron is surrounded and supported by the glial cells like a Buddha sitting in a cage; his tail is the axon. The cross-hatched areas surrounding the axon and arranged in nodal fashion comprise the myelin sheath. (Redrawn from Peele, T., *The Neuroanatomic Basis for Clinical Neurology,* New York, McGraw-Hill, 1961.)

Because much of the educational endeavor is directed toward improving intellectual performance and motor performance (e.g., desk skills), a brief summary of some known facts concerning the structure and organization of the brain and the nervous system seem pertinent.

How the estimated 100 billion neurons (nerve cells) in the adult develop and their vast interconnections are the subject of intensive and ongoing study. In this section, only a few highlights can be summarized, but these should provide some insight into the development and workings of the nervous system and into the effects of damage to its cells and connections.

Neural Development

The development of the nervous system begins at the moment of conception. At 18 days, the formation of an embryonic disc of cells is complete, and the primitive neural plate, neural tube, and neural crest begin

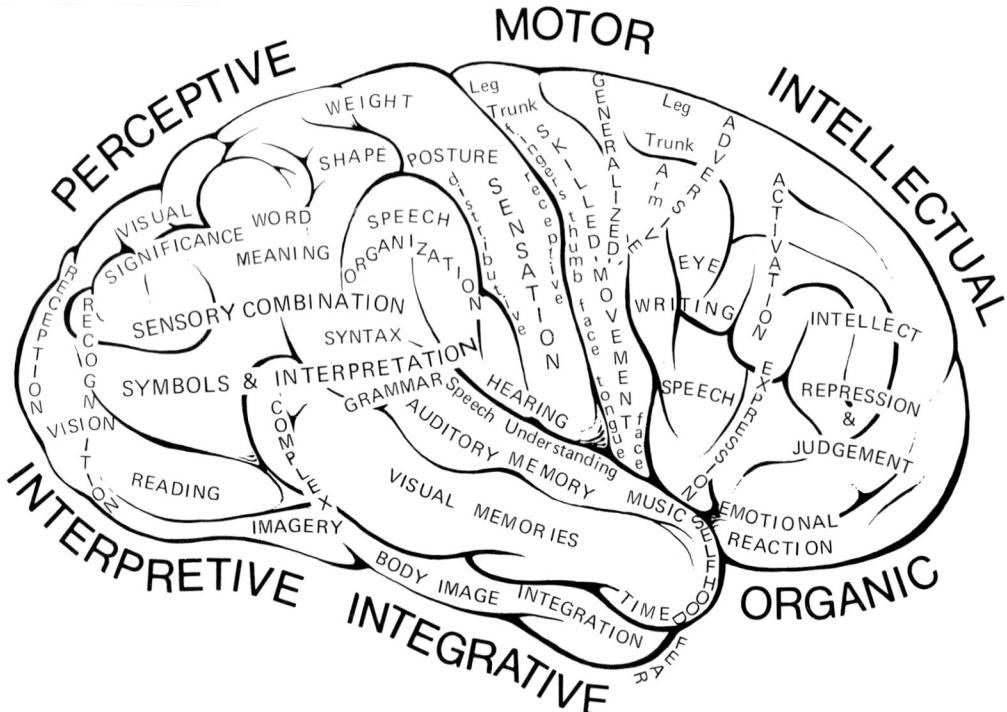

Fig. 1-6. General scheme of localization of cortical functions in the brain.

to form. By 7 weeks, the fore-, mid-, and hindbrain are differentiated. The cerebral hemispheres are recognizable by the third month. At this time, the cavities in the brain (ventricles) are clearly delineated. The two hemispheres of the brain are smooth at first but then become progressively convoluted; this allows the neurons of the cerebral cortex to increase greatly in number without requiring that the brain become larger than the skull could possibly accommodate.

Dendrites. By the sixth month of development, nearly all of the 10 billion cells of the cortex are present and in place. The growth of dendrites—treelike extensions of the nerve cell which serve to connect it with other neurons—is not complete, however. These dendritic trees arise from the neurons and continue to branch and grow until the baby is about 15 months old[3] (Fig. 1-7). During this time, each neuron becomes interconnected by dendrites to an ultimate number of 1,000 to 100,000 (average 10,000) other neurons.

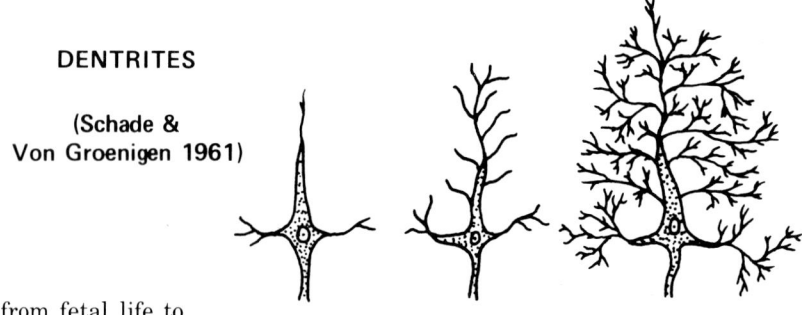

Fig. 1-7. Dendritic arborization from fetal life to age 15 months after birth.

Anatomy: Basic Parts and Terms

Neurons and myelination. Neuronal development and the covering of the nerve fibers by myelin (a fatty layer) continues until the age of 3 years[1] (Fig. 1-8). This fact helps to explain why all infants will show progressive motor improvements during the first 3 years of life. Such data should make us cautious in over-interpreting the "success" of infant programs aimed at correcting presumed ("infant at risk") cerebral damage in very young babies. In fact, despite hope for greater "plasticity" of the infant brain, the data indicate that the immature brain is even less plastic than the fully developed, mature brain.[4]

Speed of development. The brain develops rapidly and in spurts. The changes are so accelerated (neurons are generated in the fetus at a rate of more than 250,000/min) that the comparison has been made to driving an automobile on the freeway: the faster you go, the greater the stress on the controlling mechanism, and the greater the chance for disaster if these mechanisms are blocked or sidetracked.[2] Therefore, damage to the developing fetus in the first 3 months of life can result in permanent and serious defects. Because the brain is not completely developed at birth, it is easy to understand why damage to the highly developed neurons in the first 2 to 3 years of life can be so permanently destructive.

Brain Function

Modern neurobiological theory postulates that neural circuits can analyze stimuli, make decisions, and program movements. Due to current research at the cellular level, movement is thought to be not simply a chain of reflexes but, rather, the result of motor programs in the brain. These may be compared to musical scores that are written, under genetic control, during embryonic development. Such a concept would explain the spontaneous quality of actions better than would a chain of reflexes in which nerve impulses would have to enter and then exit from the brain between two quick movements. It might also explain why certain automatic functions fail to develop, despite all kinds of remedial programs, once brain damage occurs. The inability of some children with cerebral palsy to walk and of others to talk are adequate examples.

CELL GROWTH & MYELINATION

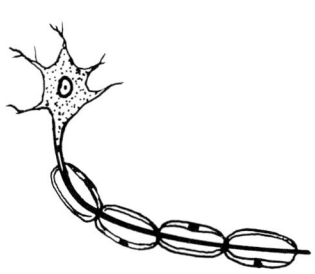
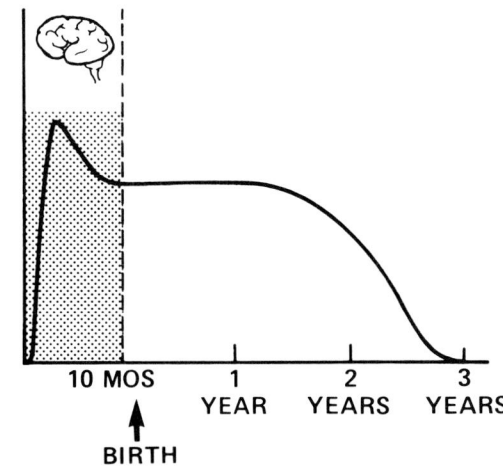

Fig. 1-8. Development of neurons and myelination from conception to age 3 years. The bumps on the "tail" of the star-like neuron schematically depict myelin, a fatty substance that covers the nerve fibers (axons) leading away from the neuron (the major cell of the brain).

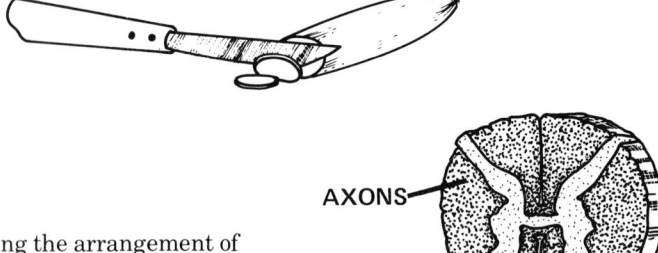

Fig. 1-9. Cross section of the spinal cord showing the arrangement of the neurons and axons. The neurons occupy what is commonly called the "gray H".

Spinal Cord

The spinal cord is a giant cable consisting of neurons and their axons, which carry impulses between the brain and the nerves that go to the limbs, trunk, bladder, and rectum. Viewed in cross section, the nerve cells in the spinal cord are arranged in the form of the letter "H" (Fig. 1-9). Because nerve cells in mass appear gray in contrast to the surrounding white fibers of the axons, we call the spinal cord neuron collection the "gray H." The spinal cord is arranged in segments that correspond to the four regions of the spinal bones (vertebrae)—cervical, thoracic, lumbar, sacral, and coccyx (Fig. 1-10). Because the spinal cord ascends during growth, the cord segments are higher than the actual vertebral bone to which they correspond. For example, the spinal cord ends at the level of the second lumbar vertebra, but the cord segment at this level is fifth sacral and coccygeal. Most of the lumbar spinal canal consists of nerve roots of the lumbar, sacral, and coccygeal segments of the cord, but not the cord itself.

The spinal cord is well protected by a thick, bony structure—the vertebral column—which is made up of individual, but contiguous, vertebrae which surround the cord. Figure 1-11 shows this in cross section. The vertebral body lies in front of (anterior to) the spinal cord, while the back part (posterior) of the spinal cord is protected by the roof of the vertebra (lamina) and its processes. Because the lamina are thinner than the bodies, it is easy to visualize that the best way to expose the spinal cord and its nerves surgically is to remove the lamina (laminectomy).

Nerves

The nerves to the limbs and trunk (peripheral nerves) arise from the spinal cord by two roots on either side—one root toward the front (anterior root) and the other toward the back (posterior root) (see Fig. 26-3). These two roots then join to make the nerve which travels to the limb and trunk muscles, joints, bones, and skin. Each nerve consists of fibers that transmit impulses to the limb muscles (called *efferent*) and those that carry sensation from the skin, muscles, joints, and bones (called *afferent*).

Where the nerve roots and their nerves join and rejoin to form the final nerves leading to the upper or lower limbs is a *plexus*. Two large plexuses, one for each upper limb, are located in the neck and shoulder on either side (brachial plexus). The two plexuses for the lower limbs are located in front of the lumbar vertebra and pelvis—again, one on either side (lumbar plexus, Fig. 1-10).

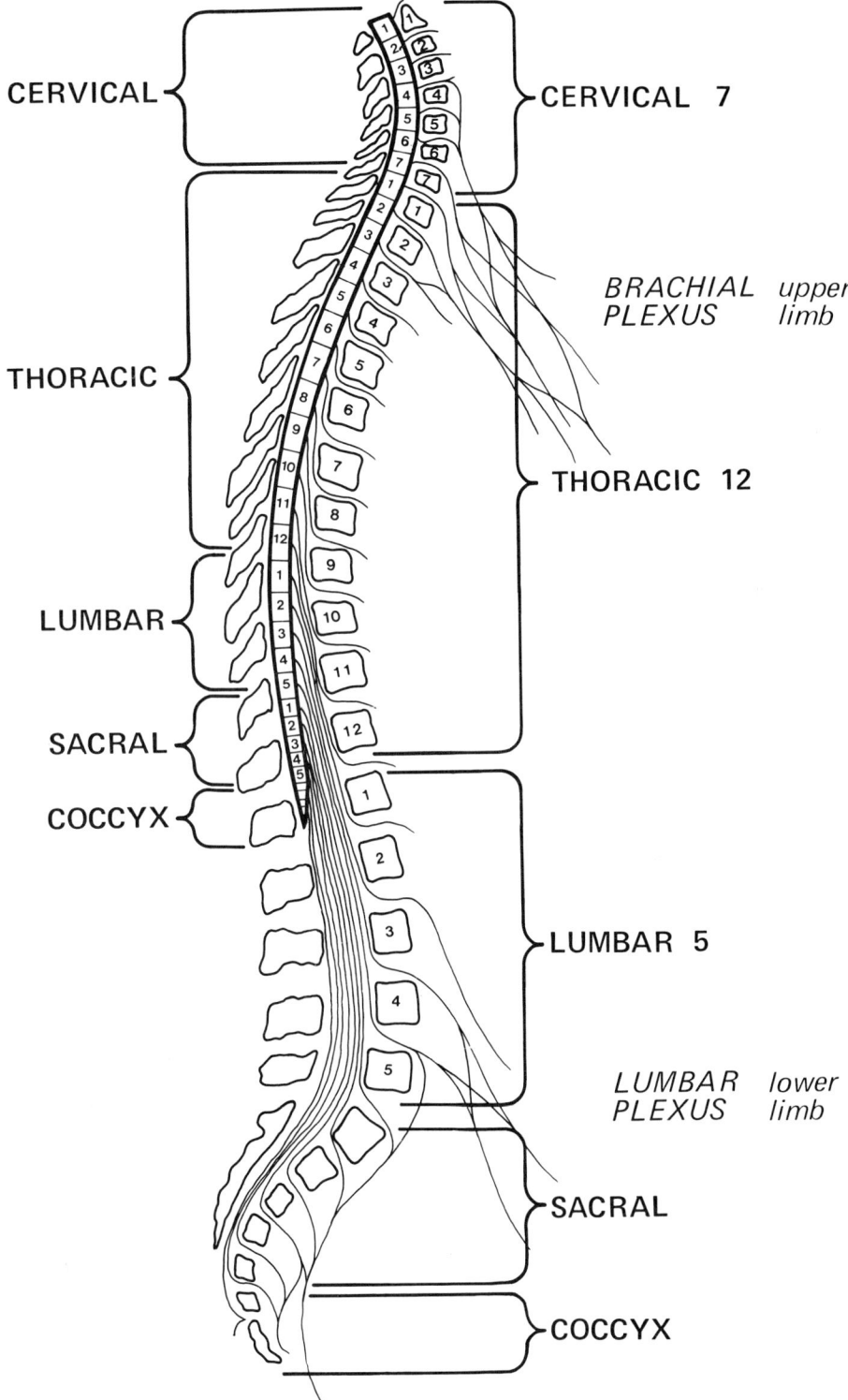

Fig. 1-10. Side view of the spinal column and the spinal cord indicating how the nerve roots emerge from the spinal cord to form the nerves to the limbs and organs. Note that the spinal cord ends at the level of the first or second lumbar vertebra. The confluence and rejoining of the nerve roots from the cervical area forms the brachial plexus, which evolves into the major nerves of the upper limb; similarly, the nerves from the lower lumbar and sacral roots converge and reform to form the major nerves of the lower limb.

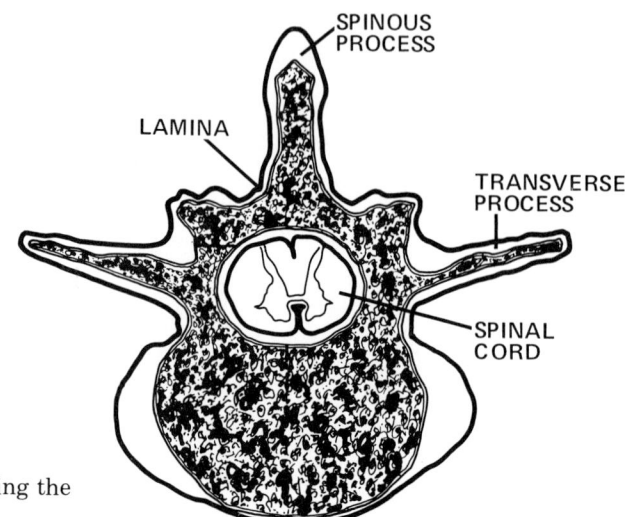

Fig. 1-11. Cross section of a vertebral body showing the bony protection to the spinal cord.

The nerves are made up of bundles of axons held together with fibrous envelopes one inside the other (*epineurium* and *perineurium*, Fig. 1-12). Each axon is surrounded by a fatty coating called *myelin* (Fig. 1-5). Myelin, which can be compared to an insulator, is important for the conduction of nerve impulses. Rapidly conducting fibers have a thick myelin sheath. Myelination is not complete at birth but proceeds as the child grows; the process is probably completed by the age of 3 years.

MUSCLES

Figure 1-13 is a schematic drawing of a typical muscle. The muscle is attached at one end, usually proximal, which is termed the *origin*. It most often terminates distally in a tough cord of fibers (tendon); this point of attachment is termed the *insertion*. The central part of the muscle is the *belly*. The entire muscle is encased in a sheath of silvery fibrous tissue (epimysium), much as a sausage is covered with its skin.

Figure 1-14 is a breakdown of the components of a muscle. The smallest unit, the *myofilament*, is ultimately responsible for the contraction of the muscle as a whole. Electron microscopy shows that the myofilaments are arranged as hexagons on cross section. the myofilaments are composed of two proteins, actin and myosin, which are thought to slide on each other. These proteins are arranged in short segments called *sarcomeres*. When the muscle is stimulated, the myofilaments shorten, the combined shortening creates tension, and the combined tensions, in turn, produce the muscle contraction. The bones move when a muscle crosses a joint.

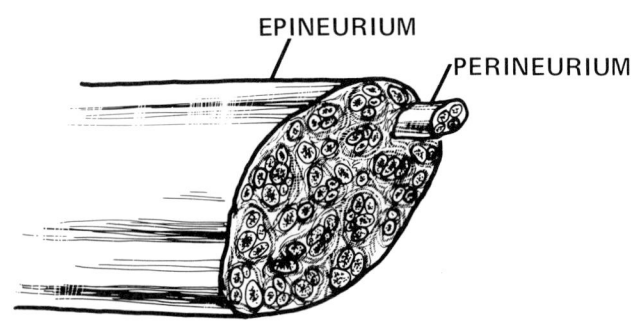

Fig. 1-12. Cross section of a peripheral nerve—nerve to the upper or lower limb. The nerve is made up of bundles of axons that are again bundled together by the *perineurium*, and, finally, these small bundles are joined and held together by another covering called the *epineurium*.

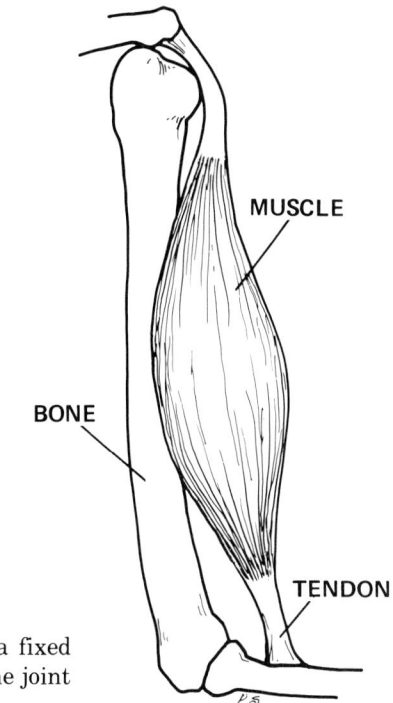

Fig. 1-13. Schematic drawing of the typical muscle. It attaches to a fixed point above the joint (the origin) and ends in a movable bone below the joint (the insertion).

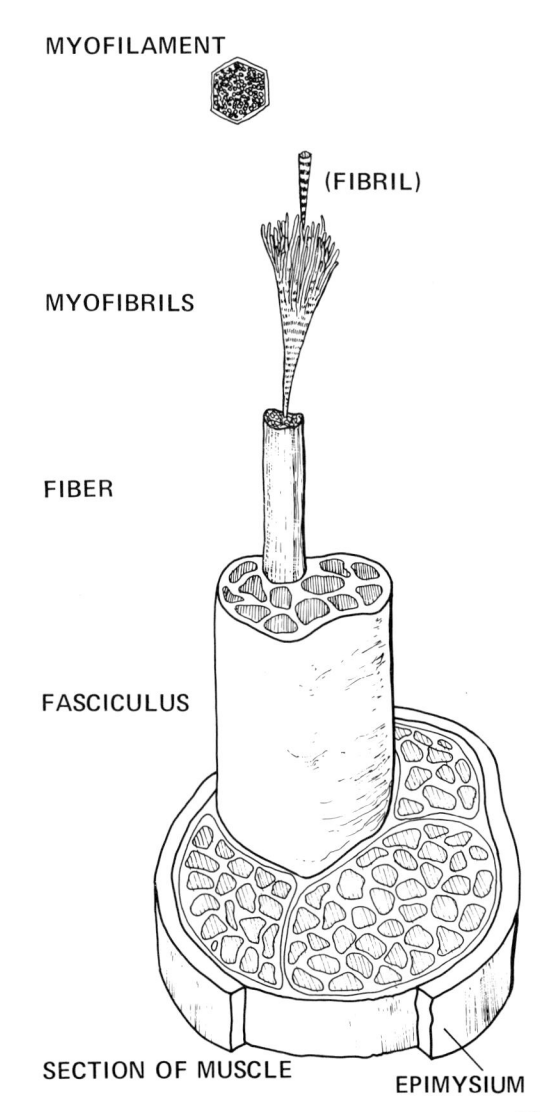

Fig. 1-14. Schematic drawing of the components of a muscle, progressing upward to its smallest elements. (Redrawn from Kelley, D. L., *Kinesthesiology,* Englewood Cliffs, N.J., Prentice-Hall, 1971. With permission.)

Fig. 1-15. Graphic representation of the electromyographic record obtained from electrodes on the skin or within the muscles, which records a pattern of muscle contraction.

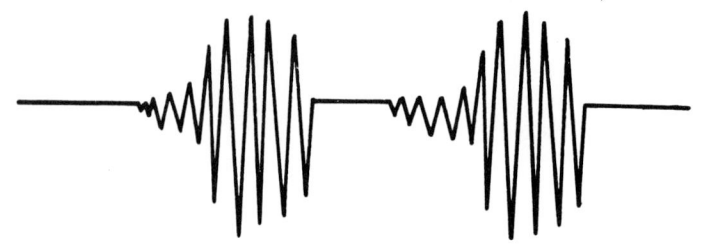

When muscles contract, electrical activity is produced. It can be recorded by placing electrodes on the skin or in the muscle and channeling the electrical activity into a cathode-ray oscilloscope. This is called *electromyographic examination* or *EMG* (Fig. 1-15).

Bone is a living tissue. Figure 1-16 delineates the essential part of a typical long bone. The outer covering is called the *periosteum*. The bone strength depends upon the thickness and density of its outer layer—the cortex. The ends of the bone, from which the bone grows in length, are the epiphyses. The epiphyseal line is the cartilage junction between the shaft and the epiphysis, and it is here that growth occurs in a child. When the epiphyseal line closes, growth ceases and the child is biologically mature. Growth of bone width occurs via the periosteum, which lays down new bone on the cortex.

Most long-bone growth in the upper limbs occurs at the ends that are furthest from the elbow joint; most growth in the lower limbs occurs at the ends nearest the knee joint (Fig. 1-17). The average age at which long-bone growth stops is 15 to 16 years for boys and 13 to 14 years for girls. Considerable variation in maturation of the skeleton is evident, however. Sometimes the child's chronological age is totally inconsistent with the skeletal age as determined by x-rays of the bones and particularly those of the wrist, for which standards have been established. In general, menstruation in girls heralds the beginning of the end of skeletal growth. The spine continues to grow for a year or two after long-bone growth stops and may contribute another inch or two to height. Only an x-ray of the pelvis and spine can determine when spinal growth has finally ceased.

Being composed of living matter, bone has an abundant supply of blood vessels which sustain the growth of the cells (Fig. 1-16). Occlusion of blood vessels to parts of the bone results in cell death (necrosis). Infection of the bone can produce such a death (septic necrosis), and the occlusion of blood vessels to the growth center (epiphysis) can produce death of that part of the bone (aseptic necrosis).

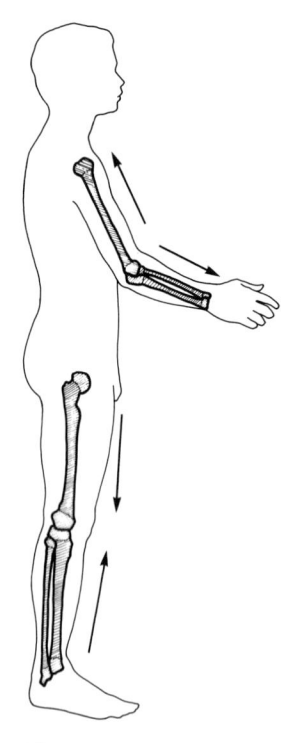

Fig. 1-17. Growth of long bones in a child. In the upper limb, the growth is away from the elbow, and, in the lower limb, it is toward the knee.

How Broken Bones Heal

A fracture is a break in the continuity of the bone. (Contrary to popular assumptions and confusions, the terms *fracture* and *break* are synonymous.) Figure 1-18 delineates the steps in fracture healing. First, a blood clot forms between the fractured ends. Cells *(osteoblasts)* from the perios-

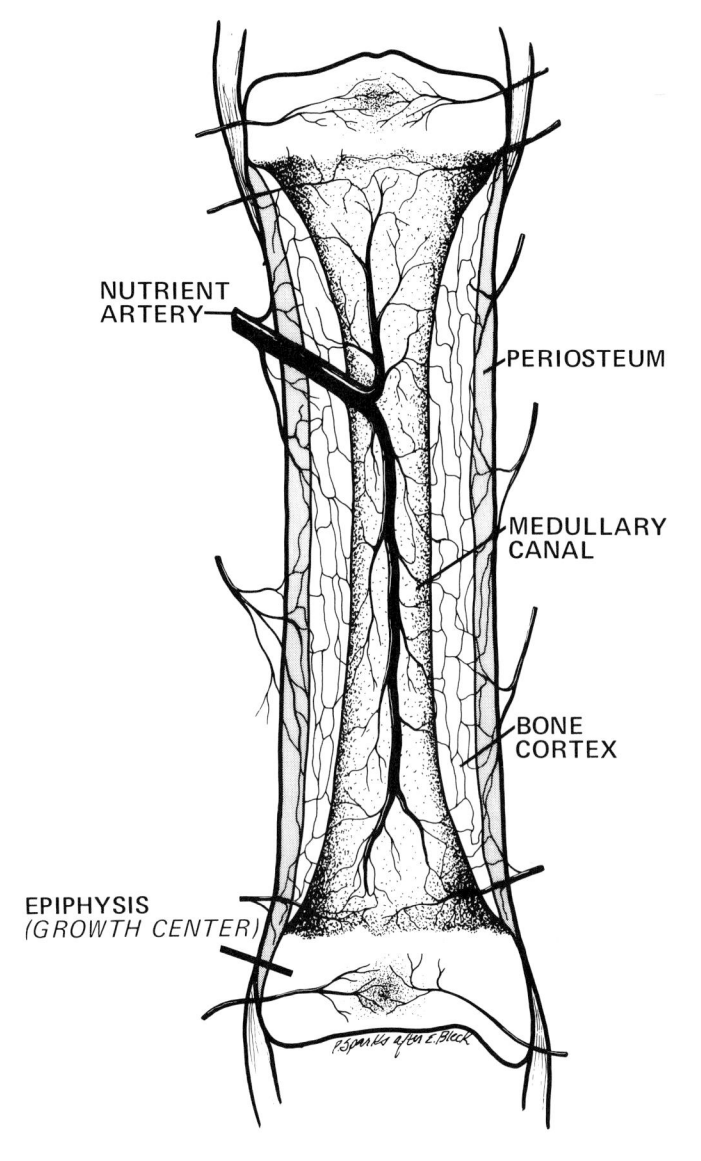

Fig. 1-16. The essential parts of a typical long bone.

teum and inner layer of the cortex *(endosteum)* then invade the blood clot and lay down new bone and cartilage. After the new bone has bridged the fracture, cells *(osteoclasts)* in the bone eat up excess new bone and remodel it. Bone is not like skin in that fractures take time to heal. In children, fracture-healing is more rapid than in adults, because the growth potential of children is greater. A fracture of a long bone in a child frequently stimulates growth, so that, when healing is complete, the healed bone (e.g., the thigh bone or femur) may be slightly longer. The greatest hazard in children's fractures is damage to the growth plate (epiphyseal line); the resultant unequal growth of that end of the bone causes a progressive deformity.

JOINTS

The junction of two bones to permit movement is called a *joint* or an *articulation.* Not all articulations move to the same degree, and joints are classified according to the degree of movement they allow: (1) *syn-*

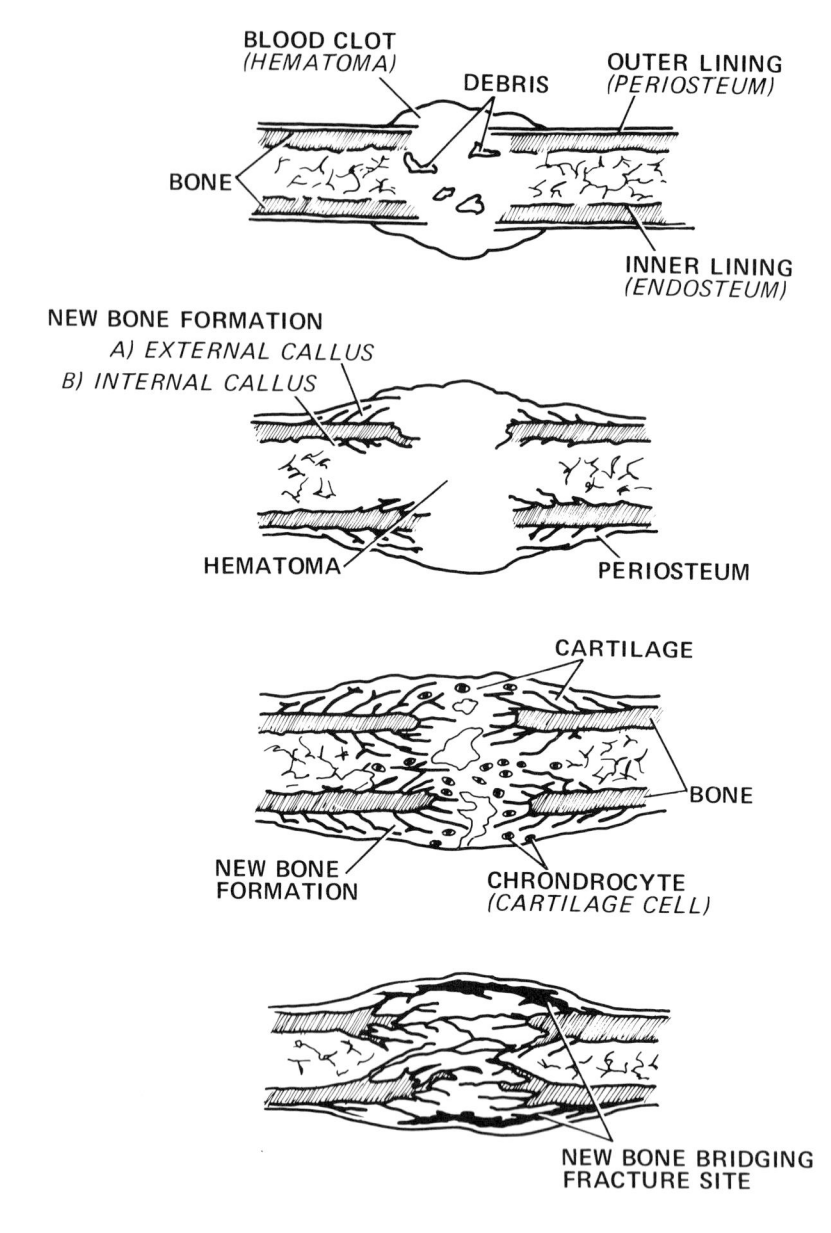

Fig. 1-18. The steps in fracture healing, reading from top to bottom. (Redrawn from Tronzo, R. G., Self-repairing, Self-renewing, *Consultant*, April 1972. With permission.)

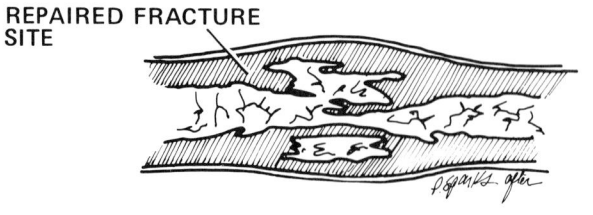

arthroses, which are immovable; (2) *amphiarthroses,* which are slightly movable; and (3) *diarthroses,* which are freely movable. The typical diarthrodial joint consists of a molded, smooth white cartilage which covers the end of each bone, a joint lining (synovium), a joint capsule, and, finally, ligaments which give the joint stability (Fig. 1-19).

Figure 1-20 depicts the interior of the knee joint and conveys the extent of the joint lining, or synovium. The function of the synovium is to

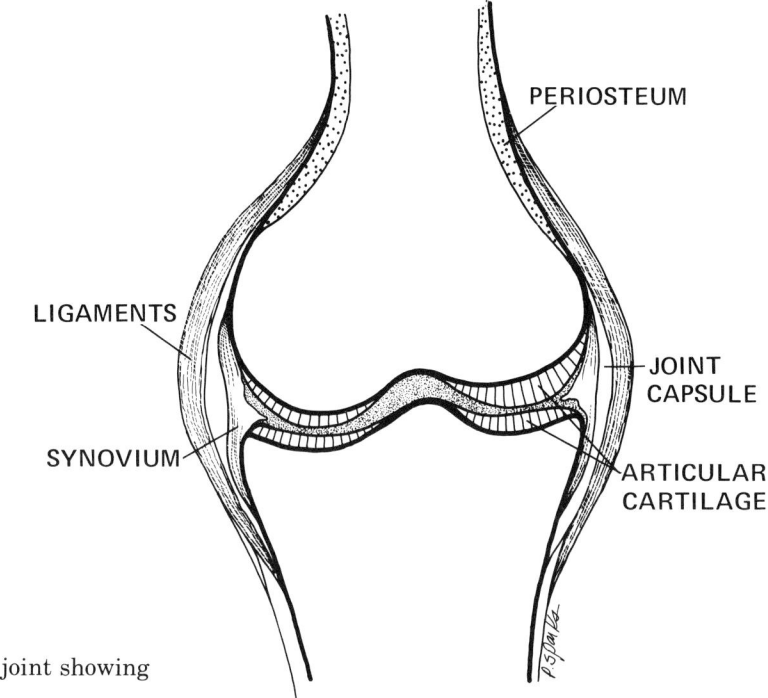

Fig. 1-19. Cross section of a typical joint showing the various parts.

provide the joint fluid that is essential for lubrication. Inflammation of a joint due to bacterial infection is *septic arthritis*. One form of nonbacterial arthritis is juvenile rheumatoid arthritis, discussed in Chapter 28. Inflammation of the joint lining is *synovitis*. A partial tear of the joint ligament is a *strain*. A complete tear or rupture of a joint ligament is a *sprain*.

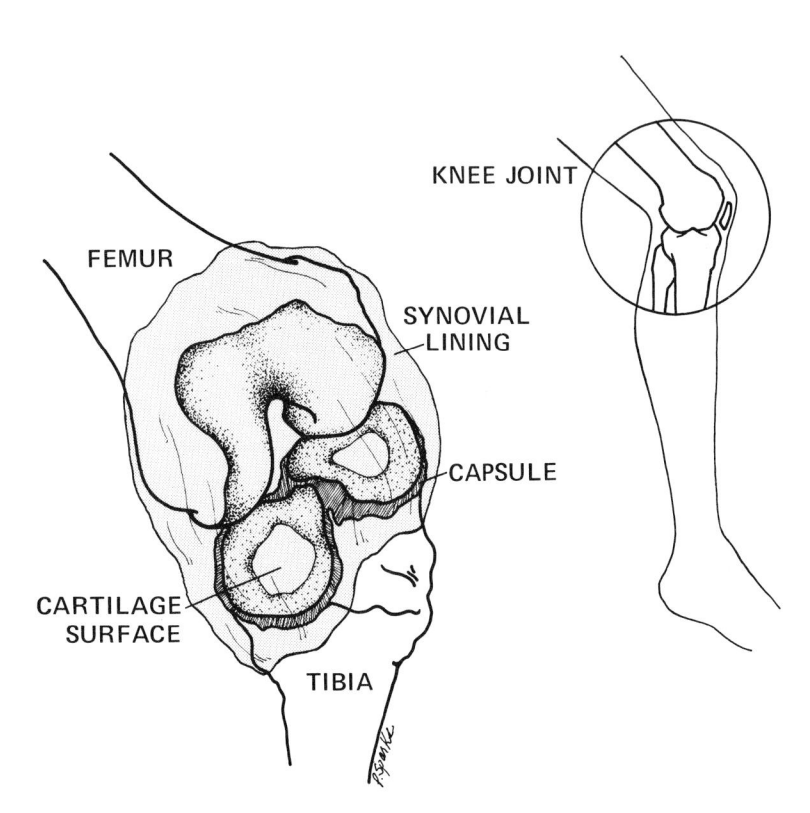

Fig. 1-20. Drawing of the knee joint showing the extent of the joint lining (synovium). The synovium excretes fluid and is responsible for the swollen joints of arthritis.

REFERENCES

1. Dobbing, V., and Sands, J., Qualitative growth and development of the human brain. *Archives of the Diseases in Childhood* 48:757–767, 1973.
2. Neligan, G. A., The human brain growth spurt. *Developmental Medicine and Child Neurology* 16:677–678, 1974.
3. Schade, V. P., and Von Groenigan, W. B., Structural organization of the human cerebral cortex. *Acta Anatomica* 47:74–111, 1961.
4. Stein, P. G., Rosen, J. J., and Butters, N., *Plasticity and Recovery of Function in the Central Nervous System.* New York, Academic Press, 1974.
5. Wire, J. The brain: What we know about it and what we don't know. *Stanford Observer,* September, 1979.

BIBLIOGRAPHY

Gardner, E., Gray, D. J., and O'Rahilly, R., *Anatomy—A Regional Study of Human Structure,* 3rd ed. Philadelphia, W. B. Saunders, 1969.

Grollman, S., *The Human Body—Its Structure and Physiology.* New York, Macmillan, 1969.

Kelley, D. L., *Kinesiology–Fundamentals of Motion Description.* Englewood Cliffs, N.J., Prentice-Hall, 1971.

Peele, T., *The Neuronanatomic Basis for Clinical Neurology.* New York, McGraw-Hill, 1961.

Warwick, R. and Williams, P., *Gray's Anatomy,* 35th ed. Philadelphia, W. B. Saunders, 1973.

The description of the neuron and of its supporting cells and function was derived from neurology lectures by Douglas Buchanan, M.D., Professor of Neurology, University of Chicago.

2

Amputations in Children

YOSHIO SETOGUCHI, M.D.

DEFINITIONS

Amputations or limb absences in children are either of acquired or of congenital origin.

Acquired amputation implies that the child was born normal but had a limb or limbs removed in part or in toto due to an accident (traumatic) or by surgery. The most common causes of traumatic amputation are automobile or other vehicular accidents, railroad accidents, accidents involving explosives, and farm accidents (not as common in California). Surgical amputations are most commonly due to malignant bone tumors but may also be due to gangrene caused by infection or to vascular disorders, congenital malformations, or other causes.

Congenital amputation means that the child is born with partial or complete absence of limb(s). In many clinics, the term *limb deficiency* is used to describe the congenital absence of a limb, since amputation implies "a cutting of a limb." Limb deficiency is thought to be due to a failure of the fetal limb bud to develop during the first 3 months of gestation. The cause(s) of limb deficiencies are still unknown in most cases. Many people still ask about the ingestion of drugs, particularly of thalidomide, but this drug as not been available for almost 20 years. Today, very few limb deficiencies, if any, are felt to be a direct result of medications taken by the mother during the pregnancy.

There are two basic types of limb deficiencies. One type resembles surgical amputation in that no normal structures, such as digits, are present distal to the missing portion (this does not mean that rudimentary finger-like nubbins may not be present, however). The other type is

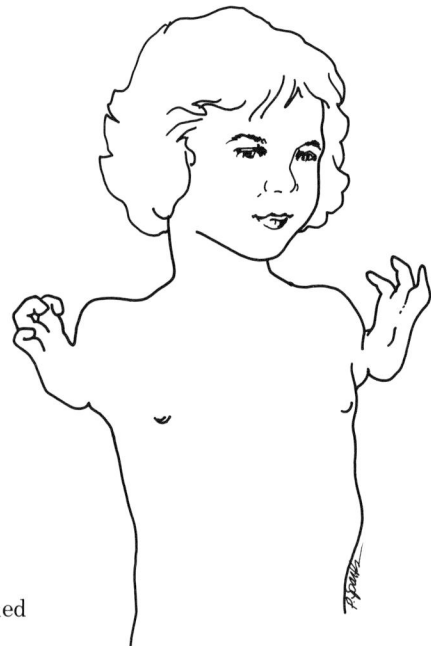

Fig. 2-1. Absence of most of arm and forearm bones, with hand attached at shoulder girdle. This condition is called *phocomelia*.

that in which a middle segment of the limb is absent, but the proximal and distal portions are intact. The classic example of this second type is the condition called *phocomelia* (from *phoco*, seal-like; *melos*, limb) in which the hands or feet are attached proximally to the shoulders or hips, with complete absence of the intervening elements of the limbs (Fig. 2-1). Some limb deficiencies are difficult to classify because they are combinations of these two basic types.

The most common limb deficiency is the below-elbow type. It is usually unilateral. The patient presents with a normal shoulder, upper arm (humerus) and elbow joint. The forearm is foreshortened, with usually two-thirds to one-half of the distal portion absent. There may be rudimentary nubbins at the distal end (Fig. 2-2).

TREATMENT NEEDS

The goal of any treatment program is to provide a habilitation plan which will allow the limb-deficient or amputee child to develop and grow as normally as possible and to enjoy life as any other child. To accomplish this objective, it is important that the treatment plan include assessment and appropriate treatment in the areas of medical, surgical, psychosocial, therapeutic, and prosthetic (artificial limbs) needs. One must also consider the specific needs that arise as the child grows older, such as school, adolescence, and vocation. In most cases, the ideal approach to the care of these children is with a multi-disciplinary team headed by a pediatrician.

Once a treatment program has begun, periodic reassessment is essential to successful habilitation or rehabilitation. It is the responsibility of the team and its members to assess the changes in need that occur with changes in the child's growth, development, interests, activities, and surroundings.

Each of the above-noted needs will be discussed briefly in the following sections.

Amputations in Children

Medical

The status of the child's total health must be considered in assessing the needs of the limb-deficient child. Any medical problem may affect the success of the habilitation program. If the child has congenital anomalies of other organ systems as well, appropriate consultations should be obtained. It should be pointed out here that, in most cases, other anomalies do not occur in persons with limb deficiencies any more frequently than they occur in the normal population. Proper medical care in areas such as nutrition, immunization, and prevention are also strongly stressed.

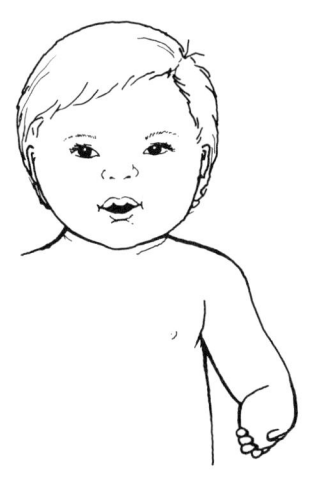

Fig. 2-2. Most common type of limb deficiency: below-elbow type. Note that part of forearm and all of hand is absent but that, rudimentary or vestigial elements are present at distal end.

Surgical

The orthopedic surgeon is an essential part of the habilitation team. Whenever there is a limb deficiency, it is important to assess the function of the remaining portion of that limb, as well as of the other extremities. In some cases, surgical procedures are indicated either to improve function or to improve the limb for ultimate prosthetic fitting.

Psychosocial

The overall success of the treatment program can be measured by how well the patient functions within his immediate environment and within the larger society. Healthy functioning depends upon adequate self-esteem. In turn, the foundation of self-esteem in the child is built during the early months and years of life, through the parents' fulfilling of the child's basic needs. Therefore, in the case of congenital limb deficiency, psychosocial treatment should begin as soon as possible after the child's birth. Treatment is initially focused upon the parents and the social and emotional needs and problems that they experience in adapting to the birth of a deformed child. The parents' painful feeling must be acknowledged and dealt with so that they may nurture the child's healthy development and invest themselves in the child's treatment plan. As the child grows, psychosocial treatment expands to include the child's own feelings, concerns and problems. Experience has shown that limb deficiency does not preclude normal development in every other respect. The key to successful development seems to be, initially, the parents' response and then, later, the response of others who are significant in the child's environment.

When amputation is required, psychosocial attention to the child, as well as to the parents, should be available before the amputation, whenever possible, and always immediately afterwards. Both the child and the family will be dealing with the trauma of sudden loss, and strong psychological support is essential. In addition, the child frequently experiences anxiety about returning to school after the loss of a limb, and the parents have concerns about how to treat a child who has suffered such a trauma. The subject of school for the limb-deficient child or the acquired amputee will be discussed later in this chapter.

Training or Therapy

When one talks about therapy for amputees, one usually means the training involved in the use of a prosthesis. In most amputee clinics, this is a major function of the occupational and physical therapists. However, some patients with congenital loss have deformed, but very functional, extremities—especially the upper ones. In such instances, the therapist may, instead, become involved in assisting the patients to achieve more effective utilization of their own extremities. Patients often find that their malformed limbs provide more function than does a prosthetic device. In other cases, the therapist may suggest and train patients in the use of assistive aids, such as special tools for feeding, pencil holders, special toileting devices, or clothing modifications. The ultimate goal is to provide patients with the opportunity to perform all tasks that are commensurate with their age and motivation.

Prosthetics

Although in most medical texts *prosthesis* refers to the replacement of any human organ or structure, in this chapter, we will use it solely to refer to artificial limbs. Artificial limbs can and have been fitted for patients with any level of amputation and limb deficiency, even patients with some digits still present. In the upper extremity, prostheses have been prescribed for providing length, prehension, and motion of various joints. The most useful function is prehension. Although the artificial device that provides the best prehensile function is the hook, this device is not the best in terms of appearance (see Fig. 2-5).

In the lower extremity, prostheses are prescribed to replace joints, to provide length, and to allow the patient to ambulate. In cases of high-level loss, i.e., at or near the hip, the patient may also need an assistive device, such as a cane or crutch.

The fabrication of the prosthesis is a highly individualized, custom process. The patients' needs in terms of both cosmesis and function must be considered before a final prescription is written.

SELECTION, TIMING, AND REASSESSMENT OF TREATMENT

When a child presents with an acquired amputation, he is generally fitted as one would fit an adult, except that the child's special needs and developmental potentials are considered in the treatment plan. The prosthesis is often altered from the standard fabrication models in order to fit the child's needs. In the lower extremity, for example, this is seen in the elimination of knee joints for the very young child with an above-knee or hip disarticulation. The child walks on a "pylon" leg. This absence of the knee joint provides a much more stable extremity on which to bear the child's weight as he or she learns to ambulate.

With the upper extremity, one may defer activating the terminal device (the patient is able to open and close the hook by means of a cable, without using the other extremity) until the child is able to understand the holding function and is able to take instruction. Thus, the hook may not be "activated" until the child reaches 1½ to 2 years of age.

In the case of congenital limb-deficient children, one must first decide whether any vestigial or rudimentary digital elements have any function and whether they would be a hindrance to prosthetic fitting. The choices for therapy are (1) therapy only—use existing limb(s); (2) no surgery—use prosthesis and therapy; (3) surgery and therapy; or (4) surgery, prosthesis, and therapy. Once a decision is made, treatment should be instituted as soon as is medically feasible so that the child's normal developmental progression is altered as little as possible. A good example of this is a child who is born lacking a fibula (the outside bone of the lower leg) and with deformity of the foot and foreshortening of the lower leg (tibia). If the foot is not functional for weight-bearing and the leg is too short, rather than fitting the child with a shoe lift, amputation and fitting with a below-knee prosthesis constitute a more effective treatment program. In order that this may be done without disrupting the patient's normal locomotor development, surgical amputation and prosthetic fitting should be performed before the child is 10 to 12 months old (Fig. 2-3).

Particularly in upper-extremity limb deficiencies, prosthetic fitting may not always be the best treatment. Although there may be weak prehensile power, lack of length, instability of joints, and less than ideal cosmesis, the patient still may derive the greatest function by the use of existing limbs, particularly when some functional hand elements are present. Therefore, the treatment plan begins with a thorough assessment of the functional potential of the limb-deficient child. The clinicians then must determine whether surgery, prosthesis, or both will most increase the functions of the patient. Surgical intervention for upper-extremity limb deficiencies is very infrequent. Prosthetic fitting is the choice for most cases in which distal structures are absent, while training and the prescription of assistive aids (adapted equipment and tools) are most often preferred for deficiencies in which functional digits remain.

Timing of prosthetic fitting is an important factor in the child's acceptance and functional use of a prosthesis. In most child-amputee clinics, the patient with an upper-extremity loss is fitted with a prosthesis when he or she develops good sitting balance—usually at 8 to 10 months of age. The exceptions are children with transcarpal deficiencies (part of hand missing) or with complete absence of the limb: because the former has so much function and the latter so little (or actually no arm function on that side), if prostheses are to be fitted for such children, the fitting is deferred until the child can make effective use of the prosthesis and is able to take proper instructions. Fitting a child at 8 to 10 months of age does not mean that the child immediately obtains maximum function from the prosthesis. In fact, the most important part of the early fitting is that it allows the child to become accustomed to the added length and weight of the prosthesis. Actual prehensile function is not obtained until after age 1 to 1½ years.

The lower-extremity limb-deficient child is fitted with a prosthesis

Fig. 2-3. Management of fibular absence: (A) deformed foot, which is unstable, with lower-leg foreshortening; (B) leg after amputation through ankle; (C) leg fitted with below-knee prosthesis.

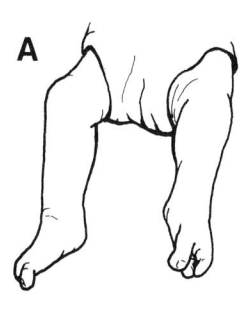

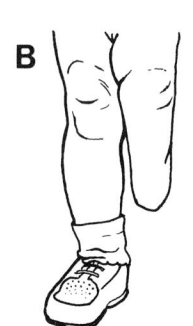

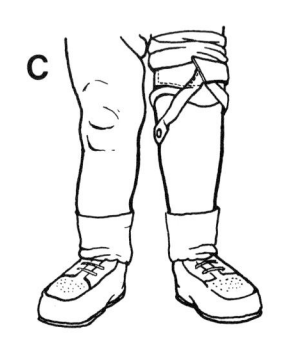

when he or she begins to pull up in order to stand (usually at 10 to 15 months of age). In order that locomotor development may progress normally, the child at that time needs equal leg lengths so that weight may be transferred easily from one side to the other. With higher levels of limb loss, many other considerations (too technical to discuss in this chapter) must be weighed in the prosthetic prescriptions.

One unique problem in the prosthetic care of limb-deficient or amputee children is the factor of normal physical growth. Even the limb which is partially absent changes in size and shape with growth. This factor requires that the child's prosthesis be checked periodically and appropriate adjustments made. Also, because the prosthesis can only be enlarged or adjusted so much, periodic replacements are needed. In most clinics, an upper-extremity prosthesis must be replaced about once every 15 to 18 months, whereas a lower-extremity prosthesis is replaced once every 12 months.

Another important consideration in prosthetic treatment is the functional needs of the child with a limb loss. Especially in the upper extremity, the demands on the prosthesis will change with growth and development. For example, in the upper extremity, the need for fine prehension usually occurs at 4 to 5 years of age. Cosmesis becomes an important factor for children in their teens.

Overall, the treatment program for the child with a limb deficiency or amputation requires careful assessment of the child's functional abilities, needs, and changing environment, as well as the family's attitudes and ability to support the program.

PROSTHETIC CONSIDERATIONS

Although there are a number of amputees or limb-deficient children who do not wear a prosthesis, the presence of a child with a prosthesis presents special concerns to the teacher. Therefore, a brief discussion of some prosthetic principles are in order.

The basic goal of any prosthetic treatment is to replace functions that are missing due to the limb loss. However, at the present state of the art, not all functions are adequately replaced or provided.

Prostheses are generally prescribed to provide prehension, length, and cosmesis. They do have some disadvantages: no sensory feedback (touch, pain, proprioception, etc.); weight; the need to wear excess paraphernalia, such as harnesses or belts; and appearance.

The prosthesis is generally fabricated to replace all missing joints and to provide proper length. Most prostheses fabricated today are "body powered," i.e., the patient is fitted with a harness and cable system that allows him to activate a component by certain body motions (Fig. 2-4). Hook and elbow function are most often so activated. In the last 10 years, considerable research has gone into externally powered prostheses. Use of electric, pneumatic, and hydraulic systems to activate prostheses have been considered. Today, external power is used primarily to activate terminal devices (prehensile devices) and elbow joints. Externally powered prostheses are expensive, often noisy, heavy, and prone to break down. For the patient with a more severe limb loss, however, such a device can provide function that the patient otherwise would not get.

The biggest problem facing the upper-extremity limb-loss child are the questions and comments generated by his "terminal device," which, in most cases, is a hook. At the present time, the hook-type terminal device is the most functional device available. In addition, the loss of the hand does not simply mean the loss of a prehensile organ: just as impor-

Fig. 2-4. Typical body-powered prosthesis for a below-elbow amputation.

tant is the loss of a sensory feedback system. Hence the patient must now substitute vision for sensory feedback in order to use a prosthesis effectively. It is therefore essential that the prosthetist or limb maker provide the patient with a device that will not obstruct the patient's view when he or she uses the terminal device for holding, manipulating, etc. If the patient and family are willing to sacrifice some function for cosmesis, a "hand-like" device can be prescribed. At the Child Amputee Prosthetics Project (CAPP), University of California, Los Angeles, a special terminal device was developed for children which provides better prehension without having a hook appearance (Fig. 2-5). Many patients and families have accepted this new device with enthusiasm.

FUNCTIONAL CONSIDERATIONS

Upper-Limb Loss

As noted previously, the decision as to whether or not a prosthesis should be prescribed depends upon many factors. The most important consideration is whether the child has the potential to perform the activi-

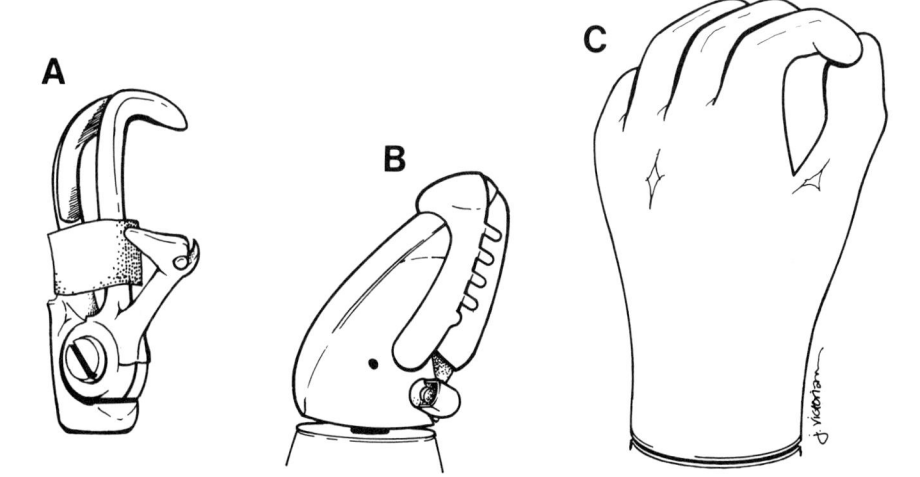

Fig. 2-5. Terminal devices currently available for children with upper-extremity limb loss: (A) a hook; (B) the CAPP terminal device; (C) a hand-like device.

ties with or without one. Unilateral absence of an upper limb is only partially compensated by a prosthesis. The degree of compensation achieved depends on the extent of limb loss and type of prosthesis required—the less extensive the limb loss and the fewer the number of prosthetic components used, the more functional the patient. The above-elbow amputee, therefore, is usually less functional than the below-elbow amputee. Many patients with high upper-limb loss, such as at the shoulder, find only limited functional benefits and so reject the prosthesis completely. If the child has had a good (re)habilitation program, under the guidance of an amputee clinic, he should have some say in whether or not he uses a prosthesis for performing various activities.

Bilateral involvement presents considerably more problems. Children with total or almost total losses of their upper limbs are often very adept with the use of their feet and toes for prehensile functions. Although this approach is unconventional, it is probably the most effective way for the child and should not disturb those who work with the child.

Prosthetic fittings and functional potentials for patients with bilateral upper-limb loss are so individualized that it is essential for the teacher to contact the clinic or the occupational therapist in order to learn how best to help the child in the school situation.

Lower-Limb Loss

Patients with unilateral lower-limb loss are able to ambulate quite well, although, as the level of loss becomes greater, the likelihood of a "limp" and the need for increased energy expenditure becomes greater. Also, if the loss is above the knee, the patient will have greater difficulty in handling stairs, inclines, and uneven terrains.

Bilateral amputees with absence of their own knee joints require, at minimum, crutches to ambulate, and many require part-time wheelchair use.

SCHOOL

Education is an important part of any child's life and this is also true for the child with limb loss(es). The limb-deficient or amputee child finds that, besides the normal anxiety of separating from parents, siblings, and home and of confronting a strange, new group of peers and adults, he or she must also face additional, unique concerns.

The first factor, the one with which parents are most frequently concerned, is that the child's limb loss or prosthesis will elicit not only curiosity but also overt reactions in the form of stares, comments and *teasing*. These reactions may impart to the child that he or she is different and, therefore, "not as good as" others.

If the child is to continue to grow along emotionally healthy lines, he or she must be prepared to deal with the crisis of entering school, as must the child's parents. The child should be made aware that at first he or she will meet with curiosity and questions from others and that, if these questions are asked simply and honestly it is best to respond to them in the same fashion.

The teacher who is well informed about the child's disabilities and abilities can help make this experience a positive one. The teacher needs to know some basic information about the prosthesis in order to assist the child in handling the questions and comments. One excellent method for demonstrating the prosthesis, at least to the child's class, is to hold a "share and tell" session.

The second factor that concerns the patient and family is function. Parents often ask: Will the physical structure of the school limit the child's capacity for independence? Will the limb loss limit his or her ability to perform independently activities required of all students, such as eating, toileting, and dressing?

Preparation of the limb-loss or amputee child for school should begin long before the critical first day. Careful assessment by the clinic therapist of the child's functional abilities, followed by the fabrication of a well-designed prosthesis, constitute the first step. The therapist should introduce those activities that the child will be required to perform in school. Hopefully, the child will thus be exposed not only to classroom activities but also to playground equipment and activities. Many children are hesitant to undertake new activities; if they are introduced to them in a supervised setting, however, they will then be prepared to enjoy them in school.

The third concern is the requirement that students take physical education. Most clinics feel that the child amputee should participate in this program. However, problems can arise if the child has to remove the prosthesis for showering. There is also some concern about dangers of the prosthesis both to the patient and to the other students, especially in contact sports. The ultimate program that is developed for each child should be based on the child's abilities and desires and on the flexibility of the school staff.

The last concern is the type of school that the child should attend and the reactions from the school personnel. For most patients, a regular school is preferred over a school for the handicapped, and, with the passage of P.L. 94-142, students and their parents now have a say in the type of school chosen. When a regular school is selected, the school personnel, especially the teacher, must be prepared to deal with the limb deficiency and the prosthesis. The teacher must know how to introduce the child and the child's limb loss and prosthesis to the class and how to minimize the child's trauma. The teacher must also be informed of the patient's functional potentials in order to provide the child with encouragement, assistance, or both, as the situation requires.

SUMMARY

This chapter has attempted to provide an overview of the problems of the limb-deficient or amputee child. Nomenclature, the treatment needs, the treatment team, some basic information on prosthetics, and the role of the school have been discussed. Although the medical team need not be directly involved in the child's education, they are a ready resource for assistance to school personnel. Close communication among the child's teacher, school nurse, physician, therapist, and social worker cannot help but make the school life of the limb-deficient or, amputee child a most positive experience.

Since the intellectual capabilities of most children with limb deficiencies do not differ from those of the general population, it is assumed that most of these children will attend regular school. They deserve the best education available.

BIBLIOGRAPHY

Aitken G. (ed.), *The Child with an Acquired Amputation*. Washington, D.C., National Academy of Sciences, 1972.

Blakeslee, B. (ed.), *The Limb Deficient Child.* Los Angeles, University of California Press, 1963.

Swinyard, C. (ed.), *Limb Development and Deformity: Problems of Evaluation and Rehabilitation.* Springfield, Ill., Charles C. Thomas, 1969.

Tachdjian, M. O., *Pediatric Orthopaedics.* Philadelphia, W. B. Saunders, 1973.

Talbot, D., *The Child with a Limb Deficiency.* Child Amputee Prosthetics Project (CAPP), University of California, Los Angeles, 1979.

3

Arthrogryposis—Multiple Congenital Contractures

EUGENE E. BLECK, M.D.

DEFINITION

Arthrogryposis (ar-throw-gry-po′-siss) is a congenital disease in which children who are affected are born with stiff joints and weak muscles. The deformities are obvious at birth. The term was derived from two Greek words: *arthro,* meaning joints, and *gryposis,* meaning curved. It was first described in 1841. Because *arthrogryposis* describes only a symptom and sign of what may be a more general, and often inherited, defect, the term *multiple congenital contractures* is preferred by some authorities.[1]

CAUSE (ETIOLOGY)

The cause of arthrogryposis is unknown. The disease process is first evident early in fetal life when, in the normal fetus, muscle development and contractions of muscles begin. In the fetus with arthrogryposis, the muscles fail to function, either because of primary muscle disease or because of primary disease of the spinal cord cells that control muscle contraction. The resulting lack of early movement of the joints in the developing fetus probably explains their stiffness and deformity at birth.

When it occurs in the absence of other defects (of the heart, lungs, urinary tract, etc.), the condition ordinarily has no family history, and no heritable factors can be discerned. Its appearance in a family thus may be sporadic. Nevertheless, a thorough search for hereditary factors should be made by chromosomal analysis and, if deemed necessary by the examining physician, by biochemical and other studies: at times arthrogryposis occurs as part of a recognizable syndrome that does have clear inheritance patterns.

An identical condition occurs in sheep, cattle, and horses, where it is caused by a virus that infects the motor cells (neurons) in the spinal cord of the fetus. This results in a loss of muscle tone in the fetus, which, in turn, leads to joint immobility. The animal is born with bent, fixed joints (contractures).

SIGNS AND SYMPTOMS

Two types of disease are described: neuropathic and myopathic. The consensus is that the myopathic form is probably a different disease and, therefore, can be discounted. The clinical picture of the neuropathic form is as follows. The children resemble a wooden marionette or Pinocchio. The limbs are fixed in almost any position, but the frequent deformities are as follows (Figs. 3-1 and 3-2):

Shoulders are turned in.
Elbows are straightened (extended).
Forearms are turned with the palm down (pronated).
Wrists are flexed and deviated inward.
Fingers are curled into the palms.
Hips are bent upward (flexed) and turned outward (externally rotated).
Knees are either bent or straightened.
Feet are usually turned in and down (equinus and varus).
Spine often shows curvature (scoliosis).
Limbs are small in circumference.
Joints appear larger and have loss of motion; hip dislocation is common.
Skin is frequently dimpled over joints that are fixed in extension.
Intelligence and speech are usually normal.

ASSOCIATED CONDITIONS

Conditions associated with the disease include congenital heart disease, urinary tract abnormalities, respiratory problems, abdominal hernias, and various facial abnormalities.

OUTLOOK (PROGNOSIS)

In general, children suffering from the disease will be deformed and stiff, with very limited joint motion. Of the three clinical types—(1) fat, (2) thin, and (3) webbed—the "fat type" has been noted to have the best prognosis for function, e.g., walking.[2] The deformities recur easily. On the positive side, these children do not deteriorate. They may or may not be able to walk, but they most often have a normal trunk. There are children who will be quite functional in a wheelchair. We should expect the child to have normal intelligence, and, if properly motivated, these children will capitalize on any opportunity given them to achieve independence.

TREATMENT

Goals of treatment are independent walking, self-care, and the ability to be gainfully employed in the future.

Surgical treatment combined with plaster casts and braces is usual for deformities, particularly of the lower limbs. Dislocation of the hip is common and is the most difficult to treat. If both hips are dislocated, many authorities recommend that they be left that way, since, despite the dislocation, the child will have a satisfactory gait. If only one hip is

Arthrogryposis

Fig. 3-1. Typical picture of a newborn with arthrogryposis: flexed, stiff elbows, flexed wrists and fingers, stiff knees.

dislocated, surgery should be attempted at an early age to replace the hip in the socket. Knee deformities are most often treated with a combination of plaster casts and surgery. Foot deformities invariably need surgery, and, frequently, it is necessary to excise the entire ankle bone (talus) to obtain a good correction. Spinal curvature (scoliosis) can be best managed by early surgical correction and spinal fusion.

In the upper limbs, the most devastating deformity is that in which the elbow is fixed in extension. Early surgery to allow the elbow to bend has been recommended, even though the range of motion thus gained

Fig. 3-2. Typical standing posture of a child with arthrogryposis. Note the wasting of the limb muscles (atrophy) and the flexed position of the wrists with flexed and crossed fingers.

might be limited. Despite growth deformities of their hands, many children are able to adapt their hands to some useful function. If the wrist is in too much flexion, surgical treatment is probably indicated.

EDUCATIONAL IMPLICATIONS

Because these children usually have normal intelligence and speech, and because physical rehabilitation is only short-term and limited, educational goals should follow the usual academic pattern. It would thus seem important to emphasize and to encourage academic achievement in such children and to direct them toward goals that don't involve hand skills or general mobility.

If handwriting is too slow, oral reporting on lessons and the use of an electric typewriter enables some of the children to keep pace with their normal peers.

REFERENCES

1. Swinyard, C. H. Lectures at the American Academy for Cerebral Palsy and Developmental Medicine and personal communication, 1979–1980.
2. Williams, P., Arthrogryposis, in *Proceedings of the Seventh Annual International Pediatric Orthopedic Seminar,* San Francisco, 1980.

BIBLIOGRAPHY

Lloyd-Roberts, G. C., and Lettin, A. W. F., Arthrogryposis multiplex congenita. *Journal of Bone and Joint Surgery* 52-B:494, 1970.

Mead, N. G., Lithgow, W. C., and Sweeney, H. J., Arthrogryposis multiplex congenita. *Journal of Bone and Joint Surgery* 40-A:1285, 1958.

Tachdjian, M. O., *Pediatric Orthopedics.* Philadelphia, W. B. Saunders, 1973.

4

Asthma

BIRT HARVEY, M.D.

Asthma, one of the most common chronic diseases of childhood, is frequently encountered in the classroom. Asthma may be best described as a labored, wheezing breathing caused by interference with the normal flow of air in and out of the lungs. The most pronounced noise accompanies exhalation, and the time required for exhalation is prolonged. There may be shortness of breath, and cough is often present. The discussion in this chapter will be limited to allergic asthma and thus will not consider other nonallergic causes of wheezing.

The wheezing of asthma is caused by a combination of events occurring in the lungs. First there is a tightening of the muscles that surround the inner walls of the bronchial tubes. Second, swelling of the tissues lining the air tubes occurs. This swelling is caused by extra fluid in the cells of the walls and by dilation of the blood vessels which course through the walls. Third, there is an increase in the amount and thickness of secretions within the tubes. Together, these three factors cause a decrease in the airway diameter. As air passes through the narrowed bronchial tubes, a whistling noise—the asthmatic wheeze—results (Fig. 4-1).

HISTORY

Asthma is at least as old as history. Dr. Albert D. G. Blanc has written an excellent account of the historical aspects of the disease. The word is derived from the Greek for "panting" or "gasping." Many of the observations made years ago hold true today, and it is surprising how little our

Fig. 4-1. (A) Normal bronchus. (B) Asthmatic bronchus. The bronchial tube becomes narrowed from tightening of the muscles, increased fluid, and distension of blood vessels in the walls. Within the narrowed lumen of the bronchus, increased mucous production results in further obstruction to the passage of air.

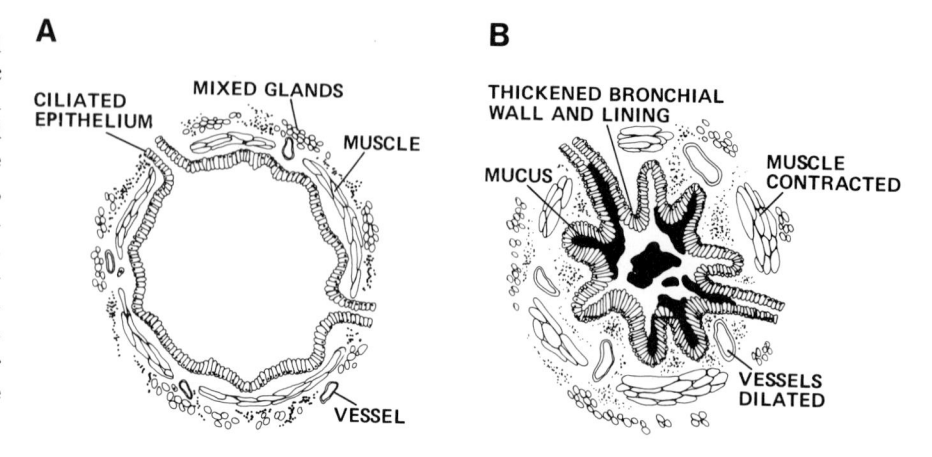

knowledge has actually increased beyond what was taught centuries ago. Prescriptions for asthma are in records of Egyptian medical knowledge extending back to 3000 B.C. Hippocrates, writing in about 400 B.C., mentioned emotions, cold, and dampness in connection with this disease. Aurelianus, a fifth-century Roman, not only skillfully described an attack of asthma, but also offered several suggestions for treatment which might well be used at the present time. Avicenna (980–1037) mentioned the effect of nerves and food on breathing. Maimonides (1135–1204) advocated living in suburbs rather than cities, moderation in diet and treatment, and individualization of treatment. Van Helmont (1577–1644) cited cases where dust or food reactions precipitated an attack of asthma, noted seasonal differences, and noticed hives in patients or their families. Willis (1621–1675) recognized that some people are predisposed to asthma and wrote that the lungs are thrown into spasm due to influences passing down the "pneumonic" nerves to the lungs.

INCIDENCE

A survey done in the state of Washington mentioned asthma as the fifth most common reason for which children see a physician. A United States Public Health Service survey done in 1960 showed the rate of prevalence of asthma in children to be 2.58 percent. More recent studies in Colorado and Texas have shown a similar incidence. Fourteen million of the approximately 70 million children in the country had some type of chronic disease, and over 1.5 million had asthma. The single chronic condition causing the highest percentage of days lost from school was asthma. It was responsible for 20 percent of days lost because of chronic conditions. This survey probably underreported, so the true incidence may be even higher.

CAUSES

The basic causes of asthma are little understood. Our knowledge of them is expanding rapidly, so we may hope for more effective therapy and prevention based on better understanding of causation.

The individual with "allergy" was at one time felt to have a deficiency in antibodies, which allowed substances such as pollens, house dust, animal danders, molds, and foods to react against his own tissues. Our present belief is just the opposite. The allergic individual has an overabundance of antibodies to certain substances, and these antibodies react in heightened response whenever the allergy-producing substances (allergen or antigen) are inhaled or ingested into the body. The union of

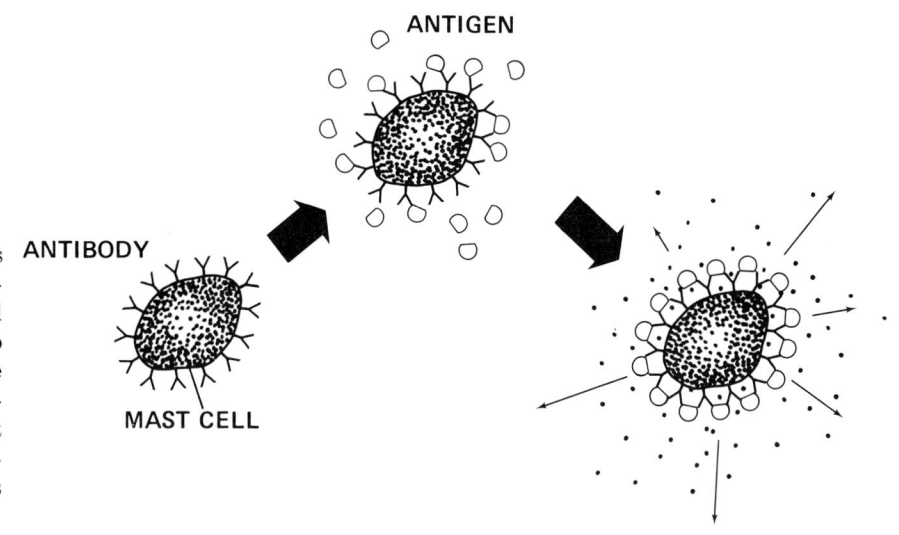

Fig. 4-2. Antibodies against various substances to which the child is allergic are attached to the mast cells. When the offending substance (antigen) comes in contact with the antibody, the release of various chemicals occurs.

the antigen and antibody leads to an explosive reaction and release of chemicals from the mast cells of the body (histamine, serotonin, bradykinin, SRS-A). These chemicals, in turn, produce the symptoms we call allergy (Fig. 4-2). The allergic reaction can take place in various parts of the body, such as the nose (allergic rhinitis or hay fever), lungs (asthma), eyes (allergic conjunctivities), and skin (eczema or hives). One of the most serious reactions occurs in the lungs.

It is still not clear why the allergic individual reacts so explosively to substances that, in a nonallergic individual, are inoffensive and tolerated. The original term "allergy," coined by Clemens von Pirquet in 1906, classified the response as "altered reactivity." This is still the accepted definition today.

Two basic factors are at work when asthma occurs. First, there is a constitutional predisposition on the part of the individual to form allergy antibodies, and second, he must have contact with offending substances (allergens) to which he will react. The substances to which a predisposed person may become allergic and against which he will make antibodies can be divided broadly into ingestants and inhalants. Younger children are more prone to have asthma from ingestants. Some of the most common offenders in early childhood are milk, eggs, nuts, chocolate, wheat, and citrus fruits. As a child grows older, he generally tends to develop greater tolerance to foods, but some people continue to have acute and severe reactions to a variety of specific foods. Another large class of ingestants is drugs. A reaction to drugs is highly variable from one individual to another. It can be very mild in some (itching or hives) and overwhelming in others (asthma or shock). The degree of allergic reaction or the intensity of asthma seems unrelated to the amount of drug ingested. One penicillin tablet can be as dangerous as 20 to the allergic individual.

Inhalants can be divided into two general classes—indoor and outdoor. The common outdoor ones are grass, tree, and weed pollens. When these substances are primarily responsible for a child's asthma, there is usually seasonal change in the severity of his disease. Tree and grass pollens tend to be most troublesome in spring, while weed pollens are more of a problem in the fall. The child is more likely to wheeze outside than in the house, and his symptoms will be exacerbated by play in areas of high-intensity exposure (such as on a freshly cut lawn in the spring).

Indoor inhalants are multiple and varied. The most common one is house dust, but substances such as wool, feathers, kapok, and animal dander may all play a role. Asthma from this type of inhalant does not usually vary as much with the seasons. Heating systems that distribute inhalants may make for more symptoms in the winter. Other inhalants that may cause much trouble are molds. They can be found indoors and outdoors at almost any time of the year, especially in coastal climates. In areas where there are hot, humid summers, the mold count is highest during that time of year. The mold count out of doors drops sharply in the winter in areas cold enough for snow to occur, but areas where rain is prominent in the winter have increasing mold counts at that time. Desert climates have the lowest mold growth.

We have discussed specific substances that may trigger an asthmatic attack in a particular child. A child's environment can affect his asthma in ways other than providing specific allergens. It has long been known that exposure to cold can precipitate attacks of asthma. In many individuals, asthmatic episodes seem to be more frequent with barometric change, dampness, wind, or very low indoor humidity. Smog—although not an allergen per se because it does not provoke an antibody reaction even in allergic individuals—can act as an irritant and flare several chronic pulmonary disorders such as asthma, emphysema, and chronic bronchitis. Severe environmental pollution (combined with inversion layers in the atmosphere) brought about the deaths of many persons with chronic respiratory disease in the tragedies of London, England, and Donora, Pennsylvania. Other irritants besides smog which may similarly provoke asthmatics include tobacco smoke, hair sprays, perfume, and chemical vapors. Environment can also play a role in asthma by exposing children to respiratory infections which may in themselves precipitate asthmatic episodes.

None of these environmental factors will produce asthma in an individual who is not predisposed. The constitutional predisposition has a strong hereditary component. One can readily elicit a history of allergies in the immediate family of most children with asthma. The allergies of the other family members may manifest themselves in disorders other than asthma and the offending substances may be different from those that trigger attacks in the asthmatic child. For example, a mother might be allergic to cats, but her son or daughter might be allergic only to dogs. All three could be allergic to cats but one might develop eczema, another allergic rhinitis, and another asthma upon exposure to the same cat. Surprisingly often, however, related individuals do react to the same substances in the same way.

Asthma can start at any age. The age of onset can, at times, give a clue as to the causative factors. The infant who wheezes because of allergies before one year of age is most likely to have a food allergy. Wheezing starting between one and five years of age is often caused by allergies to common household substances such as house dust, animal danders, and molds. The onset of allergies to tree, grass, and weed pollens usually occurs after age five.

As children grow older, they may develop greater tolerance to some allergens and seem to "outgrow" their allergic difficulties. Unfortunately, the opposite is often the case, and increasing trouble with wheezing occurs as more and more allergens provoke more frequent attacks of asthma. It is not unusual for an older child to be allergic to a combination of foods, house dusts, animal danders, molds, and pollens.

In the past it was thought that asthma was somehow produced by the presence of smoldering, chronic infection localized in the sinuses, tonsils, or teeth. Tonsils were often removed on this basis. For the most part, this theory has been discarded, and asthma is not considered a phenomenon secondary to localized infection elsewhere than in the lungs. The criteria for removing tonsils and adenoids, treating sinus infection, and dealing with dental problems should be essentially the same for a child with asthma as for any other child.

The thymus gland, which is beneath the breastbone, was once thought to cause asthma by mechanical pressure on the trachea and bronchial tubes. X-ray therapy was used to shrink the thymus. This practice has been discarded and is now condemned, since radiation can have long-term harmful results and it does not influence asthma.

EMOTIONAL FACTORS

Emotions are not the primary underlying cause of asthma, but emotional factors may play a big role in precipitating asthmatic attacks in many children. The child must have the constitutional predisposition to develop asthma, and he must have developed it on the basis of sensitization to various substances. Once asthma has been established, acute attacks may be triggered by emotions. There is a physiologic basis for some emotionally precipitated attacks, particularly when the emotional upset is accompanied by shouting, crying, and rapid breathing. In an experimental situation, one can produce spasm of the bronchial tubes by rapid breathing. We have, then, a frightening disease to which it is impossible for patient or family not to react with some degree of emotion. We have also a disease whose attacks are triggered or worsened by emotion. It is easy to see, therefore, why it becomes impossible after a time to separate problems which are precipitating asthmatic attacks from those that are secondary to the asthma. The "secondary gain" that may be derived by any child from illness can become a significant problem in asthma. Upsetting the child may produce an asthmatic attack which will bring inconvenience, concern, and perhaps guilt to those around him. It is not hard to understand why the asthmatic child often controls his family or others with whom he interacts.

SYMPTOMS

Asthma usually starts as isolated episodes of wheezing which are relatively mild and of short duration. The initial attacks are most often precipitated by respiratory infections. With time, as allergic exposures and difficulties continue, attacks become more frequent and can occur under almost any circumstances, any season of the year, day or night, indoors or outdoors. All too often the causative factors are unknown to the individual. Since the interval between exposure to allergens and the onset of an attack is quite variable and may, at times, be many hours, the precipitating factors go unrecognized.

Later, when attacks are less frequently precipitated by infection, there often will still be a clear running nose before the onset of wheezing. Rather than being a cold, this may represent nasal allergy, and, after a time varying from minutes to hours, it is followed by the onset of a characteristic, dry, hacking nonproductive cough. The cough is so typical that the parents and child both realize that wheezing will soon commence. If the attack is at all severe, the child's activity will diminish considerably. He will sit with his shoulders hunched forward, laboring hard to breathe. His whole chest moves with each respiratory effort, his nostrils may flare, and the noise of his breathing is easily audible. He may appear quite anxious and apprehensive. If the attack is very severe, there may be blueness of his fingertips and lips (Fig. 4-3).

Not all asthmatic attacks will be so marked, and some are mild

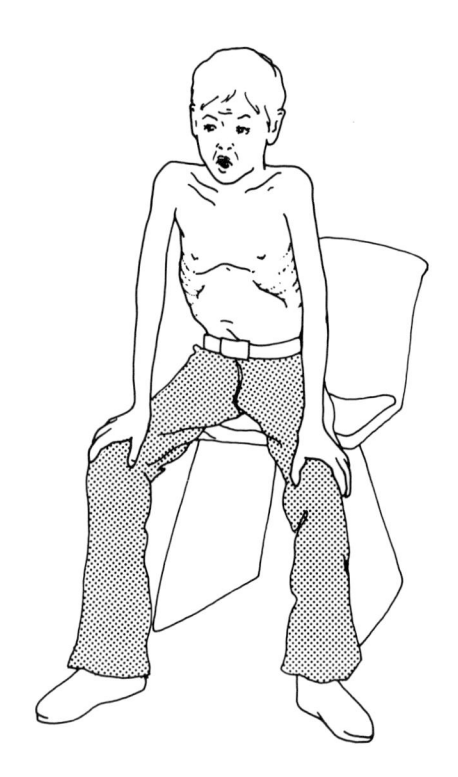

Fig. 4-3. Appearance of a child during an asthmatic attack. He may sit forward in his chair, place his hands on his knees, hunch his shoulders, and breathe through his mouth, all in an attempt to get air in and out of his lungs.

enough to require little treatment. With many children, especially early in the course of the disease, the episodes will terminate abruptly and the child will be free of any wheeze until the next acute attack occurs. In other children, especially as the duration of disease is prolonged, the wheeze will not end abruptly but will gradually decrease in severity and will persist in mild form between acute exacerbations. Thus, some children with rather marked asthma can be heard to wheeze all through the day in a very mild, almost inaudible way. Wheezing will become quite audible only in response to running, laughing, cold weather, and irritants.

TYPES OF ASTHMA

Some allergists divide asthma into two general clinical types. Although many children do not fit into either category, and some have characteristics of both, there is usefulness to the classification, since the treatment and outlook are somewhat different in the two groups. One type is called the *dermal respiratory syndrome,* or "allergic triad" of eczema, rhinitis (inflammation of mucous membranes of the nose), and asthma. These children have eczema in infancy. This is followed by frequent illnesses which appear to be colds but are usually allergic episodes involving the nose. Wheezing ensues in about 50 percent of these children within several years. The family history of allergy is quite strong, usually on both sides of the family. In addition to allergic factors, symptoms are often precipitated in these families by nonspecific irritational factors such as infection, air pollutants, emotional trauma, fatigue, chilling, and medicines. Asthmatic episodes are usually preceded by antecedent symptoms which are quite variable from one child to another, but each child tends to have his own pattern. The antecedent symptoms may include abdominal pain, headaches, constipation, diarrhea, changes in appetite, bed wetting, an itching throat, or changes in behavior, such as irritability, whining, hyperactivity, or listlessness. These variable and often complex symptom patterns have been described as the *allergy tension fatigue syndrome*. Mood changes may precede an attack by as much as twelve hours, and, since many attacks occur at night, some of these changes in disposition may be expected to come during school hours. Between episodes of wheezing, children who have this type of asthma frequently sneeze, cough, or wheeze when exposed to chemical irritants, sudden chilling, or emotional stress. The course of the disease has some relation to the nature of specific allergens, the degree of sensitivity of the child, and the amount of exposure to the particular allergens. They are generally the most difficult to treat. Their allergy problems have begun very early in life and include many allergic sensitivities. It is not unusual to find food, mold, animal dander, house dust, and pollen sensitivities intertwined in a year-round pattern of asthma, with only minimal changes in degree of severity from day to day. If these children are not treated effectively, they can become pulmonary cripples in adolescence or later life.

The second type of asthma is called *allergic rhinitis asthma*. These children have asthma associated with hay fever or, sometimes, with perennial allergic rhinitis. The nasal symptoms often precede asthma by several years, but occasionally onset is simultaneous. Approximately a third of the children with allergic rhinitis will develop asthma within a five-year period after the onset of their nasal symptoms. Children with this type of asthma usually have very specific inhalant allergens, relatively easy to identify and treat. They also have the advantage of having developed their allergy symptoms later in life, and they have generally escaped the eczema problems which are so prominent in the "allergic triad" children. Their allergens are most often airborne, and sensitivity to them can be demonstrated by skin testing. Again the severity of symptoms tends to vary with the level of the patient's sensitivity and with the frequency, duration, and amount of exposure to the offending substances. Nonspecific factors such as environmental conditions also operate in this type of asthma, but not to the degree they do in the allergic triad type. The outlook for control and improvement in this type of asthma is considerably better than in the preceding type.

OTHER CAUSES OF WHEEZING

All asthmatics wheeze, but "all that wheezes is not allergic asthma." This should also be kept in mind, because all too often the automatic assumption is that any child who is wheezing has asthma. Wheezing can be due to a variety of nonallergic causes. In the first year or two of life, because of the very small diameter of the airway, almost any disease which primarily affects the bronchial tubes may result in wheezing. Children who have respiratory problems in the newborn period or have pneumonias in the first several months of life will often wheeze during the subsequent several years whenever they have minor respiratory infections. When a child aspirates a foreign body and it lodges in the bronchial tubes, wheezing will often result. Children with cystic fibrosis, whooping cough, and birth defects of the bronchial tubes also may wheeze.

Some acute episodes of wheezing that can be mistaken for asthma are actually croup, bronchitis, or bronchiolitis. All three of these infections are self-limited acute illnesses. The only relationship with asthma is that children who have bronchiolitis appear more often to develop asthma in later years than children who do not have such an illness in early life.

CLINICAL COURSE

The course of asthma is variable and unpredictable. Some children will have attacks that are increasingly severe, while others, with the passage of time, will have milder and less frequent episodes. Attacks may start without predisposing illnesses. Duration can be minutes or hours or, on occasion, days. Some attacks have obvious precipitating factors, while other will occur quite suddenly. In childhood, asthma is more common in boys, while, after puberty, it becomes more common in girls. This is apparently due to an increased likelihood of symptoms disappearing in males at puberty rather than an increased incidence in females. It is not clear that this disappearance means permanent freedom from asthma. There is no way of knowing which children will outgrow asthma and which will have only a quiescent period that will end when their asthma flares again in their twenties or thirties. Many who are apparently asthma-free will continue to have abnormal lung-function tests for many years. It often seems that nasal allergy symptoms increase as asthma wanes, indicating a change of symptoms without a real end to sensitivity.

PROGNOSIS

The outlook for a child with asthma is influenced by factors other than sex. The longer the duration of symptoms (particularly before the onset of treatment) and the more severe the attacks, the poorer the outlook for complete clearing with no residual damage. With effective therapy, the majority of children can obtain either complete relief or, at least, a significant lessening in the severity of attacks. The child may develop a large, rounded, barrel-shaped chest from asthma in childhood, but once there is no longer obstruction to the flow of air out of the lungs these changes will gradually diminish. The chest deformity occurs because of dilation of the air sacs in the lungs. In asthma, the sacs maintain their normal elasticity and architecture and they can, over a period of time, gradually return to normal size. This is in contrast to emphysema, which gives the same outward appearance to the chest, but in which there is deterioration of the walls of the air sacs, as well as a decrease in the elasticity of the tissues between air sacs. These changes are permanent. Thus, asthma in children, even in its most severe form, does not lead to emphysema, as is too often mistakenly believed.

MORTALITY RATE

The mortality rate for asthma in childhood is much lower than in later life, but, because of the large number of children with asthma, it is a major hazard of childhood. The worldwide mortality rate gradually fell until approximately 1963, when an upward trend began to develop in the number of sudden, unexpected deaths in both adults and children. It has been suggested that the increased death rate may be related to the use of pressurized aerosol medicines that dilate the bronchial tree. Cortisone and related drugs have also been implicated as a possible causative factor in the increased death rate from asthma, but the evidence seems to implicate pressurized aerosols more strongly. Some researchers believe that the Freon propellant, by inducing abnormal heart action, is responsible for the increase in mortality. Others believe the medicine delivered by the propellant to be the cause of death. In 1967 there were in this country 159 deaths in children under 15 from asthma. Approximately 31,000 people of all ages die each year in the United States from "bronchitis, emphysema, asthma," and approximately 4,000 of these deaths are due solely to asthma.

TREATMENT

Treatment can be divided into two major intentions—that designed to prevent episodes of asthma and that designed to treat an acute attack.

The most important technique by which asthma is prevented is elimination of as many offending substances as possible from the environment. Since approximately 50 percent of a child's life is spent in his bedroom, the first efforts are directed toward making his room as allergy-free as possible. Upholstered mattresses are encased in plastic or other airtight materials or are replaced with foam rubber. Feather and kapok pillows are removed. Wool blankets are replaced by synthetic or cotton types. Synthetic fibers are used for carpets, and foam pads are used instead of those made of animal hair or felt. Bare floors without carpets or rugs are preferable. Stuffed animals containing kapok are removed and forced-air heating vents into the bedroom are closed and sealed. Elaborate (and dusty) drapes are replaced by simple cotton ones which are readily washable. Upholstered furniture is removed and an attempt is made to reduce the general clutter and as many dust catchers as possible. Similar efforts are made to keep the rest of the house as free of potential allergens as possible. Thus, stuffed furniture is avoided, pets (cats, dogs, birds, and other furry animals) are either kept outside or dispensed with, and attempts are made to correct the heating system. If forced-air heating is used, filtering devices can be added to the circulating system of the heating unit. Electrostatic precipitators are used in the child's room to remove as many allergens as possible from his nighttime environment and, if the family is to move, they are advised to find a house with radiant, rather than forced-air, heating.

Airborne pollens, house dust, and molds are extremely difficult, if not impossible, to avoid. Unless the family is to move, therapy for these types of allergens requires identification of the specific offending substances and reduction of the child's sensitivity to them by hyposensitization injections. A thorough history and physical examination with appropriate laboratory studies and diagnostic skin testing help to determine specific offending substances as closely as possible. Then an extract is prepared containing these substances. The allergic individual is injected initially with a minute amount of his allergens and, in a step-by-step process, is given increasingly higher doses of these same allergens. With each injection, his immune system forms progressively higher doses of a protective or "blocking" antibody, which renders him less allergic when the appropriate dosage is achieved (Fig. 4-4). This process usually takes several months to approach an effective antibody level. It is then continued by giving "booster" injections of the maintenance dose at regular intervals over an extended period of time. Such attempts at hyposensitization are able only to make the person less reactive and cannot cure the allergy. It is effective primarily for inhalant allergens and cannot be used for food allergy. Although hyposensitization is generally accepted in the treatment of asthma, the data are not entirely conclusive, and final evaluation of the validity of this therapy is not possible. Hyposensitization is no substitute for avoidance. A child who is allergic to grasses should not be permitted to roll around in the grass or to mow the lawn simply because he has recieved hyposensitization treatment.

Breathing exercises and mechanical drainage of the lungs are used in the long-range treatment. Children are taught how to breathe efficiently so as to get air in and out of the lungs with the least expenditure of effort. This tends to avoid panic when there is difficulty in breathing. Mechanical drainage is accomplished by placing the child in various posi-

Fig. 4-4. The antibodies against various substances to which the child is allergic are attached to the mast cells. Blocking antibodies attach to the mast cell with its antibodies. This does not result in a release of mast cell chemicals. The offending substances (antigens) cannot unite with mast cell antibodies, and the release of mast cell chemicals is thus avoided.

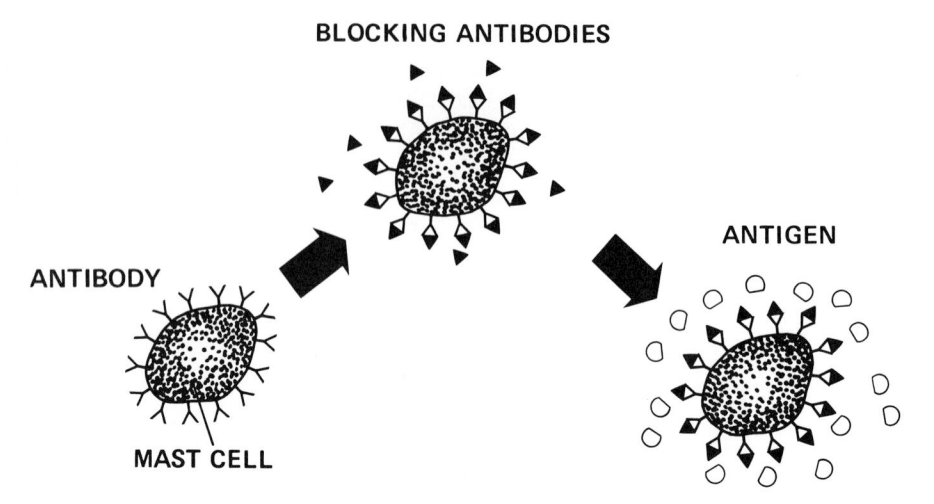

tions and pounding his chest (Fig. 4-5). This form of therapy appears to be effective in those children who have copious bronchial secretions as part of their asthma.

Since attacks of asthma can be triggered by respiratory infections, it becomes important to treat such infections early and vigorously to prevent the development of asthma. The use of drugs to control asthmatic episodes, when started early, sometimes appears to abort an asthmatic attack.

During an attack of asthma, drugs to relax the muscles of the bronchial tree are most important. Two major groups of drugs are used: theophylline drugs and adrenaline-like drugs. Because they exercise their effect by two different mechanisms, they can be used in combination. Theophylline drugs are usually given orally, except when a child is hospitalized, in which case they are given intravenously. Our ability to monitor easily the level of these drugs in the blood has made them a safe and effective first-line treatment. The second group is the adrenaline-like drugs. They are given orally, by injection, or by aerosol. Their effect may be extremely rapid or quite prolonged. When they are given by pressurized aerosol, overuse becomes easy; misuse of this form of therapy may possibly have increased the mortality rate in asthmatic children. This form of drug therapy should be used only with careful supervision.

Other drugs used for acute episodes of asthma include sedatives (for relaxation) and cough medicines (for decreasing the thickness of mucus). In very severe attacks, cortisone or related drugs may be needed. It is

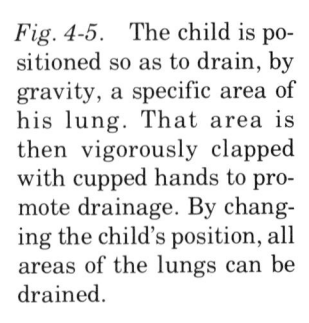

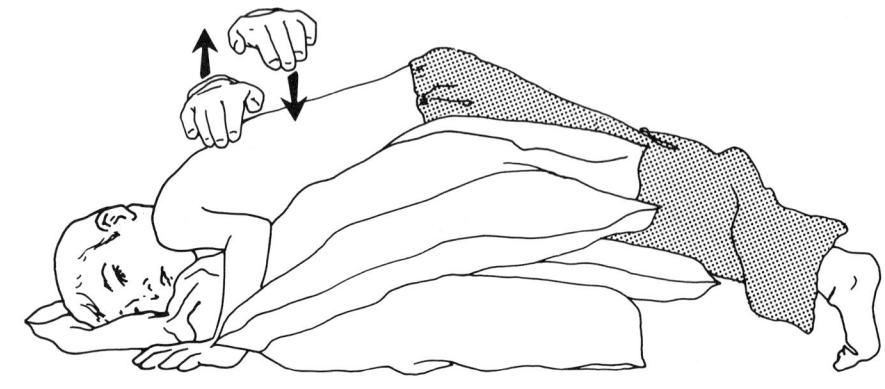

Fig. 4-5. The child is positioned so as to drain, by gravity, a specific area of his lung. That area is then vigorously clapped with cupped hands to promote drainage. By changing the child's position, all areas of the lungs can be drained.

most important to stop the use of cortisone as promptly as possible following the end of an acute attack. All too often, when cortisone is used for an extended period of time, the patient becomes unable to stop taking it without causing a flare of the asthma. Its continued use may be associated with potentially serious side-effects. Another drug for the treatment of children with asthma is called Aarane or Intal (disodium cromoglycate). It is taken by inhalation on a regular basis. Its apparent effect is to decrease the explosive release of chemical factors produced when inhalant allergens enter and react in the respiratory tract. Thus it often decreases the need for cortisone in children who have become dependent on this drug and, in general may make asthma less severe.

When a child has become dependent upon daily cortisone to keep asthma under control, weaning from this potentially dangerous therapy can be accomplished in a variety of ways. Some children may be controlled satisfactorily by long-term, continuous use of a combination of theophylline and adrenaline-like drugs. Others may function well using a poorly absorbed aerosol preparation of a cortisone-like drug, thus reaping the benefits of cortisone, while avoiding the side effects. Lastly, asthma may be controlled in some children by the use of cortisone on alternate days. Side effects are decreased in comparison to daily use, but they are still more troublesome than when a cortisone-like aerosol is used.

Tonsillectomy, adenoidectomy, the administration of gamma globulin, and other forms of therapy have had periods of vogue. They are not considered to be effective. In children who have a true sensitivity to a particular bacterium, improvement may be noted following treatment with the appropriate vaccine or extract. Although they are widely used, there is no evidence that vaccines made from general respiratory bacteria to which sensitivity has *not* been proven are helpful. There are, of course, other forms of therapy which, although not generally accepted, have enthusiastic devotees. These range from the magical to the more conventional treatment espoused by physicians who have noticed improvement in their patients.

The long-range treatment of asthma requires that careful attention be paid to the interval between attacks and that support and education be given to the child and his or her parents as to the nature of the disease and the limitations it places on the child. The patient should understand that maintaining general health and avoiding smoking are particularly important. In special cases where emotional problems appear to be playing a leading role in triggering asthmatic attacks, psychotherapy or temporary residence in a setting outside the home may be advisable. One should be careful, however, not to assume that emotional symptoms in the patient or family are the cause of asthma rather than the result.

THE ASTHMATIC CHILD IN THE CLASSROOM

Since a child with asthma may react to many substances in his environment, it is important to try to avoid bringing into the classroom potential inhalants which may trigger a child's attack. Before deciding on a class pet, for example, it is worthwhile talking with the family to find out whether the child reacts to animal danders. Pets such as turtles, fish, salamanders, and lizards, which have no dander, are essentially nonallergenic.

If foods are going to be served at class parties, attempts should be made to avoid those which might precipitate problems for an allergic student. If such avoidance is not possible, an appropriate substitute should be available for the asthmatic child.

Children with asthma may often have to take medicine in class to keep mild asthma from becoming severe. This is necessary and appropriate. However, if the child has a pressurized aerosol, it is extremely important that the teacher carefully check with the family about the frequency with which it may be used.

Exercise may readily induce wheezing. However, this must be counterbalanced by the need of the child with asthma to participate as fully as possible in physical education programs so as not to be different from his peers. In general, swimming is the best sport, and games requiring short bursts of physical activity (baseball) are better than endurance sports (soccer and running). If the child is particularly allergic to grass pollens, it may be wise to avoid having him play in grassy playground areas during physical education or recess. Some children have a form of asthma that is induced by exercise. Taking a theophylline drug or an adrenaline-like drug shortly before exercise may prevent this group from having asthma during physical activity. The child with asthma should not be permitted to use his disease as a device for getting his own way. Mild attacks may be controlled in the class by having the child sit down and rest and breathe easily, without too much attention from teacher or classmates. Some physicians advocate drinking warm water as a means of stopping mild episodes. The asthmatic child should be treated like all other children in the class whenever possible.

BIBLIOGRAPHY

Blanc, A. D. G., *So You Have Asthma.* Springfield, Ill., Charles C. Thomas, 1966.

Dees, S. *Diseases of the Respiratory Tract in Children,* vol. 1, 2nd ed. Philadelphia, W. B. Saunders, 1972, pp. 424–466.

Feingold, B. F., *Introduction to Clinical Allergy,* Springfield, Ill., Charles C. Thomas, 1973.

Gordis, L., *Epidemiology of Chronic Lung Disease in Children.* Baltimore, Johns Hopkins Press, 1973.

Kaplin, I., *The Allergic Asthmatic.* Springfield Ill., Charles C. Thomas, 1968.

5

Cancer in Childhood

MICHAEL P. LINK, M.D.

Cancer is uncommon in childhood. Despite the relative rarity, however, cancer is an important health problem in the young—second only to accidents and injury as a killer of children between the ages of 1 and 15. Recent progress in treatment has greatly improved the prognosis for children with cancer, allowing for prolonged, relatively normal survival for most patients and even long-term cure for many of them. As more children with cancer survive for longer periods of time, the adverse effects of cancer treatment on the physical and psychological maturation of the child have emerged as unforeseen problems. Modern therapy is designed to interfere as little as possible with the child's normal growth and development and to allow the usual childhood activities, especially schooling, to continue during the treatment period.

EPIDEMIOLOGY The incidence of cancer in children varies among different countries, as well as among racial groups. In the United States, the annual incidence among white children less than 15 years old is 12.45 for every 100,000. The incidence in black children is somewhat lower. Thus, nearly 7000 cases of childhood cancer are newly diagnosed in the United States each year.

DEFINITION Cancer is not a single disease but a large and heterogeneous group of diseases which share certain biological and pathological features. The many different types of cancer may arise from almost any of the diverse organs and tissues of the body. Normal body tissues are composed of billions of cells arranged in a specific architecture that is predetermined for each organ. Most tissue cells have the capacity to increase their numbers through the process of cell division. An individual cell divides into two identical daughter cells, each of which retains the capacity to divide further. This proliferation of cells allows for growth of the organ and tissues during development and for cellular renewal and repair processes in the mature individual. Under normal circumstances, cell division is carefully controlled, and cells differentiate (mature) in an orderly sequence. Neoplasia (tumor formation) represents the unrestrained, abnormal, and persistent proliferation of cells that results from a defect in the mechanisms that normally govern cell division and differentiation. The etiology of most tumors is unknown, but a variety of factors seem to interact in causing neoplasia. Genetic factors render certain individuals more susceptible to tumors, while certain environmental agents, such as chemicals, radiation, and some viruses, may be involved in stimulating abnormal cellular proliferation.

There is a great variability in the clinical course of tumors. Certain tumors grow slowly and are usually localized, without invasion of adjacent tissues and with no tendency to spread. Microscopically, such tumors are composed of well-differentiated (mature), relatively normal-appearing cells, few of which are in the process of dividing. These tumors are benign. By contrast, cancers (malignant tumors) tend to grow rapidly, invading and damaging adjacent structures. Microscopically, malignant tumors are composed of poorly-differentiated, bizarre-appearing abnormal cells (many of which are dividing) which distort and invade the surrounding normal tissues. Malignant tumors also invade the blood vessels, allowing tumor cells to break off and spread to other parts of the body where they establish additional, secondary tumors (metastases). Ultimately, overwhelming damage to particular organs caused by the primary tumor or by its metastases results in the failure of those organs and the death of the patient. The behavior of a tumor can thus be anticipated from its microscopic appearance, and the pathologic distinction between benign and malignant (cancerous) tumors is most important in determining prognosis and in planning therapy. (Rarely, a tumor that is microscopically benign may arise in a location near vital structures that is inaccessible to effective treatment, e.g., in the brain . The consequences of such "benign" tumors may be as catastrophic as those resulting from true malignancies.)

Malignant tumors are classified according to a variety of features which can be observed under the microscope. The neoplasms are named according to the normal tissues from which they are derived (e.g., rhabdomyosarcoma, connoting a fleshy tumor derived from skeletal muscle) or after the individual who first described a tumor as a clinical entity (e.g., Hodgkin's disease or Ewing's sarcoma). Cancer involving the blood-forming cells in the bone marrow is called leukemia. Specific microscopic criteria have been established for each type of tumor. Determination of the particular type of cancer is an important diagnostic step, since the behavior of the tumor—the likelihood of spread, the sites of metastases, or the response to various forms of therapy—can be predicted from the type of cancer.

The cancers seen in children are quite different from those seen in adults. Whereas tumors of the lung, breast, colon, and skin are very common in adults, these tumors are extraordinary in children. The most frequently encountered childhood malignancies are listed, with the relative incidence of each and the tissue of origin, in Table 5-1. As can be seen,

Cancer in Childhood

Table 5-1. Malignancies Encountered in Childhood

Malignancy	Tissue of Origin	Relative Incidence (%)
Leukemias		33.8
Acute lymphoblastic leukemia (ALL)	Bone marrow	
Acute myelogenous leukemia (AML)	Bone marrow	
Chronic myelogenous leukemia (CML)	Bone marrow	
Lymphomas		10.6
Hodgkin's disease	Lymph nodes	
Non-Hodgkin's lymphoma	Lymph nodes, thymus, and other sites	
Solid Tumors		
Central nervous system	Various tissues of brain and spinal cord	19.2
Glioma		
Medulloblastoma		
Ependymoma		
Neuroblastoma	Adrenal glands and sympathetic nervous system	7.7
Soft tissues		6.7
Rhabdomyosarcoma	Skeletal muscle	
Other miscellaneous soft tissue sarcomas	Various connective tissues (fat, tendons, etc.)	
Wilms' tumor	Kidney	6.0
Bone		4.5
Osteogenic sarcoma	Bone	
Ewing's sarcoma	?	
Retinoblastoma	Retina of eye	2.7
Sexual organs	Germ cells of ovary and testis	1–2
Ovary, testis		

leukemia is the most common childhood malignancy—the different types of leukemia together accounting for about one-third of all childhood cancer. Brain tumors and the lymphomas (cancer of the lymph nodes) occur relatively frequently. Wilms' tumor (cancer of the kidney) and neuroblastoma (cancer of nerve tissue) are common in infants and toddlers but rare in children over the age of 10 years. Bone cancers occur most often in adolescents and are unusual in young children.

DIAGNOSTIC TESTS

When a child is evaluated for a suspected malignancy, every effort is made to complete the diagnostic investigations promptly. The purpose of the diagnostic tests is to determine (1) whether or not cancer is present; (2) the type of cancer; and (3) the extent of the cancer. A careful physical examination is performed, with attention directed to abnormal masses (lumps), enlarged lymph nodes, or enlarged organs. Routine blood tests are done, but more sophisticated tests are usually necessary to assist in diagnosis and to follow the progress of therapy once the diagnosis is confirmed. The following list catalogs some of the diagnostic tests frequently utilized in evaluating the child with cancer; a description is given of the procedure and the purpose of each test.

1. *Biopsy.* A surgical procedure in which a piece of the suspected tumor (or, when possible, the entire tumor) is removed and prepared for examination under the microscope. The experienced pathologist can determine if the tissue is malignant and, if so, the specific type of cancer. The biopsy may be a simple office procedure if the tumor is small and superficially located, or it may involve an extensive operation if complete removal of a large neoplasm is undertaken.
2. *Bone marrow test.* An office procedure necessary to diagnose leukemia or to detect tumor metastases in the bone marrow. A small needle is inserted into one of the bones of the hip (usually posteriorly), where the bone can be felt just under the skin (Fig. 5-1). A local anesthetic is administered to minimize the discomfort. A sample of the bone marrow (which appears very much like normal blood) is withdrawn and is smeared onto slides for examination under the microscope.
3. *Lumbar puncture (spinal tap).* An office procedure to detect tumor cells (and, more commonly, leukemia cells) in the cerebrospinal fluid (CSF), a liquid, resembling water, that bathes the brain and spinal cord. The lumbar puncture is also done in order to inject drugs into the CSF. After a local anesthetic is administered to minimize the discomfort, a needle is introduced between the bones of the spine into the spinal canal (space around the spinal cord) (Fig. 5-2). The CSF is allowed to drip out through the needle, and the fluid can be examined microscopically for malignant cells.
4. *X-rays.* Standard x-rays are used frequently, as are specialized x-ray studies which provide additional information.
    a. *Tomography (laminography).* An x-ray technique which highlights details of structures lying in one body plane by blurring details of structures lying in other planes. Although specialized equipment is required, the test is simple and painless. The detailed x-ray pictures provided by tomography allow for detection of small tumors or metastases which might not be seen on conventional x-rays.
    b. *Intravenous pyelogram (IVP).* An x-ray of the kidneys and urinary tract. A radiopaque material (one which casts a shadow on x-rays) injected into a vein is concentrated and excreted by the kidneys. As the material is excreted, x-rays are taken which provide a detailed view of the kidneys and urinary tract. The IVP is useful in the diagnosis of tumors of or adjacent to the kidneys.
    c. *Gastrointestinal (GI) series (upper GI and barium enema).* A series of x-rays of the gastrointestinal tract. Barium (which is radiopaque) is swallowed or instilled by enema, and x-rays of the abdomen are taken. The gastrointestinal tract is clearly outlined, and abnormalities in or around the intestine can be detected.
    d. *Lymphangiogram.* An x-ray of the lymph nodes of the abdomen which is used to detect tumor involvement of lymph nodes. The lymphangiogram is especially useful in the evaluation of lymphomas. A special radiopaque material is injected into the tiny lymph vessels of the feet. The material spreads by lymph channels to the lymph nodes in the abdomen, and x-rays are taken which reveal detailed structure of the abdominal lymph nodes.

Cancer in Childhood

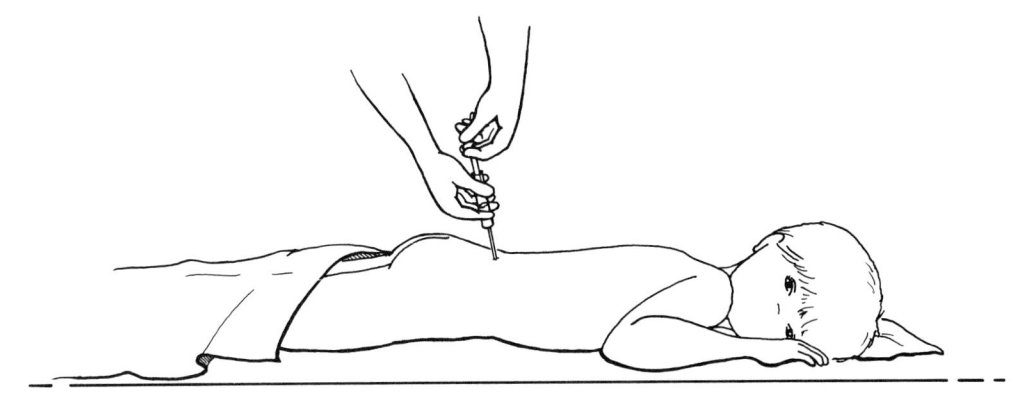

Fig. 5-1. Procedure for obtaining bone marrow for examination. The child is positioned prone, and the needle is inserted into the bones of the pelvis posteriorly. Bone marrow is withdrawn into a syringe.

      e. *Arteriogram.* A specialized x-ray study in which a catheter (plastic tube) is threaded into a specific artery, radiopaque contrast material is injected, and multiple x-rays are taken. The normal and abnormal tissues which derive their blood supply from the injected artery are highlighted. The local extent of a tumor can thus be readily ascertained.

5. *Computerized axial tomography (CAT scan).* A highly specialized technique in which the information from multiple x-ray projections—each taken from a slightly different angle—is synthesized by a computer to produce a very detailed composite representation of the organ being studied. The procedure is lengthy and expensive, but painless. CAT scanning is a new technique which has revolutionized diagnostic radiology by supplanting more invasive tests, especially for the diagnosis of brain tumors.

6. *Ultrasonography.* A technique akin to sonar, in which high-energy sound waves are propagated through tissues, and reflected sounds ("echoes") are converted to electrical signals which are projected on an oscilloscope screen. A "picture" of the internal structures is thus obtained. Ultrasonography is particularly useful in the detection of abdominal tumors. The test is simple and painless.

7. *Radionuclide scanning.* A radioactive substance which is concentrated by the organ of interest is injected into the blood stream, and the organ is scanned by a sophisticated Geiger counter. An image is produced on an oscilloscope. Normal organs and structures appear as homogeneous areas of radioactivity. Involvement of the organ by tumor appears as regions of increased or decreased radioactivity in the oscilloscope image of the organ (Fig. 5-3). Radionuclide scans of bone and liver are particularly useful in detecting tumor metastases to these structures.

Fig. 5-2. Lumbar puncture. The child is positioned curled up on his side. The needle is inserted between the bones of the spine into the spinal canal to obtain cerebrospinal fluid (CSF).

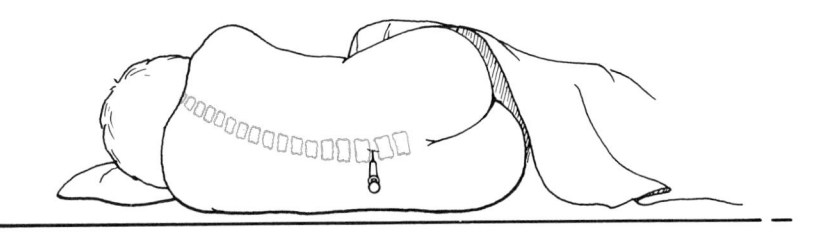

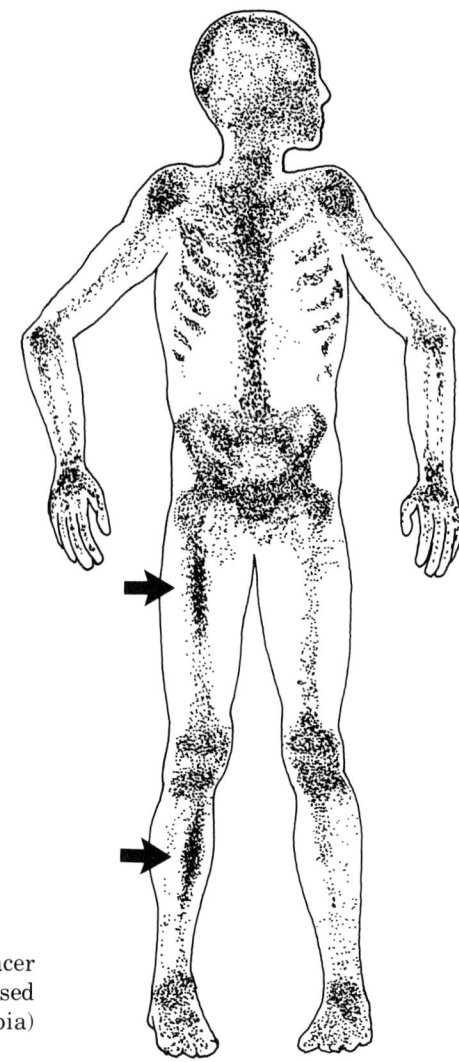

Fig. 5-3. A bone scan showing accumulation of the radioactive tracer in the bones of the skeleton. There are areas of asymmetric increased radioactivity (arrows) in the right thigh (femur) and shin (tibia) which represent metastases.

MODALITIES OF TREATMENT

The treatment of childhood cancer is a complex undertaking involving the combined efforts of many different subspecialists. Most children with cancer are cared for in centers which are equipped to handle the complicated medical, social, and psychological problems associated with the treatment of cancer. Modern cancer treatment involves surgery, radiation therapy, and chemotherapy (drug treatment), and representatives from each of these specialties are involved in planning the therapy for each patient. These specialists work with professionals from the fields of child psychiatry, social work, child development, and nutrition to provide each child with a comprehensive health management team to optimize care.

Surgery

In the past, surgery was the primary modality of therapy for cancer. Surgical removal of all tumor tissue was the only hope of cure. The operations were often extensive and disfiguring. Moreover, even radical surgery was rarely curative without additional therapy because of the tendency of malignant tumors to spread to other sites prior to diagnosis.

Cancer in Childhood

Improved understanding of cancer and tumor therapy has better defined the role of surgery. Certain tumors (e.g., rhabdomyosarcoma) are well controlled with radiation therapy and chemotherapy; thus, radical, disfiguring surgery can be avoided without compromising the potential for cure. Certain other tumors (e.g., osteogenic sarcoma) respond poorly to radiation therapy and chemotherapy, however, and radical operations are an integral part of treatment.

Radiotherapy

Less than 10 years after the discovery of x-rays by Wilhelm Roentgen in 1895, radiation was utilized in the treatment of cancer. With the dramatic advances in the understanding of radiation and the development of high-energy equipment, radiotherapy has evolved into a powerful modality for the treatment of malignancy. Radiotherapy is a technique for killing cancer cells by directing high-energy emissions at a tumor. The energy from the radiation disrupts the structure of atoms (by producing ions) and thus damages biologically essential molecules—particularly the chromosomes, which contain the genetic information of the individual cells. This damage, in turn, compromises the reproductive capacity of the cells and may produce lethal derangements in cellular metabolism. This results in the death of tumor cells and the eradication of the cancer. The radiation may be delivered in the form of electromagnetic radiation (x-rays and gamma rays) or in the form of particulate beams (neutrons and beta particles). X-rays and gamma rays are similar, but x-rays are produced by man-made generators, whereas gamma rays are naturally emitted by radioactive substances such as cobalt 60. These different radiation sources have different characteristics that can be exploited according to the specific needs of the patient. The quantity of radiation administered is carefully controlled. The dose is calculated in rads (radiation absorbed dose), which is a measurement of the amount of radiation actually absorbed by the tissues. Unfortunately, normal tissues adjacent to the tumor are also exposed to radiation, and some normal tissues in the irradiated region are unavoidably damaged. The dose of radiation that can be administered is limited by the ability of these normal tissues to withstand the effects of radiation (radiation tolerance). Certain organs (e.g., liver, kidney, lung, and intestine) tolerate radiation poorly, whereas other regions (e.g., brain and extremities) are relatively resistant to its effects. The dose of radiation required to control the tumor is often within the dose range that is likely to cause significant damage to surrounding normal structures and thus produce unacceptable complications. A technique to minimize the toxicity of radiation involves the use of *fractionated treatment,* in which the total quantity of radiation is delivered in multiple smaller doses over many days, rather than as a single large dose. The effectiveness of radiation against the tumor is not significantly compromised by the use of dose fractionation, but normal tissue tolerance is greatly improved.

When radiotherapy is utilized in the treatment of a childhood tumor, a careful plan is formulated at the outset which attempts to maximize tumor destruction, in the hopes of permanently eradicating the tumor while minimizing damage to normal tissues. A number of variables must be considered. The radiation dose required depends on the type of tumor as well as the size of the tumor, since different types of cancer respond to different radiation doses, and higher doses of radiation are required to eradicate large tumors. The exact treatment volume (region of the body to be treated) is meticulously designed. Lead shields, which block the transmission of radiation, are used to protect normal tissues, while allowing exposure of malignant tissues to the radiotherapy beam (Fig. 5-4). The most appropriate type of radiation (particles, x-rays, or gamma rays) must be selected. Occasionally, radioactive materials are surgically placed around the tumor (interstitial implants), although most radiotherapy is administered from external sources. Finally, the dose administered per fraction and the duration of therapy are outlined. Radiation treatments are typically given several days a week, and the total treatment course is administered over a week to several months, depending on the number of fractions and the total dose planned. Individual treatments last several minutes and are painless. The side effects of radiation treatment depend upon the region irradiated: nausea, vomiting, and loss of appetite complicate radiotherapy of the abdomen, while sores in the mouth may result from radiation damage to mucous membranes lining the mouth. Skin within the area irradiated may become transiently red and tender, and hair in the radiated field falls out. Radiation of the extremities causes few, if any, acute symptoms. There are also long-term side effects of the radiation because of permanent injury to normal structures. Normal tissues are able to repair much of the damage produced by radiation, but decreased growth of irradiated tissues and tanning of the skin (hyperpigmentation) in the area irradiated are frequent late side effects. Sterility results from radiation of the reproductive organs.

Chemotherapy

The era of cancer chemotherapy began in the 1940s with the demonstration by Gilman, Goodman, and Dougherty that a chemical relative of mustard gas (a chemical warfare agent used by the Germans in World War I) could be used to kill malignant cells in humans. In 1948, Farber and his associates achieved dramatic, although transient, results in the treatment of childhood leukemia with aminopterin—the forerunner of a drug used extensively in modern cancer therapy. In the three decades since these milestone discoveries, chemotherapy has emerged as a major form of cancer treatment, and many drugs are now available which have significant antitumor effects. Unlike surgery and radiation therapy, which are directed at specific regions of the body, drugs circulate in the bloodstream and are distributed to all of the tissues of the body. Thus, drugs can be used to treat tumors which have spread widely to many organs.

Chemotherapeutic agents work by entering into cells and disrupting vital metabolic processes, especially the functions necessary for cell division. The derangement of these processes causes cell death by mechanisms that are yet to be elucidated. Unfortunately, the full potential utility of chemotherapy in the treatment of childhood cancer has been limited by several practical realities. Drugs currently available are not very effective in the treatment of bulky tumors; rather, they are most useful against the residual microscopic deposits of malignant cells which persist after surgery and radiation therapy. Not all tumors respond to drugs, and certain tumors and leukemias, while responsive at first, become resistant and recur despite the continued administration of chemotherapy. Finally, the toxic side effects of drugs limit their effectiveness. Most of the drugs currently in use for the treatment of tumors are not

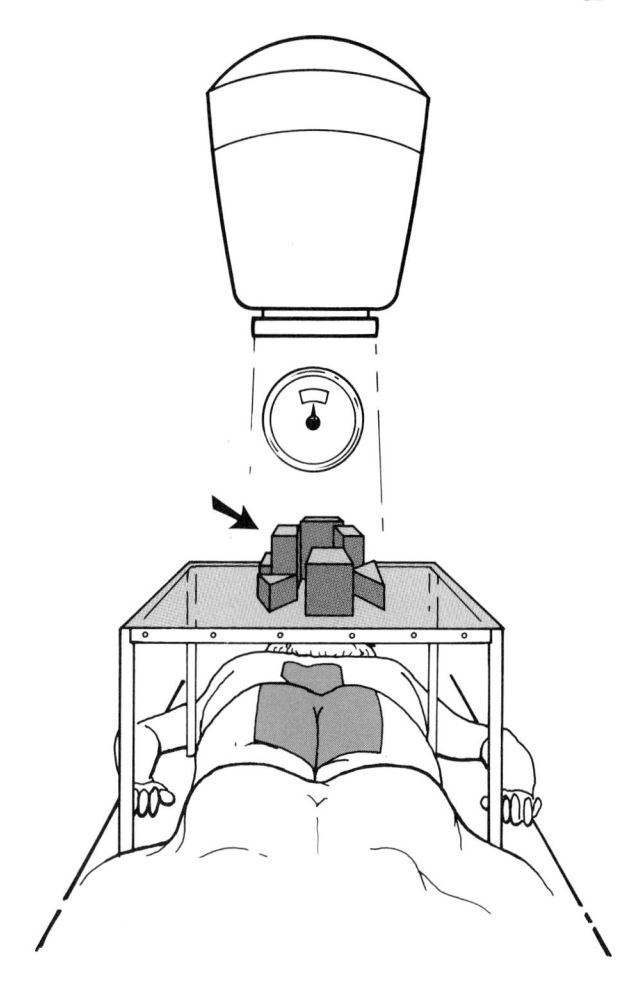

Fig. 5-4. A patient undergoing radiation treatment. The shaded area is the region to be irradiated. Meticulously shaped lead blocks (arrows) outline the radiation field and prevent radiation of normal tissues.

specifically active against cancer cells. Although malignant cells are relatively more vulnerable to the effects of chemotherapy, normal tissue cells are damaged and killed as well. The side effects of chemotherapy result from this lack of specificity. As in radiotherapy, drugs are used in a way which attempts to maximize the antitumor effects while minimizing the toxicity, but certain side effects often must be accepted as the price of therapy. Since almost all of the toxicity from chemotherapy is reversible and short-lived, the price seems small in view of the potential benefits. The most frequently encountered side effects of chemotherapy include nausea and vomiting while the drugs are administered, temporary hair loss, and reduction in the number of circulating blood cells (low blood counts). These toxicities produce varying degrees of physical and psychological disability for the cancer patient. However, the effects of chemotherapy on normal blood cells constitute the greatest threat to the patient. The normal red blood cells, white blood cells, and platelets are produced in the bone marrow and circulate in the blood stream, serving functions vital to survival. The red blood cells deliver necessary oxygen to tissues; the white blood cells protect against infection; and the platelets are tiny cells which play an important role in blood clotting to prevent excessive bleeding from tissue injury. A decrease in the number of circulating red blood cells (known as anemia) results in easy fatigability, pallor, and decreased exercise tolerance. A decrease in the number of circulating white blood cells (leukopenia) leads to increased susceptibility to severe, and potentially fatal, infections. A lowered platelet count (thrombocytopenia) results in easy bruisability and excessive bleeding with trauma. If blood counts fall excessively, children receiving chemotherapy may require blood transfusions in order to prevent these dangerous complications.

THE CHILD WITH A MALIGNANT TUMOR

Children with neoplasms are most often brought to the attention of physicians because of the appearance of a mass (abnormal growth) or because of symptoms resulting from the destruction of normal tissues by the tumor (Fig. 5-5). The most common such symptom is pain, which is especially frequent when the tumor is malignant and involves a bone. The symptoms depend entirely upon the location of the tumor and may be dramatic if the tumor is growing rapidly. On the other hand, certain tumors may produce few or no symptoms and may be detected on routine physical examination or on an x-ray taken for unrelated reasons. In the early stages of the disease, children with malignant tumors may appear remarkably well, but, in more advanced cases with widespread metastases, children appear chronically ill and may lose weight rapidly.

A biopsy is required to determine if the tumor is malignant, as well as to ascertain the type of cancer. The surgeon may remove the entire tumor at the time of biopsy if this is feasible, but malignant tumors are often inoperable. When the diagnosis has been ascertained, a thorough search for evidence of metastases (secondary tumors) is undertaken, utilizing many of the procedures listed above.

The treatment of a child with a malignant tumor depends upon a variety of factors, notably the type and extent of the cancer. Prior to the advent of effective therapy, these tumors could be expected to spread, and almost all affected children died. For some children with certain widespread tumors, there is little hope for cure even with modern treatment methods, and the goal of treatment is to keep the child as comfortable as possible (palliative therapy). For most children with cancer, effective treatment is now available, and cure is a reasonable expectation. The discomforts which may arise from aggressive therapy are acceptable in the treatment of these children because of the curative intent of the therapy. However, the therapeutic plan also aims to achieve long-term cure with a minimum of long-term sequelae and with a minimum possible disruption of normal life during therapy.

The specifics of the therapeutic plan depend upon the individual case. Many tumors are treated primarily with radiotherapy in order to avoid disfiguring surgery as much as possible; some tumors respond poorly to radiation therapy, and radical surgery (e.g., amputation) is required. In some cases, radiotherapy is administered after surgical removal of a tumor when the malignant tumor is incompletely excised.

Therapy directed entirely to the treatment of the primary tumor is rarely curative in childhood cancer. Early in the course of the disease, before the cancer can be detected, small groups of malignant cells from the primary tumor invade the bloodstream and spread to other organs. By the time of diagnosis, numerous microscopic metastases are already established which are not detectable with the diagnostic techniques now available. Untreated, these subclinical metastases progressively enlarge and are ultimately responsible for the death of the patient. Thus, most children with cancer are treated with chemotherapy, which circulates throughout the body to destroy occult metastases, in addition to the surgical and/or radiation therapy used to treat the primary tumor. The type of chemotherapy depends upon the specific tumor being treated. One to

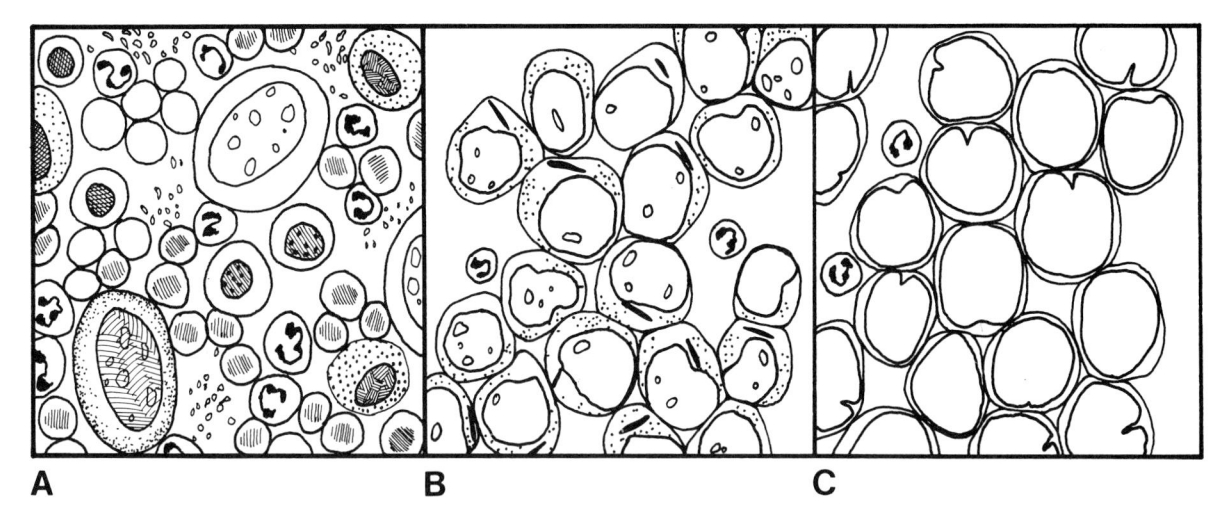

Fig. 5-5. The microscopic appearance of the bone marrow. (A) Normal bone marrow, demonstrating the many different cell types involved in the production of normal blood cells. (B, C) Bone marrow invaded by leukemia, with almost complete absence of normal blood-forming cells. (B) Artist's rendition of the blast cells in acute myelogenous leukemia. (C) The blast cells of acute lymphoblastic leukemia.

three years of chemotherapy are required to treat most childhood tumors, since experience has demonstrated that multiple courses of chemotherapy are required to destroy the residual malignant cells. Reappearance of the tumor usually results from the proliferation of tumor cells which are resistant to the drugs being used. Tumor recurrence is most likely to occur in the first 2 years after diagnosis, but later recurrences (even after chemotherapy has been completed) also occur. Recurrence of the tumor at any time is an ominous sign, and few patients with recurrent cancer can be cured.

The team approach to childhood cancer and more intensive treatment with surgery, radiation therapy, and chemotherapy have produced a gratifying improvement in the survival of children with malignancies. The prognosis for children with solid tumors is variable and depends on the type of tumor and the extent of disease at diagnosis. The majority of children with Wilms' tumor and Hodgkin's disease can be expected to do well with current treatment strategies. Improvements in therapy have brightened the outlook for children with bone tumors. On the other hand, the prognosis for children with brain tumors remains unfavorable, despite aggressive treatment.

THE CHILD WITH LEUKEMIA

Leukemia is a form of cancer in which there is a malignant proliferation of abnormal cells in the bone marrow. The bone marrow is a soft, fatty substance which fills the cavity of the bones of the skeleton and is the site of the production of normal blood cells. The invasion of the bone marrow by leukemia interferes with the production of the normal components of blood. Children with leukemia present with symptoms related to the deficiencies of normal blood cells—i.e., anemia, excessive bleeding, and infection. Leukemia may be suspected from the abnormal blood counts, but a bone marrow test is performed to make the diagnosis. The abnormal cells which fill the bone marrow in leukemia are immature blood cells referred to as *blasts*. The blast cells may also leave the marrow, circulate in the bloodstream, and invade other organs—especially

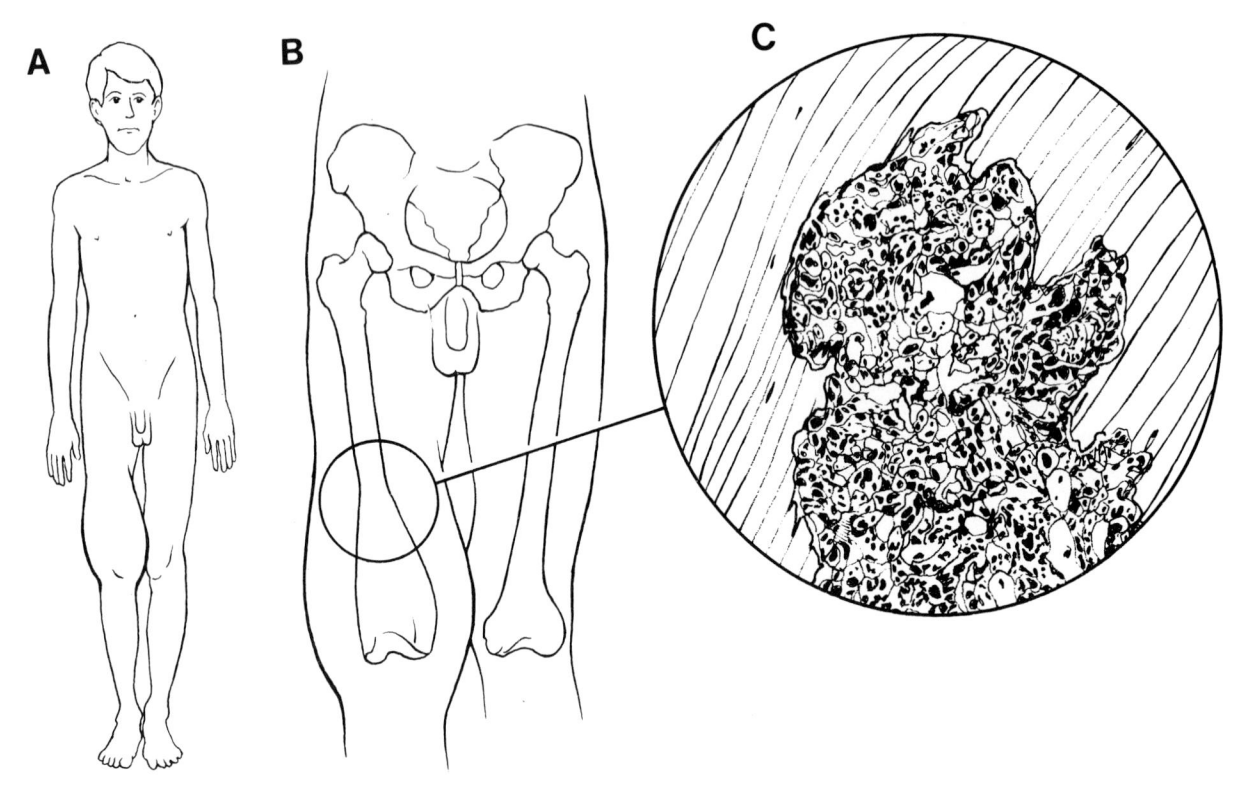

Fig. 5-6. A child with a malignant tumor of the right thigh. (A) The tumor appears as a mass above the right knee. (B) The tumor originates in the bone, causing abnormal expansion of the bone end, and extends into the soft tissues of the thigh. (C) The microscopic appearance of the malignant tumor shows it to be composed of many individual cells that invade upward into the surrounding normal bone.

the lymph nodes, liver, and spleen. The leukemic cells may also spread to the central nervous system (the brain, spinal cord, and cerebrospinal fluid).

The different types of leukemia are distinguished on the basis of the microscopic appearance of blast cells in the bone marrow (Fig. 5-6). More than 70 percent of children with leukemia have acute lymphoblastic leukemia (ALL) and 20–30 percent have acute myelogenous leukemia (AML) or one of its variants. In general, children with ALL have a much more favorable prognosis.

The principles of the treatment of leukemia in childhood are similar to those applied in treating malignant solid tumors. Leukemia is invariably widely disseminated throughout the bone marrow, bloodstream, and many organs of the body at the time of diagnosis. Treatment thus depends primarily on chemotherapy. The initial phase of therapy (called *induction*) attempts to eliminate all detectable leukemia cells from the body. *Remission* (as this return to relative normalcy is called) can be achieved within weeks in the majority of children with leukemia. It is accompanied by the return of a sense of well-being and the disappearance of the symptoms of leukemia and of the abnormal cells from the bone marrow. It is known that a significant number of undetectable leukemia cells persist during remission. In the absence of further therapy, these will proliferate, causing a reappearance of leukemia cells in the bone marrow and, ultimately, the recrudescence of all of the signs and symptoms of full-blown leukemia (termed *relapse*). Thus, after the induction of remission, further chemotherapy is given (maintenance therapy) in the hopes of destroying the residual leukemia cells and of preventing relapse.

Because of the propensity of leukemia to spread to the central nervous system, most leukemia therapy programs also incorporate a phase of central nervous system treatment during the month after the completion of induction therapy. Central nervous system therapy usually involves a series of drug injections into the cerebrospinal fluid, with or without concurrent irradiation of the brain.

In most treatment protocols for leukemia, children receive 2½ to 3 years of maintenance therapy, beyond which point the risks of toxicities from therapy appear to outweigh the benefits. Bone marrow tests are performed frequently to ascertain that therapy is effective in preventing recurrence of leukemia. Most relapses occur in the first 3 years after diagnosis. Relapse at any time is an inauspicious event, since almost all children who develop recurrence of their leukemia ultimately die despite further therapy. Newer experimental treatments such as bone marrow transplantation offer the hope of cure for some of these patients.

The prognosis for children with leukemia is improving dramatically. Before the advent of effective therapy, leukemia was uniformly fatal. With modern treatment, more than 50 percent of children with favorable types of leukemia may be cured. The prognosis is not so optimistic for children with less responsive types of leukemia. The life expectancy and quality of life for all patients with leukemia has also improved markedly with therapy, even for those not destined to be cured.

PSYCHOLOGICAL IMPLICATIONS

The diagnosis of cancer has an enormous psychological impact on the child and his family. Most parents and older children who are unaware of recent progress in treatment are cognizant of the serious implications of cancer, and the diagnosis is usually perceived as a near certain death sentence. Even in cases where cure is a realistic goal, the disruption of the normal day-to-day life by the demands of treatment further stresses the mental health of the family. A great deal has been published regarding the psychological aspects of cancer. The issues are important because the emotional consequences of cancer may be as disabling as the physical effects.

At the time of diagnosis, the cancer patient and his family are confronted by the threat of a potentially fatal disease, the disfigurement that may be necessary as the price of therapy, and the disruption of daily existence and future plans. The anxieties and stresses generated may be overwhelming. Each child develops his own coping mechanisms, but variable degrees of anger, denial, and depression are usually evident. For older children, many of whom are able to comprehend fully the connotations of cancer, the diagnosis creates seemingly insurmountable problems. Adolescence is a period during which body image, conformity with peers, and future planning are especially important issues, and adolescents with cancer may have particular difficulty contending with the implications of the diagnosis. If the initial phases of therapy are successful and treatment settles into a routine, the diagnosis may become more readily acceptable and the patient and family may be encouraged to return to as normal a life as possible. Thereafter, a new set of stresses may emerge. The discomfort of therapy and diagnostic procedures, a new dependence on physicians and other health care personnel, and a sense of isolation felt by most cancer patients contribute to the depression which afflicts children with chronic disease. School performance and participation in other activities may suffer, further threatening self-esteem. Resumption of normal life activities may thus be a difficult process.

The uncertainty of the outcome of treatment is a constant source of anxiety for patients and their families. Even in the most favorable cases, families live with the fear that the therapy may not be successful, and cure is perceived as a remote goal. Because of the unpredictable behavior of most cancers, families are reluctant to adopt an optimistic outlook lest their hopes are shattered by an unanticipated recurrence of the tumor. This attitude can be psychologically destructive for the patient. The child is frequently indulged excessively and may be mourned prematurely as family members begin to deal with feelings of separation. Even young children are sensitive to these emotions, and the patient may feel further isolated and bewildered in the face of his illness.

The usual coping mechanisms of the family are also stressed by the child with cancer and the demands of treatment. Families with a history of instability and difficulties in responding to stress may disintegrate under the physical, emotional, and financial strain of the serious illness. Siblings suffer to some extent because of parental preoccupation with the affected child and with the child's therapy. Marital disharmony may also be precipitated. The effects of cancer are thus felt by family members as well as the patient, and supportive therapy of the entire family is an essential part of successful treatment of childhood cancer.

EDUCATIONAL IMPLICATIONS

As stated previously, modern cancer therapy is designed to allow children undergoing treatment to pursue, as much as possible, their normal day-to-day activities. Regular attendance at school is encouraged. Classmates and the daily routine of classes are important psychological supports for the child, for whom other measures of normalcy no longer exist. Furthermore, the majority of children with cancer are approached optimistically, with a hope that they will be cured. A corollary of this hope is the expectation that their lives will return to normal at the completion of therapy. It is therefore desirable that children progress in school along with their classmates, so that the years of therapy can be remembered as a difficult period in their lives—not as lost years.

The problems produced by therapy make schooling a difficult proposition for the child with cancer. In the best of circumstances, therapy goes smoothly, with a minimum of toxicity, and the child is able to attend school regularly, save for a once-monthly visit to the clinic. Certain malignancies require more intensive treatment with greater toxicity, however. Children undergoing such therapy may have frequent absences from school because of illnesses related to therapy. Moreover, hospitalization may be required for certain types of therapy or for the treatment of therapy-related complications. It may be difficult for most of these children to keep up; but, with occasional home tutoring and close cooperation of teachers, schooling may continue successfully during the period of therapy.

It is a challenge for the teacher to make the classroom experience rewarding for any child with a chronic disease. This is especially true for the child with cancer. The unpredictable ups and downs, good days and bad, must be tolerated without disruption of classroom routine. There are other problems which confront the child in his relations with his peers which can be reconciled by the thoughtful teacher. Cancer has many connotations in our society, and children (and their parents) are likely to be frightened by the prospect of the classmate with a malignant disease. The teacher can play an important role in demystifying cancer. For example, children need reassurance that cancer is not contagious. Even young children understand the serious implications of cancer, from media exposure, and some may have had a relative who died of cancer. The patient and his classmates may ask difficult questions which should be answered compassionately and, always, honestly. Some of the visible side effects of therapy—particularly hair loss—can be psychologically devastating to children for whom conformity with peers is an important issue. In fact, many children have great difficulty returning to school because they fear ridicule by classmates. Anticipation of these problems, and plans to alleviate them before they occur, can help to avoid emotionally painful experiences for the child and schoolmates alike. Parents, patient, and teacher may wish to meet before the child's return to school, in order to discuss the anticipated questions and concerns of classmates. Early intervention by the teacher may save the patient needless suffering.

There is a tendency to be overprotective of children with cancer. This results, in part, from an appreciation of the seriousness of the illness, but mostly from ignorance of the realities of cancer therapy. Excessive sheltering may impede the normal psychosocial development of these children by unnecessarily limiting relationships with peers. In reality, few restrictions need to be placed on the activities of children with cancer. Allowances must be made for bad days, when children may limit their own physical activities. Restrictions for individual patients (especially regarding physical education) should be discussed with the child's physician. When restrictions are necessary, efforts should be made to channel the energies of the child into other fulfilling activities. The school should also be aware that children receiving chemotherapy are especially vulnerable to infection. Chickenpox, in particular, can be a catastrophic illness for children with cancer. Teachers can help prevent problems for these children by notifying parents if an illness is epidemic in the classroom.

Cancer and its therapy produce few side effects on the brain (except in the case of brain tumors), and learning skills are intact. Nevertheless, many external psychological stresses related to painful diagnostic procedures, unpleasant side effects of treatment, depression related to the diagnosis, as well as the uncertainty of the future, are likely to interfere with classroom performance. Close communication among parents, doctors, teachers, and school nurses can help keep the teacher aware of particular problems and help to devise strategies for defusing these problems in school.

BIBLIOGRAPHY

Altman, A. J., and Schwartz, A.D., *Malignant Disease of Infancy, Childhood, and Adolescence.* Philadelphia, W. B. Saunders, 1978.

Anthony, E. J., and Koupornik, C. (eds.), *The Child in His Family: The Impact of Disease and Death,* vol. 2. New York, John Wiley, 1973.

Baker, L. S., Roland, C. G., and Gilchrist, G. S., *You and leukemia: A day at a time.* Rochester, Minn., Mayo Comprehensive Cancer Center, 1976.

Binger, C. M., Ablin, A. R., Feuerstein, R. C., et al., Childhood leukemia: Emotional impact on patient and family. *New England Journal of Medicine* 280:414, 1969.

Cairns, N. U., Clark, G. M., Smith, S. D., et al., Adaptation of siblings to childhood malignancy. *The Journal of Pediatrics* 95:484–487, 1979.

Cyphert, F. R., Back to school for the child with cancer, in *Proceedings of the American Cancer Society's National Conference on Human Values and Cancer.* New York, American Cancer Society, 1973, pp. 131–134.

Gunther, J., *Death Be Not Proud.* New York, Harper & Row, 1949.

Issner, N., Can the child be distracted from his disease? in *Proceedings of the American Cancer Society's National Conference on Human Values and Cancer.* New York, American Cancer Society, 1973, pp. 127–130.

Kaplan, D. M., Smith, A., and Grobstein, R., The problems of siblings, in *Proceedings of the American Cancer Society's National Conference on Human Values and Cancer.* New York, American Cancer Society, 1973, pp. 138–141.

Koltnow, P. G., The family, in *Proceedings of the American Cancer Society's National Conference on Human Values and Cancer.* New York, American Cancer Society, 1973, pp. 122–126.

Kübler-Ross, E., *On Death and Dying.* New York, MacMillan, 1969.

Lascari, A., and Stehbins, J. A., The reactions of families to childhood leukemia. *Clinical Pediatrics* 12:210, 1973.

Lund, D., *Eric.* Philadelphia, J. P. Lippincott, 1974.

Sutow, W. W., Vietti, T. J., and Fernbach, D. J. (eds.), *Clinical Pediatric Oncology.* St. Louis, C. V. Mosby, 1977.

vanEys, J., Supportive care for the child with cancer. *Pediatric Clinics of North America* 23:215, 1976.

Young, J. L., and Miller, R. W., Incidence of malignant tumors in U. S. children. *Journal of Pediatrics* 86:254, 1975.

6

Cerebral Palsy

EUGENE E. BLECK, M.D.

DEFINITION

The term means brain *(cerebral)* paralysis *(palsy)*. Although ancient descriptions and depictions of cerebral palsy can be found, its modern history dates from 1861, when William J. Little, an English surgeon, described the disorder. Later, in 1937, Dr. Winthrop Phelps, an orthopedic surgeon of Baltimore, coined the term *cerebral palsy* and described its various types in detail.

By definition and common usage, cerebral palsy is a non-progressive disorder of movement or posture that begins in childhood and is caused by a malfunctioning of, or damage to, the brain (cerebral dysfunction).

The nonprogressive nature of cerebral palsy serves as an important criterion in diagnosis. For example, a brain tumor is not cerebral palsy; rather, its effects lead to a permanent and nonprogressive movement disorder of the limbs that becomes cerebral palsy. The same holds true of skull fractures and brain hemorrhages; only the late effects of such injuries to the brain, and the resultant movement disorder, would be termed cerebral palsy. The majority of children afflicted, however, do not acquire the condition from such late childhood injuries; rather, their disorder is caused by one of a variety of diseases and disturbances occurring during pregnancy or at the time of birth. Cerebral palsy from such early causes is termed *congenital*. The relative incidence of these two types is 86 percent congenital and 14 percent acquired.[37a]

FREQUENCY OF OCCURRENCE (INCIDENCE)

Because cerebral palsy is not a reportable disease, as is syphillis, for example, absolute figures as to its incidence cannot be given. Furthermore, this incidence changes with advances in medical knowledge and their application. In the United States, for example, we have noticed a decrease in some severe forms of cerebral palsy due to the treatment and prevention of the so-called "Rh-factor baby" and also to vastly improved obstetrical care. Parallel with this development, prematurity as a cause for cerebral palsy seems to be increasing as a result of improved survival of the premature infant.

Provided these limitations are kept in mind, the 1950 data of Phelps are yet useful as approximations. According to Phelps, 7 out of every 100,000 children are born with cerebral palsy.[27] Of these seven, one dies during the first year of life; six remain. Of these six, two are so severe as to require institutional treatment, and four are left for out-patient treatment. One of these four is amenable only to home care or day (development center) care, two are moderately involved and benefit from treatment, and one is so mild that no special treatment is required.

More current data on the incidence of cerebral palsy are provided by the massive study of 40,057 single-born children by Nelson and Ellenberg.[33] This study was of children born between 1959 and 1966, all of whom were carefully examined for neurological signs at birth. The children were followed at the ages of 1 and 7 years in order to provide the basis for the diagnosis of cerebral palsy. Of these 40,057 single-born children, 128 either had moderate or severe cerebral palsy or had died of the disorder by the age of 7 years. The rate of death in the first year was 1 to 2 percent. This study was concerned only with newborn neurological signs as predictors of cerebral palsy; thus, it did not include the acquired type of cerebral palsy, such as brain damage and motor disability due to head injury. The authors of this report were quick to point out that the care of newborns has altered considerably and, no doubt, improved since 1966, so that the incidence of serious cerebral palsy has probably diminished since then.

CLASSIFICATION OF TYPES

The types of movement disorder that occur in cerebral palsy were classified by the American Academy for Cerebral Palsy in 1956[30] (Fig. 6-1). Each disorder is classified according to two factors:

1. According to the movement (physiological classification)
   a. Spasticity
   b. Athetosis
   c. Rigidity
   d. Ataxia
   e. Tremor
   f. Mixed
2. According to the limb involvement (topographical classification)
   a. Monoplegia—one limb
   b. Hemiplegia—upper and lower limb on the same side
   c. Paraplegia—lower limbs only
   d. Diplegia—major involvement in the lower limbs and minor involvement in the upper limbs
   e. Triplegia—three limbs; usually one upper limb and both lower limbs
   f. Quadriplegia—major involvement of all four limbs (tetraplegia is the same term)
   g. Double hemiplegia—rarely used; upper limbs more involved than lower limbs

Cerebral Palsy

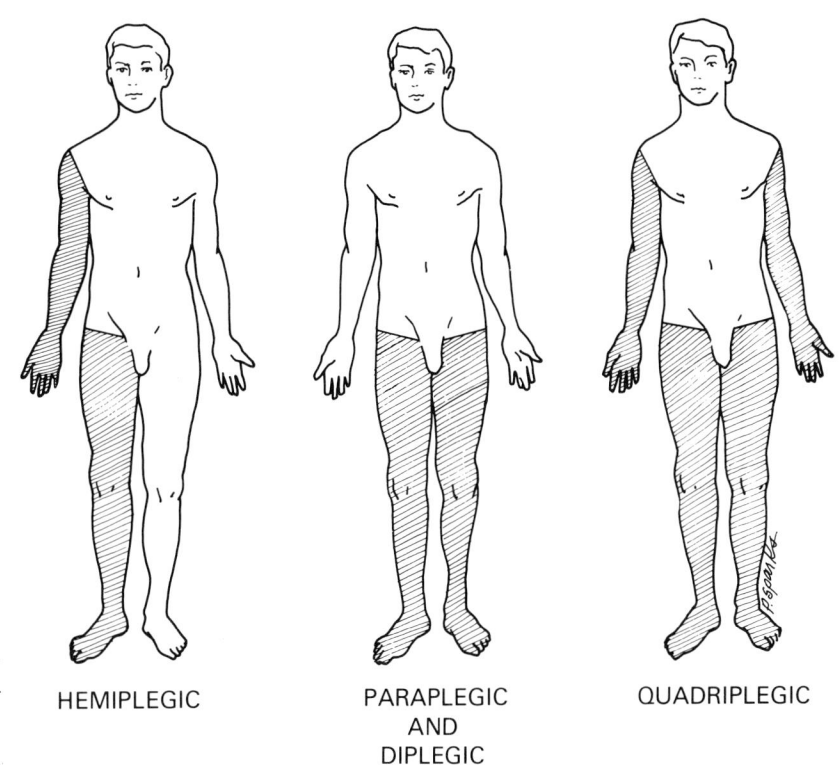

Fig. 6-1. Terminology according to limb involvement in cerebral palsy.

HEMIPLEGIC   PARAPLEGIC AND DIPLEGIC   QUADRIPLEGIC

The motor involvement and the limb involvement are both specified in the diagnosis—for example, cerebral palsy, spastic hemiplegia.

The types of cerebral palsy are distinguished by what you see and what you feel (Figs. 6-2a and 6-2b).

Spasticity

In spasticity, the limb muscle is tight and contracts strongly (increased stretch reflex) with sudden attempted movement or stretching (Fig. 6-2A). For example, tapping the heel cord (Achilles tendon) results in a quick, downward movement of the foot (plantar flexion). In spastic paralysis, this movement is exaggerated (hyperactive), even to the extent that the muscle will continue to contract repetitively (clonus). Children who have spasticity also have increased deep-tendon reflexes of the involved limbs: the ankle jerk (Achilles reflex), the knee jerk (quadriceps reflex), the elbow jerk (the biceps reflex in front of the elbow, and the triceps reflex behind), and the wrist jerk (periosteal radial reflex elicited by tapping the forearm bone—(radius)—on the thumb side of the forearm just above the wrist). An additional important reflex in spasticity is the Babinski, or plantar, response elicited by stroking the outer portion of the sole of the foot: the great toe bends upward (extends) and the other toes fan outward. Figures 6-3 to 6-6 are examples of the typical walking patterns in spastic diplegia and hemiplegia and of postures in spastic quadriplegia.

—As the child grows, the spastic muscle becomes shorter (contracture), and deformities of the limbs, pelvis, and spine may result (Fig. 6-7).

Fig. 6-2a. Top: Normal trajectory of movement from point A to B. Bottom: Spastic trajectory of movement from point A to B—overshoots but gets to point B. This type of muscle response is often referred to as "clasp knife."

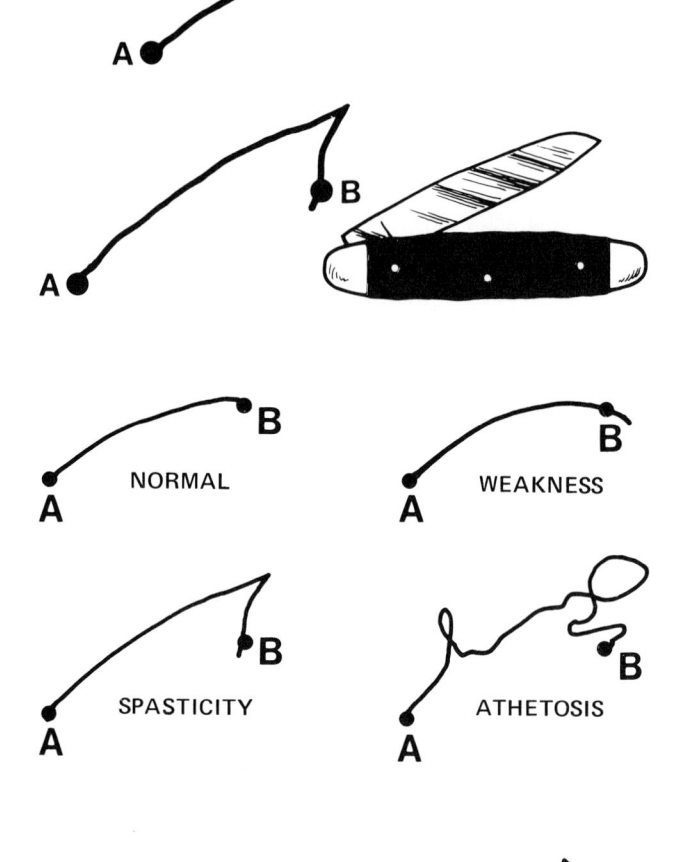

Fig. 6-2b. Graphic representation of a single movement from position A to B under the different types of cerebral palsy. (Redrawn from Gesell, A., and Amatruda, C. S., Developmental *Diagnosis,* New York, B. Hoeber, 1968.)

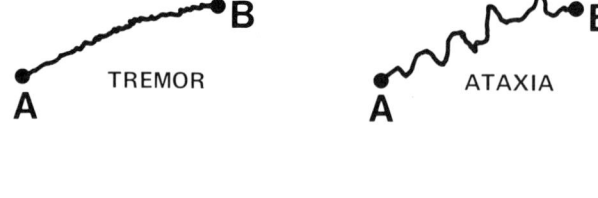

Fig. 6-3. Typical gait of child with cerebral palsy, spastic diplegia, or paraplegia. The thighs are together (adducted), turned in (internally rotated) and flexed; the knees are flexed; and the feet are in tiptoe position. (Redrawn from Ducroquet, R., Ducroquet, J., and Ducroquet, P., *Walking and Limping,* Philadelphia, Lippincott, 1968. With permission.)

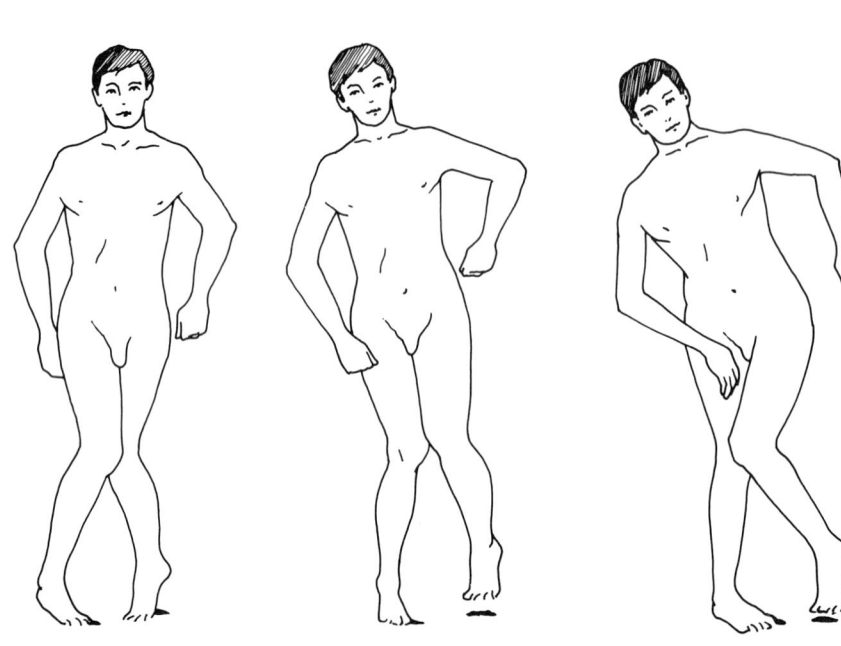

Fig. 6-4. A typical walking pattern of a child with spastic hemiplegia. The upper limb is flexed at the elbow and wrist. The foot on the same side is in the tiptoe position (equinus). (Redrawn from Ducroquet, R., Ducroquet, J., and Ducroquet, P., *Walking and Limping,* Philadelphia, Lippincott, 1968. With permission.)

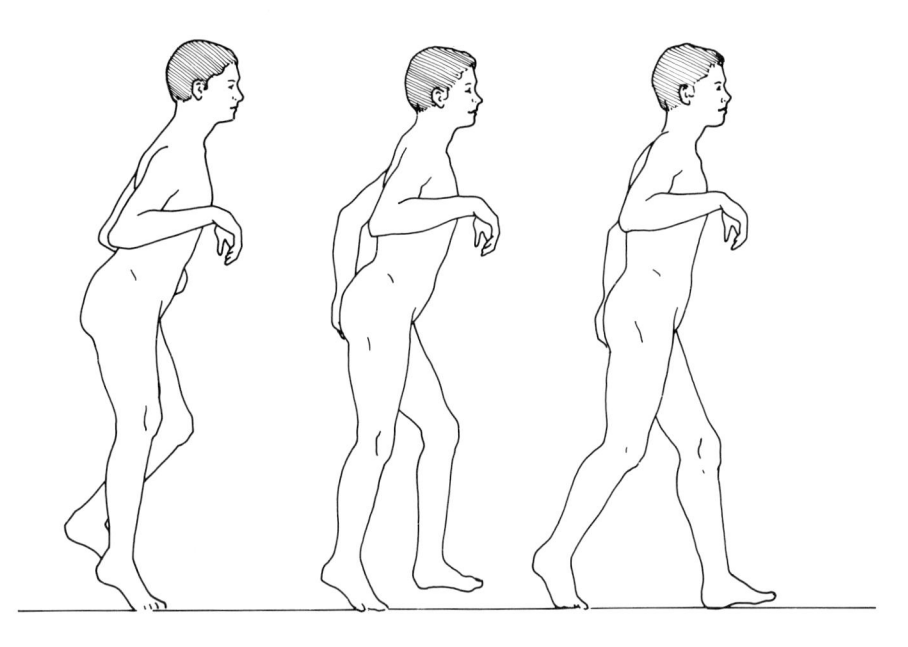

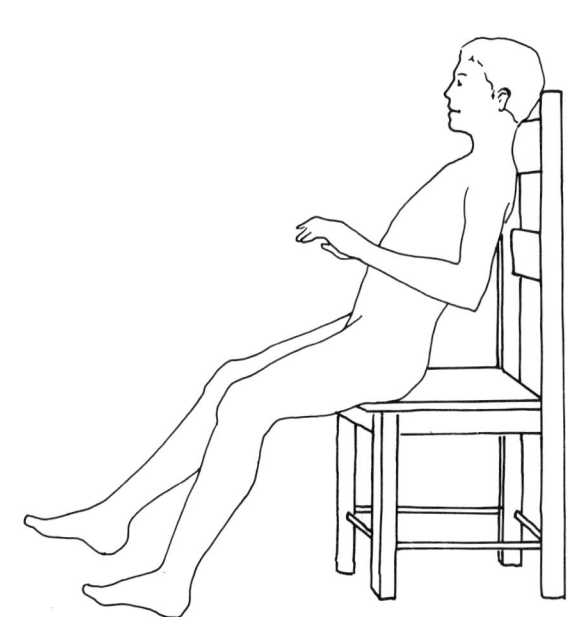

Fig. 6-5. Typical posturing of a child with cerebral palsy, spastic quadriplegia and extensor thrust.

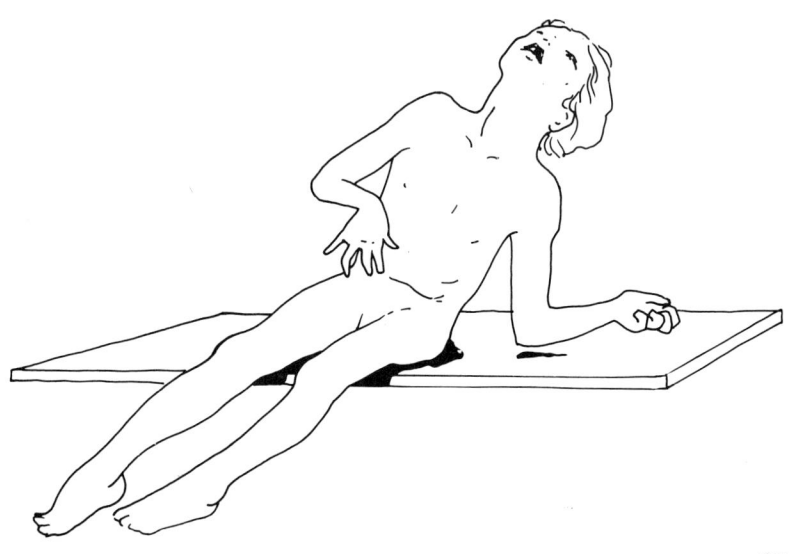

Fig. 6-6. Typical posturing of a child with cerebral palsy, severe involvement of all four limbs, with spasticity and athetosis mixed.

64   Eugene E. Bleck

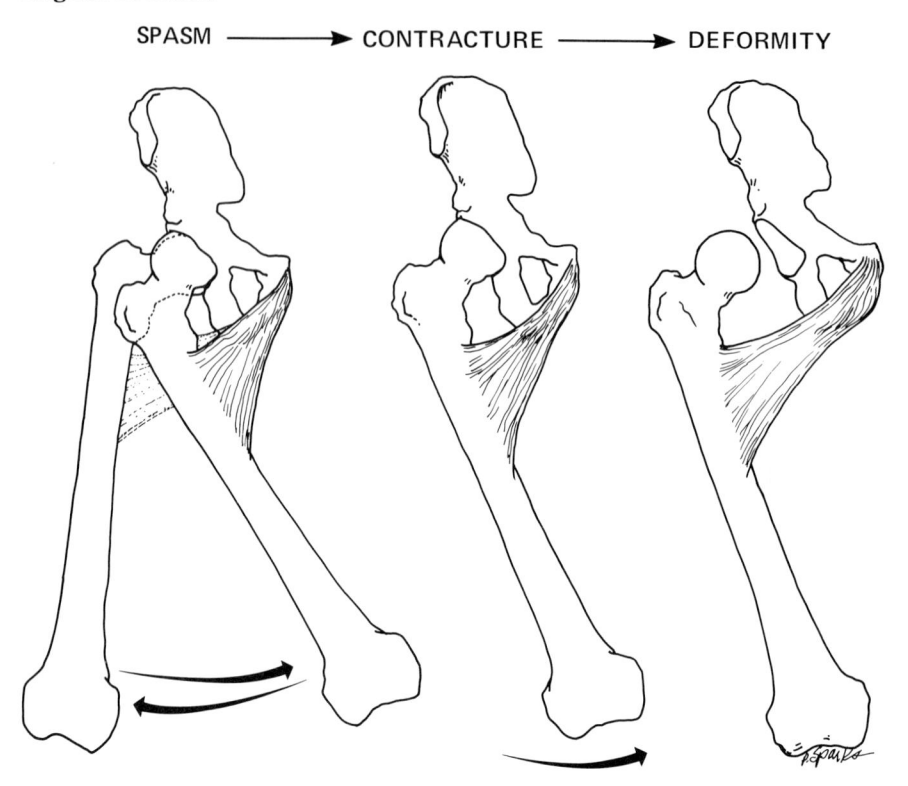

SPASM ⟶ CONTRACTURE ⟶ DEFORMITY

Fig. 6-7. Graphic representation of how a muscle spasm leads to contracture and eventually, bony deformity—in this case, dislocation of the hip.

Athetosis

In athetosis (ath-e-toe'-sis), the limbs have involuntary, purposeless movements (the muscles are normal—not spastic), and purposeful movements are contorted. There are two subtypes of athetosis. The first is nontension athetosis, in which contorted movements without muscle tightness are the main feature. These movements are, at times, rotary (rotation and twisting of the limbs), dystonic (distorted positioning of the limbs, neck, or trunk, that is held for a few seconds, then released), flailing (limbs thrashing about), or chorea "the dance"—spontaneous jerking motions, usually of the fingers or toes) (Figs. 6-8 and 6-9). The second

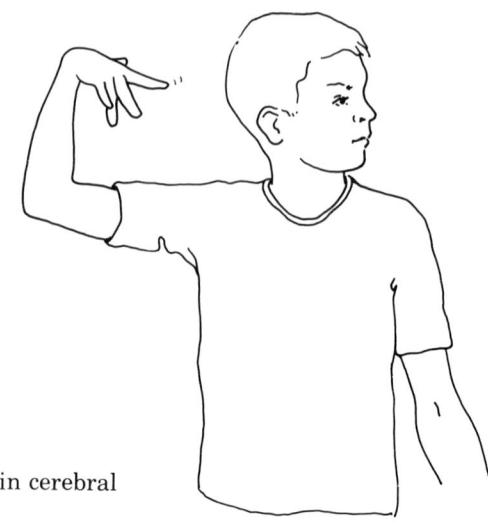

Fig. 6-8. Posturing of upper limb in cerebral palsy athetosis, dystonic type.

Cerebral Palsy

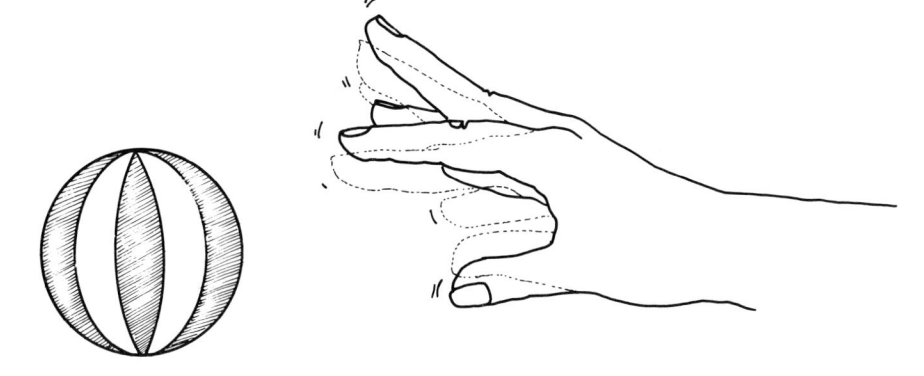

Fig. 6-9. Representation of athetosis, chorea: involuntary, jerky, and irregular movements of the fingers.

type is tension athetosis, in which the muscles are so tense that the contorted motions of nontension athetosis are blocked. Tension athetosis can be distinguished from spasticity by moving a limb joint rapidly and repetitively: with tension athetosis, the muscles become soft (flail), whereas, in spasticity, they become tighter.

Rigidity

Rigidity appears to be a severe form of spasticity—so much so that even the increased stretch reflexes are dampened. If an attempt is made to move the rigid limb, it gives way as if it were a lead pipe or a cogwheel. These children are usually quadriplegic.

Ataxia

Ataxia (ah-tak′se-ah) is a lack of sense of balance, a lack of sense of position in space, and uncoordinated movement. Such children walk as if they were sailors on a rolling ship at sea, with feet apart, trunk weaving, and arms held akimbo to maintain balance (Fig. 6-10). In the upper

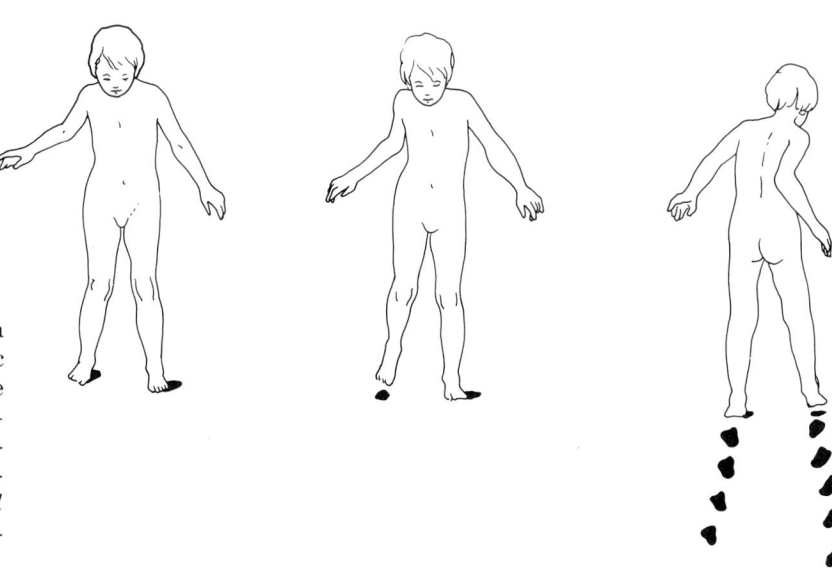

Fig. 6-10. Typical gait in a child with cerebral palsy, ataxic type. Note the broad base of the gait needed to maintain balance. (Redrawn from Ducroquet, R., Ducroquet, J., and Ducroquet, P., *Walking and Limping*. Philadelphia, Lippincott, 1968. With permission.)

limbs, one test of ataxia is to have the child attempt to place a fingertip at an exact, designated spot on the first try; ataxic children frequently are unable to do so.

Tremor

Tremor is shakiness of the limb involved. Tremor might be noticed only when the child attempts to use the limb (intention tremor). Continuous tremor at rest is not common in children—as it is in adults with Parkinson's disease of the brain.

Mixed*

Usually these children are quadriplegic and have both spasticity and athetosis. In addition many spastic children have deficient balance reactions (disequilibrium) (Fig. 6-11). Tremor can be observed mixed in with other types of cerebral palsy.

Atonia (meaning limp, no muscle tone, and floppy) is another type of cerebral palsy that may be found in diagnoses. However, atonia is nonexistent in schoolchildren: the atonic diplegic infant usually evolves into athetosis.

NEURO-ANATOMICAL CLASSIFICATION

I have included this classification because the terms used appear in neurological and orthopedic examinations of handicapped children, as well as in the literature. This classification attempts to sort out the types of cerebral palsy according to the area of presumed brain malfunction (Fig. 6-12).[12] Considerable evidence exists, however, that in cerebral palsy a great diffusion of brain malfunction exists, even though one movement pattern may predominate. According to this system, cerebral

*Note: Diagnosticians should try to describe the child's movement disorders in terms of the major involvement and should *not* take refuge in the "mixed" type.

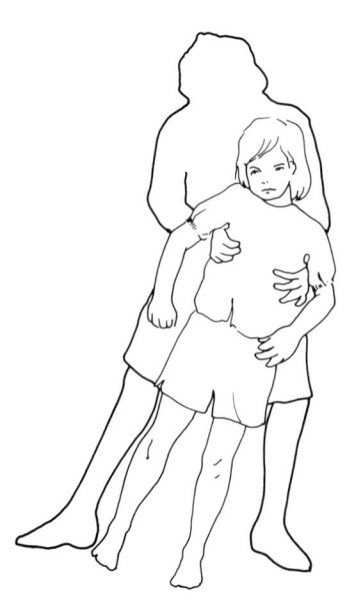

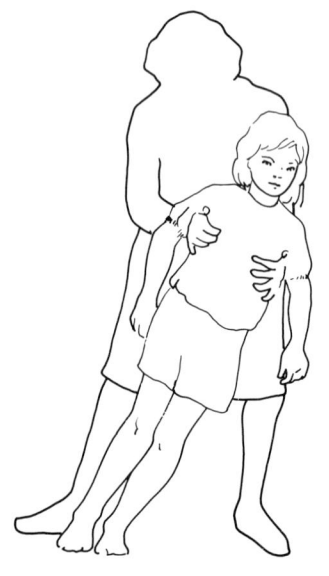

Fig. 6-11. Testing for equilibrium reactions. The child, when tilted to one side, cannot place the feet in order to maintain balance and topples over much as a felled pine tree.

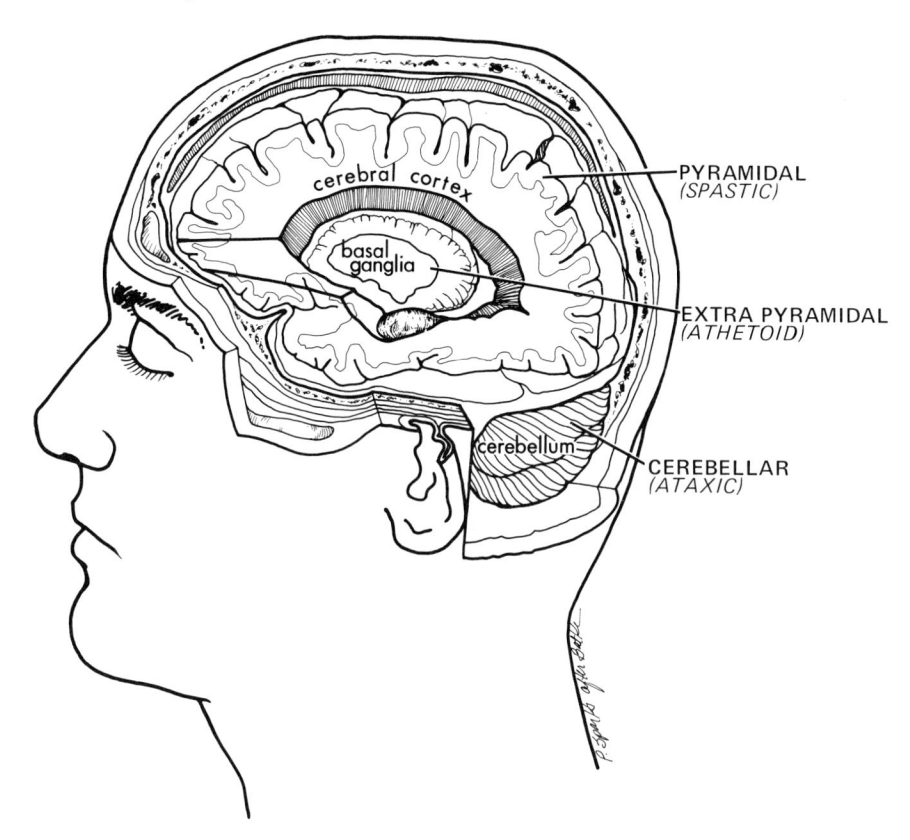

Fig. 6-12. Representation of the major portion of the brain involved in each of the three major types of cerebral palsy.

palsy is divided into three large classes: pyramidal, extrapyramidal, and cerebellar.

Pyramidal

The term *pyramidal* derives from the pyramidal arrangement of the efferent (motor) nerve fibers that descend from the brain surface (cerebral cortex) to the limbs and that function in the voluntary control of limb muscles. Damage to such cells and their nerve fibers (tracts) results in spastic paralysis.

Extrapyramidal

Extrapyramidal (eks"trah-pi'-ram-i-dal) damage is damage to any part of the brain other than that described in the preceding paragraph. The common assumption is that the damage occurs in the large collection of cells located in the central portion of the brain (basal ganglia). Such disorders (*dys*) of movement (*kinesia*) are often called dyskinetic cerebral palsy. The athetoses are in this group.

Cerebellar

The cerebellum is the "little brain" whose function is to coordinate movement, to provide sense of position in space, and to maintain equilibrium. Cerebellar (ser"e-bel'ar) cerebral palsy is synonymous with ataxia.

CAUSES OF CEREBRAL PALSY

Eugene E. Bleck

While the details of causes (etiology, e″te-ol′o-je) are beyond the scope of this chapter, an outline of the more common causes should facilitate an understanding of the disorder. These may be divided into three main groups according to time of occurrence: before birth (prenatal), around the time of birth (perinatal), and after birth (postnatal).

Prenatal Causes

1. *Inherited causes.* These are rare. The most common inherited form of cerebral palsy is familial spastic paraplegia.
2. *Infections in the mother during pregnancy.* These include german measles (*rubella*) in the first 3 months (first trimester) of pregnancy; shingles (herpes zoster virus); toxoplasmosis (a parasitic infection); and cytomegalic inclusion disease (a presumed viral infection).
3. *Lack of oxygen to the fetal brain* (fetal anoxia). This may be due to hemorrhage caused by separation of the placenta, to maldevelopment of the placenta, to shock due to blood loss (hemorrhage in the mother from injuries such as in an auto accident), or to kinking or knotting of the umbilical cord.
4. *Rh incompatability* (erythroblastosis fetalis, hemolytic anemia of the newborn, kernicterus, and hyperbilirubinemia). If the Rh factor (named from the Rhesus monkey) is present in the fetus (Rh+) but not in the mother (Rh−), the mother's immune defenses manufacture destructive agents (antibodies) that destroy the infant's red blood corpuscles (erythrocytes or red cells), and so create anemia (hemolytic anemia) in the infant. The blood-cell disintegration products (bilirubin), when combined with lack of oxygen, cause damage to the brain; yellow areas of brain destruction are found in such cases (*kernicterus,* from *kern,* brain; *icterus,* yellow). Today, most, but not all, cases of cerebral palsy due to Rh incompatability are preventable by immunization of the mother and early exchange-transfusion of the infant.
5. *Prematurity.* A child born after less than 40 weeks in the womb (gestation) and weighing less than 5 lb is considered premature.[30, 49] Prematurity accounts for 33 to 60 percent of all cases of cerebral palsy in the United States. In our own study of 119 children who had cerebral palsy, spastic diplegia, 65.5 percent were premature.
6. *Metabolic disorders.* These are predominantly diabetes in the mother and toxemia of pregnancy (occurs during the last trimester).
7. *Unknown causes.* The estimate is that 30 percent of all prenatal cerebral palsy falls in this category.[21] Most of these cases have brain maldevelopment originating in the first 12 weeks of pregnancy, during which the major part of brain development occurs (Fig. 6-13).

Perinatal Causes

1. *Birth injury* (trauma). The infant skull can be pushed out of shape during delivery possibly causing rupture of brain blood vessels or compression of the brain. Birth injury is more likely to

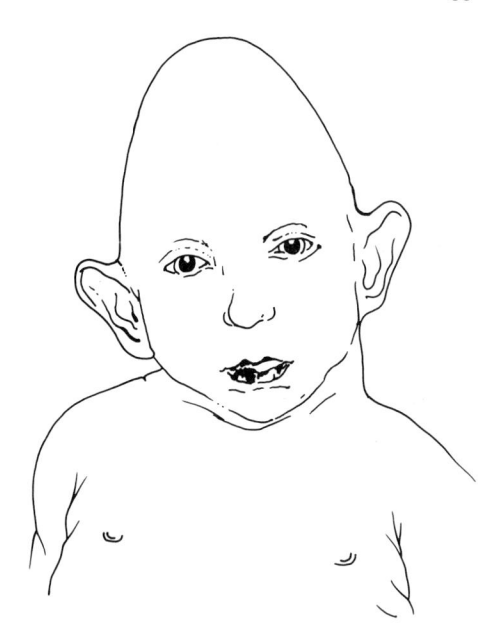

Fig. 6-13. Appearance of a child with microcephaly. The cause of the condition is unknown.

occur when the baby is very large, in difficult deliveries, in breech birth (feet first), or when labor is prolonged.

2. *Lack of oxygen* [fetal asphyxia (as-fix'-se-ah), anoxia (an-ox'-se-ah), or hypoxia (hip-ox'-se-ah)]. Damage occurs because the brain cells cannot survive prolonged oxygen lack. Possible causes of anoxia include lung collapse, pneumonia, and oversedation with drugs used to relieve labor pains (pain-relieving and sedating medications depress the respiratory centers of the fetal brain).

Postnatal Causes

1. *Head injuries.* These injuries, which include skull fractures, brain lacerations, and hemorrhages (contusions), account for approximately 18 percent of postnatal cerebral palsy.[37] Auto accidents, falling from heights, and child abuse are the leading reasons for head injuries.
2. *Brain infections and toxic conditions* [encephalopathies (en-sef"-ah-lop'-ah-thes)]. These include meningitis, viral infection (encephalitis), and toxic chemicals (e.g., lead poisoning). Together, they account for 57 percent (meningitis, 12 percent) of postnatal cerebral palsy.[37a]
3. *Brain hemorrhages or clots.* Sudden spontaneous brain hemorrhages occur in children (acute hemiplegia of childhood) and most often produce a one-sided spastic paralysis. In brain clots, a traveling blood clot or embolus (em'-bol-us) from the heart lodges in a brain blood vessel; the blood supply is thus cut off, and death of the nerve cells results.
4. *Lack of oxygen to the brain* (cerebral anoxia). Carbon monoxide poisoning, drowning, and stoppage of the heart (cardiac arrest) from electrocution are common examples.
5. *Brain tumors.* These occur after treatment when the residual movement disorder has become static.

CORRELATION OF TYPE OF CEREBRAL PALSY WITH LOCATION OF BRAIN DAMAGE (CLINICAL-PATHOLOGICAL CORRELATION)

Although the areas of the brain that control movement are quite interdependent, and although it is rare in cerebral palsy to have damage to one system alone, the presentation of some areas of identified brain damage should help us recognize the reality of brain cell destruction; see Table 6-1.* Only after this recognition, can we establish some real basis for coping with the child and his parents and for devising educational methods to compensate for his losses.

ASSOCIATED HANDICAPS

Cerebral palsy can, and often does, affect other systems controlled by the brain.[15a] These associated handicaps are sometimes more disabling than the motor disorder.

Oral-Dental

1. *Difficulty in swallowing.* If the difficulty is greater with fluids, then spasm of the pharyngeal musculature is suspected; if greater with solids, paralysis of the pharyngeal muscles may be present.
2. *Drooling.* Normal children drool from 3 to 9 months after birth. In cerebral palsy, drooling can be prolonged, excessive, and messy.
3. *Teeth grinding* (bruxism). Most often encountered in the more severely retarded.

*Experimental Cerebral Palsy. In monkeys, 8 to 12 minutes of fetal oxygen lack (asphyxia) result in temporary feeding difficulties and clumsiness; 13 to 19 minutes result in mild spasticity or athetosis; 20 to 30 minutes result in severe cerebral palsy. Certain brain cells are more sensitive to anoxia in the following order: thalamus, auditory nuclei (herein), visual system. The parietal-occipital lobes are affected first, followed by the temporal and limbic lobes, and, finally, the midbrain and brainstem.

Table 6-1. Clinical-Pathological Correlation of Cerebral Palsy

Cause	Type of Cerebral Palsy	Location of Damage (Pathology) (Fig. 6-12)
Rh incompatability	Athetosis (deaf)	Basal ganglia (collection of neurons central brain)
Prematurity	Spastic diplegia	Periventricular area (on either side of ventricles)
Birth trauma	Spasticity	Pyramidal tract
Anoxia	Spastic quadriplegia	Cortical degeneration (surface cells drop out)
Cerebral hemorrhage	Spastic hemiplegia	Porencephaly (cavity or hole in brain) (Fig. 6-14)
Postnatal encephalitis	Quadriplegia	Microgyria and enlarged ventricles (small brain convolutions—enlarged fluid cavity)

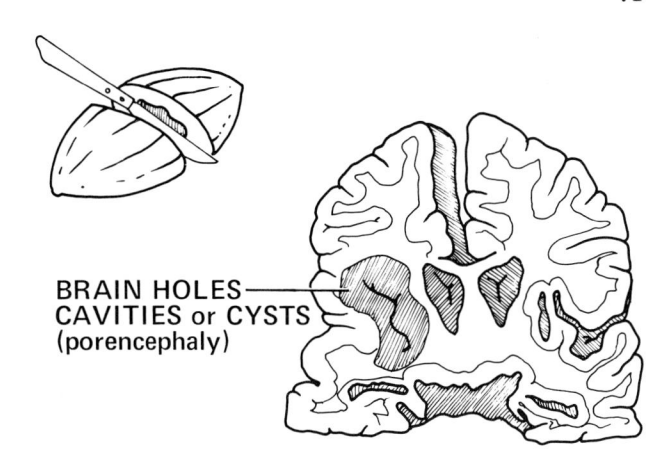

Fig. 6-14. Cross section of brain depicting large cavities or cysts—literally, holes in the brain—causing cerebral palsy (porencephaly).

4. *Dental caries.* These are more common than in normal children because of enamel dysplasia and grinding.

Speech

Some speech or language defect is present in 48 to 49 percent of children with cerebral palsy. The speech disorders might be due to paralysis or to incoordination of the speech musculature (dysarthria). Affected children may have the inability to organize and select speech (dyspraxia). (For a complete discussion of speech disorders, see Chapter 7.)

Hearing

Hearing loss is most common in athetosis that is caused by Rh factor incompatibility or rubella syndrome. Only 2 percent of the spastic children have hearing problems.

Visual

Many of these children are farsighted (hyperopia); nearsightedness (myopia) is seen mostly in prematures. Crossed eyes (esotropia) are six times more common than turned-out eyes (exotropia). Failure of the upward gaze is characteristic of athetosis due to Rh incompatibility.

Sensory Deficits

Loss of shape and texture sensation (asterognosis) of the hand is well documented, especially in spastic hemiplegia. Generally, the shorter and smaller the affected upper limb (atrophy) relative to that on the normal side, the more we suspect sensory loss.

Convulsive Disorders

Convulsive disorders occur in 86 percent of spastic patients and in 12 percent of athetoids. In postnatal cerebral palsy, seizures occur in 55 percent of the spastic hemiplegics. Seizures are rare in athetosis[11] (see Chapter 9).

Mental Retardation

When the IQ distribution of children with cerebral palsy is compared with the expected intellegence curves for the whole population, it is apparent that approximately 75 percent of children with cerebral palsy have some degree of mental retardation[22] (Fig. 6-15). In studies of large cerebral-palsy populations, serious mental retardation was present in at least 50 percent. Athetoid children are less likely than spastics to have mental retardation. Ataxics and spastic hemiplegics have a better intellectual prospect than any in the whole group. We must not forget that 25 percent of the children with cerebral palsy have normal or above-normal intellects.

Perceptual and Visual-Motor Disorders

Perceptual and visual-motor disabilities have been a concern of educators during the past two decades and still are the subject of much study. Even more popular than the studies are the treatment and educational methods designed to overcome the handicap. The literature is voluminous, and a complete exposition of the problems, the controversies, and the educational implications are far beyond the scope of this book.

But what is meant by perceptual and visual disorders? Various other names are applied as well: visuo-spatial or visuo-motor disorders, spatial inability, or constructive apraxia. Abercrombie seems to give the best definition:[1] a *perceptual disorder* is one in which the child cannot perceive spatial relationships, i.e., sees things in a distorted manner. As Abercrombie notes, however, there is little conclusive evidence that the cerebral palsied child sees things in a distorted manner, as that which

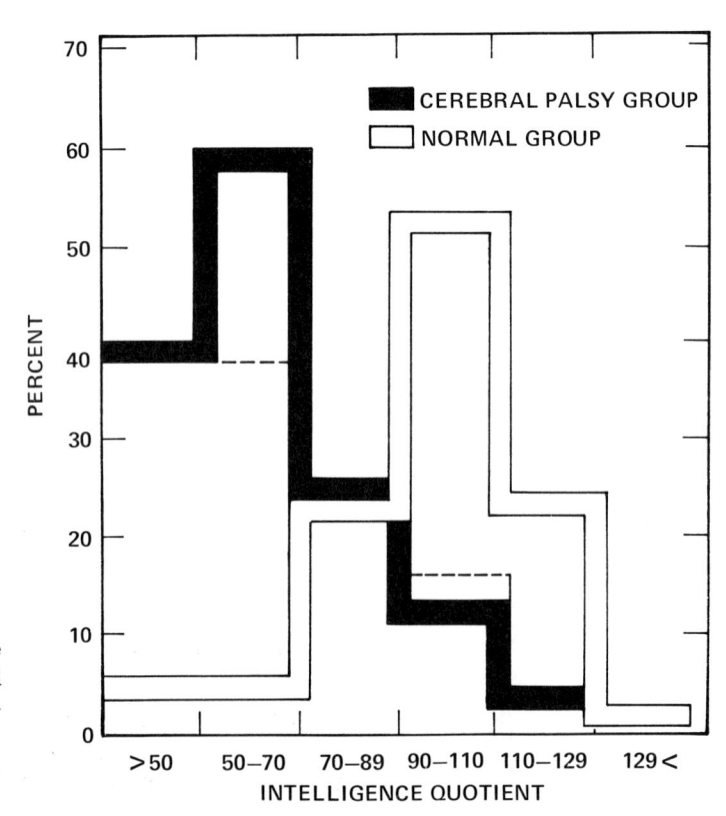

Fig. 6-15. The IQ distribution in a large group of cerebral palsied children compared with normal children of the same age. (Redrawn from Hohman, L. B., *American Journal of Physical Medicine* 32:282–290, 1953. With permission.)

Cerebral Palsy

does exist is based on tests for "perceptual disorders" that require both vision *and* movement. Thus a child who appears to have a perceptual disorder may in fact have normal perceptual abilities; he or she may simply be unable to copy what he or she perceives. Such tests measure not perceptual disorders per se but, rather, what is called *visual-motor disorder*. There is plenty of evidence that this disorder occurs frequently in cerebral palsy (Figs. 6-16 to 6-18).

Normal children improve in perceptual and visual-motor performance according to their intelligence and age. It appears that the disability that occurs in cerebral palsy is a *developmental lag*. In other words, children who have cerebral palsy cannot perform up to the norm for their age as established by the performance by their normal peers on such tests.

Incidence

Athetoids appear to have fewer perceptual and visual-motor disorders than spastics. Spastic hemiplegics often have such disorders, despite the apparently normal upper and lower limb function on one side. The question of whether or not the side involved is correlated with the disability is unresolved. What does seem evident is that the degree of motor handicap does not parallel the degree of the visual-motor or perceptual disorder. As of this writing (1981), it seems clear that, so far, no one has found a direct relationship between discernible visual system disorders (e.g., crossed eyes, nystagmus, and abnormal eye movement) and complex behavioral or learning disorders.[46]

Tests

So many different tests have been described (over 50), that the reader should consult the appropriate educational and psychological literature. We have tests for visual perception, for tactile kinesthetic perception, and for body position. Visual-motor tests include visual-perceptual, tactile kinesthetic perception, and others. These tests are in addition to the more

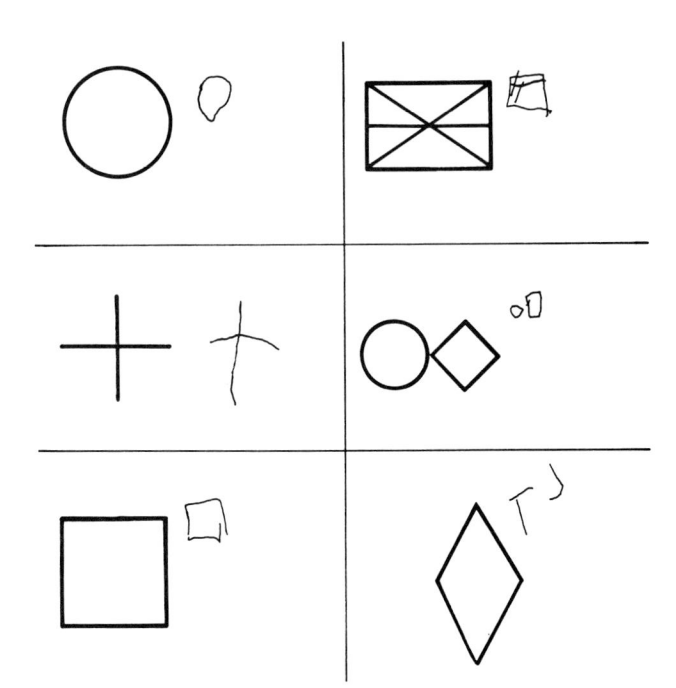

Fig. 6-16. Copy test. Attempt of a spastic diplegic child to copy simple figures. This indicates some of the problems that such children may have in perceptual and visual motor disorders. (Redrawn from Abercrombie, M. L. J., *Perceptual and Visuomotor Disorders in Cerebral Palsy*, Little Club Clinics in Developmental Medicine, No. 11, London, Heinemann, 1964. With permission.)

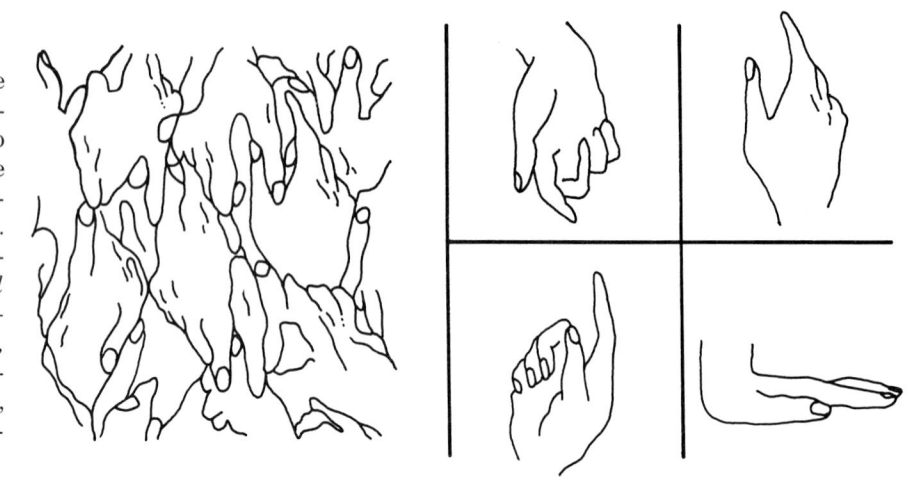

Fig. 6-17. Hidden figure tests, nonoverlapping figures. The child is asked to find which figure on the right is found in the multiple figures on the left. (Redrawn from Abercrombie, M. L. J., *Perceptual and Visuomotor Disorders in Cerebral Palsy,* Little Club Clinics in Developmental Medicine, No. 11, London, Heinemann, 1964.)

familiar intelligence tests [e.g., Stanford-Binet and WISC (Wechsler Intelligence Scale for Children)] and learning tests (e.g., Maze test).

DIAGNOSIS

The diagnosis of cerebral palsy is based almost entirely on the child's history (prenatal, perinatal, and developmental) and the physician's examination. Even though there is a strong tendency for people to be enamoured of "tests," for the most part, tests in cerebral palsy only exclude the possible progressive neurological illnesses or tell us what the brain damage and its extent might be. The following tests are used selectively:

1. *Skull x-rays.* These are used, for example, to rule out toxoplasmosis, a parasitic infection that is evidenced by calcifications (white spots) on the skull.

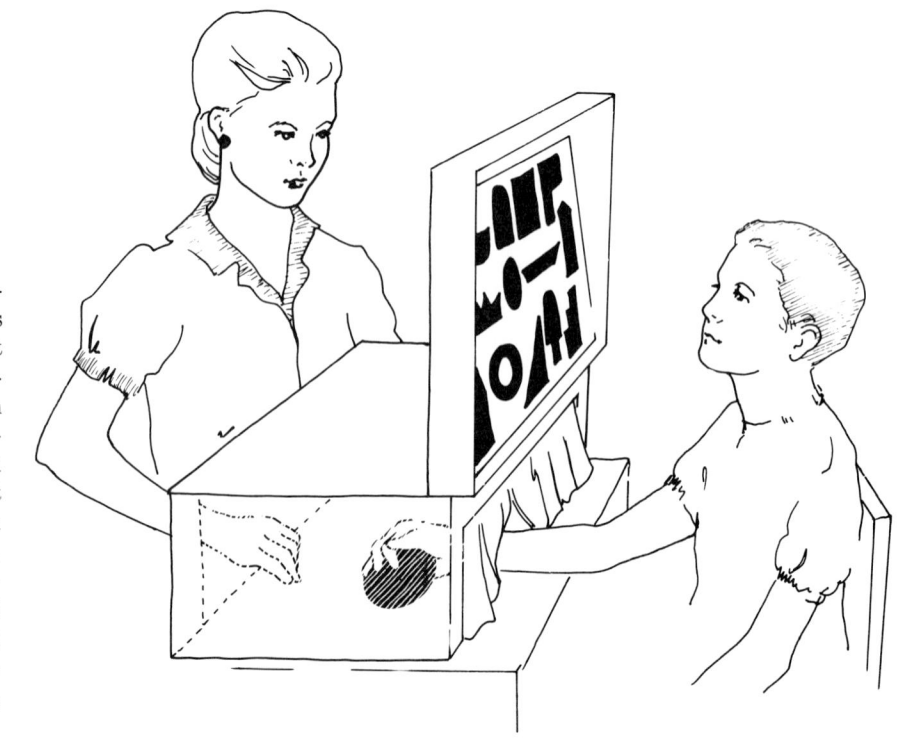

Fig. 6-18. Cross modality matching. The child is asked to feel a cut-out shape inside the box without seeing it; he is then asked to choose the corresponding figure from the visual display in front of him. (Redrawn from Abercrombie, M. L. J., *Perceptual and Visuomotor Disorders in Cerebral Palsy,* Little Club Clinics in Developmental Medicine, No. 11, London, Heinemann, 1964.)

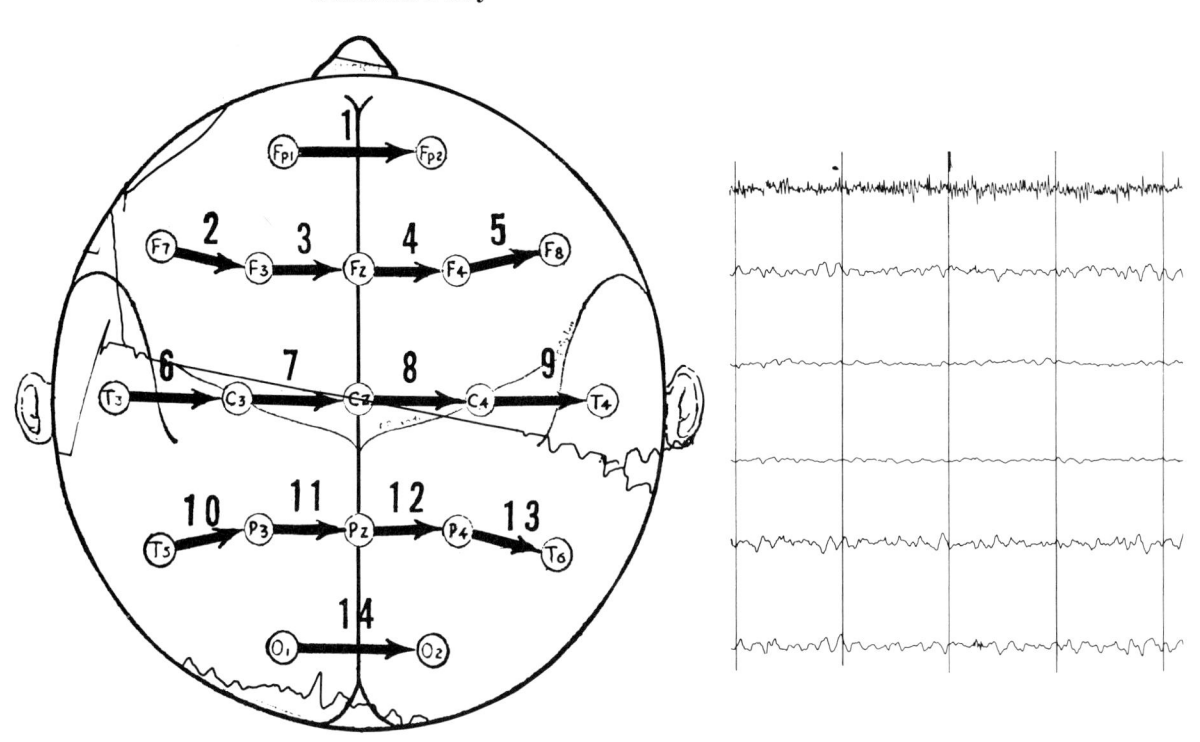

Fig. 6-19. Example of a normal electroencephalogram (EEG). The numbers on the "montage" of the skull represent the different areas sampled for electrical activity of the brain. In this figure only six of these tracings are shown. Different patterns of wave forms are the basis for diagnosis of convulsive disorders which have definite and recognizable patterns.

2. *Electroencephalogram (EEG).* This is used in the diagnosis of seizure disorders or to find focal lesions, such as brain tumor or old scars from prior brain injury (Fig. 6-19).
3. *Pneumoencephalogram.* This diagnostic test has been practically eliminated due to the superiority of the CAT scan, which demands no injections or hospitalization. In the test air is injected into the ventricles of the brain, and the resulting air shadows show up on x-ray. A displaced ventricle, suggestive of brain tumor, may be seen in this way. Cerebral atrophy (shrinkage of part of the brain) can also sometimes be diagnosed.
4. *Brain scan.* Radioactive isotopes are injected into the bloodstream. The resultant recording of radiation from brain tissue can often localize brain tumors.
5. *Cerebral arteriograms.* A dye that can be seen on x-ray (radio-opaque) is injected into the bloodstream. The x-ray of the skull will then show the blood vessels and will reveal abnormalities of the arteries in the brain—e.g., an aneurysm (local dilation of a blood vessel).
6. *Blood and urine examinations.* These may possibly reveal chemical abnormalities that might explain the cerebral palsy. For example, urine is examined for metachromatic bodies in the diagnosis of metachromatic leukodystrophy (*leuko* meaning white matter)—a progressive and severe brain-damaging disease of unknown cause.
7. *Electromyographic examinations (EMG).* The electrical activity of muscle during movement is recorded on an oscilloscope much like the EKG (electrocardiogram) or the EEG (electroencephalo-

Eugene E. Bleck

gram). Either fine wires are inserted into the muscle to record activity, or recording is from electrodes on the skin over the muscle belly. Although the EMG does not give us a diagnosis of cerebral palsy, it does discern which muscles or groups of muscles are firing normally during movement. This has significant implications for decision-making in surgical treatment and assists in the analysis of treatment efficacy (Fig. 6-20).

8. *Computerized axial tomography (CAT scan).* Multiple x-ray beams are passed through the head. Each tissue of the brain has a different density, and the computer sorts these out to give a fairly comprehensive cross-sectional image of the brain. CAT scans have almost eliminated the need for the more complex and more hazardous diagnostic procedures referred to in the previous paragraphs—pneumoencephelograms, arteriograms, and brain scans. The CAT scan has been a boon in the early diagnosis of enlargement of the brain ventricles (hydrocephalus) or of displacement of the ventricles indicative of brain tumor.

THE ESTIMATE OF THE OUTCOME (PROGNOSIS)

It should be obvious that the ability to ascertain the prospects for improvement in a particular child with cerebral palsy (based on the neurological examination, the estimate of the degree of brain damage and mental retardation, and the severity of the movement disorder) would give those working with cerebral palsied children a better perspective on the particular treatment or educational methods best suited to that child. If one starts out with only mildly hemiplegic children, the results of whatever one does might be deemed superior! In educational endeavors, speech or language therapy, physical and occupational therapy, and even orthopaedic surgery, the natural history of cerebral palsy is usually overlooked. However, there are a few things we know and should apply.

Walking Prognosis

Favorable signs are sitting by the age of 2 years and the absence or presence of a few important infantile reflexes.[9] Poor signs for walking are (1) an imposable asymmetrical tonic neck reflex (turning of the head

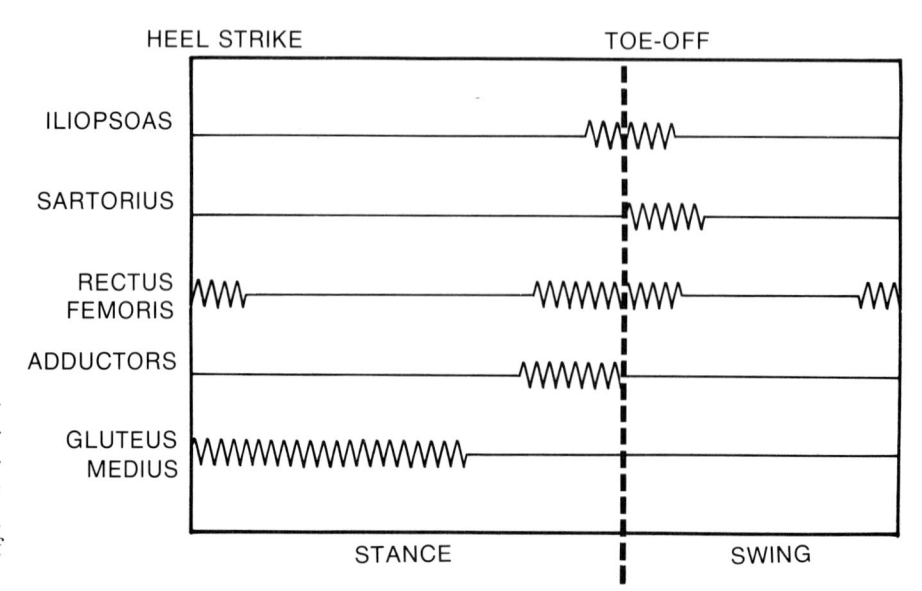

Fig. 6-20. Electromyogram of normal hip muscles. Note that the muscles fire in spurts. *Stance* means foot on the ground; *swing* is when foot is off the ground.

Cerebral Palsy

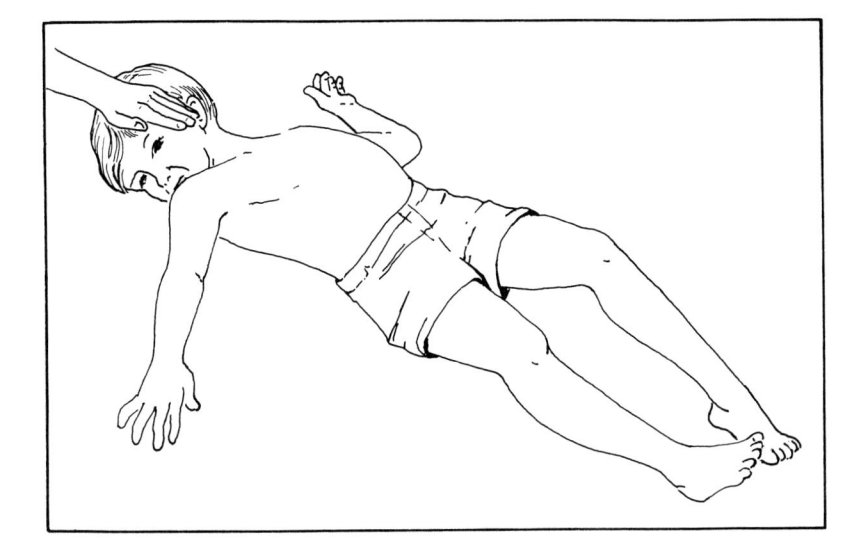

Fig. 6-21. The asymmetrical tonic neck reflex. When the head is turned, the limbs flex on the skull side and extend on the face side. The reflex is never normal if one can always impose it and if the child cannot shake loose of it. Its presence indicates severe brain damage.

causes flexion of the upper and lower limbs on the skull side and extension of the face side, Fig. 6-21; (2) a persistent Moro reflex (a loud noise, sudden jerk of the table, etc., causes the upper limbs to go out from the side of the body and then come in, Fig. 6-22); (3) a strong extensor thrust on vertical suspension (when the child is held upright by the armpits, the lower limbs stiffen out straight, Fig. 6-23); (4) a persistent neck-righting reflex (when the child is lying on his or her side, turning of the head causes the shoulders, trunk, pelvis, and lower limbs to follow in the same direction, Fig. 6-24); and (5) an *absence* of the normal parachute reaction after 11 months (when the child is lifted up horizontally by the abdomen and suddenly lowered to the table, the arms and hands normally extend

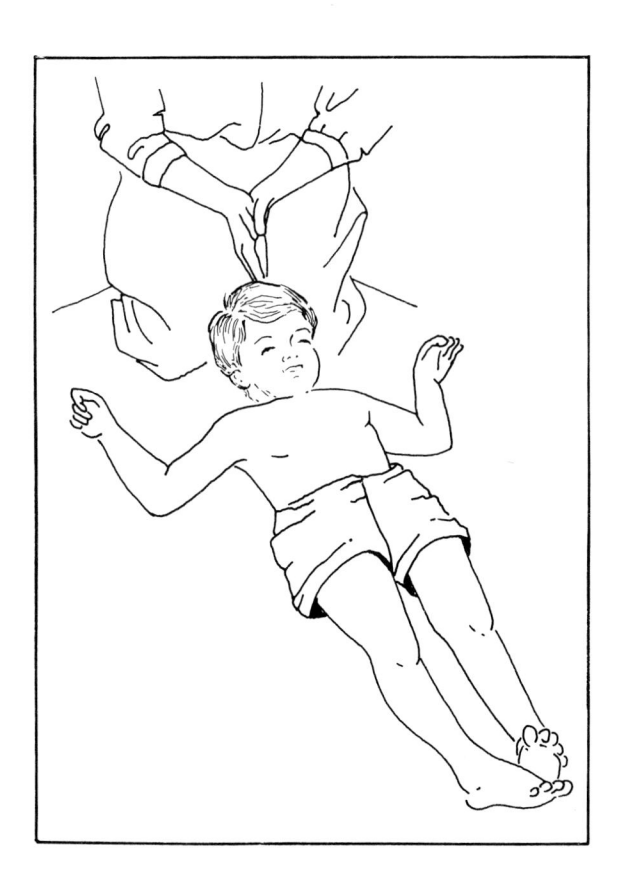

Fig. 6-22. Moro reflex. A loud noise, sudden jar of the table, or dropping the head backward 20–30° causes the upper limbs to spread apart and then come together in the embrace position. It is abnormal if present after 6 months.

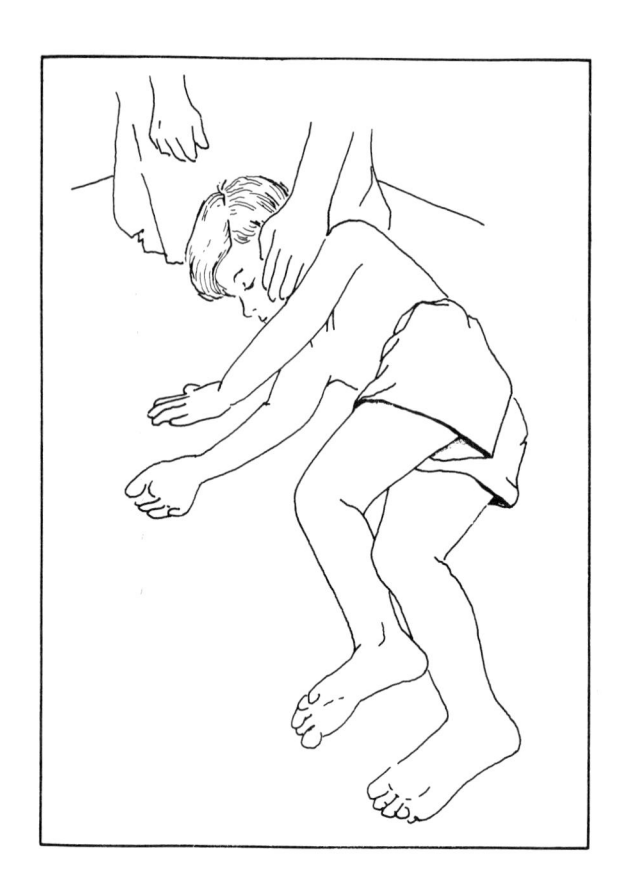

Fig. 6-23. Neck-righting reflex. When the head is turned, the shoulder girdle, trunk, pelvis, and lower limbs follow as if the child were a log being rolled. It is never normal to have a child roll over and over like a log just by turning the head.

Fig. 6-24 (left). Extensor thrust. The child is suspended from the axilla with the feet touching the ground. The positive reaction is tiptoeing, with extension of the lower limbs spreading upward to the trunk. It is never normal and often is mistaken for early standing.

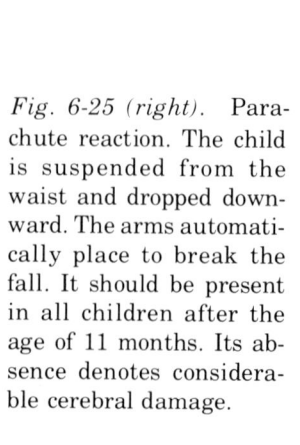

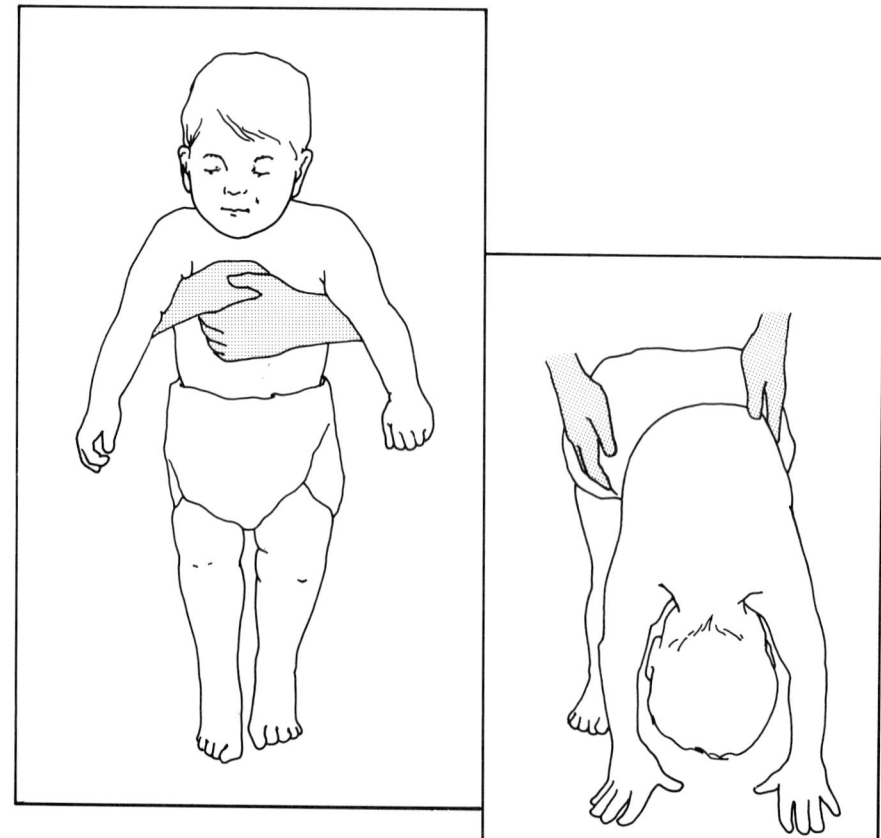

Fig. 6-25 (right). Parachute reaction. The child is suspended from the waist and dropped downward. The arms automatically place to break the fall. It should be present in all children after the age of 11 months. Its absence denotes considerable cerebral damage.

Cerebral Palsy

to the table to protect the fall, Fig. 6-25). Spastic hemiplegics usually walk by 21 months. Spastic quadriplegics and tension athetoid quadriplegics have the worst prognosis for walking and may end up in wheelchairs. Most children with cerebral palsy walk by the age of 7 years.[11]

Can treatment, then, affect the ability to walk? We hardly think so. However, treatment, whether surgical or physical therapeutic, might assist those who can walk in achieving a better-appearing and more functional walking pattern (gait). Paine found no difference between treated and untreated children with athetosis, but spastics did benefit from treatment in Paine's study of 177 cases.[36]

Does mental retardation affect the ability to walk independently? In a recent study by Shapiro, Accardo, and Capute of 152 profoundly mentally retarded children (IQ below 25) without acquired or degenerative diseases, walking began at a mean age of 30 months.[42] In those children without major neurological disability, 95.2 percent walked by the age of 72 months. Of those who had mental retardation and seizure disorders, 63.6 percent achieved walking at age 6 years. Of those who were retarded and cerebral palsied, only 10 percent were walking by this time. From these data it would appear that "cognition is a less important determinant of the ability to walk than is basic neurological integrity."[42] Of equal importance is that motor assessment, by itself, cannot diagnose mental retardation.

As was shown by Beals, walking performance in spastic diplegic children steadily improves and then plateaus at about the age of 7 years (Fig. 6-26).[9] Unless there is surgical intervention to change the spastic muscle pattern, the type of motor performance that the child will have as an adult is most likely to be the same as that at the age of 7. Physical therapy to improve the child's walking once he or she has reached 7 or 8 years is unlikely to be worth the time and effort expended, and other areas of function (like play and sports) should take precedence.

Speech Prognosis

As a rule of thumb, the uttering of recognizable sounds by the age of 2 years is a favorable sign for language development. Poor head control usually means poor speech. The spastic child is likely to develop a slow,

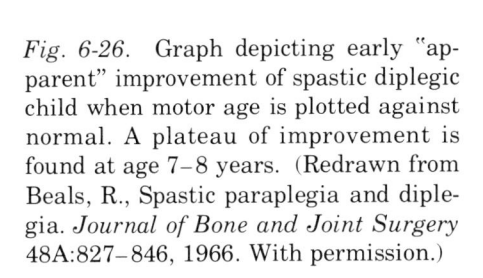

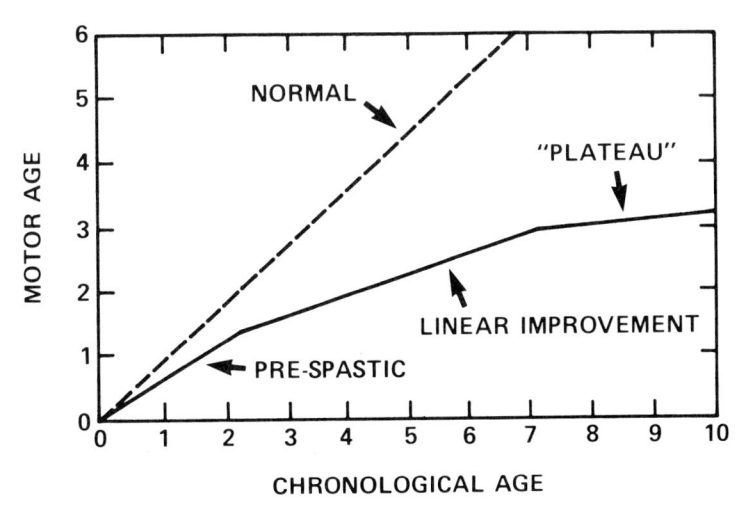

Fig. 6-26. Graph depicting early "apparent" improvement of spastic diplegic child when motor age is plotted against normal. A plateau of improvement is found at age 7–8 years. (Redrawn from Beals, R., Spastic paraplegia and diplegia. *Journal of Bone and Joint Surgery* 48A:827–846, 1966. With permission.)

labored speech; the athetoid, a jerky speech; and the ataxic, a tremorous, quavering voice.

Upper-Limb Prognosis

Early preference for use of either the right or left hand augers well for functional use of the hands. Children who do not develop hand preference or whose hands do not actively cross over the midline to the opposite side are thought to have a poorer prognosis for hand use.

Intellectual Function Prognosis

The results of psychometric tests, when properly interpreted, appear to be a valid measure of intellectual function[27] (Fig. 6-27). In counseling parents regarding this aspect of their child's future development, the graph reproduced from Bray's text (Fig. 6-28) is most helpful; the trend it depicts has been the usual experience of those who have worked a long time in this field. The graph demonstrates that, as the child matures, his or her deviation in intelligence from the normal child at the same age becomes increasingly apparent. Even though new achievements can be expected as the child gets older, the gap, unfortunately, remains and widens.

Life Expectancy

In a study of 1,416 persons with cerebral palsy under the age of 21 years, Cohen and Mustacchi found, in a follow-up study, that the cumulative survival was 83 percent—as compared with an expected 98-percent survival for the normal population.[14] The lowest mortality was found in spastic types, who had a survival of 93 percent, while the highest mortality occurred in the mixed types, who were severely involved. In another study, the mortality rate of those with cerebral palsy was 13 times the normal for males and 17 times the normal for females.[40] The death rate was greatest among the severe cases, who were probably confined to custodial institutions. In general, however, we can expect our patients in schools for the handicapped to live a fairly long life.

Cohen and Kohn reevaluated 319 patients with cerebral palsy 15 years after the initial visit.[13] Of these, 10 percent had died. Those who died were very severely involved, and, because of the relative longevity of the less disabled persons, Cohen and Kohn assessed the quality of life for the 286 survivors. These results will be discussed later in this chapter, in the section Long Term Outlook—Living With Cerebral Palsy.

PHYSICAL THERAPY

Therapy, be it conducted by a physical therapist or an occupational therapist, has come to connote a sort of specific treatment, comparable to penicillin for pneumonia. Unfortunately, it is not. The materials, methods, and results of most of the various therapies designed to improve or to alleviate the motor disorder have not been evaluated scientifically with appropriate controls. Those that have been studied show either equivocal or negative results. This point is made, not to denigrate the professional services provided by physical or occupational therapists, but

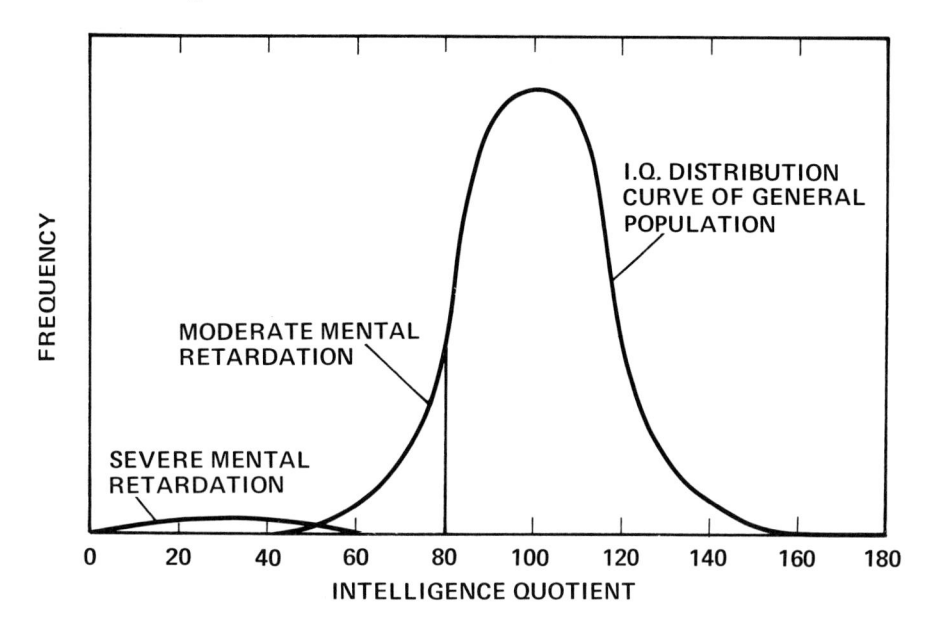

Fig. 6-27. The normal bell curve of IQ distribution of the general population and the graphic definition of severe and moderate mental retardation.

only to emphasize that the word *therapy* should not be taken to mean some sort of magical method for overcoming what is a permanent motor disorder.

Therapists serve valuable, if not essential, roles in instructing and guiding patients, parents, and teachers in the management of the motor disorder. When therapeutic exercise is indicated, a therapist becomes instrumental in motivating the patient but cannot do more than this. Passive "hands-on" therapy in cerebral palsy has not been effective and has been given up in favor of active programs that emphasize functions, fun, games, and sports for the school-age child. For some patients, the therapist may recommend compensatory devices to substitute for lost functions (e.g., walkers, wheelchairs, or crutches) and will instruct the patient in their use.

A therapist is the ideal consultant in an educational setting when it is desired to adapt games, play, and sport to a disabled child's handicap (e.g., wheelchair basketball for children who have muscular dystrophy).

Fig. 6-28. A useful graphic representation of how the retarded child lags further and further behind the normal child as time passes. The gap between the retarded child (dotted line) and the normal child (solid line) is much narrower at age 2 (gap A) than it is at age 7 (gap B). This graphic representation may help parents understand the retarded child's typical development so that unreasonable goals and expectations are not set. (Redrawn from Bray, P. F., *Neurology in Pediatrics.* Chicago, Year Book Medical Publishers, 1969. With permission.)

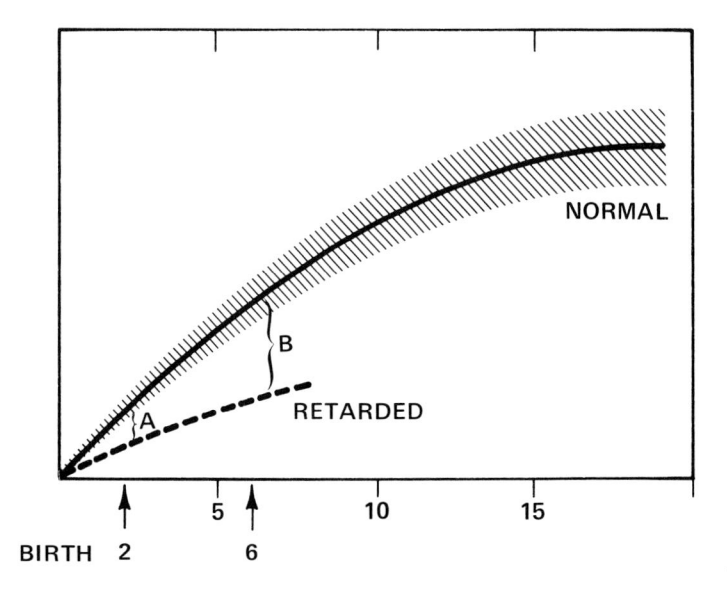

Both physical and occupational therapists are equipped to test the child objectively in order to assess motor maturity and the ability to perform all-important daily living functions.

Therapists, then, are the physician extenders, the motor-problem analyzers, and the problem solvers. But they cannot be expected to "cure" cerebral palsy. Perhaps there are exceptions to this generalization, and, on occasion, special motor-skill training may be indicated but, again, to learn a skill the patient must practice, just as any person must practice in learning to play the piano, for example. The piano teacher comes once a week to teach the lesson, but, in the interval, the student must practice. Ultimately, the success of the patient or the student will depend on his or her innate abilities and motivation to learn. Much depends, therefore, on the extent of the neurological involvement as it is reflected in the child's motor, sensory, and intellectual functions.

In a critique of physical therapy methods, David Scrutton, a physical therapist from London, England, holds that physical therapy should be "aim-oriented" and thus, the therapist should strive to:[41]

1. Ameliorate the handicap by reducing its effects to a minimum.
2. Promote the assets for the child.
3. Prevent the disability from becoming dominant.
4. Avoid any treatment method that would increase the family burden.

Summary of Physical Therapy Treatment Techniques[19]

Bobath Neurodevelopmental Treatment

The Bobath technique is probably the most commonly used method today. Briefly, it aims to inhibit abnormal reflex activity and to facilitate normal automatic movement. Before treatment is instituted, the therapist assesses the child's tonic and righting reflexes, variations in muscle tone, and general motor performance. This initial test is often referred to as the basic motor-maturity evaluation (Table 6-2). Based on this information, the therapist selects normal movement patterns consistent with the child's motor development which the child then practices. Equilibrium reactions are reinforced by shifting the child in an attempt to obtain a reflex movement toward the upright posture. The Bobaths have contributed more than any other therapy group to an improved analysis of the motor deficits and prognosis in cerebral palsy; their method has helped therapists gauge the handling of each child according to his or her developmental age.

One of the rare studies that attempted to assess the efficacy of physical therapy in cerebral palsy was that reported by Wright and Nicholson, who conducted prospective studies of 47 children under 6 years of age.[48] The children were randomly divided into three treatment groups: (1) Bobath therapy for 12 months (7 children); (2) no physical therapy for 12 months (31 children); (3) no therapy for 6 months, followed by therapy for 6 months (9 children). The study showed no significant differences between the treated and untreated children after 1 year of follow-up. Of course, such negative results are controversial, and the methods of evaluation can be questioned, but, nevertheless, this is one of the few attempts at an objective analysis and, as such, might temper the enthusiasm for any particular treatment method. This study did emphasize that the

Cerebral Palsy

physical therapists were of great value in providing continuity of care and in parent education. In no way did it denigrate their role.

Another study, by Scherzer, was a double-blind study of 24 children under the age of 18 months.[39] The experimental group had a neurophysiological program of physical therapy that was designed to achieve certain motor milestones. The control group had only passive range of motion of their limbs at school twice a week. Those who had the neurophysiological therapy showed greater improvement in motor and social functions at school, but their behaviors were no different than the controls when the children were observed at home. The extent of change was greatest in children with higher intelligence and in those who were older.

Fay-Doman Method

In this method the child is trained in a series of basic movement patterns that repeats the evolutionary progression in movement from that of fish to amphibians, to reptiles, and, finally, to anthropoids. Thus, the treatment would consist of exercises that start with swimming motions and progress onward to cross-pattern creeping. The theory postulates that the brain is comprised of evolutionary layers. Each layer coincides with a stage of locomotion that relates to a specific species, starting at the upper end of the spinal cord (the medulla) and progressing upward to the cerebral cortex. It is further postulated that cerebral dominance of one side of the brain is essential, and many of the treatment's passive exercises are directed toward this end.

This treatment for retarded children was evaluated in a controlled study by Sparrow and Ziegler,[43] who studied 45 severely retarded children and, in an exhaustive and detailed evaluation, reported negative results. Their study showed that loving care and concern were just as effective as were the complex and structured patterning methods.

Phelps and Deaver Methods

As the child grows older, these older methods, are undoubtedly used. They include facilitation of movement through exercise and relaxation, and the practice of walking activities—e.g., in parallel bars or wheelchair transfers. Braces are used to control movement and to support weak muscles. Crutches are used when necessary.

Kabat and Knott Method

The principle of this method is to develop voluntary control through the use of therapeutic exercises that increase brain excitation. One of the techniques consists of resisted mass-movement patterns: diagonal patterns of motion are used, starting from a position of extreme length and moving toward a maximal shortening of the muscles.

Rood Method

Margaret Rood's approach is to activate muscles through the sensations of heat, cold, and brushing.

Sensory-integration Method

Sensory-integration therapists emphasize the importance of tactile and vestibular (equilibrium) senses in voluntary control; this is based on the principle that sensory input always precedes motor responses and, in

Table 6-2. **Form Used for Basic Motor Maturity Evaluation (Physical Therapy Department, Children's Hospital at Stanford)**

MOTOR DEVELOPMENT: 3–12 months

Month	Supine (on back)
3	Limb posture is flexion
3	Limb and trunk postures becoming symmetrical
3	Bilateral activities at mid-line
4	Bilateral leg extension with back arching
4	(resting) Legs are in flexion abduction and outward rotation, soles may be on table
4	(active) Able to flex hips and extend legs, lifting them an inch or two
5	Rolls supine to prone (axial rotation)
5	Back arches and child raises hips (bridges, no progression)
6	Reaches forward with extended arms to be picked up
6	Lifts legs and plays with feet
7	Lifts head off table
8	Does not like supine

Month	Prone (on abdomen)
3	Holds chin and shoulder off table, weight on forearms
3	Pelvis is flat when plane of face is 45° to 90° to table
4	Head in mid-line
4	Prone swimming, jerky movements
5	Arms forward, nearly extended for support
5	Arms retracted and flexed (hands off support)
5	Support on one forearm and reaches for toys
5	Free kicking of legs
6	Rolls prone to supine (axial rotation)

Month	Prone (continued)
6	Weight bearing on both arms and hands (full extension)
7	Commando-crawls
8	Pivots
9	Goes from prone to sitting
10	Creeps on hands and knees

Month	Pull to Sitting
3	Head lag in beginning of movement, then keeps head in line with trunk
3	Head will bob forward when sit completed
3	Lower limbs are flexed
4	Slight head lag in beginning of movement, then keeps head in line with trunk
5	Assists and brings head forward, no head lag
6	Spontaneous lifting of head
6	Pulls himself to sitting (hips flex and legs extend)
6	Raises extended legs (hips are flexed, knees are extended)

Month	Sitting
3	Back somewhat rounded
3	Head mostly held up
4	Holds head steady, but set forward
4	Head wobbles when examiner suddenly sways child
4	Back shows only a lumbar curvature (slight rounding)
5	No arm support, arms retracted at shoulders with elbows flexed

Cerebral Palsy

Month	Sitting (continued)	Month	Sitting (continued)
5	Child tends to fall backwards (does not push back)	12	May shuffle on buttocks with use of hands
5	Head stable when body is mildly rocked by examiner	Month	Standing
		3	Does not accept weight
		4	Accepts some weight
6	May sit alone unsupported briefly when placed	5	Takes almost full weight
6	Arm support forward	6	Bounces
6	Sits well when propped	8	Pulls himself to standing
8	Sits unsupported, without hand support, with little overbalancing, for 1 min.	8	Readily bears whole weight when supported (not rigid)
		9	Stands holding on and lifts one foot
8	Sits erect	10	Walks holding onto furniture
8	Has arm support sideways	10	Lowers himself to floor by holding on
8	Adjusts posture to reach
9	Good sitting balance, sits for 10 min.	10	Collapses if not holding on
10	Pivots to pick up objects	12	Walks with one hand held
10	Arm support backwards	12	Attempts to stand alone
10	Leans forward and recovers	13	Stands alone well
		13	Walks alone
10	Can lean over sideways and recover	14	Gets to standing unsupported
10	Goes forward from sitting to prone	14	Stoops and recovers

addition, sensory feedback afterwards informs the neural system of the accuracy of a response.[28] Integration is the process of receiving and defining sensory input so that it may be organized for use.[2,3] The sensory-integration theory presumes that the brain and its connections after damage have a "remarkable plasticity" that allows it to "re-route, compensate, and respond to therapeutic methods that will facilitate change."[47]

A variety of specialized movements are used in this method. One objective for example, is to provide vestibular stimulation; this is done by spinning the child in a swivel chair for one minute each day. The efficacy of this method for treating children with Down's syndrome was studied by Kanter.[26] The experimental treated group in Kanter's study consisted of two children with Down's syndrome, aged 6 and 24 months. There were two control groups: (1) three normal controls between the ages of 6 and 9 months and (2) two children with Down's syndrome who received no treatment. In this, very limited, study the two untreated children with Down's syndrome showed no increase in their motor performance, whereas one normal child and one treated Down's child showed increased motor abilities.

Montgomery evaluated the effectiveness of sensory-integration therapy relative to two other treatment programs.[32] In his study, 75 retarded children (none of whom had cerebral palsy) were randomly divided into three treatment groups: (1) children who received developmental physical therapy three times each week, (2) those who received sensory-motor training three times each week, and (3) a control group who had activities of daily living and physical education, as well as crafts two and one-half times each week. Children in the sensory-motor group improved their performance in bead stringing and sit-ups, while those in the control group showed improvement in the number of steps walked on a balance beam. In all three groups the ability to ride a tricycle or kick a ball regressed over the summer vacation, possibly due to the lack of practice. This study attempted to show that sensory integration will improve motor skills and that this treatment method is more effective than the more traditional approach which emphasizes practice in skills.

The standard tests used in the aforementioned study were devised by Frostig (Frostig Movement Skills Test Battery). These included (1) the number of beads laced within 30 seconds, (2) the number of blocks transferred within 30 seconds, (3) the distance broad-jumped (cm.), (4) the number of times the body changed position in 20 seconds (control, 36; standard deviation, 29.2),* (5) the number of sit-ups performed in 30 seconds, and (6) the number of steps taken on a balance beam.[34]

Therapies for Learning Disabilities

Ayeres has reported on testing children for alternating horizontal eye movements (nystagmus) after rotating the body 10 times for 20 seconds (postrotatory nystagmus).[3] She found that children who had hyporeactive nystagmus (slow to respond with the horizontal eye movements) benefitted from sensory integrative therapy one-half hour each weekday. Children who had hyperreactive nystagmus were likely to have definite signs of cerebral dysfunction and did not benefit from sensory integrative therapy. Further, the hyporeactive nystagmus children were apt to appear more normal than other learning disabled children. It seems, then, that children with cerebral palsy will not benefit as much as apparently normal children from sensory integration. One critique of such studies has been that another form of attentive treatment, such as eating ice cream or doing sit-ups one-half hour every day, ought to be tried as a control. The beneficial effects of any ritual and of personal attention on the learning process cannot be discounted entirely, according to critics of specialized methods.

In a 12-year prospective study by Bell, Abrahamson, and McRae, there was no evidence that deficits in visual perception or motor skills had any relationship to reading retardation.[8] Robinson and Schwartz questioned whether remedial work in fine or gross motor skills was effective in helping children to learn to read.[38]

The reason for discussing in this section studies that have examined the efficacy of various methods in improving cognitive skills is to highlight the need for ongoing criticism and scholarly examination of these various therapies. They should be subject to the same type of clinical

---

*Note to reader: If you are unfamiliar with standard deviation analysis, consult a biostatistics text; very wide standard deviations in performance make such data difficult to interpret.

investigation required for the administration of drugs used to treat various conditions and illnesses.[50]

Rolfing

Rolfing is a method of deep-connective-tissue manipulation proposed as a treatment for selected musculoskeletal disorders by Ida P. Rolf. The effectiveness of this method was studied in cerebral palsied children.[25] Objective measurements of walking ability and energy costs were obtained in a kinesiology laboratory. Significant increases in walking velocity were found in 60 percent of those tested. Half of the patients were mildly involved and they improved. The other half, who were more severely involved, showed no significant or only borderline improvement. The range of motion of the knee and ankle joints during walking improved in 40 percent, but a trend toward ankle-tightness in downward (planter flexion) movement was also observed. The electromyographic changes were not impressive, nor were the foot-support patterns. This careful study indicates that, under test conditions, the results were, at best, equivocal, and that the most severely affected patients (those in greatest need of improvement) were not helped. Most importantly, the study clearly illustrates how "therapies" designed to improve walking might be objectively evaluated.

Eclectic Method

According to the author's observations, most physical therapy units in our handicapped schools follow an eclectic method, selecting what works and what is necessary for each child according to the extent and nature of the disability and the child's developmental age. If walking is a goal, we can now be fairly certain that walking patterns are set at about the age of 7 years and that, beyond this age, nothing changes appreciably. Once the child is playing on the playground and is going from place to place, this constitutes the therapy, and no more formal treatment or "intensive" physical therapy need be given. We also know that a number of the children will never walk. Certainly by the age of 7 years, those who are going to walk reasonably independently, with or without crutches, will have done so. Children in whom the prognosis for walking is poor should be allowed to be mobile in a wheelchair, and if possible, be taught how to get in and out the wheelchair in order to gain independence. To generalize further, as the child gets older (over age 8 years), locomotion treatment should become incidental. Education, self-care skills, and communication deserve the most prominent place. It is important that, eventually, the child cease being a patient and become a person.

Infant and Preschool Programs (Infant Stimulation)

Perry has questioned the value of "early intervention programs," especially when they are unwittingly projected as treatments to cure brain damage.[37b] The only benefit to the child who has been enrolled in infant stimulation programs has been in improving social interaction skills;[15b] there is no convincing data that neurological development has been altered.

These programs have been extremely valuable, however, in helping parents define and cope with the child's problem. In this respect therapists play an important role: educating parents, analyzing the motor problem, interpreting the child's development, detecting early structural changes (e.g., hip dislocation), and helping the child to achieve function through the use of compensatory technological devices (e.g., power chairs, prone boards for crawling, etc.) Most importantly, as the children reach school age, therapists may greatly facilitate the choice of the referral route that is most consistent with the child's motor and intellectual function (Fig. 6-29).

OCCUPATIONAL THERAPY

The role of the occupational therapist overlaps and compliments that of the physical therapist. Learning activities of daily living (ADL) are more important for the child than is getting over an isolated muscle tightness (Table 6-3). The occupational therapist in recent years has become a consultant for the teacher via the administration of batteries of perceptual and visual-motor tests. Prescriptions include training in perceptual skills and visual-motor coordination. As with physical therapy,

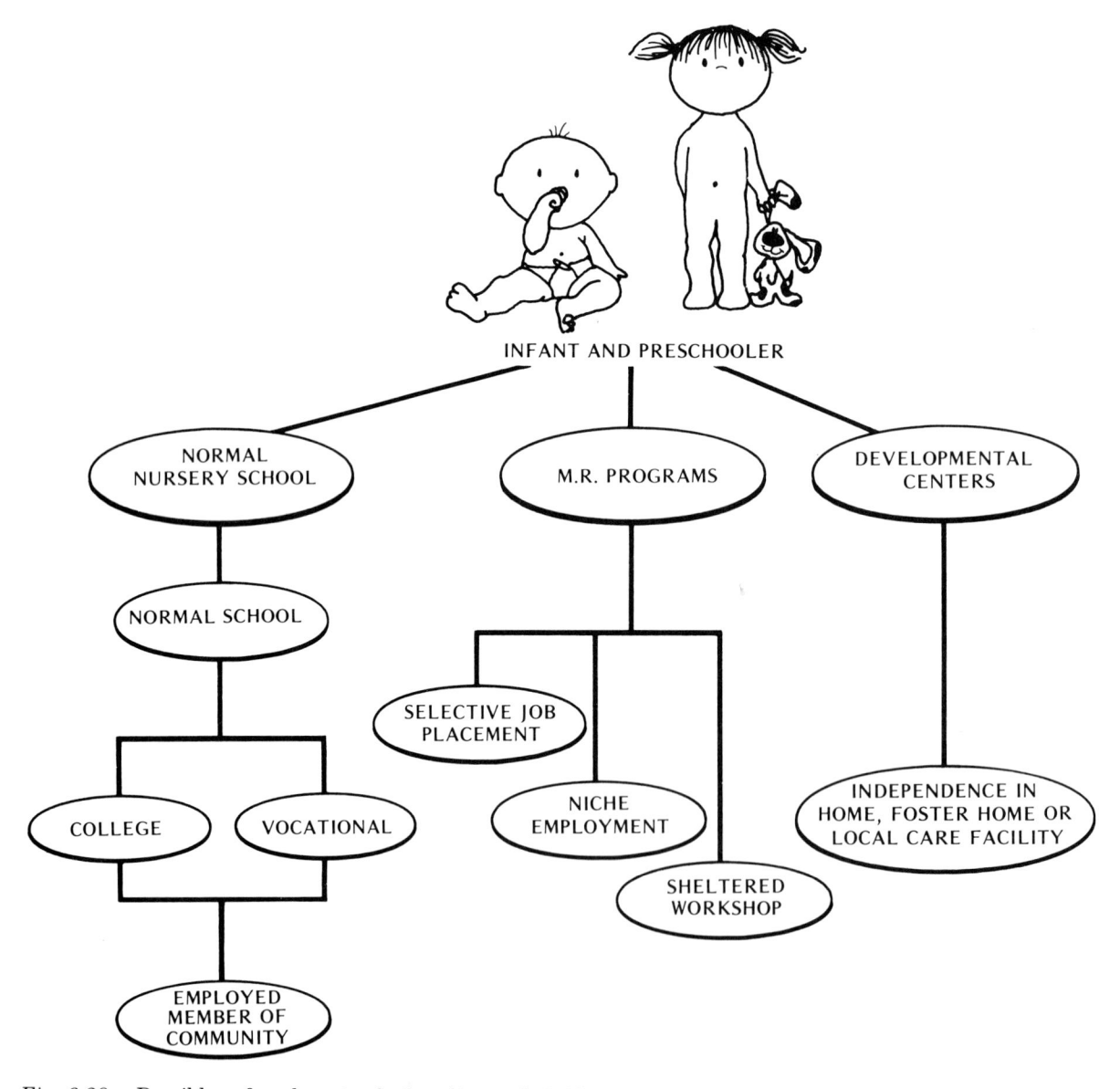

Fig. 6-29. Possible referral routes for handicapped children.

the results have not been analyzed in any definite study, but the author's impression is that, on retesting, some of the children have improved in their performance. An alternative to training in visual-motor coordination would be to develop other skills that can compensate for the visual-motor loss; for example, instead of struggling to achieve a slow, laborious handwriting, some children might benefit more from learning to use the electric typewriter. Probably not enough innovation is applied in this area of compensating for the deficits these children have. Testing and observation of the child's motor, perceptual, and visual-motor handicap can assist the teacher in defining the child's weak and strong points. The teacher can then work with the stronger points and suggest methods of compensating for the weaker ones.

A special word is necessary concerning the spastic athetoid upper limb, particularly in one-sided involvement (hemiplegia). Long experience has shown that the involved hand* is best left as a "helping hand."

PRESCRIBING "THERAPY"

Because of the impact of Public Law 94-142, which specifies entitlements to "therapy," and a consequent increase in the number of requests received for prescriptions for the Individual Educational Plan, we at the Children's Hospital at Stanford have found it necessary to develop a policy statement on prescribing. This policy is reproduced in the Appendix to this chapter.

SURGICAL TREATMENT

Surgical treatment is designed for functional and cosmetic improvement of the walking pattern.[31] Careful analysis before surgery is necessary so that, after surgery, the muscles will be balanced and a less functional walking pattern will not emerge. For example, surgery to correct spastic knee-flexion gait patterns (crouched walking with excessive lengthening of the tendons—hamstrings—behind the knee might result in overstraightening of the knees (hyperextension) and severe swayback (lumbar lordosis) (Figs. 6-30 to 6-32).

Orthopedic surgeons continue to upgrade their methods of preoperative analysis. Nothing is perfect, however. Studies examining the results of surgical treatment have been published.[5, 6, 7, 9, 17, 20, 27] Orthopedic surgery appears to have won a permanent place in the treatment of the spastic type of cerebral palsy.

REHABILITATION ENGINEERING

Rehabilitation engineering is a new field which links science and technology to the service of the physically handicapped. It encompasses the technical fields of orthotics (bracing), prosthetics (artificial limbs), robotics (mechanical devices that simulate human motion and take commands from a human who operates them with a variety of controls), mobility and seating (wheelchairs, vans, and specialized seats), interfaces and controls for the devices, and the exploding technology of microprocessing, which uses programmed computers to compensate for defects in human performance and, indeed, to enhance performance. Because cerebral palsy is the leading handicapping condition, and because rehabilitation engineering has much to offer these children, a general description

---

*Usually this hand has permanent sensory impairment of shape and texture recognition (astereognosis) as well.

Table 6-3. Form Used for Activities of Daily Living Evaluation (Occupational Therapy Department, Children's Hospital at Stanford)

CHILDREN'S HOSPITAL AT STANFORD
OCCUPATIONAL THERAPY
TIME-ORIENTED RECORD
ACTIVITIES OF DAILY LIVING ASSESSMENT

Key to Scoring:
- 4 Independent
- 3 Independent with equipment
- 2 Completes but cannot accomplish in practical time
- 1 Attempts but requires assistance to complete
- 0 Dependent—cannot attempt activity
- – Nonapplicable

The *Year-Month* vertical column represents the developmental sequence or approximate age when the child accomplishes the activity; the horizontal column represents the chronological age of the child being assessed

	VISIT NUMBER		1	2	3	4	5	6	7	8
	Julian date									
		Yr. Mo.								
	BED	Dev. Seq.								
1	Supine position	birth								
2	Prone position	birth								
3	Roll to side	1–4 wk.								
4	Roll supine to prone	0.6								
5	Roll prone to supine	0.8								
6	Sit up	0.10								
7	Propped sitting	0.6								
8	Sitting/hands props	0.7								
9	Sitting unsupported	0.10								
	Reaching									
10	to midline	0.5								
11	to mouth and face	0.6								
12	above head	—								
13	behind head	—								
14	behind back	—								
15	to toes	1.3								
	FEEDING									
16	Swallow (liquids)	birth								
17	drooling under control	1.0								
18	suck and use straw	1.6								
19	Chew (semisolids, solids)	1.6								

Cerebral Palsy

	VISIT NUMBER		1	2	3	4	5	6	7	8
	Julian date									
		Yr. Mo.								
	FEEDING (continued)	Dev. Seq.								
20	Fingerfoods	0.10								
	Utensils									
21	bottle	0.10								
22	spoon	3.0								
23	cup	1.6								
24	glass	2.0								
25	fork	3.0								
26	knife	6.0								
	TOILETING									
27	Bowel control	1.6								
28	Bladder control	2.0								
29	Sit on toilet	2.9								
30	Arrange clothing	4.0								
31	Cleanse self	5.0								
32	Flush toilet	3.3–5.0								
	HYGIENE									
33	Turn faucets on/off	3.0								
34	Wash/dry hands/face	4.9								
35	Wash ears	8.0								
36	Bathing	8.0								
37	Deodorant	10.0								
38	Care for teeth	4.9								
39	Care for hair	7.6								
40	Care for nails	8.0								
41	Care for nose	6.0								
42	Feminine hygiene	puberty								
	UNDRESSING									
	Lower Body									
43	Untie shoe bow	2.0–3.0								
44	Remove shoes	2.0–3.0								
45	Remove socks	1.6								
46	Remove pull down garment	2.6								

ACTIVITIES OF DAILY LIVING

Table 6-3. (continued)

	VISIT NUMBER		1	2	3	4	5	6	7	8
	Julian date									
		Yr. Mo.								
	UNDRESSING (continued)									
	Upper Body									
47	Remove pullover garment	4.0								
	DRESSING									
	Lower Body									
48	Put on socks	4.0								
49	Put on pull down garment	4.0								
50	Put on shoe	4.0								
51	Lace shoe	4.0–5.0								
52	Tie bow	6.0								
	Upper Body									
53	Put on pullover garment	5.0								
	FASTENERS									
	Unfastening									
	Button									
54	front and side	3.0								
55	back	5.6								
	Zipper									
56	front	3.3								
57	separating front	3.6								
58	back	4.9								
	Buckle									
59	belt or shoe	3.9								
	Tie									
60	back sash	5.0								
	Fasten									
	Button									
61	large front	2.6								
62	series	3.6								
63	back	6.3								
	Zipper									
64	front, lock tab	4.0								

ACTIVITIES OF DAILY LIVING

Cerebral Palsy

	VISIT NUMBER		1	2	3	4	5	6	7	8
	Julian date									
		Yr. Mo.								
	FASTENERS (continued)									
	Zipper (continued)	Dev. Seq.								
65	separating	4.6								
66	back	5.6								
	Buckle									
67	belt or shoe	4.0								
68	insert belt in loops	4.6								
	Tie									
69	front	6.0								
70	back	8.0								
71	neck tie	10.0								
	Snaps									
72	front	3.0								
73	back	6.0								

ACTIVITIES OF DAILY LIVING

of its application and components is presented in this chapter. All of these principles are applicable to all other handicapping conditions.

Function-oriented versus Disease-oriented Approach

Traditionally, we have taken a disease-oriented approach in the management of children with chronic disabilities. In so doing, we have failed to recognize, for example, that the child with cerebral palsy will become an adult with cerebral palsy. Disease-oriented treatment approaches can only be judged a failure when, at maturity, the child has the same disease and virtually the same disabilities. In the function-oriented approach, the problems to be resolved for a particular disabled child are assigned a priority based upon the adult's needs for optimum independence in the following areas (in order of decreasing importance):

1. Communication
2. Activities of daily living (e.g., eating, toileting, grooming)
3. Mobility (getting from here to there)
4. Walking

In general, the approach in the past was always to start with walking as the first priority, even though the prognosis for walking efficiently and independently might be very poor. Our prognostic studies indicate that the majority of children with cerebral palsy walk because the necessary

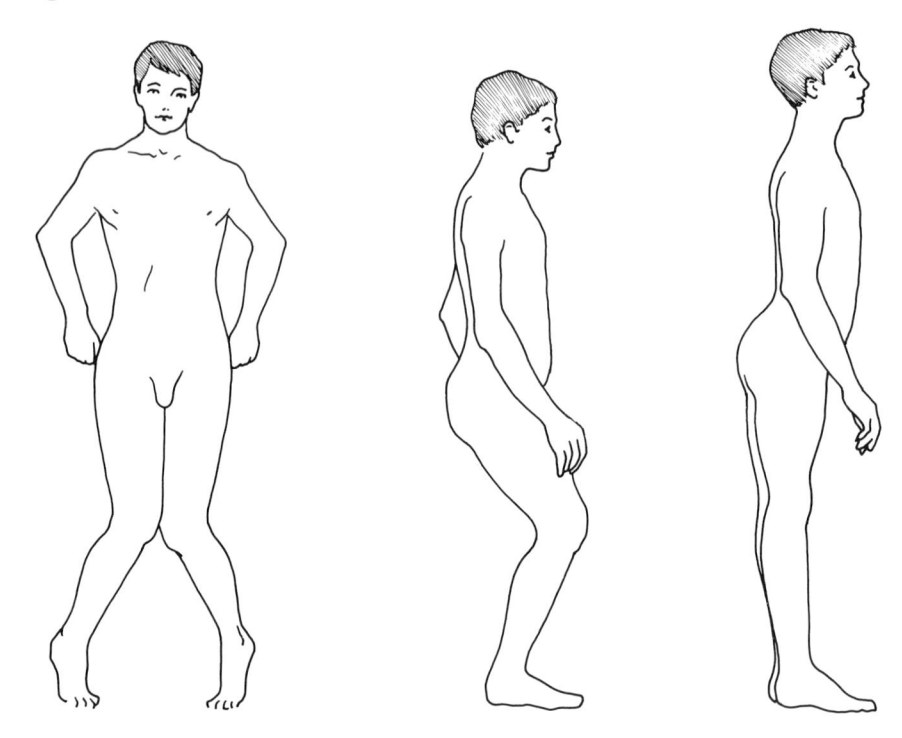

Fig. 6-30. The two figures on the left are in the typical bent-knee flexed-hip posture of a child with spastic diplegia. The figure on the right is postoperative result of weakening the muscles in the back of the thigh that flex the knee (hamstrings), either by lengthening or transfer. The resultant exaggerated swayback (lordosis) is a postural adaptation to the unrelieved hip-flexor spasm and contracture.

part of their central nervous system has remained functional, and *not* because any particular remedial method, including surgery, has been applied.

Goal Setting

In a study of 85 severely handicapped, cerebral palsied children (spastic quadriplegia or total body involved), we found that it was possible to set goals for the most important functions at an early age, and that there was no need to wait until maturity before achieving optimum inde-

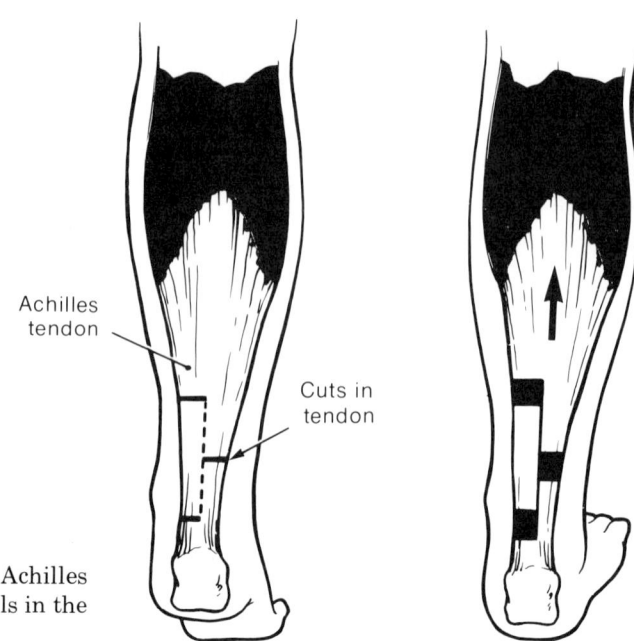

Fig. 6-31. Surgical method of lengthening the Achilles tendon. Within 6 weeks, growth of new tendon fills in the gaps.

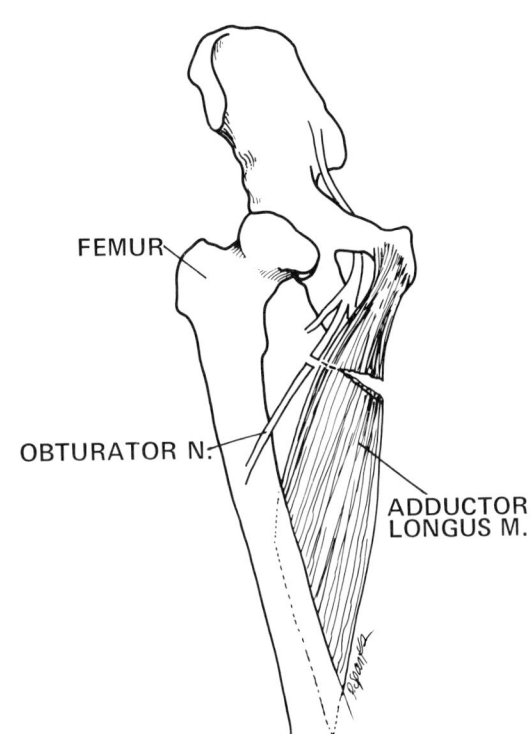

Fig. 6-32. An orthopedic operation for scissoring of the lower limbs. The adductor muscles are cut (tenotemy or myotomy), as is a branch of the major nerve (obturator nerve) supplying the spastic muscles. The muscles are thus weakened and the spasticity is reduced.

pendence and efficiency in function.[45] In particular, our study found that engineering devices consistently allowed achievement of the goals. One group of children was assessed at the age of 4 years and followed until a mean age of 16.8 years. The second group was assessed after the age of 4 years and followed for a minimum of 6 years. The results were virtually the same in both groups. We noted that, even though walking seemed to be achieved in childhood, its practicality in terms of independence and efficiency diminished during adolescence and early adulthood, when the realities of living and of independence came into focus (Figs. 6-33 to 6-36).

Orthotics (Bracing)

Orthotics is the contemporary term applied to what was called *bracing* of the limbs in the past. Contemporary orthotics are, for the most part, fabricated with thermal-setting plastics (polypropylene or polyethylene). Lower-limb orthotics are described according to the part of the limb or joint supported by the orthosis. The relevant terminology and inevitable abbreviations in common usage are as follows:

Ankle-foot orthosis (AFO): supports and immobilizes the leg below the knee, ankle, and foot.
Knee-ankle-foot orthosis (KAFO): supports the thigh, knee joint, leg, ankle, and foot.
Hip-knee-ankle-foot orthosis (HKAFO): supports and immobilizes the hip joint, thigh, knee, leg, ankle, and foot.

Figure 6-37 shows a plastic ankle-foot orthosis that is frequently used to control tiptoeing in spastic children. It is fabricated by an orthotist from a plaster mold made of the child's foot, ankle, and leg when they are held in the corrected position. A plastic sheet is heated in an oven (similar to a

Fig. 6-33. Goal and achievement—independence (IND) and efficiency (EFF) in communication—in 14 patients with spastic quadriplegia (QUAD) or total body involvement (TBI). The goal of achieving ability to initiate and to sustain a conversation was set at age 4 years and was achieved via technical aids and devices only in spastic quadriplegics. The total body involved children (dotted line) had severe mental retardation (MR) and could only give a "yes–no" response. (From Terver and Bleck.[45])

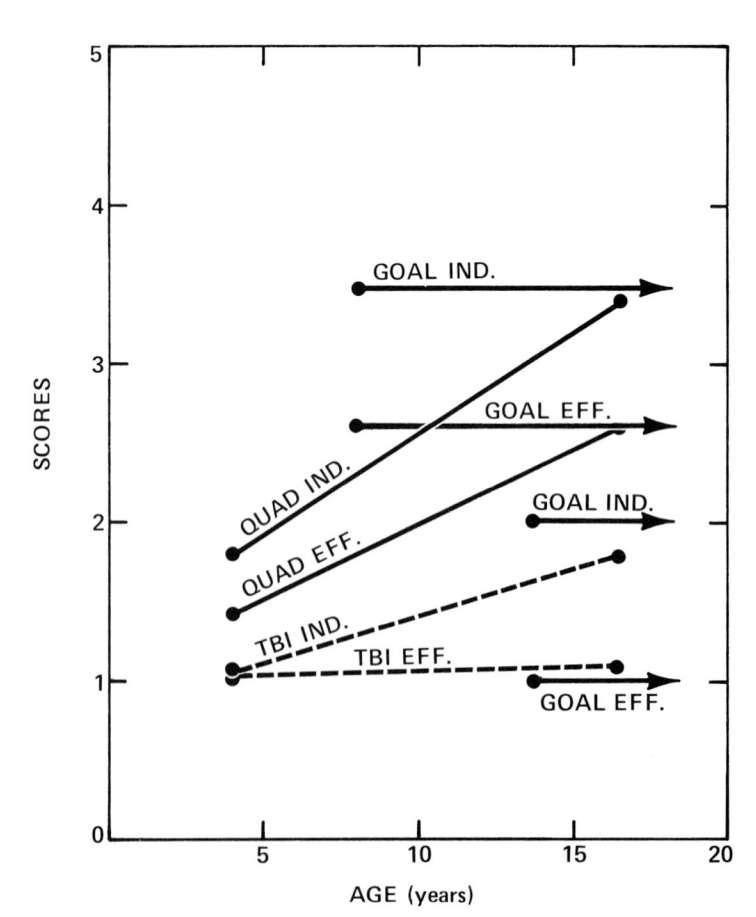

Fig. 6-34. Goals and achievements—independence and efficiency in activities of daily living—in the same patients as in Fig. 6-32. Goals were set at the age of 4 years and were almost reached by technical means at followup age of 16 years. Score 3.5, independence: can perform activities without human help but needs assistive devices. Score 2.5, efficiency: can meet own needs in feeding, toileting, and dressing (score 1); completes own care (score 2); and can perform usual household activities (score 3).

96

Fig. 6-35. Goal and achievements—independence and efficiency in mobility—in the same 14 patients as in Figs. 6-32 and 6-33. Score 3, independence: mobile without human help but needs technical devices. Score 3, efficiency: mobility sufficient to travel in community. Goals in both independence and efficiency were achieved by all spastic quadriplegic children by the age of 16.

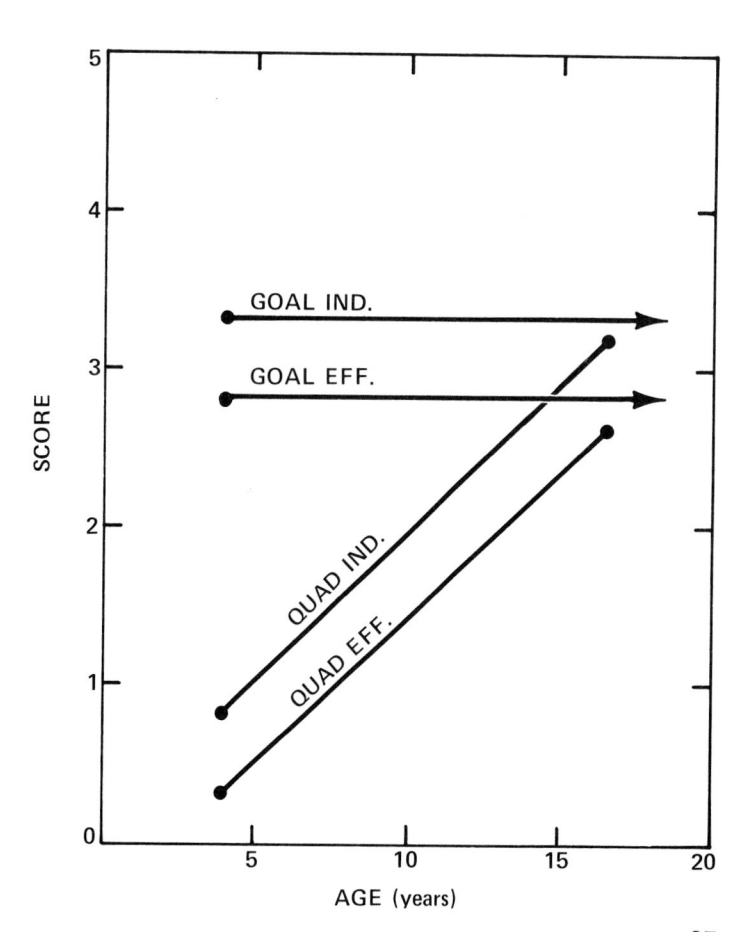

Fig. 6-36. Goals and achievements—independence and efficiency in walking—in patients with spastic quadriplegia shown in Figs. 6-32 to 6-34. Goals in independence and efficency not quite achieved by age 16 years. Score 3, independence: can walk with aid of technical devices, crutches or walker. Score 3, efficiency: household walker, limited to immediate neighborhood.

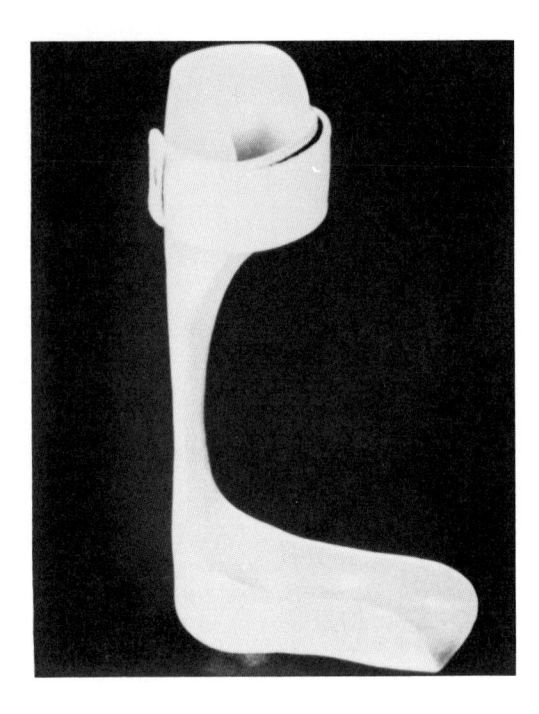

Fig. 6-37. Plastic ankle foot orthosis (AFO) used to control foot position. Worn over stockings and inside normal-appearing shoe.

pizza oven) and, when soft, is sucked over the plaster mold with a vacuum apparatus. The plastic is trimmed, and buckles and velcro straps attached.

Seating and Mobility Devices

The most common mobility device is the manual wheelchair. If the child has insufficient motor power to drive the manual wheelchair efficiently, then we recommend the use of power wheelchairs at any age. For schoolage children who definitely need mobility and independence, we have found the portable electric chair manufactured by Bec Engineering in England quite satisfactory. For larger children, adolescents, and adults, a variety of standard power chairs are available. It is very important that the wheelchair prescription include the child's exact measurements as well as a list of what acessories are necessary (such as a reclining backrest, elevating leg rests, detachable desk arms (upholstered), and trays upon which the child's limbs can rest while driving the chair). Clear polycarbonate lap trays are functional because they allow the child to see where he or she is going and, at the same time, provide a desk or platform from which the child can work particular devices (Fig. 6-38). Special electronic switches and controls may be necessary to operate a powered chair for those children who have inadequate upper-limb control and dexterity. Electric chairs can be driven with puff controls, head tilt, or a foot or big toe motion (Fig. 6-39). The assessment for and prescription of mobility equipment can be made by the occupational therapist working in conjunction with the rehabilitation engineer.

Many spastic quadriplegic children do not have adequate sitting balance because of loss of the central nervous system functions that control trunk stability. When such children are put unsupported, into a chair or on a bench, they will topple over; they constantly need to use their upper limbs to maintain balance and a sitting position. This, then, precludes the use of the upper limbs in activities of daily living such as in the opera-

Cerebral Palsy

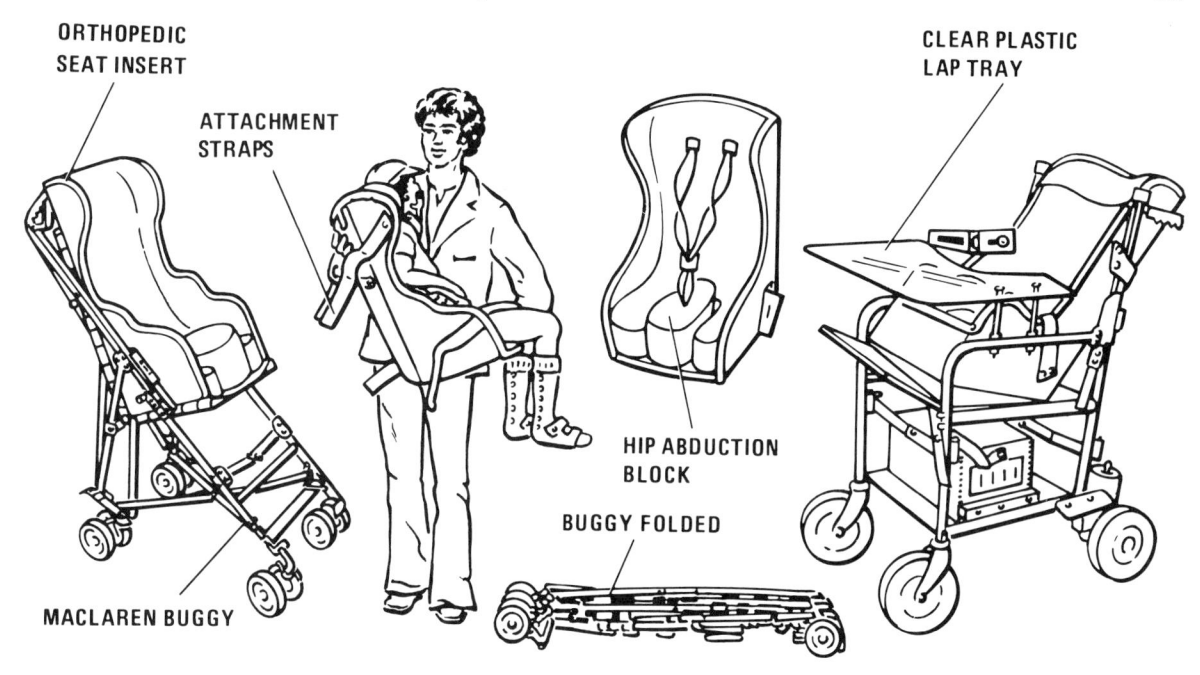

Fig. 6-38. Mobility systems and seat inserts.

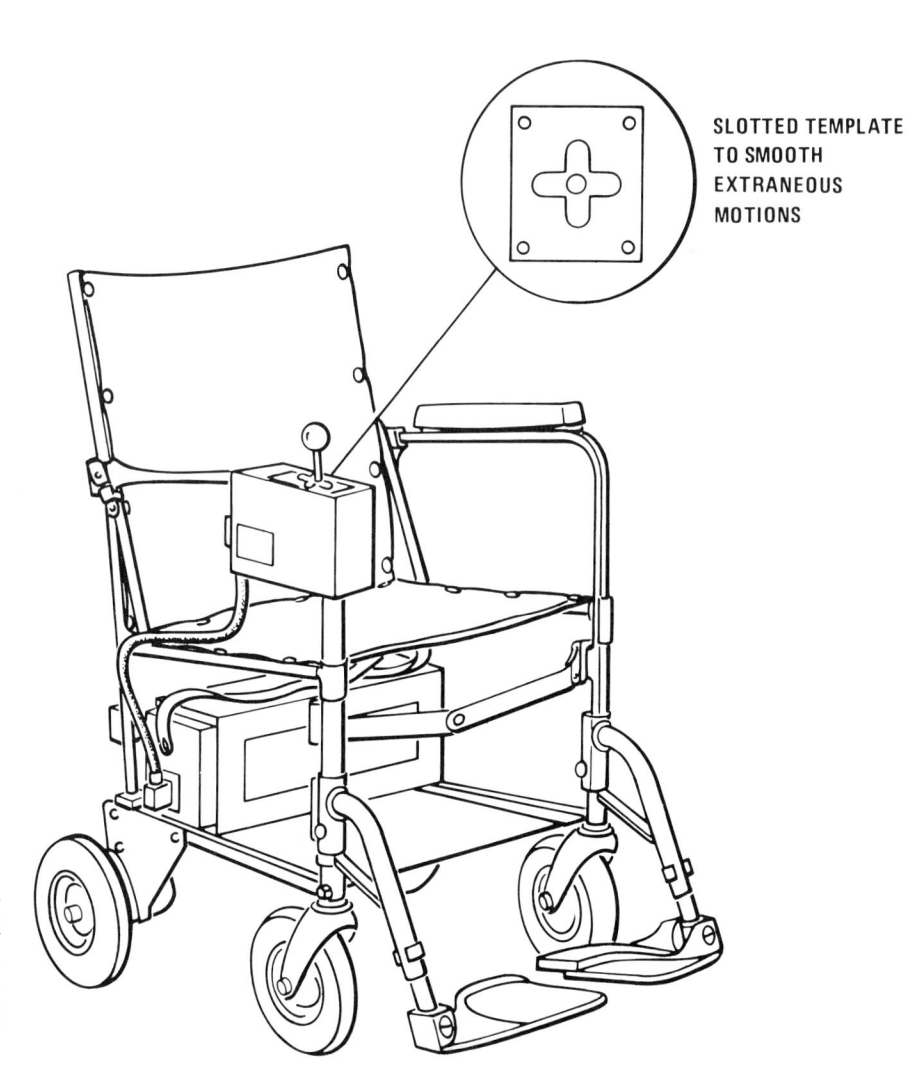

Fig. 6-39. Portable electric chair with slotted template for joystick. Template nearly eliminates need for fine control by hands.

tion of the controls of a communication or mobility device, or both. The first step, then, in the management of such children is to provide trunkal stability by means of a contoured wheelchair insert. Currently, we prefer an insert that captures the child's sitting posture in the most relaxed position (generally, tilted backwards slightly, with hips and knees flexed) (Fig. 6-37). The seat is carved out of foam plastic to support the trunk, shoulders, and head (if necessary) and then is upholstered with fabric. We have found that vinyl is uncomfortable for prolonged sitting because of increased perspiration and retention of body heat.

Activities of Daily Living

One of the most difficult activities of daily living is self-feeding, and devices have been made to compensate for impairments of this function. Their use is still limited, however, and much work is needed in research and development before automatic feeding devices may be applied on a broad basis. One feeder that is applicable for children who have no manual dexterity but who can make a fist and push down on a knob and have head contol is the Ontario Crippled Children's Feeder (see Chapter 22). Feeding devices, as well as devices that assist in dressing and toileting, can be found in the medical equipment catalogs of companies that specialize in aids for the handicapped. Such catalogs are readily available in practically all occupational therapy departments.

Communication Devices

The place for nonoral communication and the devices available are delineated in Chapter 8 of this text.

Microprocessors

The technology of microprocessing and miniaturization of circuitry is advancing daily and rapidly. One application of the microprocessor has been an environmental control system, in which functions such as turning on electric lights, television, or radio, and answering the telephone can be controlled by the totally handicapped person from the bedside or wheelchair. Breath controls, head controls, tongue controls, and foot or toe controls can be easily and effectively used by the person who has inadequate hand or upper-limb control (Fig. 6-40). Microprocessors are already functionally operative in commercially available synthetic voice devices (see Chapter 8). Microprocessors for educational use by the handicapped and in robotics can be expected to make further contributions to the quality of life for the disabled.

Walking Aids

In setting goals for cerebral palsied persons we can classify their mobility as follows:

1. Community walker: can get about the community independently, with or without crutches.

Fig. 6-40. TV monitor display of electronic maze game in microprocessor used to test child's ability to manipulate controlling switches.

2. Household walker: can get about in the household but needs a wheelchair outside of it.
3. Physiological walker: can walk only in the physical therapy department for exercise, usually with the aid of parallel bars. This person needs a wheelchair for household and community mobility.
4. Nonwalker: incapable of functional walking and will need a manually operated or power wheelchair.

The nonwalker can be further subdivided according to the method of transfer in and out of the wheelchair:

1. Independent: can get in and out of the wheelchair without assistance.
2. Assistive: needs the assistance of one person to get out of the chair but does not need to be lifted.
3. Dependent: needs to be lifted out of the wheelchair.

The usual walking aids are crutches—either the standard axillary type or the forearm crutches. Various types of walkers are available, the most functional being the aluminum pick-up walker, usually with small wheels in the two front legs.

DRUG THERAPY

Other than for the control of seizures, drug therapy has been notably unsuccessful, particularly in the control of spasticity. Diazepam (Valium) has been helpful in relieving some of the excessive motions and tension in some athetoid patients.[16] It is thought to act through exerting a tranquilizing effect on the brain. Athetosis is well known to be augmented by stress and anxiety; consequently, some adult athetoids have found alcohol beneficial in controlling symptoms.

A drug recently released for use in spastic cerebral palsy is Dantrolene sodium. The drug is thought to reduce the excitability of the muscles and, thereby, the spasticity. We at the Children's Hospital evaluated this drug and found that its side effects outweighed any relaxation achieved. In general, we now use Dantrolene sodium only for relief of spasticity in some postoperative patients. Its major side effect is drowsiness, but it can also affect liver functions; consequently, liver function must be monitored at regular intervals in patients taking the medication.

The late Meyer Perlstein, in discussing new drugs for cerebral palsy, would, whenever he had a chance, inevitably come back to alcohol, and especially wine, as the best drug yet devised—readily available, relatively inexpensive, and, possibly, good-tasting. Whether or not chronic alcoholism has been experienced by athetoids has not been reported. However, it seems prudent to consider this side effect before recommending this particular form of pharmacological relaxation.

It is well known that barbituates (phenobarbital), which sedate the normal person, might well make brain-damaged patients more excitable. Paradoxically, the brain-damaged are sometimes calmed by the stimulant, dextroamphetamine.

Because, as William Osler has said, "the desire to take medicine is perhaps the greatest feature which distinguishes men from animals," the search for medications has much appeal. A word of caution, then, is in order regarding any "new" drug that may be promoted for cerebral palsy. The efficacy of any such medication should be carefully tested in a double-blind study—in which neither the examiner nor the patient knows which is the real drug and which is the fake (placebo)—using objective methods of measuring the extent of motor disorder before and after drug use. Unfortunately, most drug studies have not met these criteria.

LONG-TERM OUTLOOK—LIVING WITH CEREBRAL PALSY

What happens to the child with cerebral palsy after leaving school? This is a matter of concern not only to teachers but to society as a whole. A recent study by O'Reilly[35] examined a population of cerebral palsied children born prior to 1964. At the time of the report, in 1971, 33 percent were found to be mentally normal, essentially self-sufficient, and assimilable into the general population. The borderline and retarded children with a minor physical problem were in sheltered environments or custodial care. About 5 percent had normal intelligence but needed social and intellectual stimulation and were precluded from full employment or functioning because of severe physical involvement.

A study by Hassakis entailed a follow-up analysis of 68 patients who at follow-up were between the ages of 18 and 31 years.[18] Thirty-five percent of the hemiplegics, 56 percent of the spastic quadriplegics, 50 percent of the athetoids, and 17 percent of those with mixed forms were retarded. A functional analysis was done on all patients, including whether or not they could drive a car. None of the patients who had IQs below 50 were fully functional. Of the remaining patients, 73 percent of the spastic hemiplegics, 33 percent of those with mixed forms, and 13 percent of the spastic quadriplegics were fully functional; none of the patients with athetosis were functional. Mental retardation was the main limiting factor in one-third, and physical handicaps were the main limiting factor in two-thirds of patients. Twenty-one of 40 patients studied in detail were employed: 5 in competitive employment and the rest in niche or workshop employment. Nineteen were unemployed. Fifty percent

Cerebral Palsy

of the patients had restricted social lives, and 60 percent were not dating or married.

Ingram et al. studied the long-term outcomes of children with cerebral palsy in Scotland, mainly in the cities of Edinburgh and Dundee and the counties of Perth, Angus, and Kinross.[23] An examination of their social lives showed that 21 percent led a normal social life; 25 percent led a restricted social life; 11 percent attended only clubs for the disabled or had only disabled friends; 27 percent led a social life confined to the family; 4 percent never left their homes; and 12 percent were in institutions for the mentally handicapped. About 45 percent were unemployed. Those in smaller towns had a higher percentage of niche employment (one job only for which they were suitable): 31 percent in the smaller towns versus 14 percent in the cities or Edinburgh and Dundee. Females seemed to be employed for relatively more skilled jobs than males. Hemiplegics had a higher rate of employment (48 percent) than diplegics (33 percent) or athetoses (20 percent). The severity of the handicap and the degree of mental retardation are important factors in obtaining employment (Fig. 6-41). Another factor in obtaining employment and in social adjustment to adult life was an overprotective attitude exerted by parents in early life. A more favorable outcome regarding employment was found in those who had attended regular school or at least had the opportunity of even-

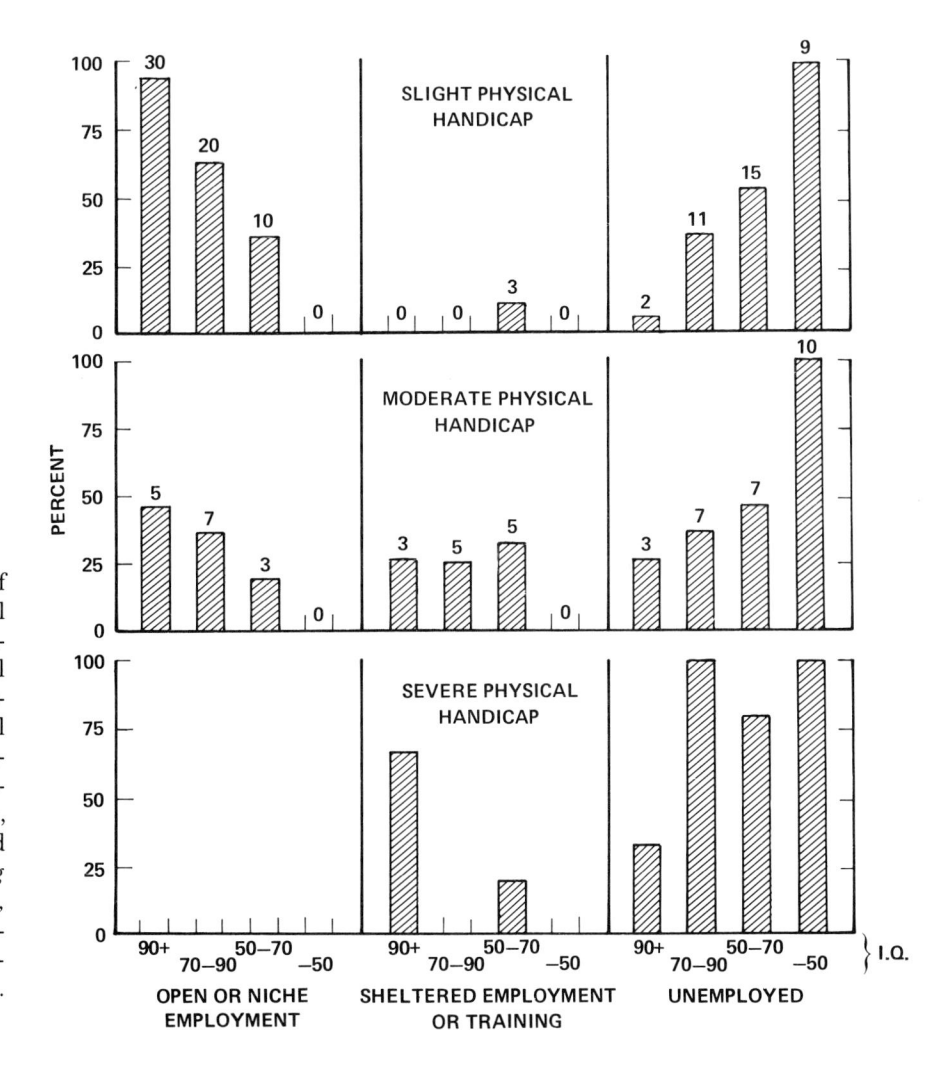

Fig. 6-41. Percentage of persons with cerebral palsy employed in Edinburgh, Dundee, and small towns, according to the severity of the physical handicap and the intelligence. (Redrawn from Ingram, T. T. S., Jameson, S., Errington, J., and Mitchell, R. G., *Living with Cerebral Palsy*, Clinics and Developmental Medicine, No. 14, London, Heinemann, 1964. With permission.)

tually attending regular school. Those who had gone to normal schools but had failed to obtain work were often emotionally disturbed.

More recent studies have confirmed those just quoted. O'Reilly found that the more severe the intellectual retardation, the lower the capacity for employment; regular schooling and completion of secondary school was important; and spastic paralysis was more favorable than athetosis.[35] A follow-up study of patients with cerebral palsy by Cohen and Kohn (296 living patients) again demonstrated that intelligence was positively correlated with independent functioning.[13] The more severe the mental and physical disability, the less likely that there would be a favorable outcome. One group with IQ scores over 80 who had severe physical disability continued to be dependent despite their higher intellectual capability because their physical disability precluded the use of the mental capabilities. Cohen and Kohn also found that the psychological evaluations of all patients did not change significantly over the years, especially in the lower (IQ less than 50) and upper ranges (IQ more than 80). Their conclusion was that parents of children who have severe physical disabilities and lower intellectual capabilities, should not be encouraged to have unrealistic expectations when the indications are towards dependency. Mental energies might be better devoted to the task of planning and preparing for a stimulating and comfortable environment. For children to achieve optimum independence at maturity, it appears necessary that the families accept the child's disability and not let it act as a barrier to the assumption of responsibility.

Despite these somewhat discouraging statistics, one should remember that the population of children with cerebral palsy varies from one country to another, and that the type and severity of cerebral palsy continues to change, hopefully for the better. The demands on the professional team for rational analysis and direction of the cerebral palsied child continue to be great.

The changing causes of cerebral palsy and the improved outlook for children with cerebral palsy due to prematurity will affect follow-up statistics. As causes of the severest types of cerebral palsy are eliminated, it is likely that the employment and social follow-up statistics will be much improved. Most of the follow-up studies now available include large groups of patients who had severe cerebral damage due to causes which have been declining with improved medical diagnosis and treatment.

In our own study of the outcomes of 119 children with spastic diplegia (65.5 percent of which were associated with prematurity), we found that 90 percent could enter regular school by the age of 8 years. These children did not need physical therapy after entering regular school, except following orthopedic surgery, and then for maximum duration of 12 months. Only 16 percent deteriorated in function, only 8.4 percent were not walking, none were in a development or day care center, and none were in institutions. Of those over age 21 years, 3 percent were in a sheltered workshop. The rest were either in school, advanced education, or working. This study probably confirms that one needs to be concerned about the extent of the specific motor and mental handicap in a particular child when directing an educational program. Children who have spastic diplegia have a good prognosis for social integration, do not need ongoing physical therapy, and do not need a long-term passage through special schools. This is in marked contrast to the spastic quadriplegic and the total body involved who need appropriate goal setting in terms of function rather than disease, and who need compensatory technical aids for optimum function.

EDUCATIONAL IMPLICATIONS

Winnie H. Bachmann's study of 216 persons who had attended orthopedically handicapped schools in California (63 percent of whom had cerebral palsy) indicated that "traditional objectives for normal children may be inappropriate and unachievable for some handicapped students."[4] As a result of her study, she concludes that the use of a team approach for each student cannot be overemphasized. It appears particularly important that the educational unit be in synchrony with and support the medical therapy unit. Because physical abilities were one of the main causes for unemployment in her study, it is recommended that much time be spent in learning the activities of daily living, in mastering a method of communication, and in achieving independent mobility. Work experiences in school are highly recommended, as they provide the student with an opportunity to earn self-reliance, to cooperate with others, and to take direction and criticism from others. In addition to strictly academic subjects, it would appear that many students should learn about and be tested for the various vocational roles open to the handicapped.

The teacher must recognize that there are some cerebral palsied children who will go on to college, and that these differ from others who will only be able to enter the vocational work force or to work only in a sheltered environment. Some, unfortunately, will be able to do neither and will have to be prepared for home or sheltered-environment living. Careful analysis of the whole child, taking into account the complexity of his disability and capitalizing on his strong points, is the most demanding but also the most important task for the teacher and the medical therapy unit.

Integration of many of the cerebral palsied children into the regular schools, provided such children are intellectually capable, has been pushed forward by Public Law 94-142, which requires that the child be placed in the least restrictive environment. An early definition of the child's capabilities and neurological function is extremely important. Compensatory devices for function, such as nonoral communication devices and mobility equipment, will allow many children to be integrated into regular schools. In order to achieve this integration, it is essential that special schools for the handicapped offer function-oriented rather than disease-oriented treatment, as the latter tends to segregate the handicapped permanently from the community.[29, 44]

To achieve integration, demands for "therapy" for the child in regular school or in other educational settings should be based not on mere legal entitlement for such services but, rather, on functional aims that are consistent with a careful, objective analysis of the extent of the child's neurological disorder and on data regarding the results and efficacy of such therapies. To do otherwise will restore once again the medicalization and segregation of the child from "the least restrictive environment."

FUNCTIONAL DEVELOPMENTAL ASSESSMENT

In addition to understanding normal infant motor development, it may assist the teacher to refer to the norms of functional development for children at various ages. Table 6-4 is a functional developmental assessment prepared by Claudia Brower of the Children's Hospital at Stanford. The assessment test is reproduced on a time-oriented record so that serial testing might be done (space for eight tests is provided on the forms). The first page is a summary of the total scoring for gross motor development, fine motor development, language, and personal-social development. The pages that follow the summary sheet are the details of the testing in each broad area.

Table 6-4

CHILDREN'S HOSPITAL AT STANFORD
Occupational Therapy
TIME-ORIENTED RECORD
FUNCTIONAL DEVELOPMENTAL ASSESSMENT

FUNCTIONAL DEVELOPMENTAL ASSESSMENT—SUMMARY

Key to Scoring: (Years and/or months) child passed all items thru this age.
(Years–years) child failed some items within these ages.
(–) not asked, no functional tasks available to evaluate.

The norm is listed for each task at which 90% of the children passed.
The age is noted as follows: year:month

VISIT NUMBER	1	2	3	4	5	6	7	8
Julian date								
Chronological age								
GROSS MOTOR DEVELOPMENT								
Coordination/Strength								
Balancing								
Locomotion								
Visual Motor—Upper Limbs								
Visual Motor—Lower Limbs								
FINE MOTOR DEVELOPMENT								
Reach/Carry/Bilateral Coordination								
Grasp/Placement/Release/Eye Hand Coordination								
Prehension/Thumb-Finger Manipulation								
Visual/Visual-Motor/Visual-Discr./Spat. Relations								
Graphics/Drawing/Writing								
LANGUAGE								
Auditory Discrimination/Memory								
Expressive Language								
Receptive Language/Non-Verbal Language								
Quantitative Concepts								
Reading								
PERSONAL-SOCIAL								
Social Response/Home/Community								
Play/Work								
Self/Family								
Body Scheme								
Eating/Drinking/Food Preparation								
Dressing/Undressing								
Hygiene/Toileting								

Cerebral Palsy

CHILDREN'S HOSPITAL AT STANFORD
Occupational Therapy
TIME-ORIENTED RECORD
FUNCTIONAL DEVELOPMENTAL ASSESSMENT

FUNCTIONAL DEVELOPMENTAL ASSESSMENT

Key to Scoring:
- 4 Passes
- 3 Passes with equipment and/or adaptive technique.
- 2 Accomplishes, but not in practical time.
- 1 Attempts, but requires assistance to complete.
- 0 Fails, cannot attempt activity.
- – Nonapplicable

The norm is listed for each task at which 90% of the children pass.
The age is noted as follows: Year:month

VISIT NUMBER		1	2	3	4	5	6	7	8
Julian date									
Chronological Age									
	Norm Yr:Mo								
GROSS MOTOR DEVELOPMENT									
Coordination/Strength									
1. Lifts head—prone	0:1								
2. Lifts head 45°—prone	0:2.6								
3. Lifts head 90°—prone	0:3								
4. Chest up—arm support	0:4								
5. Rolls—supine to prone	0:5								
6. Rolls—prone to supine	0:6								
7. Sits—hands free for manipulation	0:8								
8. Pulls to stand	0:10								
9. Gets to sitting—from prone	0:11								
10. Gets into chair 16 in. high	1:3								
11. Pulls toy on string	1:6								
12. Squats in play	1:9								
13. Seats self	2:0								
14. Pedals trike 10 ft. with aid	2:6								
15. Pedals trike 10 ft.	3:0								
16. Somersaults	4:0								
17. Somersaults over 6 in. object	5:0								
18. Rides bike trainer wheels	5:6								
19. Carries object with both hands down steps	5:6								
20. Carries liquid 8 ft. without spilling	6:0								

VISIT NUMBER		1	2	3	4	5	6	7	8
Julian date									
Chronological Age									
	Norm Yr:Mo								
GROSS MOTOR DEVELOPMENT (continued)									
Coordination/Strength (continued)									
21 Bends, touches floor	7:0								
22 Leg lifts	7:0								
23 Carries chair	7:0								
24 Rides bike	9:0								
Balancing									
25 Steadies head—sitting	0:4								
26 Sits without support	0:8								
27 Stands, holding-on	0:10								
28 Stands momentarily	0:11								
29 Stands well alone	1:2								
30 Stoops and recovers	1:2								
31 Stands on one foot with aid	2:6								
32 Tiptoes—1 second	2:6								
33 Walks line	3:0								
34 Stands on one foot—1 second	3:3								
35 Stands on one foot—5 seconds	3:4								
36 Walks balance beam	4:6								
37 Walks line—heel-toe	5:0								
38 Stands—heel-toe	6:0								
39 Stands on one foot—10 seconds	6:0								
40 Walks backward—heel-toe	6:3								
41 Stands on one foot—15 seconds	7:0								
42 Lies on back, stands, maintains balance	7:6								
43 Balances on toes of one foot for 5 seconds	8:6								
44 Tiptoes—10–12 seconds (eyes closed)	9:0								
45 Balances on one foot—10 seconds (eyes closed)	10:0								
46 Tiptoes—15 seconds (eyes closed)	11:0								
47 Tiptoes—1 ft., 10 seconds	12:0								
48 Tiptoes—squatting (eyes closed)	12:0								

FUNCTIONAL DEVELOPMENTAL ASSESSMENT

VISIT NUMBER		1	2	3	4	5	6	7	8
Julian date									
Chronological Age									
	Norm Yr:Mo								
GROSS MOTOR DEVELOPMENT (continued)									
Locomotion									
49 Rolls over	0:5								
50 Bears weight	0:6								
51 Commando crawls	0:7								
52 Creeps on hands and knees	0:10								
53 Walks with one hand held	0:12								
54 Walks holding onto furniture	0:12								
55 Walks alone	1:1								
56 Walks, rarely falls	1:3								
57 Log rolls	1:6								
58 Walks backwards	1:6								
59 Upstairs—nonreciprocal feet with aid	1:9								
60 Runs 8 ft.	2:0								
61 Downstairs—nonreciprocal feet with aid	2:6								
62 Upstairs—alternate feet with aid	3:0								
63 Downstairs—alternate feet with aid	3:3								
64 Skips	3:3								
65 Upstairs—alternate feet	3:6								
66 Downstairs—alternate feet	4:0								
67 Runs 50 ft.—avoids obstacles	4:6								
68 Skips—alternate feet	5:3								
69 Runs 50 yd. in 12 seconds	6:0								
70 Marches	6:0								
71 Gallops	6:6								
72 Skips backwards	7:6								
73 Runs 50-yd. dash in 9 seconds	8:0								
Visual Motor—Upper Limbs									
74 Offers ball	0:9								
75 Hurls ball	1:0								

FUNCTIONAL DEVELOPMENTAL ASSESSMENT

Table 6-4. (continued)

	VISIT NUMBER		1	2	3	4	5	6	7	8
	Julian date									
	Chronological Age									
		Norm Yr:Mo								
	GROSS MOTOR DEVELOPMENT (continued)									
	Visual Motor—Upper Limbs (continued)									
76	Throws ball	1:6								
77	Rolls 9 in. ball—sitting	2:3								
78	Bounces 9 in. ball—1–3 ft.	2:3								
79	Throws tennis ball overhand	2:6								
80	Throws 9 in. ball—4–5 ft.	2:6								
81	Throws 9 in. ball—6–7 ft.	2:9								
82	Catches 9 in. ball, arms and body	3:0								
83	Throws 9 in. ball underhand	3:0								
84	Bounces 9 in. ball—4–5 ft.	3:4								
85	Throws tennis ball 5 ft.	3:6								
86	Throws 9 in. ball—8–9 ft. from chest	3:8								
87	Catches 9 in. ball, hands and body	4:6								
88	Throws 9 in. ball, 12–13 ft.	4:9								
89	Catches bounced tennis ball with hands	5:5								
90	Throws 9 in. ball—14–15 ft.	5:5								
91	Catches 9 in. ball with hands	5:6								
92	Throws 9 in. ball—16–17 ft.	6:0								
93	Throws tennis ball 25 ft.	6:0								
94	Catches tennis ball with one hand	7:0								
95	Bats tennis ball	7:0								
96	Dribbles ball	8:0								
97	Throws tennis ball 50 ft.	9:0								
	Visual Motor—Lower Limbs									
98	Kicks 9 in. ball (demonstration)	1:0								
99	Kicks 9 in. ball (command)	2:0								
100	Walks up, kicks 9 in. ball	2:3								
101	Jumps down 8 in.—both feet	2:6								

VISIT NUMBER		1	2	3	4	5	6	7	8
	Julian date									
	Chronological Age									
		Norm Yr:Mo								
	GROSS MOTOR DEVELOPMENT (continued)									
	Visual Motor—Lower Limbs (continued)									
102	Jumps in place	3:0								
103	Broad jumps	3:2								
104	Jumps 10 or more steps	3:6								
105	Broad jumps—1 ft.	3:9								
106	Hops on one foot—4 ft.	4:5								
107	Broad jumps—2 ft.	4:9								
108	Hops on one foot—8 ft.	5:0								
109	Broad jumps—2½ ft.	5:0								
110	Jumps over 6 in. rope—both feet	5:3								
111	Kicks 9 in. ball—2-step start	5:6								
112	Hops on one foot—16 ft.	5:6								
113	Hops in a pattern	6:0								
114	Runs and kicks a rolled 9 in. ball	7:6								
115	Kicks a dropped ball	9:0								
116	Kicks ball in midair	10:0								
	FINE MOTOR DEVELOPMENT									
	Reach/Carry/Bilateral Coordination									
117	Thrusts arms in play	0:1								
118	Symmetrical arm movements	0:3								
119	Hands come to midline	0:4								
120	Unilateral lead in reaching	0:7								
121	Transfers object hand-to-hand	0:7								
122	Bilateral reach	0:8								
123	Reciprocal reach	0:10								
124	Holds object bilaterally	0:10								
125	Pulls apart pop-beads	1:0								
126	Turns doorknob	2:0								

FUNCTIONAL DEVELOPMENTAL ASSESSMENT

Table 6-4. (continued)

	VISIT NUMBER		1	2	3	4	5	6	7	8
	Julian date									
	Chronological Age									
		Norm Yr:Mo								
	FINE MOTOR DEVELOPMENT (continued)									
	Reach-Carry-Bilateral Coordination (continued)									
127	Stirs	2:0								
128	Turns crank-handle (egg beater)	3:0								
129	Opens doors	3:6								
130	Puts paper clip on paper	4:6								
131	Sharpens pencil	5:0								
132	Sweeps with household broom	6:0								
133	Uses hammer to drive headed nail	6:0								
134	Draws line with ruler	7:0								
135	Opens and closes hand alternately	8:0								
136	Saws	10:0								
137	Arm rotations	11:0								
	Comment:									
	Hand dominance									
	Grasp/Placement/Release/Eye Hand Coordination									
138	Reflex grasp	0:2								
139	Involuntary release	0:2								
140	Hands predominantly open	0:4								
141	Grasps rattle	0:4								
142	Ulnar-palmer grasp	0:6								
143	Radial-palmer grasp	0:7								
144	Crude voluntary release	0:10								
145	Waves bell	0:10								
146	Mature grasp	1:0								
147	Places block in box	1:0								
148	Unwraps loose-wrapped object	1:3								
149	Places pellet in cup	1:3								
150	Builds 2-block tower	1:6								
151	Inserts pellet in bottle	1:6								

FUNCTIONAL DEVELOPMENTAL ASSESSMENT

VISIT NUMBER			1	2	3	4	5	6	7	8
	Julian date									
	Chronological Age									
		Norm Yr:Mo								
	FINE MOTOR DEVELOPMENT (continued)									
	Grasp/Placement/Release/Eye Hand Coordination (continued)									
152	Unscrews 3 in. lid	2:0								
153	Builds 4-block tower	2:2								
154	Unscrews 1 in. lid	3:0								
155	Builds 8-block tower	3:0								
156	Screws 1 in. lid	4:0								
157	Creases paper	4:6								
158	Inserts letter in envelope	5:6								
159	Uses eraser	6:0								
160	Sews with straight stitch—6 in.	6:0								
161	Threads needle	7:0								
162	Builds straight 8-block tower	7:0								
163	Unlocks door with key	8:0								
164	Uses screwdriver	9:0								
	Prehension/Thumb—Finger Manipulation									
165	Pats, slaps	0:6								
166	Rakes pellet	0:8								
167	Pokes	0:10								
168	Apposed pinch	0:11								
169	Squeezes squeaking toy	1:0								
170	Opposed pinch	1:4.7								
171	Turns page	1:6								
172	Holds crayon with fingers	2:3								
173	Opens and closes scissors	2:3								
174	Snips	2:6								
175	Strings 1 in. beads	2:6								
176	Cuts 6 in. paper in two	3:0								
177	Strings ½ in. beads	3:0								
178	Winds up toy	3:6								

FUNCTIONAL DEVELOPMENTAL ASSESSMENT

Table 6-4. (continued)

	VISIT NUMBER		1	2	3	4	5	6	7	8
	Julian date									
	Chronological Age									
		Norm Yr:Mo								
	FINE MOTOR DEVELOPMENT (continued)									
	Prehension/Thumb—Finger Manipulation (continued)									
179	Cuts 6 in. line within ½ in.—15 seconds	3:6								
180	Grasps pencil with finger	4:0								
181	Cuts 2 in. triangle within ½ in.—45 seconds	4:0								
182	Cuts 6 in. square within ¼ in.—45 seconds	4:6								
183	Cuts 6 in. circle within ¼ in.	5:0								
184	Squeezes tube	5:0								
185	Opens and closes safety pin	6:0								
186	Dials telephone	6:0								
187	Cuts cardboard and cloth	6:6								
188	Picks up small objects with tweezers	6:6								
189	Cuts paper doll	7:0								
190	Presses typewriter keys	8:0								
	Visual/Visual—Motor/Visual—Discr./Spat. Relations									
191	Symmetrical eye movements	0:1								
192	Regards person momentarily	0:1								
193	Follows midline	0:1								
194	Follows past midline	0:3								
195	Follows 180°	0:4								
196	Fixation during distraction	0:6								
197	Search technique	0:8								
198	Eyes track object 78 in. away	1:0								
199	Places round object in round hole	1:6								
200	Looks at book right-side-up	1:9								
201	Nests three boxes	2:0								
202	Matches red-yellow	3:0								
203	Builds bridge (imitation)	3:4								
204	Stacks 6 blocks by size	3:6								
205	Places 3 forms in form board	3:6								

VISIT NUMBER		1	2	3	4	5	6	7	8
Julian date									
Chronological Age									
	Norm Yr:Mo								
FINE MOTOR DEVELOPMENT (continued)									
Visual/Visual—Motor/Visual—Discr./Spat. Relations (continued)									
206 Sorts dissimilar objects (nuts from bolts)	4:0								
207 Builds 5-block gate (imitation)	4:0								
208 Picks longer line	4:4								
209 Recognizes 3 colors	4:6								
210 Builds 5-block train (imitation)	5:0								
211 Builds block stairs—base of 3	6:0								
212 Sorts similar items by size, shape, or color	6:0								
213 Builds block stairs—base of 4	7:0								
214 Locates 13 basic colors	7:3								
Graphics/Drawing/Writing									
215 Makes incidental marks with crayon/pencil	1:1								
216 Makes purposeful marks with crayon	1:3								
217 Scribbles, but marks may go off page	1:6								
218 Scribbles, confined to page	2:1								
219 Imitates vertical line	3:0								
220 Imitates horizontal line	3:5								
221 Traces along line	4:0								
222 Copies + (cross)	4:4								
223 Copies ○ (circle)	4:4								
224 Colors within lines	5:0								
225 Draws three-part man	5:2								
226 Prints first name	5:3								
227 Draws six-part man	6:0								
228 Copies square	6:0								
229 Copies some printing	6:0								
230 Prints first and last name	6:0								
231 Copies triangle	6:6								
232 Writes numbers to 20	6:6								

FUNCTIONAL DEVELOPMENTAL ASSESSMENT

Table 6-4. (continued)

	VISIT NUMBER		1	2	3	4	5	6	7	8
	Julian date									
	Chronological Age									
		Norm Yr:Mo								
	FINE MOTOR DEVELOPMENT (continued)									
	Graphics/Drawing/Writing (continued)									
233	Writes own phone number	6:9								
234	Copies diamond	6:9								
235	Prints ABC's	7:0								
236	Prints simple words	7:0								
237	Prints between lines	8:0								
238	Writes name in cursive writing	8:6								
239	Prints full address	8:6								
240	Writes in cursive	9:0								
241	Addresses envelopes	9:6								
242	Writes letter including heading and closing	9:6								
	LANGUAGE									
	Auditory Discrimination/Memory									
243	Responds to bell	0:1.2								
244	Eyes locate source of sound	0:6								
245	Turns to voice	0:8								
246	Listens selectively to familiar words	0:8								
247	Repeats single syllables (ba, da, ba)	1:6								
248	Repeats two-syllable word or phrase	2:0								
249	Repeats 3–4 syllable sentence	2:3								
250	Repeats 2 digits	2:6								
251	Repeats 5 syllable phrase/sentence	2:9								
252	Repeats 3 digits in series	3:0								
253	Delivers one-item verbal message	3:6								
254	Produces loud and soft sounds	4:6								
255	Delivers two-item verbal message	5:6								
256	Says: Bub, tub, stub, flub	6:0								
257	Repeats 4 digits in a series	7:6								
258	Delivers 3-item verbal message	7:6								

FUNCTIONAL DEVELOPMENTAL ASSESSMENT

VISIT NUMBER			1	2	3	4	5	6	7	8
	Julian date									
	Chronological Age									
		Norm Yr:Mo								
	LANGUAGE (continued)									
	Expressive Language									
259	Vocalizes pleasure sound (ah)	0:2								
260	Vocalizes two different vowel sounds (ah, uh)	0:3								
261	Laughs	0:3								
262	Squeals	0:5								
263	Combines vowel sounds (i.e., oo)	0:7								
264	Uses single consonant (baba, gogo)	0:8								
265	Babbles, using several consonants (ba, da, mm)	0:9								
266	Says MaMa, DaDa—nonspecific	0:10								
267	Imitates speech sounds	0:11								
268	Imitates words	1:0								
269	Says DaDa, MaMa—specific	1:1								
270	Says two words	1:2								
271	Names object desired	1:6								
272	Says three other words other than Mama, Dada	1:8								
273	Uses noun phrase with adjective (big boy)	1:9								
274	Uses verb phrase (lie down, go home)	1:9								
275	Uses subject-predicate phrase (dog run, car go)	1:9								
276	Names object shown	2:0								
277	Uses noun phrase with article (a/the boy)	2:0								
278	Uses possessive noun phrase (my ball, daddy car)	2:0								
279	Names one picture	2:5								
280	Says single short sentence	2:6								
281	Adds "ing" ending to words	2:6								
282	Asks questions	2:6								
283	Refers to self by pronoun rather than name (I, me)	2:6								
284	Uses past tense	2:9								
285	Refers to others by pronoun	3:0								
286	Selects correct pronoun (him, he, his)	3:0								

FUNCTIONAL DEVELOPMENTAL ASSESSMENT

Table 6-4. (continued)

VISIT NUMBER		Norm Yr:Mo	1	2	3	4	5	6	7	8
	Julian date									
	Chronological Age									
	LANGUAGE (continued)									
	Expressive Language (continued)									
287	Uses negative phrases (can't, don't like)	3:0								
	Receptive Language/Nonverbal Language									
288	When name is called, momentarily stops activity	0:9								
289	Attends to simple commands	0:9								
290	Shakes head for "No"	0:10								
291	Waves "bye-bye"	0:10								
292	Performs gesture command, "pick me up"	1:0								
293	Indicates wants by gesture	1:2								
294	Attends to adult voices speaking	1:2								
295	Points to familiar object when requested	1:5								
296	Performs simple command	1:6								
297	Imitates gestures involving an object	1:6								
298	Points to object according to function	2:3								
299	Points to familiar object in picture	2:6								
300	Regulates action to verb	2:6								
301	Follows directions	2:7								
302	Points to picture according to function	2:9								
303	Demonstrates use of familiar objects	3:0								
304	Locates above, below, behind	4:5								
305	Selects objects by comparative adjective (big, bigger, biggest)	5:0								
306	Pantomimes described actions	6:0								
307	Selects objects from verbal description	7:0								
308	Follows written direction	9:0								
309	Selects items based on written description	9:6								
	Quantitative Concepts									
310	Knows "one more"	1:5								
311	Counts to one	2:6								

VISIT NUMBER			1	2	3	4	5	6	7	8
	Julian date									
	Chronological Age									
		Norm Yr:Mo								
	LANGUAGE (continued)									
	Quantitative Concepts (continued)									
312	Counts out one object	3:0								
313	Counts to three	3:6								
314	Counts to five	4:0								
315	Counts to nine	4:6								
316	Counts 3 objects	5:0								
317	Counts to 19	5:3								
318	Counts to 39	6:0								
319	Identifies coins	6:0								
320	Counts out 9 objects	6:6								
321	Tells time to the hour	6:6								
322	Counts out 19 objects	6:9								
323	Counts to 59	6:9								
324	Tells time to quarter-hour	7:0								
325	Counts to 99	7:0								
326	Counts to 39 objects	7:0								
327	Adds 2 digits totaling ten	7:0								
328	Combines two coins to equal larger one	7:6								
329	Names days of week in succession	7:6								
330	Subtracts two digit numbers	8:0								
331	Tells time to 5 minutes	8:0								
332	Relates today, tomorrow, yesterday to the days of the week	8.0								
333	Names current month	8:0								
334	Matches coins to written symbol	8:3								
335	Tells time to minute	9:0								
336	Divides 2-digit number	10:0								
	Reading									
337	Helps turn pages	1:0								
338	Turns several pages at a time	1:8								

FUNCTIONAL DEVELOPMENTAL ASSESSMENT

Table 6-4. (continued)

	VISIT NUMBER		1	2	3	4	5	6	7	8
	Julian date									
	Chronological Age									
		Norm Yr:Mo								
	LANGUAGE (continued)									
	Reading (continued)									
339	Looks at a picture book, correctly-oriented	1:9								
340	Looks selectively at pictures	2:0								
341	Turns pages singly	3:0								
342	Follows sequentially a series of pictures	4:0								
343	Reads numerals to 3	5:0								
344	Reads numerals to 9	5:6								
345	Reads numerals to 19	6:0								
346	Reads letters	6:6								
347	Reads numerals to 39	6:6								
348	Reads numerals to 59	7:0								
349	Reads words: to, see, cat, big	7:0								
350	Reads numerals to 99	7:3								
351	Reads cursive writing	7:6								
352	Reads numerals over 100	7:9								
353	Reads story aloud	8:0								
354	Reads want ads	8:6								
355	Uses TV Guide	11:0								
356	Uses Telephone Book	11:0								
357	Reads front page of newspaper	12:0								
	PERSONAL-SOCIAL									
	Social Response/Home/Community									
358	Regards face	0:1								
359	Smiles spontaneously	0:5								
360	Stranger reaction	0:10								
361	Smiles responsively	1:9								
362	Takes direction from nonfamily member	2:0								
363	Responds to and makes verbal greetings	3:0								
364	Remains quiet when adults are talking	3:0								

VISIT NUMBER		1	2	3	4	5	6	7	8
Julian date									
Chronological Age									
	Norm Yr:Mo								
PERSONAL-SOCIAL (continued)									
Social Response/Home/Community (continued)									
365 Shows interest in conversations of others	3:6								
366 Responds to conversation queries	3:6								
367 Acknowledges compliments/service with thank you	4:0								
368 Waits to be acknowledged before speaking	4:0								
369 Says "excuse me" when disruptive/to interrupt	4:6								
370 Separates from mother easily	4:7								
371 Answers telephone	5:0								
372 Refrains from unattractive actions in public	5:6								
373 Participates at commun. recreation programs	6:6								
374 Attends community spectator events	7:6								
375 Uses private recreation facilities (movie)	8:0								
376 Travels by taxi, tells driver destination	9:0								
Play/Work									
377 Works for toy out of reach	0:9								
378 Plays peek-a-boo	0:10								
379 Resists toy pull	0:10								
380 Plays pat-a-cake	1:1								
381 Plays ball	1:4								
382 Imitates housework	1:6								
383 Works with adult—1 minute	1:6								
384 Entertains self with toys	2:0								
385 Plays alone, in presence of other children	2:0								
386 Works with adult—5 minutes	2:0								
387 Plays cooperatively (shares) with other children	2:6								
388 Works in small group—5 minutes	2:6								
389 Works with adult—15 minutes	3:0								
390 Takes turns	3:5								
391 Works in small group—15 minutes	3:6								

FUNCTIONAL DEVELOPMENTAL ASSESSMENT

Table 6-4. (continued)

	VISIT NUMBER	Norm Yr:Mo	1	2	3	4	5	6	7	8
	Julian date									
	Chronological Age									
	PERSONAL-SOCIAL (continued)									
	Play/Work (continued)									
392	Cleans up toys	4:0								
393	Plays table games with supervision	4:0								
394	Occupies self unattended	5:0								
395	Plays 2–3 table games	5:6								
396	Works in small group—30 minutes	6:0								
397	Plays cooperatively in large group game	6:0								
398	Remains at task when distractions are present	7:0								
399	Pursues a hobby	7:6								
400	Performs useful tasks in leisure time	8:0								
	Self/Family									
401	Recognizes mirror image	1:0								
402	Responds to name	1:6								
403	Identifies self by first name	2:0								
404	Tells number of family members	2:9								
405	Tells own sex	3:0								
406	Tells full name	3:0								
407	Tells age	3:0								
408	Names siblings	3:9								
409	Tells street address	4:0								
410	Tells street and town address	4:6								
411	Tells month of birth	4:6								
412	Tells month and day of birth	5:0								
413	Tells first and last names of parents	5:6								
414	Tells father's job	6:0								
415	Tells complete birthdate	6:6								
416	Tells complete address	6:6								
417	Tells father's employer/place of work	6:6								
418	Tells phone number	7:0								

FUNCTIONAL DEVELOPMENTAL ASSESSMENT

VISIT NUMBER		1	2	3	4	5	6	7	8
Julian date									
Chronological Age									
	Norm Yr:Mo								
PERSONAL-SOCIAL (continued)									
Self/Family (continued)									
419 Tells birthplace	8:0								
Body Scheme									
420 Points to one named body part	1:5								
421 Points to mouth, eyes, nose, feet	1:6								
422 Points to hair, hands, ears, head, legs, arms	2:6								
423 Points to fingers, toes, stomach, back, knee, chin	3:0								
424 Points to teeth, heels, finger nails	4:0								
425 Points to elbows, ankles	4:6								
426 Shows right hand	5:6								
427 Shows left hand	5:9								
428 Knows right/left side of body parts	6:0								
429 Knows right/left side of objects	6:0								
Eating/Drinking/Food Preparation									
430 Swallows soft foods	0:3								
431 Eats soft foods from spoon held by adult	0:6								
432 Feeds self cracker	0:8								
433 Drinks from glass/cup held by adult	0:9								
434 Feeds self finger-foods	0:10								
435 Holds own bottle to drink	0:10								
436 Controls drooling	1:0								
437 Holds glass to drink when adult places it in hand	1:5								
438 Sucks from straw	1:6								
439 Drinks from cup	1:6								
440 Chews (semisolids; solids)	1:6								
441 Drinks from glass held in one hand	2:0								
442 Uses spoon in fist, spilling	2:0								
443 Uses spoon in fist, no spilling	3:0								
444 Uses fork in fist	3:0								

FUNCTIONAL DEVELOPMENTAL ASSESSMENT

Table 6-4. (continued)

VISIT NUMBER		1	2	3	4	5	6	7	8
Julian date									
Chronological Age									
	Norm Yr:Mo								
PERSONAL-SOCIAL (continued)									
Eating/Drinking/Food Preparation (continued)									
445 Pours cup/pitcher	3:9								
446 Holds spoon in fingers; solid foods	4:0								
447 Holds fork in fingers	4:3								
448 Uses knife to spread	5:0								
449 Uses knife to cut	6:0								
450 Pours from 2 quart container	6:0								
451 Sets controls on stove	6:0								
452 Prepares dry cereal	6:5								
453 Uses appropriate feeding utensils	7:0								
454 Prepares sandwich	7:0								
455 Opens can manually	7:0								
456 Cuts or slices with sharp knife	7:6								
457 Removes hot items from stove	7:6								
458 Sets controls on oven	8:0								
459 Peels with knife	8:3								
460 Removes hot items from oven	8:6								
Dressing/Undressing									
461 Cooperates in dressing	1:0								
462 Removes socks or shoes	1:6								
463 Removes unfastened garment (coat)	2:0								
464 Unbuttons front buttons	2:6								
465 Removes pull-down garment (pants)	2:6								
466 Puts on shoes	3:0								
467 Dresses with supervision	3:5								
468 Buttons—series of 5	3:6								
469 Buckles	3:9								
470 Removes pullover garment	4:0								
471 Zips	4:0								

FUNCTIONAL DEVELOPMENTAL ASSESSMENT

VISIT NUMBER		1	2	3	4	5	6	7	8
Julian date									
Chronological Age									
	Norm Yr:Mo								
PERSONAL-SOCIAL (continued)									
Dressing/Undressing (continued)									
472　Laces shoes	4:0								
473　Puts on pullover garment	5:0								
474　Dresses unsupervised	5:0								
475　Ties bow	6:0								
476　Polishes shoes	6:6								
477　Selects clothes appropriate to weather	8:0								
Hygiene/Toileting									
478　Bowels controlled	1:6								
479　Bladder controlled	2:0								
480　Turns faucets on/off	3:0								
481　Washes hands	3:2								
482　Flushes toilet	3:3								
483　Arranges clothing in toileting	4:0								
484　Washes face	4:9								
485　Brushes teeth	4:9								
486　Cleanses self after toileting	5:0								
487　Blows nose without assistance	6:0								
488　Brushes teeth routinely	7:0								
489　Combs hair	7:6								
490　Bathes	8:0								
491　Bathes/showers routinely	9:0								
492　Uses deodorant daily	10:0+								

FUNCTIONAL DEVELOPMENTAL ASSESSMENT

REFERENCES

1. Abercrombie, M. L. J., *Perceptual and Visuomotor Disorders in Cerebral Palsy.* Little Club Clinics in Developmental Medicine, No. 11. London, William Heinemann, 1964.
2. Ayeres, A. J., Characteristics of types of sensory integrative dysfunction. *Journal of Learning Disabilities* 5:336–343, 1972.
3. Ayeres, A. J., Learning disabilities and the vestibular system. *Journal of Learning Disabilities,* 1:18–29, 1978.

4. Bachmann, W. H., Variables affecting post-school economic adaptation of orthopaedically handicapped and other health-impaired students. *Rehabilitation Literature* 33:98–102, 1972.
5. Baker, L. D., A rational approach to the surgical needs of the cerebral palsy patient. *Journal of Bone and Joint Surgery* 38-A: 313–323, 1956.
6. Banks, H. H., and Green, W. T., Adductor myotomy and obturator neuroectomy for the correction of adductor contracture of the hip in cerebral palsy. *Journal of Bone and Joint Surgery* 42-A: 111–126, 1960.
7. Bassett, F., Surgery of the foot and ankle, in *American Academy of Orthopaedic Surgeons Instructional Course Lectures*. St. Louis, C. V. Mosby, 1971.
8. Bell, A. E., Abrahamson, D. S., and McRae, K. N., Reading retardation: twelve year prospective study. *Journal of Pediatrics,* 91:363–370, 1977.
9. Bleck, E. E., *Orthopaedic Management of Cerebral Palsy*. Philadelphia, W. B. Saunders, 1979.
10. Bobath, B., *Abnormal Postural Reflex Activity Caused by Brain Lesions*. London, William Heinemann, 1965.
11. Carothers, B., and Paine, R. S., *Natural History of Cerebral Palsy*. Cambridge, Mass., Harvard University Press, 1959.
12. Christensen, E., and Melchior, J., *Cerebral Palsy–A Clinical and Neuropathological Study*. Clinics in Developmental Medicine, No. 24. London, William Heinemann, 1967.
13. Cohen, P., and Kohn, J. G., Follow-up study of patients with cerebral palsy. *Western Journal of Medicine* 130:6–11, 1979.
14. Cohen, P., and Mustacchi, P., Survival in cerebral palsy, *Journal of the American Medical Association* 195:642–644, 1966.
15a. Denhoff, E., *Cerebral Palsy and Related Disorders*. New York, McGraw-Hill, 1960.
15b. Denhoff, E., Current status of infant stimulation or enrichment programs for children with developmental disabilities. *Pediatrics* 67:32–37, 1981.
16. Denhoff, E., *Drugs in Cerebral Palsy*. Clinics in Developmental Medicine, No. 16. London, William Heinemann, 1964.
17. Evans, E. B., Surgery of the knee, in *American Academy of Orthopaedic Surgeons Instructional Course Lectures*. St. Louis, C. V. Mosby, 1971.
18. Gesell, A., and Amatruda, C. S., *Developmental Diagnosis*. New York, Harper and Row, 1947.
19. Gillette, H., *Systems of Therapy in Cerebral Palsy*. Springfield, Ill., Charles C. Thomas, 1969.
20. Goldner, J. L., Surgery of the upper limb. *American Academy of Orthopaedic Surgeons Instructional Course Lectures*. St. Louis, C. V. Mosby, 1971.
21. Hassakis, P. C., Outcomes of Cerebral Palsy Patients. Paper read at the Annual Meeting of the American Academy for Cerebral Palsy, Denver, Colo., 1974.
22. Hohman, L. B., Intelligence levels in cerebral palsied children. *American Journal Physical Medicine* 32:282–290, 1953.
23. Ingram, T. T. S., Jameson, S., Errington, J., et al., *Living with Cerebral Palsy*. Clinics in Developmental Medicine, No. 14, London, William Heinemann, 1964.
24. Jones, M., *Syllabus of Instructional Courses of the American Academy for Cerebral Palsy*, 1972.
25. Jones, M. H., and Rolf, I. P., *Evaluation of Functional Changes in Cerebral Palsied Subjects Following Rolfing Techniques*. Downy, Calif., Rancho Los Amigos Research Reports, 1979, pp. 43–45.
26. Kanter, R. M., Clark, D. C., Allen, L. C., and Chase, M. A., Effects of vestibular stimulation on mystagmus response and motor performance in the developmentally disabled infant. *Physical Therapy* 156:414–421, 1976.
27. Keats, S., *Cerebral Palsy*. Springfield, Ill., Charles C. Thomas, 1965.
28. McKibben, E. H., The effect of additional tactile stimulation in a perceptual motor treatment program for school children. *American Journal of Occupational Therapy* 27:191–197, 1973.

29. Milani-Compretti, A., in Study group in integrating the care of multiply handicapped children. Meeting of The Spastics Society Medical Education and Information Unit, Durham, England, 1977.
30. Minear, W. L., A classification of cerebral palsy. *Pediatrics* 18:841, 1956.
31. Miranda, S., Outcomes of spastic diplegia. Unpublished study, Palo Alto, Calif., Children's Hospital at Stanford, 1979.
32. Montgomery P., Effect of sensory integrative theory on the neuromotor development of retarded children. *Physical Therapy* 57:799–806, 1977.
33. Nelson, K. B., and Ellenberg, J. H., Neonatal signs as predictors of cerebral palsy. *Pediatrics* 64:225–237, 1979.
34. Orpet, R. E., *Frostig Movement Skills Test Battery*. Palo Alto, Calif., Consulting Psychologists Press, 1972.
35. O'Reilly, D. E., The future of the cerebral palsy child. *Developmental Medicine and Child Neurology* 13:635–640, 1971.
36. Paine, R. S., On the treatment of cerebral palsy: The outcome of 177 patients, 74 totally untreated. *Pediatrics* 29:605–616, 1962.
37a. Perlstein, M. D., and Barnett, H. E., Natural history and recognition of cerebral palsy in infancy. *Journal of the American Medical Association* 148:1389–1397, 1952.
37b. Perry, P. C., On growing new neurons: Are early intervention programs effective? *Pediatrics* 67:38–41, 1981.
38. Robinson, M. E., and Schwartz, L. B., Visuo-motor Skills and Reading Ability. *Developmental Medicine and Child Neurology* 51:281–286, 1973.
39. Scherzer, A. L., Mike, V., and Olson, J., Physical therapy as a determinant for change in the cerebral palsied infant. *Pediatrics* 58:47–51, 1976.
40. Schlesinger, E. R., Allaway, N. C., and Peitin, S., Survivorship in cerebral palsy. *American Journal of Public Health* 49:343–354, 1959.
41. Scrutton, D., Aim-oriented physical therapy. Paper read at the Annual Meeting of the American Academy for Cerebral Palsy and Developmental Medicine, San Francisco, 1979.
42. Shapiro, B. C., Accardo, P. J., and Capute, A. J., Factors affecting walking in a profoundly retarded population, *Developmental Medicine and Child Neurology* 21:369–373, 1979.
43. Sparrow, S., and Zigler, E., Evaluation of patterning treatment for retarded children. *Pediatrics* 62:137–149, 1978.
44. Taft, L. T., Are we handicapping the handicapped? *Developmental Medicine and Child Neurology* 14:703–704, 1972.
45. Terver, S., and Bleck, E. E., Goal setting and factors influencing independence in severely involved cerebral palsied children. Unpublished study, Palo Alto, Calif., Children's Hospital at Stanford, 1979.
46. Touwen, B. C., *Examination of the Child with Minor Neurological Dysfunction*, 2nd ed. Philadelphia, J. B. Lippincott, 1979.
47. Vizie, M. B., Sensory integration: A foundation for learning. *Academic Therapy*, 10(3), 1975.
48. Wright, T., and Nicholson, J., Physiotherapy for the spastic child: An evaluation. *Developmental Medicine and Child Neurology* 15:146–163, 1973.
49. Wright, F. H., Blough, R. R., Chamberlin, A., et al., A controlled follow-up study of small prematures born from 1952 through 1956. *American Journal of Diseases of Children* 124:506–521, 1972.
50. Yule, W., Issues and problems in remedial education. *Developmental Medicine and Child Neurology* 18:674–682, 1976.

Eugene E. Bleck

APPENDIX

May 1, 1980

Name of Patient _____

SUH# _____

Birthdate _____

Children's Hospital at Stanford
POLICY STATEMENT

On Requested Prescriptions for Occupational Therapy and Physical Therapy for Handicapped Children as Part of the Individual Education Plan Mandated (Public Law 94-142) and Authorization for Above Patient.

The Reasons for Policy

Current and Continuing Experience

We have been progressively inundated by requests for prescriptions for physical and/or occupational therapy and/or evaluations in children who are attending various schools and development centers in California. The explicit reason for such prescription is to fill a slot in the individual educational plan (IEP) with a period of "therapy." These requests usually originate from various nonmedical sources: school teachers, school authorities, parents, and legal rights advocate organizations.

With increasing frequency, the usual route of request is via the parents, who obtain this request from the school authorities, usually with great urgency for a proposed planning meeting with the teacher. The parents then go to the California Children's Services (CCS) Medical Therapy Units, and either the parents or the therapist then write or phone us to give them a prescription.

We have been asked to state that the child receiving physical or occupational therapy should have a specified period of time allotted during the week for physical and/or occupational therapy, e.g. 30 minutes one time per week, two times per week, etc., and that the therapy should be specific and should accomplish a definite goal.

Experience with Handicapped Children's Programs

From 1955 to 1979, the way that the system worked was that, when a patient was seen in orthopedic consultation, the referring physician was given our report, and, if an agency was involved, copies of the report were sent to it as well. We would, in general, suggest occupational and/or physical therapy, orthotics, rehabilitation engineering equipment, or surgery, or any combination of these, depending upon the particular needs of the patient. This was sufficient. If we believed that occupational or physical therapy evaluation and/or management were required, we would so state. If we operated on a patient and initiated the postoperative therapy program, we transmitted information pertaining to this therapy to the therapist who was to assume responsibility for the patient's treatment.

What has happened since 1980, however, even in patients whom we have seen for only one-time consultation, or whom we have seen repeatedly in follow-up, is that we are getting an increasing number of requests to write "therapy" prescriptions.

Cerebral Palsy

Effect of Public Law 94-142

Since this law went into effect, we have been asked, on top of our normal consultations, to write additional prescriptions. This appears to be medical direction from the outside and is similar to a request for drug therapy when we have seen no indication for such therapy in our original request and see none now. Frequently, the patients have had physical and occupational therapy evaluations and therapy in the past and have moved on to higher ground, which usually involves "mainstreaming" and participation in athletic endeavors or desk activities. They are at that point attempting to cope with their disability, rather than continue on the pathway of remediation (which most authorities have given up in favor of the use of compensatory methods).[6] In this connection, an occupational therapy evaluation can be helpful in selecting and implementing the use of methods and tools that compensate for the deficit. The same could be said for physical therapy evaluations; the evaluation may show, for instance, that walking has become so laborious and energy-consuming that a wheelchair (either manual or powered) may be the most efficient way for the patient to become socially integrated into the community and at school.

Cost Control by Physicians

Finally, it is claimed repetitively that physicians have the key to the control of health care costs because we are the ones who are doing the ordering and prescribing. This is true not only of the physicians in the private sector, but in the public sector as well. In this regard, then, we must have adequate justification for prescribing any type of therapy, be it drugs, physical or occupational therapy, or surgery.

What is "Therapy"?

Unfortunately many people, including physicians and therapists, have a misconception of what these valuable and highly skilled paramedical professionals called physical and occupational therapists can accomplish with "therapy." This has led, no doubt, to the current demands for treatment by therapy (even as a legal right) to cure chronic, handicapping conditions such as cerebral palsy or other musculoskeletal conditions.

During the past 30 years various systems of therapy have come, gone, and then returned—for example, neurodevelopmental therapy and the Bobath, Phelps, Deaver, Rood, and patterning methods. New ones, such as sensory integration, have also arisen. All of these methods were largely directed toward improving motor performance by means of positioning and passive exercises and were based upon the principle of providing passive input to the brain in order to alleviate the condition. The results in walking ability, however, have been shown to be highly dependent upon the extent of the original damage to the brain in patients with cerebral palsy.[3, 6, 10] Similarly, in conditions such as muscular dystrophy, the walking ability and mobility depend highly on the extent of the muscle disease as it progresses, while, in traumatic paraplegia, the motor ability depends on the extent of original disruption of the spinal cord at various levels.

The success of therapy systems in remediating cerebral palsy and mental retardation have been shown to be negative when treated patients were compared with control groups.[11,13] Parenthetically, even the application of perceptual, visual motor, and coordination methods in remedial programs for reading retardation were shown to have negative results in a well controlled study.[1]

By 1977, it was apparent that the disease-oriented approach to chronic handicaps had not worked and moreover, had resulted in medicalization and permanent segregation of the handicapped child from society. Integration, therefore, became the solution. (This policy was implemented in the San Mateo County special schools in 1957 and was successfully carried out.[7]) As described below, our experience with cerebral palsied children and with children who have other handicapping conditions confirms the experience of other authorities.

Children by the age of 7 or 8 years actively resist, for the most part, a passive physical therapy program. We have, however, found that intensive, short-term specific therapy programs are useful when carried out between 3 and 12 months postoperatively.[9] We concur with the experiences of Campos de Paz Jr. of Brazil and Bauman of Basel, Switzerland, that a passive physical therapy in the school-age child is generally useless, and, instead, that therapists should design programs for play, fun, games, and sports that help the child in mobility and social integration.[2,5]

We have recently studied the factors that account for independence and efficiency in 85 severely involved cerebral palsied children, who were followed in one group for 12.8 years and in another for 16 years. All had reached the age of 16 years at the time of the study.[12] What we found was that goals for achieving optimum adult independence and efficiency in their three major needs—communication, activities of daily living, and mobility—were consistently met with the help of technical aids and adaptive equipment that were carefully selected by a team of physicians and therapists in conjunction with orthotists and specialists in rehabilitation engineering. We found that reasonable goals for function could be set as early as the age of 4 years in the children.

Therapy is not specific, as is penicillin for pneumonia, nor is it magic. The therapist who sees the patient once a week for one hour, or even once every day (if such were feasible), acts as analyzer of the defect, a physician extender. He or she suggests ways of compensating for the defect through the use of equipment, tools, and clothing and instructs the patient, family, and school staff on the best positioning, play, exercises and means of relief for the patient. The constant goal is to help the patient achieve optimum independence and social integration. This is now being called the "holistic" approach.

In infancy and preschool programs the therapist continues to play an important role. He or she instructs in how to help the child attain various motor milestones, suggests ways of handling the child at home, and provides ongoing analysis of the motor problem and of the total child. The objective of these efforts is to direct and place the child in the best possible learning environment during the school years, whether this be in regular school, a handicapped school, a development center, or a trainable mentally retarded program, etc.[3]

Rather than confront parents, school authorities, and, sometimes, therapists about the realities of therapy, it's aims, and what can be accomplished in a given time frame, most physicians would, no doubt, prefer to sign a generalized prescription, let it run for 6 months, and then renew it repeatedly until the child reaches maturity or is no longer in school or in the developmental center after age 21. Especially in view of our responsibility for cost containment, it seems unwise to impose such open-ended treatment programs when they were not suggested or recommended by us on a reasonable scientific basis in the first place.

We would no more prescribe unevaluated, open-ended therapy than we would prescribe unevaluated drugs or surgery. If we did, we would need an informed consent by parents. If a clinical trial were to be conducted, we would seek an appropriate control system and approval by the human subjects investigation committee of the institution. Furthermore, we would publish the results in official publications.[7]

In view of the above state of the problem and because we cannot continue to spend valuable resources on writing prescriptions, we are sending this formal statement of policy in the interests of efficiency, of rational care for the child, and, possibly, the education of well-intentioned persons who have not looked at "therapy" from the same perspective.

Policy

1. Patients on whom we have a complete medical record, whom we have seen in medical consultation and/or follow-up, who have not occupational or physical therapy evaluations and/or therapy requested by us, and who have a request coming in via the school authorities to the parents and then to the medical therapy program, are hereby authorized for an occupational or physical therapy *evaluation* if none has been done within the past *12 months*. This evaluation should include objective testing for activities of daily living, hand and mouth function, and mobility. Standard functional test forms are available (see Bleck, E. E., and Nagel, D., *Physically Handicapped Children—A Medical Atlas for Teachers,* 2nd ed., New York, Grune & Stratton, 1981). We should emphasize that, according to regulations of the California Childrens' Services, CCS Medical Therapy Units have the prerogative to evaluate the patients.

2. Therapists should then state what lacks there are and what could reasonably be accomplished with remediation and compensatory methods such as specialized occupational therapy or mobility equipment. Management should be aim-oriented and should take place within a definite time frame. Results should be evaluated at least at the end of 1 year, if not at 6 months. Only CCS patients whose conditions make them eligible will be served in the CCS medical units.

3. *Consultations by therapists* are always in order and *are hereby authorized* for the patient, be they in handicapped school, in regular school, or in developmental centers.

4. Requests for sensory motor integration treatment, visual perceptual treatment, sensory motor treatment, or whatever, are designed for "learning disabilities;" because these are purely educational functions, prescriptions from us for them cannot be honored. To our knowledge, there have been no consistent data analyses of the end results of such treatments. Therefore, we would have to consider such prescriptions similar to those for drug therapy that has been unevaluated and unapproved by the FDA—except when given under an exceptional investigational

license which entails testing according to the usual scientific method of materials, methods, and results with appropriate controls. If a time should arrive when appropriate data indicate that the methods are efficacious and appropriate criteria for selection and warnings of complications and contraindications are given, we would undoubtedly write the prescriptions for medical treatment.

Eugene E. Bleck, M.D.

Lawrence A. Rinsky, M.D.

REFERENCES

1. Ball, A. E., Abrahamson, D. S., and McRae, R. N., Reading retardation: A twelve year prospective study. *Journal of Pediatrics* 91:363–370, 1977.
2. Bauman, J., The Swiss experience in cerebral palsy. Instructional course lecture, Annual Meeting of the American Academy for Cerebral Palsy, New Orleans, 1975.
3. Bleck, E. E., and Headley, L., Treatment and parent counseling for the preschool child with cerebral palsy. *Pediatrics* 27:1026–1032, 1961.
4. Bleck, E. E., Locomotor prognosis in cerebral palsy. *Developmental Medicine and Child Neurology* 17:1825, 1975.
5. Campos de Paz, A., Jr., Management of cerebral palsy in Brazil. Lecture, Children's Hospital at Stanford, Palo Alto, California, 1980.
6. Crothers, B., and Paine, R. S., *Natural History of Cerebral Palsy.* Cambridge, Harvard University Press, 1959.
7. Ford, L. F., Bleck, E. E., Collins, F. J., et al., Efficacy of Dantrolene sodium in the treatment of spastic cerebral palsy. *Developmental Medicine and Child Neurology* 18:770–783, 1976.
8. Milani-Compretti, A., in Study group in integrating the care of multiply handicapped children. Meeting of The Spastic Society Medical Information Unit, Durham, England, 1977.
9. Miranda, S., and Bleck, E. E., Outcomes of 119 children with cerebral palsy, spastic diplegia. Fellowship dissertation, Palo Alto, Calif., Childrens Hospital at Stanford, 1979.
10. Shapiro, B. K., Accardo, P. J., and Capaute, A. J., Factors affecting walking in a profoundly retarded population. *Developmental Medicine and Child Neurology* 21:369–373, 1979.
11. Sparrow, S., and Zigler, E., Evaluation of a patterning treatment for retarded children. *Pediatrics* 62:137–149, 1978.
12. Terver, S., and Bleck, E. E. Goal setting and factors affecting independence in severely involved cerebral palsied children, Fellowship dissertation, Palo Alto, Calif., Childrens Hospital at Stanford, 1979.
13. Wright, T., and Nicholson, J., Physiotherapy for the Spastic Child: An Evaluation. *Developmental Medicine and Child Neurology* 15:146–163, 1973.

7

Communication Disorders: Speech and Hearing

KATHRYN R. BEADLE, Ph.D.

The most complicated of all learned behaviors is the understanding and use of speech. It requires the integration and coordination of the entire neurophysiological system. Although speaking begins with the translation of thought into words (linguistic symbols), man is still totally ignorant as to exactly how this first step is accomplished. Nevertheless, our chosen words somehow become electrical impulses (brain waves) which serve as messengers to our muscles of articulation. These messages from the brain move the vocal cords and muscles to produce acoustical energy (sound waves) which travels through the air to enter the ears of a listener. The sound waves are then reconverted into electrical impulses which travel to the listener's brain, where the message is interpreted. A simplified schematic diagram of this process is shown in Fig. 7-1.

When the message in the form of electrical energy reaches the listener's brain, it is understood as speech. Sending and receiving these messages takes only a few seconds, but this accomplishment is the most complex and least well understood of all human phenomena. Nevertheless, most of us take speaking entirely for granted.

Communication may break down as the result of hearing, language, or speech disorders at a number of levels. The first level of breakdown is deafness. If a child enters life with little or no hearing, normal learning is impossible. If he is profoundly deaf, his vocabulary will be severely limited, and this, in turn, will interfere with his conceptual development. Additionally, because lack of hearing precludes the monitoring of speech, speech development will also be severely affected. Less severe hearing

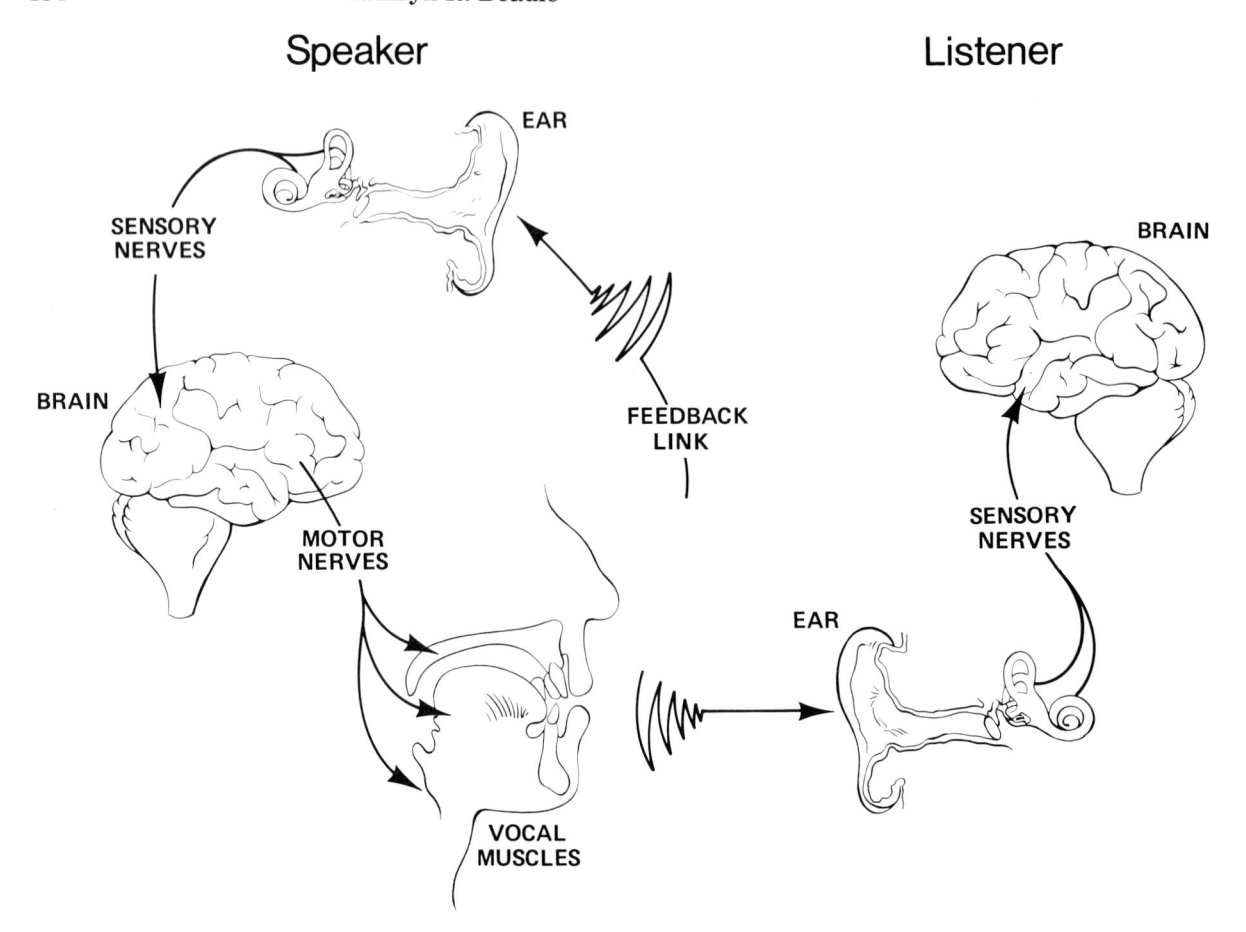

Fig. 7-1. The communication process.

losses can also play a significant role in a wide variety of developmental areas. These include auditory perceptual breakdowns, articulation disorders, linguistic deficits, and specific learning disabilities. Research in this area has indicated that even intermittent hearing losses may have far-reaching effects. A number of studies have shown that children with a history of mild, intermittent hearing losses associated with middle-ear pathologies show a significantly higher incidence of speech and language disturbances and of subsequent academic failures.[1-4] Special attention must therefore be given to these children in order to provide supplemental help when it is necessary.

The second level of disruption is in the understanding and use of language. Like deafness, this disruption may result from developmental or acquired dysfunctions of the central nervous system. Hearing may be normal, but the affected individual cannot adequately understand what he hears. The resulting language disorder is called *aphasia* in adults and has been referred to as *developmental,* or *childhood, aphasia* in children.[5-10]

The third major area of communication breakdown occurs at the level of speech production. Although the hearing and linguistic systems are intact, the individual lacks the muscle control or the anatomical structures necessary for normal speech. Deficits in these areas result in a speech or voice disorder.

In order to understand and to deal effectively with individuals who

HEARING DISORDERS

have communication disorders, it is necessary to have a basic understanding of the processes involved.

Hearing Mechanisms

A sectional diagram of the human ear is shown in Fig. 7-2. The part of the ear that we see (pinna) may be of cosmetic value, but it serves no purpose in hearing. The eardrum (tympanic membrane) is the first important structure involved in sound transmission. Sounds set up air vibrations, and, when these vibrations enter the ear canal, they cause the eardrum to move. These vibrations are transmitted to a set of three tiny bones (ossicles) located in the middle ear. The innermost ossicle, which is shaped like a stirrup, is connected to the membrane (oval window) that seals the opening into the inner ear (cochlea). Movements of the ossicle against the oval window set up a current within the liquid which fills the cochlea (endolymphatic fluid). The base of the cochlea is lined with auditory receptor cells, called hair cells; these connect with the nerve endings that join together and exit from the cochlea as the auditory nerve (VIIIth cranial). Motions in the fluid of the ear move the hair cells, and the vibrations stimulate electrical impulses which are carried to the brain by the auditory nerve. When the sounds thus transmitted are speech sounds, they are relayed through the brainstem to the cortex, where they are interpreted. Because this system of sound transmission is so intricate, it may be interfered with in a number of ways.

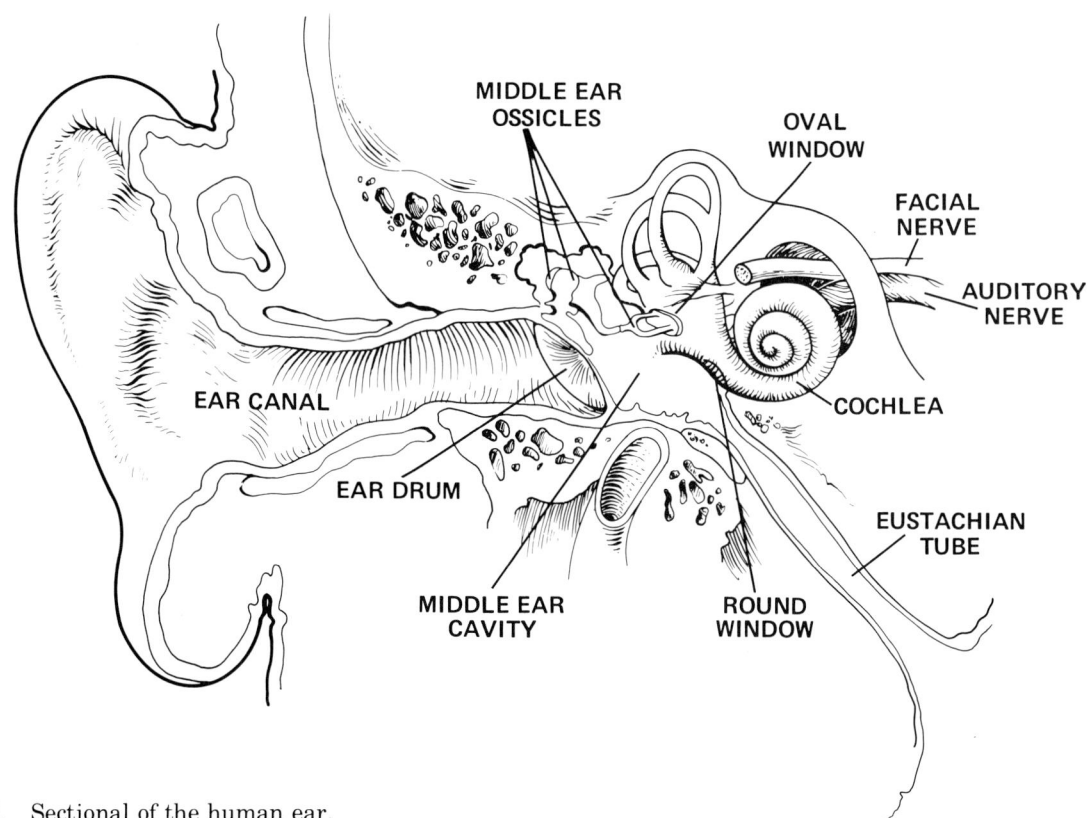

Fig. 7-2. Sectional of the human ear.

Types of Hearing Losses

Hearing losses may be classified into three major categories according to the site of interference: conductive, sensorineural, and central.

Interference with sound transmission in the outer or middle ear is termed a *conductive* hearing loss. With this type of loss, hearing may be improved simply by making speech loud enough to compensate for the reduced conductivity. Acquired hearing losses in children are almost always of a conductive nature.[11]

Conductive pathology may occur in either the outer auditory canal or the middle ear. In the outer auditory canal, the accumulation of wax is the most common problem, although foreign objects may also sometimes enter the auditory canal. Once discovered, outer ear problems are easily remedied.

The major cause of conductive hearing loss related to middle ear pathology is *otitis media,* an inflammation or infection within the middle ear. If not treated, it may become chronic and cause a build-up of fluid within the middle ear, which can lead to a ruptured eardrum. Chronic otitis media is the most frequent cause of conductive hearing loss. There are many causes of hearing losses related to middle-ear infections or pathology,[16] but conductive hearing loss can usually be resolved if the individual receives the proper medical treatment as soon as possible.[12-14]

When the loss of hearing is due to dysfunction of the inner ear or along the pathway from the inner ear to the brainstem, the loss is called *sensorineural*. A "pure" sensorineural loss exists when the outer and middle ear are normal in every way. Sound reaches the inner ear, but it cannot be transmitted normally to the brain. The recognition of different consonants depends upon high-frequency information within the speech signal; it is these sounds that are lost with a sensorineural deficit. As a result, sensorineural losses may seriously impair the ability to understand speech, even when the sounds are amplified with a hearing aid.

Most babies born with impaired hearing have sensorineural losses, but this type of pathology may also be acquired during life by disease, injury, toxic drug effects, prolonged exposure to noise, or simply in the process of aging. Adequate treatment often involves educational as well as medical intervention. Sensorineural losses are usually irreversible, but a great deal may be accomplished in the direction of compensation for the loss.

It is important to note that some hearing losses contain both conductive and sensorineural components. These are referred to as *mixed* losses. Also, if a loss is confined to only one ear (unilateral), the normal ear enables the individual to overcome the effects. Only bilateral hearing losses can produce serious handicaps.

Any interference with sound transmission from the brainstem to the auditory cortex, or within the cortex itself, produces a *central* hearing loss. This may be caused by a brain tumor or abscess, by vascular changes in the brain (stroke), or by any form of congenital or acquired brain damage. With central deafness, the patient can "hear" but does not understand what he hears. Central deafness, therefore, falls within the realm of the neurologist and the speech pathologist, and is generally treated as a form of receptive language disorder (aphasia).

Complete descriptions of the symptoms, causes, and treatment of hearing disorders are available in a number of textbooks.[11-14,25]

LANGUAGE DISORDERS

Language Mechanisms

Most people have a general idea of what *language* is, yet this word is frequently used interchangeably with the term *speech*. Wood[15] has pointed out that language consists of the total system of symbols used in communication, including speaking, reading, and writing. Speech (pronunciation) is simply the final end-product of the language process. Although people from different countries use different sound combinations to express ideas, the use of verbal symbols and the development of language is universal. The initial use of first words, then phrases, and then syntactical combinations occurs in a predictable sequence and at set ages in children, regardless of where they live. In addition to providing a method of communication, normal language development also stimulates our thinking, helps us to interpret and to store experiences, and enables us to organize our ideas. Without "inner" language, the learning process would be considerably less efficient.

Normal language function requires a complex integration of both sensory and motor information and is, therefore, dependent upon an intact peripheral and central nervous system. Developmental or acquired deficits of varying degree may occur at any point within this system.[5,6,8,14-16] Figure 7-3 provides a simplified model of language transmission.

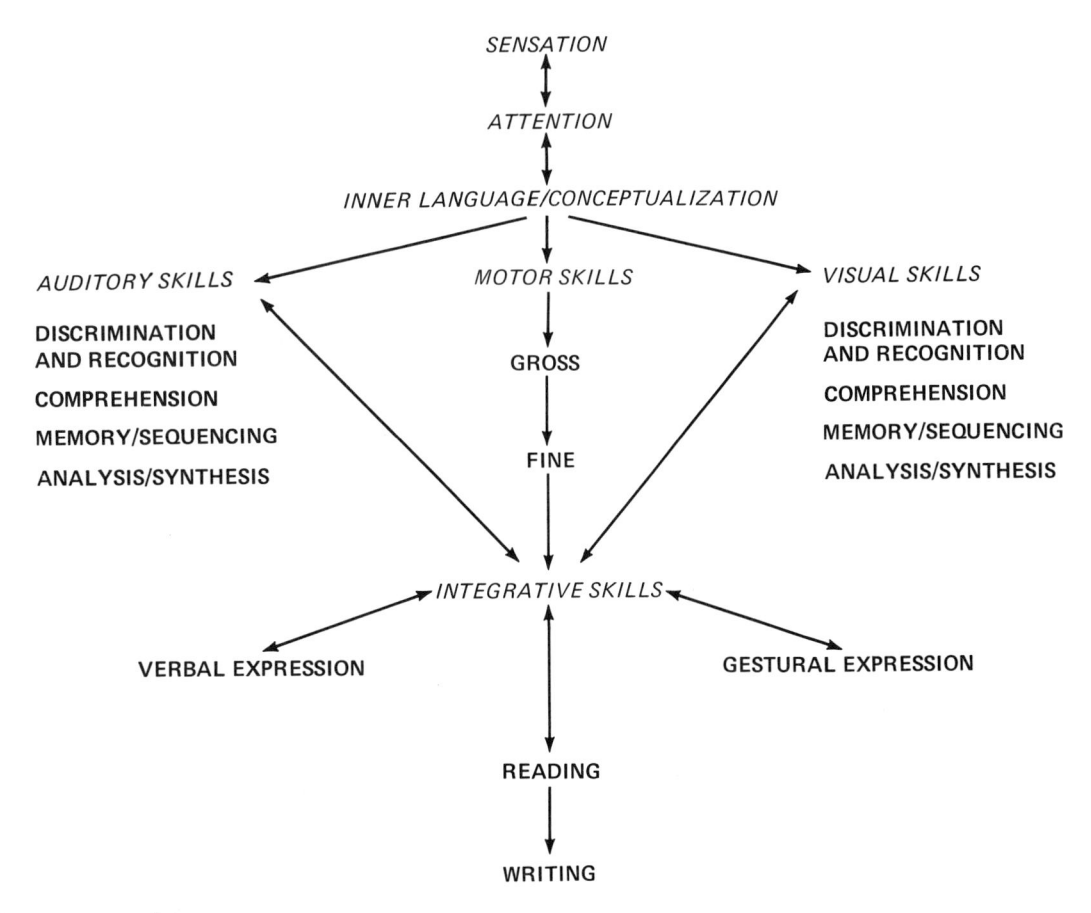

Fig. 7-3. Language model.

Types of Language Disorders

Language disorders almost always result from some degree of congenital or acquired asphasia, although, occasionally, they are related to environmental deprivation or severe emotional disturbance.

In children, language deficits generally reflect a developmental breakdown in the ability to use and to understand symbols. Subsequent deficits in auditory memory and perception lead to inadequate understanding of speech and limited verbal expression. Because this type of disorder (dysphasia or childhood aphasia) is secondary to central nervous system dysfunction, these children will often show other developmental deviations as well. Children with limited vocabularies will have difficulty in forming concepts appropriate for their age and in regulating and planning their behavior.[17-18] A limited attention span and inappropriate behaviors often result from the inability to process verbal information or to use inner speech to evaluate and organize responses. These behavioral difficulties must be considered in the light of the linguistic breakdowns, and remediation strategies should include methods for helping the child deal with both the language and the behavioral problems.

Unremediated language disorders often result in severe learning disabilities. Early identification is therefore crucial, and careful differential

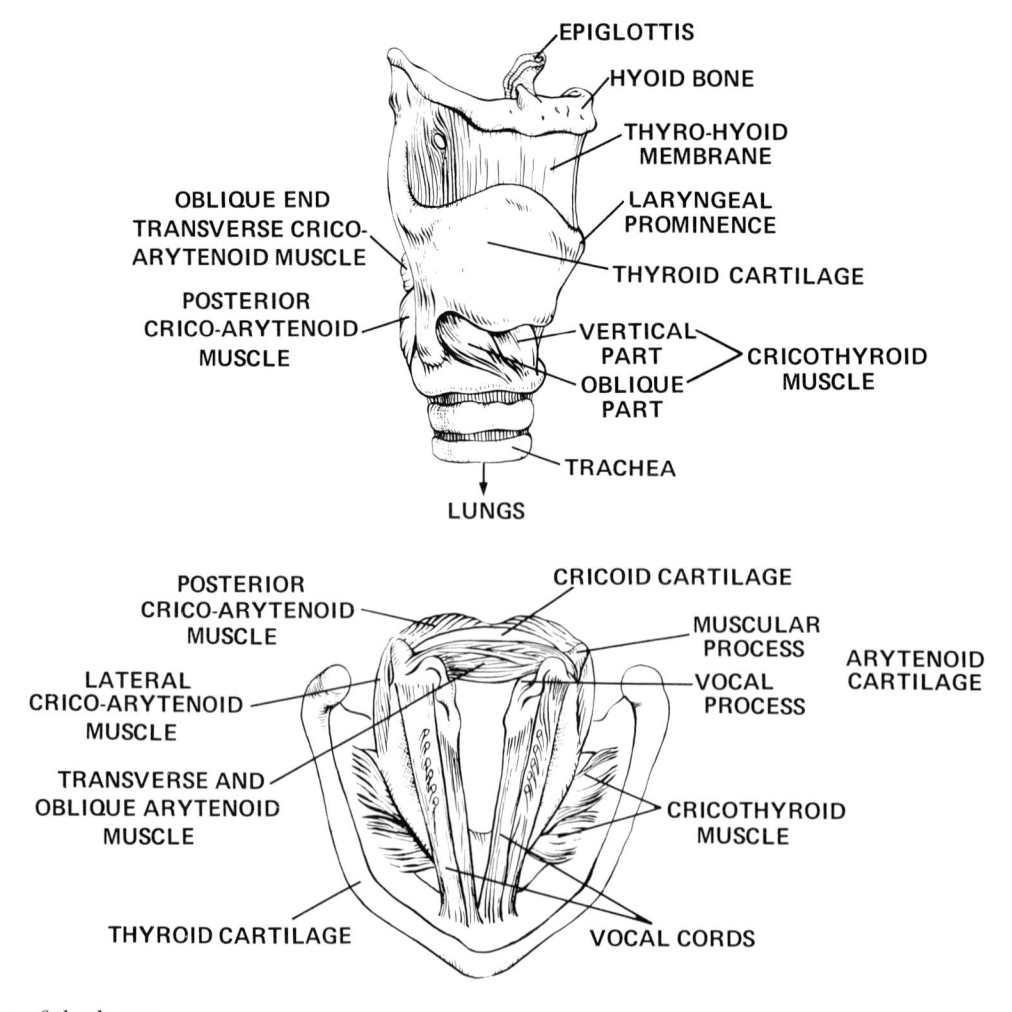

Fig. 7-4. Anatomy of the larynx.

diagnosis designed to determine areas of strength and weakness and to locate the point of breakdown in the developmental sequence requires the combined efforts of experts from a number of specialists.[6,8,16] The diagnosis should establish the best approach for remediation for each individual child. Because these children, like normal children, are constantly learning and developing, decisions concerning academic and educational placement must be flexible and must be reevaluated at regular intervals. Although children with mild to moderate language disorders may learn differently or more slowly than normal children, they should not be classified as mentally retarded. By definition, they must show normal or above-normal ability in some other area in order to be classified as having a language disorder or childhood aphasia. This type of disorder is now well recognized as a separate entity. Special remedial and sophisticated diagnostic techniques are rapidly being developed to treat these children,[8,9,19-21] and most school systems now offer special classes for the linguistically handicapped.

SPEECH DISORDERS

Vocal Mechanisms

Once our thoughts are organized into the appropriate grammatical, syntactical, and sentence forms, the words must then be produced by the larynx and the muscles of articulation (Fig. 7-4). Speech disorders or voice disorders, as opposed to aphasia or language disorders, refer to problems in output only. Breakdowns in communication at this level may occur in the absence of any hearing deficit or central nervous system dysfunction. When speech or voice disorders occur in isolation, they are generally the result of inadequate muscle control or structural anomalies, such as cleft palate or poor tooth alignment (malocclusion).

Phonation

The speech production process begins at the level of the larynx, where our vocal cords are housed (Fig. 7-4, top). The larynx is a continuation of the windpipe (trachea) and is formed by cartilages and paired muscles. The bottom sketch in Fig. 7-4 shows the interior of the larynx. The paired vocal cords are attached to the thyroid cartilage at the front and to two prominences of the paired arytenoid cartilages (muscular process and vocal process) at the back. The cords may be opened and closed by rotating and compressing the arytenoid cartilages. When the vocal cords are brought together and air from the lungs is forced through them, they open and close rapidly (vibrate) to produce voice (phonation). The number of times the cords open and close within a second determines how high or how low our voice is. When we hum middle C, for example, our cords are opening and closing 256 times per second. Both the pitch and loudness of our voice are controlled by changes in the vocal cords *(mass adjustments)*, in the amount and rate of airflow through the cords, and in the tension of the vocal cords.

Voice disorders may result from illnesses or injuries which lead to paralysis of the muscles (hypofunction), but this is relatively rare compared to the number of vocal pathologies which result from vocal abuse or misuse (hyperfunction).[22,23] Because the vocal mechanism is so finely balanced, even minor variations in speaking habits, not to mention excessive shouting or vocal usage, can disturb this balance. If detrimental habits continue over a long period of time they can produce pathological changes such as vocal ulcers, nodules, and polyps. Vocal retraining generally eliminates problems of this nature. If the growths are large and have been present for some time, surgical removal followed by voice therapy is the preferred method of treatment. In order to rule out progressive disease, individuals with voice disorders should always be seen by a physician for laryngoscopic evaluation before treatment begins.

Articulation

When we phonate, the sound we produce travels through the vocal tract (Fig. 7-5), which consists of the throat (pharynx) plus the nasal and oral cavities. The shape of the vocal tract can be modified by moving the tongue, opening or closing the soft palate, moving the lips, and opening and closing the mouth. This flexibility enables us to shape (or selectively resonate) the voice into any of the many different sounds (phonemes) in our language. Most children are able to form all the phonemes of the language by the age of four, even though they may not do so consistently for another year or two.[19]

Obviously, when the structures within the vocal tract are abnormal, the resonating characteristics may be dramatically changed. The result is poor pronunciation or an articulation disorder. For example, individuals with cleft palates are often unable to close off the nasal cavity adequately. This not only alters their voice quality, but also affects their pronunciation because it destroys pressure relationships within the oral cavity that are necessary for precise articulation. Similarly, alterations of dental alignment may change the shaping characteristics of the oral cavity in such a way that the accurate articulation of some sounds is not possible. Fortunately, advances in surgical, orthodontic, and prosthodontic techniques have improved the outlook for individuals with problems of this nature. Medical and dental procedures, in combination with speech therapy to maximize compensatory adjustments, are now quite successful in treating articulation disorders associated with structural deviations.

A large proportion of developmental articulation disorders are the result of delayed neurological maturation. Because the demands on fine coordination and timing are probably greater for accurate speaking than for any other daily activity, children with immature physiological systems cannot meet these demands. Careful diagnostic workups will identify these children, and maturation may then be enhanced through the selective stimulation provided by speech therapy. It is important to treat these children as early as possible, before improper productions become overlearned and the child becomes seriously disturbed by his inability to communicate.

Muscle incoordination may also stem from a more serious cause, such as neurological disease or damage. Cerebral palsy, Parkinson's disease, multiple sclerosis, and damage to any of the motor speech areas within the central nervous system can affect articulation in various ways. In these cases, the muscles of articulation may be partially paralyzed, and the articulation disorder which results is called *dysarthria*. There are many different types of dysarthria[6] but, in general, speech therapy is designed to help the patient obtain maximum accuracy within the limits of his neuromuscular ability. Although it is relatively rare, a child may occasionally maintain infantile articulation patterns for emotional (or

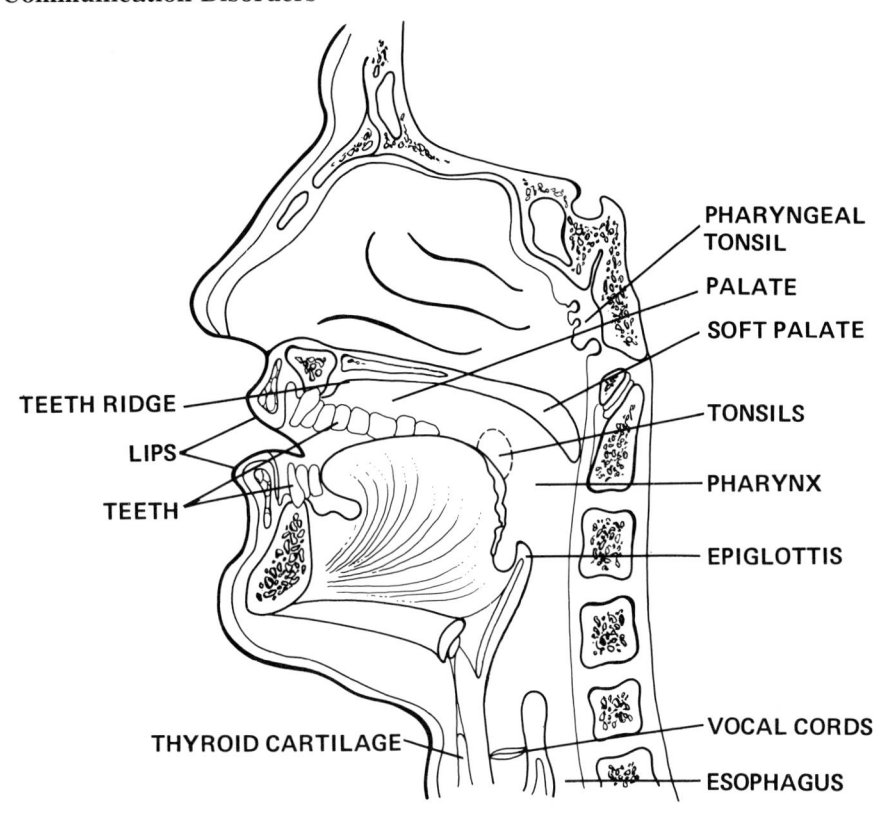

Fig. 7-5. The vocal tract.

manipulative) reasons. However, because muscle incoordination is a part of an overall neurophysiological immaturity, the children described above may also be emotionally immature.[24] Careful differential diagnosis is therefore necessary before basic causation can be determined. In the developing child, behavioral control or emotional maturity depends upon physical and neurological maturation, as well as on environmental factors.

Stuttering

More than any other speech disorder, stuttering is an enigma. Despite years of extensive research,[25] the cause or causes of stuttering are still unknown. Investigators even have difficulty in agreeing upon a definition of stuttering, but most would concur that it is an involuntary interruption in the rhythm of speaking, which may manifest itself in a number of ways. In general, research has shown that people who stutter are no different in terms of emotional adjustment or intelligence from those who do not. In addition, no discernible physical, perceptual, or chemical differences have been found in this group. The therapeutic approach, therefore, is to treat stuttering as learned behavior, and behavioral modification techniques have proved to be very effective in reducing dysfluency. The treatment of young stutterers varies somewhat from that for adults,[6,24] and children with this problem should be referred to a speech therapist. Despite the unknown quality of the disorder, therapy for stuttering can be very effective.

CONCLUSION

Communication is a multistage process which may break down at any level. Because this process is so crucial to social, academic, and professional interactions, the problems associated with a speech, language, or hearing disorder can be devastating. Early recognition and understanding of these problems can be crucial in reducing frustration and minimizing their effect on behavior and performance.

REFERENCES

1. Holm, V. A., and Kunze, C. H., Effect of chronic otitis media on language and speech development. *Pediatrics* 43:833–837, 1969.
2. Katz, J., The effects of conductive hearing loss on auditory function. *ASHA: A Journal of the American Speech, Hearing, and Language Association* 20:877–886, 1978.
3. Lewis, N., Otitis media and linguistic incompetence. *Archives of Otolaryngology,* 102:387–390, 1976.
4. Webster, D. B., and Webster, M., Neonatal sound deprivation affects brain stem auditory nuclei. *Archives of Otolaryngology* 103:392–396, 1977.
5. Barry, H., *The Young Aphasic Child.* Washington, D.C., Alexander Graham Bell Association for the Deaf, 1961.
6. Darley, F. L., *Diagnosis and Appraisal of Communication Disorders.* Foundations of Speech Pathology Series. Englewood Cliffs, N.J., Prentice-Hall, 1964.
7. Eisenson, J., *Aphasia in Children.* New York, Harper & Row, 1972.
8. McGinnis, M., *Aphasic Children.* Washington, D.C., Alexander Graham Bell Association for the Deaf, 1963.
9. Myklebust, H., *Auditory Disorders in Children.* New York, Grune & Stratton, 1964.
10. Schuell, H., Jenkins, J., and Edward J. P., *Aphasia in Adults.* New York, Harper & Row, 1965.
11. Newby, H. A., *Audiology.* New York, Appleton-Century-Crofts, 1964.
12. Davis, H., and Silverman, S. R. (eds.), *Hearing and Deafness,* Rev. ed. New York, Holt, Rinehart, and Winston, 1964.
13. Shambaugh, G. E., *Surgery of the Ear.* Philadelphia, W. B. Saunders, 1959.
14. Travis, L. E. (ed.), *Handbook of Speech Pathology and Audiology.* New York, Appleton-Century-Crofts, 1972.
15. Wood, N. E., *Delayed Speech and Language Development.* Foundations of Speech Pathology Series. Englewood Cliffs, N.J., Prentice-Hall, 1964.
16. Mecham, M., Berko, M. J., Berko, F. G., and Palmer, M., *Training in Childhood Brain Damage.* Springfield, Ill., Charles C. Thomas, 1969.
17. Beadle, K. R., Clinical interactions of verbal language, learning, and behavior. *Journal of Clinical Child Psychology,* Fall 1979, pp. 201–206.
18. Beadle, K. R. Disturbances in speech behavior, in Darby, J., (ed.), *Speech Disturbances in Medicine and Psychiatry,* vol. 2. New York, Grune & Stratton, 1981.
19. Battin, R. R., and Haug, C. O. (eds.), *Speech and Language Delay: A Home Training Program.* Springfield, Ill., Charles C. Thomas, 1968.
20. Scott, L. B., *Developing Communication Skills: A Guide for the Classroom Teacher.* Manchester, Mo., Webster/McGraw-Hill, 1972.
21. Sperry, V., *Of Course I Can: Auditory Skills.* Englewood Cliffs, N.J., Responsive Environments, 1973.
22. Greene, M. C., *The Voice and Its Disorders.* New York, Macmillan, 1957.
23. Boone, D., *The Voice and Voice Therapy.* Englewood Cliffs, N.J., Prentice-Hall, 1977.
24. Winitz, H., *Articulatory Acquisition and Behavior.* New York, Merdith, 1969.
25. Van Riper, C., *Speech Correction: Principles and Practices.* Englewood Cliffs, N.J., Prentice-Hall, 1972.

BIBLIOGRAPHY

Bateman, H., *A Clinical Approach to Speech Anatomy and Physiology.* Springfield, Ill., Charles C. Thomas, 1977.

Denes, P. B., and Pinson, E. N., *The Speech Chain.* Holmdel, N.J., Bell Telephone Laboratories, 1968.

Ladefoged, P., *Elements of Acoustic Phonetics.* Chicago, University of Chicago Press, 1962.

8

Nonoral Communication

Edited by
EUGENE E. BLECK

Handicapped children who are nonverbal do, despite this handicap, possess language ability. This chapter highlights methods by which such children may achieve some form of self-expression. Children who were formerly thought to be retarded because they could not speak have, with the use of these methods, been able to communicate needs, emotions, concepts, and desires. Surely this marks a major breakthrough in the management of the nonverbal child.

Augmentative Communication System: Blissymbolics

SHIRLEY McNAUGHTON

Interacting is communicating.

Interacting is teaching and learning.

Interacting can be USING BLISSYMBOLS.

AUGMENTATIVE COMMUNICATION SYSTEM

Children who lack functional speech have always presented a special challenge to the educator. Their need to interact with accepting persons and with a stimulating environment is as strong as that of the speaking child, yet they are deprived of speech, the usual communication system by which this interaction occurs. Until recent years, teachers had little option but to assume a dominating role in their interaction with the nonspeaking student, communicating with and teaching a child who was, essentially, a noninitiating "receiver." This is no longer the case, however. Throughout the 1970s, innovative clinical and educational programs, together with research in cognition, language, and communication, have led to a new approach for interacting with nonspeaking persons. The expanded communication capability is described as the Augmentative Communication System. As outlined by the American Speech-Language-Hearing Association,[1] an Augmentative Communication System has three components: (1) technique, or means of transmitting an idea; (2) symbol set/system, or means of representing the idea; and (3) communication/interaction behavior, or the behavior necessary for making the idea received and understood.

Preliminary to the advancement of the Augmentative Communication System concept, there has been growing acceptance by many professionals that:

1. Communication is more than speech and can best be dealt with by considering all modes of communication along with all modes of interaction.[5,7]
2. The use of an Augmentative Communication System will not hamper the development of speech.[8,12,15,17,18]
3. Language and cognition have a reciprocal relationship, each interacting with the other in the course of their development.[2,4] Hence, deprivation in the area of language may have a damaging effect upon cognitive development.
4. Language has both communicative and noncommunicative functions. Since speech fulfills both these functions for the speaking

child, the Augmentative Communication System should do likewise for the nonspeaking child.
5. When the instructional program expands beyond the development of speech to the development of an Augmentative Communication System, the responsibility previously assumed by the speech pathologist needs to be shared with professionals from several disciplines, one of which is education.

The role of the teacher in instructing the nonspeaking student is a challenging one. Through the use of an Augmentative Communication System, the teacher has the opportunity to facilitate the student's interacting with others within the educational setting. Moreover, the teacher is instrumental in developing the student's ability to interact successfully at home and in the community.

BLISSYMBOLICS

History

The value of Blissymbolics* as a symbol system that can be used within an Augmentative Communication System has been widely demonstrated.[8,10,18] The system was first applied in 1971 with cerebral palsied children at the Ontario Crippled Children's Centre, Toronto, Canada. Its use within the Augmentative Communication System for physically and mentally handicapped persons gained acceptance in 14 countries over the next 8 years.†

To support the use of Blissymbolics within Augmentative Communication Systems, the Blissymbolics Communication Institute (BCI) was established in Toronto, Canada.‡ BCI offers training programs and instructional materials and provides its associate members with ongoing information regarding developments in the symbol system and in its application.

Symbols

Blissymbolics is a graphic, meaning-based system that is capable of representing a wide range of meaning.§ Blissymbols are constructed from a small number of basic geometric shapes:

☐ △ ⊿ ○
♡) | ~

Because many Blissymbols are pictographic, they are easily learned by children at the early developmental level:

---

*Blissymbolics was originally designed by Charles K. Bliss in the 1940s as an international language.[3]
†Australia, Canada, Denmark, Finland, France, Holland, Iceland, India, Israel, New Zealand, Norway, Sweden, United Kingdom, United States of America (Blissymbolics Communication Institute, *Bulletin* 5(1), 1979).
‡Blissymbolics Communication Institute, 350 Rumsey Road, Toronto, Ontario, Canada, M4G 1R8 (originally named Blissymbolics Communication Foundation).
§For comprehensive descriptions of BCI Blissymbolics, see.[9] For information relating to the system and its application within Augmentative Communication Systems see.[8] For a full exposition of the system and the rationale for each Blissymbol see.[3]

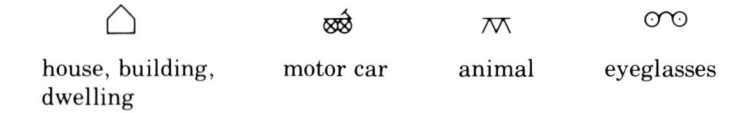

house, building, dwelling   motor car   animal   eyeglasses

Many Blissymbols are ideographic and thus can be used to represent complex ideas:

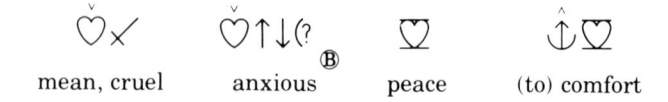

mean, cruel   anxious   peace   (to) comfort

Some Blissymbols are arbitrary, providing a means of representing functional words:

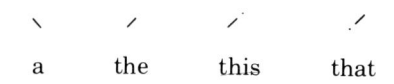

a   the   this   that

Each Blissymbol "spells" in meaning units; that is, the concept is represented by the total symbol:

teacher is: person (who) gives knowledge

Blissymbols appear as single units, either in the form of simple symbols:

ear   eye   (to) smell   (to) speak

or as compound, superimposed symbols:

deaf   blind   (to) taste

They may also appear as several units (compound, sequenced symbols):

soft   salty   beautiful, attractive   school

BLISSYMBOLICS AND THE FUNCTIONS OF LANGUAGE

The structure of Blissymbolics is of particular value to the teacher, for the system has capabilities that permit it to be used for learning as well as communicating and teaching. Blissymbolics serves well both the noncommunicative and the communicative functions of language. Taken from lists compiled by Chapman[14] and Tough,[16] these functions include:

Augmentative Communication System

Noncommunicative Functions

- to form concepts
- to reason logically
- to imagine
- to establish a self image
- to examine the language code itself (metalingual function)
- to focus on the linguistic form for its own sake

Communicative Functions

- to give information
- to get the listener to do, believe, or feel something
- to express one's intentions, beliefs, feelings
- to solve problems
- to make and maintain social contact

Noncommunicative Functions

With respect to the noncommunicative functions of language, Blissymbolics contributes in subtle but constructive ways:

1. Blissymbols help the child in the formulation of concepts as he or she strategically uses the several special symbols contained in the system. For example, use of the opposite-meaning symbol gives the student experience with the concept, opposite:

   big   little   young   old
          (opposite   (opposite
           of big)   of young)

2. Blissymbols support logical reasoning. For example, use of the combine symbol allows the student to construct logically his or her own personal symbol expression through sequencing the meaning components that he or she selects as relevant. *Interacting,* for instance, might be represented by the symbol:

   which combines the following components:

   reference   reciprocal   action
   line   motion   indicator

   The symbol represents reciprocal action between defined points of reference. Enclosure of the symbol elements between the combine indicators, ⊚ , indicates that that particular symbol expression is not at present part of the standard BCI Blissymbol vocabulary.

3. Blissymbols provide symbols that stimulate the imagination:

   make-believe   monster   ghost

4. Blissymbols offer symbols that assist in the development of self-image:

selfish considerate self-control smart

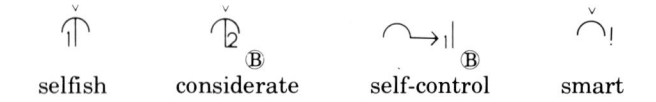

5. The logic and simplicity of Blissymbols allow the student to examine the system's structure. For example, the indicators signal grammatical categories:

action indicator   plural indicator   description (evaluation) indicator

6. Blissymbols encourage a unique "poetic" function through the meaning-shape relationships of the symbols. "Growing up," for example, involves slight visual differences:

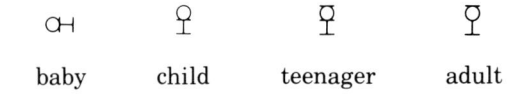

baby child teenager adult

Communicative Functions

Serving the communicative functions of language, Blissymbols are selected sequentially to construct a message.

1. New information can be given:

    Daddy will be returning home tomorrow.

2. Requests can be made:

    Please give (a) drink to him.

3. Feeling and ideas can be expressed:

    I love you.

4. Problems can be defined and tackled:

    If I give (the) map to her,

    she can find (the) correct street.

5. Social interaction can be maintained:

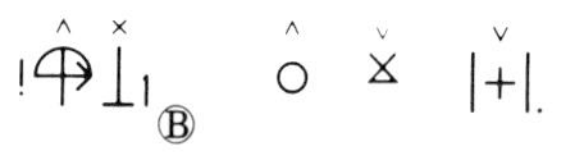

Let's talk more together.

For communication purposes, Blissymbols are organized into Blissymbol displays (Fig. 8-1). Displays range in size from a few to over 800 symbols.

For both teacher and student, the use of Blissymbolics offers a further opportunity. As the teacher records the Blissymbol messages initiated by the student and writes messages to serve as models, and as the student derives meaning from this Blissymbol print, the student participates in the process of reading. Much remains to be learned as to how this activity relates to the development of later reading skills, but many teachers are developing exciting reading programs, as they explore the ways in which the reading of Blissymbolics can facilitate the reading of traditional orthography.

THE USE OF BLISSYMBOLS

Blissymbols may be displayed for students' use in many ways. For some users, symbol displays are mounted on wheelchair trays. For others, displays may be carried in menu-type folding displays, inserted in wallet and purse-type folders, worn as aprons, affixed to walkers, or displayed on walls in frequently used rooms. Blissymbols may also be incorporated into electromechanical and electronic displays for students who are unable to point directly at the desired symbol. And we are just beginning to see the utilization of Blissymbols within personal computers—an exciting new development!

The techniques by which Blissymbols are used are as varied as are the types of displays. Blissymbols can be targeted directly on a symbol display, in which case the user points at the desired symbol with a finger or other body part. In these instances, the receiver must be present and

Fig. 8-1. Display that can be used in introducing adults to Blissymbol communication.

respond immediately. Blissymbols can also be selected by the user from symbols displayed on a technical aid, with the desired symbol indicated either by a small light,[13] a print-out of the symbol,[11] or a presentation of the symbol on a television screen.[6] When such technical aids are used, the receiver need not be present. In the latter instance, the Blissymbol message can be transmitted from one computer terminal to another by telephone communication lines. Whichever technique is used, words always appear with the symbol, making the system functional whether or not the receiver understands Blissymbols.

Communication/Interaction

The communication/interaction behavior necessary for successful Blissymbol interaction is typical of the behavior required for all Augmentative Communication Systems. The *receiver* must be accepting of the different system, must take time to interact in a new and different way, and must remain open to discovering the benefits that may be derived from communicating through a nonspeech system. The *user* must develop all the communication/interaction skills required of those who speak, and in addition, must become adept at putting the receiver at ease, meeting the receiver's special communication needs, and orienting new acquaintances to a different way of interacting.

THE TEACHER'S ROLE

The teacher makes a valuable contribution in providing a learning situation that allows the Augmentative Communication System to become functional. The teacher's role includes teaching the system, developing the means and techniques by which the system will be used, and providing the student with experiences which allow him or her to develop the necessary communication/interaction behaviors. "Given the state of the art regarding the development and use of communication techniques, there is no nonspeaking person too handicapped to be able to utilize some augmentative communication system."[1]

Teachers, then, have an important part to play in facilitating the interaction of their nonspeaking students with others through use of an Augmentative Communication System. Using Blissymbolics is one effective way in which this may be done.

REFERENCES

1. American Speech-Hearing-Language Association (ASHA), Non-speech Communication: A Position Paper. *ASHA Journal* 22: 267–272, 1980.
2. Bates, E., Benigni, L., Bretherton, I., et al., From gesture to the first word: On cognitive and social prerequisites, in Lewis, M., and Rosenblum, L. A. (eds.), *Interaction, Conversation, and the Development of Language*. New York, Wiley, 1977.
3. Bliss, C. K., *Semantography/Blissymbolics*. Sydney, Australia, Semantography Publications, 1965.
4. Bowerman, M., Semantic and Syntactic Development, in Schiefelbusch, R. L. (ed.), *Bases of Language Intervention*. Language Intervention Series, vol. 1. Baltimore, University Park Press, 1978.
5. Chapman, R. S., and Miller, J., Analyzing language and communication in the child, in Schiefelbusch, R. L. (ed.), *Nonspeech Language and Communication: Analysis and Intervention*. Baltimore, University Park Press, 1980.
6. Giddings, W., Norton, J., Nelson, P., et al., Development of a Blissymbol terminal: An interactive TV display to enhance communications for the

physically handicapped. *Proceedings of the Sixth Man-Computer Communications Conference,* Ottawa, Ontario, Canada, 1979. [Available from Peter Nelson, National Research Council, Ottawa, Ontario, Canada, K1A OR8.]
7. Harris, D., and Vanderheiden, G. C., Enhancing the development of communication interaction, in Schiefelbusch, R. L. (ed.)., *Nonspeech Language and Communication: Analysis and Intervention.* Baltimore, University Park Press, 1980.
8. Harris-Vanderheiden, D., Lippert, J., Yoder, D. E., et al., Blissymbols: An augmentative/symbol communication system for nonvocal severely handicapped children, in York, R., and Edgar, E. (eds.), *Teaching the Severely Handicaped,* vol 4. Seattle, American Association for the Education of the Severely and Profoundly Handicapped, 1977.
9. Hehner, B. (ed.), *Blissymbols for Use.* Toronto, Blissymbolics Communication Institute, 1980.
10. Kates, B., and McNaughton, S., *The First Application of Blissymbolics.* Toronto, Blissymbolics Communication Institute, 1975.
11. Kelso, D., and Silverman, H., The Bliss-com: A portable symbol printing communication aid. *Proceedings of Fourth Annual Conference on Systems and Devices for the Disabled,* Seattle, Washington, 1977, p. 99.
12. McDonald, E., and Schultz, A., Communication boards for cerebral palsied children. *Journal of Speech and Hearing Disorders* 38: 73–88, 1973.
13. McNaughton, S., Blissymbolics and technology. *Proceedings of the Workshop on Communication Aids for the Handicapped,* Ottawa, Ontario, Canada, 1977. [Available from Peter Nelson, National Research Council, Ottawa, Ontario, Canada K1A OR8.]
14. Miller, J. F., Assessing children's language: A developmental process approach, in Schiefelbusch, R. L. (ed.), *Bases of Language Intervention.* Language Intervention Series, vol. 1. Baltimore, University Park Press, 1978.
15. Schaeffer, B., Spontaneous language through signed speech, in Schiefelbusch, R. L. (ed.), *Nonspeech Language and Communication: Analysis and Intervention.* Baltimore, University Park Press, 1980.
16. Shafer, R. E., The Work of Joan Tough: A case study in applied linguistics. *Language Arts* 55(3):308–314, 1978.
17. Silverman, F. H., *Communication for the speechless.* Englewood Cliffs, N.J., Prentice-Hall, 1979.
18. Silverman, H., McNaughton, S., and Kates, B., *Handbook of Blissymbolics.* Toronto, Blissymbolics Communication Institute, 1978.

Blissymbolics are © 1981 by Blissymbolics Communication Institute, Toronto, Canada.

Ⓑ indicates —1) a symbol which differs from the C. K. Bliss version either in symbol form or accompanying wording or —2) a new BCI symbol authorized in absence of requested comment from C. K. Bliss.

BIBLIOGRAPHY The Use of Blissymbols

Harris-Vanderheiden, D., Lippert, J., Yoder, D. E., et al., Blissymbols: An augmentative/symbol communication system for nonvocal severely handicapped children, in York, R., and Edgar E. (eds.), *Teaching the Severely Handicapped,* vol. 4. Seattle, American Association for the Education of the Severely and Profoundly Handicapped, 1977.

Hehner, B. (ed.), *Blissymbols for Use.* Toronto, Blissymbolics Communication Institute, 1980.

McDonald, E., *Teaching and Using Blissymbolics.* Toronto, Blissymbolics Communication Institute, 1980.

McNaughton, S., and Kates, B., The application of Blissymbolics, in Schiefelbusch, R. L. (ed.), *Nonspeech Language and Communication: Analysis and Intervention.* Baltimore, University Park Press, 1980.

Silverman, H., McNaughton, S., and Kates, B., *Handbook of Blissymbolics.* Toronto, Blissymbolics Communication Institute, 1978.

Augmentative Communication Systems

American Speech-Language-Hearing Association (ASHA), Non-speech Communication: A position paper. *ASHA Journal* 22:267–272, 1980.

Goldenberg, E. P., *Special Technology For Special Children.* Baltimore, University Park Press, 1979.

Schiefelbusch, R. L. (ed.), *Nonspeech Language and Communication: Analysis and Intervention.* Baltimore, University Park Press, 1980.

Silverman, F. H., *Communication for the Speechless.* Englewood Cliffs, N.J., Prentice-Hall, Inc., 1979.

Eulenberg, J., and Vanderheiden, G., We are a community. *Communication Outlook*, 1:1, 1978.

Sign Language: Examples of Classroom Survival Signs*

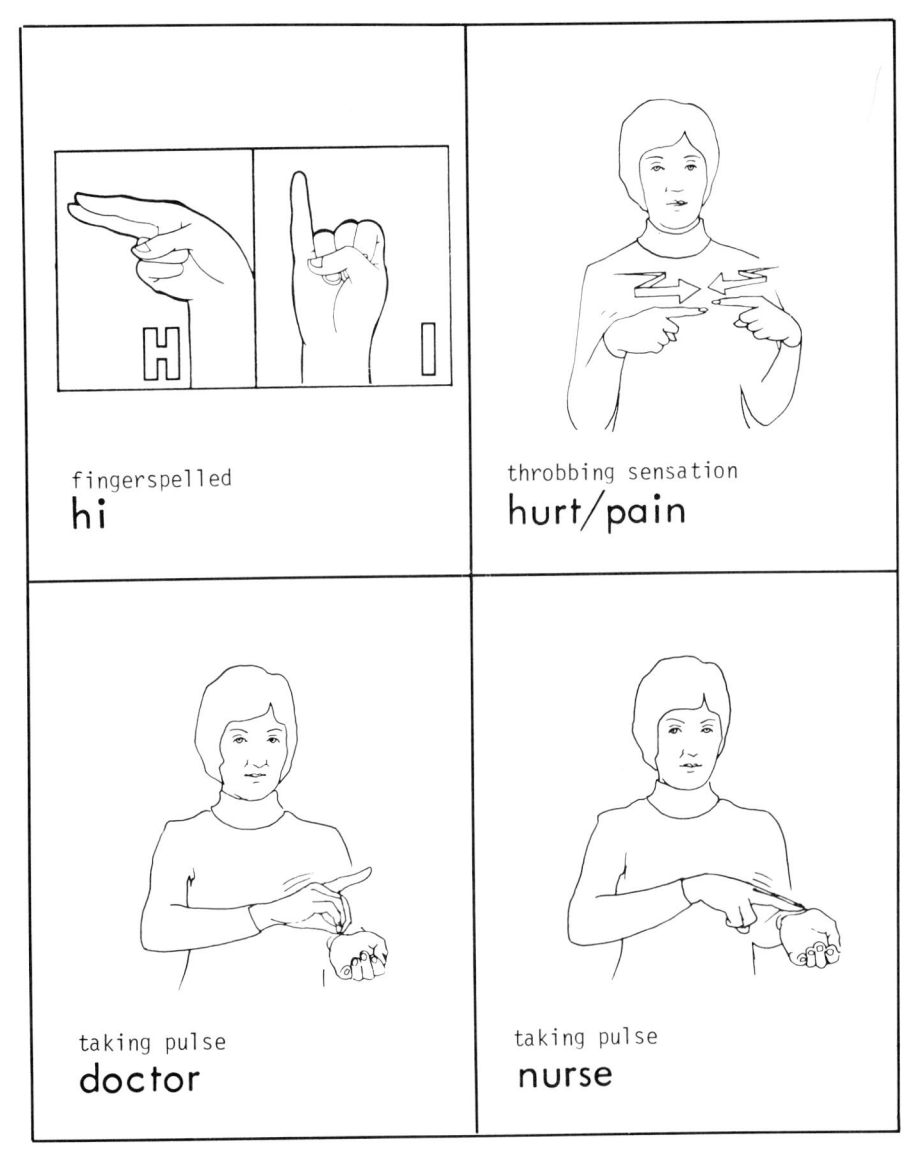

fingerspelled
hi

throbbing sensation
hurt/pain

taking pulse
doctor

taking pulse
nurse

*Reproduced from *100 Medical Survival Signs,* © Joyce Media, P.O. Box 458, Northridge, CA 91328. With permission.

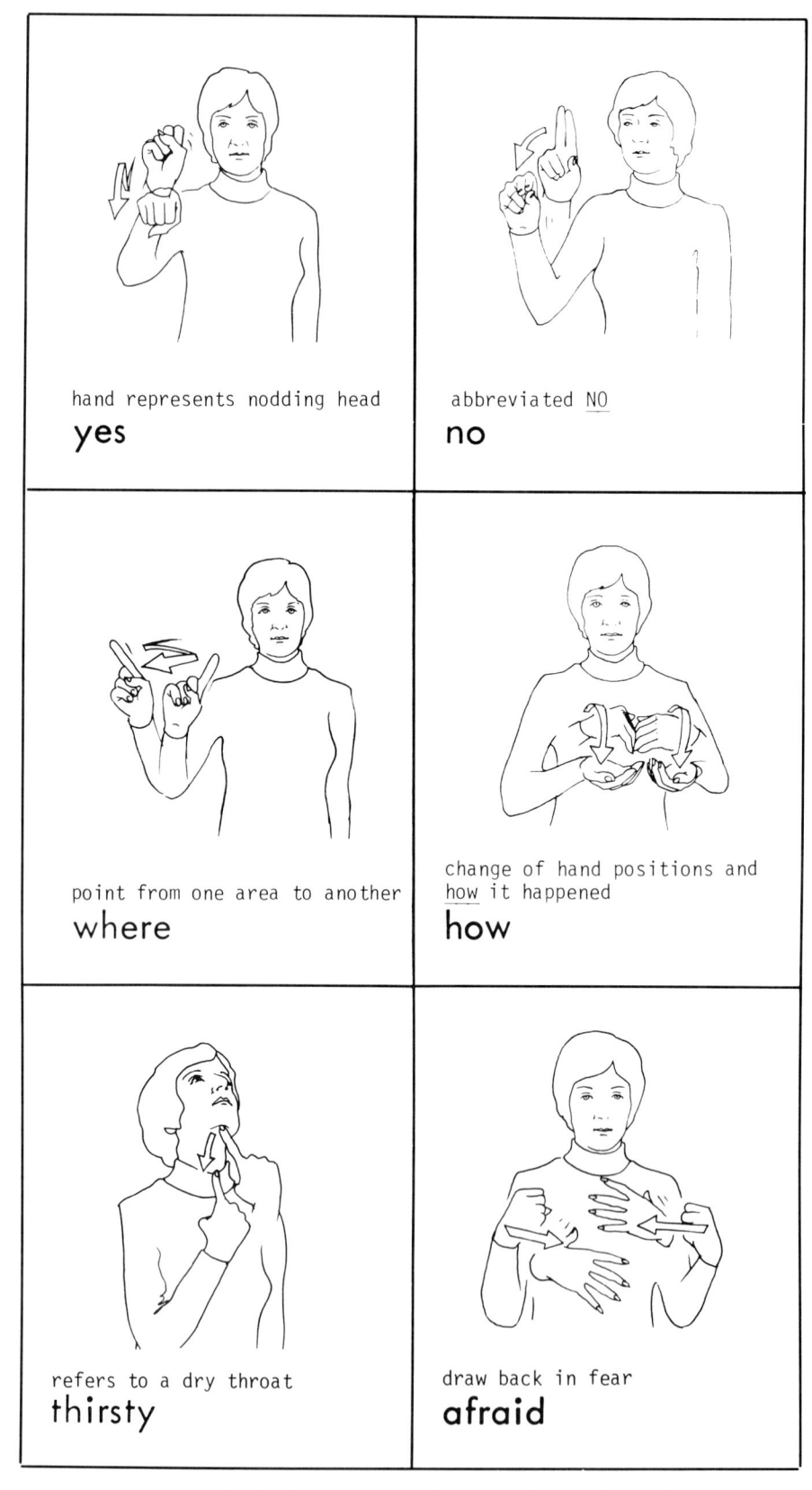

Eugene E. Bleck

hand represents nodding head **yes**	abbreviated NO **no**
point from one area to another **where**	change of hand positions and how it happened **how**
refers to a dry throat **thirsty**	draw back in fear **afraid**

Reproduced from *100 Medical Survival Signs*, © Joyce Media, P.O. Box 458, Northridge, CA 91328. With permission.

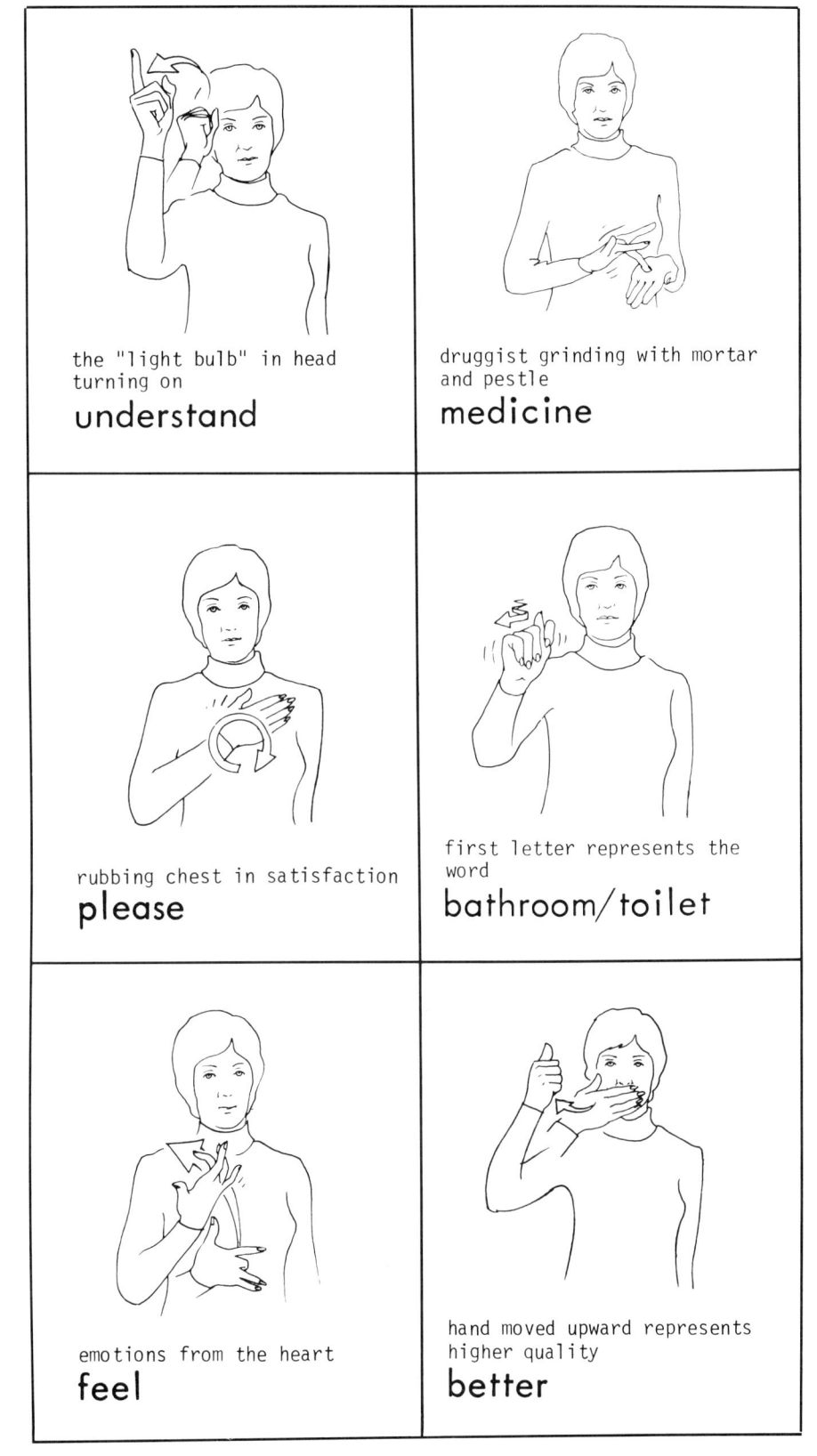

Sign Language: Classroom Survival Signs 157

the "light bulb" in head turning on **understand**	druggist grinding with mortar and pestle **medicine**
rubbing chest in satisfaction **please**	first letter represents the word **bathroom/toilet**
emotions from the heart **feel**	hand moved upward represents higher quality **better**

Reproduced from *100 Medical Survival Signs*, © Joyce Media, P.O. Box 458, Northridge, CA 91328. With permission.

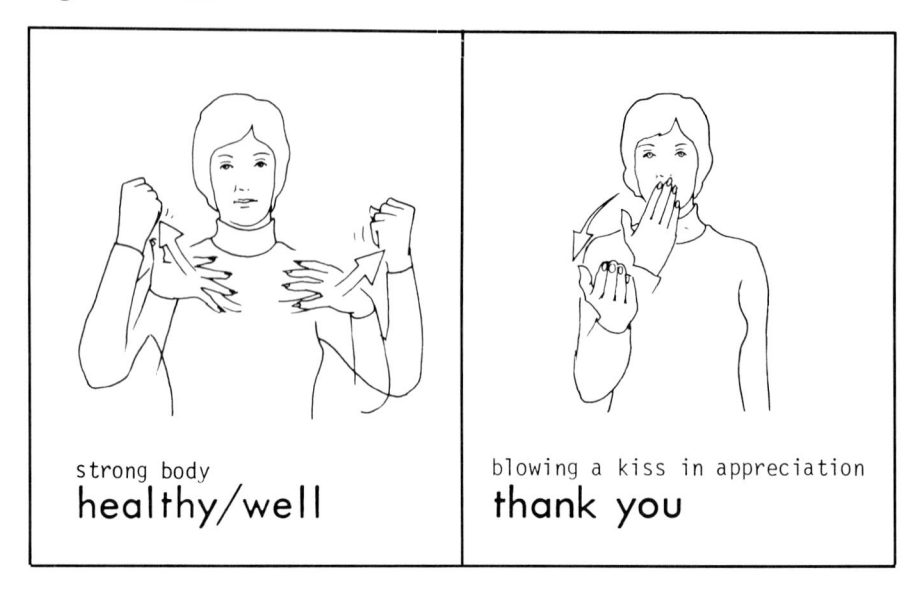

| strong body
healthy/well | blowing a kiss in appreciation
thank you |

Reproduced from *100 Medical Survival Signs*, © Joyce Media, P.O. Box 458, Northridge, CA 91328. With permission.

Systems and Devices for Nonoral Communication

MAURICE LeBLANC, C.P., M.S.

Children who cannot speak can often compensate for this inability by writing, typing, and using their hands in order to communicate. Some children are multiply or severely involved, however, and for them such means of communicating are not available.

Many of these children who cannot communicate by normal means are, nevertheless, intellectually capable. They have receptive, although not expressive, language and therefore can benefit from some sort of substitutive communication system. They comprise the largest group of children needing communication assistance seen in developmental centers, special education schools, and normal classrooms, and are the focus of the following discussion.

DEFINITIONS

Communication devices may be grouped into two general categories. *Substitutive aids,* with which we are concerned here, are those that replace the speech that a child lacks: an example would be a voice prosthesis.* The second group, *augmentative aids,* are those that assist what speech a child already possesses: examples are speech amplifiers† and speech clarifiers.‡

Some confusion exists regarding the meaning of the terms, *nonverbal* and *nonvocal.* For this reason, the terms *nonoral* and *nonspeaking* are used (interchangeably) in the following discussion to mean the functional loss of speech as a practical means of communication.

POPULATION

Various estimates[1,2] suggest that there are approximately 1½ million people in the United States who can potentially benefit from communication assistance of one form or another. This includes persons with cerebral palsy, head injury, spinal cord injury (quadriplegia), aphasia resulting from stroke, or progressive neuromuscular disease. Most of the nonoral children who are seen in schools are cerebral palsied, and it is estimated that, of the 750,000 persons with cerebral palsy in the United States, approximately 20 percent are nonoral.[1]

Persons whose primary disability is deafness or blindness, or both, are excluded from these estimates.

---

*Voice prosthesis: such as HandiVoice, manufactured by H. C. Electronics, Inc., Mill Valley, California, and Form-a-Phrase, manufactured by Scitronics, Inc., Bethlehem, Pennsylvania.
†Speech amplifier: such as the Rand Voice Amplifier, manufactured by Lumirand, Mentor, Ohio, and Speech Amplifier T-F2, manufactured by A B Specialinstrument, Stockholm, Sweden.
‡Speech clarifier: such as available from the National Institute for Rehabilitation Engineering, Pompton Lakes, New Jersey.

PRIORITY OF NEEDS

Surveys of persons with severe physical handicaps have indicated a priority of needs as follows:

1. Communication
2. Independence in activities of daily living
3. Mobility
4. Ambulation

If one ponders the above list, one can see that it is easier to start at the bottom and work up, rather than at the top and work down. Daniel Webster once said, "If all my possessions were taken from me with one exception, I would choose to keep the power of communication, for by it I would soon regain all the rest."

A NEW FIELD

The endeavor to provide communication assistance to people who are nonspeaking or nonwriting, or both, began in the 1970's. Over the past 5 years, there has developed significant momentum towards effecting a national program centered around these efforts.

The TRACE Center at the University of Wisconsin in Madison has developed a resource book[4] that is essentially a catalog of communication aids. Another relatively new development is the publication of *Communication Outlook,* a periodical that focuses on communication aids and techniques. Edited and published by the Artificial Language Laboratory at Michigan State University, with assistance from the TRACE Center, it forms the nucleus for an International Action Group for Communication Enhancement. In addition, a number of local, multidisciplinary communication groups have been formed in major cities throughout the country, to share information and develop services for their communities.

National advocacy for people requiring communication assistance also moves forward. Such advocacy is important both because the disabled cannot speak for themselves and because the population of such people is so diverse, consisting of people with different disabilities, among whom the need for communication assistance is the sole common denominator.

SELECTION AND USE OF A COMMUNICATION SYSTEM

The successful use of a communication system depends upon (1) a keen and complete assessment of a child's needs and circumstances, (2) the provision of an appropriate aid and means of control, and (3) adequate training and follow-up. Each of these three areas will be addressed in this chapter.

Assessment

Ingredients

A good place to start in the assessment of children who require communication assistance is simply to list the information one needs in order to make a proper judgment. This should include such factors as:

1. Mental capabilities
2. Educational level and program

3. Physical abilities and limitations
4. General medical picture
5. Status of vision and hearing
6. Status of speech and related therapy
7. Needs at home as well as at school
8. Role of a wheelchair and of seating support in the child's life
9. Personal desires and preferences
10. Role of parents and school in use and implementation of communication system
11. Aids and controls available
12. Funding available for purchase of system

While this list of "ingredients" is by no means complete, it does illustrate the variety of factors that must be considered for a satisfactory assessment of a child's needs and the best means of meeting those needs. Some of the data will be subjective, because it is difficult to test a nonoral child. Very beneficial insights can sometimes be gained from family, attendants, and friends: although they may lack medical or professional training and experience, such persons spend a lot of time with the child and thus often have gained insight into the child's needs, abilities, and so forth.

Team Approach

The extensive list of factors to be considered suggests that a team effort is essential for the satisfactory assessment of each child. The composition of the team is frequently as listed below. Naturally, not all need be present at one place at one time:

Parents/family	Occupational therapist
Physician	Rehabilitation engineer
Speech pathologist	Advocate/social worker
Teacher	Third party payer

Establishing Goals

Since the acquisition of language begins before speech, it is important to start communication assistance early on, thus allowing the child's development to proceed as normally as possible. From this point onward, the child's communication needs will change as he or she grows. Hence, it is important to recognize that the child may have to "graduate" from one communication system to another, or, at least, may require modification of an existing system.

It is therefore worthwhile to establish both short-term and long-term goals for communication enhancement. For example, two short-term goals might be to teach the child the alphabet and words and to train him or her in manual control and dexterity; both would be intermediate steps toward the long-term goal of teaching the child to type as a means of communication. Such goals are helpful, even though they may require reevaluation at a later date, after more experience and testing. Indeed, sometimes a full evaluation is not possible until the child has mastered at least a modest communication system.

Maurice LeBlanc

Choosing a Communication System

The communication system involves the child, the method the child uses for control, and the device which provides the desired output. The young child seen in school is most likely a child with cerebral palsy, severe involvement (quadriplegic), who is limited to a wheelchair with seating support. The types of controls and devices which complete the communication system for such a child are the subject of the following discussion.

*Controls**

Most of the children seen for communication assistance are so severely involved as to be nonspeaking and nonwriting. In such cases, finding a good, functional, and reliable control for operation of a device presents a challenge. The guidelines for arriving at a suitable control are as follows:

*The Rehabilitation Engineering Center, Children's Hospital at Stanford, Palo Alto, California, has developed a catalog of controls, which is made available to teachers and clinicians.

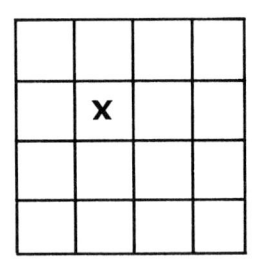

Fig. 8-2. Direction selection. Child simply points at what he or she wants to say.

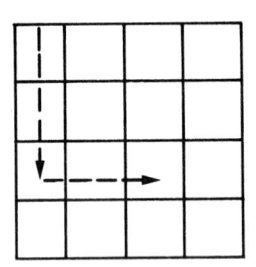

Fig. 8-3. Scanning selection. Child operates a moving light which makes a row and column scan to indicate what he or she wants to say.

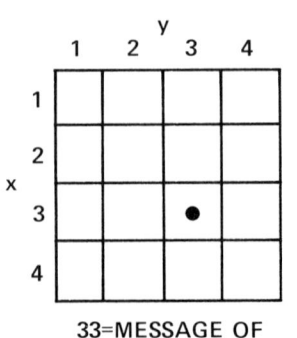

Fig. 8-4. Encoding selection. Child somehow indicates X and Y coordinates to designate the row and column that indicate what he or she wants to say.

33=MESSAGE OF SELECTION

1. Determine which of the child's body motions is best suited for operating a control.
2. Try to use that body motion in the operation of a device. When the device is a typewriter, for instance, we first try using the hands or fingers, then a typing stick, then a headwand, and so forth.
3. Employ the KISS (Keep It Simple Stupid) method whenever possible. The more simple and straightforward the design, the lower the cost and the greater the reliability.
4. Simple manual control usually means a direct-selection type of operation. An example would be a board on which the child directly points to what he or she wishes to say.
5. When a child cannot point and select with his or her own body motion, then one must consider other means of control. Alternate methods usually involve some sort of scanning or encoding scheme. Such methods are usually slower, more complex, and costlier, but, nonetheless, allow a child to operate a communication device when this would otherwise not be possible.

Examples of control methods are shown in Figures 8-2 to 8-4.[†]

Devices[4]

Many different communication aids are now commercially available, and more will be available in the future. All of them provide essentially one or more of the following outputs:

1. *Visual output.* A visual display that shows what one wants to say. Such a display can be matrix of messages on a lap board or a deck of "vocabulary" cards from which the child may choose the appropriate one. This method requires that the "listener" be present in order to see what the child is saying, and therefore is appropriate when a child has parents or teachers around with whom to converse. It also is useful for teaching pictures, words, spelling, and so forth, and thus is an education aid as well.
2. *Printed output.* As opposed to a visual display, which is "soft copy," "hard copy," or written output, is appropriate for sending or storing information. Because the information is retrievable, this method allows the child, when alone, to compose a message at leisure, which may be read by the "listener" later on: the listener does not have to be present during construction of the message. The communication aid in this case can also serve as an educational or vocational aid.
3. *Speech output.* Since it is primarily the production of oral communication that these children lack, a speech prosthesis is psychologically very rewarding. Such a device is also appropriate for classroom conversation, group activities, and telephone talk, where visual and printed outputs would not be as effective. Present speech output communication aids are generally of two types: (1) those which record real speech on tape and then search the tape and play out the desired message and (2) those which store word sounds, or phonemes, and produce synthesized speech.

[†]Nomenclature from the TRACE Center, University of Wisconsin, Madison.

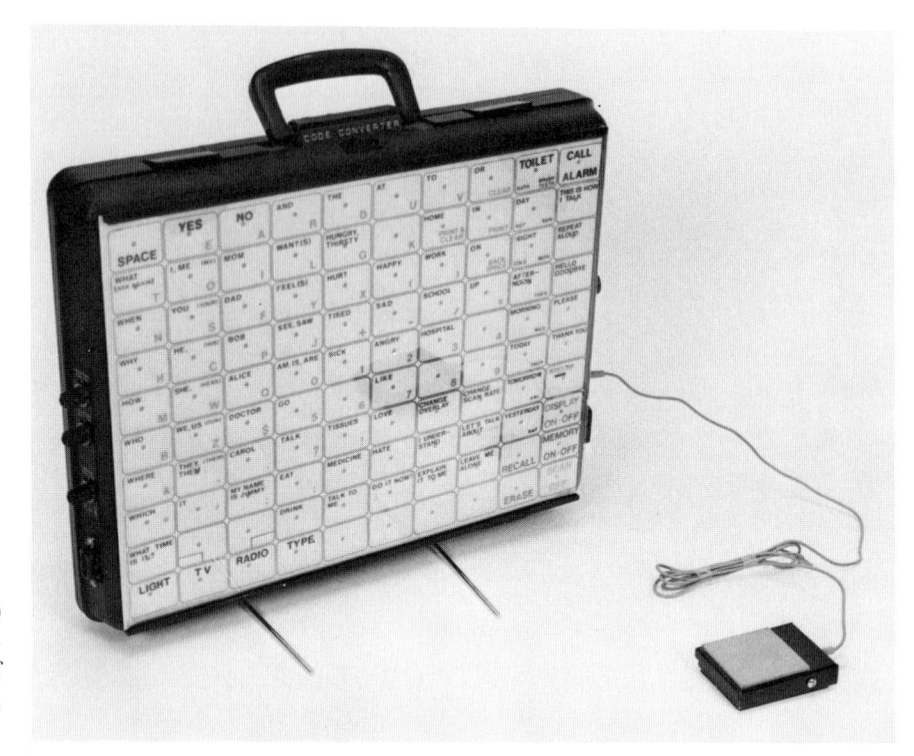

Fig. 8-5. Zygo Model 100 visual output communication device. (Courtesy of Zygo Industries, Inc., Portland, Oregon.)

With the former, vocabulary is limited to what can be stored on tape; with the latter, vocabulary is unlimited because only the sounds need to be stored.

Examples of communication devices are shown in Figures 8-5 to 8-7.

Future Trends

Most of the communication aids developed to date give only one of the above types of output. They generally are made as flexible for use as possible, so that different visual overlays can be inserted, vocabulary can be changed, and so forth. Because only one type of output is possible,

Fig. 8-6. Canon Communicator printed output communication device. (Courtesy of Telesensory Systems, Palo Alto, California.)

Systems and Devices—Nonoral Communication

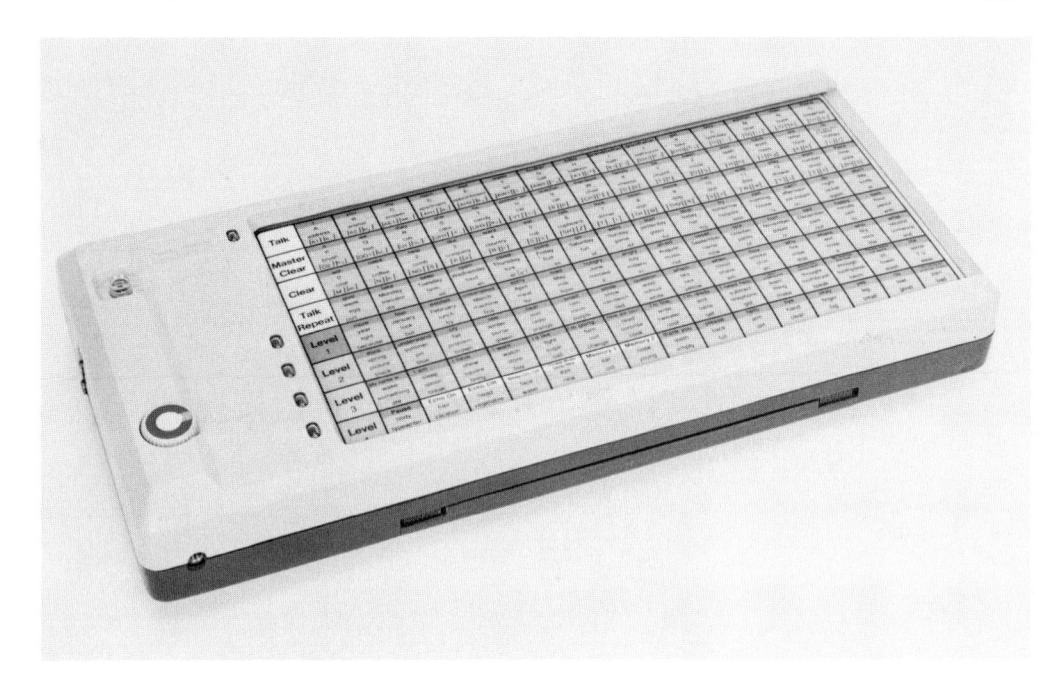

Fig. 8-7. HandiVoice speech output communication device. (Courtesy of H. C. Electronics, Inc., Mill Valley, California.)

however, the child will most likely need a different aid as his or her needs change and as he or she develops educationally and vocationally.

An increasing number of microprocessor-based communication aids, such as the Autocom,* Express,† and TIM,‡ are being developed. These offer multiple types of output and, in addition, have:

1. A "smart" aid that can be programmed to do what you want it to do
2. The ability to accept different types of control
3. The ability to change the informational content of the aid
4. The ability to produce different kinds of output simultaneously or separately
5. Smaller packaging because of miniaturization of electronic parts

The above factors lend themselves to an aid that is more flexible and adaptable and can "grow" with the child. It is conceivable that the child would then need only one aid in a lifetime, provided the aid could be that durable. The Autocom, Express and TIM are shown in Figures 8-8 to 8-10.

Implementation

Progression

There is a hierarchy of communication which is helpful as a guide in both the assessment and the implementation of communication assistance for a child.

*Telesensory Systems, Inc., Palo Alto, California.
†Prentke-Romich, Co., Shreve, Ohio.
‡Computers for the Physically Handicapped Inc., Huntington Beach, California.

Fig. 8-8. Autocom microprocessor-based communication device. (Courtesy of Telesensory Systems, Palo Alto, California.)

1. Before implementing any communication system it is necessary to insure that the child has two-way communication, such as a "yes–no" system, that allows the child to respond to a question asked. This indicates that the child has a receptive language, is mentally processing information, and is responsive.
2. Once a "yes–no" system is established, the next step is to implement a system whereby a child can initiate his or her own conversation and thoughts.

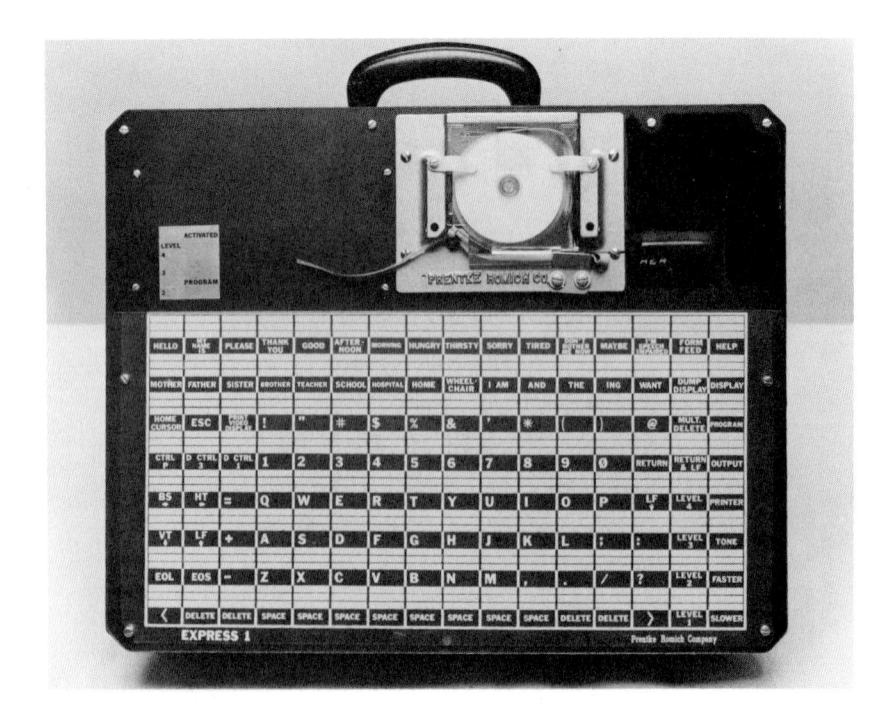

Fig. 8-9. Express I microprocessor-based communication device. (Courtesy of Prentke Romich Co., Shreve, Ohio.)

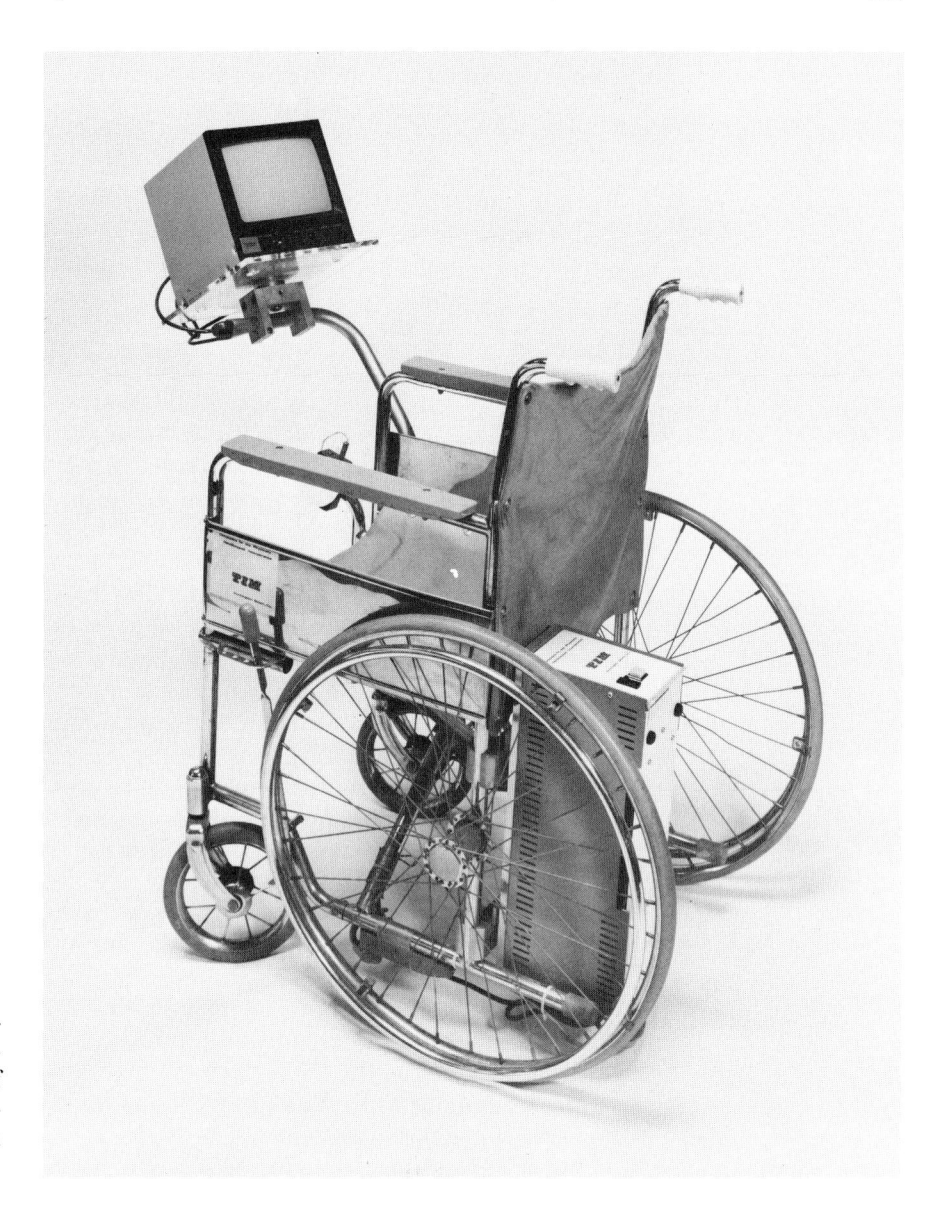

Fig. 8-10. TIM microprocessor-based communication device. (Courtesy of Computers for the Handicapped Inc., Huntington Beach, California.)

3. The next step or goal is to implement a progressively larger vocabulary as the child grows. A common occurrence is to see a child go from a 4-square to a 16-square to a 100-square matrix-type visual display.
4. The final goal is to enhance the child's communication potential as much as possible by any methods possible, such as by increasing speed of output, adding different types of output, and so forth.

Importance of Training and Follow-up

This final stage of implementing a communication system is extremely important. It is easy to feel that the job is over once the child has received an aid. In many ways, however, the job has only just begun. The child must learn how to use the new communication system (including the control and the device), learn what to do if something goes wrong, and learn how to charge and change batteries, among other technical details. In addition, an educational plan for the child must be developed.

Another necessary action is follow-up. One study has shown that active parents will get repairs done and initiate actions when there is a problem. In contrast, passive parents tend to do nothing: a communication system may be put in the closet simply because a switch or wire is broken. Some correlation has been demonstrated between "success" with active parents and "nonsuccess" with passive parents. The same can be said for any member of the professional team. Some program of follow-up and evaluation is therefore essential.

DISCUSSION AND SUMMARY

The question is often asked, "Is a new aid a crutch for speech?" In fact, aids have been found to promote speech development. The rationale for this result is that: (1) Doing something is better than doing nothing; the whole mental-motor system, speech included, is stimulated in the use of the aid. (2) Through the mechanical expression of basic needs, a child develops the ability to relate and to feel relaxed in normal conversation. (3) Because some of the aids are so slow in output, a child will often attempt to out-speak them.

To summarize, the experiences at several centers providing communication services for nonspeaking and nonwriting people allow certain conclusions and guidelines to be drawn:

1. Professionals formerly thought that the optimum time to implement a communication system was when the child entered school, at age 5 or 6 years. We now believe, however, that it is best to start as early as possible, since the acquisition of language starts very early, before the acquisition of speech. By the age of 4 a child normally has a vocabulary of 4000 words.
2. It is better to do something than to do nothing at all. Whatever the system implemented, the stimulation gained through its use enhances the child's growth and development.
3. It is beneficial to have both short-term and long-term goals of action, insofar as these are possible.
4. Proper assessment, provision of a communication system, and implementation require a team effort.
5. Although the communication device itself is important and tends to be the focus of all effort, it is not an end in itself. Equally important are proper training, use, and follow-up.

REFERENCES

1. Bureau of Education for the Handicapped, *Conference on Communication Aids for the Non-Vocal Severely Physically Handicapped Person,* Alexandria, Virginia, 1976.
2. Number of disabled people by selected types of impairment and age, in *Rehabilitation Engineering: A Plan for Continued Progress, II.* Charlottesville, University of Virginia, 1978.
3. Preston, J., Jr., *Assessment of Needs for Controls and Interfaces to Operate Assistive Devices for the Severely Disabled.* Palo Alto, California, Rehabilitation Engineering Center, Children's Hospital at Stanford, 1979.
4. Vanderheiden, G. C. (ed.), *Non-Vocal Communication Research Book.* Baltimore, University Park Press, 1978.

BIBLIOGRAPHY

Bigge, J. L., and O'Donnell, P. A., *Teaching Individuals with Physical and Multiple Disabilities.* Columbus, Ohio, Charles E. Merrill, 1976.

Communication Outlook (Newsletter). Published quarterly by the Artificial Language Laboratory, Computer Science Department, Michigan State University, East Lansing, MI 48824.

Communications Resources for the Developmentally Disabled. Washington, D. C., Job Development Laboratory, George Washington University, 1977.

Copeland, K. (ed.), *Aids for the Severely Handicapped.* New York, Grune & Stratton, 1974.

Equipment for the Disabled: Communication. Headington, Oxford, England, Oxford Regional Health Authority, 1975.

Golbin, A. (ed.), *Cerebral Palsy and Communication: What Parents Can Do.* Washington, D. C., Job Development Laboratory, George Washington University, 1977.

Lloyd, L. L. (ed.), *Communication Assessment and Intervention Strategies.* Baltimore, University Park Press, 1976.

Lundman, M. (ed.,), *Technical Aids for the Speech Impaired: An International Survey on Research and Development Projects.* Stockholm, Swedish Institute for the Handicapped, ICTA Information Center, 1978.

A Manner of Speaking. Toronto, Ontario, Canada, Blissymbolics Communication Institute, 1979.

Nelson, P. J. (ed.), *Proceedings of the Workshop on Communication Aids for the Handicapped.* Ottawa, Ontario, Canada, Canadian Medical and Biological Engineering Society, 1977.

Vanderheiden, G. C., *Non-Vocal Communication Resource Book.* Baltimore, University Park Press, 1978.

Vanderheiden, G. C., and Grilley, K., (eds.), *Non-Vocal Communication Techniques and Aids for the Severely Physically Handicapped.* Baltimore, University Park Press, 1976.

Vicker, B. A. (ed.), *Non-Oral Communication System Project, 1964–1973.* Iowa City, University Hospital School, University of Iowa, 1974.

9

Convulsive Disorders

BRUCE O. BERG, M.D.

A convulsion is one of the most dramatic events in human experience, even to physicians. It is not too surprising that throughout the ages patients with convulsions were regarded as supernatural or inspired by the gods, and that they were usually not accepted as "normal" humans. Hippocrates titled his monograph describing patients with convulsions "On The Sacred Disease," and seizures were called the "falling sickness" by others.[1] Today, many people, even those considered "modern" and "sophisticated," still regard the epileptic with awe or as a "different" kind of human being. This should not be the case. Clearly, all of us should know something about the disorder of epilepsy.

DEFINITIONS

We have used the terms *convulsions, seizures,* and *epilepsy,* but what does each of these really mean? A convulsion is the same as a fit or seizure, and epilepsy is a recurrent convulsive disorder. Many laymen commonly equate the generalized seizure with epilepsy, but this is erroneous, for the variability of convulsive phenomena is vast and there are many types of convulsive manifestations other than the generalized fit. Because of this variability, one's definition of a convulsive disorder is necessarily broad. A convulsive disorder can be defined as a paroxysmal, transient alteration of brain function that begins and ends spontaneously and has a tendency to recur.

INCIDENCE

The true incidence of epilepsy (or convulsive disorders) is not well known. Estimates based on Selective Service statistics indicate that at least 0.5 percent of the United States population, or over one million people, have convulsive disorders. The highest incidence occurs in children under 5 years old (152/100,000) and the lowest incidence occurs between the ages of 20 and 70 years (4–20/100,000).[2] In one prospective study of 18,500 children it was found that, by the age of 5 years, 2 percent of the group had one or more febrile fits and 1 percent had fits not associated with fever.[3] There appears to be a preponderance of males with seizure disorders, and it is felt that this higher incidence in the male may be related to the greater likelihood of head trauma. Lennox and Lennox found a male:female ratio of 100:77 in noninstitutionalized patients.[2]

If one considers only those children who are included in the broad category of cerebral palsy, the incidence of epilepsy is quite high, ranging from 12 percent to 86 percent, depending on the type of motor disorder. Aird and Cohen, for example, reported seizures in 34 percent of patients with athetosis and 66 percent of those who were spastic.[4] Perlstein et al., on the other hand, reported seizures in 11 percent of athetotics and in 86 percent of spastics.[5]

CAUSES (ETIOLOGY)

A convulsive disorder, or epilepsy, is not a specific disease; rather it is symptomatic of some abnormality of brain function. Seizures are caused by a variety of factors, including brain anomalies, vascular malformations or bleeding into the cerebral substance, trauma, brain tumors, inflammation of the brain (encephalitis) or of its membranous coverings, the meninges (meningitis), and metabolic disorders such as low blood calcium, low blood sugar, or low blood magnesium. In over one-half of patients with epilepsy, no specific cause can be found for the seizures; this group has been called *cryptogenic* or *idiopathic*.

The role of heredity in the etiology of convulsive disorders is not yet well understood, and one cannot speak in terms of "all or none" or use the common genetic labels of "recessive" or "dominant." Rather, we are confined to the consideration of families, or large groups of related people, and the "likelihood" of one's having seizures. In one large study of family members (parents, siblings, and children) of epileptics, Lennox found a 2.7 percent incidence of recurring fits.[6]

Part of the problem in understanding the heritability of epilepsy has been related to the lack of uniform definitions, or lack of agreement as to what constitutes a fit, and the failure to identify specifically the relationships of affected relatives to the epileptic patient. Another factor is variability in interpretation of the electroencephalogram.

CLASSIFICATION

The classification of any biological phenomena is arbitrary and must be viewed in that light. For example, the categorization of convulsive disorders has been based upon clinical, presumed anatomic, or neurophysiological grounds, or combinations thereof. The classification presented herein (Table 9-1) is principally based on clinical manifestations of the convulsions. It must be pointed out, however, that an International Classification of Epilepsy has been adopted by the World Health Organization.[7] These two classifications are compared in Table 9-2.

Table 9-1. Classification of Convulsive Disorders

I. Grand Mal (generalized)
II. Focal epilepsy
   A. Motor, sensory
   B. Temporal lobe (psychomotor)
III. Petit mal epilepsy
   A. Typical (lapse or absence attack)
   B. Atypical
      1. Myoclonic
      2. Akinetic
IV. Infantile spasms
V. Autonomic epilepsy
VI. Mixed epilepsy

TYPES OF CONVULSIVE DISORDERS

Grand Mal

The grand mal, or generalized fit, is a dramatic, awe-inspiring event. The patient may be aware that a seizure is about to occur because of an unusual sensory perception (the aura), which is actually the beginning of the convulsion. That perception may include abdominal cramping, a feeling of nausea, an unpleasant odor, such as of burning rubber, or some pervasive, nondirected fear. Often the patient can only say, "it just feels funny." The patient may suddenly appear strange or bewildered, stop all activity, and then lose consciousness. The arms are extended or flexed, the legs are extended with generalized stiffening, and the patient falls to the ground. As the muscles contract, air may be forced from the lungs through the vocal cords, resulting in a peculiar eerie, sometimes frightening cry, and there may also be a loss of bowel or bladder control, or both. This is the *tonic* (stiff) phase that usually progresses to the *clonic* (jerking) phase.

As the clonic phase begins, the patient commonly becomes less rigid, and quivers or becomes tremulous. The arms or legs, or both, begin to jerk synchronously. The jerking decreases in frequency and severity and then suddenly stops—the entire episode, including both tonic and clonic phases, lasting less than several minutes.

During the seizure, the patient's pupils may constrict and then dilate, and, because of inefficient swallowing of saliva and movement of the lips and mouth, there may be a "froth," or bubbling, about the lips. Regular respiration ceases, and the patient often becomes cyanotic. Soon after termination of the spell, when regular respiration has resumed, the color returns to normal. The patient may have postictal confusion or headache at this time, or may fall into a deep sleep that lasts from minutes to hours.

Focal Fit

It is believed that a focal fit originates in an abnormal electrochemical (epileptic) discharge from a localized group of neurons in the brain. The seizure pattern is usually the same from one spell to the next, with

Table 9-2. Comparison of Clinical and International Classifications

Clinical Classification	International Classification

Focal epilepsy	I. Partial seizures (beginning locally)
	  A. With elementary symptomatology (generally without impairment of consciousness)
	    1. Motor symptoms
	    2. Sensory symptoms or somatosensory symptoms
	    3. Autonomic symptoms
	    4. Compound forms

Temporal lobe (psychomotor)	B. With complex symptomatology (generally with impairment of consciousness)
	    1. Impairment of consciousness only
	    2. Cognitive symptomatology
	    3. Affective symptomatology
	    4. Psychosensory symptomatology
	    5. Psychomotor (automatisms) symptomatology
	    6. Compound forms

	C. Partial seizures secondarily generalized
	II. Generalized seizures (symmetrical and without local onset)
Petit mal	A. Absence
Grand mal	B. Tonic and clonic
Grand mal, limited	C. Tonic only D. Clonic only

Atypical petit mal (petit mal variant, minor motor epilepsy)	E. Bilateral massive epileptic myoclonus
	  F. Atonic
	  G. Akinetic

Salaam, or jacknife, seizures	H. Infantile spasms
	III. Unilateral seizures
	IV. Unclassified seizures

stiffening and/or jerking of only one arm or leg or of the ipsilateral (the same side) arm and leg. The focal fit may be only a twitching on one side of the face or, more commonly, about the corner of the mouth, with concomitant twitching of the ipsilateral thumb and fingers. Occasionally, the fit will start in one place and spread to involve other ipsilateral muscles and then muscles on the contralateral side, resulting in a generalized convulsion. This has been called "march" epilepsy, or Jacksonian epilepsy (in recognition of a British neurologist, John Hughlings Jackson). Although the conscious state is altered during the focal seizure, the patient may not lose consciousness completely but, instead, may be aware of

Convulsive Disorders

his surroundings although unable to speak or respond normally to the environment.

Some convulsive phenomena that are consistently related to one area of the brain have been named for that cerebral location, as in the case of temporal lobe (or psychomotor) epilepsy. Temporal lobe fits are characterized by their seemingly purposeful, automatic nature. The patient appears to have an altered conscious state but, at the same time, is able to carry out complex, coordinated acts. The variability of temporal lobe fits is great, and the patient may later recount vivid ictal, visual, auditory, or gustatory hallucinations. During the spells he may perform such complex acts as walking about, undressing, or repeating a phrase or sentence over and over. If one attempts to restrain the patient during the spell, the patient may vigorously resist or become obstreporous, or both.

Petit Mal Triad

Three different types of seizures are considered under the category of petit mal epilepsy: the typical variety, or staring spell, and two atypical forms, or petit mal variants. The *typical petit mal* spell is the momentary suspension of all activity—a staring spell, or, as some have called it, a lapse or absence attack. Such spells are often overlooked initially, as the child is assumed to be daydreaming, and, indeed, it may well appear to be so. Minor movements of the eyes or slight fluttering of the eyelids have been observed to accompany some of the staring spells. The entire episode lasts less than 5 to 10 seconds.

The *atypical petit mal,* or *petit mal variant,* may take one of two forms: the myoclonic or the akinetic attack. *Myoclonic epilepsy* is a disorder in which the patient has paroxysmal, brief contractions of part of a muscle or group of muscles. There may be a brief, sudden neck flexion or extension, in which the head suddenly drops forward or backward, and other muscles or muscle groups may be involved, causing the arms or legs to jerk or the trunk to bend sharply upon itself.

The *akinetic attack* is also known as *astatic* or *inhibition* epilepsy. These spells are characterized by sudden-drop attacks, in which the patient suddenly loses muscle tone and plummets to the ground, only to rise again shortly thereafter. Some patients appear to have an aborted akinetic attack, as if they have "caught themselves" before falling to the ground, and look as if they are nodding or having a sudden momentary jolt.

These three different kinds of seizures—typical petit mal, myoclonic, and akinetic—were included in what Lennox called the *petit mal triad.* He brought the spells together in a triad, realizing that, although there was no good common denominator for the spells, they had somewhat similar electroencephalographic patterns and were treated with similar types of anticonvulsant medications, and that patients with myoclonic attacks not uncommonly had akinetic or staring spells as well. It must be pointed out that Lennox also had recognized a more ominous prognosis for those patients with myoclonic and/or akinetic attacks; the seizures were more likely to be recalcitrant to treatment and the patients not uncommonly became mentally retarded.[1] The atypical petit mal, or petit mal variant, has more recently been called the Lennox-Gastaut syndrome.

Infantile Spasms

Infantile spasms are a convulsive disorder that is seen only during the first few years of life and that is probably related to the immaturity of the brain. Infantile spasms have been called by many different names, including West's syndrome, salaam seizures, jactitation, massive myoclonia, or jackknife seizures. They have been associated with a variety of different disease states, including tuberous sclerosis, phenylketonuria, and hypoglycemia. The onset of spells occurs before the first birthday in approximately three-quarters of all patients with infantile spasms.

The infant may initially have focal or generalized spells but, with the passing of time, the fits seem to "mature" to a state in which there is a massive, synchronous muscle contraction. The infant, with arms flexed and elevated, suddenly flexes the neck and trunk forward or extends the trunk backward. The spells commonly occur in a series, one after the other, and the infant may utter an eerie cry between each of the massive jerks. Occasionally, because of the "doubling up" appearance of the infant, a diagnosis of colic is incorrectly made and the patient is treated inappropriately with some intestinal relaxant. At the onset of this convulsive disorder, the patient often becomes less responsive and less aware of his environment.

Autonomic Epilepsy

This category of convulsive disorder includes patients with recurring paroxysmal abdominal cramping (abdominal epilepsy) with or without vomiting and often followed by postictal lethargy. Other convulsive manifestations include recurring episodes of headache, skin flushing, pupillary dilation, and olfactory sensations, as well as other, less common, symptoms of autonomic nervous system dysfunction. It is essential that the patient be most carefully examined so that there is no possibility of overlooking other pathological states that could produce similar symptoms.

Mixed-type Epilepsy

Patients with different types of seizures are included in this category. The child, for example, who has generalized as well as petit mal convulsions is said to have a *mixed convulsive disorder*.

PATIENT EVALUATION

If there is any question as to whether a child has a convulsive disorder, he should be referred to a physician for evaluation. The doctor should spend a great deal of time eliciting the details of the history, for that information describes the nature of the disorder. Since the patient is not aware of what actually happens during the spell, one must rely on the parent, a teacher, or some other observant witness to recount the details. For example, when do the seizures occur? How often and how long do they last? And what actually happens to the patient during the convulsion?

It is important that the physician be tactful and kind, because relating the details of the seizure can be frightening and embarrassing to the child and to his family. For example, in describing the event the physician should use words with which the child and family are comfortable;

only later, once a good patient–physician relationship has been established, should the other synonyms be used in a matter-of-fact manner. The physician should always be gentle with the patient so that the patient will not be afraid to ask questions, even those he may believe are silly.

A careful general examination, including a complete neurological assessment, must be carried out to determine if there is evidence of some physical abnormality that could be related to the convulsive disorder. It should be remembered that the physical examination may be completely normal, even if the patient has a severe seizure disorder.

Laboratory studies should be completed next in order to rule out the possibility of any metabolic abnormality, such as low blood sugar, low blood calcium, or low blood magnesium, causing the seizures. Skull x-rays are obtained only as necessary, and, occasionally, a lumbar puncture (spinal tap) is required to obtain more information about the central nervous system. A computerized tomographic brain scan may be indicated if abnormalities are found on the neurological examination or if structural abnormalities of the brain are strongly considered.

The electroencephalogram (EEG), a graphic record of the electrical activity of the brain, recorded from wires attached to the various locations overlying the brain, is an essential part of the initial evaluation. Although a somewhat crude diagnostic tool, the EEG can be very helpful by providing electrical correlates to clinical data regarding the convulsive disorder.

When all studies have been completed, the physician is usually able to identify the type of convulsion and to determine whether there is a known etiological agent. As noted earlier, epilepsy has been shrouded in mystery and superstition for centuries, and the physician must thoughtfully and realistically discuss the entire matter with the patient and his or her family. Treatment with anticonvulsant medication (Table 9-3) is required in almost every convulsive disorder, and the medication must be taken daily, usually for at least 3 or 4 years of seizure-free activity.

TREATMENT

A few general principles relating to the treatment of convulsive disorders should be followed:

1. Initial treatment should be a single drug.
2. Drug dosage should be increased slowly to tolerance levels.
3. In patients with seizures that are difficult to control, additional drugs are added in a careful, systematic way.
4. Physical examinations, and blood and urine studies should be performed at regular intervals.
5. EEGs are obtained as part of the initial analysis but, later on, are obtained only as individually indicated.
6. The motor vehicle laws must be studied in each state. In California, for example, all epileptic patients 14 years or over must be reported to the Department of Motor Vehicles, and all such patients must have periodic reports on their condition sent to the Department.

CONCLUSIONS

The essential factor in good patient management is a sound patient–physician relationship, with support and encouragement given to the family and to the patient so that the patient may resume normal activi-

Table 9-3. Anticonvulsant Drugs*

Drug	Use	Comment
BARBITURATES		
Mephobarbital (NF) (Mebaral)	Same as phenobarbital	A drug with fewer sedating and anticonvulsant properties than phenobarbital; nonetheless, effective in seizure control. Contraindications are the same as for phenobarbital.
Metharbital (NF) (Gemonil)	Generalized	Not used as a first choice anticonvulsant drug. Given for generalized seizures; some physicians claim effectiveness in control of myoclonic attacks. Contraindications are same as for phenobarbital.
Phenobarbital (USP)	Generalized Focal epileptic equivalent Occasionally petit mal	Most effective and cheapest anticonvulsant medication. Particularly useful in generalized or focal fits, but occasionally used in other convulsive types. Side effects are few but include skin rash and irritability or lethargy. Contraindicted in severe renal or hepatic disease or porphyria.
Primidone (USP) (Mysoline)	Generalized Focal	Effective in control of generalized as well as focal seizures, particularly temporal lobe epilepsy. Should be given in gradually increasing dosage to maintenance level. Side effects include lethargy, ataxia, dizziness, and occasional headaches.
HYDANTIONS		
Diphenylhydantoin (USP) (Dilantin)	Generalized Focal epileptic equivalent	A most useful drug for controlling generalized or focal seizures and occasionally other types of seizure attacks, e.g., akinetic or myoclonic attacks. It can be given as a single daily dose or divided into two doses. Side effects include gingival hyperplasia, dermatitis, hirsutism, lymphadenopathy, megaloblastic anemia, and leukopenia. Pulmonary fibrosis, hepatitis, and polyarthropathy have been reported. Nystagmus, ataxia, and lethargy are seen in drug overdosage. Diphenylhydantoin is contraindicted in patients with known hypersensitivity to hydantoins.

*Adapted from Berg, B. O., Convulsions, in Pascoe, D. J., and Grossman, M. (eds.), *Quick Reference to Pediatric Emergencies*, Philadelphia, J. B. Lippincott, 1978, Chap. 4. With permission.

Drug	Use	Comment
OXAZOLIDINES		
Trimethadione (USP) (Tridione)	Petit mal—occasionally myoclonic	Trimethadione has been used for treatment of petit mal seizures refractory to other drugs. Adverse side effects include nausea, vomiting, anorexia, and weight loss. Drowsiness, headache, and visual disturbances have also been reported, as well as blood dyscrasias and lupus erythematous syndrome. Other reactions include hepatitis, precipitation of generalized fits, a myasthenia gravis–like syndrome, hair loss, and nephrosis.
SUCCINIMIDES		
Ethosuximide (USP) (Zarontin)	Petit mal—occasionally myoclonic	Drug of choice for control of petit mal attacks. Gastrointestinal complaints, headaches, restlessness or drowsiness, and hiccups have been reported as side effects. Adverse reactions include leukopenia, agranulocytosis, aplastic anemia and lupus erythematosis.
OTHERS		
Diazepam (NF) (Valium)	Status epilepticus Myoclonic	Drug of choice for treatment of status epilepticus. Occasionally useful in treating myoclonic or akinetic seizures. Side effects include drowsiness, fatigue, and ataxia; paradoxical reactions including hyperexcited states, anxiety, hallucinations, insomnia, rage, and sleep disturbances have been reported. Contraindicated in acute narrow angle glaucoma.
Carbamazepine (Tegretol)	Generalized epilepsy—tonic and/or clonic Temporal lobe epilepsy	Drowsiness, unsteadiness, nausea, or vomiting. Some hematologic disorders have been seen.
Valproic Acid (Depakene)	Generalized epilepsy Petit mal—myoclonic or akinetic	A useful drug for treating generalized epilepsies, e.g., Lennox-Gastaut syndrome, absence or myoclonic fits. Patient may initially have gastrointestinal complaints, drowsiness, transient hair loss. Incoordination has been noted. Isolated cases of severe liver toxicity have been reported.

ties insofar as this is possible. Parents must learn to support and guide the child quietly and to understand how he views the problem. Attempting to overlook or to ignore the seizures is as dangerous as becoming oversolicitous of the child's activities. Teachers must also know something about epilepsy so that they will not, incorrectly and unjustifiably, regard the child as strange or as someone to be feared and convey this attitude to the patient's classmates.

Convulsions have been a common part of human existence from the dawn of the race. Members of a civilized society must recognize that a fit is a symptom of abnormal brain function and not a manifestation of some mystical or mysterious affectation. Most children with convulsive disorders are well controlled by the daily administration of anticonvulsants, and they must be encouraged and supported so that they may live as normal a life a possible.

REFERENCES

1. Temkin, O., *The Falling Sickness*. Baltimore, Johns Hopkins Press, 1945.
2. Lennox, W. G., and Lennox, M., *Epilepsy and Related Disorders*. Boston, Little, Brown, 1960.
3. Van den Berg, B. J., and Yerushalmy, J., Studies on convulsive disorders in young children. *Pediatric Research* 3:298–304, 1969.
4. Aird, R. B., and Cohen, P., Electroencephalography in cerebral palsy. *Journal of Pediatrics* 37:448, 1950.
5. Perlstein, M. A., Gibbs, E. L., and Gibbs, F. A., The EEG in infantile cerebral palsy. *Proceedings of the Association for Research in Nervous and Mental Disease* 26:377, 1947.
6. Lennox, W. G., Heredity of epilepsy as told by relatives and twins. *Journal of the American Medical Association* 146:529, 1951.
7. Gastaut, H., Clinical and electroencephalographic classification of epileptic seizures. *Epilepsia* 11:102–113, 1970.

10

Counseling: Perspectives and Resources

Edited by
EUGENE E. BLECK, M.D.

The professional's job is to help the parent and child deal with the child's handicap. Each family and each child has its own mix of physical, intellectual, psychological, social, economic, educational, community, religious, and ethnic characteristics. Given so many variables, it obviously is not possible to generalize from one family or individual to the next. Multiple sources of counseling and information are therefore necessary. Ultimately, each person must cope with the disability in his or her own way, and each family and each disabled person is thus the best judge of their own needs: professionals can only offer the information and resources necessary for coping. In recognition of this reality, this chapter on *Counseling* presents a number of different viewpoints and includes a listing of reading materials and organizations that offer services for the handicapped and their families.

Counseling: A Developmental Approach

JUDY HOWARD, M.D.

If your high school or college had offered courses entitled How to Parent a Handicapped Child or How to be a Successful Handicapped Person, would you have enrolled? Probably not, as no one anticipates the need to use such information. Yet, learning to parent a handicapped child and learning to be a competent handicapped adult are essential for the parents and children we serve. As professionals who work with handicapped children and their families, we need to have in mind a "curriculum" that attempts to fulfill these course titles—a "curriculum" based on our knowledge of normal development and on information learned from these families we serve, as well as on an evaluation of the pros and cons of past treatment regimens.

Throughout the following discussion it is assumed that what constitutes the best services to these individuals we serve is ultimately, that which will contribute most effectively to a base on which a successful life can be built.

In developing an Individual Education Plan (IEP) it is not easy to select for each child those short-term goals that will most facilitate the best possible long-term outcome. The importance of doing so, however, has been increasingly come. The importance of doing so, however, has been increasingly recognized in recent years. In 1975 Dr. Elliot O'Reilly, an orthopedic surgeon and then President of the American Academy for Cerebral Palsy and Developmental Medicine, presented the results of 20 years of clinical experience with 336 physically handicapped adults. Treatment consisted of careful orthopedic management, appropriately supervised physical and occupational therapy programs, and medical follow-up by Dr. O' Reilly. Comparing his patient population to those who had been treated during the previous 20 years, he found *no* difference between the two groups in terms of their station in life: 30 percent were employed, 30 percent were in institutions or had died, and 40 percent were at home without productive activity.[12] Then, in 1979, Dr. Eugene E. Bleck advocated that treatment be reoriented so as to take into account the handicapped child's nonorthopedic needs as well and to give top priority to improving the person's communication skills and mobility.[2] In view of the prime importance of these skills for achieving success in this world, such an emphasis, indeed, makes sense. The late Dr. Ronnie MacKeith, a pediatrician, emphasized yet another important aspect of the care of the handicapped child: "Children develop in *families,* and parental attitudes and functioning are consequently of great importance, especially when the child has a handicap" (p. 285).[8]

Routine medical and therapy treatments, then, are not in themselves effective in changing significantly a handicapped person's life. Perhaps, however, if we emphasize patients' behavioral strengths, provide opportunities for mobility, and improve family understanding and support, more of these youngsters will succeed.

Fig. 10-1. "Children develop in families, and parental attitudes and functioning are consequently of great importance, especially when the child has a handicap" (p. 285).[8]

PARENTING A HANDICAPPED CHILD

"We want a normal child, not a handicapped one" (p. 517),[1] writes Rod Ballard, the parent of a mentally handicapped child and a lecturer in social work. Planning, conceiving, and giving birth to a child is one of the most creative tasks that two human beings can engage in. More often than not, parents hope that their newborn infant will contribute basic attributes to the family: intelligence, physical prowess, beauty, immortality for the family name, and so forth.

Soon after birth, the stage is set for the beginning of a two-way communication system between parent and child. Young infants have the capacity to see, to hear, and to move in rhythm to their parent's voices.[3] Some like to refer to this as a time for "bonding."[7] It is a joyous period for most parents.

"We Wanted a Normal Baby."

During the early months of a handicapped infant's life, what do parents feel as they begin to digest the reality of their child's handicap? Mr. Ballard[1] expresses it this way: "All parents experience grief at the "loss" of a child they thought would be normal, and their feelings about the child are bound to be ambivalent" (p. 517). As Ballard notes, the emergence of feelings of love and affection is accompanied by the simultaneous emergence of feelings of anger, despair, worthlessness, and frustration, particularly in the initial period after the diagnosis of a handicapping condition. Not unfrequently, a specific diagnosis is not available, giving

Fig. 10-2. "All parents experience grief at the 'loss' of a child they thought would be normal, and their feelings about the child are bound to be ambivalent" (p. 517).[1]

rise to doubts and fantasy in parents that must be addressed.[1] Freeman and Pearson have aptly conveyed the overriding anxiety of parents who have not received an adequate assessment and explanation of their child's condition: to such parents, "their child is 'not a person but a question mark'" (p. 36).[4]

Each parent responds to this situation as an individual, and counselors must therefore expect that emotional responses and means of coping will vary from one family member to the next. It is not unreasonable for parents to ask for time to try to understand what has happened to their child. They need time to cry, time to be alone, and time to be angry; these are normal feelings in people experiencing a sad event.

"Our Baby Needs us to Help Him."

Such a statement is a clue that the parents are mustering their strength to proceed with a plan to help their handicapped child. Parents desiring assistance in caring for their handicapped child will want to find help, whether it be through community agencies, private pediatricians, or self-referral.

During the initial visit, many parents expect the professional to focus entirely on the infant's deficit areas. Most are pleased if, instead, attention is given as well to what is right about their child. To establish credibility, it is important to verify to parents that the problem areas so carefully described to them by the specialists are indeed present; it is just as important, however, to stress that each infant has his or her areas of skill. For instance, a crying baby who is soothed by his parent's voice, or one who visually fixates on his parent's smile (even though his own facial muscles are too weak to smile back), gives evidence of strength; commenting on such behaviors is one way of directing attention toward a child's assets. Occasionally parents will comment about the difficulty they have in looking for their child's good points, one reason for this being that they fear this will give rise to unrealistic hopes that their child will be normal. Initially, then, many parents need to be helped to realize that it is their child's strengths, not weaknesses, which will allow for future successes.

Counseling: A Developmental Approach

The counselor never errs in taking time to listen and to explore such open-ended questions as, "What is the best time of the day for your child? What do you enjoy doing with him? Have you taken time for yourself? What are your priorities as we plan a program together? Such questioning helps parents to focus gradually on their child's abilities.

"Teacher, My Child is Vocalizing to His Toys."

Does this sound like an observant parent? Too often professionals overlook parents' need to feel competent in parenting their handicapped child.[4] Attempts should be made to reassure parents in this respect, calling their attention to the fact that even the most experienced of their group frequently have self-doubts about their ability to deal with the special problems of a handicapped child. Such support is especially important when a child is seriously disabled, since the parents of such children do not receive the feedback regarding their parenting decisions that parents of normal children receive (for example, a hug and kiss from a repentant 24-month old following a scolding for breaking an object reminds a mother that setting of limits is necessary).

The anxiety arising from this lack of cues is frequently compounded by professionals whose advice, however well intended, draws attention to the child's shortcomings: that the child is not gaining enough weight, is not improving as expected in the motor milestones, should wear glasses in order to correct the vision in a weak eye, should wear nighttime braces in order to stretch his heel cords, and so forth.

Parents are asked by professionals to assess their child's needs objectively and to plan accordingly. As Freeman and Pearson have noted, "Parents of the handicapped are sometimes expected to be more 'realistic' than would be considered reasonable for the parents of normal children. Few people are entirely realistic about matters which affect them deeply" (p. 44).[4]

Fig. 10-3. One of the most important parts of the professional's role is to help parents develop a sense of competence in caring for their handicapped child. When the focus is on the child's disability, this function is all too often overlooked.

Acting as a "builder of competence" in these parents is often difficult, not because the parents themselves are difficult, but because those about them are.

"I Cannot Control the Deep Depression I Feel When Told My Handicapped Child Has a New Problem."

Adjusting to the fact that one's infant is handicapped is not easy. Those early years are fraught with many stressful experiences—finding out that one's child is handicapped, feeling unable to carry on intelligently, and becoming increasingly isolated from old friends whose children are "normal." During the ensuing years, parents must master the ins and outs of an extensive service-delivery system, tolerate the confusing and often impersonal jargon of pediatric neurologists, orthopedic surgeons, therapists, and educators, and prepare for the next important phase in their child's life—entrance into the elementary school system. Parents often look forward to this next step. Their child has become more socially independent and, at the same time, they have learned to trust others in caring for their child; this frees parents to pursue new or old interests. On the other hand, however, they often feel some trepidation as they plan the move from a predictable setting to a new one, often asking, "Will the new school be the right one for our child?"[11] Supportive replies to such questions are needed: for instance, "You have explored several possibilities, and this program seems right for now," or, "You do not need to feel that all decisions are permanent ones, but give this one a fair try."

With the introduction of a new staff, new "curricula" are introduced and, possibly, new problems are recognized. No matter how carefully and sensitively discussed, these new-found problems each evoke a similar response. Emotions that occurred at the time of the initial diagnosis are revived, with parents often asking, "What else will be found wrong with my child?" or "Does this mean he has more brain damage than was thought?" Depression ensues. This is again followed by a resurgence of parental strength.

The professional needs to anticipate these and other such crisis periods. To this end, MacKeith has described four predictable times of crisis during the growth of a handicapped child. The first develops when parents initially learn about or suspect their child's handicap. The second occurs around the time, usually when the child is 5 years old, when parents and professionals plan the child's placement in school. If the child enters an "ordinary" school, parents often have expectations of success. A third crisis period may occur when the handicapped person leaves school and the permanence of the disability becomes obvious to all. The final crisis develops as the parents grow older and, eventually, are unable to care for their handicapped son or daughter.[7]

Following each of these crisis periods, most parents are more open to receiving helpful guidance. In order to offer effective support at this time (as well as times of calm), it is important to remember that, "While the professional is learning about the parent, the parent is deciding whether the professional is someone who can be trusted" (p. 39).[4] The attributes necessary to establish such trust are not unique to this situation: compassion, empathy, patience, and the ability to project a sensitive, personalized concern. "Parents of handicapped children are still people . . . people with a serious problem, a great sorrow—a living sorrow" (p. 41).[4]

Fig. 10-4. Predictable crisis periods in the lives of the handicapped and their families: (1) when the handicap is first suspected or diagnosed, (2) when the child enters school, (3) when the child leaves school, (4) when the aged parents are no longer able to care for their handicapped son or daughter.

"The Great Strength of Your Program Was the Opportunity I had to Meet Other Parents in a Similar Situation."

When parents who have participated in the UCLA Intervention Program for Handicapped Children are asked what in the program was most beneficial to them, they invariably discuss their sincere joy at having the opportunity to meet other parents of handicapped children. This experience lessens their lonesome burden. Years afterward, they continue to stress their need for such contact and the opportunity it offers for sharing common concerns and triumphs. When their children are bussed to school such contact becomes difficult. Efforts to meet new parents of handicapped children frequently fail for a variety of reasons—working parents, lack of interest, or lack of encouragement and support from educational personnel.

The reasons for continuing such parent interactions are many. Parents are innundated with details about their child's educational and therapy programs and periodically need to stand back in order to assess the current situation and where it is leading. Other parents can often help

Fig. 10-5. Parents can often gain much support from interacting with other parents of handicapped children—sometimes even one parent touching another is all that is needed.

them in gaining the needed perspective. As choices are made as to which short-term goals (such as completing a simple puzzle or signing a single word in order to communicate thirst) will lead to an optimum long-term outcome, the opportunity to compare notes with parents of older handicapped children is important. Together, parents and counselor can then begin to match short-term goals with long-term results that are acceptable to parent and child.

Contact with other parents is helpful in another way as well. As was stressed earlier, children grow up in *families,* and parental attitudes and functioning greatly influence how other family members cope with the child's handicap.[9] Parents like to hear how other parents have managed siblings' questions such as, "Why did this happen to my little sister?" "Will it happen to my children?" or "What do you do when people on the street ask over and over, 'What is wrong with him'?"[6,10]

Even if one parent simply touches the other, that may be all the support that is needed at that time. Most parents have an ongoing need to share their experiences with others who are in a similar situation. This is not to imply however, that parents of handicapped children need or desire to end their friendships with parents of nonhandicapped children: both kinds of friends are important.[11]

A CHILD'S GROWING PERCEPTION OF HIS OR HER HANDICAP

"Our son rarely thinks about his handicap." I once accepted that statement from a parent of an adolescent young man with cerebral palsy, until I talked to the son himself. Contrary to his parents' belief, he thought about his disability each time he tried to dress, shave, brush his teeth, toilet himself, and eat. The thoughts were brief, but he did think about his condition; he simply did not vocalize these thoughts. This experience led me to reconstruct what I know about growing cognitive awareness of one's disability.

Dr. A. H. Parmelee, has encouraged professionals to focus their energies on the *child* who happens to be disabled rather than on the disability that happens to be in the child. To this end, he advocates a developmental framework as allowing a better understanding of the children we treat.[13] This will be the basis for my discussion.

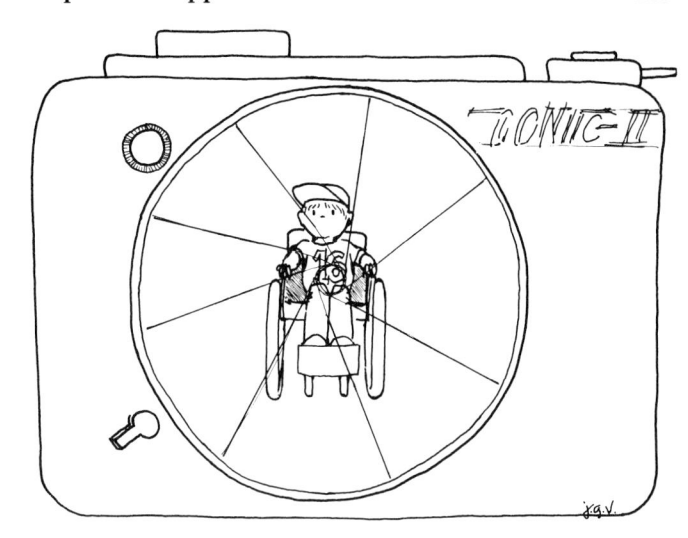

Fig. 10-6. The professional's focus should be on the child who is disabled rather than on the disability that happens to be in the child.[13]

Infant and Toddler Years

Generally speaking, nonhandicapped and handicapped infants under 9 months of age do not project a need for independence. They can be placated by adult attention and prefer a close proximity to their parents. Between the ages of 9 and 18 months, however, the independent spirit emerges. Temper tantrums, the use of "no," the throwing of objects, and frequent periods of frustration normally appear. These infants are at the center of their own universe, and this egocentricity shows in their behavior. For example, infants at this age love to build block towers and knock them over with glee. Should an attentent adult then pick up the blocks, the game will start all over, with the infant in charge. A slight variation will occur with the infant who has motor problems and therefore cannot perform this task independently: he (or she) allows an adult to assist and even to release his tightly flexed fingers from around each cube, his attention holding firm. He then knocks the tower down with the same sense of pride of accomplishment and independence as the infant who was unaided.

Between 18 and 30 months, children begin to demonstrate verbal and/or behavioral responses to difficult tasks. "I can't," is frequently

Fig. 10-7. Infant and toddler years—at the center of their own universe, infants at this age love to build block towers and knock them over with glee.

heard when new tasks are presented. Anger and sadness are realistic responses of both nonhandicapped and handicapped toddlers to failing at tasks that, intellectually, they are capable of performing—for example, turning the pages of a book in anticipation of the story line or moving from one area to another to secure a favorite toy. All are readily comforted, however, by concrete solutions to their problem. Gently assisting the child in turning the pages for instance, or supporting the hips so that the child can "walk," gives him or her a sense of success at the task at hand. Handicapped and nonhandicapped children share many new and challenging tasks at this age, and all respond positively when assisted.

Preschool Years

The preschool period, between 3 and 5 years of age, is a time when children begin to become conscious of the differences between themselves and others. "Easy answers" are accepted as explaining these differences, however; for example, "I can't walk because my muscles aren't strong," or, "I'm special because I'm adopted." Such simple, comforting answers are sufficient to limit additional introspection. Children at this age rarely complain about the quality of their abilities, such as clumsiness, the need for a walker, an inability to dress oneself, or an inability to articulate words perfectly.

School Years

A rather dramatic change in self-perception occurs at about the age of 6 years. Children begin asking questions such as, "Where did I come from?" or "Who do I look like?" Competition to succeed in school—to be the best reader or the fastest runner—becomes important as each child begins to assess where he or she fits into the surrounding "known" world.

In a study comparing the self-concept of young physically handicapped children to that of nonhandicapped controls,[14] a colleague and I were impressed by the similarities between the two groups. Handicapped children between 3 and 6 years did not express concern or make many inquiries about their disability. The 6- and 7-year-olds, however, frequently related experiences, made comments, or asked questions that revealed much sensitivity on their part as to how others perceived their differentness. The specifics may be different but, just like others of their age, handicapped children, have problems with how they perceive themselves:

> A 6-year-old girl came home from school and asked, "Am I disabled or handicapped?"
>
> Another articulate 6-year-old girl described in detail how her premature birth was the cause of her cerebral palsy: "I was a teensy weensy baby and was put in an incubator and almost died." Later, when asked what her response was to being teased by her classmates because she could not walk, she replied, "I want to tell tham I hate their guts, but then the teacher would bench me."
>
> A 7-year-old handicapped boy, who had also been teased by classmates, had a successful experience in a rocket-making course during summer school, where he was the youngest and yet the most knowledgeable in the class. Commenting on this experience, he said, "For the first time the kids really like me."

Fig. 10-8. School years—at a time when handicapped children begin to be sensitive to their differentness and how it is perceived by others, achievements that win the friendship and respect of peers assume a special importance.

One 5-year-old asked his mother, "Why did you make me this way?"

A 6-year-old boy became withdrawn at school and cried for hours at home because he could not run and climb like his classmates.

A 5-year-old with cerebral palsy adamantly refused to play with two of his "old" chums who were his classmates in a program for disabled children. His mother was stymied by this sudden outburst. Shortly after, his sister expressed interest in becoming a teacher of handicapped children. He commented with much seriousness, "You don't want to work with those funny-looking kids!"

One 6-year-old boy was participating in a baseball game when a nonhandicapped classmate approached him and said, "You sure look funny when you run." Upon hearing this, another nonhandicapped classmate ran up and said, "You're my friend and I don't care how you look."

Adolescence

Handicapped children initially are not concerned about the permanency of their handicaps, feeling that they will get better in time. Within a few years, however this expectation may change. In a study by Dr. Klaus Minde, a child psychiatrist from Toronto who interviewed 41 children with cerebral palsy, 50% of the 10-year-olds interviewed demonstrated a depressed affect relating to their understanding that a cure for their disability was not forthcoming.[11]

A tendency toward withdrawal also may appear in handicapped adolescents. In the 14-year-olds he interviewed, Minde observed that a withdrawal of parents and siblings from the handicapped adolescents had occurred.[11] Similarly, Harper and Richman investigating the personality profiles of adolescents with cleft lip or palate or with orthopedic disabilities, found both groups to be behaviorally inhibited. Those with cleft lip or palate displayed greater self-concern and ruminative self-doubt over interpersonal interactions, while the orthopedically impaired group exhibited a sense of isolation, a passive orientation to interpersonal interaction, and generalized feelings of alienation.[5]

SUMMARY

These are observations of adolescents who had participated in traditional treatment programs that focused on improving their disability.

Let us reflect a minute about the possible cause for withdrawal from society by many of these handicapped adolescents. Is the diagnosis of cerebral palsy the culprit? Not entirely. What about those short-term goals that focused on correction of their problem areas and the many failures the children experienced when those goals were never achieved? Or what about the inability of parents to encourage development of the child's strengths because the professionals advising them focused on the disability rather than the child? No one knows the answers to these questions. One parent has commented to me time and time again, "I always try to remember that my child must have a successful experience each day, be it ever so small, if he is going to learn to respect himself."

Can the handicapped child learn to feel important, feel confident enough to try new experiences and to build on his strengths in order to compensate for his areas of need? The answer may depend on whether a parent can feel worthy as a person and competent as a parent, can recognize the child's behavioral strengths, and can consider the child's current and future needs within the context of the family.

These may be long-term goals worth considering.

BIBLIOGRAPHY

1. Ballard, R., Help for coping with the unthinkable. *Developmental Medicine and Child Neurology* 20:517–521, 1978.
2. Bleck, E. E., *Orthopaedic Management in Cerebral Palsy.* Philadelphia, W. B. Saunders, 1979.
3. Condon, W., and Sander, L., Neonate movement is synchronized with adult speech: Interactional participation and language acquisition. *Science* 183:99–101, 1974.
4. Freeman R. and Pearson, P., Counselling with parents, in Apley, J. (ed), *Care of the Handicapped Child.* Clinics in Developmental Medicine, No. 67. London, William Heinemann Medical Books, 1978, pp. 35–47.
5. Harper, D., and Richman, L., Personality profiles of physically impaired adolescents. *Journal of Clinical Psychology* 34:636–642.
6. Howard, J., The influence of children's developmental dysfunctions in marital quality and family interaction, in Lerner, R., and Spanier, G., *Child Influence on Marital and Family Interaction: A Life-Span Perspective.* New York, Academic Press, 1978, pp. 275–298.
7. Klaus, M., and Kennel, J., *Maternal Infant Bonding.* St. Louis, C. V. Mosby, 1976.
8. MacKeith, R., The feelings and behavior of parents of handicapped children, *Developmental Medicine and Child Neurology* 15:524–527, 1973.
9. MacKeith, R., The restoration of the parents as the keystone of the therapeutic arch. *Developmental Medicine and Child Neurology* 18:285–286, 1976.
10. Miller, N., Parents of children with neurological disorders: Concerns and counseling. *Journal of Pediatric Psychology* 4:297–306, 1979.
11. Minde, K., Hackett, J., Killou, D., et al., How they grow up: 41 physically handicapped children and their families. *American Journal of Psychiatry* 135:1344–1349, 1972.
12. O'Reilly, E., Care of the cerebral palsied: Outcome of the past and needs for the future. *Developmental Medicine and Child Neurology* 17:141–149, 1975.
13. Parmelee, A. H., The doctor and the handicapped child. *Children* 9:189–193, Sept./Oct. 1962.
14. Teplin, S., and Howard, J., Self concept in young physically handicapped children (in press).

Take It Easy When Evaluating the Mentally Retarded Child*

GUNNAR B. STICKLER, M.D.

Nobody questions the need for careful evaluation of a mentally retarded child. However, the physician's responsibility is to detect the condition promptly, to study the child adequately, and to inform the parents fully.

What is meant by "adequate study" of the child? I suspect that the term "adequate" varies from one institution to the other, and that the types and numbers of diagnostic tests recommended will depend upon the particular interest of the staff experts in the research aspects of mental retardation. As so often happens in pediatrics, methods of research tend to be accepted in clinical practice as constituting proper diagnostic management. Consequently, parents and the referring physician may consider the examination incomplete if the child does not have an electroencephalogram, an echoencephalogram, a pneumoencephalogram, or some other "gram," along with biochemical investigations that include both screening tests of the urine for metabolic disorders and a diversity of blood tests. Included also may be chromosome analysis. All these may be followed by consultations involving the ophthalmologist, psychologist, speech pathologist, audiologist, pediatric neurologist, and child psychiatrist.

Without question, in specific instances, many of these testing and consultation procedures are necessary. But the injudicious use of these technics, the automatic requesting of all these consultations, and the congregating of a team to discuss the multiple aspects of a child's problem can lead to a huge waste of manpower and a very large bill.

Sanity should prevail. The pediatrician should lead the effort to come to useful conclusions about the diagnosis and the management of every mentally retarded child. The pediatrician should decide on the needs for testing procedures and the specific consultations. The needs differ from one patient to the next; routines should be avoided.

In pediatric training programs the intern and resident should have exposure to children with the various metabolic and focal and progressive neurologic diseases. Personal observations of the biochemical disturbances in these disorders will give them the necessary training and experience, so that later in their careers they can make decisions for referrals in the investigation of the child who has mental subnormality.

*Reprinted from *Clinical Pediatrics,* 11:373–374, 1972. By permission of the author and publisher.

Counseling Parents

JOYCE KELLNER, M.S.W., L.C.S.W.

In their dealings with parents, teachers often find themselves acting in the role of counselor. This happens for a variety of reasons: they may be aware of potential problems which they feel obligated to discuss, or parents and others may seek their advice as "experts" on a variety of topics related to child development. This is true for teachers of nonhandicapped as well as those of handicapped, but in the latter situation it is important that *special* thought be given as to how to handle the specific issues that may arise. Besides understanding the special nature of the problems with which disabled children and their families may be struggling, a teacher, ideally, should be able to decide when such problems need the attention of another professional. This chapter will attempt to delineate some typical issues of concern and will discuss when and how to refer families for professional counseling, and to whom they should be referred.

PARENTAL REACTIONS

It has often been said that perhaps the most crucial factor in a child's adaptation to a disability is the reaction of his or her parents to the disability.[1] The parents' feelings color and shape their reaction both to the child and to others with whom they discuss their child.

Response to Diagnosis

Just as parents of disabled children start out with the same hopes and expectations for their children as do parents of nondisabled children, so also they have many of the same needs and concerns. They have the need to love and nurture, the need to be loved, and the need to feel good about themselves as parents. They desire, as do most parents, that their child will grow up to be well-adjusted, happy, and productive. Unlike other parents, who are apt to take such things for granted, they may worry about whether or not their disabled child will ever be independent and self-supporting, have friends, and be able to marry and rear offspring. The ways in which these many needs and concerns manifest themselves will depend, at least in part, on the parents' feelings, which cause them to act and react in special ways.

Denial

What then might be some of the predictable feelings of parents of a disabled child? At the time of diagnosis, parents are often shocked and disbelieving. This response may occur whether the diagnosis is made at birth or later in a child's life. Even the parent of an older child, who has suspected a disability for some time, may have an extreme reaction. The shock may be so overwhelming that parents may seem not to have heard the diagnosis. Likewise, they may not be able to accept what they have heard. This reaction can result in *denial,* which is a defense against that which seems unbearable. Extreme denial can produce the phenomenon of "doctor (or other service) shopping," in hopes of finding a magical solution to the problem. Such denial may render the parent unable to act effectively on behalf of his or her child because so much energy is being expended maintaining the defense.

Ambivalence

Ambivalence is a state of mind which is probably experienced by all parents to a greater or lesser degree. Parents of the nondisabled certainly have mixed positive and negative feelings about their children, at least some of the time. For all parents the positive side of ambivalence is manifested in tender, nurturing, and protective feelings toward their young. Where these feelings are colored by related (but less adaptive) feelings of pity, there may develop a tendency to infantilize a child to the point of inhibiting his or her intellectual, social, and emotional growth. An overly close attachment between parent and child may create pathologic dependence of each on the other. Such dependence is characterized by parental inability to foster or tolerate autonomy in the child, with the child being unwilling (or psychologically unable) to pursue independent activities and relationships. For the parents of disabled children, the negative side of ambivalence may involve actual revulsion, aversion, and dislike. This is especially apt to be the case for the parents of a disabled newborn, where there is no backlog of love or positive prior experiences with the child to mitigate the parents' negative feelings. Extremely strong aversive feelings may cause parents to reject their child. MacKeith states that "Rejection may show itself as *cold rejection, rationalized rejection,* [in which] the parents suggest that the child should be in a home with specially trained people to care for him; *dutiful caring* without warmth; or *lavish care* from overcompensation of the feeling of rejection."[1] Such rejection may lead a family to give up the handicapped child for out-of-home placement or adoption (although, of course, such decisions may also be made for practical or other more positive reasons). Feelings of rejection which are extreme and do not resolve or find a satisfactory outlet may lead to inconsistency, punitiveness, or even outright abuse.

Anger

Anger is another emotion which parents of disabled children may experience but have difficulty verbalizing. Socially and culturally, it may not be considered "nice" or otherwise acceptable for a loving parent to resent a child (or the needs of that child). This is especially true if the child is "sick" or disabled and therefore, expected to evoke a compassionate response. But disabled children can be incredibly needy, in both a psychological and a pragmatic sense, and their needs pose extreme demands on parental resources. On the psychological side, it should not be surprising that handicapped children may become inordinately emotionally dependent on their caretakers. Children who must rely indefinitely on others to do for them what they are unable to do for themselves may eventually have problems with their self-esteem. There can develop a vicious circle in which greater physical dependence leads to a sense of inadequancy, which, in turn, reinforces dependence. A child who feels inadequate may be shy or socially awkward and may have difficulty making friends. The more deficient the child's relationships with peers are, the more likely it is he or she will turn increasingly to parents for satisfaction of these needs. This can create a severe strain on parents, who may not even realize what is happening.

The practical burdens posed by caring for a handicapped child can be enormous. There may be unmanageable expenses posed by ongoing medical needs. Parents may lose time from work or other important activities because of doctors' visits, school conferences, etc. Extra time and energy may be spent in arranging transportation or child care or in finding specialized services. In addition, while one parent may be struggling with all these tasks, other members of the family may show signs of feeling neglected. In trying to attend to everyone's personal needs (including one's own), parents sometimes feel overwhelmed, resentful, and angry. Although such anger is normal, it tends to provoke a guilty reaction in parents who may confuse anger at their situation with anger at the child himself. This guilt may make them intensify their efforts to take care of everything and everyone, which may create a vicious circle of increased frustration, exhaustion, anger, and yet more guilt.

Feelings of Inadequacy

Another powerful feeling the parents of disabled children may struggle with is that of inadequacy. This has two dimensions: (1) feelings of inadequacy at reproduction; and (2) feelings of inadequacy at the demands of rearing a special child. With regard to reproduction, it is normal to want and to expect to have a healthy, "perfect" child. When such desires and expectations fail to be fulfilled, particularly in genetically inherited illnesses, it is often experienced as a tremendous blow to one's self-esteem. The resultant sense of having failed not only oneself, but also the others who shared those expectations (spouse, family, and friends) can create severe depression. Often this is accompanied by feelings of guilt over real or imagined "sins," i.e., unacceptable thoughts or behavior which are felt to have contributed, if not actually caused, the disability. It is very common for even the most rational people to entertain such notions, although they may never discuss them. Related to guilt is the feeling of shame, which is an embarrassed response to the reactions of others. It may cause parents to withdraw from social contacts and produce an isolation which is debilitating for all concerned. If feelings of anger, inadequacy, guilt, and shame are so strong as to be intolerable to the individual, they may be projected as blame onto others—one's spouse, relatives or doctor. These feelings may be expressed as hostility and unreasonableness in dealing with professionals, whose mere presence may serve to remind the parents of their "failings."

Feelings of inadequacy in parenting may develop from focusing too exclusively on the extraordinary needs of the disabled child, while failing to recognize the "ordinary" needs that he or she shares with all children. Trying to anticipate and deal with these special needs can create overwhelming anxiety, which may result in avoidance measures or, even, immobilization. Self-doubt creates inconsistencies in parental behavior, which, in turn, produce mixed messages to the child about what is expected of him or her and what he or she may expect in return.

Bereavement

It is crucial that parents acknowledge and deal with feelings of bereavement early on. If parents do not grieve the normal child they did not have (or who they once had but who now is irrevocably changed), it is unlikely that they will ever really accept the child they do have. Anger and sadness are natural reactions to any loss and they must be experienced if a more positive adaptation is ultimately to take place. Parents need to express their feelings, to explore the sources of these feelings, and, hopefully, to try to anticipate what the behavioral implications of these feelings may be. As parents come to accept their situation more fully, they may eventually want to channel their feelings into action. This may mean talking with other parents to learn how they cope, or reading about the particular disability, or becoming politically active on behalf of the handicapped. The action taken may not specifically relate to the child's disability: undertaking a hobby, returning to school, or starting a job may just as well signal the end of mourning. It should be noted, however, that just as mobilizing oneself into purposeful activity can be adaptive response, it can also be a means of avoiding confronting important issues directly. Whether the behavior is adaptive or is aimed at avoiding certain realities depends on whether or not, and how, the individual handled the needed time of initial bereavement.

Besides the initial mourning which normally follows a diagnosis of disability, there is a related phenomenon which bears mentioning. That is the chronic sorrow which has been associated with having a handicapped child. Although the concept of *chronic sorrow* was developed to explain parental response to having a mentally retarded child,[2] it would also seem to apply to other handicaps. Chronic sorrow does not necessarily mean protracted, unremitting depression; rather, it may be recurring feelings of loss and sadness. These feelings are apt to arise whenever parents have occasion to confront how their child is "different" from the child they had hoped for. For example, any time there is a developmental milestone, such as when a child is about to enter school, parents are likely to experience anew their feelings of grief and mourning. If parents appear to be chronically immobilized by grief or anger, they may need professional help. (Immobilization may be indicated by an ongoing inability to make decisions, plan effectively, or set limits on behalf of the child.) It is also indicated by being unable to focus on anything about the child besides the negative aspects of his or her situation. Chronic neglect of one's own needs, or the needs of a spouse or the other children, is also an indication that a parent is "stuck" and help is needed.

IDENTIFICATION OF A PROBLEM

What are some of the other indicators that a family is in need of outside professional help? Parents will rarely ask directly for a counseling referral, even when they recognize that they are in psychological distress. They are more likely to ask the teacher for advice on problem solving; for example, how to handle particular issues such as oppositional behavior or the development of self-help skills. Often the "presenting problem" will be something the child does (e.g., thumb sucking or hitting) or doesn't do (e.g., reading or dressing self) that the parent finds unacceptable. It can be helpful to find out to whom the behavior is a problem and why. Never assume that, because a behavior is offensive to you, you know why it bothers a parent. Their "why" can give you important information as to what is significant and emotionally loaded for the parent. If two parents disagree about how a behavior should be dealt with (or if, indeed, it should be dealt with at all), it may be very hard to implement a corrective stragegy. Finding out when and in what circumstances a problem arose, as well as what has been tried in the way of remedies, is important in deciding what the next step should be. For example, a kindergarten-age child who was completely toilet trained and then, after a sibling was born, began to wet the bed at night, more than likely has a different problem than a child of the same age who has never established bladder control. When considering problems that may have a physiological component (e.g., headaches in a child with hydrocephalus), it is always wise to recommend that the child be seen first by his or her pediatrician so that physiological causes can be ruled out.

PROBLEM SOLVING

In considering seeming behavioral problems (e.g., a 2-year-old who is called "selfish" because she doesn't like to share), sometimes all that is required is educating a parent as to what may reasonably be expected of a child at a given developmental level. Parents (especially new parents) often do not know what a child is physically or mentally capable of at a given stage, and, therefore, they do not know when they are demanding too much or too little. It can be particularly confusing if a parent has a child who is one age chronologically, but who functions at a much different level in cognitive, social, or emotional areas. Pinpointing behavioral management strategies that have worked in the classroom or developing strategies jointly with parents—to arrive at consistent approach—can be very helpful.

Once suggestions have been made and an approach has been decided on, it is important to check on the results. If a parent does not follow through, gives up too easily, or seems inconsistent, and if the problem is such that it seriously interferes with the child's or the family's functioning, it may mean that the parents' feelings are blocking the "desired" change. Both interpersonal and internal conflicts can make it difficult for anyone to act on good advice. Such conflicted feelings need to be expressed and, ultimately, resolved in order for a parent to give clear and consistent messages to a child. This is an area teachers and other non–mental health professionals often feel inadequate in evaluating. The critical thing is not to feel a need to probe into the parental psyche oneself, but, rather, to be sensitive to the extent of the parents' distress and, thereby, to know when a referral should be made.

WHEN TO REFER

But what if parents are not asking for help? In what kinds of situations should a teacher consider suggesting professional counseling? It is not uncommon for teachers to identify behaviors or personality traits in a student which are cause for concern, but which parents may have overlooked. Disturbances such as learning problems and disruptive, aggressive, or anti-social behavior are obvious, and most schools have their own psychologists or other professionals available to assess these. But children may also exhibit other, more subtle, kinds of disturbances which require professional attention. Withdrawal from social interaction, unattentiveness, listlessness, poor appetite, poor grooming (especially in the adolescent), or self-stimulating behavior may be indications that a child is unhappy or depressed. In examining such behaviors, it is very important to determine in what situations they occur—whether at home, at school, in reaction to some particular occurrence, or at a particular time. It is also important to try to determine what factors outside of school may be contributing to a problem that manifests itself in the classroom.

It is probable that, with a little forethought, at least some adjustment problems at school can be avoided. If a child with a newly diagnosed handicap is returning to his or her regular class, or if a child with a pre-existing handicap is entering a new class, preparation of everyone involved can ease the transition. Helping a child who misses school frequently to keep up with his or her work is important. Teachers may reassure parents by calling to find out what their concerns are and what, if any, special management of the child is needed, and by offering to work closely with the child and his or her family to insure optimal adjustment. The anxiety of entering an unfamiliar environment can be lessened by having a new child visit the school and classroom in advance. Similarly, by orienting the child's classmates in advance as to the particular nature of the child's handicap, and by encouraging questions, the teacher can promote a positive and supportive response. Finally, with the parents' permission, the teacher may call the child's pediatrician to find out how the child's disability will affect his or her performance at school. This can provide a wealth of useful information and can help one avoid creating frustrating experiences for the child.

It seems relevant to comment at this point on members of the handicapped child's family, besides the child and the parents, who may show signs of stress. The siblings of handicapped children not uncommonly experience their own set of difficulties in adaptation. They may have unusual responsibilities thrust upon them prematurely by overburdened parents. They may be emotionally neglected by parents who are preoccupied with struggling with their own feelings in addition to a multitude of tasks. They may feel guilty that their own jealous feelings or "bad" behavior somehow caused their sibling to be handicapped. And they may be depressed for any or all of the foregoing reasons. Teachers of nonhandicapped children who know that one of their students has a handicapped sibling, especially one with a recently diagnosed handicap, should be alert to such reactions.

REFERRAL RESOURCES

To whom, then, should one refer a family when counseling seems indicated? The family pediatrician is often a good place to start. He or she may know of community resources which may be of help to the family. Most communities have county of local mental health agencies which offer a variety of mental health services. County welfare departments often have information and referral services which can provide names of local public mental health agencies. There are also a variety of private agencies which offer counselling to families and individuals. And, of course, there are private psychiatrists, clinical psychologists, and social workers in private practice who may be of help. The discipline of the individual therapist is, perhaps, not as important as the extent of his or her experience in working with the families of handicapped children. When one is at a loss as to how and where to locate such a person, contacting a hospital or diagnostic center that serves the handicapped would be a logical place to inquire.

THE REFERRAL PROCESS

Finally, how does one actually go about making a referral? The place to begin is to point out, frankly, to parents the perceived need. This can be a very delicate task, because parenting is an emotionally sensitive issue for most people, and parents of handicapped children are especially vulnerable to criticism. One may start by exploring with parents the general notion of asking for outside help. Have they ever considered it? What would they think of such a suggestion? Such discussion can ease the way into a more direct statement about what one feels is indicated. Stressing the positive—by appealing to the parents' desire to do what's best for the child or to minimize their own conflicts—is a legitimate and often effective approach. It is also helpful to acknowledge the parents' difficulty in acting, while indicating a feeling of optimism that positive change is possible. No matter how strong one's own conviction that professional help is indicated, it is wise not to be dogmatic. Raising the issue for consideration and giving a parent time to think about it is apt to be much less threatening than a more insistent approach. Don't be discouraged if, the first time counseling is brought up, the suggestion is not met with enthusiasm, and don't hesitate to come back to it if the problem persists. Once there is an indication of interest, however, offering to help find a resource (or at least find someone else who can do that) is an important step in completing the process. Finally, one should follow up to see whether or not a referral "took," and, if it didn't, why not. Such continued, nonjudgmental interest and support can be a significant factor in eventually moving the family to utilize professional counseling.

SUMMARY

Teachers need to be aware of parental reactions, as these reactions influence the way in which parents relate to their child and have a bearing on the child's functioning in school. Possible reactions include *denial, ambivalence, rejection, anger, feelings of inadequacy,* and *bereavement. Guilt, shame* and *depression* may also be present. Any of these feelings, if not dealt with and resolved, can immobilize the person experiencing them and cause sufficient distress to warrant professional intervention. Teachers should be able to identify potential problems in the student or family that can impede the student's development. Teachers may intervene by problem solving with families when this is possible, but will also need to know when and where to refer parents for professional counseling.

REFERENCES

1. MacKeith, R., Feelings and behaviors of parents of handicapped children. *Developmental Medicine and Child Neurology* 15:525–527, 1973.
2. Olshansky, S., Chronic sorrow: A response to having a mentally defective child. *Social Casework* 43:191–194, 1962.

BIBLIOGRAPHY

Barnard, K., and Erickson, M. L., *Teaching Children with Developmental Problems: A Family Care Approach*. St. Louis, C. V. Mosby, 1976

Noland, R. L. (ed.), *Counseling of Parents of the Ill and Handicapped*. Springfield, Ill. Charles C. Thomas, 1971.

Pless, I., and Pinkerton, P., Chronic Childhood Disorders: Promoting Patterns of Adjustment. Chicago, Henry Kimpton, 1975.

Travis, G., *Chronic Illness in Children: Its Impact on Child and Family*. Palo Alto, Stanford University Press, 1976.

Spock, B., and Lerrigo, M., *Caring for Your Disabled Child*. New York, MacMillan, 1965.

Understanding the Atypical Child: How I Learned to Live with My Handicapped Daughter*

PATRICIA CRAVEN

I saw Pat Craven's daughter only once in orthopedic consultation. I've learned from Pat Craven, and other parents like her, not to generalize or to prejudge the feelings of parents of handicapped children. Her calm and certain acceptance of the realities of her daughter's severe mental and physical handicap has allowed the loving care of her child as a human being.

Not all parents can immediately achieve the emotional state of this mother; for some, it may take years to see the person behind the handicap. Pat Craven's responses to what some might label a "tragedy" seemed worth sharing with a wider readership who might thereby gain greater insight into parental dealing and coping.

Eugene E. Bleck, M.D.

My daughter, Robyn, has Cornelia de Lange Syndrome. When she was born, I was initiated into a completely different realm of mothering than I had previously been used to with my eldest daughter, Jody, who was then 5 years old. The world of the handicapped child is distinctly unique. Having Robyn in my life was an even deeper dive into an unknown ocean of responsibilities, feelings, and disciplines.

During the pregnancy, I had dreams and intuitive feelings that the child I was carrying was not normal. As Robyn emerged from me at birth, I heard a voice I recognized to be my new child saying, "My body doesn't reflect my spirit, look deep and you'll see me." That, of course, was exactly what I needed to hear—that her spirit was whole, even though her body was missing parts. She was telling me to look deep, to come to her as she was coming to me, with a receptive heart and an open mind.

Her message also confirmed that my intuition was right. My child was indeed handicapped. Her primary disability was obvious immediately. She was born with only one finger on each wrist. Her second major disability is her cleft palate, which required that I use special feeding techniques for the first year of her life. In addition to this, she is mentally retarded and her hearing is impaired. Her vision is excellent, and she has legs and feet and is expected to walk someday. She is very alert, responsive, and even, I feel, telepathic. At 2 years of age, she weighs just 15 pounds, which is small for a child of her age.

Her birth took place at home, attended by a midwife, my dear friend Marilyn, and my daughter. A hospital birth could have meant that Robyn and I would have been denied our bonding experience. It is not unusual for the hospital attendants to whisk an abnormal infant away to the nursery before the mother is shocked by his or her appearance or condition.

*Reprinted from *Well-Being* 36:36–42, 1978. By permission of the author and Well-Being Productions.

Understanding the Atypical Child

Over the next 2 hours after her birth, we all took turns holding Robyn. We were all in a tender place between acceptance and disbelief.

Those first hours that Robyn and I spent looking at each other were the most vital hours of our relationship. All of the intuitive knowing that came to me about being her mother, accepting her as a gift, and having faith that our lives merging was not accidental would have been missed if we'd been apart. For the first time in my life, I was conscious of connecting up with a person on the spiritual plane first, instead of making her pass inspection on the physical, mental, and emotional levels. Robyn didn't seem surprised to see me at all. I think she had made previous reservations!

She came to the right place. I knew a child like this needed a mother who was not afraid to assert herself and who would do her best to care for her in truly beneficial ways. Robyn needed me, with my boldness, courage, strength, and determination. I was to be her life support. Living with her from the very beginning taught me how to want to be that for her. We created a strong, sure bond during those critical first weeks, as we struggled with the deepest issues two people who are making a commitment to each other must deal with. We constantly sent messages to each other—from her heart to my heart, and back again. We grew in each other's faith and trust. We saw each other and, together, learned the meaning of looking deep.

I have a tremendous honor and respect for Robyn. No one can accurately call her life an accident or tragedy. To automatically hold the opinion that a person with a weird body is a less valuable creation is to greatly limit the nature of the universe.

In keeping with my philosophy of living in a simple, natural, and practical way, I wanted to breastfeed my children. With Jody this was no problem, and for 15 months she was a healthy breastfed baby. When Robyn was born without the desire or ability to suck properly, my plans to breastfeed had to be revised. I set about to find an electric breastpump which I had to pay the La Leche League $1.50 a day to use. (The pumps are now available, free, from the Nursing Mother's Counsel in my county). I pumped my milk out six times a day at first—once every 3 hours, except during the middle of the night. I stored the milk in sterile bottles provided by the hospital where I took Robyn when she was 3 hours old. They were kept for Robyn's feedings in the refrigerator in the nursery. I had plenty of milk and no difficulties.

Robyn was fed by tube for the first year and a half of her life. This procedure is basically simple, but not without the hazards of aspiration or choking. I learned how to do it from the nurses in the hospital.

There were many tears during this period in our life together. Most of them were from me as I tried to keep myself together, emotionally. I didn't know what to expect from all of this. The ground I was breaking was new to most everyone. Cornelia de Lange children are rare, and their lives are unpredictable. I had plenty of "professionals" giving me advice, but I found that the only way I was going to make it was to live from day to day, using the information and experience that came to me from Robyn herself.

A typical child will respond to her environment with easily understood signals and language. It is not difficult to communicate with a typical child's mind and heart, because perceptions usually come and go clearly. Affection and physical responsiveness is readily available with a typical child, who understands the meaning and intent of his experiences. With an atypical child, the realms of the mind and the emotions must be touched from the outside, through the physical body, in order to have meaning to the child's mind. Through stimulation of sensory and motor systems, the child will be encouraged to explore and to participate in his total environment.

Psychological and intellectual development depends on inspiration. For a typical child this is not a problem, because there is usually a sufficient increase in interest in everything from the moment of birth. An atypical child needs a tremendous amount of positive exposure to inner and outer environments before he can find his foundation in this world and move with it.

A typical child will cry when hungry, for example, and smile when joyful. Often a child who is handicapped will not initiate this type of interaction. She may not cry to let you know she's hungry. When played with, she may show no obvious signs of pleasure. Depending on the nature and degree of the disability, the appearance of characteristic responses may be extremely delayed, or may not appear at all.

Robyn has a downturned mouth, which is typical of the de Lange syndrome. When she smiles, her mouth does not turn up at the corners. Her eyes sparkle, she gets dimples in her cheeks, and she chuckles, but this is not an easily recognizable expression to those who are unfamiliar with her body language.

The body language of a child who cannot send or receive familiar signals of communication has, at first, a unique idiosyncratic language of her own. This language is learned together by parent and child. It is not something which the parent teaches the child. Typical children imitate the faces and actions they see. They can connect the meaning to facial expressions and corresponding actions, objects, and sounds. But the child who cannot comprehend the connections does not learn the meaning of what he sees, or how to interact with it, much less communicate in the traditional ways.

A parent of a handicapped child watches her child closely and can be alert to the ways the child uses her face and body. A perceptive person can use this information to call the child's attention to herself. Being open to the unique possibilities of each child provides the ideal atmosphere for a truly creative exchange.

It is really important for parents to know that the child is expressing love, or discomfort, and that he does recognize his parents. Parents who think their child is rejecting them or doesn't know them can become deeply discouraged and are not easily consoled. But although the handicapped child may not jump for joy when a loved one walks into the room, they do feel. Every child has an opening that you can look through to see his feelings. That's what a body is for—to give the essence of life a vehicle for this world. A parent and child touch each other by looking deep, by seeing deep.

After a firm foundation has been established between parent and child, new, more traditional, forms of language, such as sign language, can be learned together. Provisions must be made for hearing and speech disabilities, but the important thing to remember is that there must be a language of some sort. Using the hands gives an obvious sign to the child that someone thinks he is worth communicating with. Signing gives the child a consistent input of meaningful symbols. It gives the child something to listen to and make sense out of his world with.

The openness and acceptance of the child the way he is at the beginning is the first essential step towards integrating his world with yours. That means a parent has to let go of wishes and desires for the child to be normal and progress as typical children do. It is hard, but not impossible.

As I mentioned earlier, physical contact is the first way in which a parent can initiate a positive relationship with her child. Cuddling a baby is such a natural way of expressing mutual appreciation and love. With a handicapped child, it is often more difficult to achieve a level of closeness that is fulfilling to both child and parent. Specifically, there are many disabilities which involve uncontrolled body movements or postures which make physical contact extremely awkward or uncomfortable. It is very frustrating when body-to-body contact is interfered with.

When a child demonstrates a tendency towards tactile defensive behavior, i.e., emotional or physical resistance to touch, it can be even more disillusioning to those caring for him. Body contact must be rewarding to everyone. There are some basic things a parent can do to facilitate positive contact.

The most soothing and sensuous touch besides the human hand is water. Baths in lukewarm water are extremely effective in reorienting a person to his or her center.

Exploration of one's own body is usually the first introduction a person gets to the physical plane on a conscious level. Thumbsucking in early infancy is a common way children discover themselves. A breastfed child will have most, if not all, of his sucking needs met through breastfeeding. But a mentally or physically handicapped child characteristically does not know how or have a desire to suck. If he can suck, the suck reflex may be very weak and ineffectual. Bottle feeding is easier, but still is no simple feat for a child who has weak face or mouth muscles, inability to swallow, or difficulty breathing. To inspire a positive experience associated with the face, lips, and tongue, a parent must employ a massage technique for those areas.

Feeling, kissing, and fondling the child should be done freely and without inhibition, especially with the child who cannot or will not do it for himself. Lotions, various textures of cloth, and other bodies are all quite beneficial in stimulating the nerve endings in the body to produce pleasurable sensations.

Materials which provide unique tactile stimulus are fur, grass, hair, feathers, terry cloth, velvet, beans in a tub, styrofoam pellets, mud, sand, cornmeal, bubbles, carpeting, paper.

For motor development, there are specific exercises which aid the child's exploration. Swinging in a hammock gives a feeling of space as well as support. Moving around in different directions while in the hammock adds depth to perceptions and a sense of self in space. It also stimulates sensory centers in the ear, which serves to promote listening and communication. A balance board tilted forward, backward, and sideways will encourage the development of balance and strength in the back, stomach, leg, and arm muscles. A huge ball can be used for rolling the child around—to facilate comprehension of up and down, as well as to give unique views of the world.

A mirror is one of the best tools for introducing the child to himself. Being propped up on a triangular wedge of foam stimulates the child to hold his head up and use arms and legs for locomotion. A board with wheels on the bottom is very useful when the child is on her stomach and can push or pull herself around the room. For bouncing, standing, and strengthening the feet, legs, hips, and back, the child can be placed in a seat which is suspended securely from a door jam or ceiling. In this, she can turn herself around, stand, or straighten her legs. For a child who spends a lot of time on her back, this type of equipment provides beneficial experience of the world right side up.

Most important for the first 6 months or year (or longer) is a baby carrier that can be worn in the front or back, in which the baby can be carried about the home, yard, or out for walks, while resting on the body of the person caring for her. (My personal recommendation is the "Baby Bundler," handmade by Cathy Flicker of Woodacre, California, for $30.00. She will custom-design and make Bundlers for children with special needs.) A playpen, infant seat, crib, or high chair need only be used for a minimum period of time, if at all. These appliances limit the child's environment and can stifle development. They each serve their own purpose but cannot be expected to provide adequate stages for the evolution of the whole child.

Color therapy is of great value to children with handicaps. A woman I know who has a couple of hyperkinetic foster children uses blues and greens in their baths for a soothing effect. Also, she sees that their clothes are not visually overstimulating (reds, oranges, and yellows), because this could overcharge their already oversensitive nervous systems. On the other hand, children who have difficulty paying attention to their surroundings may benefit by the use of vibrant colors to encourage their interest. Muted yellows and oranges may be helpful to those who have digestive disturbances.

For visual stimulation, a child needs a mobile hanging over his crib. Cutout faces from magazines taped up for him to look at inspires appreciation and attention to faces. A disabled child may not be interested in eye contact. It is very important, if you want to share this with your child, that you be persistent and consistently provide eye contact in every way available.

Make it worthwhile for your child to look at you. First by using your eyes as channels of love—just like faucets—turn on the love and know your child is getting it. This means you have to aim. It takes a while to get the flow right, but your heart knows how and it will do all the work.

Another way to share seeing with your child is to make your face interesting by making different expressions, or painting it like a clown.

A child that is blind can still benefit from eye contact. Kissing the eyes lightly, touching them with a feather, gently washing them with a cotton ball, stroking the lashes, all these touches communicate love. He will literally feel it in his eyes.

The vital thing here is that he be exposed to your face and eyes continuously and be encouraged to use his face and eyes to explore the world. Positive reinforcement for being with you adds another dimension to the relationship promoting togetherness.

A typical child will use sight on his own without the imposed incentive of food, affection, or toys. All the senses are usually working together to integrate what's happening. A typical child just naturally wants to be involved. There are naturally occurring rewards for the participation that is required. For the handicapped child, all the senses may or may not be working properly. Some of the senses may be lacking entirely. Coordinating everything so it works efficiently to send congruent messages about life to the child may take years.

To discourage withdrawal and encourage involvement, a child needs auditory stimulus as well. Patterns of solitary behavior start very young if there is difficulty perceiving and being harmonious with your world. With mental retardation, neurological dysfunction, or hearing impairment, it is not always guaranteed that your child will hear sufficiently and, if he does hear, that he will always listen. Again, it is something a parent has to make worthwhile if he wants his child to participate.

Some ways to attract attention consist of the following: use a music box that has something to watch along with the music, or call attention to household noises, such as the telephone, blender, doorbell, animals, clocks, water running, records with children's voices, any music with a beat, dancing, clapping.

Toys that make noises, such as squeaks, clicks, rings, toots, or beeps, are easy to find. The important thing here is to convince the child that sounds are meaningful. Again, positive reinforcement when the child acknowledges the sound is essential to making the experience something the child will want to repeat.

Talking to the child, even if you know she can't hear, sends lots of messages that are vital to her growth and adjustment on all planes. The physical and mental planes need the vibration of sound to stimulate the nervous system into functioning just for the very basic reason of survival.

Talking in a low, soothing voice with much intonation right near the ear will provide excellent audio nourishment. It actually causes the bones in the inner ear to vibrate and stimulate the auditory nerve, even if the child cannot distinguish what he is hearing. Tell your child how you feel about him. Whisper endearments. Tell your child what you love about life.

Whenever I am near my daughter's ears, I can't resist nibbling her earlobes. I remember when she was just 3 hours old the pediatrician we brought her to at the hospital was telling me how all the de Lange babies have upturned earlobes. I said, "At least she has earlobes. I love to suck on earlobes." A look of astonishment came over the doctor's face. She couldn't believe I'd want to get that intimate with my "deformed" baby.

I have mentioned the importance of giving positive reinforcement to the child when he displays a receptive response to people and things. In raising Jody, I was strongly opinionated against using a system of reward and punishment as a method of teaching or discipline. I wanted her to reap internal rewards in the form of heightened self-esteem, direction, and discipline. This has proven to be an effective way of guiding her. But, for a mentally retarded child who is not yet aware of the significance of her internal or external world, I have found that I must call her attention to its meaning. I do this by creating tangible actions and reactions involving her basic senses; I call it positive reinforcement. I am inclined to express my enthusiasm by kissing, hugging, talking to her happily, and squealing with joy. I also use her favorite foods, special toys, and other imaginative devices to give positive reinforcement.

At any rate, it is necessary to provide him or her with a very obvious reason to think productively about just being.

I discourage slapping, spanking, or other forms of physical discipline for the typical and atypical child alike. In my opinion, there is no point in using parts of the child's body, particularly the butt, to try to communicate disapproval or direction. This is negative reinforcement, which I believe does just that—supports negative behavior. The punishment and guilt suffered for the moment in the process of physical discipline is often perceived by the child to be all that is required of him in terms of responsibility for his action.

In the matter of encouraging a child to get to know his body and to use it to expand his horizons, negative reinforcement serves to create varying degrees of unpleasant associations with the body. I believe it inhibits healthy development. A normal infant feels things in his body and, after a few months, learns to recognize and differentiate the origin and meaning of the feelings. A handicapped child may not even have an awareness of body sensation at first. If she does, she may not be able to determine its source. She could be very confused or totally unable to communicate its meaning. Even if all this if overcome, she may not be aware or able to express her perceptions and integrate her experience into a consistent and recognizable pattern of behavior.

It is hard enough with a normal body and mind to keep from tuning out and neglecting parts of our bodies which we associate with negative experiences or attitudes. For a handicapped child, who needs to tune into his body in the first place, tuning out and turning off his responses is too easy.

How, then, do you teach a handicapped child self-discipline? The same sensible way as you would with any other child. There are no pat answers, of course, but there are some very basic guidelines which can be observed and tailored to fit individual circumstances. First and foremost, the attitude that must be eliminated in order for any kind of guidance to be successful and enriching is that a severely handicapped child does not understand the concept of discipline. This is blatantly false.

Self-discipline does not rely on thoughts or principles that are learned as much as it relies on the intuitive knowing that we must survive, that we want to survive. Handicapped people most certainly are equipped with this necessary desire. Recognizing this, we can, as parents, make a point to inspire our children to listen to their intuition to simply take good care of themselves. For this, example is the best teacher. The values in the home life need to be carefully and consciously born and nurtured together. And they must be honored and believed in by every member of the family.

For specific interactions and ways of communicating with one another in a family situation, I suggest Parent Effectiveness Training. The concepts of Active Listening and "I" Messages are highly valuable tools in working with others, children, and adults as well.

Real communication is an art. It must be taught and practiced. Very few of us receive training for parenthood before we are right in the middle of it, up to our kneecaps in breastpads and bicycles. It is of utmost importance, then, if our children are to become healthy, responsible adults, that we do not leave their rearing to chance trial and error. What we communicate to them on all levels is the water which nourishes their growth.

Our children are not the reason we "didn't finish our education" or "didn't do anything but take care of the home." Our children are our education and our home, if we are appreciative of their presence. That is not to say that we are our children, or that they are extensions of us, but simply that one prospers considerably when one blooms where one is planted. Many parents feel that they must let the child know who is "boss" or engage in some sort of a battle of wills. Many falsities are cherished with these ideas. In Parent Effectiveness Training, light is shed on all of these attitudes and constructive solutions are explored. I strongly urge parents of handicapped children to approach discipline and guidance with adequate preparation.

All in all, what I see to be a wholistic approach to raising a severely handicapped child is just being there, being near, and having it be okay for you and your child to be together. It's opening up new possibilities for loving and caring. It's exploring the deepest parts of yourself with compassion. It's looking deep inside one another—touching and being touched, listening, being led, being taught—being one for the sustenance of two.

Another Parent's Experience: Letting Handicapped Children Do Things for Themselves*

Dear Ann Landers: As a stepmother to a young man with a cerebral palsy handicap who cannot speak, I would like to tell parents how important it is to let *all* children do as much for themselves as they possibly can.

My stepson, Barry, could not walk until age 5. Until that time, he crawled and got around on a homemade skateboard. Through strict discipline and his own self-determination, Barry has learned to cook, to vacuum, to make his bed, to do dishes, and to wash clothes. He is able to read and write and use sign language. He graduated from the eighth grade of a public school at age 18 and received a standing ovation from his fellow students when he received his diploma. Barry took it upon himself to study for the G.E.D. test and finish high school. Of course, he made it. Having been taught the value of money, he saved and paid for private driving lessons. Now he has his own car. He works at a handicapped-sponsored job and maintains his own apartment.

Had his parents not had the fortitude to let him do for himself, Barry might still be sitting in a wheelchair or lying in a bed, being waited on hand and foot instead of enjoying life and dating girls.

It is heart-breaking to watch a child struggle with his twisted hands to get a bite of food to his mouth or a glass of water—or tie a shoe, or pick himself up after falling from a bicycle. But you must remember, even though it would be so easy to do it for him, he is stuck with those limbs for the rest of his life and he must learn to do for himself. If you, as parents, take away his chance to learn and do everything for him, you are denying that child the opportunity to learn to take care of himself. —A Proud Mother

Dear Mother: You have a right to be proud. I wonder how many able-bodied kids can point to a record like Barry's. Please say hello to that stepson of yours. He sounds like a real winner.

*Reprinted from Ann Landers and the Field Newspaper Syndicate, Sept. 9, 1980. With permission.

Society Versus the Wheelchair: The Experiences of a Handicapped Child*

ROSE MARIE MacELMAN
CHARLES E. BURDEN, M.D.

Rose Marie became a patient of mine at the age of 2½, just one month after I began practicing pediatrics in July of 1962. She had typical childhood illnesses and seemed otherwise normal until March of 1965, when on her preschool physical exam I picked up mild ataxia and a positive Romberg's sign. This showed slow, but steady progession, so a year later I referred her to a neurologist. He felt she had a progessive degenerative cerebellar disease of unknown etiology. At that time, her only problems were an unsteady gait and "shaky" handwriting. In 1971 her sister, 5 years younger, was noted to have an identical disability.

By 1972, Rose Marie had ECG abnormalities consistent with Friedreich's ataxia. By that time she was confined to a wheelchair, had slurred speech, and a progessive scoliosis. In five more years she had developed diabetes mellitus (felt to be unrelated), occasional choking spells, and marked weakness and ataxia of her upper as well as lower limbs, distally more than proximally. She has absent deep tendon reflexes and loss of position and vibratory sensation in the lower limbs.

Despite her problems, Rose Marie is a B student and a very personable young lady. In the spring of 1978, a few months before she was to graduate from high school, I was sent a form from the state vocational rehabilitation director regarding her potential and prognosis. Although I felt I knew Rose Marie as well as any of my patients, my immediate reaction was, "Rehabilitation? For a progressive neurologic disease with marked disability?" She was already also being followed by a neurologist, orthopedic surgeon, and physical therapist. I felt nothing more could be done to improve her potential. To me, sending her to business school seemed a "waste" of taxpayers' money, especially if she continued to become weaker (her father had died from a heart condition several years ago and her mother lived on social security with help from her family).

Soon after my "sentence" concerning rehabilitation was handed in, a sensitive visiting nurse, who had been helping the family with Rose Marie's diabetes and general care, brought to my office the following essay that Rose Marie had typed for a school assignment. On reading the essay, I was moved by Rose Marie's capability and enthusiasm. She does have the potential for many years of useful life, and her aspirations certainly deserve as much support as man's aspiration to reach Mars. I have been able to reverse my original pronouncement, which I now view with chagrin. Because of this articulate expression of Rose Marie's own viewpoint, I have had to reassess my own attitudes towards the handicapped.

*Reprinted from *Pediatrics* 63:576–579, 1979. By permission of C. E. Burden and the publisher. © 1979 by the American Academy of Pediatricians.

Society Versus the Wheelchair

I would like to share Rose Marie's "Society vs the Wheelchair" with physicians caring for young people everywhere, hoping that others, who, like myself, have had a "practical," hardline approach to rehabilitation of the handicapped, may become more sensitive to the desires of the handicapped to be contributing members of society.

Charles E. Burden, M.D.

My name is Rose Marie MacElman. I'm a senior at Brunswick High School. I have been brought up in public life and not "hidden" as people did to so many of the handicapped in years past. Living in public life as I have, I can give you some of my first-hand experiences of how society treats the handicapped person.

My handicap is a disease called cerebellar ataxia. It is not a communicable disease. My parents noticed when I was 5½ years old that my coordination was not what it should be. At first the doctors thought the problem was in my feet, but, after many series of tests and a brain wave, they found that the problem was not my feet at all but the part of the brain that controls all motivation, the cerebellum. Gradually, I started getting weaker and weaker until, at the age of 12, I found myself relying totally on a wheelchair.

When I first went into the wheelchair I was very shy and afraid of people. I didn't want to be the center of attention. I didn't want people to notice me at all. Because of being so shy, I didn't have any friends my own age. My only friends were my family and close friends of the family who were a lot older than I.

When I got into the outside world, I found that people say and do things unintentionally. Sometimes people will stare out of curiosity. Young children who don't understand will ask, "Why are you sitting in that chair?" and "Why can't you walk?" I explain to these young children that my legs won't walk. They accept this explanation without further questioning.

I have two small cousins who, at first, were very scared of me. When they would come to visit, they wouldn't get near me at all until we all sat down together and my family explained to them that there was no need to be frightened. I was just like them except I couldn't walk and have to use my wheelchair to move around. Now they are not afraid, and they play with my wheelchair when I'm not in it.

In grammar school I had very few friends. Most of the children my own age didn't understand my disability and thought I was odd, so most of my friends were limited to teachers and faculty. In junior high school I had more friends, because they understood that I wasn't that much different from them. Now that I am in high school, it seems that everyone is my friend. They look for my personality rather than my handicap. Even still, there are a certain few who choose to ignore me completely.

Most of my friends have problems of their own. My best friends enjoy my company and want me to go places with them and participate in activities that they enjoy.

I find teachers at school have any different views on how to instruct me in my studies. Some realize that I cannot work as fast or as accurately as the other students, and they let me work on my own and at my own pace. Others won't accept the fact that I'm not able to keep up with the other students and ask me to drop the course rather than try and help me grasp what I can. I want so much for teachers to help me as much as they can, because I am interested and I am willing to learn. Some teachers smother me, and I feel that this is as bad as not bothering with me at all. They make me feel incapable. What they don't seem to realize is that just because I am physically handicapped doesn't necessarily mean that I am mentally handicapped as well.

Adults who know me treat me with compassion and kindness, but they also realize that I don't want to be treated like a special type of person or be treated like a child. They encourage me and make me feel like I have a chance like any other person, despite my handicap.

When I go into shopping centers or restaurants, lots of people stare and ask questions, such as, "Did you injure your legs in an accident?" I hate it when elderly people with canes and walkers stare at me. I feel more at ease when people care enough to stop and ask what my handicap is.

What embarrasses me most is when priests, nuns, or ministers stop and say a prayer or bless me. In a way it makes me feel warm inside, but it embarrasses me.

I have found since there have been more facilities for the handicapped, society is accepting us as normal individuals.

Pine Tree Camp (an Easter Seal facility in Maine) has been a part of my life for 5 years now. I go there for 8 weeks every summer. I find camp life most enjoyable. About 100 handicapped children and adults are able to enjoy the many activities there, such as swimming, nature hikes, arts, crafts, music, and drama. It gives each of us a chance to participate at his or her own level and to enjoy things that the walking would takes for granted.

Just recently, I was accepted at a business college. I am hoping this experience will broaden my knowledge in business education, and some day I would like to become an accountant.

So far I have talked about all the disadvantages of being handicapped; but it does have its advantages, too, such as not having to stand in lines, having people open doors for me, having people make way for me in crowded places, and being the first in a group to view exhibits.

Environmental barriers prevent many handicapped people from gaining access to places of employment, transportation systems, private homes, schools, restaurants, shopping centers, and even bathroom facilities. Some people say, "We cannot change the whole structure of society just for a few people." Such people are concerned with the expense of installing elevators, ramps, enlarging bathrooms in public places, and making curb cuts in sidewalks. They may claim, "It's their problem, so why should I do anything about it, and why should I pay for special services for them?"

The cost of altering environmental obstacles is not the only objection made. The nonhandicapped majority is upset or depressed by the sight of the handicapped in public restaurants and other public places. They are likely to nudge their wife or husband and shake their head with sorrowful eyes, while thinking or whispering under their breath, "That poor thing." Therefore, high curbs, stairs, narrow bathrooms (and bathrooms at the bottom of a set of stairs), revolving doors, and turnstiles serve not only to limit the freedom and mobility of handicapped persons but also to protect the public from seeing something *they* feel uncomfortable with.

When ramps or elevators are installed for the benefit of handicapped individuals, they are usually in such buildings as hospitals, clinics, and service institutions. For example, two years ago, on the University of Kansas campus, a new geologic center was built to honor a famous scientist, Dr. Moore. On the day that the building was to be dedicated, Dr. Moore, who happened to be in a wheelchair, had to use the service entrance to get into his own building. Why? Well, no one thought that a person in a wheelchair would ever need to use a university building. Even in hospitals there are often stairs in the business offices and research laboratories. Therefore, handicapped people can go to a hospital or a doctor, but they cannot be the secretaries or the scientists.

Ramps and curb cuts do not benefit only people in wheelchairs. After the University of Kansas installed curb cuts in the sidewalks and parking lots, the students and staff were asked why they thought the curb cuts were needed. Ninety percent of the students thought the curb cuts were built for the bicycle riders on campus. The delivery men thought curb cuts were there to help them move their paper towels and cases of pop bottles in and out of buildings. The people in charge of the physical plant thought they were built to help them move their gardening and snow removal equipment up and down the sidewalks. Thus, many groups benefited from the curb cuts.

Many handicapped children and adults feel frustrated and helpless in public places with the countless stairs and the endless stares. Many stay within their own homes to avoid the hassles. They may have accepted their handicap, but the point is that others have not. Handicapped individuals must not give in to the negative stereotypes and negative expectations of others. They must maintain positive self-esteem. They must demand entrance to public places because they are entitled to it. Many have the ability to work, to teach in a public school system, to enjoy movies and recreational facilities, and to do all the things that other people can do. The only problem is that people with handicaps are denied the right to participate in many activities because the environment does not allow them access.

When handicapped people do go into the outside world, they are often seen as totally helpless. The clerks in stores or waitresses in restaurants often ask the other person with me (the person pushing the wheelchair), "What would she like?" or "What is her size?" or "Would she like to order?" or "Can I help her?" Being in a wheelchair does *not* mean that I cannot speak for myself and that I should be treated like a child. Handicapped people rarely need interpreters; questions should be addressed directly to them.

I must emphasize that I am speaking not only for myself. Of the more than 220 million people in the United States, 30 million are disabled in one way or another. Many are unemployed, restricted from recreational activities, and confined to their homes. There has been some progress in services and attitudes toward the handicapped in recent years. Many medical and technologic discoveries have aided handicapped people, such as special typewriters, elaborate hearing equipment, automobiles driven by only manual controls, and electric wheelchairs. Also, recent legislation states that children with handicaps must be integrated into the public school system. There are efforts being made to hire the handicapped across the entire country. In addition, any public building being built with federal funds must include ramps or elevators so that wheelchairs can enter easily.

Nevertheless, much still needs to be done to educate the public in regard to the handicapped and to change their fearful attitudes. One way in which attitudes are being changed is through the Miss Wheelchair America Pageant. Beverly Chapman of Florida was chosen to be Miss Wheelchair America of 1977. She tours the entire country in a van with the help of others and makes speeches and public appearances to stimulate public interest and concern about the many everyday problems faced by users of wheelchairs. She attempts to help "close the gap" between the wheelchair world and the walking world. The Miss Wheelchair America Pageant has grown rapidly each year. Last year there were entrants from 30 states, and next year they hope to have representatives from every state in the country.

Interesting projects have been started to help other children understand handicapped children. Perhaps children can, in turn, teach their parents. A project in Massachusetts works with teachers, children, parents, nurses, and others to do away with the prejudices surrounding handicapped children. They encourage young children to talk openly about handicapped people they know and to invite people (both children and adults) with handicaps to visit their classroom, talk with them, and let them experiment with hearing aids, crutches, and wheelchairs. One little girl brought to class her infant brother, who had suffered birth injuries. She proudly described the attempts of her family to help him. As her classmates became aware of the amount of time she devoted to her brother, they became more understanding of why she was unable to play at times. The children who participated in frustrating experiments (e.g., going to the school bathroom in a wheelchair when the halls were crowded) became more sensitive to the difficulties of those with a handicap. The frustration of a blind person can be experienced by putting on a blindfold and then trying to eat a snack or drink water from a water fountain. Field trips to rehabilitation centers and special schools also can help to do away with negative stereotypes. The children involved in the program in Massachusetts became more curious, concerned, accepting, and comforting of others with handicaps. Most importantly, they learned that people with handicaps have feelings, likes, and dislikes similar to their own.

In conclusion, there are many ways in which attitudes of the public toward the handicapped can be changed and the negative attitudes that exist must be changed. Environmental obstacles also must be changed. Not only will the 30 million handicapped benefit from positive change but the nonhandicapped majority will benefit as well. In personal terms this can be expressed as follows: I am anxious to be able to go into stores, restaurants, movie houses, and bathrooms freely, and to do so without stares and condescending looks of others. Others will learn and benefit from my being able to do so, because I, Rose Marie MacElman, have much to offer.

BIBLIOGRAPHY

Cleary, M., Helping children understand the child with special needs. *Children* 12:6–10, July/August 1965.

Cohen, S., Integrating children with handicaps into early childhood educational programs. *Child Today* 4:15–17, January/February 1975.

Gentile, F., Getting unstuck. *Journal of Rehabilitation* 43:29–30, November/December 1977.

Harris, R., Harris, C., A new perspective on the psychological effects of environmental barriers. *Rehabilitation Literature* 38:75–78, March 1977.

Nelson, D., The ladies room: An experience in personal rehabilitation. *Journal of Rehabilitation* 43:15–16, September/October 1977.

Rehabilitation news. *Journal of Rehabilitation* 43:4–5, January/February/March/April 1977.

Literature for Parents and Professionals

Most professionals underestimate the level of a parent's understanding of their child's handicap. When first told about their child's condition, many parents are unable to assimilate information that, emotionally, they are not ready for. Written materials may be read and reread as acceptance grows and as the need to know more increases.

Professionals such as teachers, physicians, students, and others concerned with counseling parents will often gain more insight from literature expressly written for lay persons than from scientific texts.

Children and adolescents might find hope and motivation from reading "success" stories about and by handicapped persons. Therefore, a list of biographic literature is also included in this section.

Table 10-1. Health Education Literature for Parents of Handicapped Children

Title	Target*	Source†
ALLERGIES		
Allergic Diseases	P, D, O	Allergy Foundation of America
Allergy in Children	P, D, O	Allergy Foundation of America
Cosmetic Allergy	P, D, O	Allergy Foundation of America
Drug Allergy	P, D, O	Allergy Foundation of America
Food Allergy	P, D, O	Allergy Foundation of America
Hay Fever	P, D, O	Allergy Foundation of America
Hay Fever: The Facts	P, D, O	American Lung Association
Hay Fever Holiday	P, D, O	Abbott Laboratories
Insect Stings	P, D, O	Allergy Foundation of America
Mold Allergy	P, D, O	Allergy Foundation of America
Respiratory Problems and Related Allergies	P, D, O	Riker Laboratories
The Skin and Its Allergies	P, D, O	Allergy Foundation of America
What Do We Know About Allergies?	P, D, O	Public Affairs Pamphlets, No. 486
Allergies	P, D, O	American Medical Association
ASTHMA		
Asthma, Climate, and Weather	P, D, O	Allergy Foundation of America
Handbook for the Asthmatic	P, D, O	Allergy Foundation of America
El Asma-Como Sobrellevarla	P, D, O	Public Affairs Pamphlets, No. 437
Asthma: How to Live with It	P, D, O	Public Affairs Pamphlets, No. 437
Asthma: A Practical Guide for Physicians	D	American Lung Association
BIRTH DEFECTS		
Birth Defects: The Tragedy and Hope	P, D, O	National Foundation—March of Dimes
Birth Defects: Questions and Answers	P	National Foundation—March of Dimes
The Child with a Missing Arm or Leg	P	Children's Bureau Folders
The Child with Spina Bifida	P, D, O	Foundation for Child Development
Congenital Malformations	P	National Foundation—March of Dimes
Chromosome 21 and Its Association with Down's Syndrome	P	National Foundation—March of Dimes
Tay Sachs Disease and Birth Defects Prevention	P, D, O	National Foundation—March of Dimes
Are You His/Her Type?	P, D, O	National Foundation—March of Dimes
Rubella Robs the Cradle	P, C	National Foundation—March of Dimes

Title	Target*	Source†
Sarampion Aleman: Tragedia que Acecha La Cuna	P, C	National Foundation—March of Dimes
Spina Bifida—A Birth Defect: Hope Through Research	P, D, O	Superintendent of Documents, PHS No. 1023
CEREBRAL PALSY		
Cerebral Palsy: What You Should Know About It	P, D, O	United Cerebral Palsy Associations, Inc.
Cerebral Palsy: Hope Through Research	P	Superintendent of Documents, PHS No. 713
What is Cerebral Palsy?	P	United Cerebral Palsy Associations, Inc.
Cerebral Palsy: More Hope Than Ever	P, D, O	Public Affairs Pamphlets, No. 401
Spastic Cerebral Palsy	P, D, O	The Spastics Society
The Early Years	P, D, O	The Spastics Society
The Basic Motor Pattern	P, O	The Spastics Society
CLEFT PALATE AND LIP		
Research Explores Cleft Palate	P, D, O	Superintendent of Documents, PHS No. 1487
The Road to Normalcy	P, D, O	Mead Johnson Laboratories
Your Cleft Lip and Palate Child	P, D, O	Mead Johnson Laboratories
Steps in Habilitation	D, O	Mead Johnson Laboratories
Bright Promise	P, D, O	National Easter Seal Society for Crippled Children and Adults
CONGENITAL HEART DISEASE		
If Your Child Has a Congenital Heart Defect	P, D	American Heart Association
COOLEY'S ANEMIA		
Cooley's Anemia and Birth Defects Prevention	P, D, O	National Foundation—March of Dimes
CYSTIC FIBROSIS		
Your Child and Cystic Fibrosis	P	National Cystic Fibrosis Research Foundation
Questions and Facts about Cystic Fibrosis	P, D, O	National Cystic Fibrosis Research Foundation
A C/F Child is in Your Class (Teacher's Guide)	O	National Cystic Fibrosis Research Foundation
Living with Cystic Fibrosis: A Guide for the Young Adult	P, C	National Cystic Fibrosis Research Foundation
Directory of Cystic Fibrosis Care, Teaching, and Research Centers	P, D, O	National Cystic Fibrosis Research Foundation
DIABETES		
An Instructional Aid on Juvenile Diabetes	P, C, D, O	Pediatrics Department, University of Texas

Table 10-1. (continued)

Title	Target*	Source†
DIABETES (continued)		
Care of the Child with Diabetes	P, D, O	Ames Company, Division of Miles Laboratories, Inc.
Diabetes Teaching Manual	D, O	State University of New York, Upstate Medical Center
What is Diabetes?	P, D, O	Eli Lilly and Co.
Keith and Tommy Climb to a New Life	C	Eli Lilly and Co.
EPILEPSY		
Epilepsy: Hope Through Research	P, D, O	Superintendent of Documents, PHS No. 05-938
The Child with Epilepsy	P	Children's Bureau Folder, No. 35
Epilepsy: Today's Encouraging Outlook	P, D, O	Public Affairs Pamphlets, No. 387
Answers to Most Frequent Questions People Ask about Epilepsy	P, D, O	Epilepsy Foundation of America
Because You Are My Friend	C	Epilepsy Foundation of America
Epilepsy School Alert	O	Epilepsy Foundation of America
Medical and Social Management of the Epilepsies	P, D, O	Epilepsy Foundation of America
Pharmacopoeia of the Epilepsies	D	Epilepsy Foundation of America
Recognition and First Aid for Those with Epilepsy	O	Epilepsy Foundation of America
HANDICAPS—GENERAL		
A Handicapped Child in Your Home	P, D, O	Children's Bureau Folder, No. 73-29, Superintendent of Documents
Helping the Handicapped Teenager Mature	P, D, O, C	Public Affairs Pamphlets, No. 504
Handy Helpful Hints for the Handicapped	P	National Easter Seal Society for Crippled Children and Adults
Caring for Your Disabled Child	P	Collier-MacMillan Paperback Division
Helping the Crippled Child Reach Attainable Occupational Goals	P, O	National Easter Seal Society for Crippled Children and Adults
HEARING		
Helping the Child Who Cannot Hear	P, D, O	Public Affairs Pamphlets, No. 479
Language and Education of the Deaf	P, C, D	National Association for the Deaf
Training Opportunities: A Guideline for Professionals, Deaf Persons, and Parents	P, C, D, O	National Association for the Deaf

Title	Target*	Source†
JUVENILE RHEUMATOID ARTHRITIS		
Arthritis in Children	P, D, O	The Arthritis Foundation
Home Treatment Program for Children with Rheumatoid Arthritis	P, D, O	Texas Children's Hospital
The Truth about Aspirin for Arthritis	P, C, D, O	The Arthritis Foundation
When Your Child Has Rheumatoid Arthritis	P, C, D, O	National Foundation—March of Dimes
KIDNEY DISEASE		
Kidney Disease	P, C	Superintendent of Documents, PHS No. 1307
MUSCULAR DYSTROPHY		
A Guide to Parents	P	Muscular Dystrophy Group of Great Britain
Muscular Dystrophy Fact Sheet	P, D, O	Muscular Dystrophy Associations of America, Inc.
Muscular Dystrophy: Hope Through Research	P, D, O	Superintendent of Documents, PHS No. 06-996
The Inheritance of Muscular Dystrophy	P, C, D, O	Muscular Dystrophy Group of Great Britain
These Are the Facts	P, C, D, O	Muscular Dystrophy Group of Great Britain
NEUROLOGY		
Suggestions for Parents	P, C, D, O	Lovelace-Bataan Medical Center
OSTOMY		
All about Jimmy (Coloring Book)	C	United Ostomy Association
My Child Has an Ostomy	P, O	United Ostomy Association
SICKLE CELL ANEMIA		
Answers to Common Questions about Sickle Cell Disease	P, D, O	Superintendent of Documents, PHS No. 73-364
Fast Facts about Sickle Cell Anemia	P, C, D, O	National Foundation—March of Dimes
Sickle Cell Anemia: A Medical Review	D, O	Superintendent of Documents, PHS No. 72-5111
Sickle Cell Anemia: What It Is, What Can Be Done	D, O	Superintendent of Documents, PHS No. 72-5108
Where's Herbie? A Sickle Cell Coloring Book	C	Superintendent of Documents, PHS No. 21-102:H41
SPEECH		
Helping Your Child Speak Correctly	P, D, O	Public Affairs Pamphlets, No. 445
The Child with a Speech Problem	P, D	Children's Bureau Folder, No. 52, Superintendent of Documents

Table 10-1. (continued)

Title	Target*	Source†
VISION		
How Does a Blind Person Get Around?	P, D, O	American Foundation for the Blind
Living with Blindness	P, D, O	Public Affairs Pamphlets, No. 473
Parents' Guide to Children's Vision	P, O	Public Affairs Pamphlets, No. 339
Storytelling and the Blind Child	P, O	American Foundation for the Blind
The Preschool Child Who is Blind	P	Children's Bureau Folder, No. 39, Superintendent of Documents
The Preschool Deaf, Blind Child	P	American Foundation for the Blind
What Can We Do about Limited Vision?	P, D, O	Public Affairs Pamphlets, No. 491
Who Is the Visually Handicapped Child?	D, O	American Foundation for the Blind

Reproduced from Van Vechten, D. V., Satterwhile, M. A., and Pless, B., Health education literature for parents of physically handicapped children, *American Journal of Diseases of Children* 131: 311–315, 1977. With permission. © 1977 by the American Medical Association.
*P indicates parents; C, children; D, doctors; and O, other professionals.
†Complete addresses are provided in the list of additional references.

Table 10-2. Addresses for Literature Cited in Table 10-1.

Abbott Laboratories
14th St. and Sheridan Rd.
North Chicago, IL 60064

Allergy Foundation of America
801 Second Ave.
New York, NY 10017

American Foundation for the Blind
15 W. 16th St.
New York, NY 10010

American Heart Association
44 E. 23rd St.
New York, NY 10010

American Lung Association
1740 Broadway
New York, NY 10019

American Medical Association
535 N. Dearborn St.
Chicago, IL 60610

Ames Co.
Division of Miles Laboratories, Inc.
Elkhart, IN 46514

Arthritis Foundation
1212 Avenue of the Americas
New York, NY 10036

Children's Bureau Folders
Superintendent of Documents
US Government Printing Office
Washington, DC 20402

Collier-MacMillan Paperback Division
Collier Books
866 Third Avenue
New York, NY 10022

Eli Lilly & Co.
Indianapolis, IN 46206

Epilepsy Foundation of America
1828 L St. N.W.
Washington, DC 20036

Foundation for Child Development
345 E. 46th St.
New York, NY 10017

Lovelace-Bataan Medical Center
5200–5400 Gibson Blvd. S.E.
Albuquerque, NM 87108

McGraw-Hill Book Co.
1221 Avenue of the Americas
New York, NY 10020

Mead Johnson & Co.
Evansville, IN 47721

Muscular Dystrophy Associations of America, Inc.
1790 Broadway
New York, NY 10019

Muscular Dystrophy Group of Great Britain
26 Borough High St.
London SE1 9QG England

National Association of the Deaf
905 Bonifant St.
Silver Springs, MD 29010

National Cystic Fibrosis Research Foundation
3379 Peachtree Rd. N.E.
Atlanta, GA 30326

National Easter Seal Society for Crippled Children and Adults
2023 W. Ogden Ave.
Chicago, IL 60612

The National Foundation—March of Dimes
Box 2000
White Plains, NY 10602

Pediatrics Department
University of Texas Medical Branch
Galveston, TX 77550

Public Affairs Pamphlets
381 Park Ave. S.
New York, NY 10016

Riker Laboratories
19901 Nordhoff St.
Northridge, CA 91314

The Spastics Society
12 Park Crescent
London W1 N4 EQ England

State University of New York
Upstate Medical Center
Syracuse, NY

Superintendent of Documents
US Government Printing Office
Washington, DC 20402

Texas Children's Hospital
Texas Medical Center
Houston, TX

United Cerebral Palsy Association, Inc.
66 E. 34th St.
New York, NY 10016

United Ostomy Association, Inc.
1111 Wilshire Blvd.
Los Angeles, CA 90017

MAGAZINE SUBSCRIPTIONS

Accent on Living, Inc.
PO Box 726
Gillum Rd. and High Dr.
Bloomington, IL 61701

The Exceptional Parent
PO Box 964
Manchester, NH 03105

Reprinted from Van Vechten, P. V., Satterwhite, M. A., and Pless, B., Health education literature for parents of physically handicapped children, *American Journal of Diseases of Children* 131:311–315, 1977. With permission. © 1977 by the American Medical Association.

Table 10-3. Literature on Counseling, Communication, and Parents

Ashley, J., *Journey Into Silence*. London, Bradley Head, 1973.
Ayrault, E. W., *Helping the Handicapped Teenage Mature*. New York, Association Press, 1971.
Bruhn, J., Hampton, J., and Chandler R., Clinical marginality and psychological adjustment in hemophilia. *Journal Psychosomatic Research,* 15:207–213, 1971.
Charney, E., Patient–doctor communication: Implications for the clinician. *Pediatrics* 54:779–785, 1972.
Featherstone, H., *A difference in the Family: Life with a Disabled Child*. New York, Basic Books, 1980.

Table 10-3. (continued)

Francis, V., Korsch, B., and Morris, M., Gaps in the doctor–patient relationship. *New England Journal of Medicine* 280:535–540, 1969.

Garson, A. J., Williams, R. Jr., and Reckless, J., Long-term follow-up of patients with tetralogy of Fallot: Physical health and psychopathology. *Journal of Pediatrics* 85:429–433, 1974.

Gordon, S., *Living Fully: A Guide for Young People with a Handicap, Their Parents, Their Teachers, and Professionals.* New York, John Day Company, 1975.

Hofmann, R., *How to Build Special Furniture and Equipment for Handicapped Children.* Springfield, Ill. Charles C. Thomas, 1974

Kanthor, H., Pless, I. B., Satterwhite, B., et al., Areas of responsibility in the health care of multiply handicapped children. *Pediatrics* 54:779–785, 1974.

Lagos, J. C., *Seizures, Epilepsy, and Your Child: A Handbook for Parents, Teachers, and Epileptics of All Ages.* New York, Harper and Row, 1974.

McAnarney, E., Pless, I. B., Satterwhite, B., et al., Psychological problems of children with chronic juvenile arthritis. *Pediatrics* 53:523–528, 1974.

Massie, R., and Massie, S., *Journey.* New York, Alfred A. Knopf, 1975.

Mattar, M., Markello, J., and Yaffe, S., *Pharmaceutic factors affecting pediatric compliance. Pediatrics* 55:101–108, 1975.

Pless, I. B., and Satterwhite, B., Chronic illness in childhood: Selection, activities, and evaluation of non-professional family counselors. *Clinical Pediatrics,* 2:403–410, 1972.

Pless, I. B., and Satterwhite, B., The family counselor, in Haggerty, R. J., Roghmann, K., and Pless, I. B. (eds.): *Child Health and the Community.* New York, John Wiley, 1975.

Pless, I. B., and Pinkerton, P., *Chronic Childhood Disorder: Promoting Patterns of Adjustment.* London, Henry Kimpton, 1975.

Plummer, B., *Give Every Day a Chance.* New York, Putnam, 1970.

Schoonover, M., *Letters to Polly.* Grand Rapids, Mich., W. B. Erdmans, 1971.

Splaver, S., *Your Handicap: Don't Let It Handicap You.* New York, Julian Messner, 1974.

Stein, S. B., *About Handicaps: An Open Family Book for Parents and Children Together.* New York, Walker, 1974.

Steinhauer, P., Mushin, D., and Rae-Grant, Q., Psychological aspects of chronic illness: Symposium on chronic disease in children. *Pediatric Clinics of North America* 21:825–840, 1974.

Tagliacozzo, E. M., and Kenju, I., Knowledge of illness as a predictor of patient behavior. *Journal of Chronic Disease* 22:765–775, 1970.

Weiner, F., *Help for the Handicapped Child.* New York, McGraw-Hill, 1973.

Wentworth, E., *Listen to Your Heart: A Message to Parents of Handicapped Children.* Boston, Houghton Mifflin, 1974.

West, P., *Words for a Deaf Daughter.* New York, Harper and Row, 1970.

Williams, T. F., Martin D., Hogan, M., et al., The clinical picture of diabetic control studied in four settings. *American Journal Public Health* 57:441–451, 1967.

Wilson, D., *Hilary: The Brave World of Hilary Poe.* New York, McGraw-Hill, 1971.

Wolf., B., *Don't Feel Sorry for Paul.* Philadelphia, Lippincott, 1974.

Reprinted, with additions, from References in Van Vechten, D., Satterwhite, M. A., and Pless, B., Health education literature for parents of physically handicapped children. *American Journal of Diseases of Children* 131:311–315, 1977. With permission. © 1977 by the American Medical Association.

Literature for Parents and Professionals

Table 10-4. Biographical Literature

BLINDNESS

Chevigny, H., *My Eyes Have a Cold Nose*. New Haven, Conn., Yale University Press, 1946.
Criddle, R., *Love Is Not Blind*. New York, W. W. Norton & Company, 1953.
Fraser, I., *Whereas I Was Blind*. London, Hodder, 1942.
Keller, H., *Story of My Life*. Garden City, N.Y., Doubleday, 1954.
Ohrstad, K., *The World at My Finger Tips*. Indianapolis, Bobbs-Merrill Company, 1942.
Russell, R., *To Catch an Angel*. New York, Vanguard Press, 1962.

CEREBRAL PALSY

Carlson, R., *Born That Way*. New York, John Day, 1941.
Killilea, M., *Karen*. Englewood Cliffs, N.J., Prentice-Hall, 1952.

DEAFNESS

Greenberg, J., *In This Sign*. New York, Avon, 1978.
Warfield, F., *Cotton in My Ears*. New York, Viking Press, 1948.

MENTAL RETARDATION

Buck, P. S., *The Child Who Never Grew*. New York, John Day, 1950.
Junker, K. S., *The Child in the Glass Ball*. Nashville, Abingdon Press, 1954.
Nichols, P., *Joe Egg*. New York, Grove Press, Inc., 1968.
Seagoe, M. V., *Yesterday was Tuesday. All Day and All Night*. Boston, Little, Brown, 1964.

MISCELLANEOUS

Henrich, E., and Kriegel, L., *Experiments in Survival*. New York, Association for the Aid of Crippled Children, 1961.
Hunt, P., *Stigma: The Experience of Disability*. London, Geoffrey Chapman, 1966.
Lukens, K., and Panter, C., *Thursday's Child Has Far To Go*. Englewood Cliffs, N.J., Prentice-Hall, 1969.

PHYSICAL HANDICAPS (ORTHOPEDIC)

Baker, L., *Out on a Limb*. New York, McGraw-Hill, 1946.
Barton, B., *And Now to Live Again*. New York, Appleton-Century-Crofts, 1944.
Brickhill, P., *Reach for the Sky*. W. W. Norton & Company, 1954.
Brown, A. A., *The Log of a Lame Duck*. New York, Macmillan, 1939.
Brown, C., *My Left Foot*. New York, Simon & Schuster, 1955.
Burgess, P., *Who Walk Alone*. New York, Holt, Rinehart & Winston, 1940.
Goldman, R. D., *Even the Night*. New York, Macmillan, 1947.
Hathaway, K. B., *The Little Locksmith*. New York, Coward-McCann, 1943.
Hoopes, G., *Out of the Running*. Springfield, Ill., Charles C. Thomas, 1939.
Lawrence, M., *Interrupted Melody*. New York, Appleton-Century-Crofts, 1949.
Lindsey, M., *Courage!* New York, E. P. Dutton, 1938.
Linduska, N., *My Polio Past*. Chicago, Pellegrini & Cudahy, 1947.
Martin, B., *Miracle at Carville*. Garden City, N.Y., Doubleday, 1950.
Murray, J. M., (ed.), *Katherine Mansfield's Letters to John Middleton Murray*. New York, A. Knopf, 1951.
Russel, H., and Rosen, V., *Victory in My Hands*. New York, Creative Age Press, 1949.
Viscardi, H., Jr., *A Man's Stature*. New York, John Day, 1952.

Reprinted from Pless, I. B., and Satterwhite, B., Health education literature for parents of handicapped Children. *American Journal of Diseases of Children*, 122:206–211, 1971. With permission. © 1971 by the American Medical Association.

Table 10-5. Books for Parents and Professionals

CEREBRAL PALSY

Finnie, N., *Handling the Young Cerebral Palsied Child at Home*. E. P. Dutton—Sunrise, 201 Park Ave., S., New York, NY 10003. Revised Edition, Pub. 1975.

Joel, G. S., *So Your Child Has Cerebral Palsy*. University of New Mexico Press, Albuquerque, NM 87108. Pub. 1975.

CHILD DEVELOPMENT

Accardo, P. J., and Capute, A. J., *The Pediatrician and the Developmentally Delayed Child*. University Park Press, 233 E. Redwood St., Baltimore, MD 21202. Pub. 1979.

Brazelton, T. B., *Infants and Mothers–Differences in Development*. Dell Publishers, 1 Dag Hammarskjold Plaza, 245 E. 47th St., New York, NY 10017. Pub. 1972.

Brazelton, T. B., *Toddlers and Parents—A Declaration of Independence*. Delacorte Press, 1 Dag Hammarskjold Plaza, 245 E. 47th St., New York, NY 10017. Pub. 1976.

Caplan, F. (ed.), *First Twelve Months of Life*. Bantam Books, 414 E. Golf Rd., Des Plaines, IL 60016. Pub. 1978.

Gasell, A., *The First Five Years of Life*. Harper & Row, Keystone Industrial Park, Scranton, PA 18512. Pub. 1940.

Holt, K. S., *Developmental Paediatrics*. Butterworth Publishers, Inc., 19 Cummings Park, Woburn, MA 01801. Pub. 1977.

Illingworth, R. S., *Development of the Infant and Young Child*. Longman, Inc., Churchill-Livingston Medical Division, 19 W. 44th St., New York, NY 10036. 7th Edition, Pub. 1980.

Knobloch, H., and Pasamanick, B. (eds.), *Gessell & Amatruda's Developmental Diagnosis*. Harper & Row, Medical Department, Keystone Industrial Park, Scranton, PA 18512. 3rd Edition, Pub. 1974.

Siffert, R. S., *How Your Child's Body Grows*. Grosset and Dunlap, Inc., 51 Madison Ave., New York, NY 10010. Pub. 1980.

CLEFT PALATE

Team Management for Cleft Lip and Cleft Palate Patient. H. K. Cooper Institute for Oral-Facial Anomalies and Communication Disorders, 24 N. Line St., Lancaster, PA 17602. Pub. 1974. (Blue book for parents; tan book for professionals.)

CONVULSIONS

Baird, H. W., *The Child with Convulsions–A Guide for Parents, Teachers, Counselors, and Medical Personnel*. Grune & Stratton, Inc., 111 Fifth Ave., New York, NY 10003. Pub. 1972.

DIABETES

Kipnis, L., and Adler, S., *You Can't Catch Diabetes From a Friend*. Triad, Scientific Publishers, Gainesville, FL. Pub. 1979.

EDUCATION

Hobbs, N., *The Futures of Children*. Jossey-Bass, 615 Montgomery St., San Francisco, CA 94111. Pub. 1974.

Kephart, N., *Slow Learner in the Classroom*. Charles Merrill, 1300 Alum Creek Dr., Columbus, OH 43216. 2nd Edition, Pub. 1971.

Levy, H. B., *Square Pegs, Round Holes (The Learning Disabled Child in the Classroom and at Home)*. Little, Brown & Co., 34 Beacon St., Boston, MA 02108. Pub. 1973.

ETHICS

Swinyard, Chester A., *Decision Making and the Defective Newborn*. Charles C. Thomas, 301–327 E. Lawrence Ave., Springfield, IL 62717. Pub. 1978.

Literature for Parents and Professionals

GENERAL—SOCIAL OVERVIEW

Gliedman, J., Ruth W., *The Unexpected Minority: Handicapped Children in America* (The Carnegie Council on Children). Harcourt Brace Jovanovich Inc., 757 Third Ave., New York, NY 10017. Pub. 1980.

MENTAL RETARDATION

Smith, R. M., *An Introduction to Mental Retardation*. McGraw-Hill Book Co., 330 W. 42nd St., New York, NY 10036. Pub. 1971.

PARENTING

Austin, G., *The Light Touch to Eating, Sleeping, and Toilet Training* (Brochure). ECR Collection, PO Box 615, Los Altos, CA 94022. Pub. 1980.

Austin, G., *The Parent's Guide to Child Raising*. ECR Collection, PO Box 615, Los Altos, CA 94022. Pub. 1980.

Austin, G., *The Parent's Medical Manual*. ECR Collection, PO Box 615, Los Altos, CA 94022. Pub. 1980.

Kenihan, K., *How to be Parents of a Handicapped Child—And Survive*. Penguin Books, 625 Madison Ave., New York, NY 10022. Pub. 1981.

Markel, G., and Greenbaum, J., *Parents Are to be Seen and Heard*. Impact Publishers, PO Box 1094, San Luis Obispo, CA 93406. Pub. 1979.

Markun, P. M. (ed.), *Parenting*. The Association for Childhood Education international, 3615 Wisconsin Ave. N.W., Washington, DC 20016. Pub. 1973

Turnbull, A., and Rutherford, H., III, *Parents Speak Out–A View from the Other Side of the Two-Way Mirror*. Charles E. Merrill Publishing Co., Columbus, OH 43216. Pub. 1978.

PRADER-WILLI SYNDROME

Neason, S. A., *Prader-Willi Syndrome: A Handbook for Parents*. Prader-Willi Syndrome Association, 5515 Malibu Drive, Edina, MN 55436. Pub. 1978.

PREGNANCY AND BIRTH DEFECTS

Apgar, V., and Beck, J., *Is My Baby All Right?*. Trident Press, 1230 6th Ave., New York, NY. Pub. 1972.

RECREATION AND PHYSICAL EDUCATION

The following books can be ordered from AAHPER Publications, 1201 18th St., N.W., Washington, DC 20036.

Physical Activities for Impaired, Disabled and Handicapped Individuals, 1976.

Dance for Physically Disabled Persons: A Manual for Teaching Ballroom, Square, and Folk Dances to Users of Wheelchairs and Crutches. 1976.

Involving Impaired, Disabled, and Handicapped Persons in Regular Camp Programs, 1976.

Challenging Opportunities for Special Populations in Aquatic, Outdoor, and Winter Activities, 1976.

Aquatic Recreation for the Blind, 1976.

Special Fitness Test Manual for Mildly Mentally Retarded Persons, 1976.

Adapted Physical Education Guidelines: Theory and Practices for 70s and 80s, 1976.

Physical Education and Recreation for Cerebral Palsied Individuals, 1976.

Physical Education, Recreation, and Sports for Individuals with Hearing Impairments, 1976.

Physical Education, Recreation, and Related Programs for Autistic and Emotionally Disturbed Children, 1976.

Early Intervention for Handicapped Children Through Programs of Physical Education and Recreation, 1976.

Annotated Listing of Films: Physical Education and Recreation for Impaired, Disabled, and Handicapped Persons, 1976.

Values of Physical Education, Recreation, and Sports for All, 1976.

Dance Therapy. Focus on Dance VII, 1974.

Table 10-5. (continued)

RECREATION AND PHYSICAL EDUCATION (continued)

Integrating Persons with Handicapping Conditions into Regular Physical Education and Recreation Programs, 1975.
Materials on Creative Arts for Persons with Handicapping Conditions, 1975.
Physical Education and Recreation for Impaired, Disabled, and Handicapped Individuals: Past, Present, Future, 1975.
Physical Education and Recreation for Individuals with Multiple Handicapping Conditions, 1975.
Physical Education and Recreation for the Visually Handicapped, 1973.
Practical Guide for Teaching the Mentally Retarded to Swim, 1969.
Programming for the Mentally Retarded in Physical Education and Recreation, 1968.
Recreation and Physical Activity for the Mentally Retarded, 1966.
Resource Guide in Sex Education for the Mentally Retarded, 1971.
Special Olympics Instructional Manual–From Beginners to Champions, 1972.
Testing for Impaired, Disabled, and Handicapped Individuals, 1975.

REHABILITATION

Downey, J., *The Child with Disabling Illness: Principles of Rehabilitation.* W. B. Saunders, W. Washington Square, Philadelphia, PA 19105. Pub. 1974.

SPINA BIFIDA

Swinyard, C. A., *The Child with Spina Bifida.* Information Series, Spina Bifida Association of America, 343 S. Dearborn St., Chicago, IL 60604. Pub. 1977.

Community, State, National, and International Resources for Recreation and Leisure*

Table 10-6. Local, State, National and International Organizations

The organizations listed herein offer a variety of services to individuals with physically handicapping conditions: for example, sports, architectural accessibility, travel, consumer advocacy, horseback riding, and governmental assistance. These are local, state, national, and international organizations, and they are listed alphabetically.

Adapted Sports Association, Inc.
6832 Marlette Rd.
Marlette, MI 48453

American Alliance for Health,
  Physical Education, and
  Recreation
1201 16th St., N.W.
Washington, DC 20036

American Coalition of Citizens with
  Disabilities
Room 308
1346 Connecticut Ave. N.W.
Washington, DC 20036

American Institute of Architects
1735 New York Ave. N.W.
Washington, DC 20006

American Special Recreation
  Association
c/o John Nesbitt, Ed.D.
Recreation Education Program
University of Iowa
Iowa City, IA 52240

American Wheelchair Bowling
  Association
2424 N. Federal Highway, #109
Boynton Beach, FL 33435

Architectural and Transportation
  Barriers Compliance Board
330 C Street, S.W.
Washington, DC 20201

Arts, Inc.
850 Third Ave.
New York, NY 10022

Association of Handicapped Artists
1134 Rand Building
Buffalo, NY 14203

Association of Mouth and Foot
  Painting Artists, Worldwide
Fl. 9490 Vaduz
Kasperigasse 7 Switzerland

Avenues: A National Group for
  Arthrogryposis Multiplex
  Congenita
5430 East Harbor Heights Dr.
Port Orchard, WA 98366

Berkeley Outreach Recreation
  Program
2020 Milvia St., Suite 460A
Berkeley, CA 94704

Boy Scouts of America
Scouting for the Handicapped
  Division
PO Box 16030, Dallas–Ft. Worth
  Airport
Dallas, TX 75261

Bureau of Education for the
  Handicapped
Recreation Division
400 Maryland Ave., S.W.
Washington, DC 20202

California Association for Health,
  Physical Education, and
  Recreation
401 S. Hartz Ave., Suite 306
Danville, CA 94526

*Reprinted, with minor changes, from Christiason, M. A., *Directory of Recreation and Leisure Services for the Physically Handicapped Within the Greater Los Angeles Area*. With permission. Original version available from the author at 11066 Gonsalves Place, Cerritos, CA 90701. © 1979 by the author.

Table 10-6. (continued)

California Association of the
 Physically Handicapped
PO Box 22552
Sacramento, CA 95822

California League of Cities—
 Recreation Committee
c/o 1108 O St.
Sacramento, CA 95814

California Parks and Recreation
 Society
1400 K St., Suite 302
Sacramento, CA 95814

California State Department of
 Architects
1500 Fifth St.
Sacramento, CA 95814

California State Department of
 Parks and Recreation
PO Box 2390
Sacramento, CA 95811

California State Department of
 Rehabilitation
830 K St. Mall
Sacramento, CA 95814
Attn: Mobility Barriers Section

California Wheelchair Athletic
 Association
260 Montecillo Dr.
Walnut Creek, CA 94595

Committee for the Promotion of
 Camping for the Handicapped
2056 South Bluff Rd.
Traverse City, MI 59684

Community Access Network—
 Mobility Barriers
c/o Department of Rehabilitation
830 K St. Mall
Sacramento, CA 95814

Creative Growth
c/o Mr. and Mrs. Elias Katz
2505 Broadway
Oakland, CA 94012

Do-It-Leisure Cooperative
621½ Mangrove
Chico, CA 95926

Educational Facilities Laboratories
850 Third Ave.
New York, NY 10022

Environmental Therapeutic
 Systems, Inc.
PO Box 6421
Vero Beach, FL 32960

Environmental Traveling
 Companions
PO Box 131
Vallecito, CA 95251

Gametime
900 Anderson Road
Litchfield, 49252
Attn: Therapeutic Consultant

Girl Scouts of the USA
Scouting for Handicapped Girls
 Program
830 Third Ave.
New York, NY 10022

Handicapped Artists of America,
 Inc.
8 Sandy Ln.
Salisbury, MA 01950

Handicap Horizons
3250 E. Loretta Dr.
Indianapolis, IN 46227
Handicapped Flyers International
Mr. Bill Blackwood
1171 Rising Hill
Escondido, CA 92025

Handicapped Travel
PO Box 1123
Pacific Palisades, CA 90272

Handicapped Travel Club
3319 Avalon St. Space 42
Riverside, CA 92509

Handicapped Travlers Association
1291 E. Hillsdale Blvd.
Forster City, CA 94404

Heritage Conservation and
 Recreation Service
1951 Constitution Ave. N.W.
Washington, DC 20240

Indoor Sports Club
A National Club for the Physically
 Disabled
1145 Highland St.
Napoleon, OH 43535

International Handicapped Network
PO Box B
San Gabriel, CA 91778

Mainstream
1200 15th St. NW
Washington, DC 20055

Resources for Recreation and Leisure

Mainstreaming Handicapped
 Children and Youth in
 Community Settings
Attn: Recreation and Park
 Administration
604 Clark Hall
University of Missouri
Columbia, MO 65211

Minnesota Outward Bound School
 Program for the Disabled
308 Walker Ave.
South Wayzata, MN 55291

Mobility International USA
c/o John Sullivan
Friendship Facilities Rt. 4
1718 W 2525 Rd.
Ottawa, IL 61350

Momentum Talent Management
228 E. 89th St.
New York, NY 10026

Ms. Wheelchair California
PO Box 74605
Hollywood, CA 90004

Muscular Dystrophy Association of
 America, Inc.
810 Seventh St.
New York, NY 10019

National Amputation Foundation
 (Golfing)
12–45 150th St.
White Stone, NY 11357

National Amputee Golf Association
24 Lakeview Terr.
Watchung, NJ 07060

National Amputee Skiing
 Association
3738 Walnut Ave.
Carmichael, CA 95608

National Archery Association
2833 Lincoln Highway E
Ronks, PA 17472

National Arts and the Handicapped
 Informaion Services
Box 2040, Grand Central Station
New York, NY 10017

National Association of the
 Physically Handicapped, Inc.
76 Elm St.
London, OH 43140

National Association of Sports for
 Cerebral Palsy
c/o United Cerebral Palsy
 Association of Connecticut
One State St.
New Haven, 06511

National Center for a Barrier Free
 Environment
1140 Connecticut Ave. N.W., Suite
 1006
Washington, DC 20036

National Center for Law and the
 Handicapped
1236 N Gody St.
South Bend, IN 40017

National Cerebral Palsy Games
c/o Ray Clark, Chairman
Detroit Recreation Department
1710 Water Board Building
735 Randolph St.
Detroit, MI 98226

National Committee, Arts for the
 Handicapped
1701 K St. N.W., Suite 801
Washington, DC 20006

National Consortium on Physical
 Education and Recreation for the
 Handicapped
1201 16th St. N.W., Suite 610E
Washington, DC 20036

National Council for Therapy and
 Rehabilitation Through
 Horticulture
Mount Vernon, VA 22121

National Endowment for the Arts
2401 E St. N.W.
Washington, DC 20506

National Easter Seal Society for
 Crippled Children and Adults
2023 W. Ogden Ave.
Chicago, IL 60612

National Handicapped Sports and
 Recreation Association
c/o Fred Nichol, President
Penn Mutual Building, 3rd Floor
4105 E. Florida Ave.
Denver, CO 80222

National Information Center for the
 Handicapped
1201 16th St. S.W.
Washington, DC 20036

Table 10-6. (continued)

National Institute on New Models For Community Recreation and Leisure for Handicapped Children and Youth
Dr. John Nesbitt
Recreation Education Program
University of Iowa
Iowa City, IA 52240

National Institute on Special Recreation
c/o 362 Koser Ave.
Iowa City, IA 52240

National Paraplegia Foundation
369 Elliot St.
Newton Upper Falls, MA 02164

National Paraplegia Foundation
Southern California Chapter
PO Box 65885
Los Angeles, CA 90065

National Park Service
United States Department of Interior
1100 L St. N.W.
Washington, DC 20240

National Rehabilitation Information Center
308 Mullen Library
Catholic University of America
Washington, DC 20004

National Therapeutic Recreation Society (A Branch of the National Recreation and Park Association)
1601 N. Kent St.
Arlington, Va. 22209

National Wheelchair Athletic Association
40-24 62nd St.
Woodside, NY 11377

National Wheelchair Basketball Association
c/o Office of Commissioner
110 Seaton Building
University of Kentucky
Lexington, KY 40506

National Wheelchair Marathon Committee
369 Elliot St.
Newton Upper Falls, MA 02164
Attn: Bruce Marquis

National Wheelchair Softball Association
PO Box 737
Sioux Falls, SD 51101

North American Recreation
PO Box 758
Bridgeport, CT 06601

North American Riding for the Handicapped Association
Route 1
Medland, GA 31820

Paralyzed Veterans of America
4330 E. West Highway, Suite 300
Washington, DC 20014

People-to-People Program
Committee for the Handicapped
LaSalle Building, Suite 610
Connecticut Ave. and L St.
Washington, DC 20036

Playground Corporation of America
29-16 40th Ave.
Long Island City, NY 11101

Play School Associates, Inc.
111 E 59th St., 13th Floor
New York, NY 10022

President's Committee on Recreation and Leisure
Washington, DC 20210

President's Committee on Employment of the Handicapped
Washington, DC 20210

Progressive Architecture Barrier Free Buildings Workshop
PO Box 643
Menominee Falls, WI 53051

Project Aquatic Mainstreaming
PO Box 698
Longview, WA 98632
Attn: Grace Reynolds

Rancho Kumbya—Recreation Ranch for the Handicapped
c/o Highway 58
Oreston, CA 93432

Recreation Center for the Handicapped
207 Skyline Boulevard
San Francisco, CA 94132

Rehabilitation International— Information Service
c/o Stiftung Rehabilitation
69000 Heidelberg 1
PO Box 101
409, Federal Republic of Germany

Resources for Recreation and Leisure

San Jose Parks and Recreation Department
155 W Mission St.
San Jose, CA 95110
Attn: Therapeutic Recreation Section

Self-Improvement Through Riding Education
c/o Hamburg Cove
Lyme, CT 06371

Ski for Light
c/o 2305 White Tail Ct.
Reston, VA 22091

Society for the Advancement of Travel for the Handicapped
3600 Wilshire Blvd., Suite 1230
Los Angeles, CA 90010

Southern California Wheelchair Aviators
Mr. Harry Eckelberger
135 Montecito
Shell Beach, CA 93449

Target Access
Department of Recreation and Leisure
San Jose State University
San Jose, CA 95192

Theraplan, Inc.
PO Box 1244
Manhattan, KS 66502

Theraplay Products
2924 40th Ave.
Long Island City, NY 11101

United Cerebral Palsy Association, Inc.
66 E 34th St.
New York, Ny 10016

United States Department of Agriculture
Division of Recreation
United States Forest Service
Washington, DC 20250

United States Department of Health, Education, and Welfare
Rehabilitation Services Administration
Social Rehabilitation Services
330 C St. SW
Washington, DC 20210

United States Ski Association, Central Division
Handicapped Skiers Committee
6832 Marlette Rd.
Marlette, MI 48453

United States Table Tennis Association
PO Box 815
Orange, CT 06477

United States Wheelchair Sports Fund
40-24 62nd St.
Woodside, NY 11377

Washington, DC, Therapeutic Recreation Center for the Handicapped
G and 31st St. S.E.
Washington, DC 20010

Wheelchair Motorcycle Association
101 Torrey St.
Brockton, MA 02401

Wheelchair Pilots Association
11018 102nd Ave. N.
Largo, FL 33540

Zonka and Associates—Facility Planners for the Handicapped
2501 Virginia
Park Ridge, IL 60008

Eugene E. Bleck

Table 10-7. General Resource Information Regarding Recreation and Use of Leisure for Individuals with Physically Handicapping Conditions

The literature listed herein covers a wide variety of subject headings. The sources are listed alphabetically by subject topic and in bibliographic fashion. The major topics covered are as follows:

>   Architectural Accessibility: General Information
>   Architectural Accessibility: Playground Design and Play Equipment
>   Arts and Crafts
>   Assistive Devices and Equipment
>   Aquatics and Swimming
>   Community Colleges—Adaptive Physical Education Classes
>   Community Recreation Programming
>   Consumer Organizations
>   Financial Assistance
>   Leisure Counseling
>   Journals, Magazines, and Newsletters
>   Outdoor Recreation and Camping
>   Recreation for the Handicapped and Therapeutic Recreation
>   Travel
>   Wheelchair, Adapted Sports, and Physical Activities
>   Miscellaneous

ARCHITECTURAL ACCESSIBILITY: GENERAL INFORMATION

American Institute of Architects, Buildings for all to use. *American Institute of Architects Journal,* March 1969.

American National Standards Association, Inc., *Specifications for Making Buildings and Facilities Accessible to, and Usable by, the Physically Handicapped.* New York, 1971, 12 pp.

Architectural and Transportation Barriers Compliance Board, *Resource Guide to Literature on Barrier-Free Environments, With Selected Annotations.* Washington, DC, 1977, 223 pp.

Austin, R., *Resources Handbook on Barrier Free Design.* Manhattan, Kan., Theraplan Publications, 1978, 80 pp.

Barrier-free Design—Report of United Nations Experts. *International Rehabilitation Review.* 26(1): 1–36, 1975.

Bednar, M., *Barrier-Free Environments.* Stroudsburg, Penn., Dowden, Hutchinson and Ross, Inc., 1977, 278 pp.

California State Department of Rehabilitation, *California Access Laws: A Compendium of Laws Governing Architectural and Transportation Accessibility for Handicapped Persons.* Sacramento, Mobility Barriers Section, 1977, 24 pp.

California State Department of Rehabilitation, *Community Accessibility.* (brochure). Sacramento, Mobility Barriers Section, 1977, 16 pp.

California State Department of Rehabilitation, *Is Your Community Accessible to the Physically Handicapped? How Does Your Town Compare?* Sacramento, Mobility Barriers Sechon, 1976, 16 pp.

California State Department of Rehabilitation, *Parking for Physically Handicapped Persons.* Sacramento, Mobility Barriers Section, 1977, 7 pp.

Capitol Development Board, *Accessibility Standards Illustrated.* Springfield, Ill., 1978, 217 pp.

Cary, J. R., *How to Create Interiors for the Disabled.* New York, Pantheon Press, 1978, 127 pp.

Easter Seal Society, *Current Materials on Barrier-Free Design.* Chicago, 1978, 8 pp. (#A-200).

Easter Seal Society, *Tooling Up For Accessibility.* Chicago, 1978, 34 pp.

General Services Administration, *Day on Wheels.* Washington, DC, 1975, 120 pp.

Harkness, S., and Groom, J., *Building Without Barriers for the Disabled.* New York, Watson-Guptill Publications, 1976, 80 pp.

Mace, R. L., *Applications of Basic Design Specifications.* Fayetteville, N.C., Barrier Free Environments, Inc., 1978, 45 pp.
National Academy of Sciences, *Mobility of Spinal Cord Impaired People.* Washington, D.C., 1975, 193 pp. (Final Report).
National Arts and the Handicapped Information Service, *Architectural Accessibility.* New York, 1977, 23 pp.
National Center for a Barrier Free Environment, *Accessibility Assistance: Directory of Barrier Free Design Consultants.* Washington, D.C., 1978, 186 pp.
National Center for a Barrier Free Environment, *Tools for Accessibility of United Nations Experts-A Selected List of Resources for Barrier Free Design.* Washington, D.C., 1978, 8 pp.
National Center for Law and the Handicapped, Moving towards a barrier-free society. *Amicus* 3 (4): 25–48, 1978
Nugent, T. J., *The Problem of Access to Buildings for the Physically Handicapped.* Farmington, Conn., Stanly Magic Door Company, 1978, 9 pp.
President's Committee on Employment of the Handicapped, *The Disabled and Elderly: Equal Access to Public Transportation.* Washington, D.C. 1975, 67 pp.
Seidenbaum, A., Barriers and the disabled. *Los Angeles Times,* April 20, 1976, p 17.
Shaw, J. and Tica, P., *Barrier-Free Design Accessibility for the Handicapped.* New York, Institute for Research and Development in Occupational Education, 1976, 31 pp.
Smith, A. Joicoeur, R., and Leet, M., *Wheelchair-manship Project.* Minneapolis, American Rehabilitation Foundation, 1971.
Snyder, M., *Laws and Regulations for Barrier-Free Design.* Manhattan, Kan., Theraplan Publications, 1977, 55 pp.
U.S. Department of Health, Education, and Welfare, Office of Handicapped Individuals, *Resource Guide on Architectural Barriers Removal.* Washington, D.C., 1979, 50 pp. (#79-22006).
U.S. Department of Health, Education, and Welfare, *Design for All Americans: Report of National Commission on Architectural Barriers to Rehabilitation of the Handicapped,* Washington, D.C., 1968, 54 pp.
Wachter, P., Lonenc, J., and Lai, E., *Urban Wheelchair Use, A Human Factors Analysis.* Chicago, Access Chicago Rehabilitation Institute of Chicago, 1976, 21 pp.

ARCHITECTURAL ACCESSIBILITY: PLAYGROUND DESIGN AND PLAY EQUIPMENT

Austin, D., *Design of Recreation Facilities for Special Populations.* Lawrence, Kan., Division of Independent Studies, University of Kansas, 1977, 42 pp.
Austin R., *Playgrounds and Play Spaces for the Handicapped.* Manhattan, Kan., Theraplan Publications, 1974, 62 pp.
Bowers, L., *Play Learning Centers for Preschool Handicapped.* Tampa, Fla., University of South Florida, 1975, 97 pp.
Bowers, L., State of the art—An analysis of the status of research on play apparatus for handicapped children, *Physical Education and Recreation for Impaired, Disabled, and Handicapped Individuals.* Washington, D.C., American Association of Health, Physical Education, and Recreation, 1976, pp. 341–354.
Goldsmith, S., *Designing For the Disabled.* Great Britain, Riba Productions Limited, 1976, 524 pp.
Gordon, R., *The Design of a Preschool Therapeutic Playground: An Outdoor Learning Laboratory.* New York, Institute of Rehabilitative Medicine, New York University Medical Center, Rehabilitation Monograph #97, 1972, 52 pp.

Table 10-7. (continued)

Gutierrez, R., *Park Planner, Designer for Handicapped.* Available from the author: 413 B Howland Canal, Venice, Calif. 90291.

Kliment, S., *Into the Mainstream–A Syllabus for a Barrier-Free Environment.* Washington, D.C., Rehabilitation Services Administration, 1975, 44 pp.

Playground Corporation of America, *Frustration vs. Spontaneity–Planned Playgrounds for the Handicapped.* Long Island City, N.Y., 1969, 15 pp.

Playground Corporation of America, *Helping Rehabilitate the Handicapped Child Through Successful Physical Play.* Long Island City, N.Y., 1969, 9 pp.

Playground Corporation of America, *The Handicapped Child Playscape and the Instructor.* Long Island City, N.Y., 1969, 17 pp.

Play Learning Centers for Preschool Handicapped Children. Tampa, Fla., University of South Florida, Division of Educational Resources (16mm film, 30 minutes).

Silverstein, B. M., *Where to Find What! A Selected Annotated Bibliography on Playgrounds and Playgrounds for Handicapped Children.* Tampa, Fla., University of South Florida, Division of Educational Resources, 1976, 38 pp.

Singh, S., *Mainstreaming Handicapped Individuals: Parks and Recreation Design Standards Manual.* Springfield, Ill., Department of Conservation, 1978, 50 pp.

U.S. Department of Housing and Urban Development, *Barrier-Free Site Design.* Washington, D.C., 1975, 82 pp. (#023-000-00291-4).

U.S. Department of Interior, *Planning and Operating Facilities for Crippled Children.* Washington, D.C., Bureau of Outdoor Recreation, 1967, 34 pp.

ARTS AND CRAFTS

Alan Short Center, *Arts for the Handicapped.* Available from the center: 521 Acacia Street, Stockton, Calif., 95202.

Alkema, C. J., *Art for the Exceptional.* Boulder, Colo., Pruett Publishing Company, 1971, 110 pp.

American Alliance for Health, Physical Education, and Recreation, *Dance for Physically Disabled Persons—A Manual for Teaching Ballroom, Square, and Folk Dances to Users of Wheelchair and Crutches.* Washington, D.C., 1976, 128 pp.

American Alliance for Health, Physical Education, and Recreation, *Materials on Creative Arts (Arts, Crafts, Dance, Drama, and Music) for Persons with Handicapping Conditions.* Washington, D.C., 1975, 104 pp.

Anderson, F. E., *Art for All the Children. A Creative Sourcebook for the Impaired Child.* Springfield, Ill., Charles C. Thomas, 1978, 304 pp.

Craft Techniques in Occupational Therapy. Washington, D.C., U.S. Government Printing Office, 1971, 290 pp. (#008-020-00397-2).

Educational Facilities Laboratories, *Arts and the Handicapped—An Issue of Access.* New York, 1976, 78 pp.

The Family Creative Workshop-Workbook Series. New York, Plenary Publications International, 1976, 25 volumes.

Kay, J. G., *Crafts for the Very Disabled and Handicapped—For All Ages.* Springfield, Ill., Charles C. Thomas, 1977, 201 pp.

Lee, C. C. and Lee, M., *Christopher Puppet Theater—Puppetry of/for the Disabled.* Available from the United Cerebral Palsy Association, Inc., New York, N.Y.

Lindsay, Z., *Art and the Handicapped Child.* New York, Van Nostrand-Reinhold, 1972, 144 pp.

Rich, M. K., *Handcrafts for the Homebound Handicapped.* Springfield, Ill., Charles C. Thomas, 1960, 116 pp.

Rickard, J., *Art as Therapy, Recreation, and Rehabilitation for the Handicapped.* San Jose, Calif., Lansford Publishing Company (Audio Visual Program).

Rubin, J., *Child Art Therapy.* New York, Van Nostrand-Reinhold, 1978, 288 pp.

Schatter, R., *Creative Dramatics for Handicapped Children.* New York, John Day Company, 1967, 100 pp.

Taylor, F., Artuso, A., and Hewett, *Creative Art Tasks for Children.* Denver, Love Publishing Company, 1977, 73 pp.

Ulman, E., and Dachinger, P., *Art Therapy in Theory and Practice.* New York, Schocken Books, 488 pp.

Williams, G. H., and Wood, M. M., *Developmental Art Therapy.* Baltimore, University Park Press, 1977, 198 pp.

ASSISTIVE DEVICES AND EQUIPMENT

Accent Special Publications, *Single Handed? Special Aids, Techniques and How-To Ideas.* Bloomington, Ill., 1978, 40 pp.

American Alliance for Health, Physical Education, and Recreation, Adapted equipment for physical activities. Washington, D.C., *Practical Pointers* 1(5), 1977, 6 pp.

American Parking Equipment, Inc., *Wheel-Ski, Model XP101.* Madison Heights, Mich., 1978, 6 pp.

Cowart, J., *Teacher-Made Adapted Devices for Archery, Badminton, and Table Tennis.* Washington, D.C., American Alliance for Health, Physical Education, and Recreation. *Practical Pointers,* 1(13), 1978, 16 pp.

Easter Seal Society, *Sources of Information on Self-Help Devices for Persons with Disabilities.* Chicago, 1978, 6 pp. (#L-6).

Lowman, E., and Klinger, J., *Aids for Independent Living: Self-Help for the Handicapped.* New York, McGraw-Hill, 1969, 796 pp.

Maddak, Inc., *Total Function Recreation Equipment for the Disabled.* Pequannock, N.J., 1977, 6 pp (Brochure).

May, E. E., *Independent Living: For the Handicapped and the Elderly.* Boston, Houghton Mifflin, 1974, 271 pp.

National Fund for Research into Crippling Disease, *Equipment for the Disabled: Leisure and Gardening.* London, Manton Limited, 1973, 54 pp.

Rosenberg, C., *Assistive Devices for the Handicapped.* Minneapolis, American Rehabilitation Foundation, 1968, 185 pp.

Self Help Items: For Independent Living. Rocky Hill, N.J., Fashion Able Catalog, 1979, 12 pp.

Soshe, M., *Handbook of Adapted Physical Education Equipment and Its Use.* Springfield, Ill., Charles C. Thomas, 1972, 210 pp.

AQUATICS AND SWIMMING

American Alliance for Health, Physical Education, and Recreation, *Aquatics for the Impaired, Disabled, and Handicapped.* Washington, D.C., 1972, 28 pp.

American Alliance for Health, Physical Education, and Recreation, *Challenging Opportunities for Special Populations in Aquatic, Outdoor, and Winter Activities.* Washington, D.C., 1976, 128 pp.

American National Red Cross, *Adapted Aquatics: Swimming for Persons with Physical Impairments.* Washington, D.C., 1977, 254 pp. (#321107).

American National Red Cross, *Methods in Adapted Aquatics—A Manual for the Instructor.* Washington, D.C., 1977, 48 pp. (#321-236).

American National Red Cross, *Swimming for the Handicapped—A Manual for the Aide.* Washington, D.C., 1974, 36 pp. (#321-225).

American National Red Cross, *Swimming for the Handicapped—Instructor's Manual.* Washington, D.C., 1960, 67 pp. (#321-218).

Anderson, W., *Teaching the Physically Handicapped to Swim.* Levittown, Transatlantic Arts, Inc., 1968, 84 pp.

Annand, V., *Aquatics for the Handicapped.* Arlington, Va., National Therapeutic Recreation Society, 1975, 49 pp.

Easter Seal Society, *Swimming for the Handicapped Child and Adult.* Chicago, 1973, 13 pp.

Easter Seal Society, *Teaching Persons Who Are Handicapped to Swim.* Chicago, 1977, 10 pp.

Table 10-7. (continued)

National Council of the Young Men's Christian Association. *"Project PAM—Mainstreaming in Aquatics"* (Workshop). Write PO Box 698, Longview, WA 98632.

National Therapeutic Recreation Society, Aquatics for the Handicapped. *Therapeutic Recreation Journal,* 10(2):33–76, 1976.

COMMUNITY COLLEGES—ADAPTIVE PHYSICAL EDUCATION CLASSES

Chancellor's Office
California Community Colleges
Academic Affairs
1238 S St.
Sacramento, CA 95814

Cerritos College
11110 E. Alondra Blvd.
Norwalk, CA 90850

Chaffey College
5885 Haven Ave.
Alta Loma, CA 91701

Cypress College
9200 Valley View
Cypress, CA 90630

East Los Angeles College
1301 E. Brooklyn Ave.
Monterey Park, CA 91754

El Camino College
16007 Crenshaw Blvd.
Torrance, CA 90506

Long Beach City College
4401 E. Carson
Long Beach, CA 90808

Mission College
1101 San Fernando Rd.
San Fernando, CA 91340

Pasadena College
1570 E. Colorado Blvd.
Pasadena, CA 91100

Rio Hondo College
3600 Workman Mill Rd.
Whittier, CA 90608

Santa Monica College
1900 Pico Blvd.
Santa Monica, CA 90406

California Intercollegiate Conference
c/o Hugh Smith
Chaffey College
Intercollegiate Athletic Department
Alta Loma, CA 91701

COMMUNITY RECREATION PROGRAMMING

Adaptive Recreation Unit, *Understanding the Handicapped.* Los Angeles, City Recreation and Parks Department, 1976, 22 pp. (Mimeographed).

American Alliance for Health, Physical Education, and Recreation, *Guide to Information Resources: Programming for Persons with Handicapped Conditions Through Physical Education, Recreation, and Related Disciplines.* Washington, D.C., 1973, 21 pp.

American Alliance for Health, Physical Education, and Recreation, *Integrating Persons with Handicapping Conditions into Regular Physical Education and Recreation Programs.* Washington, D.C., 1975, 60 pp.

American Alliance for Health, Physical Education, and Recreation, *Physical Education and Recreation for the Impaired, Disabled, and Handicapped Individuals: Past, Present and Future.* Washington, D.C., 1976, 424 pp.

Avedon, E., *Activating Community Resources for Therapeutic Recreation Service.* New York, Comeback, Inc., 1970, 101 pp.

Bureau of Education, *New Models for Community Based Recreation for Handicapped Children and Youth.* Iowa City, Recreation Education Program, University of Iowa, 1976, 420 pp. (Final Report).

Bushnell, S., and Kelley, J. O., *Providing Community Recreational Opportunities for the Disabled.* Urbana, Ill., Office of Recreation and Park Resources, Department of Recreation and Park Administration, University of Illinois, 1974, 23 pp.

Christiason, M. A., Recreation for the physically handicapped person. *California Parks and Recreation,* Dec. 1975–Jan. 1976, pp. 33–35.

Easter Seal Society, *Year Round Recreation Programs for the Handicapped.* Chicago, 1973, 13 pp. (#CT-22).
Fairchild, E., and Neal, L., *Common-Unity in the Community: A Forward-Looking Program of Recreation and Leisure Services for the Handicapped.* Washington, D.C., Hawkins and Associates, 1975, 149 pp.
Froehle, M. J., *How to Find the Physically Handicapped Residents of Your Community.* Anaheim, Calif., Parks, Recreation, and Arts Department, 1977, 3 pp. (Mimeographed).
Graduate students, *Recreation for the Handicapped—Activities and Training Factors.* Northridge. Calif., California State University at Northridge, Recreation and Leisure Studies Department, 1975, 20 pp. (Mimeographed).
Hawkins, D., *A Systems Model for Developing a Leisure Education Program for Handicapped Children and Youth.* Washington, D.C., Hawkins and Associates, 1977, 438 pp.
Henderson, D. D., *Therapeutic Recreation Center.* Washington, D.C., Department of Recreation, 1977, 5 pp.
Michauk, L. A., *The Physically Handicapped and the Community.* Springfield, Ill., Charles C. Thomas, 1970, 132 pp.
Moskalik, C. J., Owen, S. L., Deem, B. A., Joos, S., and Scott, S., *Therapeutic Recreation Services: Why Recreation for the Handicapped in a Municipal Setting?* San Jose, Calif., Parks and Recreation Department, Therapeutic Recreation Section, 1974, 15 pp.
National Parks and Recreation Association, Open the windows of your mind, *Proceedings 1974 NRPA Regional Forum, San Diego, Calif.,* Arlington, Va., 1974, 140 pp.
Neal, L. L., *Leisure Services: Selected Surveys of Services for Special Groups.* Eugene, Oregon, University of Oregon, Department of Recreation and Park Management, 1970, 87 pp.
Nesbitt, J. A., *Recreation for the Handicapped: A Social Right, A Rehabilitation Necessity.* Washington, D.C., President's Committee on Employment of the Handicapped, 1972, 8 pp.
Patrick, G. D., *Obtaining Use of Community Facilities for Special Populations.* Carbondale, Ill., 1973, 7 pp.
Pomeroy, J., State of the art in community recreation for the handicapped. *Physical Education and Recreation for the Impaired, Disabled and Handicapped Individual: Past, Present and Future.* Washington, D.C., American Alliance for Health, Physical Education, and Recreation, 1976, pp. 239–290.
President's Committee on Employment of the Handicapped, *Recreation and Handicapped People—A National Forum on Meeting the Recreation and Park Needs of Handicapped People.* Washington, D.C., Subcommittee on Recreation and Leisure, 1974, 63 pp.
President's Committee on Employment of the Handicapped. *Proclamation—The Leisure Needs of Handicapped People.* Washington, D.C., Subcommittee on Recreation and Leisure, 1975, 1 p. (Brochure).
President's Committee on Employment of the Handicapped, *Recreation is for Handicapped People.* Washington, D.C., Subcommittee on Recreation and Leisure, 1974 (Brochure).
Recreation Therapy Department, *At Your Service—Access to Recreation.* Boston, Massachusetts Rehabilitation Hospital, 1976, 38 pp.
Strake, R., The Role of the Therapeutic Recreator in Relation to the Community Recreator, *Therapeutic Recreation Journal* 3(1):25–28, 1969.
Wilson, G., *Community Recreation Programming for Handicapped Children.* Arlington, Va., National Therapeutic Recreation Society, 1974, 37 pp.
Witt, P., *Community, Leisure Services and Disabled Individuals.* Washington, D.C., Hawkins and Associates, 1977, 134 pp.

Table 10-7. (continued)

CONSUMER ORGANIZATIONS

California Association for the Physically Handicapped

PO Box 22552
Sacramento, CA 95822
(Architectural Barrier Committee, etc.)

Therapeutic Recreation Consultant
11060 Gonsalves Pl.
Cerritos, CA 90701

Southern California Regional Director
Ms. Roxanne Bent
21673 Dirigo Circle
Huntington Beach, CA 92646

Beachwood Chapter
Mrs. Theresa Mtero
5417 Blackthorne Ave.
Lakewood, CA 91712

East Los Angeles Chapter
Ms. Mark Avbel, President
6431 Easton St.
Los Angeles, CA 90022

East San Gabriel Valley Chapter
Mr. Jim Schoonover
316 S. Astell
West Covina, CA 91740

Glendale-Burbank Chapter
Mr. David Walsh, President
430 N. Adams St.
PO Box 9426
Glendale, CA 91206

Los Angeles Chapter
Mr. Dale Williams, President
834 22nd St.
Santa Monica, CA 90403

Pasadena Chapter
Ms. Martha Griswold, President
2364 Ganesha
Altadena, CA 91001

Rancho Chapter
Mr. Mike Morrione, President
5737 Florence Ave.
South Gate, CA 90280

San Fernando Valley Chapter
Mr. Shawn Solomon, President
6330 Rhea Ave.
Reseda, CA 91335

South Bay Chapter
Ms. Molly Berry, President
705 W. 36th St. Apt. #1
San Pedro, CA 90731

Committee for the Handicapped, *Directory of Organizations Interested in the Handicapped.* Washington, D.C., People-to-People Program, 1976, 48 pp.

Darrel McDaniel Independent Living Center
14354 Haynes St.
Van Nuys, CA 91401

Disabled Resources Center
330 East Broadway
Long Beach, CA 90802

Indoor Sports Club—A National Club for the Physically Handicapped

1145 Highland St.
Napoleon, OH 43545

President, District I
Mr. Dave Nevenschwander
4926 Denver
Montclair, CA 91762

Hondo Chapter
Mr. Rex Strohmeier, Director
7902 Genesta
Van Nuys, CA 91406

Huntington Park Chapter
Mr. Les Harrington, Director
10634 Reichling Ln.
Whittier, CA 90606

Long Beach Chapter
Mr. Clayton Benson, Director
20315 S. Denker
Torrance, CA 90501

Los Angeles Chapter
Ms. Mildred McMillan, Director
7328 Bairnsdale
Downey, CA 90242

Indoor Sports Club—A National Club for the Physically Handicapped (continued)

San Fernando Chapter
Mr. Lou Hasquet, Director
9665 Arleta
Arleta, CA 91331

Wilmington Chapter
Ms. Helen McWilliams
2315 Harding
Long Beach, CA 90805

Long Beach Commission on the Handicapped
City Hall
333 W. Ocean Blvd.
Long Beach, CA 90802
Attn: Recreation Committee

Los Angeles City Council on the Handicapped
City Hall, Room 2100
200 North Main
Attn: Recreation Committee

Los Angeles County Commission for the Handicapped
383 Hall of Administration
500 W. Temple St.
Los Angeles, CA 90012
Attn: Recreation Committee

Western Law Center for the Handicapped
849 S. Broadway, Suite 206
Los Angeles, CA 90014

Westside Community for Independent Living
11687 National Blvd.
Los Angeles, CA 90066

FINANCIAL ASSISTANCE

American Alliance of Health, Physical Education, and Recreation, *Guide for Financial Assistance and Program Support for Activities in Physical Education and Recreation for Impaired, Disabled, and Handicapped Participants: Foundation Programs*. Washington, D.C., 1973, 99 pp.

American Alliance of Health, Physical Education, and Recreation. *Guide for Financial Assistance and Program Support for Activities in Physical Education and Recreation for Impaired, Disabled, and Handicapped Participants: Innovation and Success Stories*. Washington, D.C., 1977, 6 pp.

Architectural and Transportation Barriers Compliance Board, *Funding Guide for the Removal of Environmental Barriers*. Washington, D.C., 1976, 22 pp.

Eckstein, B. J., Handicapped Funding Directory. Oceanside, N.Y., Research Grant Guides, Inc., 1978, 163 pp.

Leisure Information Service, *Fund Development and Technical Assistance Report*. Washington, D.C., Hawkins and Associates (Bi-weekly Newsletter).

U.S. Department of Health, Education, and Welfare, *Federal Assistance—For Programs Serving the Handicapped*. Washington, D.C., 1977, 333 pp. (#DHEW-OHD-77-22001).

LEISURE COUNSELING

Campbell, M., Hurtubise, D., Poirier, A., and Witt, D., *Leisure Counseling and Leisure Education—Resource Kit*. Ottawa, Ontario, Canada, Department of Recreology, University of Ottawa, 1973.

Christiason, M. A., *Recreation Activity Inventory*. Cerritos, Calif., 1975, 5 pp. (Unpublished paper).

Compton, D. M., and Goldstein, J. E., *Perspectives of Leisure Counseling*. Arlington, Va., National Therapeutic Recreation Society, 1978, 199 pp.

Table 10-7. (continued)

Edwards, P. B., Leisure Counseling Techniques, in *Individual and Group Counseling Step-by-Step.* Los Angeles, Calif., University Publishers, 1975.

Edperson, A., Mirenda, J., Overs, R., and Wilson, G. T., *Leisure Counseling Kit.* Washington, D.C., Alliance for Health, Physical Education, and Recreation, 1975.

Gunn, S. L., Leisure counseling—An analysis of play behavior and attitudes using transactional analysis and gestalt awareness. In Robb, G., and Hitzhusen, J., (eds.), *Expanding Horizons in Therapeutic Recreation, III.* Columbia, Mo., Technical Educational Services, 1976.

McDowell, C. F., Emerging leisure counseling concepts and orientations. *Leisurability* (2)4:19, 1974.

McDowell, C. F., Toward a healthy leisure mode: Leisure counseling. *Therapeutic Recreation Journal,* 8(3):96–124, 1974.

McDowell, C. F., *Leisure Counseling Selected Life Style Processes.* Washington, D.C., Hawkins and Associates, 1976, 156 pp.

O'Morrow, G. S., Recreation counseling—A challenge to rehabilitation. *Rehabilitation Literature* 31:226, 1970.

Overs, R. P., A model for avocational counseling. *Journal of Health, Physical Education, and Recreation* 4(2):36, 1970.

Overs, R. D., Taylor, S., and Adkins, C., *Avocational Counseling Manual: A Complete Guide to Leisure Guidance.* Washington, D.C., Hawkins and Associates, 1977, 203 pp.

Overs, R. D., O'Connor, E., and De M. Arco, B., *Avocational Activities for the Handicapped: A Handbook for Avocational Counseling.* Springfield, Ill., Charles B. Thomas, 1974, 178 pp.

Thompson, G., Outline for development of a recreational counseling program. *Therapeutic Recreation Journal* 6(2):83, 1972.

Weiner, A., The recreation advocate—Your leisure insurance agent, *Therapeutic Recreation Journal* 9:63, 1975.

JOURNALS, MAGAZINES, AND NEWSLETTERS

Accent on Living
PO Box 700
Bloomington, IL 61701

Achievement
925 N.E. 122nd North St.
North Miami, FL 33161

American Journal of Art Therapy
6010 Broad Branch Rd. N.W.
Washington, DC 20015

Arise
c/o Brooklyn School for Special Children
376 Bay 44th St.
Brooklyn, NY 11214

California Rehab
California Department of Rehabilitation
830 K Mall, Rm. 318
Sacramento, CA 95841

California Wheelchair Athletic Association Newsletter
260 Montecillo Drive
Walnut Creek, CA 94595

Challenge
American Alliance for Health, Physical Education, and Recreation
1201 16th St. N.W.
Washington, DC 20036

Challenge Magazine
c/o Ms. Wheelchair California
PO Box 74605
Hollywood, CA 90004

Closer Look—National Information Center for the Handicapped
Box 1492
Washington, DC 20013

Disabled–USA
President's Committee on Employment of the Handicapped
Washington, DC 20210

Journal for Therapy and Rehabilitation
Theraplan Publications
2301 Timber Creek
Manhattan, KS 66502

Resources for Recreation and Leisure

International Rehabilitation Review
219 E. 44th St.
New York, NY 10017

Journal of Leisurability
281 Station A
Ottawa, Ontario, Canada
Kln8V2

Journal of Physical Education and Recreation
c/o American Alliance of Health, Physical Education, and Recreation
1201 16th St. N.W.
Washington, DC 20036

Mainstream Magazine
861 6th Ave. Suite 610
San Diego, CA 92101

National Association of the Physically Handicapped Newsletter
6473 Grandville Ave.
Detroit, MI 48228

National Wheelchair Athletic Association Newsletter
40–24 62nd St.
Woodside, NY 11377

New World Magazine
c/o California Association of the Physically Handicapped
PO Box 22552
Sacramento, CA 95822

Newsletter—Committee on Recreation Free Design
c/o President's Committee on Employment of the Handicapped
Washington, DC 20210

Newsletter—Committee on Recreation and Leisure
c/o President's Committee on Employment of the Handicapped
Washington, DC 20210

Newsletter—National Council for Therapy and Rehabilitation Through Horticulture
Mount Vernon, VA 22121

Paraplegia Life
National Paraplegia Foundation
333 N. Michigan Ave.
Chicago, IL 60601

Paraplegia News
Paralyzed Veterans of America
c/o 5201 North 19th Ave., Suite 108
Phoenix, AZ 85015

Polling
United Cerebral Palsy Association of New York
122 E. 23rd St.
New York, NY 10010

Programs for the Handicapped
c/o Office for Handicapped Individuals
Switzer Building, Room 3517
330 C St. S.W.
Washington, D.C. 20201

Rehabilitation Gazette
4502 Maryland Ave.
St. Louis, MO 63108

Rehabilitation Literature
c/o Easter Seal Society for Crippled Children and Adults
2023 W. Ogden Ave.
Chicago, IL 60612

Rehabilitation World
c/o Rehabilitation International—USA
20 W. 40th St.
New York, NY 10018

Report
c/o National Center for a Barrier Free Environment
8401 Connecticut Ave.
Washington, DC 20015

Sigma Signs
Rehabilitation Education Center, Room 130
Oak St. and Stadium Dr.
University of Illinois
Champaign, IL 61820

Sports-N-Spokes
5201 N. 19th Ave., Suite 108
Phoenix, AZ 85015

The Independent
Center for Independent Living
2539 Telegraph Rd.
Berkeley, CA 94704

Therapeutic Recreation Journal
c/o National Therapeutic Recreation Society
1601 N. Kent St.
Arlington, VA 22209

Wheelchair Competitor
925 N.E. 122nd St.
North Miami, FL 33161

Table 10-7. (continued)

OUTDOOR RECREATION AND CAMPING

Books and Brochures

Bowers, L., An overview of the status of camping for the handicapped in the United States. *Physical Education and Recreation for the Impaired, Disabled, and Handicapped Individuals: Past, Present and Future.* Washington, D.C., American Alliance of Health, Physical Education, and Recreation, 1976, pp. 373-421.

Easter Seal Society, *Guide to Special Camping Programs.* Chicago, 1968, 107 pp. (#E-45).

Easter Seal Society, *Maximum Utilization of Camp Facilities.* Chicago, 1973, 41 pp.

Easter Seal Society, *Directory of Resident Camps for Persons with Special Health Needs.* Chicago, 1977, 71 pp., #E-41.

Goodwin, V., and Uloth, R., *Outward Bound and the Physically Disabled.* Wayzata, Minn., Minnesota Outward Bound School, Grant Final Report, 1979, 45 pp.

Hawkins, D., Vinton, D., and Pantzer, B., *Camping and Environmental Education for the Handicapped.* Washington, D. C., Hawkins and Associates, 1978, 170 pp.

Heritage Conservation and Recreation Service, *Outdoor Recreation Planning for the Handicapped.* Washington, D.C., 1967, 34 pp.

Heritage Conservation and Recreation Service, *Recreation for Special People.* Washington, D.C., 1977, 48 pp.

Heritage Conservation and Recreation Service, *1978 Nationwide Outdoor Recreation Plan, Recreation Needs of the Handicapped.* Washington, D.C., 1978, 40 pp.

Lions Club, Mammoth Lakes, *Recreation for the Handicapped.* Mammoth Lakes, Calif., 1978, 4 pp. (Brochure).

National Forest Service, *Planning a Facility for the Handicapped—Mammoth Lakes Campground.* Washington, D.C., 1968, 22 pp.

Nesbitt, J., Hanson, C., Bates, B., and Neal, L., *Training Needs and Strategies in Camping for the Handicapped.* Eugene, Oregon, University of Oregon, Center for Leisure Studies, 1972, 241 pp.

New York Department of Conservation, *Outdoor Recreation for the Physically Handicapped. A Handbook of Design Standards.* Albany, N.Y., State Council of Parks and Outdoor Recreation, 1967, 16 pp.

Schoenbohm, W. B., *Planning and Operating Facilities for Crippled Children.* Springfield, Ill., Charles C. Thomas, 1962, 311 pp.

Shea, T., *Camping for Special Children.* St. Louis, C. W. Mosby, 1977, NA.

United Cerebral Palsy Association, *Day Camping for the Cerebral Palsied.* New York, 1958, 227 pp.

Facilities

Project Torch
Robb Gary, Director
c/o Camp Allen, Inc.
RFD 5
Manchester, NH 03102

REACH—Resources for the
  Expansion and Advancement of
  Camping for the Handicapped
c/o Elizabeth M. Farley, Ed.D.
University of Kentucky
405 Bradley Hall
Lexington, KY 40506

White Oak Village Recreational
  Facilities for the Handicapped
c/o Mountwood Park
PO Box 208
Parkersburg, WV 26101

Wilderness Expeditions
c/o Ken Sleight
349 South 600 East
Salt Lake City, UT 84102

RECREATION FOR THE HANDICAPPED AND THERAPEUTIC RECREATION

American Alliance for Health, Physical Education, and Recreation, *Publications Catalog*. Washington, D.C., 1978, 38 pp.

American Alliance for Health, Physical Education, and Recreation, *Guidelines for Professional Preparation Program for Personnel Involved in Physical Education and Recreation for the Handicapped*. Washington, D.C., 1973, 72 pp.

Architectural and Transportation Barriers Compliance Board, *Access to Recreation*, Washington, D.C., 1977, 70 pp.

Avedon, E., *Therapeutic Recreation—An Applied Behavior Science Approach*. Englewood Cliffs, N.J., Prentice Hall, Inc., 1974.

Axline, V. M., *Play Therapy*. New York, Ballantine Books, 1969, 379 pp.

Christiason, M. A., *Recreation Therapy Programming in a Rehabilitation Setting*. Cerritos, Calif., 1977, 8 pp. (Unpublished paper).

Clark, V. L., and Clark, E. B., *Recreation in the Therapeutic Play*. Hicksville, N.Y., Exposition Press, 1972.

Cleverdon, D., et al., *Play in a Hospital: Why and How*. New York, Play Schools Association, 1971, 54 pp.

Denure, M., and Kidd, J., *Recreation Educators Institute—Workshop*. Santa Monica, California Community Colleges, 1970, 62 pp. (Workshop report).

Delta Sigma Omicron, *Wheelchair Square Dancing*. Champaign, Ill., Rehabilitation Center/University of Illinois Publications, 1963, 17 pp.

Dunn, D. R., *Guidelines for Action: Developing Opportunities for the Handicapped in Recreation and Leisure Services*. Arlington, Va., National Therapeutic Recreation Society, 1971, 62 pp.

Easter Seal Society, *Recreation for the Handicapped*. Chicago, 1978, 11 pp., #L-12.

Fain, G. S., and Hitzhusen, G., *Therapeutic Recreation: State of the Art*. Arlington, Va., National Park and Recreation Association, 1978, 168 pp.

Faye, V., and Peters, M., *Therapeutic Recreation: Its Theory, Philosophy, and Practice*. Harrisburg, Pa., Stockpole Books, 1972, 223 pp.

Geba, B., *Therapeutic Recreation in a Medical Setting*. San Diego, San Diego State University Press, 1975, 156 pp.

Gunn, S. L., *Pertinent Terminology for Therapeutic Recreation*. Urbana-Champaign, Ill., University of Illinois Press, 1974, 64 pp.

Harris, M. S., *Leisure Time Skills in Rehabilitation Services*. San Diego, Region IX, Rehabilitation Continuing Education Program Grant Final Report, 1978, 87 pp.

Haun, P., *Recreation: A Medical Viewpoint*. New York, Columbia University, Teachers College, Bureau of Publications, 1965, 98 pp.

Hunt, V. V., *Recreation for the Handicapped*. Englewood Cliffs, N.J., Prentice Hall, 1955, 340 pp.

Jaretzki, F., *Guidelines for Recreational Therapy*. New York, Health Sciences Publishing Corporation, 1972, NA.

Jordon, J., Dayton, B., and Brill, K. *A Process Analysis Approach to the Development of a Competency-Based Curriculum in Therapeutic Recreation at the Masters Degree Level*. Philadelphia, Temple University Press, 1978, 440 pp.

Jordon, J., Dayton, B., and Brill, K. *Theory and Design of Competency-Based Education in Therapeutic Recreation*. Philadelphia, Temple University Press, 1978, 244 pp.

Kelly, J., et al., *Therapeutic Recreation: Guidelines for Competency-Based Entry Level Curriculum*. Arlington, Va., National Therapeutic Recreation Society, 1976, 163 pp.

Kraus, R., *Therapeutic Recreation Service—Principles and Practices*. Philadelphia, W. B. Saunders, 1973, 234 pp.

Langdon, G., *Your Child's Play*. Chicago, Easter Seal Society, 1957, 25 pp., #E-18.

Table 10-7. (continued)

Martin, F., *Therapeutic Recreation Information Center (TRIC)*. Sacramento, California State University at Sacramento, Recreation and Leisure Studies Department, 1977.

McCowan, L., *It's Ability That Counts—A Training Manual on Therapeutic Riding for the Handicapped.* Olivet, Mich, Olivet College Press, 1972, 87 pp.

National Center for Law and the Handicapped, Reaching for new heights in recreation for handicapped people. *Amicus* 3(3): 24–27, 1978.

Nesbitt, J., *Educating the Handicapped Child for Leisure Fulfillment.* Iowa City, University of Iowa, Recreation Education Program, 1977, 197 pp.

Nesbitt, J., *New Concepts and New Processes in Special Recreation.* Iowa City, University of Iowa, Recreation Education Program, 1978, 156 pp.

Nesbitt, J. A., *Seminar on Professional Cooperation and Development in Therapeutic Recreation Service.* San Jose, Calif., San Jose State University, 1969, 20 pp.

North Carolina Recreation Commission, *The Doctors and Recreation in the Hospital Setting.* Raleigh, N.C., North Carolina Recreation Commission, 1962, 78 pp.

O'Brien, S. B., *More Than Fun: A Handbook of Recreational Programming for Children and Adults with Cerebral Palsy.* New York, United Cerebral Palsy Association, 1967, 47 pp. (Mimeographed).

O'Morrow, G. S., *Therapeutic Recreation: A Helping Profession.* Reston, Va., Reston Publishing Company, 1976, 288 pp.

Park, D., Recreation Awareness Paper. *Awareness Papers,* vol. 1. Washington, D.C., White House Conference on Handicapped Individuals, 1977, pp. 119–132.

Peterson, C. A., and Gunn, S. L., *Therapeutic Recreation Program Design: Principles and Procedures.* Englewood Cliffs, N.J., Prentice Hall, 1978, 345 pp.

Pomeroy, J., *Recreation for the Physically Handicapped.* New York, The MacMillin Company, 1964, 382 pp.

Recreation Center for the Handicapped, *Publication List.* San Francisco, 1972, 8 pp.

Rehabilitation Services Administration, *Access to Recreation—A Report on the National Hearing on Recreation for Handicapped Persons.* Washington, D.C., Department of Health, Education, and Welfare, 1977, 66 pp.

Robinson, F., Jr., *Therapeutic Recreation—Ideas and Experiences.* Springfield, Ill., Charles C. Thomas, 1974, 181 pp.

Roma, L., *Play Helps: Toys and Activities for Handicapped Children.* New York, International Ideas, 1977, 108 pp.

Schiffer, M., *Therapeutic Play Group.* New York, Grune & Stratton, 1969, 214 pp.

Shivers, J. S. and Fait, H. F., *Therapeutic and Adapted Recreation.* Philadelphia, Lea and Febiger, 1975, 366 pp.

Stadler, M., *Syllabus Recreation 194: Introduction to Therapeutic Recreation.* San Jose, Calif., California State University at San Jose, Spartan Bookstore, 1972, 251 pp.

Stein, T. A., and Sessoms, H. D., *Recreation and Special Populations.* Boston, Holbrook Press, 1974, 430 pp.

U.S. Department of Health, Education, and Welfare, Office of Handicapped Individuals, *Recreation and Handicapped Youth—4-H Recreation Leader's Guide.* Washington, D.C., 1979, 10 pp., #2M478.

TRAVEL

Books and Brochures

ABT Associates, *Travel Barriers: Transportation Needs of the Handicapped.* Springfield, Va., 1969, 300 pp.

Amtrack Public Affairs, *Access Amtrack.* Washington, D.C., 1977, 5 pp. (Booklet).

Annano, D. R., *The Wheelchair Traveler.* Milford, N.H., Annano Enterprises, 1977, 144 pp.

Resources for Recreation and Leisure

Architectural and Transportation Barriers Compliance Board, *Access Travel: A Guide to Accessibility of Airport Terminals.* Washington, D.C., 1977, 10 pp.

Atwater, M. H., *Rollin' On: A Wheelchair Guide to U.S. Cities.* New York, Dodd, Mead, 1978, 290 pp.

California State Parks and Recreation Department, *The California State Parks System Guide.* Sacramento, 1976, 23 pp.

California State Parks and Recreation Department, *A Guide for the Handicapped to the California State Park System.* Sacramento, 1976, 38 pp.

Department of Transportation, *Travel Barriers.* Washington, D.C., U.S. Government Printing Office, 1970, 46 pp.

Easter Seal Society, *Airline Transportation for the Handicapped and Disabled.* Chicago, 1971, 45 pp.

Funk, D., *Guidelines for Transportation for the Handicapped.* Washington, D.C., Hawkins and Associates, 1979, 50 pp.

Gutman, E., *Travel Guide for the Disabled.* Springfield, Ill., Charles C. Thomas, 1967, 133 pp.

Holiday Inn Directory (including accessible hotels). Available from Executive Offices, 3792 LaMar Avenue, Memphis, TN 38118.

Junior League of Los Angeles City, *Around the Town with Ease.* Los Angeles, 1974, 56 pp. (English and Spanish).

Laus, M. D., *Travel Instructions for the Handicapped.* Springfield, Ill., Charles C. Thomas, 1977, 164 pp.

National Park Service, *Access National Parks.* Washington, D.C., 1978, 197 pp.

National Park Service, *National Park Guide for the Handicapped.* Washington, D.C., 1972, 79 pp.

Nelson, J., *Wheelchair—Vagabond.* Santa Monica, Calif., Project Publishers, 1975, 132 pp.

President's Committee on Employment of the Handicapped, *A List of Guidebooks for Handicapped Travelers and Interstate Rest Area Directory.* Washington, D.C., Subcommittee on Recreation and Leisure, 1975, 21 pp.

President's Committee on Employment of the Handicapped, *Highway Rest Areas for Handicapped Travelers.* Washington, D.C., Subcommittee on Recreation and Leisure, 1974, 72 pp.

Reamy, L., *Travel Ability—A Guide for Physically Disabled Travelers in the United States.* New York: MacMillan, 1978, 298 pp.

Transworld Airways, *Consumer Information about Air Travel for the Handicapped.* New York, 1976, 12 pp. (Brochure).

Travel for Physically Disabled, Their Family and Friends. Hallandale, Florida, Rambling Tours, 1976, 15 pp.

Weiss, L. *Access to the World, A Travel Guide for the Handicapped.* New York, Chatham Square Press, 1977, 178 pp.

U.S. Government Printing Office, *Access National Parks—A Guide for Handicapped Visitors.* Washington, D.C., 1978, 200 pp. (#024-005-00691-5).

Travel Agencies Serving the Handicapped

Dimar International Tours
18662 MacArthur Blvd., Suite 450
Irvine, CA 92715

Evergreen Travel Service
19429 44th St.
Lynwood, WA 98036

Flying Wheels Travel
143 W. Bridge St.
Box 382
Owatonna, MN 55060

Getz International Travel Agency
640 Sacramento St.
San Francisco, CA 94119

Nova Travel, Inc.
1027 N. Coast Highway
Laguna Beach, CA 92651

Rambling Tours, Inc.
PO Box 1304
Hallandale, Florida 33099

Table 10-7. (continued)

The Travel Place
3600 Wilshire Blvd., Suite 1230
Los Angeles, CA 90010

Travel Teck, Inc.
33 Dartmouth St., Suite 100
Walden, MA 02148

Travel Services

Continental Trailways
Good Samaritan Plan
1512 Commerce, Suite 500
Dallas, TX 75201

Pinetree Transportation
(Charter Bus Service for Handicapped)
P.O. Box 16005
1175 E. Spring St.
Long Beach, CA 90806

Helping Hand Service—For the Handicapped
Greyhound Bus Lines,
208 E. 6th St.
Los Angeles, CA 90013

Universe Travel Agency
3611 Long Beach Blvd.
Long Beach, CA 90807

Rehabilitation International USA
Access to the Skies Program
20 W. 40th St.
New York, NY 10018

Ruth Lusby
(Consultant on Travel and the Handicapped)
1338 Mountain St.
Glendale, CA 91207

WHEELCHAIR, ADAPTED SPORTS, AND PHYSICAL ACTIVITIES

Adams, R. C., Daniel, A. N., and Rullman, L., *Games, Sports, and Exercises for the Physically Handicapped,* 2nd ed., Philadelphia, Lea and Febiger, 1975, 254 pp.

American Alliance for Health, Physical Education, and Recreation, *Competitive Athletic Programs for Impaired, Disabled, and Handicapped Persons.* Washington, D.C., 1973, 18 pp.

American Alliance for Health, Physical Education, and Recreation, *Physical Activities for Impaired, Disabled, and Handicapped Individuals.* Washington, D.C., 1976, 128 pp.

American Alliance for Health, Physical Education, and Recreation, *Physical Education and Recreation for Handicapped Children: Proceedings of a Study Conference on Research and Demonstration Needs.* Washington, D.C., 1970, 81 pp.

Beeman, M., *Scuba Diving for the Handicapped Project.* Irvine, Calif., Veterans Affairs Office, University of California, Irvine, 1978, 21 pp.

Cesario, J., *Scuba Diving for Physically Handicapped Program.* New York, Institute of Rehabilitative Medicine.

Collingwood, T. R., *Therapeutic Recreation and Adapted Physical Education within Rehabilitation.* Hot Springs, Ark., Arkansas Rehabilitation Research and Training Center, 1971, 44 pp.

Craig, T. T., *The Humanistic and Mental Health Aspects of Sports, Exercices, and Recreation.* Chicago, American Medical Association, 1977, 137 pp.

Cratty, B. J. and Breen, J. E., *Educational Games for Physically Handicapped Children.* Denver, Love Publishing Company, 1972, 91 pp.

Cratty, B. J., *Developmental Games for Physically Handicapped Children.* Palo Alto, Calif., Peek Publications, 1971, 52 pp.

Exceptional Games—For Physically Handicapped. c/o Acampar Programs, Inc., 2422 Pacific Coast Highway, Hermosa Beach, CA 90254.

Fait, H. F., *Special Physical Education—Adaptive, Corrective, Developmental.* Philadelphia, W. B. Saunders, 1978, 414 pp.

Geddes, D., *Physical Activities for Individuals with Handicapped Conditions.* London, C. V. Mosby, 1974, 108 pp.

Guttman, L., *Textbook of Sport for the Disabled.* Great Britain, Alden Press, 1976, 184 pp.

Grzymro, J., and Seaman, J., *To Teach Adapted Physical Education: A Resource Manual for Physical Educators and Classroom Teachers.* Indiana University, 1971, 51 pp. (Mimeographed).

Hedley, E., *Recreational Boating for Physically Handicapped.* Albertson, Long Island, Human Resources Center, 1978, 42 pp.

Labanowicz, S., The psychology of wheelchair sports, *Therapeutic Recreation Journal* 11(1):11–17, 1978.

Labanowicz, S., *Wheelchair Basketball: A History of National Association and an Analysis of the Structure and Organization of Teams.* Urbana-Champaign, Ill., University of Illinois, 1975, 378 pp. (Unpublished doctoral thesis).

Lipton, B. A., The role of wheelchair sports in rehabilitation, *National Rehabilitation Review,* Vol. 21:15–19.

Los Angeles County Department of Parks and Recreation, *New Games for the Handicapped.* Los Angeles, Calif., Rehabilitation Unit.

National Amputee Skiers Association, *National Amputee Ski Technique.* Carmichael, Calif., 1970, 91 pp.

National Fund for Research into Crippling Disease, *Equipment for the Disabled,* Vol. 6, Leisure and Gardens, 3rd ed. Sussex, Great Britain, 1973.

National Wheelchair Athletic Association, *Constitution and Rules, Training Techniques and Records.* Woodside, N.Y., 1977, 131 pp.

Owen, E., *Playing and Coaching Wheelchair Basketball.* Champaign, Ill., University of Illinois Press, 1979, 400 pp.

Paralyzed Veterans of America, *Competitive and Recreational Wheelchair Sports.* Washington, D.C., 1978, 8 pp. (Brochure).

Savitz, H. M., *Wheelchair Champions.* New York, Thomas Y. Crowell, 1978, 117 pp.

Sherrill, C., *Adapted Physical Education and Recreation: A Multi-Discipline Approach.* Washington, D.C., Hawkins and Associates, 1978, 690 pp.

Sports benefit handicapped, *Long Beach Independent-Press Telegram,* February 27, 1977.

Stieler, W. E., *Kick the Handicap, Learn to Ski: A Handbook of Information for the Physically Handicapped.* Marlette, Mich., Adapted Sports Association, 1977, 123 pp.

Vannier, M. H., *Physical Activities for the Handicapped.* Englewood Cliffs, N.J., Prentice Hall, Inc., 1977, 338 pp.

Vodola, T. M., *Individualized Physical Education Program for the Handicapped Child.* Englewood Cliffs, N.J., Prentice Hall, 1973, 308 pp.

Weisman, M., and Godfrey J., *So Get On With It.* Garden City, N.Y., Doubleday and Company, 1977, 159 pp.

MISCELLANEOUS

Accent on Living. *1978 Buyers Guide.* Bloomington, Ill., Cheever Publishing Company, 1978, 74 pp.

Achtenberg, J., *Legal Aid for the Disabled.* Washington, D.C., President's Committee on Employment of the Handicapped, 1975, 52 pp.

Baskin, B. H., and Harris, K. H., *Notes from a Different Drummer: A Guide to Juvenile Fiction Portraying the Handicapped.* New York, R.R. Bowker Co., 1977, 375 pp.

Becker, E., *Female Sexuality Following Spinal Cord Injury.* Bloomington, Ill., Accent Special Publications, 1978, 380 pp.

Table 10-7. (continued)

Boy Scouts of America, *Scouting for the Physically Handicapped.* New Brunswick, N.J., 1976, 64 pp. (3039).

Bruck, L., *Access—The Guide to a Better Life for Disabled Americans.* New York, Random House, 1978, 251 pp.

California Advisory Council on Vocational Education, *Barriers and Bridges.* Sacramento, 1977, 149 pp.

California Department of Rehabilitation, *Proceedings of the 1976 California Conference on Handicapped Individuals.* Sacramento, 1976, 281 pp.

California State University at Dominguez Hills, *Friends—Resource Booklet.* Dominguez Hills, Calif., Handicapped Students Office, 1976, 239 pp.

Center for Independent Living, *Report—Conference on Independent Living Movement.* Berkeley, Calif., 1976, 60 pp.

Community Planning Council, *Directory of Health, Welfare, and Recreational Services—Long Beach Area.* Long Beach, Calif., 1970, 59 pp.

Cook, M., *To Walk on Two Feet.* Philadelphia, Westminster Press, 1978, 91 pp.

Dibner, S., and Dibner, A., *Integration or Segregation for the Physically Handicapped Child.* Springfield, Ill., Charles C. Thomas, 1973, 201 pp.

Disabled Student Service Center, *Resource Catalog for Independent Living.* San Francisco, San Francisco State University, 1977, 162 pp.

Eareckson, J., *Joni.* Grand Rapids, Mich., Zondervan Publishing House, 1976, 228 pp.

Eareckson, J., and Estes, S., *A Step Further.* Grand Rapids, Mich., Zondervan Publishing House, 1978, 192 pp.

Easter Seal Society, *An Exceptional View of Life—The Easter Seal Story.* Chicago, 1977, 64 pp.

Easter Seal Society, *A Library on the Rehabilitation of the Physically Handicapped.* Chicago, 1978, 17 pp. (#L-1).

Easter Seal Society, *Publications List.* Chicago, 1978, 26 pp. (#A-226).

Easter Seal Society, *Selected List of Periodicals that Publish Articles Concerning Persons who are Handicapped.* Chicago, 1978, 13 pp. (#L-10).

Easter Seal Society, *Selection of Recent Books About Handicapped Persons—A Check List of Popular Fiction.* Chicago, 1978, 20 pp. (#L-3).

Everest and Jennings, Inc., *Many Roads—A Guide for Wheelchair Users.* Los Angeles, 1975, 6 pp. (#90075575).

Galbreath, P., *What You Can Do For Yourself—Hints for the Handicapped.* New York, Drake Publishers, 1974, 272 pp.

Girl Scouts of the United States of America, *Handicapped Girl Scouts—A Guide for Leaders.* New York, 1968, 94 pp. (#19-171).

Goldenson, R. M., Dunham, J., and Dunham, C., *Disability and Rehabilitation Handbook.* New York, McGraw-Hill, 1978, 846 pp.

Gregory, M., *Sexual Adjustment: A Guide for the Spinal Cord Injured.* Bloomington, Ill., Accent Press, 1976, 73 pp.

Henscheid, H., *View of Life.* Chicago, Easter Seal Society, 1975, 16 pp. (#1075-0019).

Heslinga, K., *Not Made of Stone: The Sexual Problems of Handicapped People.* Springfield, Ill., Charles C. Thomas, 1974, 208 pp.

Information and Referral Service of Los Angeles County, *Director of Health, Welfare, Vocational, and Recreation Services in Los Angeles City and County.* Los Angeles, 1975, 284 pp.

Jones, R., *The Acorn People.* Des Plaines, Ill., Bantam Books, 1977, 33 pp.

Lippman, L., *Attitudes Towards the Handicapped.* Springfield, Ill., Charles C. Thomas, 1972, 136 pp.

Los Angeles County Department of Public Social Services, *Community Resource Information Bank (CRIB).* Los Angeles, 1976, 154 pp. (Recreation Booklet).

Los Angeles County Department of Public Social Services, *Community Resource Information Bank (CRIB)—Programs for the Handicapped.* Los Angeles, Ca., 1977, 218 pp.

Michaux, L. A., *The Physically Handicapped in the Community*. Springfield, Ill., Charles C. Thomas, 1970, 134 pp.

Miers, E. S., *Why Did This Have to Happen?* Chicago, Easter Seal Society, 1957, 28 pp. (#1073-110).

Mooney, T. O., Cole, T. M., and Chilgren, R. A., *Sexual Options for Paraplegics and Quadriplegics*. Boston, Little Brown, 1975, 111 pp.

Moore, C., Morton, K., and Mills, J., *A Readers Guide for Parents of Children with Mental, Physical and Emotional Disabilities*. Washington, D.C., U.S. Department of Health, Education, and Welfare, 1976, 144 pp. (#(HSA)-77-5280).

President's Committee on Employment of the Handicapped, *Employment in Recreation, Parks, Leisure, or Cultural Services of the Handicapped*. Washington, D.C., Subcommittee on Recreation and Leisure, 1972, 8 pp.

President's Committee on Employment of the Handicapped, *A Handbook on the Legal Rights of Handicapped People*. Washington, D.C., U.S. Government Printing Office, 1977, 103 pp. (#040-000-00355-0).

Programs for the Handicapped, *Directory of National Information Sources on Handicapping Conditions and Related Services*. Washington, D.C., U.S. Government Printing Office, 1977, 405 pp., (#017-000-00196-5).

Pyramid Films, *Get It Together*. Santa Monica, Calif. (16 mm film, 20 minutes).

Robinault, I. D., *Sex, Society, and the Disabled*. New York, Harper and Row, 1978, 273 pp.

Savitz, H. M., *Consider: Understanding Disability as a Way of Life*. Minneapolis, Sister Kenny Institute, 1975, 35 pp.

Stubbins, J., *Social and Psychological Aspects of Disability*. Baltimore, University Park Press, 1977, 617 pp.

Trieshmann, R. B., *The Psychological, Social, and Vocational Adjustment to Spinal Cord Injury—A Strategy for Future Research*. Washington, D.C., Rehabilitation Services Administration, Department of Health, Education and Welfare, 1978, 222 pp.

Veterans Administration, *A Source Book—Rehabilitating the Person with Spinal Cord Injury*. Washington, D.C., 1972, 58 pp. (#5100-00063).

White House Conference on Handicapped Individuals, *Proceedings of the 1977 White House Conference on Handicapped Individuals,* 3 vols. Washington, D.C., 1978.

Wright, B. A., *Disabling Myths About Disability*. Chicago, Easter Seal Society, 1977, 17 pp. (#A-207).

Table 10-8. An Example of Community Resource Creation by Parents

I. TASK—TEAM ADVOCATES FOR SPECIAL KIDS

Who Are "Special Kids"?

Special kids are children with extra physical, educational, or emotional needs. They are the blind, the deaf, the orthopedically handicapped, the learning disabled, the mentally retarded, and the emotionally disturbed—children with handicapping conditions but children who laugh, cry, feel pain, and hope, and have the same right to a full life as any child does.

What Is TASK?

TASK is parents helping parents—a nonprofit corporation that serves as a central source that a parent of a special child can turn to for assistance and support in seeking and obtaining needed educational, medical, or support services for their child. Some of the services provided by TASK are:

1. Central resource center for available service, literature, and educational materials.
2. Legal rights information

Table 10-8. (continued)

3. Trained educational advocates to assist parents.
4. Parent education—workshops and 2-day advocacy training course
5. Newsletter
6. Community awareness and sensitization programs—"Let's Be Friends"
7. Parent library
8. Bilingual services
9. Peer counseling
10. Consumer advocacy

When Are You Qualified to Receive These Services?

NOW! Any special child and those special people in his or her life need only call and ask for assistance. Services are offered at no cost, but donations are welcome.

Where Are Services Provided?

Services are provided in all of Orange County [California].

Why TASK?

Special kids and their families have had unmet needs in a variety of areas for many years. Parents have often felt alone in trying to find a way in which to provide for the maximum development of their child. They have had to try to cope with the pressures and diverse priorities of various agencies, educational and medical professionals, and special interest groups. The frustration of trying to deal with a program so segmented is disturbing to all parents and devastating to some parents. Current statistics indicate that 35 percent of all high-risk newborns return to the hospital abused, and that the divorce rate for parents of handicapped children is not the usual 50 percent but rather 75 percent. These results are terrifying to the child and the family, and result in tremendous costs to the state for institutionalization, welfare, delinquency, and society as a whole.

TASK has been formed by a group of parents who realize that these problems have reached levels that can no longer be overlooked. At last parents helping parents is a reality in Orange County. There is one number, 951-TASK, that any parent can call to gain support of any kind—moral, consumer, medical, or educational. PLEASE CALL!

TASK
1800 East La Veta Avenue, Suite 234
Orange, CA 92666

II. LET'S BE FRIENDS

Let's Be Friends is

- A 45-minute program designed for the kindergarten to third grade level.
- A positive program to help the typical classroom child learn about handicaps and feel more comfortable with their handicapped peers.

- Two dolls, one handicapped and one non-handicapped, discussing their friendship, their difficulties, and their feelings.
- Hands-on time for each child to learn about and try a variety of equipment used by disabled people (e.g., wheelchair, crutches, walkers, braces, casts, prosthesis, hearing aid, Braille book, and white cane).
- Follow-up for teachers with coloring sheet, books, book bibliography, simulated activities, and, in the future, suggested movies.

The program is designed to build a better understanding about handicaps by

- Building an awareness in the child without a handicap of what it is like to be handicapped.
- Answering questions young children have about handicaps.
- Minimizing fears and anxieties so friendships between children can be freely developed.
- Recognizing qualities which are the same in *all* children.

A *Let's Be Friends Kit is*

A packet offering a summarization of how to organize your own Let's Be Friends program in your community.

It includes samples of

volunteer registration form	sample letter to teacher and parents
doll instructions	coloring sheet
publicity forms	teacher questionnaire
equipment check list	bibliography
script	simulated activities list

For a copy of a Let's Be Friends kit or further information, please contact:
TASK
8100 Garden Grove Blvd.
Garden Grove, CA 92641
c/o Jean Turner
(714) 898-9571

For information regarding the inner workings of a Let's Be Friends program, please contact either of the following:

Saddleback Valley Pilot Program	Gretchen Watz
Betty Momoda	26031 Via Viento
25805 Via Viento	Mission Viejo, CA 92691
Mission Viejo, CA 92691	(714) 837-6424
(714) 586-7323	

11

Cystic Fibrosis

BIRT HARVEY, M.D.

The most common, and usually fatal, hereditary disease of childhood, cystic fibrosis, was not described until 1936. By 1938 it was recognized as a significant entity that affects many children. At that time Dorothy Andersen, a pathologist, reported a series of infants, all of whom died by 1 year of age from lung disease. She showed that there was involvement of the pancreas as well as the lungs and theorized that some disorder of the pancreas prevented absorption of vitamin A, which, in turn, caused lung changes. Because the diseased pancreas had many cysts and much fibrous scarring, Dr. Anderson named the disease *cystic fibrosis of the pancreas*. In subsequent years, the name has been changed several times by researchers who demonstrated involvement of other organs. Most people still use the original name, however, and probably shall continue to do so until the basic mechanisms of the disease are better understood.

FREQUENCY

It is estimated that one in every 500 children is born with this hereditary disorder, and approximately one in every 25 Caucasians carries the gene. Cystic fibrosis is the most common cause of death from a genetic disorder in the United States and the most common cause of chronic lung disease in Caucasian children. It occurs much less frequently in blacks and is very rarely reported in Oriental children.

POSSIBLE CAUSES

One of the most popular alternate names for cystic fibrosis is *mucoviscidosis*. This is a descriptive term which means the widespread presence of abnormally thick, viscid mucus. This name came into use once it was apparent that various aspects of the disease could be attributed to an abnormal mucus secreted, not only in the pancreas and the lungs, but in other organs as well. Various workers were able to show that the walls of the stomach, the intestine, the salivary glands, and the liver all secrete abnormal mucus. Numerous studies have defined more precisely the properties of this mucus, but the basic reason for the abnormality has not been found. In 1952 it was discovered that children with cystic fibrosis have an abnormal concentration of salt in their sweat. This peculiarity of the sweat glands was the first evidence that non–mucus-secreting glands were also involved in this disorder. Cystic fibrosis is now considered to involve all the secreting glands of the body, except those that secrete into the bloodstream.

Work by some investigators has implicated abnormal concentrations of calcium in secretions from various glands as a possible causative factor. Other workers have shown an abnormal protein in the blood of children with this disorder and in their parents. The lack of absorption of certain fats or deficiencies in trace metals have also been suggested to play a role. However, we do not as yet know the basic underlying cause.

MODE OF INHERITANCE

Cystic fibrosis is considered to be a simple recessive genetic disorder. Each parent of an affected child must carry one c/f gene, and, to be affected, the child must inherit two c/f genes, one from each parent. Persons who have only one c/f gene and one normal gene are carriers of the disorder, but there are no significant abnormalities associated with being a carrier.

Whenever two parents carrying the gene for c/f produce a child, there is a one-in-four chance that the baby will have cystic fibrosis. There are two chances in four that he will be a carrier of the disease, and one chance in four that he will not carry the gene. Figure 11-1 illustrates how the disease is transmitted by two carrier parents. Because each pregnancy has the exact same one-in-four risk of producing a child with the disorder, some carrier parents, by the laws of chance, may have two or three successive affected children, whereas others may have one affected child and numerous normal children. No matter what has occurred in any preceding pregnancy, each subsequent pregnancy has the same one-in-four chance of producing a child with the disorder.

The discovery of an abnormal protein isolated from the blood of children with cystic fibrosis and from carriers of this gene may become the basis for carrier identification.

BODY ORGAN CHANGES

It is not difficult to relate the abnormalities that occur in children with cystic fibrosis to the changes that can be demonstrated in their organs.

In the periphery of the pancreas are small glands which secrete into narrow channels. These channels unite into larger and larger ducts until, finally, they empty into the intestine. One might liken this to a river formed by many small tributaries. In cystic fibrosis, an increasing number of these tiny tributaries become blocked because of thickened secretions. When complete blockage occurs, the glands continue to secrete, but the secretions cannot be released. The glands swell and become cysts with

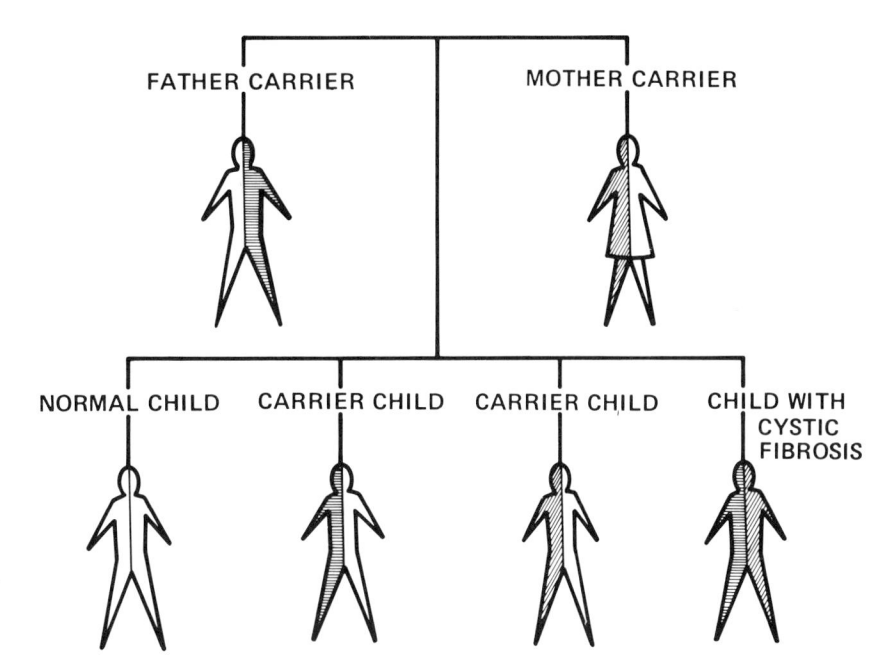

Fig. 11-1. Transmission of the cystic fibrosis gene from two carrier parents.

scarred fibrous tissue surrounding them. As fewer and fewer pancreatic secretions reach the intestine, there is less breakdown of food, and more symptoms of disease appear.

A somewhat analogous but milder process in the liver results in damage to that organ.

In the normal lung, cells lining the bronchial tubes and trachea secrete mucus. These cells also have fine hairs, called cilia, which function in carrying the mucus away from the periphery of the lungs. Rhythmic waving motions of the cilia move the mucus, which rides on the cilia in a layer as thick as a sheet of paper. The mucus is thus moved inward and upward from the periphery of the lungs, eventually reaching the upper end of the trachea, where it is swallowed. Inhaled particles are trapped in this mucus and expelled in this manner.

In children with cystic fibrosis, the mucus does not move effectively, and the lungs are poorly cleared. As time goes on, more mucus remains, and areas of the lungs become blocked. The lung can be thought of as a large tree, with the trachea being the main trunk and the bronchial tubes the branches. The abnormalities we see in cystic fibrosis are due to accumulated mucus in many of the small peripheral branches (Fig. 11-2).

As we inhale, the lungs expand, and the bronchial tubes show a corresponding dilation (Fig. 11-3). When we exhale, the lungs, including the bronchial tubes, tend to decrease in size. It is therefore easier for air to get into the lungs than out of them, since the diameter of the bronchial tubes is larger on inspiration than on expiration. When mucus partially obstructs the opening of a bronchial tube, this difference in diameter between inspiration and expiration becomes very important. The mucus can act as a "ball valve," trapping air in the periphery of the lung and resulting in overinflation of many areas of the lungs.

If enough mucus accumulates in the opening of a small bronchus, it may occlude the opening so completely that air can pass neither in nor out of the portion of the lung peripheral to the mucus. The air trapped beyond the obstruction will gradually be absorbed into the body, and that area of lung will collapse. This collapse is called *atelectasis*.

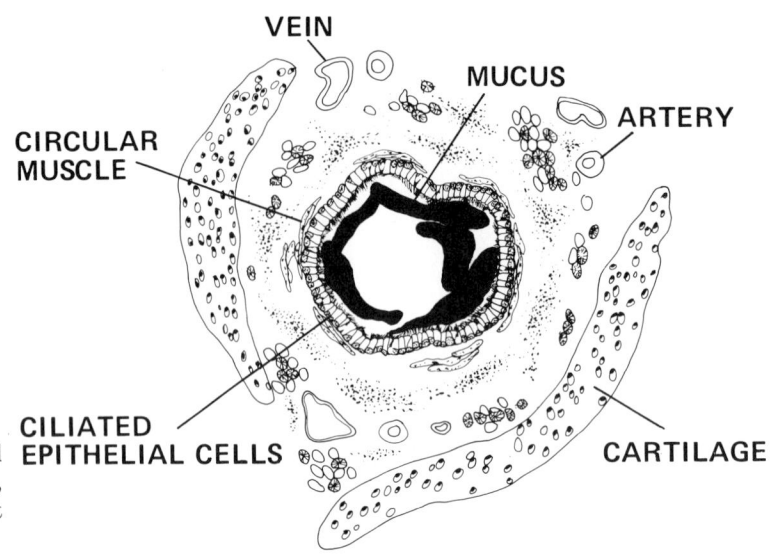

Fig. 11-2. The bronchus of a child with cystic fibrosis. It has much thick, viscid mucous; this tends to obstruct passage through the lumen.

Infection in many small bronchial tubes occurs as a result of poor clearance of inhaled material plus damage to areas of lung tissue. The pathology of the lung in cystic fibrosis consists of hyperinflation, atelectasis, and infection (Fig. 11-4).

Under a microscope, it is possible to see evidence of disease in other mucus-secreting glands of the body. Although the secretions of the sweat glands are abnormal, no anatomic changes can be found.

SYMPTOMS

A child with cystic fibrosis may come to a doctor's attention in a variety of ways. The disease may be evident at birth in those children whose predominant abnormality is of the intestinal tract. A lack of the normal

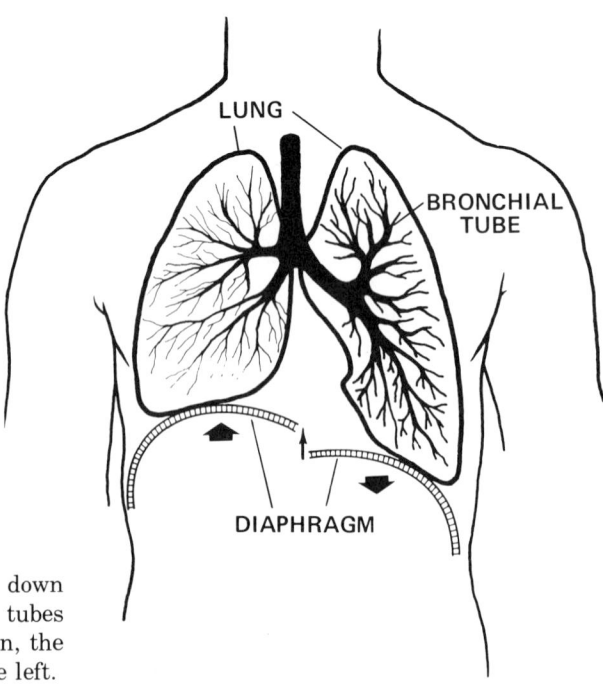

Fig. 11-3. On inhalation, the diaphragm moves down and the chest wall out, thus opening the bronchial tubes more widely, as seen on the right. With expiration, the bronchial lumen become narrower, as shown on the left.

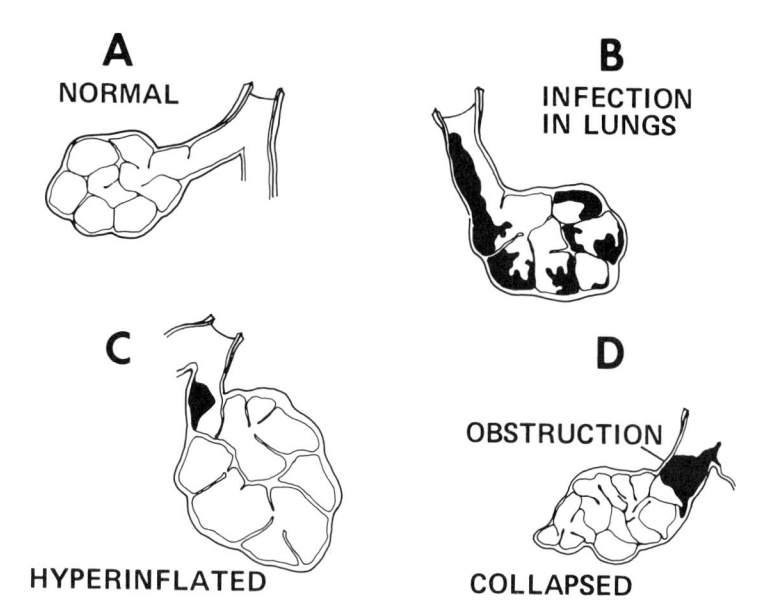

Fig. 11-4. The air sacs of the lung. (A) Normal appearance. (B) Sacs are partly filled with pus from infection; this leads to poor air exchange. (C) Obstruction of the small bronchus permits air to enter the lungs more readily than it exits, resulting in overinflation of the air sacs. (D) The obstruction is complete and, as air is absorbed into the blood, the air sacs collapse.

pancreatic juice during fetal life can result in a grossly thickened material replacing the normal stool that babies pass in the first day or two of life. Inability of the child to pass this material causes obstruction of the intestine, and surgery is required to relieve it.

Intestinal involvement is often not severe enough to manifest itself at birth, but it will be evident later, when the child's stool shows the effect of insufficient pancreatic juice. Pancreatic juice supplies enzymes that break down ingested proteins, carbohydrates, and fats. Fortunately, other organs of the intestinal tract also supply enzymes that break down proteins and carbohydrates, as well as some fats. A child with cystic fibrosis with significant involvement of the pancreas will have stools that are frequent, bulky, greasy, and very foul in odor, due to the excretion of undigested fats. The child may lose calories in his stool, so that either he will have a voracious appetite to make up for the calorie loss, or he will fail to gain weight adequately.

Involvement of the lungs results in an increased frequency and more prolonged course of respiratory infections. The child who develops a cold is subsequently apt to have a persistent cough for several months or to develop an episode of pneumonia or bronchitis secondary to this cold. Once infection is firmly lodged in the chest, one can expect cough to become chronic and to be present most of the time. Cystic fibrosis should be considered, therefore, in children with chronic cough or frequent episodes of bronchitis or pneumonia.

Since plugs of mucus in the bronchial tubes can partly obstruct the flow of air, particularly on expiration, wheeze may occur secondary to this type of obstruction. Consequently, some children are initially diagnosed as asthmatic, before the correct diagnosis of cystic fibrosis is considered.

The high salt content of sweat can cause problems in the summertime, particularly for the active child who perspires freely. If enough salt is lost in the sweat, the child may become acutely ill and require hospitalization in order to receive the needed rapid, intravenous replacement of the salt lost.

DIAGNOSIS

The symptoms of this disease can mimic those of many other disorders. Involvement of the lungs may be mistaken for pneumonia, bronchitis, or asthma. Involvement of the intestine may be confused with celiac disease or other somewhat similar intestinal disorders.

Before the discovery of high levels of salt in the sweat of children with cystic fibrosis, the diagnosis had to be established by passing a tube through the mouth and stomach into the intestine. The juice from the pancreas was aspirated and analyzed for its enzyme content. Low levels of enzymes, together with symptoms of lung and intestinal involvement, were the basis for a firm diagnosis.

Since the discovery of high levels of salt in the sweat, the diagnosis of cystic fibrosis has become much easier and less traumatic for the child. A small area on the forearm is chemically stimulated to induce sweating. This sweat is collected, and the concentration of salt determined. This type of test is almost always conclusive in either confirming or ruling out the diagnosis.

PHYSICAL APPEARANCE

The physical appearance of children with cystic fibrosis varies, depending on the severity of the disease. Often, because of the hyperinflated lungs, the chest has a big, rounded appearance. Since there is a larger stool quantity and more gas, the abdomen may be distended and protruding. The extremities may be thin, and there may be a thickened, bulbous rounding to the ends of the fingers and toes. Treatment sometimes results in a dark discoloration of the teeth. (Fig. 11-5).

TREATMENT

Children who have loss of pancreatic function can be given, as a substitute, extract of animal pancreas in either tablet or powder form at meal times. The diet may be modified to decrease the quantity of fatty food. Since children with cystic fibrosis have some difficulty absorbing fat-soluble vitamins (A, D, E, K) from foods, vitamin supplements are given.

In warm weather, salt intake should be increased and, for children who are particularly active and perspiring quite freely, salt tablets are often recommended.

The prime emphasis in treatment is directed toward the most serious manifestation of this disease—involvement of the lungs. It is important to keep the lungs as clear of mucus and as free of infection as possible, so that an optimum airway can be maintained. This is accomplished in several ways. Postural drainage is a principal method of clearing the lungs. The child is placed in various positions to drain different areas of the lungs. While each area is draining, that portion of the chest is clapped vigorously and vibrated in an attempt to dislodge and move mucus (see Fig. 4-5). This can be compared to a ketchup bottle that one tilts and then bangs sharply so as to move the ketchup. Many physicians precede percussion and vibration of the lungs with an aerosol treatment. The child breathes through a mask or a mouthpiece an aerosolized solution that is intended to help liquify the secretions and to widen the bronchial tubes so that percussion is more effective (Fig. 11-6). Sometimes antibiotics are also given in this way.

Probably the most important single factor in modifying the course of this disease has been the use of antibiotics to fight infection in the lungs.

Cystic Fibrosis

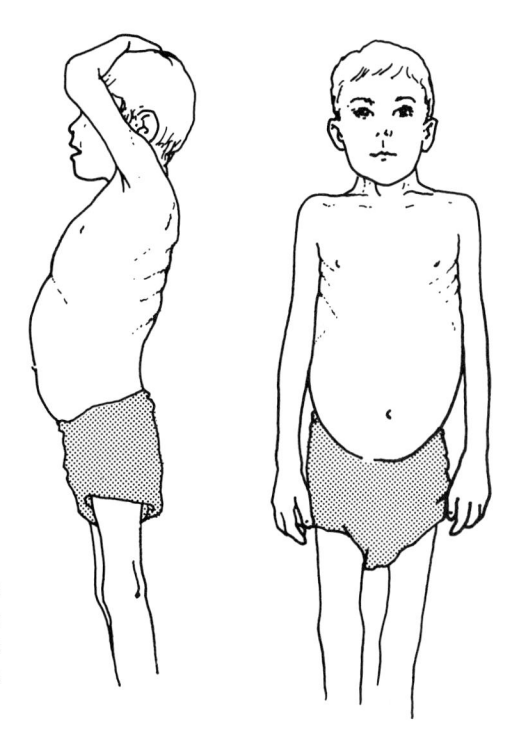

Fig. 11-5. Appearance of the child with cystric fibrosis. The lack of muscle makes the ribs stand out. The overinflated chest is wider from front to back and gives a square appearance around the shoulders. Note the marked abdominal protuberance and the thin, wasted buttocks, arms, and legs.

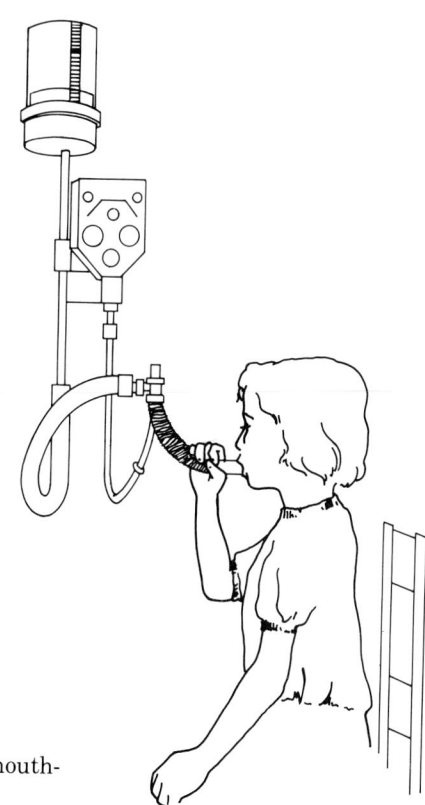

Fig. 11-6. The child breathes an aerosolized medicine through the mouthpiece.

Antibiotics are usually given by mouth and sometimes by aerosol. On occasion, if infection becomes severe, it may be necessary to hospitalize the child and give him antibiotics intramuscularly or intravenously.

PROGNOSIS

The course of cystic fibrosis is progressive and relentless, but proper treatment can affect the rate of progression. If the rate can be slowed enough, the child may grow to lead a normal adult life, with only minimal limitation. Early diagnosis and effective treatment are of paramount importance.

In some children, the disease will continue to progress at a relatively fast rate, in spite of intensive therapy. The most common cause of death is lung damage leading to insufficient oxygen to support life.

As treatment becomes more effective in minimizing the destruction of the lung, more children are dying from heart failure secondary to involvment of the lungs. Disease of the lungs makes it difficult for the heart to pump blood through them. Occasionally, children die from involvement of the liver, and deaths have also been reported from shock following the rapid loss of salt with excessive physical activity in hot weather.

In the initial reports of this disease, almost all deaths occurred before 1 year of age, primarily from overwhelming lung infection. With the advent of antibiotics in the 1940s and early 1950s, the average age of death gradually rose. During the 1960s, more effective means of cleansing the lungs of mucus were developed, and there was further improvement in longevity. Also contributing to this were greater physician awareness of the disease, earlier diagnosis, and earlier treatment. The average age of death is now approximately 19 years, with a definite upward trend, so that we can expect that a very large percentage of children will arrive at adulthood, many of them functioning well. Some adult women with cystic fibrosis are capable of having children. Adult males with cystic fibrosis are almost always sterile.

EDUCATIONAL IMPLICATIONS

There are several things which the teacher of a cystic fibrosis child might bear in mind that can help improve the quality of the child's experience at school: (1) The child with cystic fibrosis may cough frequently. The lung disease is not communicable, however, and the child need not be kept away from other children for fear of exposing them to the cough. The child may frequently try to hide the cough or to avoid coughing, since it brings attention. This is bad, because it is most important that the child cough out the mucus and not keep it in the lungs. The less the attention paid to the child's coughing and the more it is accepted, the freer the child will feel to cough when needed. (2) The student with cystic fibrosis will have an increased appetite and may well take seconds and thirds during times when the class is eating. This should be encouraged, and attention should not be focused on it. If the child is on a diet which has a modified fat intake, it is well to encourage adherence to the diet. If this would require eating foods other than those that the remainder of the class eats, however, it is better that the child be allowed dietary indiscretions so as not to feel set apart from his or her peers. (3) Children with cystic fibrosis will have an increased number of stools, so that they may have to leave the class more often than other children. (4) They may be on multiple medicines, for both pancreatic and lung involvement, and may need to take medicines during class hours. They should be helped to do this as unobtrusively as possible. (5) Although physical stamina may be somewhat impaired because of lung involvement, children with cystic fibrosis should be permitted to engage as fully as possible in all activities. They need to be watched, however, to insure that they do not try to go beyond their limits in an effort to hide the disease. In particularly hot weather, they should not play so heartily that they perspire excessively, unless they receive adequate quantities of added salt. (6) Children with this disease are neither more nor less intelligent than their peers, although they may appear brighter because their orientation tends to be more intellectual than physical. (7) Children with cystic fibrosis should be treated as much as possible like the other children in a class.

It is important to realize the psychological as well as the physical and the economic load that this disease places on the cystic fibrosis child and his family. Time and energy must be spent in giving and receiving treatments. Vacations are limited. Money may not be available for normal family activities. The cystic fibrosis child is aware of the added burden he places on his family. He realizes his differences from his peers in physical size, limitation of activities, the need to take medicines and treatments, his chronic cough, and in countless other ways. All this must be considered in deciding how best to treat a cystic fibrosis child in your class.

BIBLIOGRAPHY

Guide to the Diagnosis and Management of Cystic Fibrosis. Atlanta, National Cystic Fibrosis Research Foundation, 1971.

Shwachman, H., *Diseases of the Respiratory Tract in Children,* vol. 1, 3rd ed. Philadelphia, W. B. Saunders, 1972.

12

Dermatomyositis

JOHN J. MILLER, III, M.D., Ph.D.

Dermatomyositis is a rare disease which occurs in several forms in adults, but appears to be a different disease in children. The cause is unknown. There is some evidence that it is an "autoimmune" disease (see chapter on Juvenile Rheumatoid Arthritis), in which abnormal antigen–antibody complexes are deposited in the walls of small blood vessels, producing inflammation and occlusion of the blood flow to skin, muscle, and intestine. However, there is other evidence to suggest that a direct attack on muscle cells by abnormal lymphocytic cells may be the cause of muscle destruction.

In adults the disease is usually progressive, ending in death after a long period of time. One variation of the disease is associated with the presence of cancer and will disappear if the cancer can be removed and cured. In contrast, it is generally felt that most children have a self-limited illness that lasts about 2 years. It is becoming apparent, however, that some children do develop chronic disease following an acute phase. Children may die either during the acute stage or of chronic residua, but most respond well to modern treatment. Children do have more serious skin problems than adults and have greater disease in their intestinal tracts, but do not develop kidney or heart disease. They may have involvement of the central nervous system, but this is not yet well documented or understood.

ONSET AND COURSE

Usually there is an insidious onset of weakness, which is most noticeable in the major muscles of the trunk, shoulders, and hips. The children have difficulty in climbing stairs and in getting up from the floor or out of chairs. They cannot do push-ups or knee bends. In a few, the onset is very sudden and the progression of weakness is very rapid. Skin changes appear at the same time, sometimes in subtle forms but usually in a fairly florid rash. Most characteristic is a reddening, shininess, and dry scaling over knees, elbows, knuckles, and tips of fingers. The lesions over the knuckles are so typical that they almost give proof of the diagnosis. Most children also develop rash on the face, neck, and chest (Fig. 12-1). This rash has a very characteristic "heliotrope" or violet hue. The eyelids are often swollen (Fig. 12-2), and swelling may also occur on the backs of hands and feet. A few children do not have skin involvement, and are said to have "polymyositis." There is probably no real difference in the muscle disease in these children, however. Some children also develop arthritis. Intestinal bleeding or perforation can occur in the early stages and is a major cause of death in this period. The other major early problem is pneumonia caused by aspiration of food or saliva. This happens because of the loss of strength in the muscles of the upper airway and throat. This type of weakness may be evident in school because the child will have nasal speech, and will be unable to pronounce *k*s, *h*s, or *r*s because he cannot move his soft palate.

Obviously it is best to reverse the weakness with therapy before serious complications occur. Before the advent of modern glucocorticosteroid (cortisone) treatment, about one-third of the children died, one-third were crippled by the progressive muscle disease, and one-third ended up functionally near normal. We now expect almost all children to respond to drug treatment. Very few should die, and most should return to near normal condition. In those in whom there is an incomplete response to therapy, progression of the disease leads to scarring within muscles. As the scars mature, the muscle becomes thinner and shorter, producing contractures and stiffness. This leads to immobility and crippling. A year or so after onset, some children develop plates or knobs of calcium under the skin and around and in muscles. This hard material extrudes itself through the skin and may be so extensive as to create almost an insect-like exoskeleton which cracks with movement. Sores produced in this way become infected and are constantly painful. The scarring of the skin may become as bad as that within the muscle. Children who are severely affected will be virtually immobile and may develop chronic pneumonias and eventually die. The muscle and the skin disease usually stabilize after a period of 2 years. Some people feel that most children will have no further problems. However, several centers have now reported that some children continue to have slow progression of their disease for 5 to 10 years. Muscle specimens have shown continued inflammation in biopsies taken as long as 9 years after onset. Arthritis may persist and may take on the appearance of rheumatoid joint disease. Calcium deposits last for many years and may remain painful problems. Relapses may occur many years after the onset.

TREATMENT

The medical treatment of dermatomyositis in children is largely limited to glucocorticosteroids. At the Children's Hospital at Stanford, all children so treated have responded, although other medical centers have not had uniformly good results. Very high doses have to be given, and these produce many unwanted side effects (see chapter on Juvenile Rheu-

Dermatomyositis

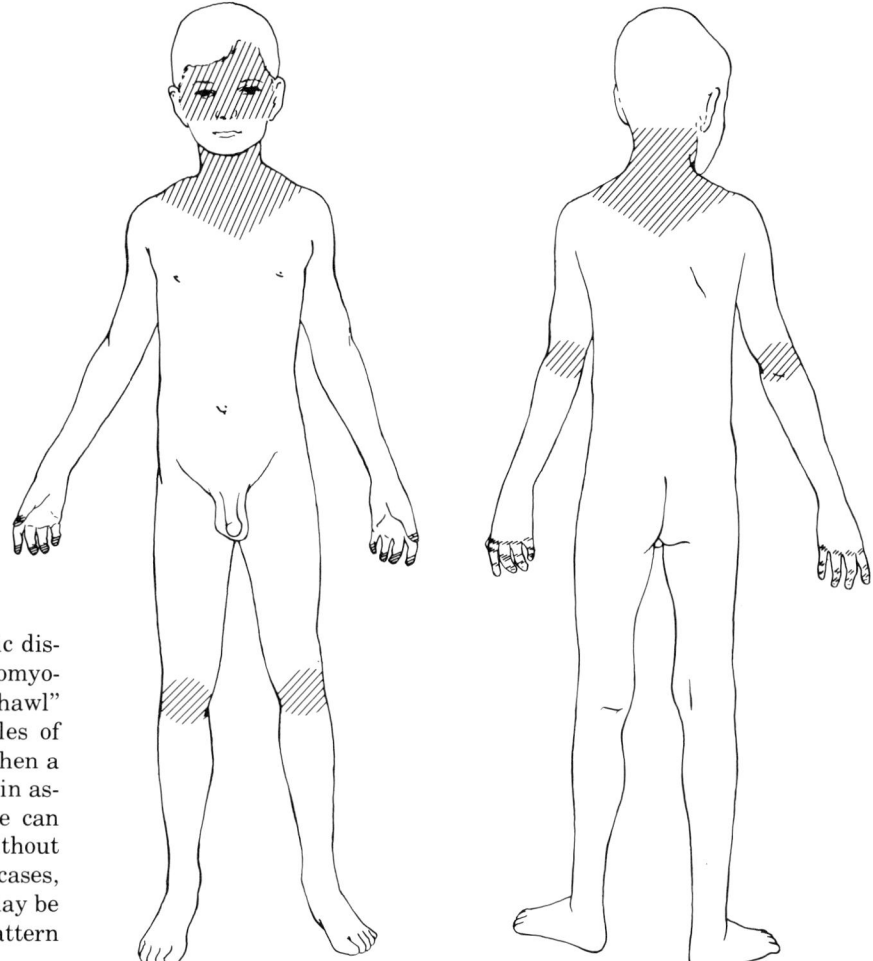

Fig. 12-1. The characteristic distribution of rash in dermatomyositis: cheeks and forehead, "shawl" area, elbows, knees, knuckles of the hands, and fingertips. When a history of weakness is found in association with this rash, one can make the diagnosis even without laboratory tests. In severe cases, the entire trunk and limbs may be involved in rash, but the pattern shown here is most typical.

matoid Arthritis). The worst problem that occurs is intestinal bleeding. This is also a complication of dermatomyositis, and it may be impossible to know whether the disease or the treatment is causing the bleeding. The dose of steroid is slowly tapered as the disease improves. Some drug is usually required for years. Relapses of the disease may occur as the drug dose is tapered, or after it stops, but these relapses will respond to

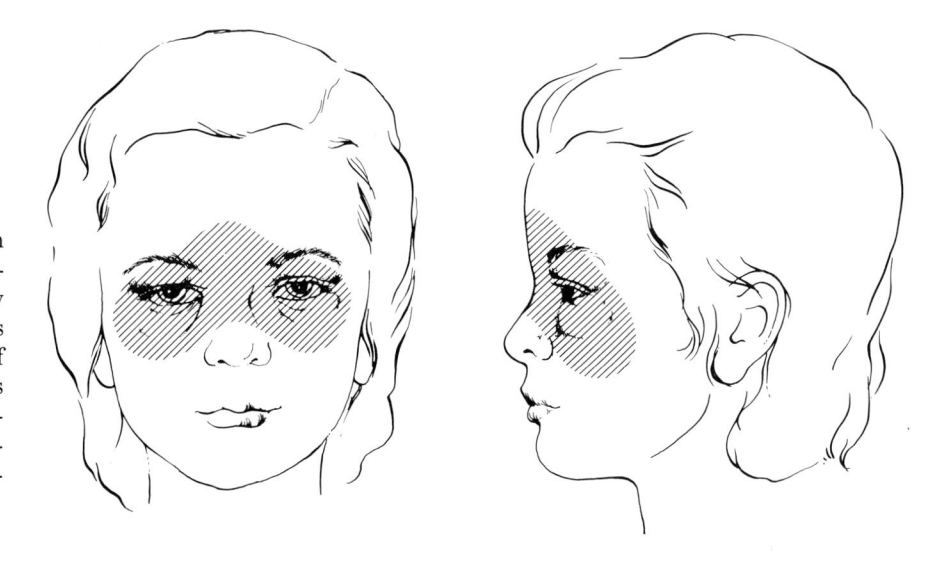

Fig. 12-2. The rash on the face may be widespread, but it is usually localized to the cheeks and the central portion of the forehead. The eyelids are often swollen and discolored, with a characteristic "heliotrope" hue (violet).

treatment as well as the original attack. In some medical centers, patients who don't respond are treated with methotrexate, an anti-cancer drug. We at Stanford use high doses of intravenous steroids when oral drugs are less effective than desired.

During this period, a careful physical therapy program is required. Initially, the child needs to have exercises that stretch his muscles and thereby prevent tightening and contractures. This must be performed by a physical therapist, since it will be painful for the child to perform himself once contractures have started to form. As the disease comes under control, exercises to rebuild strength become important. These must be done by the child himself. Although the problems are most apparent in the trunk, shoulders, and hips, the disease hits all muscles, and the therapist must be alert for changes requiring help in other parts of the body as well. The most common late problem is contractures of the flexors of the fingers, producing a claw-like hand that cannot fully open or bend backwards.

In children with severe residual skin problems, it may be necessary to avoid soap and to use special lotions to keep the skin soft. Infection in sites of calcium extrusion must be anticipated. Special bedding may be required to prevent sores from developing.

SCHOOL PROBLEMS

Most of these children should not present any particular problem in school. Some of the children do react with depression and anger at the limitations produced by the disease. Although most will have sufficient residual strength and mobility to perform general activities, few will be able to keep up with their classmates in any physical education program. This produces further anger and frustration. A common problem is falling. The weakness does not allow the children to catch themselves or to prevent a fall after even a mild push or shove in a school hallway or yard. They may not be able to climb stairs. For most of these children, noncompetitive physical activities designed to maintain mobility and increase strength are best, particularly in the period close to their acute episode. Severe acting-out behavior and delinquency has occurred in two children seen at Stanford. Counseling which anticipates and accepts the children's limitations may be helpful in preventing such reactions.

One child seen at Stanford showed a marked change in school performance after the acute phase had been successfully handled. Psychological testing indicated poor acute memory, which possibly was evidence that the disease had affected the brain as well. Only a few similar problems have been reported in other children with dermatomyositis, but it may be more common than currently guessed. Significant changes in performance or behavior should be examined by psychologists and physicians.

BIBLIOGRAPHY

Hanson, V., and Kornreich, H., Systemic rheumatic disorders ("collagen disease") in childhood, Part II. *Bulletin on the Rheumatic Diseases* 17:441, 1967.

Miller, J. J., III, Late progression in dermatomyositis in childhood. *Journal of Pediatrics* 83:543, 1973.

Miller, J. J., III, and Koehler, J. P., Persistence of activity in dermatomyositis of childhood. *Arthritis and Rheumatism* 20 (suppl):332, 1977.

Sullivan, D. B., Cassidy, J. T., Petty, R., et al., Prognosis in childhood dermatomyositis. *Journal of Pediatrics* 80:555, 1972.

13

Juvenile Diabetes Mellitus

ROBERT O. CHRISTIANSEN, M.D.
RAYMOND L. HINTZ, M.D.

Diabetes mellitus is a disorder of carbohydrate, protein, and fat metabolism, which may become apparent anytime between early infancy and old age. In juvenile diabetes mellitus, the body's main energy source, a sugar known as *glucose,* cannot be used normally because the body cannot make a hormone known as *insulin.* While the discovery that a child has diabetes mellitus may come as a great shock to both child and parents, a thorough understanding of the nature of the disease and its method of treatment can allow the child to lead a life that is as normal in almost every aspect as it was before the onset of diabetes. Juvenile diabetes mellitus is an unusual disease in that it is one of the few diseases in which the patients can be made into "miniphysicians" equipped to provide their own care. Only in this way can these children achieve the degree of freedom from diabetes required for living a normal and useful life.

NORMAL METABOLISM

The human body can be thought of as a type of energy-consuming machine, similar in nature to the automobile. In humans, the energy source—analogous to gasoline in the car—is the simple sugar, glucose. Glucose can come directly from carbohydrates in our diet, or it can be made by the liver from other types of food substances. All of the tissues in the body, such as muscle, brain, heart, liver, and kidneys, can use glucose as their major energy source. Glucose is consumed inside the cells of the body, where it is converted into the energy used for daily activity (Fig. 13-1). For glucose to enter certain cells, the hormone insulin is required.

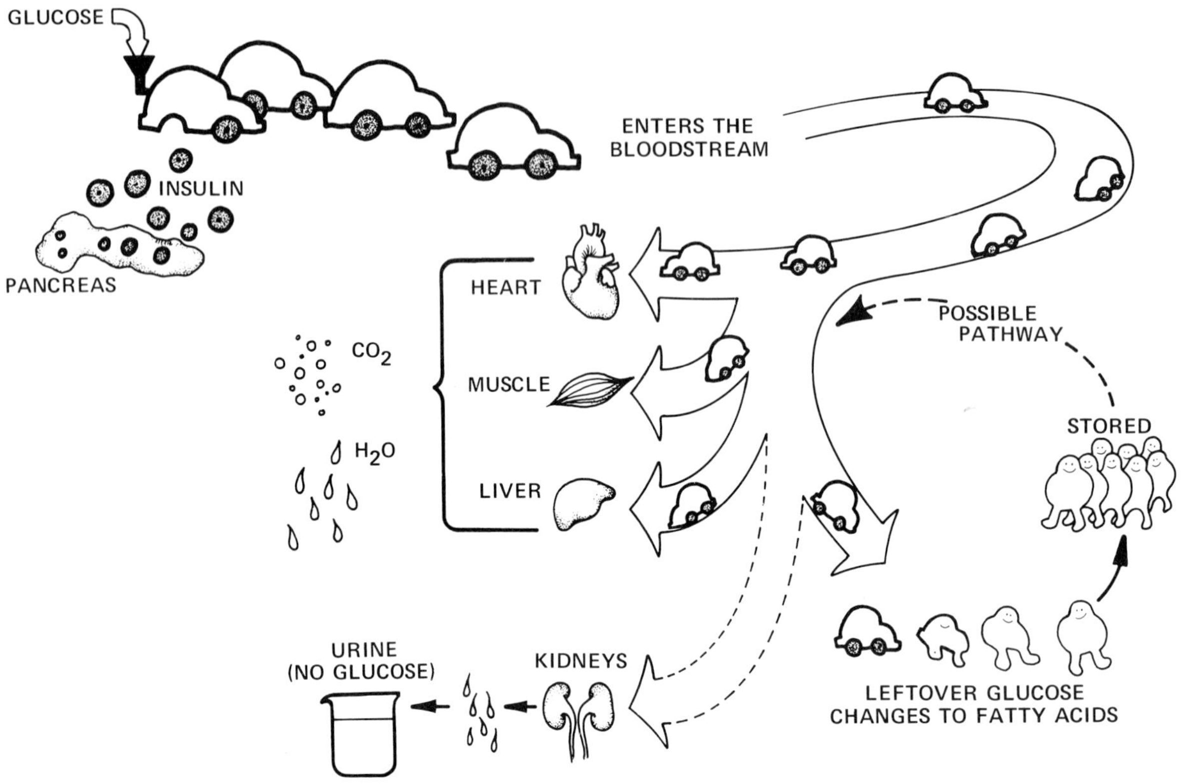

Fig. 13-1. Normal metabolism.

(A hormone is a substance that is made at one point in the body and is transported in the bloodstream to other sites in the body, where it exerts its action.) Insulin is made in the pancreas, in a special cell known as the beta cell. When a person ingests food, the amount of glucose in the blood rises; in the normal person this rise signals the pancreas to release insulin into the bloodstream. The insulin travels in the bloodstream to various parts of the body, where it exerts its action by allowing the glucose to enter cells where it will be used to provide energy for walking, playing, and so on. When we take in more food than is required for energy, the extra food is converted to fat and stored in special fat cells. If we do not eat for a relatively prolonged period of time, this fat will be broken down in the fat cell and released to the body in the form of fatty acids. Many tissues in the body, such as muscle and heart, can utilize fatty acids in place of glucose as an energy source. There are some differences, however, in how the body metabolizes, or burns, glucose and fatty acids. When glucose is used as a fuel source, it is burned very efficiently, leaving only carbon dioxide (which is expired into the air) and water. When fatty acids are metabolized, however, the endproducts, known as ketone bodies, must be excreted into the urine. Three ketone bodies are formed from fat metabolism; for simplicity, however, only one of them, acetone, will be used as an example in the discussion that follows.

METABOLISM IN DIABETES MELLITUS

In juvenile diabetes mellitus, the pancreas is unable to make insulin. It follows that the use of glucose as an energy source will be disturbed (Fig. 13-2). When there is no insulin, the glucose cannot move into the cells as fast. Moreover, the resulting shortage of glucose in the cells indi-

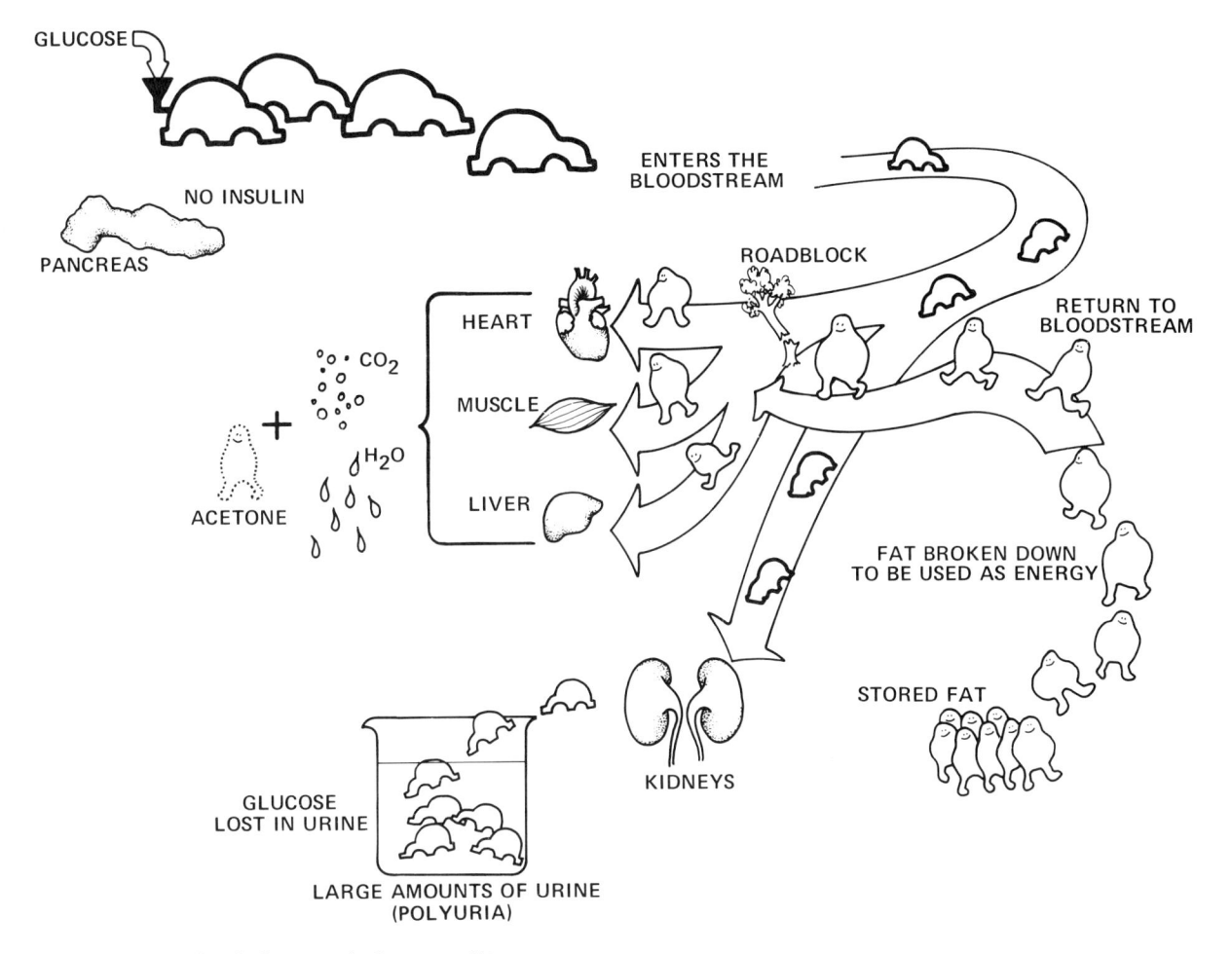

Fig. 13-2. Metabolism in diabetes mellitus.

rectly stimulates the liver to produce even more glucose. The amount of glucose present in the blood thus rises, and the amount of glucose passing through the kidney in the blood also is increased. The function of the kidney is to make urine out of blood. Normally, the kidney completely extracts the glucose from the blood, so that no glucose appears in the urine. When the amount of glucose delivered to the kidney reaches a certain level, however, the kidney suddenly finds itself unable to extract the excess glucose, and glucose begins to appear in the urine. As this happens, the amount of urine increases, because the glucose carries water with it. Thus, one of the first signs of diabetes is polyuria (the production of large amounts of urine). The diabetic who is producing too much urine now compensates by polydipsia (drinking large amounts of liquids). Since glucose in the blood cannot enter the cells, the body acts as if no food were being ingested, and fat is broken down for energy, just as in starvation. The patient now experiences polyphagia (the eating of excessive amounts of food) and weight loss. Tiredness and weakness also develop. If nothing is done, the diabetic will soon develop diabetic coma (technically known as ketoacidosis) and, if untreated, may die. When diabetes first appears, the development of these symptoms may take several weeks. Later, once the diabetic is being treated, the omission of insulin will result in the same symptoms, but their development will now require only a day or two. If an individual is going to develop diabetes, there is nothing that will forestall its development. Nothing that the individual did or ate caused the diabetes to appear. Likewise, it is not true that eating sweets will bring on diabetes.

In addition to juvenile diabetes, there is a form of the disease known as adult-onset diabetes. In adult-onset diabetes, the pancreas is able to make some insulin, but the amount produced is insufficient for normal glucose metabolism. Adult-onset diabetes may be precipitated by pregnancy, obesity, or certain medications, and is usually controlled more easily than juvenile diabetes, often by diet alone.

GENETICS

The development of juvenile diabetes mellitus is strongly influenced by heredity, but the degree to which it is an inherited trait is not yet known. The issue is further complicated by the fact that diabetes is not apparent at birth and may take months to decades to appear. Therefore, only a few generalizations can be made about the inheritance of juvenile diabetes. Diabetes is much more prevalent in children whose close relatives have the disease. A child is more likely to develop diabetes if both parents have diabetes than if just one parent has diabetes, is more likely to develop diabetes if a parent has the disease than if an aunt or uncle has diabetes, and is more likely to develop diabetes if an identical twin has the disease than if a brother or sister had diabetes. However, even if an identical twin develops juvenile diabetes, it is not certain that the other twin will get it. This fact and other evidence makes scientists think that some other factors, perhaps viral, are needed—in addition to heredity—to produce juvenile diabetes mellitus. Since diabetes appears any time between a few months and several decades after birth, and since there are many ways in which diabetes can present (juvenile diabetes, adult-onset diabetes, obesity-associated diabetes, etc.), it is not possible to predict who will or will not develop diabetes and what type of diabetes he will have.

TREATMENT

At this point, it should seem obvious that the way to treat juvenile diabetes is to replace the insulin that is lacking. This is precisely what is done. Since insulin is a protein hormone, its administration by mouth would result in its being digested by the intestine and, therefore, it would be rendered inactive. Insulin, then, must be injected to be effective. Once insulin therapy is embarked upon, insulin must be given daily for the rest of the diabetic's life. While pills may be used in some forms of adult diabetes, experience has taught us that pills are useless for the treatment of juvenile diabetes mellitus.

There are several kinds of insulin which are commonly used for the treatment of diabetes. One of these is called *regular insulin*. This insulin is extracted from the pancreas of the pig or cow and is not altered in any way. Its action begins within a half hour following its injection; its activity peaks at about 2 hours; and almost all of it is gone by 4 to 6 hours. This type of insulin is handy for quick results, but it would have to be given about four times a day to be useful for treatment. This drawback is overcome by the use of longer-acting insulins, such as NPH insulin or Lente insulin. *NPH insulin* is modified after its extraction so as to have a longer duration of action; its maximum action occurs 8 to 10 hours after injection. *Lente insulin* is even slower acting and has its peak activity 14 to 16 hours after injection. The action profiles of the various insulins are compared in Table 13-1. Mixtures of insulins are sometimes used to get the

Table 13-1. Relative Efficiency of Different Types of Insulin

Type of Insulin	Onset of Action (hours)	Peak Activity (hours)	Duration of Action (hours)
Regular insulin	½–1	2–3	4–6
NPH insulin	1–1½	8–10	20–24
Lente insulin	1–1½	14–16	24–26

desired results. In these cases, regular insulin is mixed with NPH insulin, or semi-Lente insulin is mixed with Lente insulin.

Almost all insulin now used in the United States is in the U-100 strength. U-100 insulin contains 100 units of insulin per cubic centimeter. Two special U-100 syringes are made for use with U-100 insulin. One contains up to 100 units of insulin and is usually used by larger children and adults. The other contains only up to 50 units of insulin. Since it is easier and more accurate to measure small amounts of insulin with this syringe, it is usually used by smaller children. Since there are still other strength insulin syringes available (U-40 and U-80), it is very important to make sure that only the U-100 syringe is used to inject U-100 insulin. Otherwise, a serious error in the dosage of insulin can be made.

TESTING THE URINE

One way to judge whether or not the patient is receiving enough insulin it to test the urine for sugar and acetone. The amount of sugar in the urine can be tested by using Clinitest tablets. Five drops of urine and 10 drops of water are measured into a test tube and a Clinitest tablet is dropped in. The solution begins boiling. Once the boiling stops, the test tube is shaken and compared against a color chart supplied with the Clinitest tablets. A deep blue color indicates that no sugar is present in the urine; the urine is said to be negative. The color gradually changes to green and then to orange as the amount of glucose in the urine increases. Each color has a specific value, such as 1+, 2+, 3+, and 4+. A value of 4+ is assigned to urine that turns bright orange; this signifies that the maximum amount of glucose measurable is present. Acetone is measured in the urine by the use of Acetest tablets. A drop of urine is placed on the tablet, and, after 30 seconds, the color is compared against a chart supplied with the Acetest tablets. No color is read as negative; light lavender signifies moderate acetone; and deep purple signifies strong acetone.

Urine results are always recorded by giving the glucose content first, followed by the acetone content. Thus, a urine might be said to be 2+ and negative (containing 2+ glucose and no acetone) or 4+ and moderate (containing 4+ glucose and moderate acetone). The amount of glucose in the urine is an indirect measure of how much glucose is present in the blood and reflects the level of insulin activity. Normally, no acetone is present in the urine. When acetone begins to appear in the urine, this signifies that fat is being broken down for energy; hence, insulin must not be present in adequate amounts. Normally, one likes to keep the urine showing 1+ to 3+ glucose and no acetone. Urine testing is generally carried out four times per day: first thing in the morning, before lunch, before dinner, and at bedtime. If a urine is to be representative, it must be "double-voided." This means that the diabetic urinates and discards the urine, then urinates again in a few minutes, testing this second voiding. This is that the urine tested is not urine that has remained in the bladder for a long time. With schoolchildren, it is often possible to dispense with before-lunch testing; having to test the urine at school may be embarrassing for the diabetic child.

INSULIN REACTIONS

While enough insulin must be given to allow the cells to utilize glucose for energy, too much insulin may be harmful. When an excessive dose of insulin is given, the amount of the sugar in the blood falls drastically. Certain organs in the body, and particularly the brain, cannot utilize fatty acids and thus have an absolute requirement for glucose as their sole energy source. If not enough glucose reaches the brain, then certain symptoms appear: headache, dizziness, irritability or other changes in personality, blurred vision, nausea, vomiting, profuse sweating, fast heart rate, cold hands and feet, and eventually, convulsions, coma, and death. These are the symptoms of an insulin reaction, or a hypoglycemic episode (low blood sugar). An insulin reaction is more likely to occur at the time of peak action for the insulin. If a diabetic receives too much NPH insulin at 7:30 A.M., for example, an insulin reaction would be likely to occur some 8 hours later, or at 3:30 P.M. The symptoms of insulin reaction, unlike those of ketoacidosis, are rapid in onset. Thus, they must be recognized and treated promptly if serious problems are to be avoided. Normally, the administration of concentrated sugar in some form will terminate the insulin reaction in a matter of 2 to 3 minutes. Sweetened fruit juices (such as orange juice), nondietetic carbonated beverages, or fruit-flavored hard candies (such as Charms or Life-Savers) are the best sources of rapid sugar. If the diabetic does not respond promptly to sugar or vomits what is given, medical aid must be sought immediately to avoid further problems.

Since it is important to distinguish between symptoms caused by too little insulin and those caused by too much insulin, these two situations are contrasted in Table 13-2.

CONTROL OF DIABETES

When a child first develops diabetes, he or she is usually hospitalized for 5 to 7 days in order to be taught those things that are necessary for self-care. The child must learn about diabetes, must learn how to test for urine glucose and acetone, must learn how to self-administer insulin, and must learn how to adjust the insulin dosage so that the amount taken is just right for him or her. Once the child leaves the hospital and is at home and attending school, he or she must be in control of the diabetes.

What does control of diabetes mean? Four criteria of control are commonly used.

1. Growth must be normal. The child's growth in both height and weight should be similar to that of other children of the same age and size who do not have diabetes.
2. The child must not have acetone in the urine. Ketones in the urine mean that the diabetes is sufficiently out of control that the body must utilize fat for energy; when diabetes is properly controlled, this is not necessary.
3. The child must not have insulin reactions, which are potentially dangerous and indicate that too much insulin is being administered.

Table 13-2. Effects of Too Much and Too Little Insulin

	Insulin Reaction	*Ketoacidosis*
Onset	Rapid (matter of minutes)	Gradual (matter of hours)
Symptoms	Headache Nausea Vomiting Palpitations Tremulousness	Tiredness Fatigue Polydipsia Polyphagia Polyuria
Skin	Cold and moist	Warm and dry
Breathing	Normal or shallow	Deep (air hunger)
Urine tests	Negative glucose Negative acetone	4 + glucose Positive acetone
Treatment	Sugar	Insulin

4. The amount of sugar in the child's urine should be sufficiently low that there is no increase in urine volume. The child should not have to get up at night to urinate.

Normally, the urine tests should yield values of between 1+ and 3+ for glucose. The test should not be negative (which would make an insulin reaction likely), nor should it be 4+ (which would signal an insulin deficiency). It is not always possible to accomplish this type of control, and many diabetics seem to alternate between negative and 4+ for glucose, with no tests ever in between. This latter situation is acceptable, so long as the amount of glucose in the urine is not sufficient to cause large urine volumes.

ROLE OF DIET AND EXERCISE

Careful control of diabetes mellitus requires that attention be paid to two other matters which profoundly influence the amount of insulin required: diet and exercise. Everyone should eat a healthy diet, and this is true of the diabetic as well. But there are other dietary requirements for the diabetic. The diet must be constant from day to day, both in the amount and types of foods eaten and in the times that they are eaten. This does not mean that the diabetic must have a special diet, or eat special foods, or be forbidden special foods, or eat the same thing from day to day. Diet is usually taught by the exchange system. By this system, the diabetic learns to substitute foods of like content for one another. He is free to choose what he is going to eat, but he must choose according to some sort of plan. This, then, allows him to select foods that are to his liking and still keep a constant diet. Most diabetics eat five meals per day: breakfast, lunch, dinner, and two snacks—one in the afternoon and one at bedtime. If a child is going to a birthday party, he or she can choose foods from among those offered that can substitute for his normal afternoon snack. The key to diet—and, therefore, to the control of diabetes—is regularity. If a child eats two eggs, two slices of bacon, a slice of buttered toast, and a glass of milk for breakfast one day and then a peach and a glass of water the next, it is unlikely that the diabetes will be kept under control and the child probably will not feel well. Likewise, eating dinner at 6 P.M. one evening and at 9 P.M. the next will adversely affect the diabetes. For the diabetic to feel his or her best, dietary regularity is essential.

Exercise, like insulin, increases the uptake of glucose by the cells. Thus, when a diabetic exercises, he or she burns glucose, while sparing insulin. A certain amount of exercise daily is necessary for all human beings. Again, the watchword is regularity. If the child with diabetes has roughly the same amount of exercise at the same time each day, it will be easier to control the diabetes. But this is not always possible. Some days it rains, and the child cannot participate in outdoor activities. In general, the amount of exercise should be roughly equivalent from day to day. Should a child wish to engage in more acitivity than usual, say on the weekend, then this is easily handled. If the child were to play continuously for a prolonged period, a hypoglycemic episode might develop; to prevent this, the child need only stop after each half-hour to an hour of play and eat a snack to cover the energy that has been expended. This simple measure will almost always prevent hypoglycemic episodes.

EFFECT OF INFECTION

One of the problems that the diabetic must face is the effect that illness or infection (such as sore throat, ear infection, or bronchitis) may have on his diabetes. Infection tends to make diabetes worse. Often a diabetic who has been in good control will start to have acetone in the urine during an infection. This means that the child with an infection will need more insulin for a day or two until the infection is cured. Extra insulin may be administered either by increasing the number of doses of regular insulin taken or by increasing the amount of NPH or Lente insulin taken in the morning. Once the infection has cleared, it is important to remember to lower the dose of insulin back to the preinfection level.

ADJUSTMENT PROBLEMS

Diabetes comes as a great shock, both to the child with the disease and to the parents. It may take time to adjust to having the disease, but, in general, the better the diabetic understands the disease, the fewer problems he or she will have in making this adjustment. It is important not to single out the child as being special and to avoid having the child's whole life center around his or her diabetes. Whether or not a child wishes to tell other children that he or she has diabetes is his or her own decision and should be handled on an individual basis. It is best that the diabetic child in school be treated the same as everyone else, with as little attention as possible focused on the fact that he or she has diabetes.

While the previous discussion has stressed the significant role the child may perform in administering self-care, age obviously modifies the role a child can play. Most 8- or 9-year-olds can test their own urine and record the results. Many children at this age can also be taught to measure and to inject their own insulin (with parental supervision, of course). Prior to the inception of puberty, all diabetic children should be performing complete self-care: selecting the diet, testing the urine, administering the insulin, and changing the insulin dose. When they are delayed in this regard, problems may result.

EDUCATIONAL IMPLICATIONS

The educator who deals with the child with juvenile diabetes should strive to achieve two goals. The first is to remain alert to the special needs of the diabetic youngster. This includes being able to recognize and respond to the sometimes subtle early signs of an insulin reaction—signs that can consist of only a change in personality or alertness. Prompt ingestion of glucose (e.g., a lifesaver) at this stage can prevent a more severe reaction. It is important to realize that recurrent behavioral problems or lapses in attention, particularly before lunch, in the midafternoon, or during physical activity, may be due to insulin reactions. If this is suspected, the child's parents and doctor should be informed so that an adjustment can be made in the insulin or diet. Other special problems that the diabetic youngster may have include polyuria (increased urination), with a need to visit the restroom more often, and polydipsia (increased thirst).

The second goal is to recognize that the diabetic youngster can lead an active, normal life, and to incorporate this child completely into all classroom activities so that he or she is not singled out as being different.

SUMMARY

Juvenile diabetes mellitus is an inherited disorder in which the body cannot use glucose normally because the pancreas does not produce insulin. The disease may be controlled by the administration of insulin. Good control depends upon maintaining a careful balance in insulin intake, diet, and exercise. The better the diabetic understands the nature of diabetes and its mode of treatment and can apply this knowledge to his or her own care, the more he or she may free himself from his diabetes. Under these circumstances, there is no reason why the diabetic child's life need be different in any way from that of the child who does not have diabetes.

BIBLIOGRAPHY

Paulsen, E. P., and Colle, E., Diabetes mellitus, in Gardner, L. (ed.), *Endocrine and Genetic Diseases of Childhood*, 2nd ed. Philadelphia, W. B. Saunders, 1975.

Renold, A. E., Stauffacher, W., and Cahill, G. F., Jr., Diabetes Mellitus, in Stanbury, J. B., Wyngaarden, J. B., and Fredrickson, D. S. (eds.), *The Metabolic Basis of Inherited Disease*, 4th ed. New York, McGraw Hill, 1978.

14

Down's Syndrome

LIEBE S. DIAMOND, M.D.

Mongolism, or Down's syndrome, is probably the most widely occurring and most easily recognized form of mental retardation. The disorder occurs in 1 out of every 770 live births among Caucasians, American Blacks, and Japanese. The incidence is strongly dependent on maternal age. The rate is approximately 1 in 200 live births for mothers 20 years of age or under and 1 in 55 for mothers over 45 years of age, with the rate climbing steeply after maternal age of 35. Paternal age does not appear to be significant. The prevalence of Down's syndrome (an indicator of the number of affected persons in the population) is 1 in 1000 among infants under 1 year old, 1 in 1400 among school-age children, and 1 in 2200 among those 10 to 14 years old. In the general population, the prevalence may reach 1 in every 3300 persons.

The underlying abnormality in Down's syndrome is the presence of a third Group G chromosome (trisomy 21).* Normally, there are only two chromosomes in the 21 position. In some patients, the extra chromosome material (chromatin) is not separate but is attached directly to one of the two regular Group G chromosomes as a result of the sticking together (translocation) of genetic material (Fig. 14-1). There are also patients who have more than one cell line; in these patients, only some cells contain the extra chromatin material, while other cells are normal. Such patients are called *mosaic* because of this difference in chromosomal content between the cell lines. Mosaic patients may demonstrate a complete

---

* See Appendix of chapter for details on genetics.

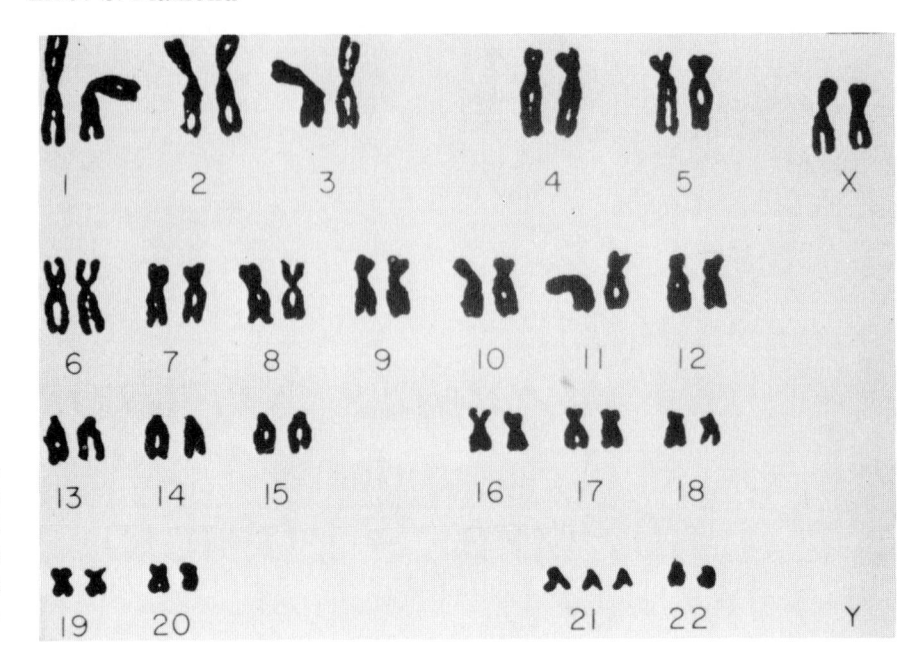

Fig. 14-1. Trisomy 21. An extra chromosome in the 21st group in classical Down's syndrome. Three chromosomes, rather than the normal two, are in location 21.

disorder of Down's syndrome, may be completely normal, or may show an intermediate level of affectation.

Females with Down's syndrome are fertile, and 50 percent of their offspring will have the disorder. No clear evidence is available regarding the sexual activity or fertility of males with the syndrome. The risk of having a second child with Down's syndrome is 1 percent for about 96 percent of all patients. It rises to 5 to 20 percent in that 4 percent of patients with a balanced t(21q22q) translocation in one parent. In this situation, a piece of chromatin material from one of the number 22 chromosomes is stuck onto a normal number 21 chromosome. The total amount of chromatin material is not increased, as it is in true trisomy. The affected individual is a translocation carrier, however, and can give to an offspring a more than normal amount of chromatin, causing the child to have Down's syndrome. The risk of having a child with Down's syndrome is also 5 to 20 percent for a parent with trisomy 21–normal mosaicism. The risk reaches 100 percent for the less than 1 percent of patients with a parent who has an isochromosome with t(21q21q) translocation. Such a chromosome is made of two identical partial pieces of the number 21 chromosome that are stuck together to form an unusually long chromosome that has double the amount of chromatin material for some characteristics and no chromatin material for others.

Carriers of balanced translocations, in whom the total amount of chromatin material is normal, but chromosomes are stuck together, are usually detected only after having a child with Down's syndrome. For unknown reasons, mothers with balanced translocations between the D and G groups of chromosomes are at a greater risk of having an affected child (10 to 20 percent risk) than are fathers with the same translocation (2 to 5 percent risk). If the balanced translocation occurs within the G Group itself, the risk approaches 100 percent if the parents have no normal children, but drops to the level of the risk for the D–G translocation if a normal child has been born.

Diagnosis can best be made by combining clinical findings with laboratory confirmation of the chromosomal abnormalities. Historically,

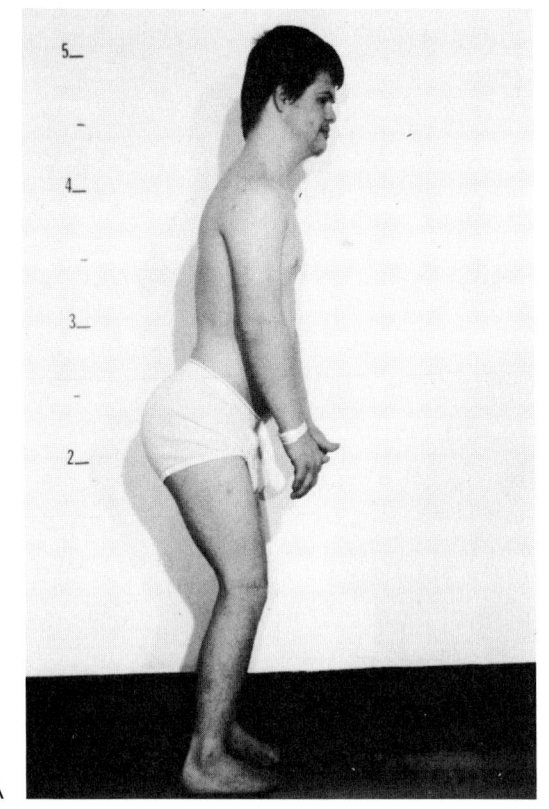

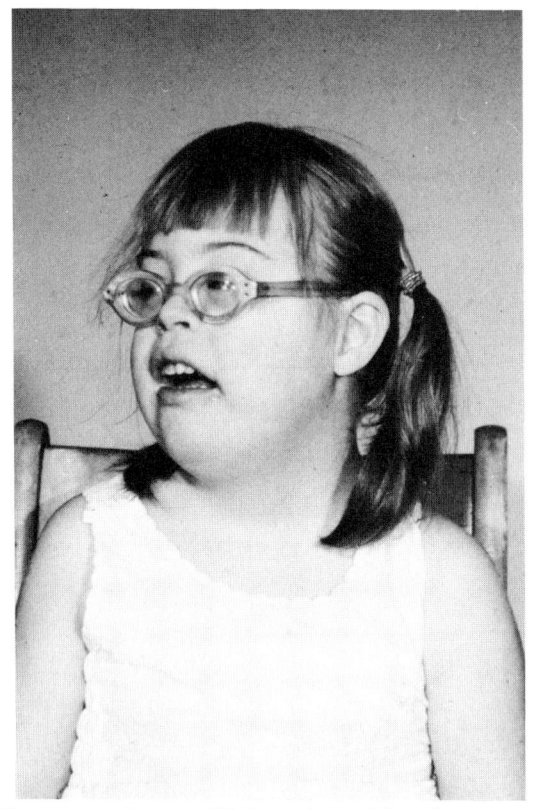

Fig. 14-2. Physical features chracteristic of children with Down's syndrome. (A) Round-shouldered stance, flattened face, small nose, small skull (brachycephaly), flat occiput, low-set ears, and excess skin at nape of neck. (B) Small nose, epicanthic folds, oblique palpebral fissures, and open mouth with high palatal vault.

mathematical manipulation of measurements of the skull and pelvis were used, but these were discarded when chromosomal analysis became available following discovery of the specific genetic abnormality involved.

CLINICAL FEATURES

The clinical features of the syndrome include:

1. Flattened facial features, slanting eyes (oblique palpebral fissures), a skin fold in the inner corner of the eye (epicanthic fold), a flattening of the back of the skull, a short, wide head (brachycephaly), and a small nose with a depressed nasal bridge and a high, arched, and narrow palate (Fig. 14-2).
2. Low ear position, with abnormally shaped ear lobes.
3. Eyes—problem in visual acuity, speckled iris (Brushfield spots), cross-eyes (strabismus), and inflammation of the eyelids (blephoritis).
4. Short limbs, round-shouldered stance.
5. Hands—short and broad, a curved fifth finger (clinodactyly), occasionally, extra fingers (polydactyly), a transverse palmar crease (simian line), abnormal and characteristic finger prints (abnormal dermatoglyphics), and a single flexion crease in the fifth finger (Fig. 14-3).
6. Feet—increased space between first and second toes, with a groove in the skin between the toes (plantar furrow). Severe

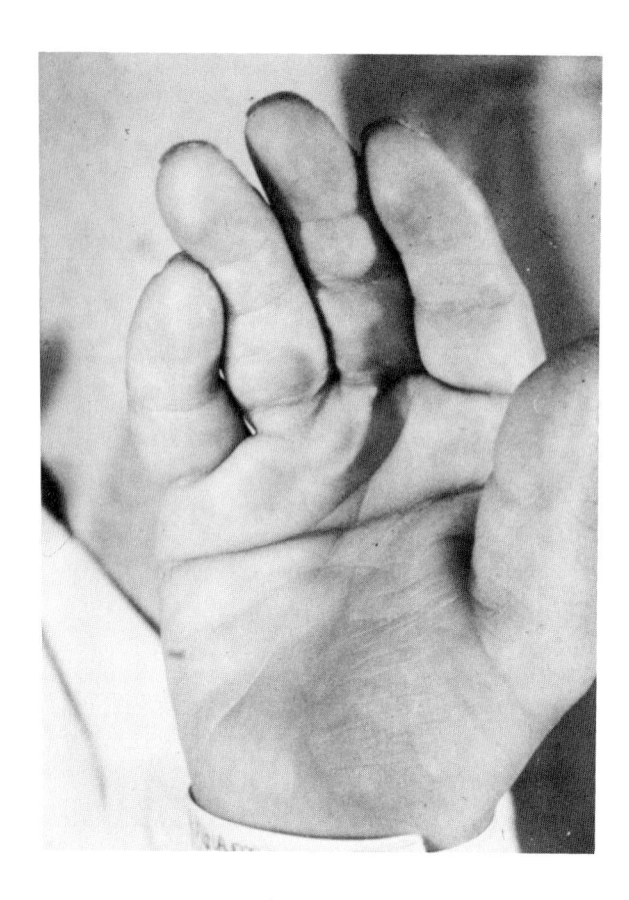

Fig. 14-3. Typical hand of child with Down's syndrome. Short and broad, with curved fifth finger due to trapezoidal middle phalanx. Note transverse palmar crease (simian line).

flatfeet, inward displacement of the front of the foot (metatarsus primus varus), very prominent big toes (hallux varus), and abnormal dermatoglyphics (Fig. 14-4).
7. Very poor muscle tone (hypotonia, hyperextensibility, or hyperflexibility of joints).
8. Absent startle (Moro) reflex at birth.
9. Excess skin at nape of neck.

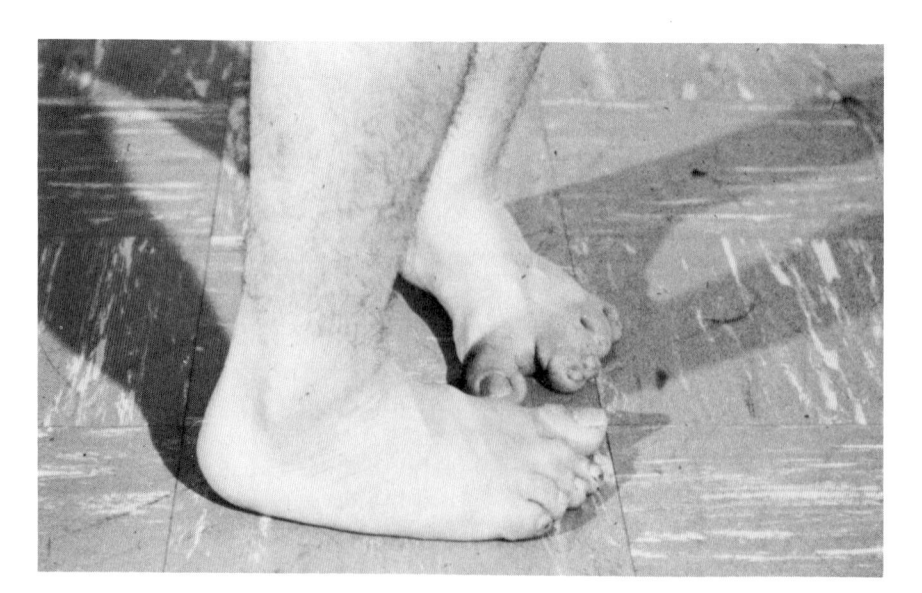

Fig. 14-4. Hallux varus. Big toe separated from other toes as thumb is from fingers.

Down's Syndrome

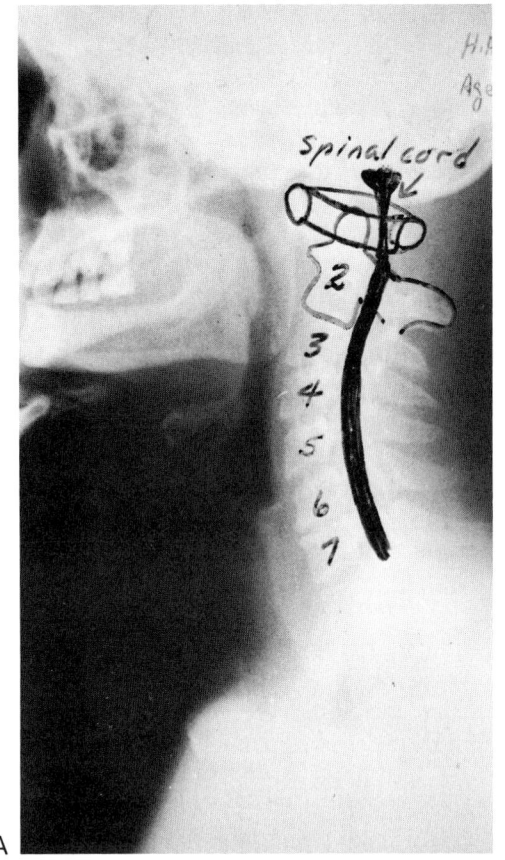

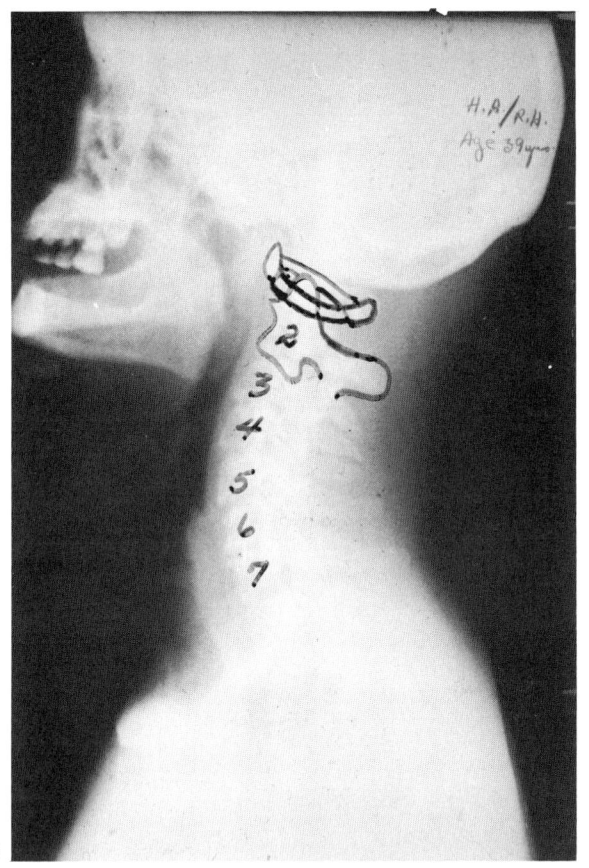

Fig. 14-5. X-ray side (lateral) views of the neck of a 39-year-old with Down's syndrome. There are 7 neck (cervical) vertebrae. The top, ring-like one is the first vertebra (atlas); the knob of the second vertebra (odontoid) extends inside of this ring. (A) When the head is bent forward, the ring of the atlas slips backward, pinching the spinal cord (unstable atlantoaxial joint). (B) When the head tilts backward, the ring closes in front and opens in back to give space to the spinal cord.

10. Mental retardation with delayed motor and intellectual development.
11. Furrowed tongue with dental abnormalities. The mouth is held open with fissures (rhagades) around the lips.
12. Congenital heart disease.
13. Leukemia.
14. High incidence of serious infectious disease, including pneumonia, sinusitis, ear infections (otitis), and bronchitis.

X-RAY FEATURES

The x-ray features are:

1. The skull is small (microcrania) and is flattened from front to back. The pharynx and nasopharynx are also flattened. The bones of the base of the skull are rotated upward and backward, and the cribriform plate, which lies at the top of the nasal passages, is located high in the cranial cavity. The upper jaws are poorly formed, and portions of the skull are lacking in fine bony structure. The sinuses are delayed in development, and the sutures of the skull are slow to close. The cartilaginous bones that form the very base of the skull are poorly developed (Fig. 14-5).

2. The long bones are shorter than normal, but stature is proportionate with normal annual incremental gains.
3. The growth centers at the ends of the long bones become joined to the main body of the bone at a delayed rate (delayed fusion of epiphyses).
4. The end-points of the skeleton, including nose, jaws, fingers, and toes, are poorly developed (acromicria).
5. Pelvis—in the first year of life, the shape of the pelvis can be diagnostic of Down's syndrome and, in fact, was used as the primary method of detecting the disease before the chromosomal analysis evolved.
6. The middle bone of the fifth finger is shaped as a trapezoid.
7. Severe flatfeet, accompanied by distortion in the normal angles between the tarsal bones (talus and calcaneus).
8. Abnormalities of the cervical and thoracolumbar spine, including, in 10 percent of patients, partial displacement of the first and second cervical vertebrae, as seen in radiographs taken in the side view.

MANAGEMENT

Trisomy 21 patients vary widely in their intellectual capacity and range from marginally literate to severely deficient. The vast majority are able to live at home or in foster care; only the severely affected require institutionalization. Immobile retarded persons do not long remain in the general community, however, and physically disabled adult retardates are rarely able to live outside an institution. For this reason, early and considerate management of the orthopedic affectations of Down's syndrome becomes important.

The severe flatfeet (pes planus) of the Down's patient can be managed in young children with arch supports and protective but flexible foot gear that will not produce pain. These children are relatively weak and are unable to flex a stiff or rigid sole. Even adults with symptomatic flatfeet, callus formation, and dropping of the ankle bones (talus) may respond to arch supports, provided that the deformity is not severe and arthritis has not yet appeared. In young children with severe symptomatic flatfoot, surgical fusion of the joint between the ankle and heel bone (talocalcaneal, subtalar joint) is an effective means of providing foot support and improving weight-bearing alignment. In older patients, more complete bony fusion (triple arthrodesis) is needed.

Bunion formation is a major problem in patients with Down's syndrome. It is important to correct the deformity when it interferes with shoe fitting or when it becomes painful. Patients in public institutions who have problems with shoe fitting are generally given sneakers to wear. In cold, wet weather, chronic skin changes occur in such patients because of the lack of protection given by these shoes. In warmer climates, patients who constantly wear sneakers are susceptible to foot injuries caused by objects dropped from above. Patients who are sufficiently educable to live outside an institution need to obtain proper footgear so that they can function in the general community and have pain-free feet. The underlying deformities of the Down's bunion are the inward displacement of the front of the foot and outward displacement of the great toe (metatarsus primus varus and hallux valgus; Fig. 14-6); these are best treated by surgical realignment. Simple bunion removal has not been satisfactory for long-term management. The "hitch-hiker's" great toe

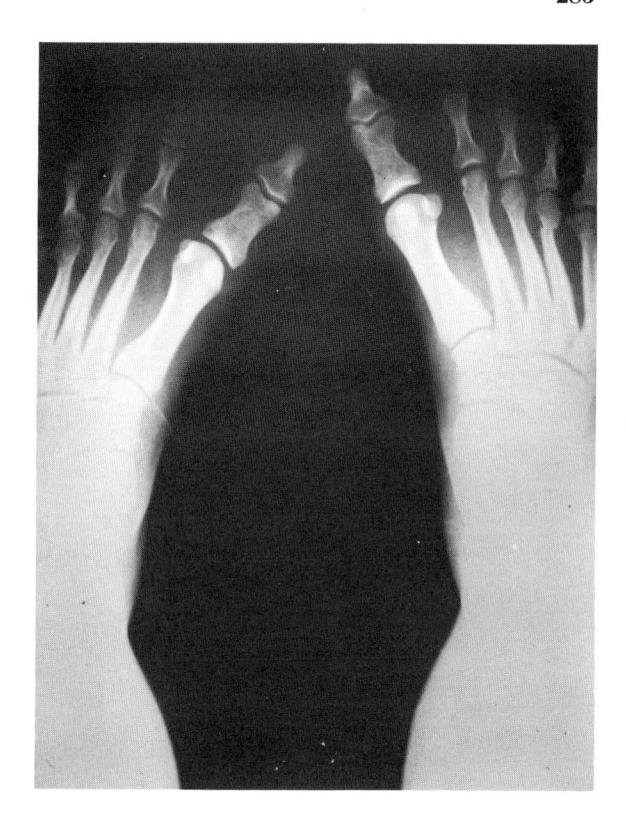

Fig. 14-6. Radiograph of feet with severe hallux varus and metatarsus primus varus. Big toes assume position of hitch-hiker's thumb.

(hallux varus) seen in young Down's patients makes shoe fitting almost impossible. The toes are cramped into whatever shoe is available, giving rise to the secondary bunion (hallux valgus). For this reason, severe hallux varus in the very young ought to be corrected by surgical realignment. Early surgical realignment is a simple operation which heals rapidly in the young child.

Among the most troublesome and difficult orthopedic problems are

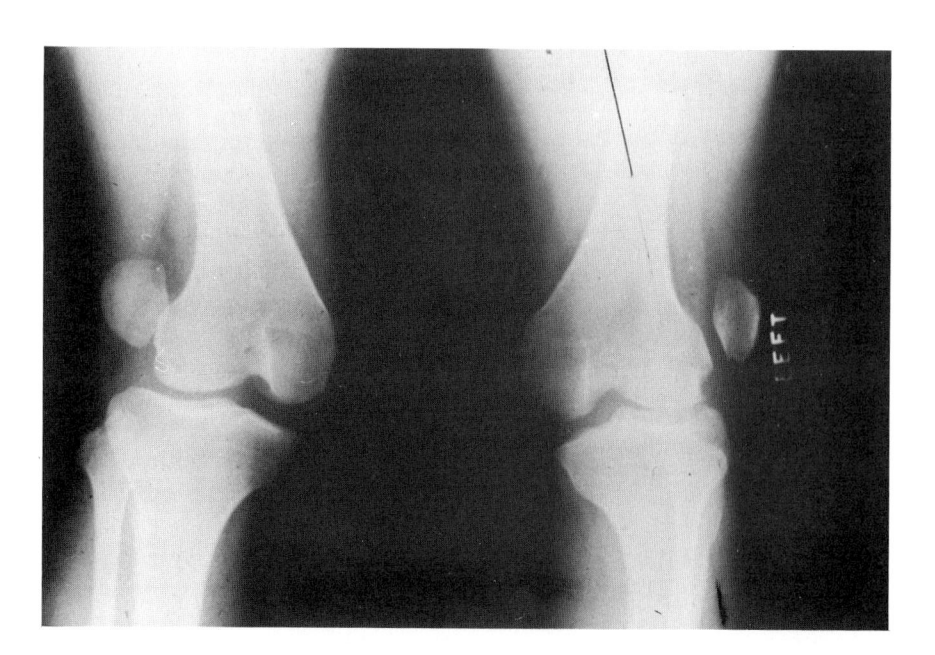

Fig. 14-7. Complete lateral disloction of the patellae with subluxation (partial dislocation) of the knees.

partial and complete dislocation of the knee cap (patella) (Fig. 14-7). These problems should be treated surgically; the specific procedure used should depend on the age of the child. In many patients, however, the softening of the cartilage of the patella (chondromalacia), or total absence of a suitable notch for the patella together with severe laxity of the restraining tissues, make removal of the patella the treatment of choice. When displacement of the patella has been very long-standing, the knee may be unstable. Knee fusion may be used satisfactorily in such cases, although all knee motion is then sacrificed.

Spinal curvature (scoliosis) is only rarely of major clinical importance in children with Down's syndrome, but these patients do respond well to spine fusion. There is no data available on the use of brace treatment in patients with Down's syndrome, but spinal brace acceptance is generally poor among severe retardates.

Patients with partial or complete dislocation in the first and second neck vertebrae (cervical) are at high risk for sudden onset of paralysis because of pinching of the spinal cord. There is evidence in the literature that patients seen early with slipping (subluxation) but without neurological signs frequently progress to four-limb paralysis (quadriparesis) or sudden death. This is particularly true in an institutional setting, where scuffles amongst the patients can produce unexpected injuries.

An ambulatory patient can live in the general community. If in an institution, he can be taught to carry out routine self-care and can have a more interesting life with his peers. A paralyzed patient requires total care, however, whether at home or in an institution. Therefore, patients with neck instability but without neurological signs are best managed by bony fixation performed before the onset of quadriplegia. It is helpful to use skull (halo) traction and to incorporate the halo into the postoperature cast. This minimizes the risk of loss of position in uncooperative patients. Because 10 percent of all persons with Down's syndrome have unstable first and second cervical vertebral joints, x-rays should be obtained in all patients with Down's syndrome to determine the status of the cervical spine.

Displacement of the growth center of the upper thigh bone (slipped capital femoral epiphysis) can occur at the hip and is a major problem because of the high incidence of death of the growth center (femoral head) and of the resulting secondary complications (Fig. 14-8). Early and careful pinning and close observation are required in the management of this difficult problem.

Dislocation and subluxation (partial dislocation) of the hip should be cared for by early conservative methods in plaster and bracing in infancy. If subluxation persists, tucks (imbrication) in the joint capsule, change in the angle of the upper thigh bone (varus derotation osteotomy of the femur) and alteration of the shape of the socket by cutting the pelvic bones may be utilized.

Many Down's patients adopt an abnormal sitting posture, and an effort should be made to prevent this. These patients sit with the sole of the foot placed under the chin with the knee resting on the floor, as one would rest an elbow on the table, while supporting the head with the hand.

Bilateral dislocated hips have generally been treated by watchful inaction (Fig. 14-9). In intellectually adept Down's patients, treatment

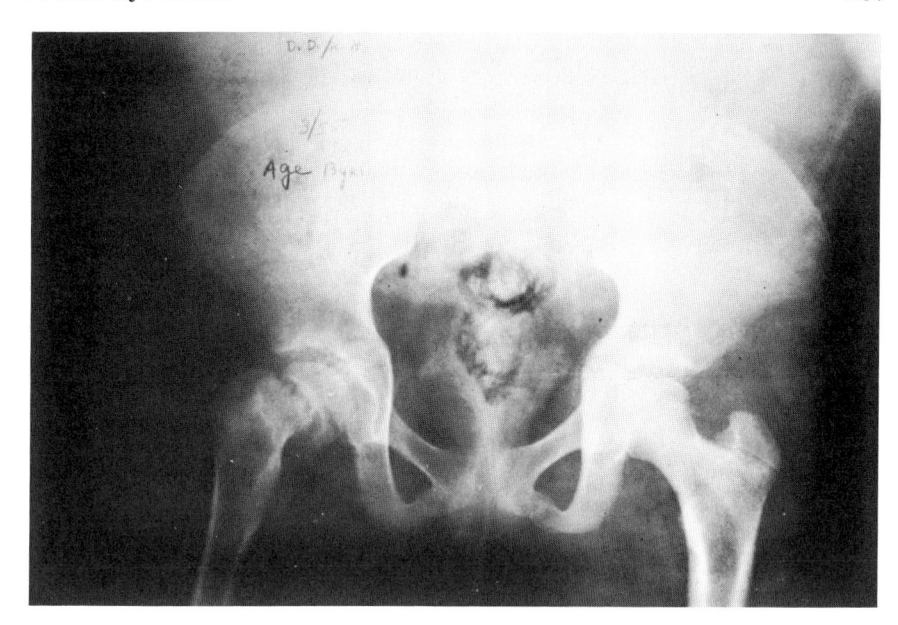

Fig. 14-8. Right hip growth center (epiphysis) has slipped on neck of femur. Slipped capital femoral epiphysis.

probably ought to be undertaken on a more aggressive level. It is not unusual, however, to have the femoral heads simply drop out of perfectly normal-appearing sockets because of the extreme laxity of the joint capsule. In such situations, it may be impossible, in spite of all efforts, to maintain satisfactory reduction of the hips.

Appropriate treatment should be given for clubfeet, polydactyly, rheumatoid arthritis, and the other scattered orthopedic diagnoses to which these children are susceptible, in order to prevent discomfort, improve function, and improve the appearance of those patients who are

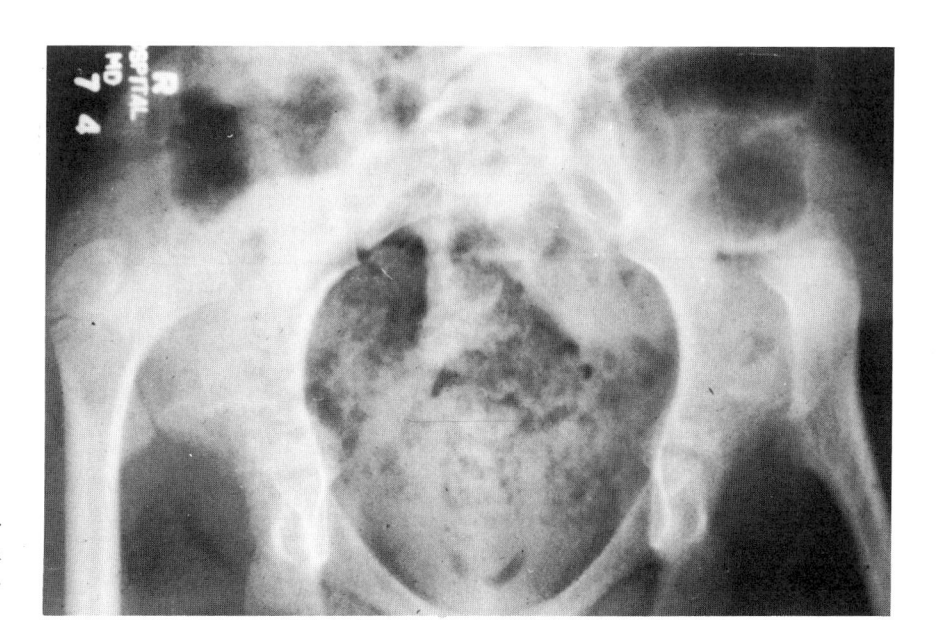

Fig. 14-9. Complete dislocation of both hips in spite of competent acetabula (sockets).

able to live in the general community. Because patients with Down's syndrome are generally pleasant and cooperative, they are ideal persons for rehabilitative care and respond readily to kind and considerate treatment by both physicians and ancillary personnel. Those who require prolonged hospitalization for major problems can be entered into the hospital school system without great difficulty.

APPENDIX: INTRODUCTION TO HUMAN GENETICS

There are a large number of handicapping conditions that are transmitted from one generation to the next as inherited characteristics. Long before the formal laws of inheritance were elucidated, men recognized the patterns of transmission of hair color, eye color, extra fingers, and bleeder's disease (hemophilia). In 1860, the monk Mendel, working with sweet peas, discovered the laws governing the inheritance of dominant and recessive traits. This information was lost and then rediscovered about 1900.

A *dominant trait* is a characteristic that is always visible in a child who received the trait from a parent. It is represented in genetic diagrams by a capital letter, i.e., "A." Common examples are achondroplastic dwarfism and extra digits.

A *recessive trait* is one that will not be visible unless the child receives the trait from *both* parents. The sole exception to this is a sex-linked recessive trait, which is revealed in the presence of only one donor parent because of the influence of sex. Recessive traits are represented in genetic diagrams by a lower case letter, i.e., "a." A well recognized recessive trait is the possession of red hair.

The chromosomes which carry the genetic information are located in the nucleus of the cells of all plants and animals. The chromosomes themselves consist of many small units, called *genes*, which are made of DNA (deoxyribonucleic acid) and protein. It is the DNA which contains the genetic code. Although chromosomes may be seen using special techniques of light microscopy, genes are so much smaller that even electron microscopy can only give a hint as to their location on a chromosome.

Most human cells have a total of 46 chromosomes. These consist of 22 pairs of *autosomes*, which determine the general characteristics of the individual, and 2 *sex chromosomes*, which determine whether the individual is male or female. A female has two X chromosomes and no Y chromosomes, whereas a male has one X and one Y. The presence of a recessive gene on the X chromosome produces a sex-linked disorder in males, because there is no countering gene on the Y chromosome. An autosomal dominant trait is carried by a gene on one of the autosomes, as is an autosomal recessive trait. The following sections diagram the patterns of inheritance for such traits.

Autosomal Inheritance

A = Dominant trait, e.g., brown hair
a = Autosomal recessive trait, e.g., red hair

An individual may carry traits such that he or she:

AA Carries brown hair gene on both chromosomes for hair color (homozygous).* Hair will be brown.

Down's Syndrome

Aa   Carries both brown and red genes (heterozygous).† Since brown is the dominant trait, hair color will be brown.

aa   Carries only red genes (homozygous). Hair will be red.

If AA mates with AA,

```
      AA × AA
  ┌────┬──┴──┬────┐
  AA   AA   AA   AA
```

All children will be homozygous for the dominant trait and will have brown hair.

If Aa mates with AA,

```
      Aa × AA
  ┌────┬──┴──┬────┐
  AA   Aa   Aa   AA
```

Two children will be homozygous and two heterozygous, but all will have brown hair. The two heterozygotes will carry the red hair trait.

If Aa mates with aa,

```
      Aa × aa
  ┌────┬──┴──┬────┐
  Aa   aa   aa   Aa
```

Two children will have red hair (homozygous for recessive trait). Two will have brown hair, will be heterozygous, and will carry the red trait.

If Aa mates with Aa,

```
      Aa × Aa
  ┌────┬──┴──┬────┐
  AA   Aa   Aa   aa
```

One child will have red hair and three will have brown hair. The two heterozygotes will carry the red hair trait.

If aa mates with aa,

```
      aa × aa
  ┌────┬──┴──┬────┐
  aa   aa   aa   aa
```

All will have red hair and be homozygous for the recessive trait.

Sex-Linked Inheritance

X = Normal female sex chromosome
X̄ = Female sex chromosome carrying abnormal trait, e.g., hemophilia
Y = Male chromosome

An individual may carry traits such that he or she is a:

XX   Normal female—no disease, no carrier state
XX̄   Female carrier of hemophilia
XY   Normal male
X̄Y   Male with hemophilia

If XX̄ mates with XY,

```
      XX̄ × XY
  ┌────┬──┴──┬────┐
  XX   XY   XX̄   X̄Y
```

There will be one noncarrier normal female, one normal male, one carrier female, and one male with hemophilia.

If XX mates with X̄Y,

```
      XX × X̄Y
  ┌────┬──┴──┬────┐
  XX̄   XY   XX̄   XY
```

There will be two carrier daughters and two normal males.

*Homozygous: Both chromosomes of a pair contain identical genes for a trait.
†Heterozygous: Each chromosome of a given pair has a different gene, e.g., one has gene for red hair, the other has the gene for brown.

Liebe S. Diamond

If X**X** mates with **X**Y,

$$X\underline{X} \times \underline{X}Y$$
$$X\underline{X} \quad XY \quad \underline{XX} \quad \underline{X}Y$$

There will be a carrier daughter, a normal son, an affected female, and an affected male.

Gene-Level Disorders

A brief list of gene-level disorders, transmitted according to the Mendelian laws of inheritance, follows.

1. *Autosomal dominant inheritance*
   a. Achondroplastic dwarfism
   b. Apert's syndrome—tower skull and fused fingers and toes
2. *Autosomal recessive inheritance*
   a. San Fillipo syndrome—profound retardation, with an abnormal substance excreted in the urine
   b. PKU—a well-known disorder of profound mental retardation, with excretion of phenylketones in the urine
   c. Red hair—an attractive trait, not abnormal, but transmitted by the autosomal recessive mode
   d. Sickle-cell anemia
   e. Diastrophic dwarfism
3. *Sex-linked recessive inheritance*
   a. Hemophilia
   b. Lesch-Nyan syndrome—increased uric acid, severe mental retardation, and self-abuse
   c. Color blindness

Chromosome Disorders

A karyotype is a map of an individual's chromosomes which is prepared in the laboratory in order to detect the presence of any gross abnormality of chromosome structure. In man, it is usually prepared from a culture of white blood cells. Possible abnormalities are omission of a chromosome, partial omission of a chromosome, or the sticking together of pieces of two different chromosomes (translocation). These accidents take place either (1) during the formation of the original ovum or sperm cell (each of which contains half the number of chromosomes necessary to form an individual) or (2) during the first few cell divisions that occur after fertilization, when the embryo is just starting to form. When the error takes place in the second, or subsequent, division of those original cells, there will be two or more cell lines with either normal or abnormal chromosome numbers. Such patients are said to be mosaic for the trait.

A brief description of some common chromosome disorders are found below:

1. *Turner's syndrome.* These patients have one X chromosome and no Y chromosome; that is, their chromosome type (genotype) is XO. They have only 45 chromosomes. They are ferile but appear female in body type. They do not mature sexually and require medication to develop the normal characteristics of an adult female.

2. *Klinefelter's syndrome.* These are males who have, in addition to their normal X and Y sex chromosomes, an extra X chromosome. They have large breasts and female body types but male anatomy. With their clothing on, many can be mistaken for females. They are sterile and may be retarded to a degree.
3. *Trisomy 21—Down's syndrome.* These children have an extra chromosome in the number 21 position on the karyotype. They are the classical Mongoloid children.
4. *Cat-cry syndrome (cri du chat).* These children are missing a part of the number 5 chromosome. They are severely retarded and have a high-pitched cry which sounds rather like a cat, hence the French name for this disorder.

15

Physically Disabled Driver*

Edited by
EUGENE E. BLECK, M.D.

One of life's activities often affected by motor or sensory impairment is the ability to operate a motor vehicle. Due to the resulting lack of mobility, persons with disabilities are often deprived of meaningful vocational opportunities, participation in community and cultural events, and recreational activities. Being able to drive offers the home-bound person independence and greater self-sufficiency. However, if these potential drivers are to operate their vehicles safely, not only is adequate equipment necessary but also proper training.

PROGRESS IN AUTOMOTIVE SYSTEMS

Much attention is now focused on mass transit for handicapped persons and on various para-transit and taxi transportation schemes. However, these alternatives only partially meet the transportation needs of disabled people. In addition, they need a convenient and economical means of getting to work and performing the many functions associated with daily living. A practical solution is to have many of these disabled persons operate motor vehicles independently.

*Reprinted from *Rehabilitation Brief,* 3(9), June 25, 1980, by permission of the Rehabilitation Research Institute. This study was prepared by RRI, College of Health Related Professions, Gainesville, FL 32010, and was supported by Research Grant No. 105-78-4014 from the National Institute of Handicapped Research, Department of Education, Washington, DC 20202.

Some of the difficulty encountered by disabled drivers can be overcome by providing information on opportunities already available. For example:

1. Selecting the type of vehicle most appropriate for their functioning capabilities;
2. Purchasing the most appropriate options and adaptive devices;
3. Arranging for installation of special devices;
4. Locating training facilities;
5. Evaluating driving tasks;
6. Employing appropriate operating procedures;
7. Assuring proper maintenance of equipment, particularly adaptive equipment; and
8. Taking precautions against problems encountered outside the car.

Early Progress

Paraplegics were among the first disabled group to be assisted with adapted driving devices—hand controls. These devices are used to depress brake and accelerator pedals by moving levers or knobs located near the steering wheel. At first, some of the hand controls were crude, makeshift devices, often fabricated by local garages out of sticks, rods, bolts, and wires. They were generally flimsy, unreliable, and often unsafe.

Recognizing this safety problem, the United States Congress authorized the Veterans Administration (VA) in 1976 to develop safety standards for adaptive driving aids which manufacturers must meet if these aids are to be purchased for veterans at government expense. As helpful as these standards are, they affect only a relatively small group of actual or potential disabled drivers. The VA has estimated that there are approximately 60,000 veterans who have vehicles equipped with adaptive driving aids. The National Academy of Sciences estimates that, for every veteran who drives with adaptive aids, there are ten disabled nonveterans who could benefit from similar devices. This suggests that approximately 500,000 or more additional disabled drivers in this country could operate vehicles using such aids.

Present Adaptions

Progress, however, has been made toward helping all disabled drivers obtain the adequate, safe equipment and proper training needed to effectively operate vehicles. Devices and vehicles that are functional, usable, available, and economically feasible are given primary consideration for adaption.

MECHANICAL CONTROLS

All known adaptive hand control systems are classified into three types: pull-push, right angle push-pull, and twist-push. In the pull-push type, the brakes are activated by applying force to the control handle in the direction away from the driver and parallel to the steering column. Control of the accelerator requires a pull in the direction towards the driver. In the right angle push-pull and twist-push types, the braking movement is the same as the pull-push, but the acceleration is accomplished either through a downward displacement or a twisting movement.

SERVO CONTROLS

Many severely disabled individuals unable to work with purely mechanical systems could probably be trained to become self-sufficient motor vehicle operators with the aid of power-augmented automotive control systems which are built into the braking and steering system. For example, to apply the brakes, the driver presses the rim of the brake-accelerator control wheel with one or both thumbs. Finger pressure of one or both hands in the reverse direction controls the accelerator. Since both the conventional steering wheel and the brake-accelerator control wheel rotate together, drivers can operate all three controls with their hands in any position on the double-wheel assembly.

VANS AND LARGE SEDANS

Today, many adaptive mechanical systems consist of rods and fasteners connecting manually-operated levers, which are mounted near the steering wheel, to the accelerator and brake pedals. Usually, these systems are installed in vans and larger-sized sedans. These type vehicles are preferred for two reasons: (1) the ease with which wheelchair users can transfer themselves from the chair to the vehicle, and (2) they provide plenty of storage room for the wheelchair.

Many disabled people cannot either transfer or pull the wheelchair into the car. Vans, therefore, become the major vehicle chosen, since entrance and exit are relatively easy when the van is equipped with a lift. A restraint system for wheelchair stability is also usually provided.

Three types of these mechanical systems with conventional mechanical hand controls for driving are now in use:

1. *Side-loading rotating lift.* Access to the vehicle is provided by a side-loading lift which rotates approximately 180° and is controlled from points both outside and inside the van. When not in use, the lift is stored in the van's cargo space.
2. *Direct side-loading lift.* This type of vehicle is also entered from the side. However, the lift is a structural part of the van. The side of the van lowers to form the lift. The driver rolls the wheelchair onto the lift, raises it completely, and closes the side door. In this case, the lift platform does not occupy cargo space. The unique feature of this system is the driver's seat, which is unique in design so that the user may independently transfer to it from the wheelchair.
3. *Rear-loading lift.* Entrance to this type of vehicle is from the rear. Controls for the lift are provided both outside and inside the vehicle—at the lift itself and the driving station.

The Unilever Control Servo System, however, has the ignition and the operation of all accessories, including lift and rear doors, actuated by pushing buttons mounted on a panel facing the driver. Actuated by a joystick, the direct connection linkage to the power brake servo valve eliminates awkward foot pedal push rods. To accelerate, the joystick is pushed forward, and to brake, it is pulled to the rear. The vehicle is steered by rotating its small, easily manipulated wheel.

A new system, zero-effort steering, has been recently developed and approved by the VA. Equipped with a fully automatic hydraulic lift, this system is fully adapted for severely disabled persons.

MODIFICATIONS FOR COMPACT CARS

Although modified vans very satisfactorily serve the needs of some drivers with disabilities, the primary goal today is economy. A suitably modified compact passenger car offers many advantages:

1. Lower initial and operating costs;
2. A savings of costly gasoline;
3. Ability to fit into ordinary residential garages; and
4. Driving a vehicle essentially the same as those driven by most able-bodied drivers.

The University of Michigan Rehabilitation Engineering Center (UM REC) is working on such a project. While the initial costs of the modified compact car may be the same as a modified van, the long-term operating costs, storage, and maneuvering problems would be reduced.

The UM Mechanical Engineering Department staff, along with colleagues in the REC, is currently developing equipment that will allow a person in a wheelchair to enter, drive, and exit an essentially standard automobile with ease. A Dodge Omni, donated by the Chrysler Corporation, is being used for this research. The Omni is particularly appropriate because it has both a relatively flat floor (due to front-wheel drive) and a large, rear hatch-back.

Preliminary studies concentrated on designing a special electric wheelchair for entering the car from a ramp at either the rear hatch door or the side passenger door. In either case, the following provisions had to be met:

1. Powered door operation with associated ramp extension and;
2. Powered seat adjustment to provide normal seating while driving and an extremely low position for entering and exiting the vehicle.

The rear entry is now a low priority project because it was found to be very expensive; the side entry was found to have several "concept" difficulties. Therefore, the most promising entry is the "door mounted access" in which a rider enters on the right-hand passenger side. The mechanics of this type of entry are more workable and can accommodate more people. As a result, two kinds of prototype chairs are also being developed: one for rear entry and exit, and one for side entry and exit.

CHAIR RESTRAINTS

UM REC has also developed a kit exhibited at the International Congress of Rehabilitation Engineering (ICRE) in Toronto, Canada, June 1980. The kit consists of a wheelchair restraint system with the following features:

1. Steel plates mounted to the frame of the chair which do not interfere with the folding of the chair nor add much weight to it;
2. Usable as either a passenger seat or a driver seat; and
3. Less expensive than other methods.

PROBLEMS OUTSIDE THE CAR

Besides driving the car, many other problems exist, such as parking, changing tires, and mechanical breakdowns. Disabled drivers need to be aware of these obstacles before venturing into traffic or before traveling alone.

Parking

Although the major parking problem is the lack of reserved spaces, many other serious problems do exist. For example, spaces may be either too far away from the building drivers need access to or may not be located next to driveways, curb ramps, or points of access to curb ramps. Also, many reserved spaces are so narrow the vehicle door cannot be fully opened to allow for the extension of ramps and electric lifts.

Changing Tires

Since personally servicing and maintaining the automobile are obviously difficult tasks for most disabled drivers, many are content to entrust these tasks to mechanics and service station attendants. However, many major problems concerning emergencies occur on the road, the most common being a flat tire. Disabled drivers should be encouraged to use self-sealing tires and also belong to a motor club. However, for persons who are capable and want to do it themselves, several suggestions may help. For example:

1. Relocate the spare tire to make it more accessible;
2. Use special aids for extracting the spare tire, raising it to the wheel, and lifting the flat tire into the car; and
3. Design or redesign tools which reduce required effort (e.g., extended jack handles). Disabled drivers should be also encouraged to carry aerosol inflators. In some cases this will enable them to take the car as far as the service station without changing the tire.

Breakdowns

Obtaining help when the car has a mechanical failure is another frequent problem. As a solution, increasing numbers of disabled drives install CB radios. Another solution is to use placards which alert passing drivers that the driver of the disabled car is physically limited. However, many drivers are reluctant to advertise their plight because of their vulnerability. (Many won't even use a disabled driver license plate or decal). Therefore, the CB radio can be the best solution to overcome their reluctance to seek help, since it (1) provides channels monitored by police and rescue services, and (2) allows the driver to talk with another driver before explaining what the problem is. Certainly any driver who plans to take lengthy trips or drive in areas where there is little traffic should use a CB radio. In fact, one report tells how one driver's wheelchair had to be pushed five miles down a dirt road after the car became stuck in the sand. (A CB radio was purchased shortly thereafter). Several other drivers reported being virtually imprisoned inside their disabled vehicles because they were unable to lower their windows to attract attention.

AUDITORY AND VISUAL PROBLEMS

Hearing Impairment

Auditory requirements for safe driving have not been established, and no state prohibits licensing of deaf individuals for passenger car operation. While certain studies have shown the possibility of overinvolvement in accidents due to hearing disorders, the evidence is inconclusive. At higher speeds, the level of hearing is unimportant, since the sound of the horn is neither loud enough nor fast enough to be a useful preventative.

Although hearing is obviously useful for driving, it may not be necessary if the hearing-impaired driver is aware of the deficiency and learns to compensate through education and training. Driver education programs specifically designed to teach the deaf driver exist and range from standard practice modifications to special car changes in dash-lighting. Often these programs include practice with simulators to miminize hazardous first-time-behind-the-wheel experiences. Also, special counseling may be necessary for some drivers, especially those suffering from the prelingual or progressive hearing loss.

Mechanical driving aids for the hearing impaired person are not elaborate. While conventional hearing aids may be of some value in operating a private vehicle, they are not usually helpful when driving a noisy passenger transport or commercial vehicle.

Probably the best aids currently available to the hard-of-hearing are the addition of both right and left outside mirrors. Also, many public information sources are available giving guidelines for compensatory activities, such as having a hearing passenger when driving unfamiliar routes or making frequent checks on possible mechanical problems. One publication which might be particularly useful is "Tips on Car Care and Safety for Deaf Drivers," available through the U.S. Department of Transportation, National Highway Safety Administration, Washington, D.C. 20590.

Low Vision

Individuals who are partially sighted or legally blind can pass the static central acuity tests (tests the ability to read road signs and to correctly identify objects) for driver licensing in some states with telescopic spectacles or "Camera lens spectacles." The bioptic telescopic spectacles consist of camera-like lens, coupled with a prism, and a high-powered eyepiece located in the upper part of a regular pair of glasses. They provide from 300- to 800-percent vision increase. They can also help patients with blind spots in the retina.

For general viewing, the driver uses regular glasses. When driving, a lowering of the head brings the telescope into focus for reading signs and spotting objects in the driving environment.

The lenses are either 2 in. in length and extend 1½ in. from the regular glasses or, in some cases, concealed. A pair of sunglasses fits over the lenses to completely shade the eyes from the sun and glare in front, on top, and on the sides.

However, not all state licensing agencies approve of these lenses. Interested persons should check with the local licensing office regarding this factor.

For additional information about these lenses, contact the nearest low-vision aid center.

DEVELOPMENTS FOR ARMLESS DRIVERS

In Heidelberg, West Germany, safety technician Eberhard Franz has driven 380,000 kilometers without an accident since 1965. Nine years before, in 1956, Franz had both arms amputated.

Twenty years old, Franz did not want to give up driving and spent the next decade working with colleagues on a system for armless drivers. In 1965, he modified a standard Renault automobile with a specially designed apparatus considered roadworthy by the German car-testing authorities. His now patented system is being built in the Volkswagen "Golf," or better known in the United States as the "Rabbit."

The system consists of a bicycle-type pedal attached to the steering mechanisms of the vehicle by a chair and gears. Turning is accomplished by rotating the pedal—forward for the right, backward for left. The use of all other vehicle controls (lights, wipers, etc.) is also adapted for foot control. The system also does not interfere with regular driving since all the standard facilities have not been changed. Conversion to regular use is possible after releasing the steering pedal and the brake lever.

These units are now available in the United States and are being distributed by Die-A-Matic, Inc., 4004 Fifth Road North, Arlington, VA 22203. The standard kit's cost, including installation, is $4433. However, special accessories are extra. For example, foot operation for the heating system is an extra $130 (including installation).

DRIVER EDUCATION: ONE MODEL PROGRAM

In 1972, the Human Resources Center (HRC) initiated an Adapted Driver Education Program. The program, which was offered free to all disabled residents of Nassau County over the age of 16, was sponsored by the Nassau County Traffic Safety Board and backed with a federal grant through the New York State Office of Vocational Rehabilitation.

Presently, HRC is setting up several statewide, regional centers for teaching this program.

These programs offer disabled drivers individualized, comprehensive training which, in turn, gives them as much time as they need to learn. They attend classes in a specially designed driving laboratory that is equipped with simulated driver's compartments and has a variety of hand controls. Each unit is wired to a movie projector showing films of potentially hazardous situations students might encounter on the highway. A nearby computer gives an automatic readout of the student's performance in reacting to the filmed hazards.

Procedures

Under the supervision of the driver education instructor, students are first taught how to get into and out of cars and vans and are then instructed in the proper use of the specific devices adapted for their functional capabilities. They are also taught how to handle emergency situations and how to compensate for functional limitations. Students are also given road training in a specially modified training car. Therefore, when the course is finished, a driver's test can be confidentially taken.

Instruction for Teachers

By law (P.L. 94-142, 1975), public schools conducting driver education must open their course to physically disabled persons. Therefore, several courses are offered which help these driver education teachers serve physically disabled persons. Some are offered at universities such as Adelphi. However, the Human Resources Center does offer an "inservice" course (at the center) for private driving instructors as well. The course includes items such as testing and licensing, evaluation and functional classification of disabilities, evaluation of automobile driving aides, adapted driver education and special problems. As part of the course, the teachers must then work with experienced disabled driver educators in schools or in the Human Resources Center for a short period of time before receiving credit and certification.

Plans are also under way for a training program for driver examiners and inspectors, since some of these state officials have limited experience in examining disabled drivers.

Directors of this program believe it will not only help many disabled people enjoy increased economic, educational, and recreational fulfillment but will also engender greater feelings of independence and general life satisfaction.

FOR MORE INFORMATION

McKnight, A. J., Greer, M. A., Marsten, F., and Koppa, R. J., *Assessment of Vehicle Safety Problems for Special Driving Populations* (Final Report No. DOT-HA-804-918). Alexandria, Va., National Public Services Research Institute, February 1979. This report is available from the National Technical Information Service, 5285 Port Royal Road, Springfield, VA 22161.

Personalized Licensed Vehicles for the Disabled: Report of a Workshop, June 1976. Copies available for $5.00 from the Publications Office, Moss Rehabilitation Hospital, 12th Street and Tabor Road, Philadelphia, PA 19141.

Pearson, J. R., and Cole, T. M. (Edited by J. Cassairt), *University of Michigan Rehabilitation Engineering Center Activities Reports,* Nos. 1 and 2. Ann Arbor, Mich., University of Michigan, 1978, 1979. The Reports, and the UM REC *Newsletter,* are available from UM REC, W. E. Lay Automotive Laboratory, Ann Arbor, MI 48109.

For a list of driving schools in the Unites States prepared to work with disabled drivers and manufacturers of special adaptive driving equipment, the American Automobile Association (AAA) has a publication, *The Handicapped Driver's Mobility Guide.*

To obtain any of the four manuals listed below or for information about Driver's Training Program, contact Mr. Edward C. Colverd, Director of Driver Education, Human Resources Center, I.U. Willets Road, Albertson, NY 11507.

Evaluating Driving Potential of Persons with Physical Disabilities ($2.75).

Teacher's Preparation Course in Driver Education for the Physically Disabled ($3.25).

Teaching Driver Education to the Physically Disabled ($3.75).

Hand Controls and Assistive Devices for the Physically Disabled Driver ($2.75).

Information on VA standards for assistive devices can be obtained by writing Mr. Anton Reichengerber, Chief, Testing and Development Division, Veterans Administration Prosthetics Center, 252 Seventh Avenue, New York, NY 10001.

Driving Systems for Independent Mobility. A monograph available for $2.50 from Elise Brown, ADL, Inc., 6 Hurlow Court, Rockville, MD 20850.

16

Emergencies

EUGENE E. BLECK, M.D.

Although many incidents can occur in the classroom that can be called emergencies, most of these can be handled by referral to the school nurse or, if needed, transfer to the nearest physician's office or hospital emergency room. Three emergencies, however—choking, respiratory arrest, and cardiac arrest—demand *immediate* measures by attendant personnel.

This chapter outlines what to do in situations of arrested breathing, heart stoppage, or both. It is meant to serve only as a refresher to those who have taken a cardiopulmonary resusitation (CPR) course conducted by the Red Cross, the local medical community, the local hospital, the local education department, or the American Heart Association and does *not* substitute for formal instruction in how to manage these urgent and life-threatening situations.

AIRWAY OBSTRUCTION (CHOKING)

Airway obstruction with secondary cardiac arrest is more common in children than is primary cardiac arrest. In children, the most frequent cause of airway obstruction is a foreign body that becomes lodged in the airway, e.g. a toy, peanut, or fruit stone. Less often, the cause is an infection, such as croup, that causes the epiglottis to swell, thereby closing off the airway to the lungs.

Universal Distress Signal

The universal distress signal for choking (Fig. 16-1) should be taught to all children so that they will be able to recognize it in themselves and in others.

Fig. 16-1. Universal distress signal for choking. Can be taught to all children and adults. [From the *Journal of the American Medical Association* 244 (suppl. 5):453–509, 1980. Copyright 1980, the American Medical Association. Reprinted with permission from the American Heart Association.]

Choking Due to Infection Versus a Foreign Body

To differentiate between obstruction caused by infection and that caused by a foreign body, the circumstances under which the emergency occurs need to be delineated. If the child has been ill, has a fever, a barking cough, and begins to wheeze and choke, the obstruction is probably due to infection; transport to a hospital emergency room or an advanced life-support facility should not be delayed. If, on the other hand, the child chokes while eating peanuts or playing with toys, then the cause is most likely a foreign body; on-the-spot measures to relieve the obstruction and cardiopulmonary resuscitation should be employed.

Disgorging a Foreign Body from the Airway

Infants and Children Ages 1 to 8 years*

In infants,

1. Straddle the baby over your arm, face down, and support the head by placing your hand around the jaw. With the other hand, give four blows to the back between the shoulder blades.
2. Sandwiching the baby between two hands, turn the infant over on its back; keeping the head down, deliver four chest thrusts in rapid succession by putting your fingers over the breastbone and pushing down.
3. If the infant is not breathing on its own, reopen the airway, put your mouth over the baby's nose and mouth, and deliver four breaths.
4. If obstruction persists, repeat steps 1, 2, and 3.

If the child is too large to be straddled over your forearm, go down on your knees and drape the child over your knee, with face and head down. Give four back blows, then roll the child over, and apply four chest compressions (see Fig. 16-9).

*Throughout this chapter, the age divisions are those used by the American Heart Association. At the time of the emergency, however, exact age is *not important,* since a slight error in either direction is not critical.

Emergencies

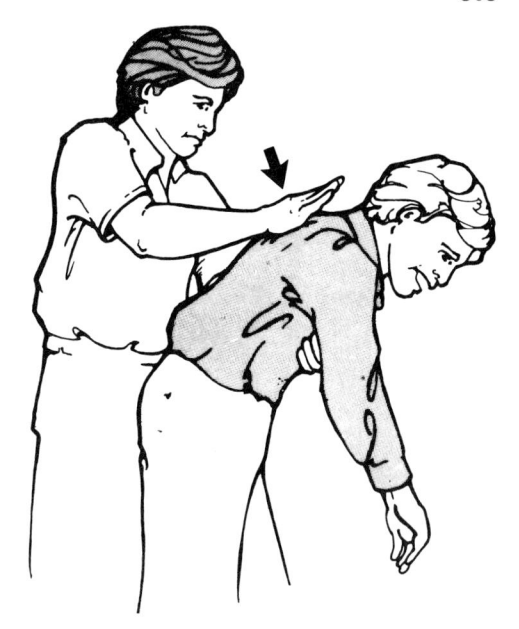

Fig. 16-2. Back blows, standing. [From the *Journal of the American Medical Association* 244 (suppl. 5):453–509, 1980. Copyright 1980, the American Medical Association. Reprinted with permission from the American Heart Association.]

Children, 8 Years, to Adults

1. *Back blows.* Deliver four sharp blows with the heel of your hand to the spine between the shoulder blades (Fig. 16-2). This can be done while standing or sitting. If the victim is lying down, kneel and roll the victim onto his or her side, facing you, with his or her chest against your thigh. Then deliver the four back blows.
2. *Abdominal thrusts.* (Use this or alternate, chest-thrust method.)
   a. *Victim standing or sitting.* Stand behind the victim and wrap your arms around the victim's waist. Make a fist with one hand and clamp the other hand over it (Fig. 16-3). Placing the thumb side of your fist over the victim's belly between the waist and rib cage, press your fist upward and inward into belly four times.
   b. *Victim lying on back* (unconscious). Straddle the victim's thigh and perform the same maneuver as in (a), thrusting upward and inward with the fist.
3. *Chest thrusts.* (Alternative to abdominal-thrust method.)
   a. *Victim standing.* Stand behind victim and place your arms directly under the victim's armpits, encircling the chest. Place the thumb side of your fist in the middle of the victim's breastbone. Make a fist with one hand, grasp it with the other and give four backward thrusts (Fig. 16-4).
   b. *Victim lying on back* (unconscious). Kneel close to side of victim's body and use same hand position as is used for closed-chest heart compression (Fig. 16-9).
4. *Finger sweeps.* With victim's head tilted back, open mouth, grasp the tongue and lower jaw between your thumb and fingers, and pull forward. Insert the index finger of your other hand into the victim's mouth and sweep it along the cheek and throat to the base of the tongue. Using the hooked finger, you may dislodge the foreign body into the mouth, where it is easily removed. *Caution:* do not push the object deeper into the airway.

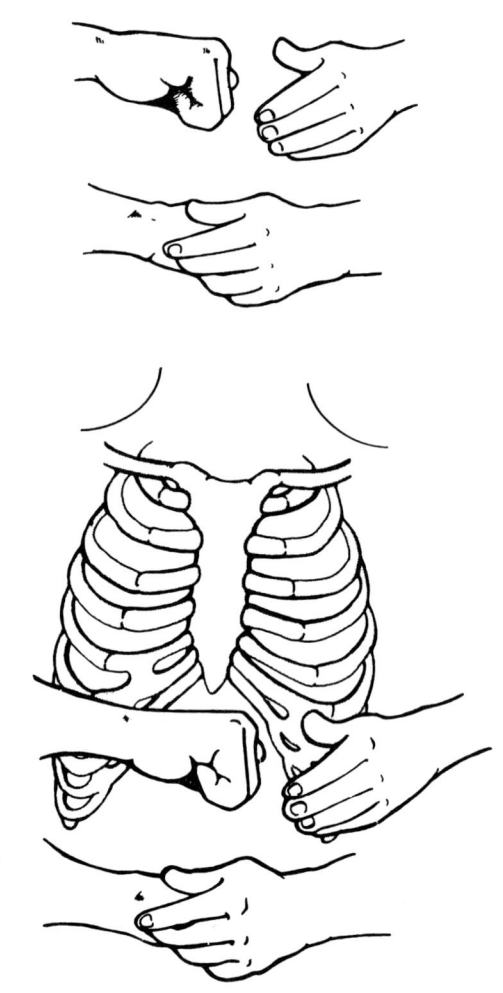

Fig. 16-3. Hand placement for abdominal thrust. [From the *Journal of the American Medical Association* 244 (suppl. 5):453–509, 1980. Copyright 1980, the American Medical Association. Reprinted with permission from the American Heart Association.]

Fig. 16-4. Chest thrust, standing. [From the *Journal of the American Medical Association* 244 (suppl. 5):453–509, 1980. Copyright 1980, the American Medical Association. Reprinted with permission from the American Heart Association.]

Emergencies

CARDIOPULMONARY RESUSCITATION (CPR)

The following steps are outlined to assist you in reviving a child or adult whose heart and breathing have stopped (cardiac and pulmonary arrest):

1. Recognize (diagnose) the CPR signs:
   a. Carotid pulse absent—feel large artery next to windpipe (trachea) in the neck (Fig. 16-5).
   b. Pupils wide open (dialated) (Fig. 16-6).
   c. Respiration absent—look at the chest to see whether it is moving (Fig. 16-7).

To make sure that the child has not merely fainted (syncope), it is important to always check for these CPR signs.

2. Mouth-to-mouth ventilation (Fig. 16-8).
   a. Clear the airway by removing any food, gum, bridges, etc., from the victim's mouth; to do this, pull the tongue out and sweep your finger inside the mouth.
   b. Hyperextend neck—tilt head backward by placing one hand behind neck and pushing up (Fig. 16-8).
   c. For a child, put your mouth over his nose and mouth and exhale; the child's chest should move (expand). For a large teenager or adult, pinch off nose with one hand, put your mouth over his mouth, and exhale.
   d. Give four quick, full successive breaths initially, followed by one breath every 5 seconds in larger children and adults and one every 3 seconds in infants and small children (ages 1 to 8 years).
3. Heart massage (Fig. 16-9).
   a. Put child flat on his back on a hard surface—the floor will do.
   b. Kneel beside or straddle the child.
   c. Locate lower half of breastbone (sternum).
   d. Keep fingers out straight.
   e. Keeping arms straight, compress the breastbone. For adults, use both hands; for children, use one hand; for infants, use two or three fingers over the sternum and one hand behind the chest.
   f. Rate of compression:
      Adults, 60/min (over 8 years)
      Children, 80/min (ages 1 to 8 years)
      Infants, 100/min (under age 1 year)
   g. Press over stomach if it is distended (bulging belly), especially in infants.
4. Combining mouth-to-mouth ventilation and heart massage: two people, one on the mouth and one on the chest. (Two people are preferred.)
   a. Give five to six effective mouth-to-mouth breaths.
   b. Check for pulse.
   c. Give chest compressions at the rate of 80/min for a child and 60/min for an adult.
   d. Stop after every fifth chest compression while partner gives one mouth-to-mouth breath, then resume compression.
   e. After 1 minute, check for return of pulse.
   f. Check pulse every 5 minutes thereafter.
   g. Watch pupils.

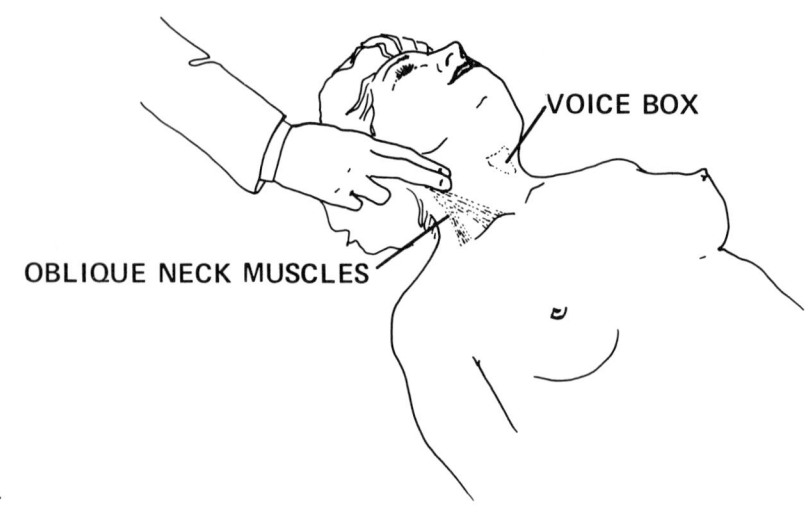

Fig. 16-5. Feel the carotid pulse.

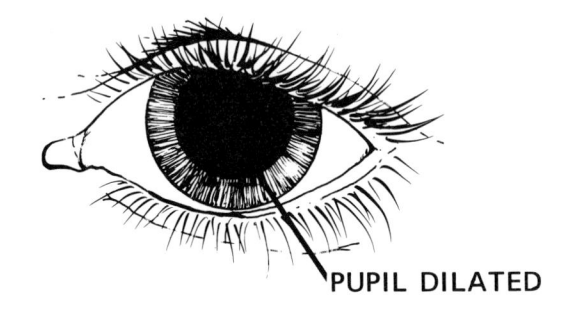

Fig. 16-6. Is the pupil dilated?

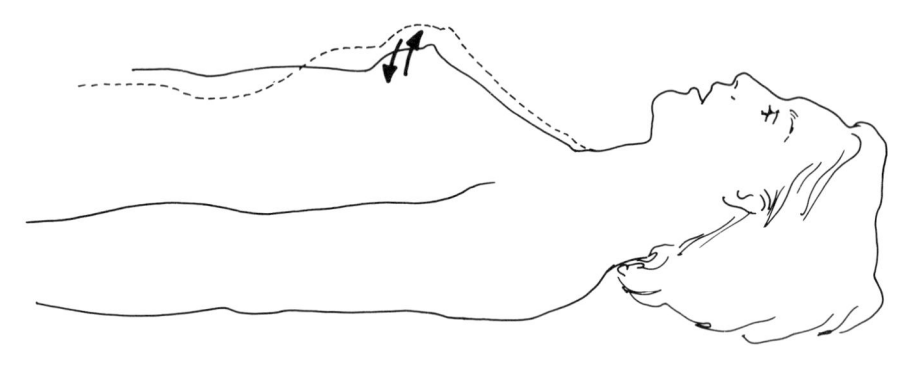

Fig. 16-7. Look at the chest. Is it moving?

      h. Feel pulse in neck (carotid pulse) to see if your cardiac massage is working. The chest compression has to be strong enough to *make a pulse*.
5. Combining mouth-to-mouth ventilation and heart massage: one person only.
      a. Give five to six mouth-to-mouth breaths.
      b. Check pulse.
      c. Give 15 chest compressions, then two mouth-to-mouth breaths. Repeat this sequence, compressing the chest at a rate of 80/min for a child and 60/min for an adult.
      d. After 1 minute check for return of pulse and check again once every 5 minutes thereafter.

Emergencies

Fig. 16-8. Method of mouth-to-mouth respiration and cardiac massage by one person: first, tilt head back and give five to six breaths, check pulse, and then give 15 chest compressions, then two mouth-to-mouth breaths and go on. [Redrawn, with permission of the American Heart Association, from Standards for cardiopulmonary resuscitation (CPR) and emergency cardiac care (ECC), *Journal of the American Medical Association* 227 (suppl 7), 1974.]

6. How long to continue?
    a. There is no definite time limit for CPR.
    b. In general, if pupils are constricted, the resuscitation efforts are working.
    c. Transport the victim by ambulance to nearest hospital. Chest compression and mouth-to-mouth breathing should continue during transport, unless the ambulance service has an artificial ventilator.

CONVULSIONS

Most convulsions are grand mal seizures and appear quite alarming. *Keep calm;* the seizure usually passes without complication.

1. Put child on floor, face up, and move him or her away from any objects that may injure him or her during the seizure.
2. Loosen clothing around the child's neck.
3. Be sure that the child's airway is open; this can be done by extending the neck (tilting head backward).

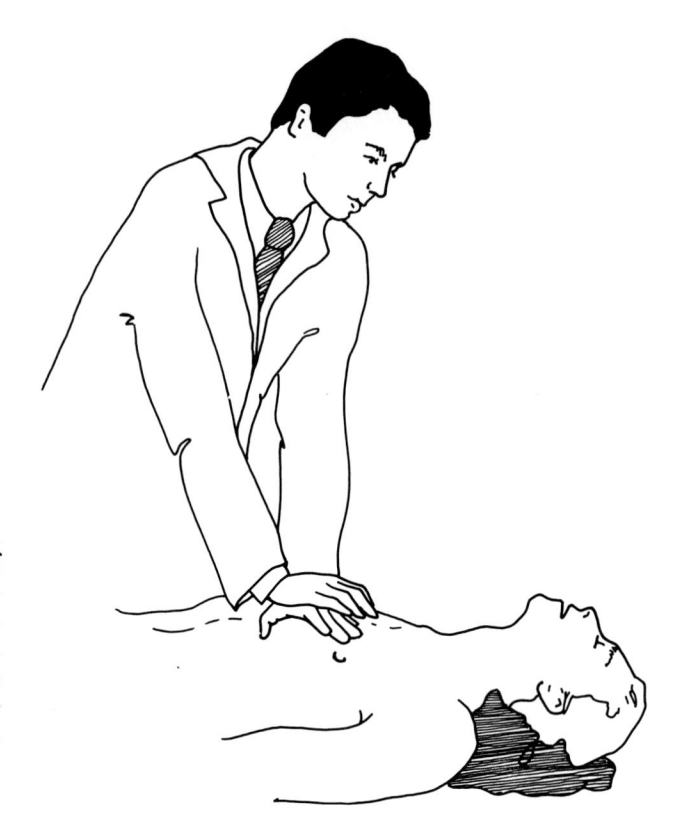

Fig. 16-9. Heart massage. Victim lies face up on a firm surface. Pressure is applied on lower half of breast bone: for adults, use both hands; children, one hand; infants, 2 fingers. Rates of compression: adults, 60/min; children, 80/min; infants, 100/min. [Redrawn, with permission of the American Heart Association, from standards for cardiopulmonary resuscitation (CPR) and emergency cardiac care (ECC), *Journal of the American Medical Association,* 227 (suppl 7), 1974.]

4. Place a padded tongue blade or similar object between the child's teeth to prevent tongue biting.

FAINTING (SYNCOPE)

To rule out cardiac and pulmonary arrest, check for the three CPR signs: carotid pulse absent, pupils dilated, and respirations absent. *Do not use cardiac massage unless the carotid pulse is absent.*

Fainting is due to a transient drop in the blood pressure, and should be handled as follows:

1. Lay the child on his or her back, face up.
2. Make sure neck is extended (head bent back) and airway is open. Using finger, remove any foreign bodies from mouth.
3. Raise the child's feet.

BIBLIOGRAPHY

American Heart Association, Standards and guidelines for cardiopulmonary resuscitation (CPR) and emergency cardiac care (ECC). *Journal of the American Medical Association* 244 (suppl. 5):453–509, 1980. Reprints available from the American Heart Association, Distribution Department, 2005 Hightower Drive, Garland, TX 75041.

CPR for Citizens. Film available from Pyramid Films, Box 1048, Santa Monica, CA 90406.

Stanford University Medical Center, Adaptation of the Santa Clara County Heart Association's *Cardiopulmonary Resuscitation Manual.*

17

Friedreich's Ataxia

JUDITH KOEHLER, M.D.

Friedreich's ataxia (FA) is an inherited (familial) disease in which there is progressive degeneration of the sensory nerves of the limbs and trunk (peripheral nerves).

SIGNS AND SYMPTOMS

The disease usually becomes evident during the first or second decade of life, although occasionally symptoms may be present in early infancy (see Fig. 17-1). Poor balance (ataxia) of the extremities and trunk is the predominant early sympton, sometimes leading to frequent falling or a wide-based, awkward, lurching, drunken-like gait. Lack of agility and clumsiness later develop. In school years, shaky, erratic, "sloppy" handwriting may become apparent due to impairment of fine motor control. Discoordination and tremor of the upper extremities may be so great that feeding becomes impossible. Speech may become slurred.

Diminished or absent knee and ankle jerks (deep tendon reflexes), loss of the ability to discern the vibrations of a tuning fork placed on the ankle (vibration sense) or of the position of a limb in space, and up-going great toes when the sole of the foot is stroked (Babinski sign) are frequently noted. Wasting (atrophy) of the distal limb muscles is present on clinical as well as on microscopic examination.

Skeletal deformities occur in a high percentage of patients.[1-3] These include clubfoot, high arches (pes cavus), or hammer toe. Spinal curvatures (kyphosis or scoliosis) is present in almost all patients by the time they reach their teen or early adult years.

Heart abnormalities are common and may become manifest at any age. Electrocardiographic (EKG) changes occur in over 90 percent of patients with FA.[4] Irregularities of heart beat, heart murmurs, and enlargement of the heart may develop. Constriction of the main aorta from the heart (subaortic stenosis)[4-6] or of the main artery to the lungs (pul-

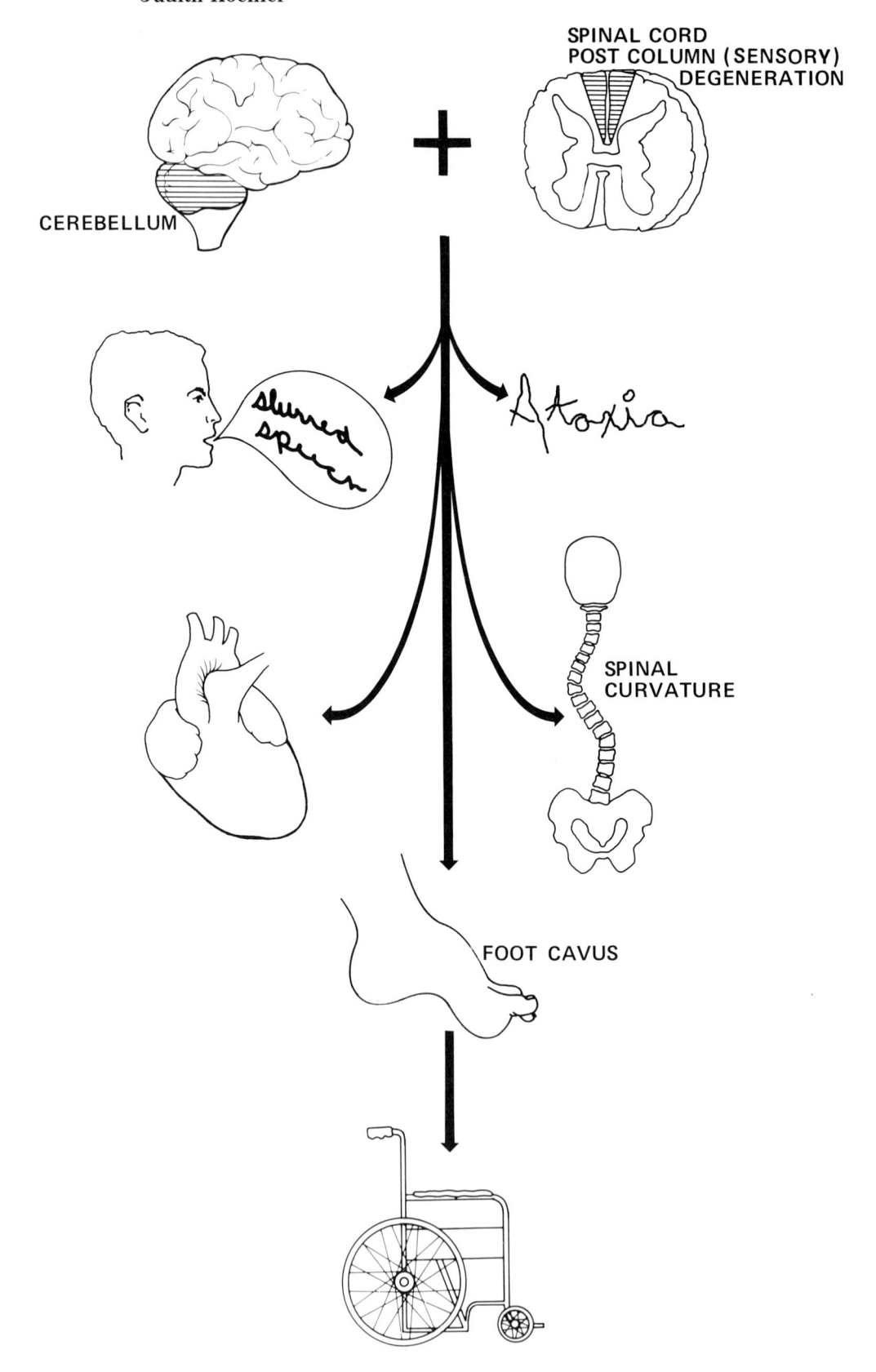

Fig. 17-1. Friedreich's ataxia. Representation of the location of the disease process in the sensory nerves and of the progressive signs and symptoms leading to eventual severe disability.

monic stenosis) have been reported in association with FA—even early in childhood, before central nervous system degeneration becomes apparent.

Eye abnormalities include paleness of the nerve to the eye (optic nerve atrophy) and degeneration of the sensory surface of the eyeball (retinal degeneration); these usually appear late in the disease course.[1,2] Involuntary side-to-side movements of the eyes (nystagmus) are almost always present. Difficulty in visual tracking, loss of normal saccadic eye movements, or diminished visual acuity may result in reluctance or inability to read.

Less common manifestations may include mental deficiency or mental deterioration.[1,2] The incidence of seizures is greater than expected.[1,2] Endocrine dysfunction may be present. Inability to control blood sugar (glucose intolerance) and abnormality of insulin secretion have been reported in FA as well as in other similar spinocerebellar degenerations.[7,8]

There are many syndromes* that may be confused with this condition, as has been outlined by Greenfield[1] and Brown.[3]

Progression of the disease may be rapid or slow. Many patients are wheelchair-bound in their late teens or early twenties, and soon thereafter are bedridden. In one study, death occurred at an average age of 26.5 years in the recessively inherited disease and at 39.5 years in a dominantly inherited form.[11] Some patients will, however, have a minimally progressive disease; as mentioned below, atypical or incomplete variants *(forme fruste)* of the disease occur commonly.

INHERITANCE

While FA is rare among the population as a whole, familial incidence is common. The disease may be inherited in an autosomal recessive pattern in which both parents, neither of whom are clinically affected, contribute a defective gene or in an autosomal dominant pattern in which only a single parent, who will be affected, need carry the abnormal gene.† It should be noted that clinically inapparent or abortive *forme frustes* of this disease, in which patients present with only one or two features of the clinical spectrum, are very common. Physicians must therefore look carefully for the presence of hammer toes, high arches, scoliosis, or tremor in all allegedly "unaffected" parents and family members. Electrical determination of the speed of nerve impulses (nerve conduction velocities) may also be indicated in some family members.

SPECIFIC THERAPY

Specific therapy is limited to correction of the orthopedic deformities and cardiac complications which develop during progression of the disease. A trial of various medications may help alleviate the intention tremor.‡ Appropriate antiseizure medications and cardiac drugs should be used when indicated. Suitable vocational training, especially with the avoidance of fine motor skills, is indicated for those with mildly progressive or static disease, since these patients will be able to function adequately in society with their fixed level of handicap.

---

*A syndrome is merely a collection of signs and symptoms observed in close association.
†See also the appendix to the chapter on Down's Syndrome for a more detailed discussion of these inheritance patterns.
‡ Tremor: shakiness of the limbs, usually noticed in the hands when attempting to do something.

EDUCATIONAL IMPLICATIONS

Children with FA should be kept in the regular classroom as long as possible. This will require additional effort on the part of the teachers, since these children will become frustrated when their muscular problems and incoordination prevent them from keeping up with the other children. Encouragement, as with every form of teaching, is of utmost importance.

If the child is no longer able to attend regular school because of the need for special physical therapy or because the loss of motor function has progressed to the point that the child can no longer get from classroom to classroom or to and from school, then the attending physician should refer the child to a school for the handicapped. Such a referral should include the diagnosis and, if at all possible, a description of what may be expected in the future with the particular child. It may not always be possible for the physician to give an accurate prediction of the future because of the variation in this and most other types of neurological diseases. Specific direction should be given for the amounts and type of physical therapy required. Special devices may be needed if the child is unable to grasp a pencil, and such devices are available. It may be necessary to use a dowel attached to various portions of the body so that the child may use an electric typewriter to write. Above all, the child will need encouragement.

REFERENCES

1. Greenfield, J. G., *The Spino-cerebellar Degenerations.* Oxford, Vincent-Baxter Press, 1954.
2. Merritt, H. H., Cerebellum, in *A Textbook of Neurology,* 4th ed. Philadelphia, Lea & Febiger, 1970.
3. Brown, J. R., Diseases of the cerebellum, in Baker, A. B., and Baker, L. H. (eds.), *Clinical Neurology,* vol. 2. New York, Harper & Row, 1971.
4. Gach, J. V., Andriange, M., and Franck, G., Hypertrophic obstructive cardiomyopathy and Friedreich's ataxia. Report of a case and review of literature. *American Journal of Cardiology* 27:436–441, 1971.
5. Boehm, T. M., Dickerson, R. B., and Glasser, S. P., Hypertrophic subaortic stenosis occurring in a patient with Friedreich's ataxia. *American Journal of Medical Science* 260:279–284, 1970.
6. Ruschhaupt, D. G., Thilenius, O. G., and Cassels, D. E., Friedreich's ataxia associated with idiopathic hypertrophic subaortic stenosis. *American Heart Journal* 84:95–102, 1972.
7. Podolsky, S., and Sheremata, W. A., Insulin-dependent diabetes mellitus and Friedreich's ataxia in siblings. *Metabolism* 19:555–561, 1970.
8. Joffe, B. I., Segal, I., and Keller, P., Insulin levels in hereditary ataxias. *New England Journal of Medicine* 283:1410–1411, 1970.
9. Spillane, F. D., Familial pes cavus and absent tendon-jerks: Its relationship with Friedreich's disease and peroneal muscular atrophy. *Brain* 63:275–290, 1940.
10. Oelschlager, R., White, H. H., and Schimke, R. N., Roussy-Levy Syndrome: Report of a kindred and discussion of the nosology. *Acta Neurologica Scandinavica* 47:80–90, 1971.
11. Bell, J. M., and Carmichael, E. A., On hereditary ataxia and spastic paraplegia. *Treasury of Human Inheritance* 4:3, 1939.

BIBLIOGRAPHY

Quebec Cooperative Study on Friedreich's Ataxia—Phase One (Symposium). *Canadian Journal of Neurological Science* 3:269–397, 1976.

18

Heart Disease in Children

DAVID BAUM, M.D.

GENERAL TYPES

When a baby is born with a structural defect of the heart or blood vessels, it is termed *congenital heart disease*. When the disorder occurs after birth, it is considered an *acquired cardiovascular disorder*.

CONGENITAL HEART DISEASE

Congenital heart disease is much more frequent in childhood than is the acquired form, whereas the opposite is true in adult life. In childhood, congenital heart disease is approximately 20 times more common than acquired disease. In the newborn, the incidence of congenital heart disease is placed at about 6 for every 1000 live births; if stillbirths were included, the incidence would be considerably higher. In reports describing long-term follow-up of untreated congenital heart disease, the incidence at 10 years of age is but 1 or 2 for every 1000. Although some of these abnormal openings close by themselves, this decline in incidence is largely the result of deaths from the more serious congenital heart defects. The largest portion of these deaths occur within the first year of life, with the majority occurring within the first few months. This fact highlights the need for early recognition, diagnosis, and appropriate therapy.

ETIOLOGY (CAUSES)

Basic development of the heart takes place very early in fetal life. The fetal heart begins to take shape toward the end of the third intrauterine week, when the embryo is but 1.5 mm long. It begins as a tube, and through a combination of differential growth, folding, and twisting, the major thoracic cardiovascular structures are formed by the end of the seventh week. Since the remaining development is largely due to growth, any severe abnormality of cardiovascular structure probably occurs before the eighth week of fetal life.

The etiology of congenital heart disease in most instances is unknown. The cause is a single mutant gene in less than 1 percent of cases, and a gross chromosomal abnormality in less than 5 percent of cases. Down's syndrome (mongolism), the best known chromosomal aberration, has a high associated incidence of congenital cardiac deformity: some 40 percent of these patients have heart defects. It is interesting to note that congenital heart disease occurs more frequently among siblings than in the general population.

Environmental influences during pregnancy have been implicated in the etiology of congenital heart disease. Mothers who develop German measles within the first 3 months of pregnancy are prone to give birth to infants with multiple congenital anomalies, including anomalies of the heart and vessels. Recent research suggests that smoking and excessive alcohol intake during early pregnancy may also play a role in causing cardiac defects.

DIAGNOSIS

Various complaints lead parents to bring a child with cardiovascular disease to a physician. The most common of these are shortness of breath, fatigue, poor growth and development, chest pain, blueness of the lips and nail beds (cyanosis), fainting, and chest deformity.

Sometimes a heart murmur is discovered when a child is being examined for other purposes, suggesting the need for cardiovascular evaluation. Although heart murmurs are abnormal heart sounds, they do not always signify heart disease.

At physical examination, the heart rate and rhythm, blood pressure, character of the heart sounds, location and timing of heart murmurs, character of breathing, liver size, and presence or absence of cyanosis (blueness of the lips and nail beds) are important. A chest x-ray is helpful because it reveals the size and configuration of the heart and the character of the blood vessels in the lungs. An electrocardiogram can reveal disorders of cardiac rhythm as well as hypertrophy (thickening) of the walls of one or more of the heart chambers. Given all this information, the physician can usually narrow down the possibilities and often makes the correct diagnosis.

If a final diagnosis cannot be made at this point, the doctor may request echocardiography, a new diagnostic technique which has proved particularly useful in children. As the name implies, information concerning cardiac structure and function is gained from sound waves reflected by the heart tissues (echoes). This non-invasive test employs a machine, the echocardiograph, that transmits high frequency sound waves through the chest wall and detects the cardiac echoes returning to the skin surface. The technique has significantly reduced our dependency on cardiac catheterization, an invasive procedure that requires hospitalization.

If still more information is necessary, as it sometimes is, the physician may recommend cardiac catheterization and angiocardiography. *Cardiac catheterization* is a hospital procedure that involves introducing a thin plastic tube, or catheter, into a blood vessel in the patient's arm or leg. The catheter is advanced through the vessel into the heart chambers and related arteries and veins with fluoroscopic guidance. The nature of

Heart Disease in Children 315

the defect is determined by measuring blood pressures as well as the oxygen saturation of blood samples obtained from the heart chambers and related vessels.

Angiocardiography is performed in conjunction with the catheterization. With angiography, a special radio-opaque fluid is injected into a blood vessel or heart chamber and x-ray films of the heart in two planes are obtained in very rapid succession as the fluid travels through the individual chambers and vessels. This specialized technique allows the structural malformations to be seen; and, in addition, supplements functional understanding of the defect.

COMMON CONGENITAL HEART DEFECTS

Patent Ductus Arteriosus

The ductus arteriosus is an open passageway between the two great arteries that arise from the heart: the pulmonary artery and the aorta (Fig. 18-1). The ductus is necessarily patent (open) during fetal life so as to allow the blood to bypass the nonaerated fetal lungs. Following the inflation of the lungs after birth, the pulmonary artery normally carries blood from the right pumping chamber of the heart (right ventricle) to the lungs to pick up a fresh supply of oxygen. This oxygen-laden blood then returns from the lungs to the heart and is delivered to the remainder of the body by the aorta.

Ordinarily, the ductus arteriosus closes within a few weeks of the baby's birth. When the ductus arteriosus remains patent, a portion of the blood passing through the aorta is shunted back to the lungs via this passage. As a result, the heart works harder to pump sufficient blood to the body while supplying that passing through the ductus. If the ductal opening is wide and the flow through it is very large, the burden on the heart may be excessive and the infant may develop heart failure. Should treatment with digitalis and other medical measures prove insufficient, surgical correction may be required. The cardiovascular surgeon accom-

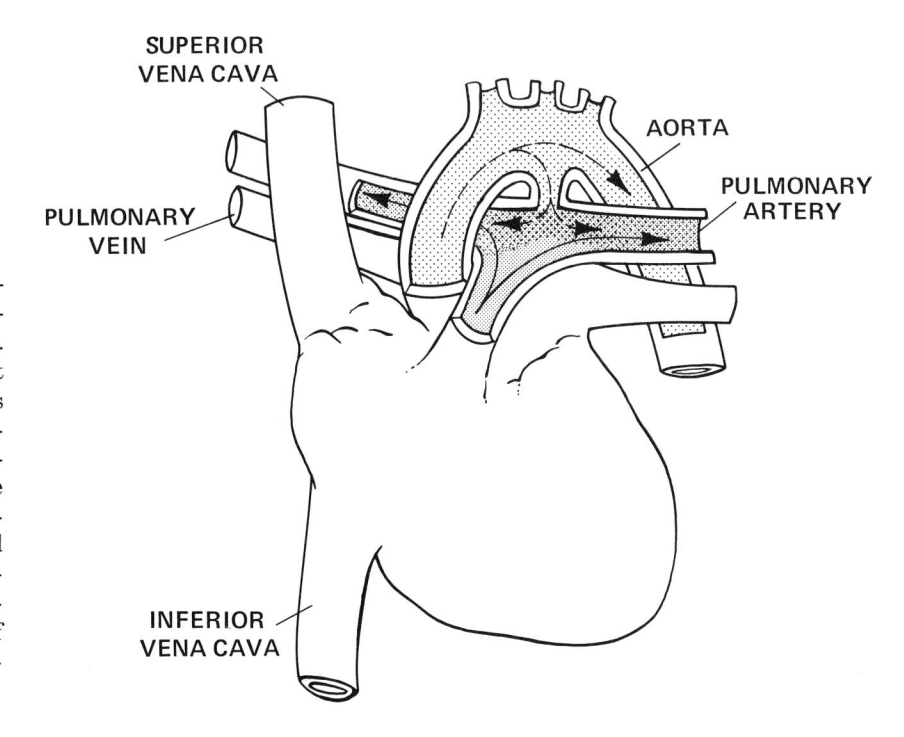

Fig. 18-1. Patent ductus arteriosus. Arrows through defect show direction of shunt. (Note labeling of heart chambers and blood vessels here and in Fig. 18-2.) Broken arrows indicate oxygenated blood returned from the lungs; continuous arrows indicate poorly oxygenated blood from the body (systemic venous return). Stippling indicates mixing of oxygenated and poorly oxygenated blood.

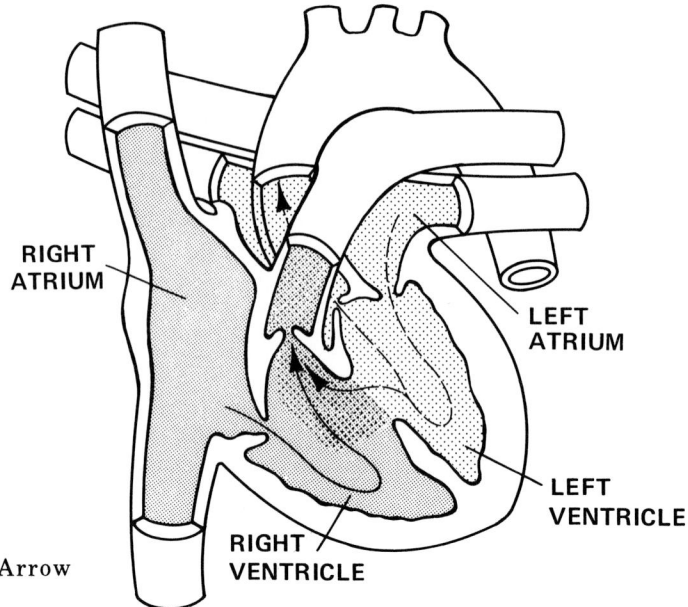

Fig. 18-2. Ventricular septal defect. Arrow through defect shows shunt direction.

plishes correction by a tieing and cutting procedure, which if there is no other malformation, results in a normal circulation. In those children with a small patent ductus arteriosus, correction is ordinarily performed after infancy. In this latter case, operation is done primarily to prevent the development of infection in the heart (bacterial endocarditis), since the defect is one of those prone to develop this complication. Until correction is performed, prophylactic antibiotics are recommended for surgical procedures involving infected tissues and for extensive dental manipulations, in the hope of preventing ductal infection.

Ventricular Septal Defect

Sometimes a baby is born with an opening in the wall of tissue (septum) that separates the left and right pumping chambers (ventricles) of the heart. As in patent ductus arteriosus, the blood that is shunted through this opening from the left to the right side of the heart is oxygenated blood which has just passed through the lungs (Fig. 18-2). The volume of blood shunted depends largely on the size of the communication between the ventricles. If the hole is small, a small amount of oxygenated blood will pass through the communication, producing little more than a loud murmur. On the other hand, if the shunt is large, both ventricles will have to pump large amounts of blood at high pressure. Over time, the heart will compensate by enlarging and hypertrophying. If these compensatory mechanisms are adequate, the patient may do relatively well, except for slow growth and undernutrition. Youngsters with large defects, however, are susceptible to the development of lung infections, or pneumonias, which usually occur during the first year or two of life. The development of pneumonia in a largely compensated infant with a large ventricular septal defect may tip the balance and produce heart failure. When heart failure cannot be managed medically, and when severely retarded growth and repeated lung infections become a problem, surgical assistance may be recommended.

Heart Disease in Children

At present, leading cardiovascular surgeons can repair ventricular septal defects successfully, even in the very young. This operation requires opening the heart with the assistance of cardiopulmonary bypass—the heart-lung machine. In small infants, body temperature may be lowered to decrease metabolism and thus protect the brain while stopping the heart for easier repair. When the defect is of sufficient size to require operation but not large enough to cause a major problem in infancy, repair is usually delayed until the child is preparing to enter elementary school. It is important to realize, however, that a large number of ventricular septal defects close spontaneously. Such spontaneous closure, when it occurs, most often takes place in early childhood.

A small number of patients with large ventricular septal defects develop a disease of the blood vessels in the lungs. If sufficiently advanced, the disease may preclude operative repair. There is no way of knowing at present which of these youngsters will develop this pulmonary vascular disease.

Children with ventricular septal defects are another group prone to develop subacute bacterial endocarditis. Therefore, they, too, require prophylactic antibiotics in circumstances in which the development of bacterial endocarditis is more likely.

Atrial Septal Defect

Holes also occur in the septum separating the two atria, or receiving chambers, of the heart (Fig. 18-3). Again, the magnitude of shunt is largely proportional to the size of the opening between the two chambers involved. In contradistinction to ventricular septal defect and patent ductus arteriosus, children with large atrial septal defects rarely present with heart failure, history of repeated pneumonia, or secondary growth failure. More often, a heart murmur is detected on a preschool or camp physical examination. Since the murmurs associated with atrial septal

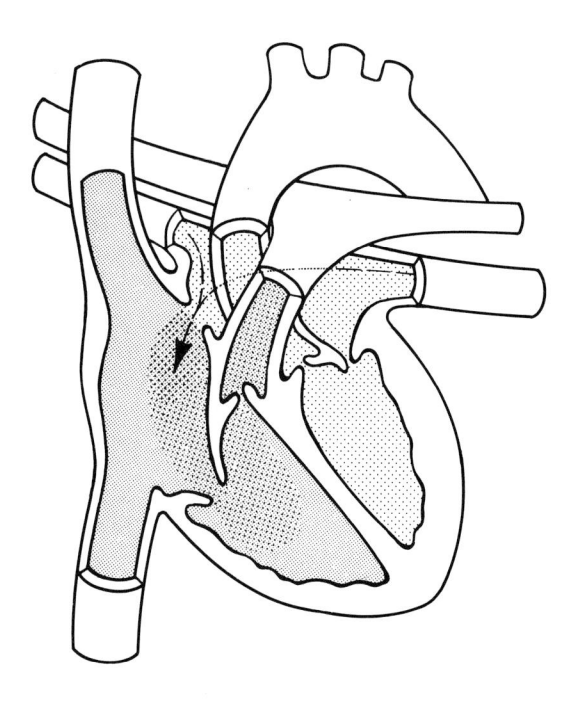

Fig. 18-3. Atrial septal defect. Arrows show shunt through defect.

defects are not usually prominent, careful examination, chest x-ray, and electrocardiogram are often required before this possibility is apparent. If the shunt is significant, total repair using the cardiopulmonary bypass is recommended sometime between 4 and 10 years of age. The possibility of developing pulmonary vascular disease is usually not a consideration until the patient reaches the second and third decades of life. Abnormal heart rhythms and heart failure become a possibility in the fourth and fifth decades if the defects are sufficiently large and have not been repaired. Patients with atrial septal defects are not usually prone to the development of bacterial endocarditis.

Tetralogy of Fallot

Tetralogy of Fallot is the commonest form of cyanotic congenital heart disease after the neonatal period. It forms three quarters of our cyanotic patients who are over 1 year old.

The tetralogy of Fallot has four components (Fig. 18-4). A large ventricular septal defect and right ventricular obstruction are basic to the physiology of the anomaly. The obstruction may be produced by narrowing or stenosis of the pulmonary valve, by subvalvular stenosis, or by both. Because the outflow of blood from the right ventricle is obstructed, a portion of the poorly oxygenated blood that returns to the ventricle from the body (systemic venous return) is diverted through the ventricular septal defect to the left ventricle. There it mixes with the oxygenated blood returning from the lungs, and this mixed blood is pumped to the body via the aorta. The arterial oxygen content is determined by the proportion of well-oxygenated and poorly oxygenated blood arriving in the aorta. When the arterial oxygen content is low, the patient appears cyanotic. The remaining two components of the tetralogy include right ventricular hypertrophy, resulting from right ventricular overwork, and overriding or straddling of the ventricular septal defect by the aorta.

Children with tetralogy of Fallot have been referred to as "blue babies." Typically, the patient with tetralogy of Fallot develops cyanosis of the lips, mucous membranes, and nail beds in infancy. However, when the defect is present in its most extreme form, patients may be cyanotic at birth. Some of these infants develop "hypoxic spells," characterized by hyperventilation, increasing cyanosis, and fainting. When these spells occur, the infant should be put on an adult's shoulder and the knees tucked up under the infant in the so-called "knee-chest" position. The physician should be notified immediately. When these patients begin having hypoxic spells, surgical relief must be considered soon, since severe spells may lead to death.

Total repair of tetralogy of Fallot is difficult in the infant but has been accomplished in a small number of the major medical centers. When total correction is not feasible, a temporizing or palliative operation can be performed. The operation provides relief by increasing the blood flow to the lungs, which is accomplished either by attaching a branch of the aorta to the pulmonary artery or by creating an opening between the pulmonary artery and the aorta itself. With the pulmonary blood flow thus increased, a larger proportion of the blood arriving in the aorta is well oxygenated, and the amount of oxygen delivered to the body is greater. This latter situation decreases the possibility of further hypoxic spells and improves the patient's overall condition.

Total repair of uncomplicated cases of tetralogy of Fallot should be

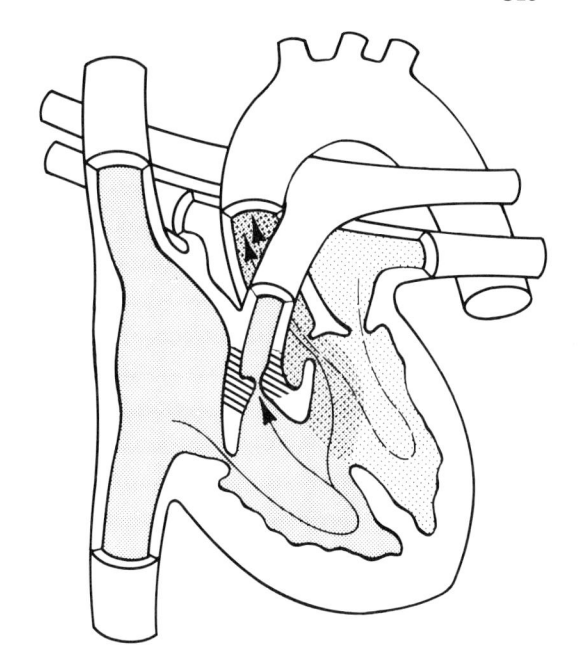

Fig. 18-4. Tetralogy of Fallot. Note that portion of systemic venous return is shunted through ventricular septal defect to left ventricle and aorta, reducing flow to pulmonary artery and lungs. Shading indicates right ventricular outflow obstruction.

performed in childhood. When growth and development have been impaired, subsequent repair often results in remarkable improvement. The surgery includes closure of the ventricular septal defect, usually with a patch of special synthetic material, and relief of the right ventricular obstruction. The constricted pulmonary valve is opened, and the obstructing muscle beneath the valve is removed. If the right ventricular outflow tract and main pulmonary artery are underdeveloped, a small patch or graft may be necessary for their enlargement, completing the repair.

Patients with tetralogy of Fallot are susceptible to bacterial endocarditis. It is quite possible that this susceptibility remains even after total repair. Thus, we recommend antibiotic prophylaxis in all of these patients whenever some particular event makes them more susceptible to the development of this dangerous infection.

Transposition of the Great Vessels

With this defect, the location of the aorta and pulmonary artery are reversed, or transposed (Fig. 18-5). The pulmonary artery originates from the left rather than the right ventricle, and the aorta is connected to the right instead of the left ventricle. Consequently, the poorly oxygenated blood returning from the body to the right ventricle is pumped right back again through the aorta, while the well-oxygenated blood returning to the left ventricle from the lungs is pumped back to the lungs through the pulmonary artery. Unless there is some communication that permits mixing of the well-oxygenated blood from the lungs with the poorly oxygenated blood from the body, the child will die very shortly after birth. Frequently, there are residual fetal communications through the atrial septum and the ductus arteriosus. A ventricular septal defect may be present, facilitating mixing between the two sides of the heart.

Although transposition of the great vessels is uncommon, it is the most frequent form of cyanotic congenital heart disease at birth. If the compensating communications between the left and right sides of the

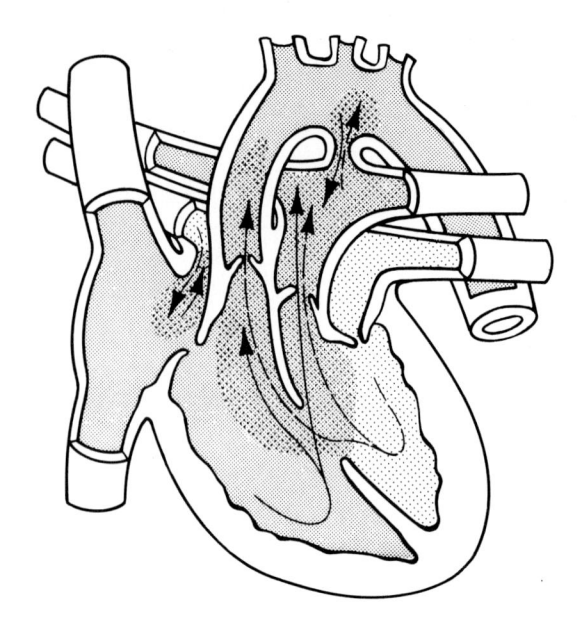

Fig. 18-5. Transposition of great vessels. Atrial and ventricular septal defects and patent ductus arteriosus are shown as potential sites of mixing. Note that aorta comes off right ventricle and pulmonary artery arises from left ventricle.

heart are inadequate or begin to close, the oxygen content of blood pumped to the body falls, and the patient becomes more cyanotic and develops congestive heart failure.

Ordinarily, cyanotic congenital heart disease is suspected early. Diagnosis is completed by cardiac catheterization and angiography. When transposition is confirmed at catheterization, an atrial balloon septostomy is frequently performed to enlarge the interatrial communication and thus, to improve the mixing of oxygenated and deoxygenated blood. This procedure is performed by passing a catheter, with a small deflated balloon at its end through the interatrial communication from the right to the left atrium. The balloon is then inflated, pulled back into the right atrium (enlarging the defect), and deflated. If this procedure is unsuccessful, the atrial septal opening can be enlarged surgically. Enlargement of the communication between the atrial chambers allows survival and often provides enough assistance to allow generalized improvement and growth. For subsequent hemodynamic repair, a baffle is inserted between the atria, which diverts the systemic venous blood to the left ventricle and pulmonary artery for oxygenation and, in addition, directs the oxygenated blood returning from the lungs to the right ventricle and aorta for distribution to the body. Although experience suggests that this operation is not an ideal procedure, it has greatly improved the outlook for patients with transposition of the great vessels. Without surgical help, almost 90 percent of patients with transposition of the great vessels die within the first year of life from hypoxia (insufficient oxygen) and heart failure.

Aortic Stenosis

Obstruction may occur in the region of the aortic valve (Fig. 18-6). If the stenosis (narrowing) is caused by deformity of the valve itself, the defect is termed *valvular aortic stenosis*. Narrowing just above the valve is called *supravalvular aortic stenosis,* while that just below the valve, within the left ventricle, is called *subvalvular aortic stenosis*. Severe obstruction forces the left ventricle to pump at higher pressures to force

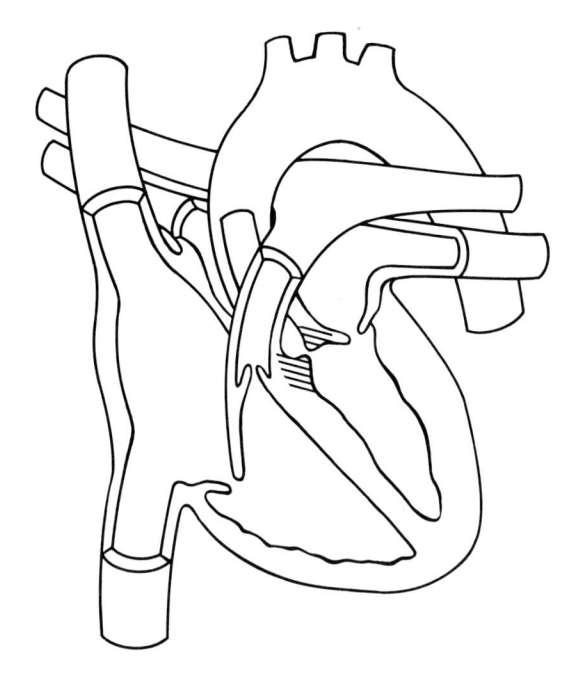

Fig. 18-6. Aortic stenosis. Shading shows stenotic valve.

blood through the narrowed area to the aorta. If sufficiently severe, the left ventricular wall hypertrophies as a compensatory mechanism. When the demands on the ventricle are too great, heart failure may develop. Frequently, severe obstruction interferes with coronary blood flow and results in exertional chest pain, providing a warning of the defect's severity.

Aortic stenosis is usually found in active children who outwardly appear perfectly well. Unless they have experienced chest pain, they are usually asymptomatic. Thus it is difficult for the child and parents to accept the presence of the defect and its potential risks. We caution against competitive athletics and advise families, schools, and playground supervisors to allow these children to rest when chest discomfort, unusual fatigue, or shortness of breath are experienced. It is advisable under any of these latter circumstances to inform the patient's physician of what has transgressed.

Relief of the obstruction can be accomplished surgically. Often the child is left with residual deformity. The opening of the valve may result in some degree of regurgitation, or leakage of blood from the aorta back into the left ventricle. Restenosis may occur. Since surgical therapy for aortic stenosis is not ideal, operation is advised only when obstruction is reasonably severe.

Patients with aortic stenosis are susceptible to bacterial endocarditis and require the usual precautions.

Coarctation of the Aorta

Occasionally the aorta is constricted in the region where the large arterial branch to the left arm arises (Fig. 18-7). If severe, this narrowing, or coarctation, interferes with the delivery of blood to the branches of the aorta beyond. Although a network of blood vessels, called *collaterals,* is normally available to bypass the coarctation, an extra work load is imposed on the left ventricle. The pulses in the legs are diminished, and

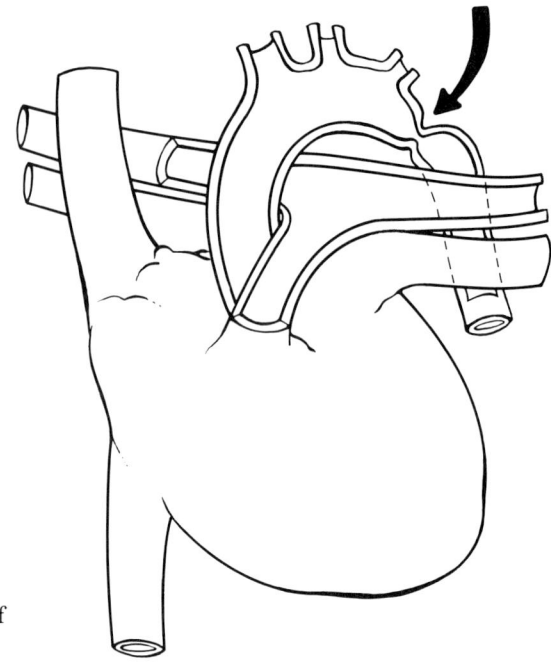

Fig. 18-7. Coarctation of aorta. Arrow points to site of narrowing.

high blood pressure may develop in the arms. Unless unmanageable heart failure ensues, surgical repair is deferred until after 4 or 5 years of age. Operation is usually performed before 10 years of age, in the hope of preventing vascular effects of high blood pressure in the aorta proximal to the area of narrowing. Preoperatively, the coarctation site is prone to infection, and, because bicuspid aortic valves (valves with two cusps, rather than the normal number of three) occur frequently in association with coarctation of the aorta, precautions for bacterial endocarditis ought to be maintained even after the coarctation has been successfully repaired.

Valvular Pulmonic Stenosis

The pulmonary valve assists in directing blood flow from the right ventricle into the pulmonary artery and thereby the lungs, where carbon dioxide is released and oxygen taken up. Narrowing of the pulmonary valve, valvular pulmonic stenosis (Fig. 18-8), is often accompanied by a muscular obstruction just below the valve, infundibular pulmonic stenosis. The extra work load of pumping blood through the obstructed valve requires the right ventricle to generate increased pressure. The walls of the ventricle compensate by thickening or hypertrophing. When the obstruction is sufficiently severe to produce high pressure, the valve is opened surgically (valvulotomy). The postoperative results of this procedure are extremely satisfactory. Pulmonary stenosis is another defect susceptible to the development of bacterial endocarditis.

ACQUIRED HEART DISEASE

Rheumatic Fever

This disease can involve many of the body's organs. It follows streptococcal infection. During an attack of rheumatic fever, various combinations of the following may be found; fever, arthritis, skin rash, subcuta-

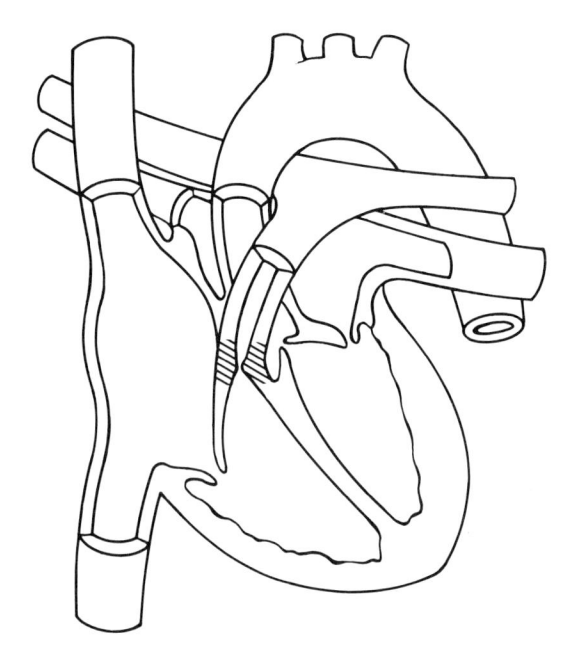

Fig. 18-8. Pulmonary stenosis. Shading indicates stenotic valve.

neous nodules, chorea, and carditis. Except for cardiac involvement, all manifestations of the illness disappear when the attack is over. However, the heart may be left with permanent damage as the result of carditis. The valves most frequently involved are the mitral (between the left atrium and left ventricle) and the aortic (between the left ventricle and aorta).

Rheumatic fever may recur. Since rheumatic fever attacks are known to follow streptococcal infections, continuous antibiotic prophylaxis is provided in the hope of preventing streptococcal infection and recurrence of the disease. Penicillin is most frequently used, unless the patient has an allergy to this antibiotic. When the latter situation occurs, an alternative antibiotic is provided.

The damage done to the heart and valves increases the patient susceptibility to bacterial endocarditis and sometimes is sufficiently severe to require surgical assistance. Surgery is rarely necessary before adulthood, however. It is particularly important to realize that these damaged hearts may limit a patient's physical capacity. Thus, the patient, his family, and others involved in his activity must understand his safe limits.

Hypertension

Hypertension, or high blood pressure, is infrequent in childhood. It usually results from kidney or endocrine (gland) disease but is sometimes essential hypertension, the causes of which are largely unexplained.

The types of medication used and the severity of the elevated blood pressure should be taken into account when considering a patient's activities.

INNOCENT MURMURS

Innocent or insignificant murmurs are unusual sounds *not* associated with organic heart disease. Ordinarily, the patient's history, physical examination, chest x-ray, and electrocardiogram allow the physician to conclude that such a murmur is of no clinical consequence. Echocardiography may occasionally be necessary to make the diagnosis.

Innocent murmurs are common in childhood. When they occur, both the family and child must understand that there is no heart disease and that the child should be treated as a perfectly normal individual.

PRECAUTIONS

Shortness of breath, chest pain, faintness, cyanosis, very rapid heart beat, and unusual fatigue are the warning signs of heart disease. When any of these signs occur, the child with cardiovascular disease, even when postoperative, should be allowed to rest and appropriate guidance ought to be obtained.

EDUCATIONAL IMPLICATIONS

Because the degree of involvement is different in each child, it is impossible to give specific limitations here for every child with a specific heart problem. However, it can be stated in general that a child with heart disease should not engage in competitive athletics or their equivalent, unless it is with the specific approval of his physician. He should be encouraged to take part in nonathletic extracurricular activities and to develop skills for earning a living that do not require physical labor. As is true for all education, the education of the child with heart disease should prepare the child to manage his future social and economic needs.

BIBLIOGRAPHY

Keith, J. D., Rowe, R. D., and Vldad, P., *Heart Disease In Infancy and Childhood.* New York, MacMillan and Company, 1978.

Moss, A. J., Adams, F. H., and Emmanouilides, G. C., *Heart Disease in Infants, Children, and Adolescents.* Baltimore, Williams and Wilkins, 1977.

19

Hemophilia

F. RALPH BERBERICH, M.D.

HISTORY

Hemophilia is an inherited disorder of blood coagulation in which a protein required for blood clotting is abnormal and, therefore, functionally deficient. Hemophilia has been recognized since antiquity and is thought to have afflicted both humans and animals for millenia. In the second century A.D., rabbis establishing rules of circumcision appreciated the lethal potential of hemophilia and observed that only males were affected. Maternal transmission of the genetic defect was clearly comprehended by the medieval rabbi and physician, Maimonides, who prohibited circumcision in the son of a mother who had had hemophilic sons by a previous husband. John Otto, an American physician writing in 1803, provided a classic description of hemophilia and noted both the persistance of the defect through generations of a New England family and the genetic pattern in which clinical manifestations skip a generation. Hemophilia has played a role in recent history, having afflicted princes in the royal houses of Europe, all of whom were descendants of Queen Victoria. Among those notables was the Czarevitch of Russia, Alexis, son of Nicolas II and Alexandra. The mystic, Rasputin, became an intimate of the court through his efforts to improve the child's health and wielded significant political power through his consequent influence over the empress. This relationship, and the family's preoccupation with the hemophilic

F. Ralph Berberich

Alexis, may have contributed significantly to the downfall of the Romanov dynasty and to the political turmoil which ensued.

GENETICS

Hemophilia is transmitted by a genetic pattern known as *sex-linked recessive inheritance*. The term *sex-linked* refers to the fact that the defective gene is located on the X chromosome, which functions in determining an individual's sex. The term *recessive* refers to the fact that the trait (hemophilia) is expressed only when the defective form of the gene alone is present. Females, who possess two X chromosomes, must therefore carry the defective form of the gene on both chromosomes in order to have hemophilia. If only one of their chromosomes bears the defective gene, they will be carriers of the defective gene and may pass it on to their offsping, but only rarely will they have bleeding difficulties. Males, on the other hand, have only one X chromosome (their second sex chromosome is a Y) and therefore require only a single dose of the defective gene to express the deficiency. This pattern of inheritance is illustrated in Figure 19-1, which also shows that each male offspring born of a carrier mother and a normal father has a 50 percent chance of having hemophilia, while each daughter has a 50 percent chance of being a carrier. Sons born to a normal, noncarrier mother and a hemophiliac father will be normal, while all daughters of such parents will be carriers.

Formerly, estimations of the chances that a relative of a hemophilic male was a carrier of the disease were made on the basis of these inheritance patterns alone. By combining such predictions with newly developed laboratory tests, it is now possible to determine this with 90 percent accuracy. Furthermore, advances have also been made toward the detection of hemophilia in utero. During early pregnancy fetal sex can be determined by an examination of cells shed into the fluid within the uterus

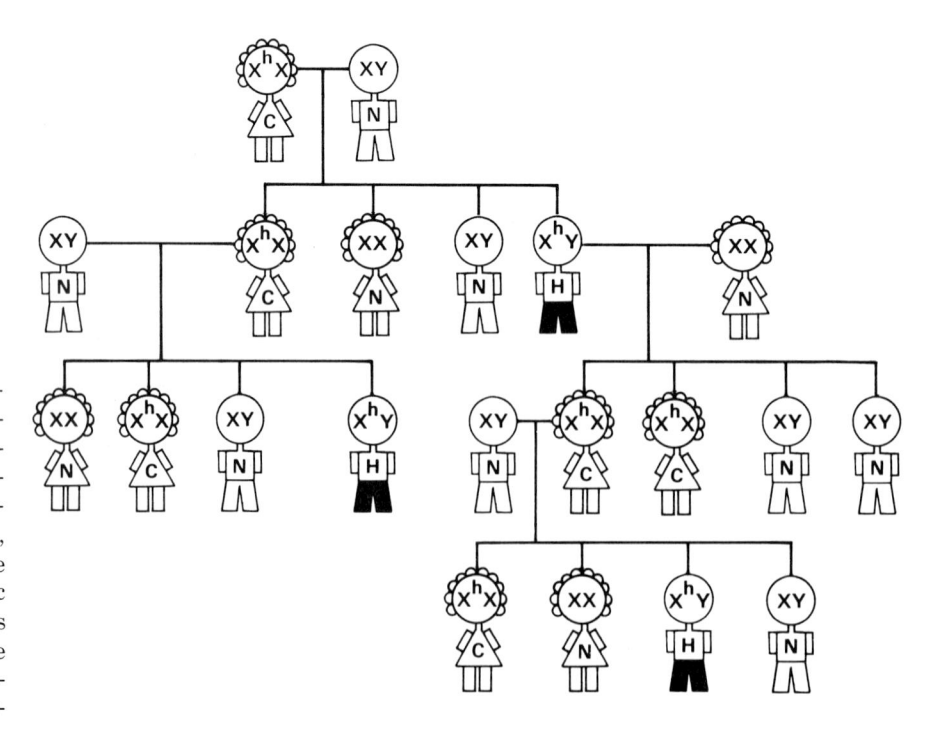

Fig. 19-1. A family pedigree illustrating the sex-linked recessive inheritance pattern of hemophilia: N, normal; C, carrier; H, hemophiliac; h, hemophilia gene. The mother of a hemophiliac carries the disorder but is not affected beause she has a second X chromosome without the defective gene.

(a procedure called *amniocentesis*). Should the fetus be a male, a recently developed technique of fetal blood sampling (fetoscopy) will make it possible to determine whether or not the fetus has hemophilia.

PHYSIOLOGY OF COAGULATION

Blood has the almost magical quality of circulating within vessels as a fluid and clotting when exposed to an abnormal surface or to the external environment. A clot acts as a seal to prevent bleeding while the disrupted tissue heals over a period of several days to 2 weeks. The delicate, but decisive, balance which the body maintains between blood fluidity and coagulation is governed by multiple factors; these include the contraction of disrupted blood vessels, the contractile action of small blood corpuscles, known as platelets, and the activation of coagulation-promoting proteins after injury. There are 13 known coagulation-promoting proteins, each of which is designated by a Roman numeral. The proteins function in a complex, integrated system to generate a mesh-like framework (fibrin) to which platelets adhere to form a plug. Two deficiency states are included in the general designation, *hemophilia*. Factor VIII deficiency (classic hemophilia, or hemophilia A) accounts for 80 percent of cases, while Factor IX deficiency (Christmas disease, or hemophilia B) encompasses the remaining 20 percent. The two disorders are indistinguishable by symptoms or by pattern of inheritance and are treated similarly, although with different therapeutic materials. An individual with a functional deficiency of one of these coagulation proteins relies on alternate mechanisms for blood coagulation. The resulting clots are poorly formed and become weak, ineffective seals. Other deficiencies of coagulation proteins or deficits in platelets can have similar consequences but are not termed *hemophilia*.

The severity of hemophilia is determined by the percentage of functioning Factor VIII or Factor IX, in the body. If this percentage is less than 1 percent of normal, then the individual will be severely affected and may have abnormal internal bleeding, usually within joint spaces, without known antecedent injury. Patients with higher percentages of functioning coagulation factors have moderate or mild hemophilia and usually exhibit abnormal bleeding following trauma, surgery, dental work, intramuscular injections, or the administration of drugs such as aspirin which interfere with coagulation. The degree of severity in hemophilia is constant over an individual's lifetime.

CLINICAL MANIFESTATIONS IN CHILDREN AND APPROACH TO TREATMENT

Sites of abnormal bleeding vary with age, activity, situational likelihood of injury, and the severity of the hemophilia.

Scrapes, cuts, and bruises may occur at any time but are especially prevalent in the school-age child. Hemophiliacs do not usually bleed excessively from minor injuries, and routine first-aid measures, such as pressure dressings, are most often adequate. A deeper cut or a more major bruise may bleed and require further treatment. Sutures and intramuscular injections should not be administered until factor replacement has been given.

Mouth, tongue, and dental bleeding occurs, especially in the preschool child, and requires treatment, even in the case of a small bleeding point. Medication that retards the dissolution of blood clots is usually prescribed in addition to factor replacement.

Head and spine injuries can be life threatening and must be reported to the parent or physician promptly, so that the child can receive appropriate factor replacement. Signs which should alert the observer to the possibility of unrecognized head or spine injuries include an overlying bump or bruise, unusual or unresponsive headaches (especially those associated with unexplained vomiting), confusion, disorientation, inappropriate sleepiness, or inability to move a limb.

Joints and muscles are the most common sites of bleeding in active, school-age children. Within the joint space is found a friable protective membrane (synovium) containing multiple blood vessels. Trauma, the wear and tear of normal activity, and the stress of weight bearing can cause disruption of these vessels and consequent bleeding into the joint space. In a severe hemophiliac, no initiating event may be found. The knees, ankles, and elbows are most commonly involved. Pain, swelling, warmth, and decreased motion are the typical signs of a joint bleed (hemarthrosis), although initial symptoms may be very subtle. Patients can sometimes sense the onset of bleeding before signs are evident and should receive treatment as early as possible. Hemarthroses are not life threatening but can cause disability and loss of limb motion if recurrent and undertreated. Pressure within the blood-filled joint, iron pigment, and blood breakdown products promote further bleeding by causing proliferation of the synovium and its blood supply. With further bleeding, the protective effect of the synovium is lost and first the cartilage, and then the bone, become subject to erosion. Over time, such patients may develop stiff, painful joints (arthritis) and a reduced arc of motion (contracture). Supportive braces, crutches, physical therapy, and rehabilitative orthopedic surgery may be required in varying degrees to ameliorate the consequences of recurrent hemarthroses. Minimization of bleeding through factor replacement at the first indication of joint bleeding is the best means of preventing these unfortunate sequelae.

Abdominal injuries are of concern, especially when the liver or spleen may have received a sharp blow. Abdominal pain, pallor, weakness, or sudden perspiration indicate potential urgency. The ribs offer some relative protection to underlying organs in the chest.

Bleeding in the *urine* or in vomited material is not necessarily a cause for alarm but should be treated as soon as is reasonably possible. *Nosebleed* should be treated with pressure and with factor replacement.

TREATMENT AND PROGNOSIS

During the past 15 years, hemophiliacs have benefited from medical and surgical innovations, notably the production from normal human blood plasma of purified, concentrated, transportable Factor VIII and Factor IX preparation. The intravenous administration of these materials provides temporary correction of the deficiency in hemophilia and can restore normal coagulation during that time. Such replacement therapy has permitted major surgery to be carried out with safety in hemophiliacs and is used to treat bleeding episodes. Regular, temporary correction can be provided (prophylaxis), but it has not been practical to provide constant, complete protection from potential bleeding. Home therapy programs, in which parents, and then the children themselves, are taught intravenous self-administration, have provided earlier, more effective treatment and have reduced the duration of disability and school and work absences (Fig. 19-2). Such therapy has provided hemophiliacs and their families with a sense of confidence and independence and has virtually eliminated midnight trips to the emergency room. The management of hemophiliacs is thus conducted by a team consisting of the patient and his family, the physician, the nurse coordinator, the physical therapist, and the social worker. The reduced reliance on physician

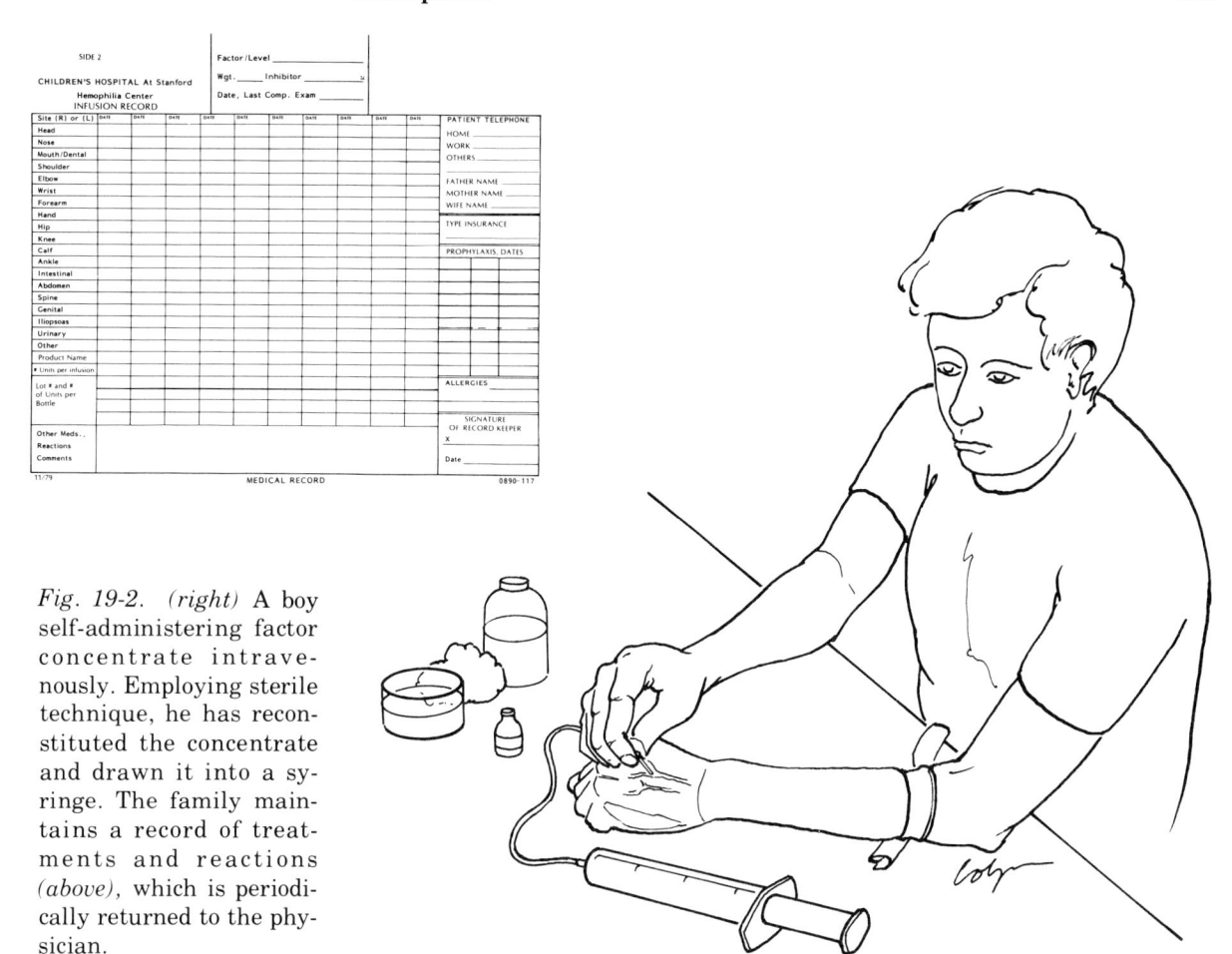

Fig. 19-2. (right) A boy self-administering factor concentrate intravenously. Employing sterile technique, he has reconstituted the concentrate and drawn it into a syringe. The family maintains a record of treatments and reactions *(above)*, which is periodically returned to the physician.

and hospital also presents potential hazards, however, since the individual's responsibility for appropriate self-care correspondingly increases. In the course of their emotional and social development, children or adolescents may be subject to erroneous judgment, embarrassment, and peer pressure which may impede prompt, effective treatment.

Problems associated with factor replacement have included the development of antibodies to administered coagulation proteins (inhibitors), liver inflammation (hepatitis), and the cost and availability of plasma products. In the presence of inhibitors, which arise in about 5 percent of patients, replacement material is immunologically destroyed as soon as it has been given. Some patients with inhibitors can be treated with alternative preparations. A hepatitis risk accompanies the administration of any blood product, especially when the material is obtained from a large group of pooled donors. A few patients who have hepatitis may develop chronic liver dysfunction. Finally, the staggering cost of hemophilia care, often thousands of dollars per year per patient, must be borne by families, insurance programs, and state government agencies. Irrespective of cost, the supply of replacement is finite and limited by the response to blood donor recruitment.

EDUCATIONAL IMPLICATIONS

It should be recognized that hemophilia is not an illness but, rather, an impairment which imposes a variable degree of physical limitation on the affected child. The goals of injury prevention, body (and, specifically, joint) preservation, and the development of maximal areas of potential productivity are emphasized in the hemophiliac, but they are not unique to him. He also has an unwelcome, but potentially beneficial, opportunity to develop judgment, tenacity, forebearance, and maturity at an early age. Teachers should be aware of the peculiar family constellation which often surrounds the hemophiliac. There may be maternal guilt owing to the nature of the genetic transmission. This tends to produce a close, protective relationship between mother and son and, sometimes, a degree of favoritism. Fathers are occasionally more distant from their sons and less attuned to the hazards of hemophilia. A push toward normality and consequent denial of limitations are common. Hemophiliacs may derive secondary gain from their disorder and use their disability or others' fear of their injuring themselves in a manipulative fashion.

Ideally, one is protective of hemophiliacs where a true hazard exists but avoids excessive sheltering. One strives to provide an environment in which the hemophiliac can develop as normally as possible in tandem with his peers. The approach to athletics may serve as an example: from an early age, the efforts of a hemophiliac should be channeled into activities in which he can achieve and be successful. Swimming is an ideal, non–weight-bearing life-long activity and should be introduced before the child is 4 years of age. A daily exercise program is essential for all hemophiliacs, and activity limitations in non-contact and water sports should be set through experience. In this way, disability or failure are less likely to arise and to reduce the benefits and enjoyment the child may derive from athletics. The only sports that are prohibited are those which carry a high risk for head or spine injury, such as tackle football, soccer, and trampoline.

Absences from school must be anticipated, although home therapy programs have reduced these dramatically. The hemophiliac may appear in school on crutches or in a brace or cast, may ask to be excused from physical activities, or may suddenly complain of pain or impending bleeding. Productive alternative activities should be provided whenever possible. Legitimate excuses or complaints should be honored, and any suspicion of manipulative behavior should be brought to the attention of parent and physician. Excessive absences that threaten academic achievement should be brought to medical attention, since they may reflect inadequate replacement therapy.

Finally, educators may be helpful in channeling vocational interests. Professions in which the individual is self-employed or independent, hours are flexible, and standing, walking, and lifting are limited are preferred. It is better to cultivate interests that may lead to such professions than to face an adolescent whose only desire is an occupation which imposes a high risk of trauma or professional failure.

SUMMARY

In summary, hemophilia is an inherited disorder of blood coagulation that may be treated by intravenous replacement of the defective clotting factor. Home therapy has decreased the crippling consequences of recurrent joint bleeding and provides the hemophiliac the security of prompt, available treatment. His goal of leading a relatively normal, productive, and fulfilling life within the limitations of his disorder is achievable through the coordinated efforts of patient, family, medical team, educators, and supporting government agencies.

BIBLIOGRAPHY Massie, R., and Massie, S., *Journey.* New York, Warner Books, 1973.
Jones, P., *Living with Haemophilia.* Philadelphia, F. A. Davis, 1974.
Boone, D. C. (ed.), *Comprehensive Management of Hemophilia.* Philadelphia, F. A. Davis, 1976.

20

Normal Infant Motor Development

FRAN FORD, R.P.T.

Why are babies so fascinating? Not because they are potentially miniature adults, but because they are constantly changing, evolving, and growing. Observing infants develop from day to day, we witness their gradual discovery of their abilities and their growing exploration of the world around them. In their first year, infants learn (among many other lessons) to control some of the manifold facets of their bodies and begin to experiment with affecting their environment.

BASIC TERMS AND THEIR MEANINGS

Concepts of Maturation

Growth, in terms of infant maturation, means an increase in physical size, whereas *development* refers to an increase in control over body movement. Both are guided by certain general laws of maturation. For example, development proceeds in a *cephalocaudal direction,* commencing in the region of the head and proceeding downward toward the feet. Thus children learn to lift first their head, later their hands, and lastly their feet. Maturation also follows a *central to peripheral direction,* beginning in the center of the body and progressing outward to the extremities; infants learn to control their shoulders and direct their arms long before they are able to grasp a toy efficiently with their fingers.

PROGRESSION OF REFLEXES AND VOLUNTARY CONTROLLED MOVEMENTS

Certain primitive reflexes emerge in anticipation of related voluntary movements, and these same reflexes necessarily become dormant before voluntary control can be practiced.[8] The *walking reflex* is a good example. It occurs when a very young baby is supported and placed in standing position; the child can bear most of his own weight and, if firmly leaned in any direction, will "walk" (rhythmical stepping of the lower limbs). All these movements take place within a flexed milieu. The walking reflex is apparent during the newborn period and for some weeks thereafter, after which it disappears—before controlled standing and walking—the goal—is achieved. In the intervening period, the baby cannot support his full weight and hence will collapse when loosely held standing. A few weeks later, the child will again support most of his weight under the same circumstances—this time mainly as a result of voluntary control, although other reflexes are now called forth to give aid. The infant's voluntary control will increase as he continues to practice standing, bouncing, and, ultimately, free walking.

The growing infant is also guided by patterns of progression characteristic of all humans. The first of these, the *phylogenetic progression pattern,* refers to the sequential emergence and appropriate modification of the primitive reflexes that dominate the baby's initial movements. Man is an antigravity being whose many diverse movements are directed contrary to the force of gravity; the baby's reflex mechanisms make possible his first move against gravity. These stereotyped first movements, or *primitive reflexes,* appear and disappear in phylogenetic sequence.

The infant is also guided by *ontogenetic progression,* which refers to the sequential development of man's ability to roll, sit, stand, and walk erect. The infant does not suddenly attain the ability to walk; rather, within this ontogenetic progression, he instinctively, and by repeated experience, modifies and practices movements provided by the primitive reflex mechanism.

Basically, these phylogenetic and ontogenetic progression patterns are characteristic of the development of all humans: all normal children, because they are members of the family of man, learn to resist gravity in very similar patterns during the varied activities of development. They learn, in sequence, to hold up their heads, to roll, to sit, to stand, and, finally, to walk. Within this general schema, however, there may be considerable individual variation. As Peiper has observed:[10]

> No two children will move in exactly the same way; sometimes the variations in the same pattern of gait may be quite considerable.... The children may be able to slide with the same skill in totally different ways.... Even though the unsupported gait always has to be learned ... other gait patterns do not necessarily have to precede it. Rather, external influences frequently determine whether one of these patterns is learned and is preferred or appears at the same time with others. Important and often deciding influences are the guidance of the mother and the example of other children ... marked fluctuations in the ages at which these various stages appear are explained by internal and external causes.

There is then, a general path of direction in an infant's development. Predictable patterns of motor behavior commence at birth, inborn patterns which exist as *potentials* and are subject to great modification by environmental forces. Each individual develops at their own rate, directed by their environment.

The developmental stages so well documented by Gesell,[3,4] Illingworth,[7,8] McGraw,[9] and Peiper[10] are but guidelines for child study. The *progression* of development is far more important than any developmental timetable to those who work with handicapped children. There is the need to know why and how a child develops as well as to understand how each sequential area of development relates to the other areas—how, together, these will compose the orderly mosaic of youthful maturation.

PRIMITIVE REFLEXES AND THE DEVELOPMENT OF GROSS MOTOR CONTROL

The developmental timetable should be used merely as a guide for direction, not as an end per se.

For infantile occupation (and often puzzlement as well), tasks of increasing complexity are woven together in interlocking stages. These tasks are founded on reflex activity which is then modified by experience. Progression from stage to stage is possible only because of the baby's strong urge toward movement, activity, and *doing* rather than just being.[10]

The young infant reacts with total movement to distress or joy. As he becomes older, however, this *global response* becomes modified to an appropriate, specific, and efficient gesture. Mass activity gives way to *specific, individual response* as the baby matures.[7]

An attempt to provide a complete list of reflexes will not be undertaken in this chapter; only a representative overall summary of the myriad events in the young child's motor evolvement will be discussed.

The diverse chain of events begins in the head and neck area, moving distally through the trunk and out to the limbs. In the baby, the distribution of muscle tone for the neck, torso, and limbs is dominated by *alert and orientation reflexes*, such as the Moro reflex and the tonic labyrinthine, tonic neck, and early supportive reactions. These orientation reflexes give the baby a template for designing and controlling his earliest movements. Presumably, the alert and orientation reflexes are controlled by low levels of the brain and brainstem. Later, as development proceeds, the *righting reactions* evolve, and, still later, these are further modified by the appearance of the *equilibrium reactions*. Apparently these later, postural responses are controlled by higher brain levels. Blending of early orientation reflexes and postural reflexes (righting and equilibrium) occurs in an interdependent, chainlike, sequential pattern; they are dependent on one another, build on each other, and modify each other.

To clarify the relationship between lower, more primitive orientation reflex action and postural reflex control, a brief discussion is warranted. The more primitive reflexes control the distribution of postural tone throughout the body. Although these unsophisticated reflexes are not totally controlling and do not produce static, unyielding positions in the normal infant, they do influence movement. Such responses may be stimulated by the position of the head or body in relation to space or to surrounding surfaces—i.e., whether the baby is lying on his stomach (*prone*) or on his back (*supine*), or is being supported in standing position (*erect*). Some reflexes are also affected by the position of the head in relation to the rest of the body, as when the baby's head is turned to one side or when it is aligned with the midline of his trunk. A normal child's muscle tone tends to be altered (increased in predictable patterns) by these various head and body positions.

Posture and movement are dynamic and constantly changing. Bobath[1,2] describes the postural reflex mechanism as consisting of two types of automatic reactions: the righting and the equilibrium reactions. The righting reactions reflect the normal position of the head in space, the alignment of the head and neck with the truck, and the alignment of the trunk and limbs (allow for head control and rotation along the body axis). Equilibrium reactions are more complex and involve shifts made in muscle tone to maintain or restore balance. Thus, the earliest reflexes afford the child a sufficient amount of muscle tone for the postural reflex mechanism to act, while, combined, the righting and equilibrium reactions permit a mobile but simultaneously stable stance against gravity. We can then superimpose voluntary movement upon static postures. In the infant, movement is random in the beginning and becomes voluntary and autodirected with experience and practice.

A simple example of the interaction among the supportive reflexes, the righting and equilibrium reactions, and the superimposition of voluntary control, is as follows: A young child is resting on his stomach (prone) on the floor. He props himself up on his elbows and holds his head from the floor. Desiring to reach out for a toy, he struggles to lift his head up (*optical and labyrinthine righting reactions* and *spinal extension*), supports himself on his elbows, and thus resists gravity (*supportive reactions of the shoulders*). Now he frees one arm and reaches out for the toy (the rest of the body accommodating him with mobile support supplied by *equilibrium and supportive reactions,* and by *body-righting acting on the body*). He secures the toy by guidance and feedback from his sensory systems.

SEQUENCE OF GROSS MOTOR CONTROL FROM NEWBORN TO TODDLER

The following discussion draws freely from the works of many sources and follows a normal child's gross motor development. Always keep in mind that gross motor development is only one area of growth, one area of control that a child must develop. Other areas are also receiving attention from the child as he matures, such as somatic growth, fine motor control, intellectual, social, emotional, and perceptual development. All of these areas that we tend to mention separately are intra-, as well as interdependent upon each other. The purpose of the following portion of the chapter is to outline the progression of a normal child so that the teacher of a handicapped child may understand how that child differs from the normal child in the area of gross motor control. The sequence of gross motor control will be traced from birth to the toddler period; developmental ages have been purposely omitted.

Newborn

The global picture of a newborn infant's gross motor control is one of *flexed* body attitude, with movements tending to be *en masse*, random, and jerky. The newborn baby, regardless of how he is held, remains in symmetrically flexed posture *(physiologic flexor hypertonus)*.

If the neonate is placed on his stomach, he keeps his head turned to one side for protection of the air passages. He can perform this head movement despite the fact that at this stage he cannot support his head in any other direction because of lack of head control. His arms are flexed and held close to his trunk and head, while his hands are usually closed (fisted), with his thumbs tucked into the palms *(adducted)*. He is capable of opening his fisted hands and of putting either hand into (or at least near) his mouth. His legs are flexed at the hips and knees; the legs hold him so that his bottom is higher than any other part (physiologic flexor hypertonus). Now if he is placed on the bed with his stomach upward (supine) or held in adult arms, he will still remain in the flexed position. The infant gives the impression that one side of his body and limbs mirrors the image of the other side *(symmetry)*. When he is thus supine, his head is held in the center. He can straighten (extend) his arms and legs (limbs) only during the *Moro reflex,* which is elicited by a sudden movement of the head or of the whole body or may be evoked by a sudden loud noise. At this stage of development, the Moro reflex causes a broad spreading of the arms to the side in a slightly upward motion *(abduction)* with extension of the elbows and wrists and extension and outward flaring (abduction) of the thumbs and fingers. The legs adopt the same pattern, but here the movement is weaker and shorter in range.

Early Infancy

Shortly after birth and for the next few weeks, other motor patterns, known as *mass primitive reflexes* emerge. For example, if the infant's trunk is supported and he is placed on his feet, he appears to stand *(primitive standing reflex);* if leaned, he will walk *(primitive walking reflex).* Both standing and rhythmical walking are performed in the flexed posture we mentioned earlier. The first righting reaction to appear is that of the *neck righting:* when the child's head is turned to one side, his whole trunk follows as though of one piece, giving the impression that he can turn over to either side during the earliest stages of lie. The turning of his head is under voluntary control, but turning of the body is controlled by reflex action (neck-righting acting upon the body).

As the baby ages, he develops increased *extension* of the body and limb musculature and loses flexion domination. As this occurs, his resting position and movement patterns become more asymmetrical *(asymmetrical tonic neck reflex).* When he is supine, the head position influences the position of the limbs. If he turns his head to one side, the arm and leg on that side extend, while the arm and leg on the opposite side flex. This movement is most noticeable in the baby's arms. A normal child tends to assume the asymmetrical position and is not dominated by the position of his head. He can willfully move his limbs into other positions but is inclined to assume the asymmetrical posture; this is useful, for it permits him to turn his head without rolling his body.

The child has benefited from his new reflexes. Because total flexion is now being resisted by increasing extension and the total symmetry and neck-righting reflexes are now opposed by the asymmetrical position, the infant is now able to explore visually the view to his side (laterally) by means of increased isolated head movements. By achieving the ability to extend his arms away from his body and look at his hands, he also is more able to interact with his surroundings.[5]

As the infant acquires still more extension power, the capacity to lift his head while prone improves. The baby begins to raise his head *(neck and spinal extension)* as though to gaze down at the place where his head had just been resting (labyrinthine and optical righting reactions and spinal extension). These reflexes increase the child's ability to raise his head and body to an upright position—i.e., to adjust his head to gravity and to the horizon. Control of head-raising is the beginning of the total extension pattern, which progresses downward through the child's trunk and limbs. Soon he will be able to lift his head higher and higher and hold it thus for longer periods. At first, when the infant elevates his head and looks about, little aid is afforded by his arms, which may be gently resting on the surface of the bed or floor, out to the side, or tucked near the shoulders.

Simultaneously, at this stage, the baby's entire body posture is becoming symmetrical once again. In addition, he is learning head control in the supine position and is able to turn his head freely and contemplate his surroundings. Improvement in head control is also apparent when the child is pulled up to sit: he can assist minimally in the beginning of the pull-to-sit motion and can hold his head a bit steadier while being supported in sitting. At the same time that he is gaining control of his head, shoulders, and arms, the capacity to flex and extend his legs emerges, tending toward mass motions which are still jerky. Generally the legs are much more mobile than the arms, moving about in total flexure or extending patterns and often producing alternating movements *(crossed extension kicking)*. Although most of the time the baby's toes are contracted into tiny claws, he is quite capable of haphazard extension and flaring of his toes.

As extension of the head and trunk increases, the earlier-mentioned rhythmical walking and reflexive standing diminish. Now if propped on his feet, the infant assists but little in supporting his weight, and will drag his feet behind him when propelled forward *(negative supporting phase)*.

At this stage, when prone, he can lift his head and fully support the weight on his extended arms *(positive supporting reaction* of the arms and shoulders). Moreover, he is able to move his head in any direction to examine all he surveys. His legs are still mobile and he moves them frequently. Also, at about this time, supported by reflex action (neck and body righting) and by accident, the infant will roll from his stomach onto his back (prone to supine position).

Although the child is now capable of supporting himself on his arms, he can also maintain his back in arched position (spinal extension) without arm support (shoulder and arm retraction), for he has developed sufficient such spinal extension to arch his trunk with his arms off the surface; his hips and legs extend, the latter separating (abduction)—the *Landau reflex*. Reminiscent of the traditional picture of a bare-bottomed baby on a fluffy bearskin rug, the child is at last completely free of the flexed posture which was his at birth. Absorbedly practicing extension, he will take his arms off the support and kick (swim) with his legs.

Rolling

The infant can now oppose gravity by controlling his head in any position. He can push up to explore the environment on straightened arms, kick freely in any direction, extend and arch his trunk, lift his legs from the support, and attempt to twist his trunk to achieve rotation between shoulders and hips (body-righting acting on the body). Ready to learn further control of rolling, he begins to roll from the supine to prone position. The child turns his head and follows either with his shoulders and arms or with his hips and legs. Controlled rolling occurs via dissolution of the asymmetrical posture by a return to symmetry and enhancement of the body's righting reflexes. These reflexes encourage axial rotation of the trunk, thereby modifying the increased extension. Along with a constantly growing rolling skill, the child is engaged in developing his prone and supine equilibrium reaction, which gives him greater latitude for rolling.

Heralded by trunk rotation (*axial rotation* between the shoulders and the hips), the control of other total movement patterns ensues, with modifications in total patterns of flexion or extension. For example, the baby, lying on his back, is able to draw up his feet to his hands and mouth; this delightful gesture not only grants him visual and tactile exploration but also enables him to practice precarious sitting long before he can balance himself while sitting or sit independently of support.

Early Sitting

At this stage of development full head control and partial trunk control have been attained, and the baby begins to sit for a matter of moments (by this time modifying the total Moro reflex). He can briefly maintain the sitting position but is not yet able to control this position independently. Because his supportive and equilibrium reactions in sitting are as yet deficient, when placed in the sitting aspect, he has a rounded back and sits without arm support, falling backward or sideways if unassisted. Later, the infant will sit with his arms stretched well forward, a reaction which is elicited by the body weight pressing the arms or legs to the surface. All of the arm muscles will then contract and so support the child, giving the onlooker the impression that he is resting on his abdomen for support, holding his hands far forward on the surface near his feet. Even though he lacks balance in sitting and topples without support, he can bear his full weight if held standing (*parachute reaction* of the legs and positive supporting reaction of the hips and lower limbs).

As the infant continues to mature, his sitting posture becomes more erect, his back now straighter due to a change in arm placement and improved spinal extension and equilibrium reactions in sitting. As he feels more secure while sitting, he props himself up with his arms more laterally, and as he gains more and more skill in sitting, there is a corresponding progression of back-arching while prone and supine (Landau reflex and *bridging*).

When the child can roll supine-to-prone, he begins to achieve independent sitting, rolling from his back to his stomach, then raising up his rotating trunk and pushing with his arms and hands. By sitting he has gained additional control of his trunk musculature and can now free one hand (and, momentarily, both hands) to play, but he still falls easily. Only after walking will he be able to use arm support to the rear while sitting, thus completing the sequence of equilibrium reactions in the sitting position. Also, beyond the stages of development covered in this chapter, he will modify again and again the manner in which he assumes the sitting posture.

Crawling

During the time the infant is rolling about and sitting supported, his equilibrium reactions in the prone and supine positions are becoming refined. Experimental crawling (stomach on the surface, with most of the movement supplied by the arms) is the logical sequel. Peiper[10] considers that at first this change of physical locale is purely accidental—i.e., that it is part of the infant's efforts to reach an object that is visible but out of reach. We have learned that the infant holds his head up to gaze forward, which initiates spinal extension. As the head departs from the surface further, the body tries to right itself in relation to the head (neck-righting acting on the body). As this takes place, the arms are brought up under the body, and the shoulder is firm to accept the support (supporting reactions of the elbows and shoulders). Often an infant in this phase of growth will reach for a toy with both hands simultaneously, causing him to fall forward. When he regains his upright position, he has moved somewhat ahead. The hands pull slightly on the surface, but in the beginning, do not assist his progression. Later, he becomes proficient at pulling himself along on his forearms. The hips and legs rest on the supportive surface and move about, but lend little real assistance in propulsion. At times, so much activity will engage shoulders and arms that the child may push himself backward and pivot on his abdomen or roll over onto his back. Here the legs become more active and give him more help.

Peiper[10] notes that after a while the child evidently loses the propelling urge and, instead, commences to support his weight on his hands and knees (*creeping position,* assisted by the supporting reactions of upper and lower limbs as well as by neck and spinal extension). The infant will rock back and forth in this position without making any apparent progress, or he may lose his balance and topple forward. Often, he will return to crawling, motivated by the desire for propulsion. His creeping movements may at first consist of moving one arm, then the other, and then flexing both legs simultaneously *hopping;* eventually a reciprocal arm and leg pattern evolves.

Standing

As the child acquires greater proficiency in creeping and sitting, he also attempts to stand and walk by hoisting himself up while holding on to furniture or an adult. Placed on his feet, the infant will stand with legs spread apart (parachute reaction and position supporting reaction of the legs) and will bounce when supported standing (*voluntary control* of the positive supporting reaction). The child progresses by creeping and practicing standing and, while sitting, continues to develop his equilibrium reactions. The equilibrium reactions therefore tend to develop just after the next, and more difficult, motor task presents itself.[6]

Supported Standing

Erect gait has been well described by both Peiper[10] and McGraw.[9] Peiper stresses that the infant's use of his arms is equally as important as the use of his legs during first attempts to stand, walk, and arise from the floor. Usually the baby is placed standing near a table, chair, or crib (for support) before he can lift himself to stand alone. After some practice in supported standing, when the infant feels safe, he dares to let go with one hand and grasp for something a distance away. Bending down is especially difficult (positive support reaction of the legs). He always keeps at least one hand on the support, and only when he is very brave (or sufficiently tempted) will he relinquish the support with one hand and reach down to the floor to pick up a toy. If the infant wants to reach the floor, he bends his knees slightly and tries to lower himself down; in the earlier stages, he usually falls and lands on his bottom. A child learns to creep to a support and pull himself to standing position before he learns to sit down unassisted from the standing position. Gradually he learns to walk sideways from support to support *(cruising).*

Early Walking

At first the infant avoids free walking whenever possible; instead, he lowers himself to the floor and creeps. If he is being "led" by an adult and the adult suddenly releases him, the infant will sit down (or at best, remain standing) but will not continue to walk (insufficient equilibrium reactions in standing). Some infants who can walk unaided move so clumsily in their excitement and fervor that they may fall. When the child achieves independent walking *ambulation*), he holds his arms in the air, up and out to the sides of his body. Now he has a wide base of support and marked flexion of the hips and legs, as he high-steps and lands flat-footed. McGraw[9] contends that some infants with lagging equilibrium reactions will run a few steps before toppling. As the child develops better equilibrium reactions and the need for firm support is lessened, his arms lower and his legs move closer together. As he walks about aided, he refines his equilibrium reactions toward the front (*anterior* equilibrium reactions); daring to let go, he proceeds alone for a short distance. He refines his *side-to-side* equilibrium reactions as he cruises.

Independent Walking

After independent walking is accomplished, the infant develops equilibrium reactions to the rear (*posterior* equilibrium reactions). If he loses his balance in the early stages of free walking, he topples forward and catches himself with his hands, or collapses to the rear and lands on his bottom (deficient posterior equilibrium reactions). Later, when he is more mature, he learns to step backward slightly as he loses his balance to the rear.

GROSS MOTOR DEVELOPMENT CHART

Table 20-1 provides an overview of the progression in gross motor development that we have discussed. It should be read in the vertical as well as the horizontal direction. The vertical direction emphasizes the variety of positions in which a child will practice his motor skills and the variety of movement patterns practiced at any one time. The horizontal direction emphasizes development of skills over time. Reading from left to right, one can follow the progression from unskilled and random to refined and purposeful movement patterns.

The reflexes and reactions are listed above the skill development patterns. The solid lines indicate strong reflex activity and the broken lines represent a weak action. One should note how closely the reflexes and voluntary movements are related.

A time scale has been purposely omitted. The development chart is designed to emphasize the general flow of development.

CONCLUSION

We must remember that gross motor development is based upon reflex control which will be modified by other reflexes as well as by experience. A baby learns to move against the force of gravity by using his reflex system; he then modifies reflex domination by experience in movement, thereby achieving coordinated, skilled mobility. As the infant attains controlled and voluntary movements, he is also developing his sense of balance and establishing his equilibrium reactions. Mature balance reactions lag behind the acquisition of gross motor skill.

Remember, too, that the need to move is inborn and that, as the child matures, he retains the inherent drive to move and to explore. Hence he will continue to practice beyond his first year of life and will thereby realize a sense of control. Likewise he will continue to tax his systems of balance and coordination until the limits of his potential are reached.

Table 20-1. Reflexes and reactions.

- primary standing
- primary walking
- Moro
- tonic labyrinthine—prone
- tonic labyrinthine—supine
- symmetrical tonic neck reflex
- asymmetrical tonic neck reflex
- neck righting acting on body
- parachute of legs
- positive supporting of legs
- plantar grasp
- labyrinthine and optical righting
- parachute—uppers
- Landau
- body righting acting on head
- equlibrium—prone
- parachute—arms—forward
- body righting acting on body
- parachute—arms—sideways
- equilibrium—supine
- equilibrium—sitting
- equilibrium—creeping
- parachute—arms—backwards
- equilibrium—standing

SKILL DEVELOPMENT

PROGRESSION
- —swimming
- —progresses a little when swimming
- —rolls side to side
- —rolls prone to supine

STANDING
- —able to hold head up more than momentarily
- —does not accept body weight
- —does not accept body weight
- —takes some of body weight
- —bears almost all weight on one hand

SITTING
- —no head control
- —back rounded
- —back rounded
- —momentarily lifts head up
- —head mostly held up, but it tends to bob forward
- —head wobbles when body is swayed
- —back curved only in lumbar region
- —no head wobble when body is swayed
- —back is straight
- —no arm support
- —sits supported
- —pulls self to sitting

PULL-TO-SIT
- —full head lag
- —almost complete head lag
- —head initially drops back, but comes forward when trunk is 30° to 40° from vertical
- —slight head lag in beginning of movement
- —no head lag
- —lifts legs (hips flexed and legs extended and then flexed)
- —lifts head off bed
- —raises extended legs and flexed hips

SUPINE
- —flexion
- —symmetrical
- —rolls over to side
- —asymmetrical
- —less total flexion
- —symmetrical body position
- —head in midline
- —symmetrical position
- —hands engage near face or over chest
- —legs flex and abduct
- —reciprocal kicking
- —bridges
- —can lift head in supine
- —reaches out to be picked up
- —lifts legs and plays with feet

PRONE
- —flexion
- —head to one side
- —knees often under abdomen
- —some kicking
- —chin intermittently off couch
- —lifts chin off bed face at 45° angle
- —head in midline
- —pelvis flat on bed
- —plane of face reaches angle of 45° to 90°
- —forearm support
- —chest off bed
- —plane of face at 90°
- —limbs stretched out in full extension
- —weight on abdomen
- —weight on forearms
- —may reach at objects
- —weight on hands with extended arms
- —chest and upper abdomen off bed

Normal Infant Motor Development

—rolls supine to prone	—pivots on stomach	—progresses backward in attempt to crawl	—crawls on abdomen —can go from sitting to prone and prone to sitting —pivots in sitting to pick up toy	—creeps on hands and knees —cruses —walks with two hands held	—creeps sole of foot intermittently on floor —cruses —walks one hand held —creeps	—walks free	
—bounces with pleasure	—stands holding onto furniture —pulls up to knees —plays on knees	—pulls to stand	—lowers himself to floor by holding on —collapses if not holding on	—lifts one foot when holding on	—attempts to stand alone		
—sits on floor with hands forward for support —tends to throw himself backwards —little balance	—sits momentarily on floor without support —sits erect —sideways arm support —adjust posture to reach for toy	—sits steady —leans forward and recovers balance	—good balance —can lean over sideways	—arm support backwards	—can twist round to pick up objects		
—can pull self to sitting holding on to person							
—does not like supine							
—may bear weight on one hand							

REFERENCES

1. Bobath, K., *The Motor Deficit in Patients with Cerebral Palsy.* Clinics in Developmental Medicine, No. 23. London, Heinemann Medical Books, 1966.
2. Bobath, K., The normal postural reflex mechanism and its deviation in children with cerebral palsy. *Physiotherapy* 57:515,1971.
3. Gessell A., and Amatsuda, C. S., *Developmental Diagnosis,* 2nd ed. New York, Hoebner, 1947.
4. Gesell, A. et al., *The First Five Years of Life–A Guide to the Study of the Preschool Child.* New York, Harper & Row, 1940.
5. Haslam, R. H. (ed.), Symposium on habilitation of the handicapped child. *Pediatric Clinics of North America* 20:1, 1973.
6. Houser, C., Lecture notes from Regional Cerebral Palsy Academy Meeting. Palo Alto, Calif., September 1972.
7. Illingworth, R. S., *An Introduction to Development Assessment in the First Year.* Clinics in Developmental Medicine, No. 3. London, Heinemann Medical Books, 1962.
8. Illingworth, R. S., *The Development of the Infant and Young Child: Normal and Abnormal,* 5th ed. Baltimore, Williams & Wilkins, 1972.
9. McGraw, M. B., *The Neuromuscular Maturation of the Human Infant:* New York, Hafner, 1969.
10. Peiper, A., *Cerebral Function in Infancy and Childhood,* trans. 3rd ed. New York, Consultants Bureau, 1963.

BIBLIOGRAPHY

Gilfoyle, E. M., Grady, A. P., Moore, J. D., *Children Adapt.* Thorofare, N.J., Charles B. Slack.

21

Myelomeningocele, Meningocele, and Spina Bifida

EUGENE E. BLECK, M.D.

DEFINITIONS

Myelomeningocele (mi-ello-men-ing'-go-seal), meningocele, and spina bifida are open defects in the spinal canal that are due to abnormal fetal development (congenital). They comprise the most serious handicapping disorder in children.

Myelomeningocele (from *myelo,* meaning cord; *meninges,* meaning coverings of the spinal cord; and *cele,* meaning sack) is an outpouching of the spinal cord through an opening at the back of the vertebral column where bone has failed to form (Figs. 21-1 and 21-2).

Meningocele is almost the same deformity as the above, except that the outpouching consists of only the coverings of the spinal cord and not the cord itself (Figs. 21-3 and 21-4).

Spina bifida occulta is a defect in which the back arches of the vertebra (i.e., the posterior elements, or spinous processes and lamina) have failed to form. There is no outpouching of the meninges or spinal cord. The bony defect is covered with skin.

FREQUENCY OF OCCURRENCE (INCIDENCE)

This deformity occurs in from 0.1 to 4.13 live births out of every 1000. No definite racial or genetic patterns are evident. Myelomeningocele is four to five times more common than meningocele.

DEVELOPMENT (EMBRYOLOGY) AND CAUSE OF THE DEFORMITY

The nervous system originates from a thickening of cells (neural plate) on the backside (dorsal or posterior) of the embryo (Fig. 21-5A). This plate then forms a groove as the cell layer thickens (Fig. 21-5B). The groove begins to close and form a tube by the 20th day of fetal life and is

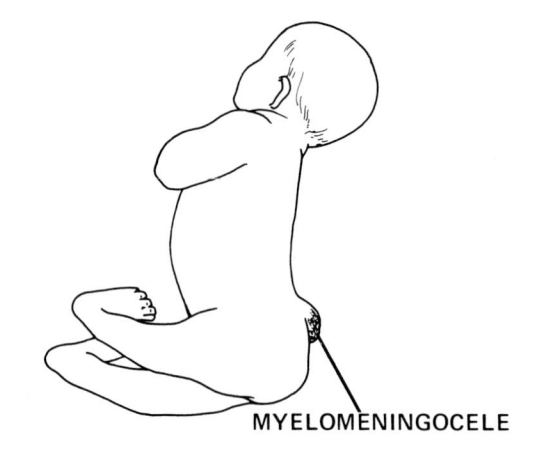

Fig. 21-1. A child with lumbar myelomeningocele. The sac is covered with a thin transparent membrane and cerebrospinal fluid oozes through it. This sac contains the portions of the spinal cord and nerve roots.

Fig. 21-2. Cross section of herniation of the spinal cord and nerve roots, and the coverings of the cord meninges—a myelomeningocele. (Redrawn from *American Academy of Orthopaedic Surgeons (AAOS) Symposium on Myelomeningocele*, St. Louis, C. V. Mosby, 1972. With permission.)

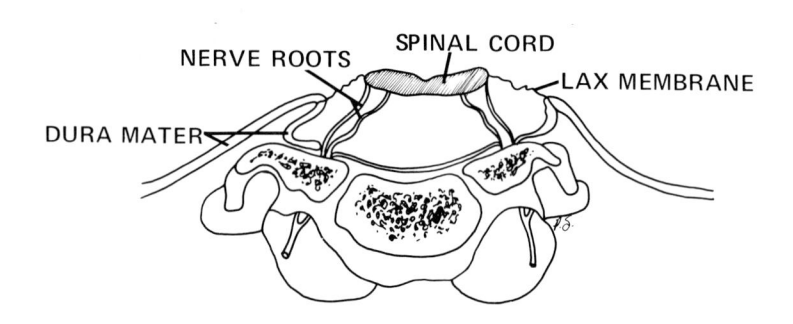

Fig. 21-3. The meningocele in a baby. No neural elements are exposed—that is, the spinal cord is not under the skin, but in its normal location.

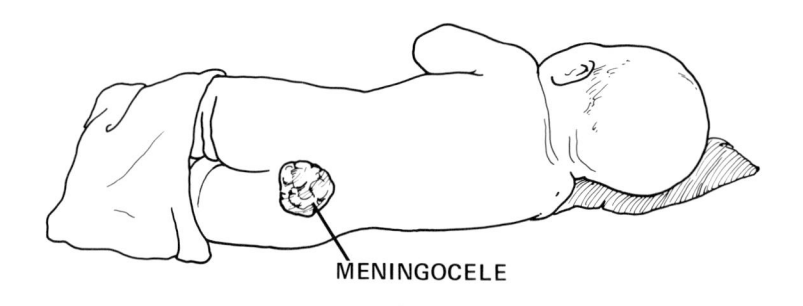

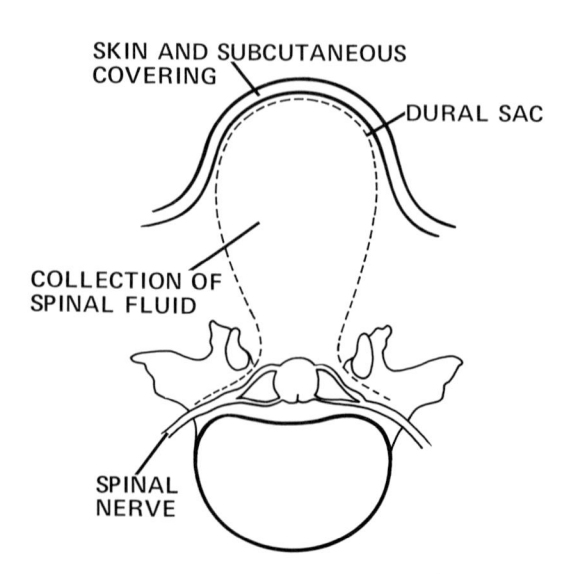

Fig. 21-4. Cross section of spinal cord and vertebra. Note herniation of the covering of the spinal cord under the skin. This is a meningocele. (Redrawn from *AAOS Symposium on Myelomeningocele*, St. Louis, C. V. Mosby, 1972. With permission.)

Fig. 21-5. Development (embryology) of nervous system. (A) Neural plate; (B) neural groove; (C) closing of groove to form neural tube.

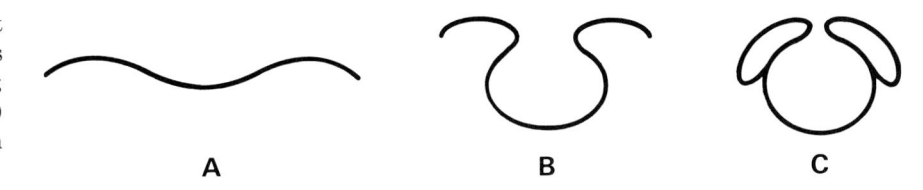

completely closed by the 30th day (Fig. 21-5C). This tube is the basic form from which the brain, brainstem and spinal cord arise. The backbones (vertebrae) are formed on either side of this tube and grow to encase it and thus protect the delicate nervous tissue inside. (See Fig. 1-9.)

In the deformity, the neural tube fails to develop completely and does not close in the first 30 days of pregnancy. The reasons for this are unknown; it is possible that viruses or other, as yet unidentified, noxious agents are responsible for thus stopping the normal development of the neural plate, groove, or tube.

DISABILITIES

Flaccid Paralysis of the Trunk and Lower Limbs

Meningoceles by definition contain no neural elements in them; therefore, paralysis is rare.

In myelomeningocele, by contrast, herniation of a portion of the spinal cord and nerve roots causes flaccid (flak'sid) paralysis of the lower limbs and trunk, the extent of which depends on the level at which the spinal cord herniation occurs. (By flaccid paralysis we mean weak, or no muscle function.) If, for example, the spinal cord is damaged at or above the eighth thoracic vertebra, trunk and total lower limb paralysis occurs, whereas if the damage occurs at the third or fourth lumbar level, the trunk muscles are spared and a part of the hip and thigh muscles are preserved (leg, foot, and ankle muscle function still are absent, however).

Bony Deformities

Because of partial paralysis in the lower limbs, muscle imbalance occurs, accompanied by the resultant bony deformities: dislocation of the hip, clubfoot (equinovarus), severe turned-in feet, or severe rocker-bottom flatfoot (calcaneal valgus) (Figs. 21-6 and 21-7). Trunk muscle weakness, combined with abnormally formed back bones (vertebrae), leads to spinal curvature (scoliosis), humpback (kyphosis), or swayback (lordosis) (Fig. 21-8).

Loss of Sensation

In addition to paralysis, complete loss of skin sensation to pain, temperature, and touch is usual with myelomeningocele. Again, the extent of loss coincides with the level of spinal cord damage. Serious skin problems, such as burns and pressure ulcers (decubitus ulcers), result. Children have to be taught to inspect their skin and to shift their position frequently to avoid gradual death of the skin due to pressure (Fig. 21-9).

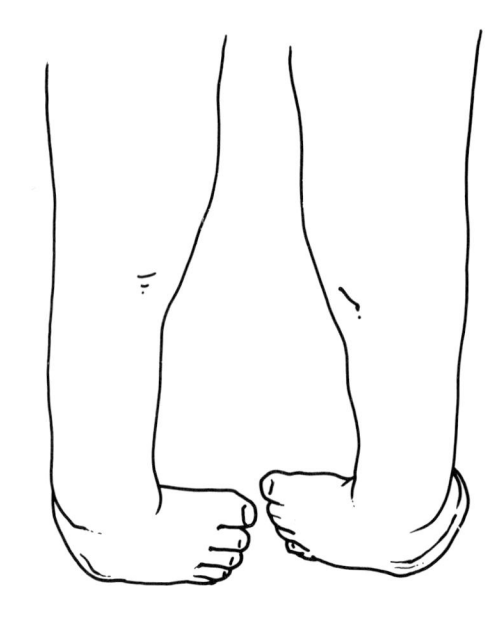

Fig. 21-6. Severe turned-in feet due to paralysis in myelomeningocele.

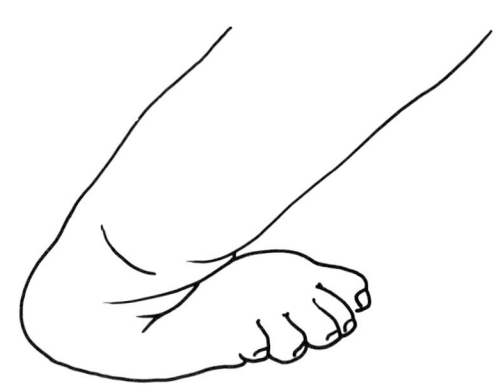

Fig. 21-7. The reversed deformity of feet in myelomeningocele—turned up and out in rocker bottom.

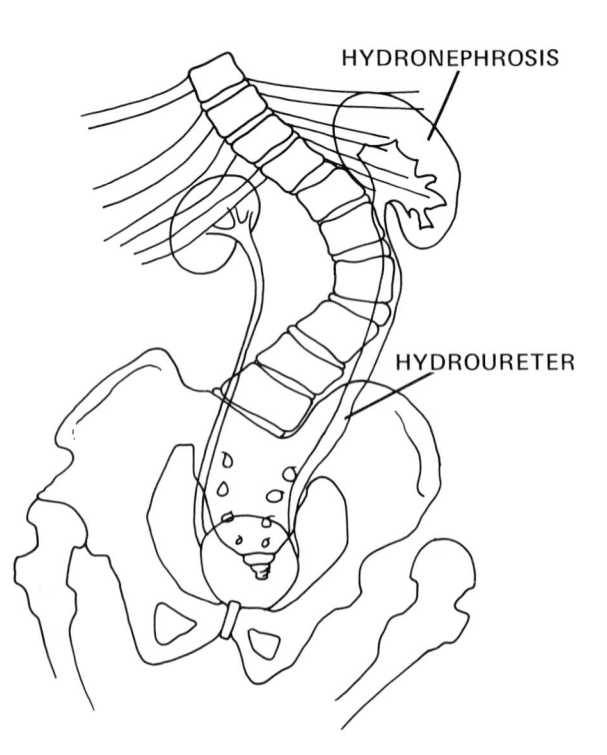

Fig. 21-8. Deformities common to children who have myelomeningocele: dislocated hips, curved spine, and hydronephrosis. In the latter, bladder paralysis caused urine to back up (reflux) into the tubes that drain the kidneys (ureters); this, in turn, causes back-up of urine into the kidney itself, causing enlargement of the kidney collecting system (renal pelvis) and destruction of kidney tissue (hydronephrosis).

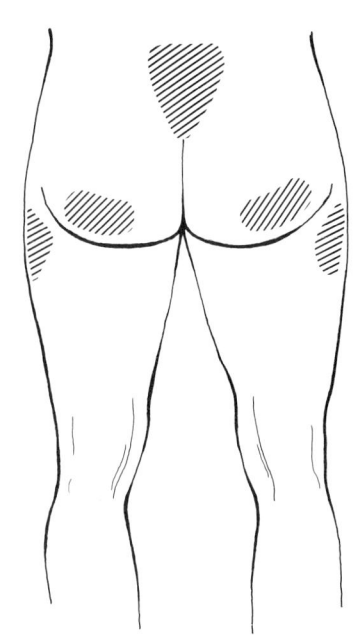

Fig. 21-9. Common sites for pressure sores (decubitus ulcers).

Bladder Paralysis

Because the myelomeningocele almost always occurs above the level of spinal cord at which the major nerve supply to the bladder exits, paralysis of the bladder and the muscles involved in urinating (micturition) inevitably occurs (Fig. 21-10). This means that these children cannot control the emptying of the bladder (incontinence). If the bladder becomes overdistended, dribbling of urine occurs (the "dam overflows") and urine stagnates (the "swamp") and begins to back up into the tubes from the kidneys to the bladder (hydroureter). If unhalted, this backup of urine will distend the collecting system of the kidney (renal pelvis), eventually causing marked enlargement of the renal pelvis (hydronephrosis) (Fig. 21-8).

Because of urine stagnation, infection easily takes hold in the bladder (cystitis) or kidney (pyelonephritis). Due to the kidney infection and subsequent loss of kidney function, death of the afflicted person would be the final outcome.

Bowel Paralysis

In myelomeningocele, bowel paralysis, particularly of the rectum and the anal muscle (sphincter), is also common (Fig. 21-10). The degree of paralysis varies. The child may have frequent, uncontrolled soiling with feces, or smearing off and on during the day due to constant dribbling of loose stools.

Hydrocephalus

Hydrocephalus (hy-dro-seph'-ah-lus), or water brain, is an associated deformity in 90 to 95 percent of children with myelomeningocele. The spinal fluid circulation in the brain is blocked (Fig. 21-11), and, because

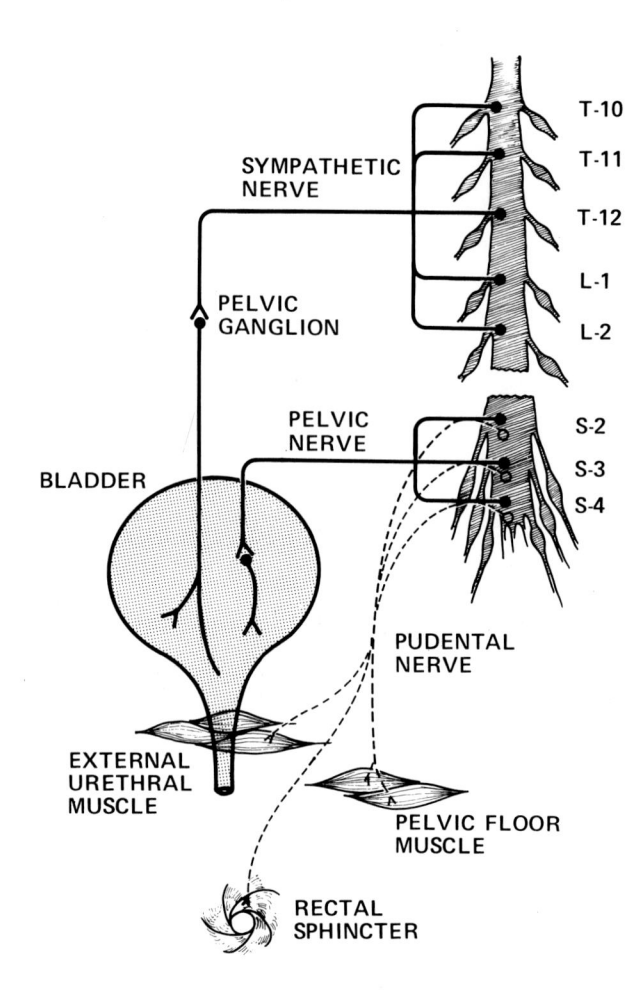

Fig. 21-10. Diagram of the nerve supply to the bladder and to the rectum showing that, with destruction of the spinal cord at a level higher than the second sacral segment (S-2), bladder and rectal paralysis result. This frequently occurs in myelomeningocele. (Redrawn from *AOSS Symposium on Myelomeningocele,* St. Louis, C. V. Mosby, 1972. With permission.)

the fluid is thus trapped in the brain cavities (ventricles) where it is formed (choroid plexus) (Figs. 1-2 and 1-3), these ventricles distend, eventually compressing the brain cells and nerve fibers (Fig. 21-12). The result is intellectual retardation and, occasionally, spastic paralysis of the lower limbs and seizures.

Children with hydrocephalus are often very verbal and have a somewhat parrotlike speech[8]. Their loquaciousness masks their low intellectual functioning in some areas.

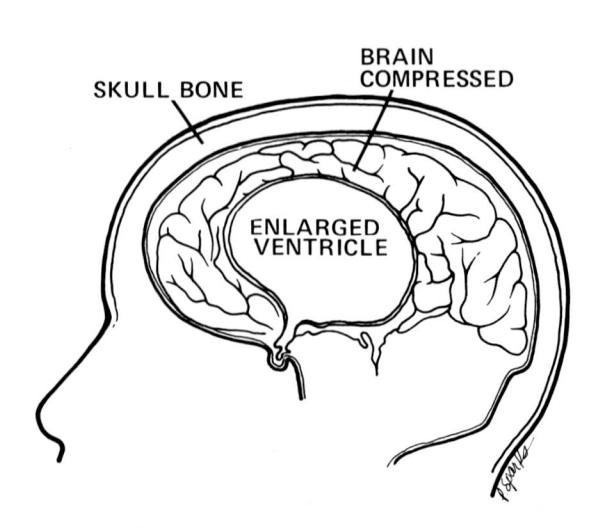

Fig. 21-11. A view of the right hemisphere inside the skull of a child who has hydrocephalus. The ventricle is enlarged, resulting in thinning of the brain. (Redrawn from *AAOS Symposium on Myelomeningocele,* St. Louis, C. V. Mosby, 1972. With permission.)

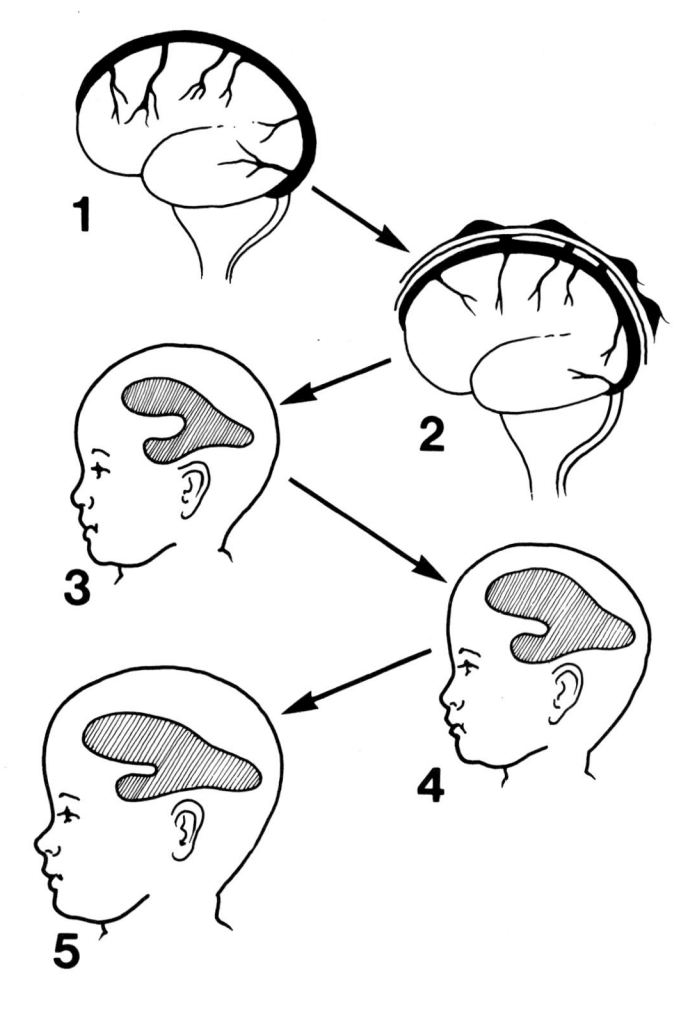

Fig. 21-12. Phases of progressive hydrocephalus. (Redrawn from *AAOS Symposium on Myelomeningocele,* St. Louis, C. V. Mosby, 1972. With permission.)

1, 2   The amount of blood in the veins of the brain is reduced and the veins of the scalp and veins communicating with the skull are enlarged.

3, 4   The fluid cavities in the brain (ventricles) are enlarged, and brain tissue is compressed. The child may show a slow development.

5   The head enlarges due to expansion of the skull bones from the enlarging ventricle. Development is slow and the IQ is low.

TREATMENT

As might be expected from the multiplicity of the defects, a team approach that utilizes professionals from a multiplicity of medical specialities is required for treatment (Fig. 21-13).

Neurosurgery

Closure of the defect of myelomeningocele early in infancy is the usual contemporary practice. Unfortunately, such early surgery does not necessarily lessen the paralysis, but life-threatening infection of the coverings of the spinal cord (meningitis) may thus be avoided.

Hydrocephalus is treated promptly by drainage of the blocked ventricles. Permanent drainage systems (shunts) have been devised. Shunts consist of plastic tubes and an interposing valve between the ventricle and the heart or the abdomen (ventriculoatrial shunt or ventriculoperitoneal shunt) (Fig. 21-14).

Orthotic Management

Orthotics is the contemporary term applied to braces and mobility equipment. Because many of these children have paralysis of the lower limbs and trunk, their mobility development can be thwarted. To com-

Fig. 21-13. The team and the child. (Redrawn courtesy of Newington Children's Hospital, Newington, Conn.)

pensate for this lack, the following orthotic system has been devised by Motloch.[1] The visual field is important in early childhood, and if at this time the child cannot get up on all fours and thus experience an expanded visual field, then a propped seat is recommended. At the point in development at which normal children can sit with their hands free, the inability to sit upright can be compensated for by a plastic foam-padded insert that allows propped sitting. Next in development the normal child will crawl and explore his or her environment for further learning. To compensate for the lack of crawling, a miniature wheelchair, termed a *caster cart,* is a valuable adjunct. Because there is a handle that can be inserted into the back of the caster cart, it can double as a stroller when the mother or father wishes to take the child on a walking excursion. At about the age of 11 to 15 months, normal children are able to stand without using their hands for support. For children who cannot, the self-standing brace called the *orthopodium,* or *A-frame brace,* has been a most useful compensatory device. And, finally, at the time when normal children achieve sit-stand

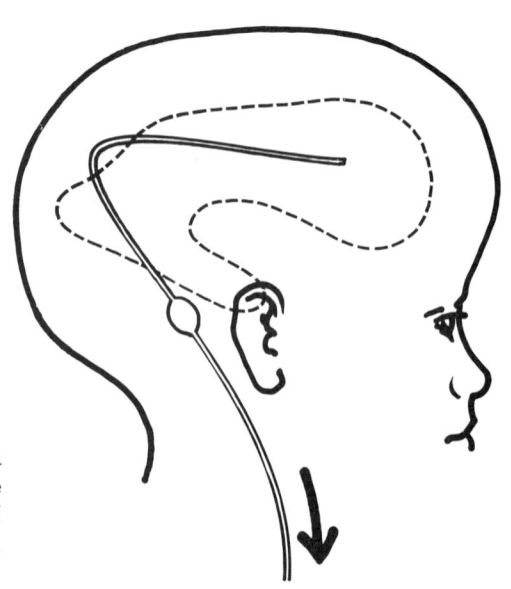

Fig. 21-14. One way hydrocephalus is relieved is by placing a tube in the ventricle and leading this out into the atrium of the heart so that the fluid is drained. This is called a *ventriculotrial shunt.* (Redrawn from *AAOS Symposium on Myelomeningocele,* St. Louis, C. V. Mosby, 1972. With permission.)

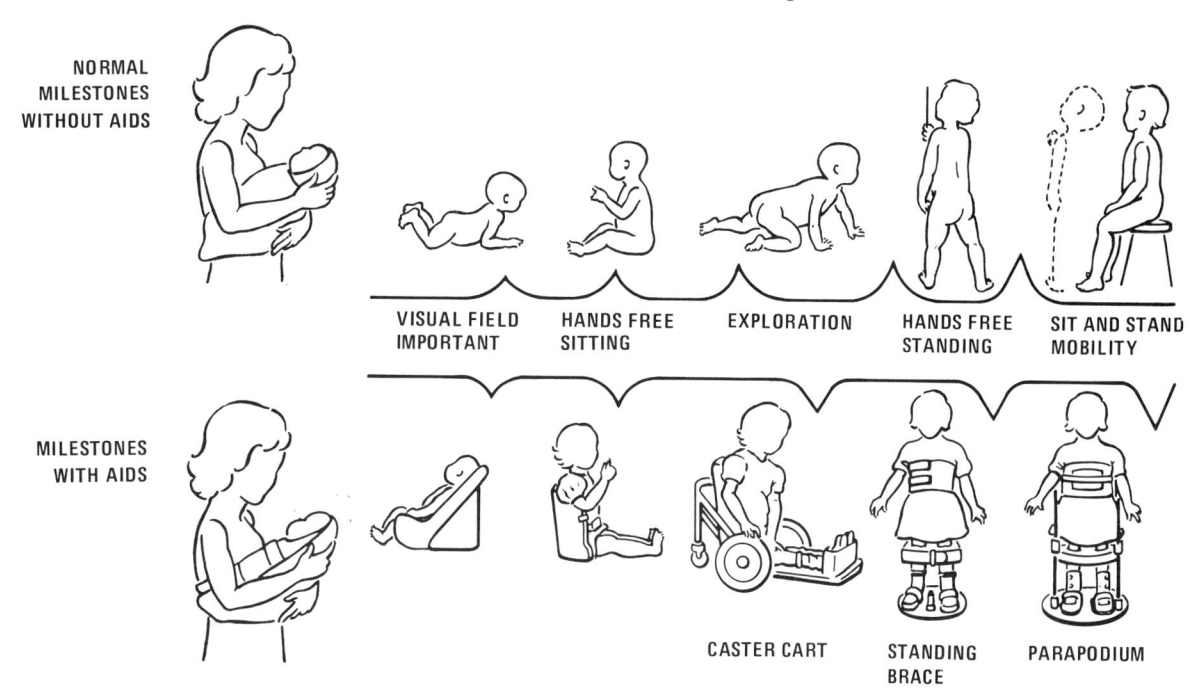

Fig. 21-15. Scheme of orthotic equipment for the child who has paralysis of the lower limbs. Equipment compensates for the child's defects in mobility and thus permits somewhat more normal development.

mobility a self-standing brace equipped with hip and knee joints (parapodium) can enable the child with myelomeningocele to sit as well as to stand. A swivel base can be attached to the platform of the brace so that rotary trunk motion propels the child forward and backward, much like "disco dancing" (Figs. 21-15 to 21-17).

Other braces can be used to give reciprocal lower-limb motion, and some patients, provided they have sufficient trunkal stability, seem to

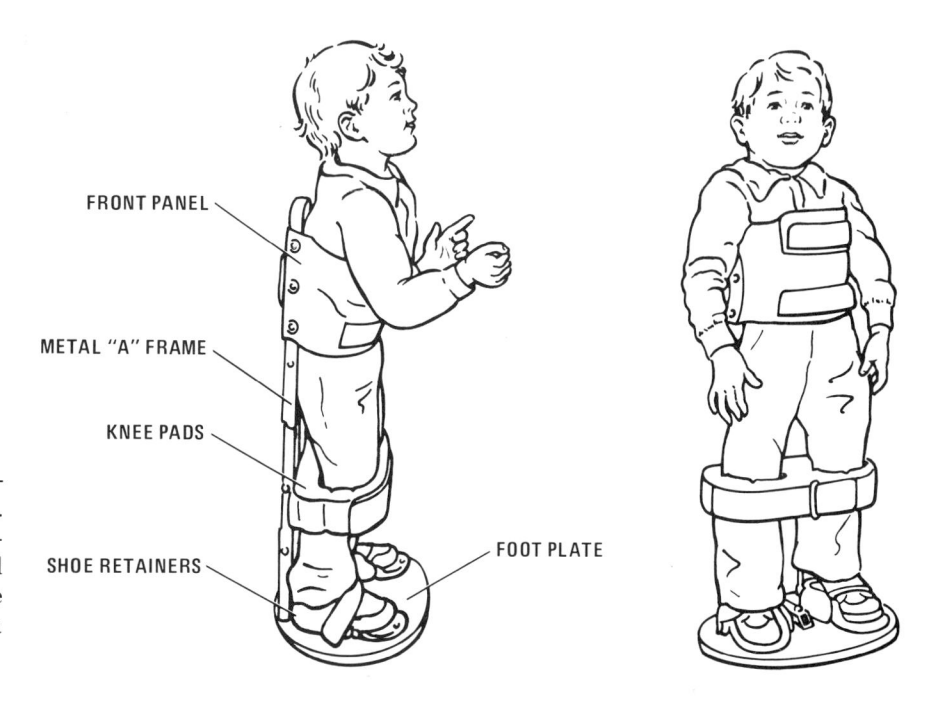

Fig. 21-16. Standing A-frame brace (orthosis). Permits hands-free standing. A child can be placed in this and have complete security in standing at a table or work station.

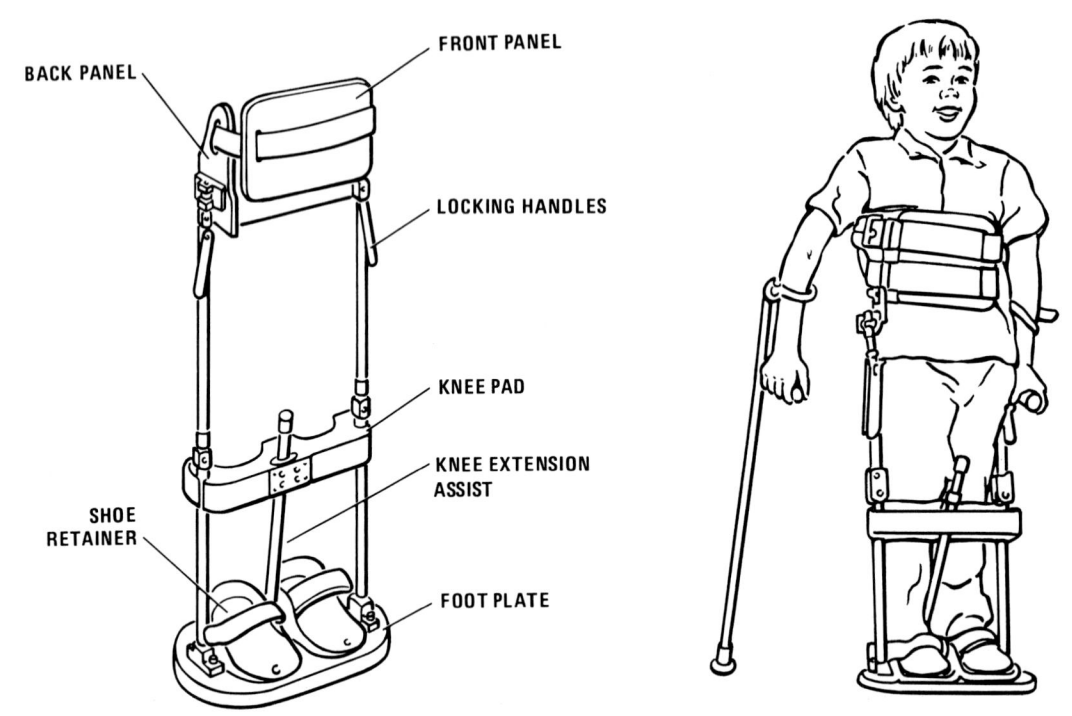

Fig. 21-17. Parapodium. Permits hands-free standing and sitting. This orthosis is similar to the A-frame (Figure 21-16), except that the hip and knee joints can flex and allow sitting.

prefer them. Two such effective orthoses are the reciprocating brace and the hip guidance orthosis.[2]

Most of the children with lower-limb paralysis will need crutches for walking and will walk either with a swing-through gait in the parapodium, or with a reciprocal gait with the reciprocating brace or the hip guidance orthosis. Those who have trunk and hip paralysis need wheelchairs for most community activities.

In general, the outlook for useful walking is related to the level of paralysis: above the 12th thoracic level, no practical walking (wheelchair); 12th thoracic to 4th lumbar level, partial household ambulation with crutches and braces; 4th lumber to 2nd sacral level, community ambulation (Table 21-1).

Orthopedic Surgery

Orthopedic surgical procedures are necessary in order to reduce and to prevent dislocation of the hip, to correct clubfeet and other foot deformities, and to correct the spinal deformities of scoliosis, kyphosis, and lordosis (Fig. 21-18, A and B).

Physical and Occupational Therapy

The role of physical and occupational therapy is to strengthen muscles and to teach crutch walking, the use of the wheelchair, and transfer to and from the wheelchair. Training in the activities of daily living and the use of adaptive equipment are most important as the child matures.

Table 21-1. Predictable Activity in Myelomeningocele

Class (Sherrard)	Motor Level Spinal Cord Segment	Critical Motor Function Present	MOBILITY-ACTIVITY RANGE School Age	Adolescent	Adult
I	T-12 (12th Thoracic)	Totally paralyzed lower limbs	Standing brace Wheelchair	Wheelchair	Wheelchair No ambulation
II	L-1-2 (1st and 2nd Lumbar)	Hip flexor muscles	Crutches Braces Wheelchair	Wheelchair Household ambulation	Wheelchair Nonfunctional ambulation
III	L-3-4 (3rd and 4th Lumbar)	Quadriceps muscles	Crutches Braces Household ambulation Wheelchair	Crutches Household ambulation Wheelchair	50% wheelchair Household ambulation with crutches
IV	L-5 (5th Lumbar)	Medial hamstrings Anterior tibial muscles	Crutches Braces Community ambulation	Crutches Community ambulation	Community ambulation with crutches
V	S-1 (1st Sacral)	Lateral hamstring and peroneal muscles	Community ambulation	Community ambulation	Community ambulation, 50% crutch or cane
VI	S-2-3 (2nd and 3rd Sacral)	Mild loss of intrinsic foot muscles possible	Normal	Normal	Limited endurance due to late foot deformities

MUSCLE DESCRIPTION

Hip flexor muscles—bend the thigh to the trunk
Quadriceps muscles—front of the thigh; straighten the knee
Hamstring muscles—back of the thigh; bend the knee
Peroneal muscles—outside of leg; bring foot upward and outward
Anterior tibial muscles—front of leg; bring the foot upward

NOTE

Coexisting preadolescent condition may affect the patient's activity and either maintain or drop it to a lower level:

1. Obesity
2. Psychosexual maturation
3. Stiff joints
4. Contracted joints
5. Brain or kidney disease
6. I.Q.
7. Spinal curvature
8. Motivation
9. Home environment

*Adapted from Banta, J. V., and Stryker, W. S., Children's Health Center, San Diego, and Orthopaedic Hospital, Los Angeles

Urology

Frequent urinalysis and culturing of the urine for bacteria is mandatory for children with myelomeningocele. A great variety of urinary antiseptic medications are available and are used according to the type of bacteria present in the urine. The urinary tract must be carefully studied at intervals by intravenous dye injection and x-rays of the abdomen; this permits visualization of the urine collecting system of the kidneys, ureters, and bladder (IV pyelogram). The urologist looks for signs of urine backup (hydroureter and hydronephrosis) (Fig. 21-8).

To keep the bladder empty and to prevent urine stagnation with subsequent serious infection, the bladder must be drained regularly. Some children can successfully empty their bladders (void) by crying, turning,

356   Eugene E. Bleck

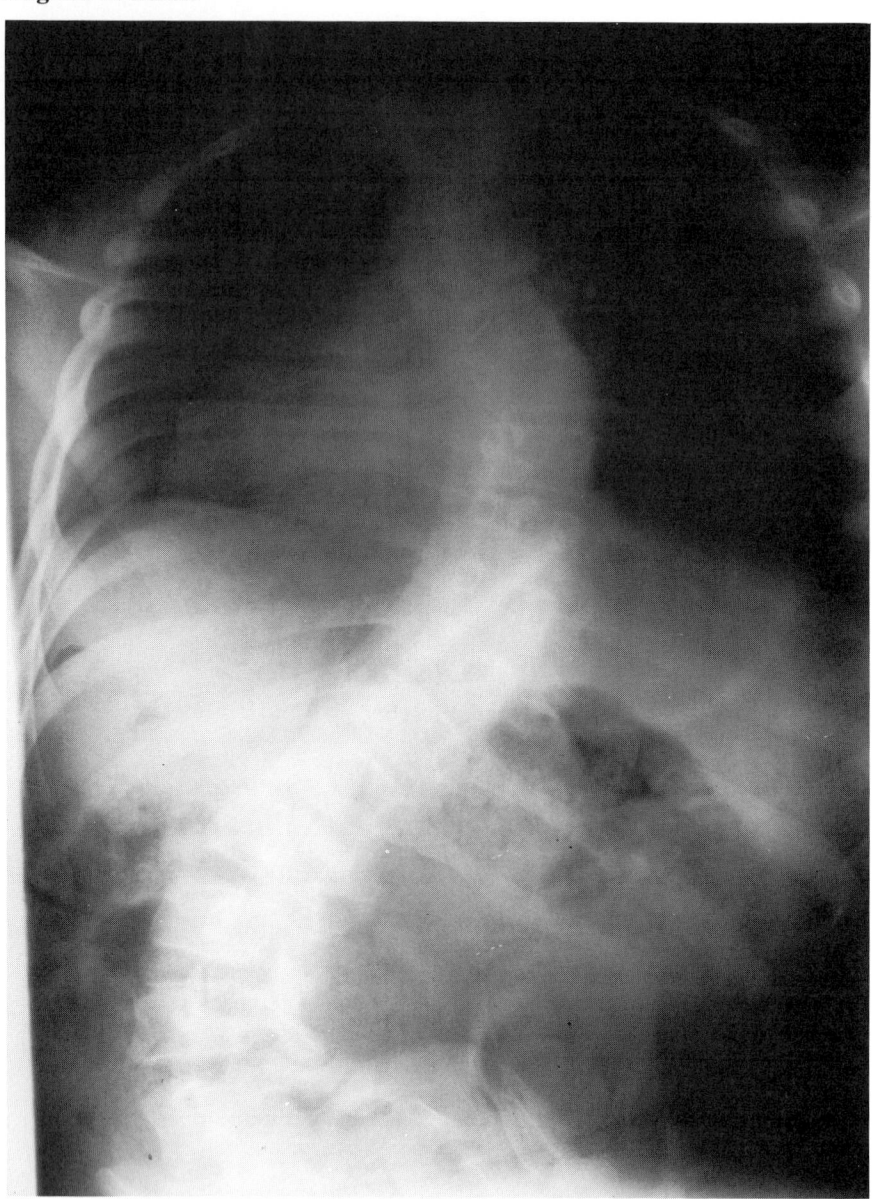

Fig. 21-18A. X-ray of severe spinal curvature (scoliosis) in a 12-year-old boy with myelomeningocele. When scoliosis is severe enough, sitting balance becomes precarious, pelvic obliquity results, and there is increased danger of pressure sores resulting from unequal weight-bearing on the buttocks.

laughing, or sneezing (Valsalva maneuver), or by manually pressing on the lower abdominal wall (Crede maneuver).

Boys have used a condom-type drainage system with the collecting bag strapped to their lower limbs. In the past, girls were offered the option of eliminating wet diapers by means of a surgical procedure that rerouted the collecting channels (ureters) from the kidney to either the small bowel (ilium) or large bowel (sigmoid colon). A piece of the bowel was then brought out to the abdominal wall, and a collecting bag was worn on the skin of the abdomen over this opening (colostomy). The procedure known as ileal loop or sigmoid loop diversion, has been used less often in the past 5 years, as the indications for it have declined.

Draining the bladder by self-insertion of a rubber tube of appropriate size through the urethra (the opening through which the urine exits—located above the vagina in females and in the penis in males) is increasingly popular and apparently quite effective in most cases. Children can be taught to do this themselves, by a variety of training methods, as early

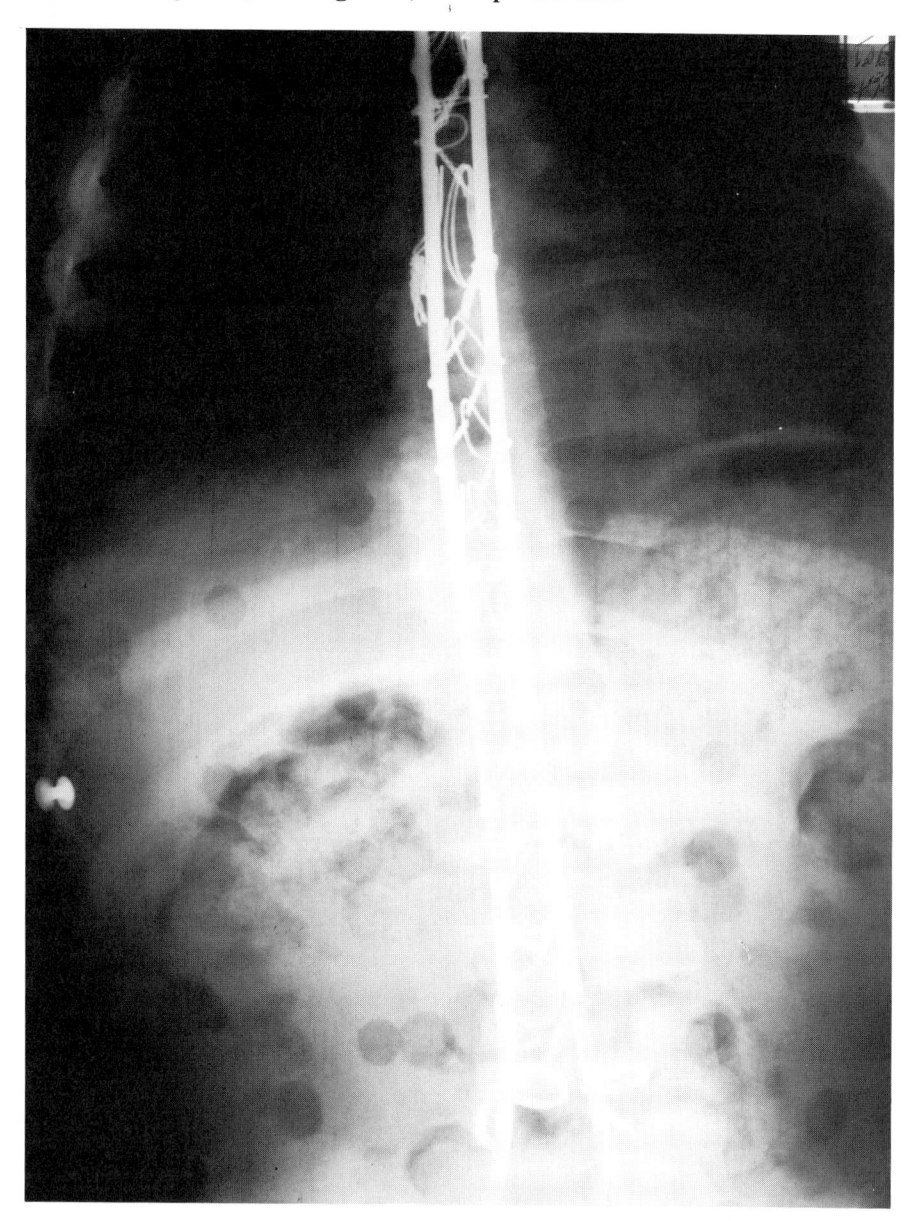

Fig. 21-18B. X-ray of spine of same patient (Fig. 21-A) after surgical correction of the spinal curvature. Segmental spinal instrumentation and spinal fusion devised by Eduardo Luque, M.D., was used. The patient can resume sitting very early postoperatively, either with no plaster cast protection or with a lightweight plastic removal jacket.

as the age of 5 years.[3] Some centers use a training doll with male or female genitalia* and a special mirror,† so that girls can see the very small opening of the urethra (urinary meatus). This technique of intermittent urinary catheterization has been assisted by many new drugs that aid in pumping the urine down from the kidneys through the ureters.

Pediatrics

In addition to being responsible for the child's general health, the pediatrician should also provide help in bowel management. This includes prescription of stool softeners (e.g., Colace or Doxinate) if hard, dry

*Horseman Dolls, Inc., Columbia, SC.
†Kinsley Mirror: Harry D. Koenig and Co., East Rockaway, NY.

stools are a problem; the establishment and reinforcement of a regular bowel pattern through the use of suppositories (Ducolax is usual); and the judicious use of enemas, when necessary. The goal is to obtain once-a-day dry, formed, and firm-to-hard stools. Diet also plays a role in accomplishing this goal.

LONG-TERM OUTLOOK

The follow-up study by Curtis, Butler, and Emerson of 100 patients with myelomeningocele over age 12 years is the best available.[4] In their study, 80 percent of patients walked, 28 percent used crutches or braces, and 20 percent used a wheelchair. Bowel control was good in 65 percent. In contrast, only 35 percent had good urinary control. Patients who had ileal conduits were the best controlled and the most satisfied. Hydrocephalus was arrested in 38 percent, and about half of the patients had ventriculatrial shunts. An IQ of 80 or above was found in 89 percent.

Seventy-nine percent had graduated from high school and 27 percent were college graduates or were in a four year college. At the time of study, of those who were considered "adults," 58 percent were employed. Social adjustment was quite high—73 percent. The marital status of 51 patients is of interest: 14 percent of the males and 41 percent of the females were married (one widow and one divorcee). "Normal" sex activity was claimed in 43 percent of the men and 24 percent of the women.

The foregoing report certainly is an encouraging one, but must be tempered by the fact that the study was begun on children with myelomeningocele who were over the age of 12 years. When one starts a follow-up study beginning at birth, as was reported by Lorber,[5,6] the overall end results are not so encouraging. In Lorber's study, the mortality rate from complications alone was 20 percent within the first 7 years of the shunt operation. Lorber reports that over half of the shunt survivors were mentally handicapped, and not more than 10 percent of survivors were likely to end up in competitive employment. Clearly, the results are better for patients with less and lower spinal cord involvement, such as lesions at the lowest level of the cord (first and second sacral segment).

SUMMARY AND EDUCATIONAL IMPLICATIONS

Myelomeningocele presents an almost overwhelming series of disabilities. Because of the need for repeat neurosurgical, urological, and orthopedic consultations and procedures, allowances for fairly frequent absences from school must be made.

Until bladder and bowel problems are under control (and this takes time), the teacher will have to put up with some odors not usually present in other children.

Many of the children will have normal or slightly below normal intellectual functions, so that, despite absences from school, learning is feasible and can possibly be compressed. Elementary-school-age children should, for the most part, be prepared for sedentary vocations, trade schools, high school, and college. All children obviously will need baseline psychometric evaluation, since verbosity in some hydrocephalic children may raise unreasonable expectations of intellectual performance.

Development of daily living skills in children with spina bifida (meningomyelocele) was assessed by Sousa, Gordon and Shurtleff.[7] The functional activities were plotted with a scoring system based on the hypothetical development of a normal child. In this study, toileting as a self-care task was delayed more than any other activity (Fig. 21-19). These children did not demonstrate interest in bowel control until long

Fig. 21-19. Graphic comparison of children with spina bifida with normal children in learning of stool and urinary self-care. Points on ordinate refer to scores obtained by a Functional Evaluation (see Table 21-2). Note change in scale between sixth and seventh years. (Redrawn from Sousa, J. C., Gordon, L. H., and Shurtleff, D. B., Assessing the development of daily living skills in patients with spina bifida, in Stark, G. (ed.), Studies in Hydrocephalus in Spina Bifida. *Developmental Medicine and Child Neurology* 18 (suppl. 37):134–142, 1976. With permission.)

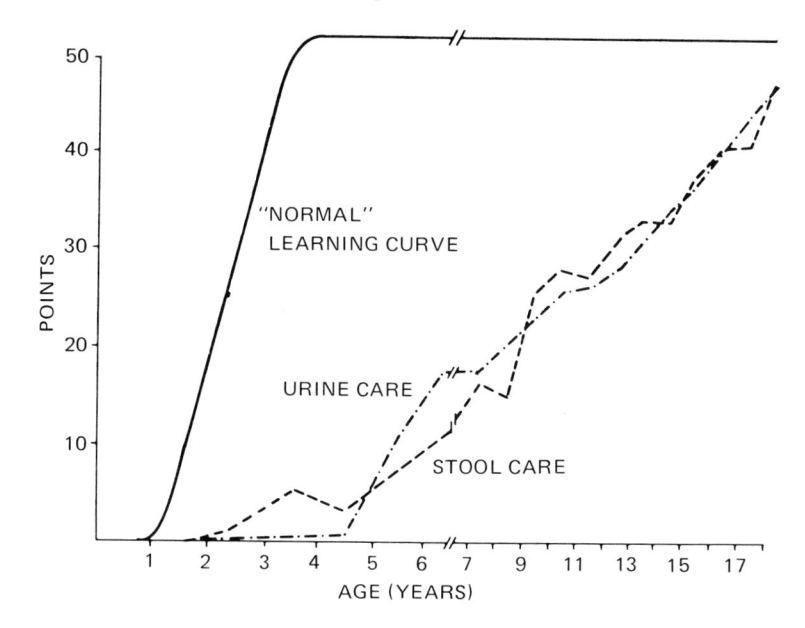

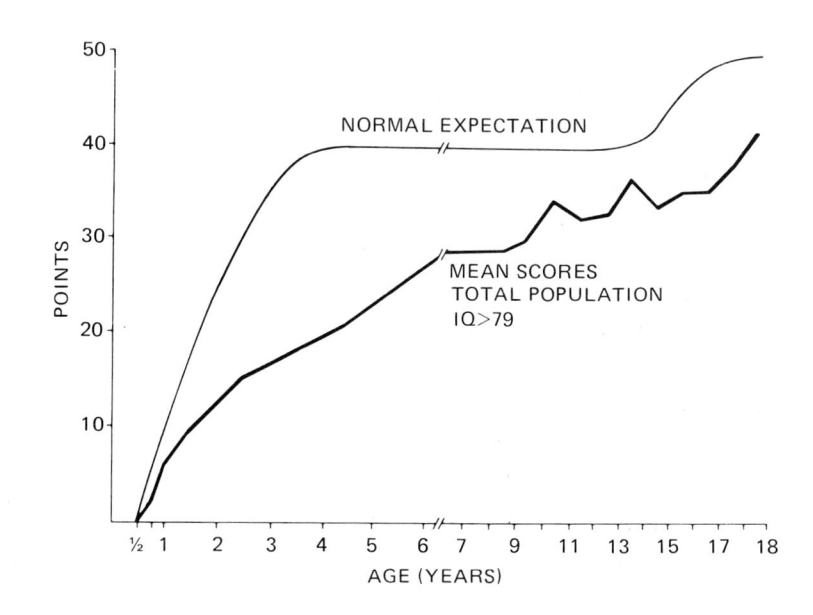

after their nonhandicapped peers. They achieved this goal on the average at the age of 17 years. This delay perhaps may be explained by the children's dependence upon the emotional and psychological readiness of their parents, who had to accept and to learn new skills in order to teach the child bowel management. Based on this report, toileting skills ought to be taught and learned earlier, by both child and parent.

In the same study,[7] most of the daily living skills showed continuing progress. The one exception to this progress was in social interaction: teenagers had *lower* social interaction scores than younger children (Fig. 21-20). In meal preparation and eating achievement the group was irregular, and scores were not related to the level of paralysis (Fig. 21-21). As a group, their development in hygiene, locomotion, and dressing was more normal: between the ages of 6 and 7 years, some were at least partly independent in these functions.

Fig. 21-20. Development of independence in eating and meal-preparation in spina bifida children compared with expectations for normal children. When compared with Fig. 21-19, these curves demonstrate that development in these skills is more normal than is development in stool and urinary self-care. (Redrawn from Sousa, J. C., Gordon, L. H., and Shurtleff, D. B., Assessing the development of daily living skills in patients with spina bifida, in Stark, G. (ed.), Studies in Hydrocephalus in Spina Bifida. *Developmental Medicine and Child Neurology* 18 (suppl. 37):134–142, 1976. With permission.)

Table 21-2. Computation of Functional Activities Score

1. *Meals*
   - 0 = totally dependent
   - 10 = finger feeds
   - 20 = feeds self with spoon
   - 30 = assists with preparation
   - 40 = independent for light snacks
   - 50 = independent: shopping, meal preparation, cleaning up

2. *Dressing*
   - 0 = incapable or independent but does not (time or motivation)
   - 10 = assists with dressing
   - 20 = dresses self with assistance
   - 30 = independent upper extremity only
   - 40 = independent after significant modification of clothes
   - 50 = independent consistently

3. *Hygiene*
   - 0 = incapable or independent or capable of assisting but does not
   - 10 = washes teeth or hands or face with assistance
   - 20 = independent in washing face, hands, teeth
   - 30 = needs minimal assistance with bath or shower
   - 50 = independent in shower or bath, could live alone

4. *Urinary Appliance Care*
   (With ileal loop, Foley catheter, or condom collector)
   - 0 = completely dependent
   - 10 = empties collecting bag when reminded
   - 20 = empties bag, is reliable
   - 30 = empties bag when reminded and assists in changing appliance; shows interest
   - 40 = empties bag, is reliable, and assists in changing it
   - 50 = completely independent
   (This is not applicable if patient does not have an appliance, unless he is older than 60 months and wearing a diaper; then, add 0 points, and add 1 to the denominator in calculating total independence.)

5. *Bowel Control Independence*
   - 0 = totally dependent
   - 10 = takes an interest; partial self-help
   - 30 = independent when reminded
   - 50 = independent and initiates

6. *Usual Means of Locomotion*
   - 0 = is carried or dependent in wheelchair
   - 10 = is carried and 'scoots'
   - 20 = uses electric wheelchair, or crawls in house and/or uses aids outside
   - 30 = independent in wheelchair at home
   - 40 = wheelchair independence in community or community-aided walker plus wheelchair for long distances
   - 50 = community-aided walker or complete function without aids, no wheelchair needed

   either

7a. *Type of Gait*
   (If locomotion is by foot)
   - 0 = standing only
   - 10 = 3-pt. hands alternate feet together, shuffle-rotate (as in standing brace)
   - 20 = swing to, or cruises on furniture
   - 30 = 4-pt. alternating, or modified 4-pt., or swing through
   - 40 = 2-pt. one aid or other gait
   - 50 = normal

   or

7b. *Transfers*
   (If locomotion is by wheelchair)
   (Points may be obtained for each of the following transfers:
   to and from bed
   to and from bath
   to and from floor
   to and from auto
   to and from auto and handles wheelchair
   - 0 = does not assist to any degree
   - 1 = needs maximum assistance, helps a little
   - 5 = uses aids or adapted equipment, needs little help
   - 10 = no aids, no help needed

8. *Method of Transportation*
   (Score only if older than 36 months)
   - 0 = does not go out
   - 10 = ambulance or other handicapped-person or special vehicle
   - 20 = passenger in private car
   - 30 = self-walk or wheelchair
   - 40 = independent public transportation
   - 50 = self-drive, auto

9. *Social Interaction*

either

a. Child or younger teen-ager
   0 = alone, few activities
   10 = plays or works actively but alone
   20 = plays or works actively with sibs or roommates, or divides time between alone and with sibs
   30 = with neighborhood children or schoolmates but prefers younger; with neighborhood children or schoolmates but prefers older
   40 = with neighborhood children or schoolmates
   50 = with neighborhood children or schoolmates, and initiates contact and play

or

b. Older teenager and adult
   0 = alone, no activities
   10 = active, mainly in special handicapped programs
   20 = is a leader in handicapped programs
   30 = active but no social ties
   40 = active, has social ties
   50 = active, has social ties and is a leader

To calculate total independence score:
1. Add all points
2. Multiply by 10
3. Divide by the number of categories contributing points

Fig. 21-21. Development of social interaction in spina bifida children compared with normal children. This is the only developmental curve that failed to progress with age. (Redrawn from Sousa, J. C., Gordon, L. H., and Shurtleff, D. B., Assessing the development of daily living skills in patients with spina bifida, in Stark, G. (ed.), Studies in Hydrocephalus in Spina Bifida. *Developmental Medicine and Child Neurology* 18 (suppl. 37):134–142, 1976. With permission.)

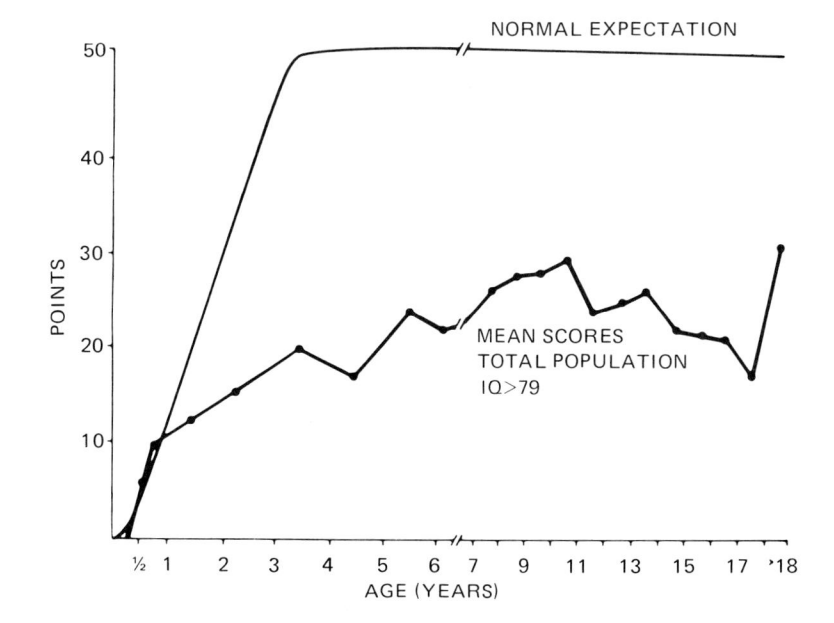

Professionals who work with such children need patience, and should consider that the children are often more capable than society allows or expects. Taking this cue, educating parents to assist the children in becoming independent seems indicated.

REFERENCES

1. Motloch, W. M., *Mobility for Spinal Cord Impaired Bifida Patients.* Paper presented at Conference on Mobility Aids for Spina Bifida Patients, Toronto, September 1974.
2. Rose, G. K., The principles and practice of hip guidance articulations. *Prosthetics and Orthotics International* 3:37–43, 1979.
3. Hanigan, K. F., Teaching intermittent self-catheterization to young children with myelodysplasia. *Developmental Medicine and Child Neurology* 21:365–368, 1979.
4. Curtis, B. H., Butler, J. E., and Emerson, C. C., in *American Academy of Orthopaedic Surgeons Symposium on Myelomeningocele.* St. Louis, C. V. Mosby, 1972.
5. Lorber, J., Early results of selective treatment of spina bifida cystica. *British Medical Journal* 4:201–204, 1973.
6. Lorber, J., Results of treatment of myelomeningocele: An analysis of 524 unselected cases, with special reference to possible selection for treatment. *Developmental Medicine and Child Neurology* 13:279–303, 1971.
7. Sousa, J. C., Gordon, L. H., and Shurtleff, D. B., Assessing the development of daily living skills in patients with spina bifida, in Stardk, G. (ed.), Studies in Hydrocephalus in Spina Bifida. *Developmental Medicine and Child Neurology* 18 (suppl 37):134–142, 1976.

BIBLIOGRAPHY

American Academy of Orthopaedic Surgeons Symposium on Myelomeningocele. St. Louis, C. V. Mosby, 1972.

Banta, J. V., and Stryker, W. S., *Exhibits on Prognosis in Myelomeningocele.* Washington, D.C., American Academy of Orthopaedic Surgeons, 1972.

Motloch, W., *Analysis of Medical Costs Associated with Healing of Pressure Sores in Adolescent Paraplegics.* Palo Alto, Calif., Rehabilitation Engineering Center, Children's Hospital at Stanford, 1978.

Reswick, J. B., and Rogers, J. E., Experience at Rancho Los Amigos Hospital with devices and techniques to prevent pressures sores, in Kenedi, R. M., Cowden, J. M., and Sclaes, J. T. (eds.), *Bed Sore Mechanics.* Baltimore, University Park Press, 1976.

Sharrard, W. J., *Pediatric Orthopaedics and Fractures.* Philadelphia, F. A. Davis, 1971.

Shurtleff, D. B., Myelodysplasia: Management and treatment. *Current Problems in Pediatrics* 10(3):1–98, 1980.

Swisher, L. P., and Pinsker, E. J., The language characteristics of hyperverbal, hydrocephalic children. *Developmental Medicine and Child Neurology* 13:746–755, 1971.

22

Multiply Handicapped Child: Severe Physical and Mental Disability

JEAN G. KOHN, M.D.

Children in classes for the severely and multiply handicapped (SMH) are, according to the guidelines for admission to these classes, severely physically handicapped and profoundly mentally retarded. In the past, such children were cared for at home or in large state institutions: only during the past 7 to 10 years have they been included in public school programs in most states.

Severe physical handicap implies that the child will have difficulty with such basic developmental tasks as sitting, standing, walking, toilet-training, feeding, and communication. These difficulties may be due to limitations in physical movement, coordination, or balance, to weakness or tightness of muscles, or, sometimes, to accompanying sensory disturbances in vision, hearing, touch, position sense, or behavior.

Profound mental retardation implies that the child will have severe deficits in adaptive behavior as compared with normal children of the same chronologic age. The revised definition of the American Association on Mental Deficiency (AAMD) (1973) reads, "Mental retardation refers to significantly subaverage general intellectual functioning existing concurrently with deficits in adaptive behavior, and manifested during the developmental period" [p. 5].[1]

According to Sontag et al.,[2] such severely involved children may include those

> who are not toilet-trained, aggress toward others, do not attend to even the most pronounced social stimuli, self-mutilate, ruminate, self-stimulate, do not walk, speak, hear, or see, manifest durable and intense temper tantrums, are not under even the most rudimentary forms of verbal control, do not imitate, manifest minimally controlled seizures, and/or have extremely brittle medical existences [p. 18].

Table 22-1. Estimated Number of Handicapped Children, 1975–1976

	Number			Percent	
	Served	Unserved	Total	Served	Unserved
Speech impaired	2,020,000	273,000	2,293,000	88	12
Mentally retarded	1,350,000	157,000	1,507,000	90	10
Learning disabilities	260,000	1,706,000	1,966,000	13	87
Emotionally disturbed	255,000	1,055,000	1,310,000	19	81
Crippled and other health impaired	255,000	73,000	328,000	78	22
Deaf	45,000	4,000	49,000	92	8
Hard of hearing	66,000	262,000	328,000	20	80
Visually handicapped	43,000	23,000	66,000	65	35
Deaf-blind and other multi-handicapped	16,000	24,000	40,000	40	60
Total aged 6–19 yr	3,860,000	2,840,000	6,700,000	58	42
Total aged 0–5 yr	450,000	737,000	1,187,000	38	62
Total aged 0–19 yr	4,310,000	3,577,000	7,887,000	55	45

U.S. Department of Health, Education, and Welfare, 1976.

A report dated June 1976 from the United States Office of Education, Department of Health, Education, and Welfare, listed 40,000 individuals in the 0- to 19-year-old age group as "deaf-blind and other multi-handicapped," while the total handicapped population in the same age group was 7,887,000 (Table 22-1). Thus, the multi-handicapped constituted but a small fraction (0.05 percent) of the total number of disabled youth in the United States. Their needs, however, are more complex and more difficult to serve. Their relatively recent inclusion into the public school system has presented problems and concerns to school administrators, teachers, and support personnel, as well as to parents and other caretakers who want to be assured of the child's safety and competence in the school setting.

The education of these severely and multiply handicapped students is geared toward teaching them the most basic developmental skills— motor control, communication at the preverbal level, and the ability to interact with others in such a way that needs are met and behavior is acceptable. In each of these three areas, the aim is to help the child achieve the maximum level of functioning of which he or she is capable.

Once the young people leave school, their quality of life will depend, in large part, upon the above three factors. Acceptance into a community facility and the degree to which such children can participate in community transportation and recreation activities will depend on their ease of transfer, social behavior, control of bladder and bowel function, and level of communication. In addition, the environment must be receptive to these individuals and there must be others around them who are capable of meeting their needs. Parents or other caretakers should be knowledgeable and well trained in the management of these young people; they should also know about their legal rights and the sources of financial support that are available for community and residential programs. Where programs do not exist, continuing pressure must be exerted on government and other institutions to provide them. The teacher of the multiply handicapped may be a valuable source of practical information to caretakers because of his or her extensive observations, experience, and practice in the classroom.

EVALUATION OF THE CHILD

The greater physical needs and more severe mental impairment of the multiply handicapped require that teachers assess such children carefully and consult with members of the helping professions.

Questions to be asked in an evaluation include: (1) If the child did not accomplish a task, why was he or she unsuccessful? (a) Was the task too difficult for this child's level of development? (b) Was the task made up of several separate skills, one or more of which was above the child's developmental level? (c) Are there other factors that singly, or in combination, compromise the child's developmental capability? (2) Did the teacher observe, assess, plan, monitor, and evaluate the child's behavior for change?[3] Or, in other words, was the teacher's preplanning appropriate for the child's developmental level?

Medical Input

For teachers involved with severely handicapped children, the medical diagnosis is often of little value unless a functional description of the child is included. For physicians, a medical diagnosis is predictive of possible accompanying problems and can thus be of use in describing and interpreting for the teacher what the child's functional difficulties may be. Too often, however, the medical diagnosis is sent to the school without any clarifying explanation, which leaves the teacher to look for interpretation from others, sometimes the school nurse, or to struggle with dictionary definitions and medical texts. Physicians can be of greater practical assistance if they explain the relevant medical terminology and indicate how the child's medical problems are apt to impact on his or her school function or behavior.

The medical diagnosis should include, first, the medical name given to the condition, together with a brief explanation of the condition named. For example, the diagnosis might read: "Cerebral palsy, spastic quadriparesis. This is a condition resulting from brain damage; it involves all four extremities with stiffness, jerkiness, and weakness."[11] Second, the diagnosis should include a statement as to whether the condition is progressive or nonprogressive. If it is progressive, the disease process is still active and the child's disability will become worse. For such a child, the teacher may need to recognize that the major effort will be to maintain function and to constantly reappraise supportive measures as the child worsens. If the condition is nonprogressive, then the disease process is no longer active and no further neurological damage is anticipated. It should be noted, however, that neither term will wholly describe the child's future development: growth factors and aspects of development that are not restricted by the medical condition will continue, causing changes in functional abilities in either direction. Thus, seeming increases in the severity of a static condition may be observed with growth, as, for example, in the child with uncontrolled muscle movements (athetosis) who becomes more functionally disabled with growth as the same muscle movements exerted over a larger muscle mass throw him or her off balance. Alternatively, the positive factors in growth and maturation may improve a child's function dramatically.

Although the physician may send a functional assessment with the medical diagnosis, more often this functional assessment must be carried out by a physical or occupational therapist, speech therapist, psychologist, nurse or other professional directly connected with the child's school. The physician, nevertheless, may offer recommendations that will be

Table 22-2. Conditions Organized by Time of Onset and Presumed Causative Factors

I. *Gestation (Prenatal)*
Developmental (i.e., malformation or failure to develop properly during gestation)
  A. Genetic disorders
    1. Chromosome disorders
      a. Down's syndrome (Trisomy 21)
      b. Trisomy 18
      c. Trisomy 13
    2. Inborn errors of metabolism
      a. Phenylketonuria (PKU)
      b. Lesch-Nyhan syndrome
    3. Multiple malformations
      a. Myelomeningocele
      b. Tuberous sclerosis
      c. Neurofibromatosis
  B. Cerebral palsy with microcephaly
    1. Spastic quadriplegia
    2. Tension athetosis, rigidity, ataxia
  C. Infections
    1. Cytomegalovirus
    2. Herpes simplex virus
    3. Toxoplasmosis
    4. Rubella virus
    5. Bacterial infections
  D. Maternal factors involving abnormalities in pregnancy, placental inadequacy, toxemia

II. *Birth (Perinatal)*
Early delivery or problems during delivery
  A. Premature delivery—small size, increased vulnerability to lack of oxygen and/or trauma in delivery
  B. Birth injury in full-term infant—breech presentation, transverse presentation, prolonged labor
  C. Infection at birth, especially herpes simplex virus and *Escherichia coli* bacteria

III. *Following Birth (Postnatal)*
Infancy, childhood and early adolescence
  A. Severe injury—near drowning, automobile accidents, child abuse/neglect, poisoning
  B. Infections—severe encephalitis, meningitis, brain abscess
  C. Progressive neurological disease

helpful in managing the child in school, may point out any physical limitations likely to prevent acquisition of new developmental skills (contractures that may prevent standing, for example), and may indicate what physical procedures or positioning may be harmful or helpful (recommending specific periods of rest and avoidance of prolonged sitting for a child with progressive scoliosis, for example).

Table 22-2 lists some of the conditions associated with multiple and severe disability. It should be emphasized however, that not all children with the diagnosis listed are severely limited in function and also that this list is not all-inclusive. Medical texts containing much more detailed lists and descriptions of neurological problems are available.[4-6]

In a review of 75 cases seen in developmental centers over a 1-year period by E. E. Bleck (personal communication), the most common diagnoses found were those identified in Table 22-3.

Table 22-3. Most Common Diagnoses in Development Center for Multiply Handicapped Children

Diagnosis*	Percentage of Patients (N = 75)
1. Cerebral palsy	32
2. Microcephaly	16
3. Rubella syndrome	3
4. Down's syndrome	6
5. Multiple congenital anomalies (heart, limbs)	10
6. Blindness	7
Total	74

*All diagnosed as severely mentally retarded.

An awareness of the differences among children who are "made wrong" (prenatal onset), those who are "born wrong" (perinatal onset), and those who are "damaged later" (postnatal onset) may be of assistance to the teacher. Children who do not develop properly during the fetal period, often have a very small head and severe involvement. They are likely to suffer from hearing impairment, visual impairment, neuromuscular problems (e.g., spasticity or athetosis), and seizures. Some may have "cortical blindness or deafness," in which the sensory apparatus is present and functional, but the recording and interpretive areas in the brain do not process the information received from the eyes or ears.

Children who sustain injury at birth to a nervous system that, until then, had developed normally may show evidence of brain damage, such as cerebral palsy, but may have residual areas of near-normal function. When their communication and learning processes are less impaired than neuromotor function, such children should be considered for classes for the orthopedically handicapped, or for regular classes with special help. Decisions about class placement may be very difficult in such cases and will require the combined observations and contributions of parents, teacher, and other professionals. A period of diagnostic observation and participation in a higher-functioning class should be available when there is sufficient doubt.

Children who are damaged later in their development usually will not have the abnormal growth and facial and physical features characteristic of the two previous groups. Islands of normal function may remain, and, sometimes, partial recovery of functional abilities lost during illness or injury may occur. These children may present a puzzle to the teacher, since some of their functions may be good, while their overall performance is poor. This is particularly true following encephalitis and severe head trauma. Children in this group who have progressive neurological disease will not be placed in SMH classes until a long slide in capability has taken place. Except in the few cerebral degenerative diseases that progress early and rapidly (such as Tay-Sachs disease) this decline will take a number of years. Maintainance of function and life support are of prime importance for such children, for whom the outlook is eventual death. Parents need to be reassured that the children are carefully and competently looked after, and good communication between school and home is crucial for an exchange of information and recommendations for care.

Table 22-4. Features Associated with Disorders Found in the Severely and Multiply Disabled

| Condition | System Involved |||||
	Neuromotor	Sensory and Other Systems	Behavioral (Including Seizures)	Communication	Cognitive
GENETIC DISORDERS					
Down's syndrome	Small size; motor delay; floppy as infants	Cataracts sometimes	Often cheerful and placid; imitative	Speech delay	Range from mild to profound
Phenylketonuria (PKU) (untreated)	Motor delay	Usually unaffected (eczema common)	Seizures in one-fourth	Related to cognitive ability	Untreated, severe; treated, range up to normal
Lesch-Nyhan syndrome	Severe spastic quadriplegia		Self-mutilation	Severe impairment	Severe
Myelomeningocele with hydrocephalus	Level of motor loss depends on location; paralysis below spinal level (osteoporosis)	Optic atrophy in some; sensory loss to touch below spinal level	Variable; seizures likely but often controllable	Variable	Mild to severe
Tuberous sclerosis	Variable; depends on location of tumors	Retinal involvement in 15%	Seizures often present and severe	Depends on cognitive ability	Mild to severe
Neurofibromatosis	Same as above	Optic-nerve tumors may result in reduction in vision due to optic atrophy	Seizures in some	Depends on cognitive ability	May progressive loss of mental ability due to tumor growth

DEVELOPMENTAL DISORDERS

Cerebral palsy with microcephaly				
Spastic quadriplegia	Severe impairment of head and trunk control; contractures; scoliosis	May be blind or deaf; may have loss of position sense	Seizures often present and severe	Severe involvement of speech apparatus	Severe to profound
Tension athetosis	Severe impairment: head control, limb control, and hand use all affected	Sensory deficits less likely than above	Seizures sometimes present	Severe involvement of speech musculature	Moderate to severe

INFECTIONS

Cytomegalovirus herpes simplex virus, toxoplasmosis	Spasticity usually	Vision impaired	Seizures	Severe impairment	Severe to profound
Rubella virus	Delayed motor development	Congenital cataracts; deafness	Sometimes autistic behavior	If deaf, speech may not develop	Moderate to severe

BIRTH TRAUMA OR ANOXIA

	Depends on area of brain damaged; spastic, athetoid, or, occasionally, ataxia	Variable	Seizures sometimes—usually controllable with medication	Depends on cognitive and motor involvement	Variable

Table 22-4. (continued)

Condition	System Involved				
	Neuromotor	Sensory and Other Systems	Behavioral (Including Seizures)	Communication	Cognitive
POSTNATAL					
Congenital hypothyroidism	Motor delay; spasticity; athetosis; inactive; infant (small size)	Sometimes deaf (thick skin; sparse hair)	Apathetic; slow in response	If deaf, do not develop speech	If untreated, severe defect; if treated late or partially, moderate defect
Child abuse with head injury	Spasticity	If intraocular bleeding occurs, have visual loss	Seizures common; behavior erratic, hyperactive	Depends on degree of injury	Depends on severity of injury
Accidental injury with head trauma	Depends on degree and location of injury	Same as neuromotor	Seizures are sometimes present; usually can be controlled with medication. Behavior disorder may be severe: restlessness, emotional lability, lack of judgement and self-restraint	Variable	Variable

Meningitis (usually bacterial)	Most recover completely unless very young or delay in treatment. Sequelae include hemiparesis, ataxia, hydrocephalus	Blindness or deafness possible	Seizures; recurrent memory loss	Variable	Varying degrees mild to profound
Encephalitis (usually viral)	No specific treatment at present; may have severe neuromotor damage	Variable	Seizures usual; behavior disorder may be severe: impulsive, uncontrollable, crying, unpredictable, and lack of judgement	Depends on age of illness and severity	Mild to severe
PROGRESSIVE DISEASE					
Friedreich's ataxia (spinocerebellar ataxia)	Progressive unsteadiness; eventual total physical incapacity	Loss of position and vibration sense	Progressive loss of mental ability with psychiatric symptoms; severe depression in adolescence	Progressive alteration in speech	Progressive loss of mental ability from normal to severe
Muscular dystrophy (not usually seen in SMH classes)	Progressive muscle weakness with contractures	No loss	Behavioral changes only in reaction to progressive weakness and loss of motor power	Unimpaired	Some are mildly retarded

ASSOCIATED DISABILITIES

Although the medical diagnosis *should* include both the major disability and any associated problems, some children come to SMH classes with incomplete assessment of multiple handicaps. This may be due to the age of the child, difficulties in assessment, a lack of the necessary diagnostic resources, or an unwillingness on the part of parents to pursue complicated or painful work-ups, such as those involving x-rays, blood studies, muscle biopsies, collection of spinal fluid, or anesthesia for eye examination. Other problems preventing full assessment may be distance from a medical center, lack of transportation, or lack of child care for other children while parents are at the medical center.

Multiply handicapped children may have a neuromotor disability and visual, hearing, cardiac, hematological, and bone problems as well. Table 22-4 presents some of the features associated with the syndromes most commonly found in children in classes for the multiply disabled. While it is helpful for teachers to have as much information as possible regarding a given child's disability, such information should not blind the teacher from observing new signs of disability and signs of *capability* as well. For instance, if the teacher observes the child paying visual attention to light and shadow, to movements of people, and to the approach of food, this often indicates that the child's residual vision can be developed and utilized. In other children, residual hearing may be encouraged and explored by a teacher using different pitch levels, sound devices, rhythms, and volume variations. Likewise, if the teacher suspects an additional disability which has not been mentioned in the records, this should be mentioned to appropriate staff, especially the school nurse, for further observation and possible ongoing assessment.[7]

MAINTENANCE OF LIFE

Life-support services may need to be incorporated into the school setting to make a child's attendance possible. The philosophy that physical disability in itself is no contraindication to school participation means that some children with severe medical problems will be in classes for the multiply handicapped. Consequently, as Haslam and Valletutti have observed, "The teacher's role in diagnosis and management will increase in complexity and in importance as more and more children with severe and profound handicaps are placed in classroom settings" [p. 6].[7] In addition to managing seizures in the classroom, life-maintenance care may include: (1) tracheostomy care, (2) gastrostomy care, (3) tube feeding (gavage) for children with feeding disorders, (4) aspiration management of children who choke easily on their food, and (5) urinary and stool collection devices, especially for children with myelomeningocele.

Parents or other caretakers who have been managing children with medical problems at home can be asked to demonstrate their procedures to the teacher prior to admission of the child to the classroom. Nursing consultation should also be available—to organize routines, to suggest modifications for the classroom situation, and to monitor performance or offer assistance when needed.

It has been suggested that all classes for severely and multiply disabled students should have nursing consultation available on-site, although this may be difficult for smaller school districts. Public health nurses can act as consultants in some areas; selection of attendants or classroom aides with practical nursing experience may also be helpful.

There are nursing texts available that describe the procedures involved in managing such students.[8-10] Elizabeth Bryan, for example, in an article entitled, "Medical Considerations for Multiple-Handicapped Children in the Public Schools" covers such topics as: First aid, emergency care, and disaster planning; Sanitation; Environment; Safety in routine activities; Safety in supplemental activities; Therapy procedures; Staff protection; Training and orientation of staff; and Special qualifications of staff.[11] In a second article, she discusses the special nature of the role of the physician who acts as a designated consultant to the school system:[12]

> Since the educator is the primary decision maker in the educational setting, the school physician must be willing and able to work in the role of advisor and consultant. Although a physician has been trained to work for the best interests of an individual patient, the school physician must always consider the interest, interaction, and welfare of children in groups [p. 486].

FUNCTIONAL ASSESSMENT

This is an essential part of the initial assessment procedure. A physical or occupational therapist should be available for this, since not only the assessment itself but also consultation regarding specific handling techniques, positioning, and activities to foster development should be available from the therapist's reports and demonstrations.

Careful observation and assessment of the child in the classroom setting—alone and with the other children, at different times of the day, and at varying levels of fatigue—help to inform the teacher of the child's capabilities. In addition, the "home caretaker" should be carefully questioned about what activities are performed outside of school, how tired the child is on returning from school, how much sleep the child needs, and what feeding adjustments are being made in the home. These and similar inquiries in other areas of function can assist the teacher in her evaluation.[13,14]

THE INDIVIDUAL EDUCATION PLAN (IEP)

Under the provisions of P.L. 94–142,* each handicapped child must have an individual plan that is prepared by the teacher, the parents or guardian, a qualified supervisor in the educational field, and, when appropriate, the child.

In preparing the IEP, some questions which the teacher may ask are: (1) What would be the next developmental step for this child? (2) What tasks would be useful for the child in his or her daily self-care and living routine? (3) What physical factors may limit these accomplishments? (4) How can allowances be made for physical and mental disabilities while support is given to identified assets?

The gains made may be small in terms of the measures of achievement for a normal child but, nevertheless, significant in the long-term outcome for a child who is severely and multiply handicapped. For example, a child who is nonambulatory but can learn to support her weight for assisted transfer may eventually be able to live in an intermediate care facility or, with attendant care, in her own parents' home, rather than in a state institution or skilled nursing care facility.

Gains may be made at a slower rate than expected, and patience and persistence are required. Particularly when support personnel are accustomed to more rapidly advancing children, special training and orientation for work in SMH classes may be needed. A special plea should be made for aides and other support personnel who are kindly, gentle, knowledgeable and comfortable with children. Firm, consistent manage-

---

*Education for All Handicapped Children Act, P.L. 94–142, November 26, 1975. Available from the Federal Register, Washington, DC 20408.

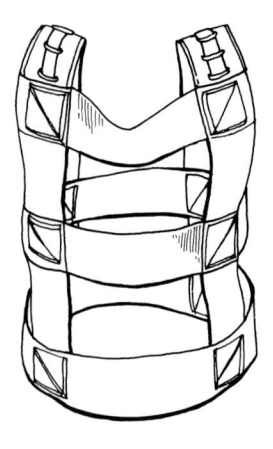

Fig. 22-1. Body harness. Made of sturdy webbing with wide Velcro closures. Offers support when trunk stability is lacking.

ment and a willingness to allow the child time to initiate and complete the required task is essential for these children. Behavioral difficulties may interfere with the acquisition of new skills, and classroom personnel need to be clear about management goals in order to function in a coordinated effort.

DEVELOPMENTAL ACTIVITIES

Many children in SMH classes are at an infantile developmental stage, due to mental retardation, physical disability, or multiple handicaps. After careful assessment, the child's present level of development can be ascertained and a plan made for proceeding to the next developmental step—allowing, of course, for physical factors which may prevent or retard progress.

Head Control and Sitting Balance

Adequate muscle support of the trunk and neck are required for sitting—a desirable position because it allows the child greater opportunity to interact, visually, with his environment. If it appears that these goals will not be achieved due to physical problems, assistive devices should be considered (Figs. 22-1 to 22-3).

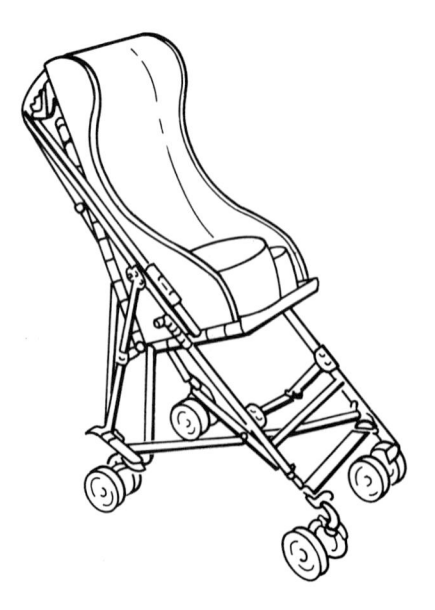

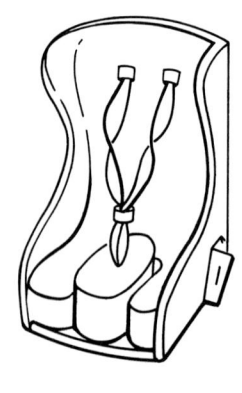

Fig. 22-2. Contoured seat insert fabricated of foam plastic and upholstered with fabric. Can be inserted into Pogom Buggy frame (Genac, Inc., Boulder, Colo.) for ease of transport.

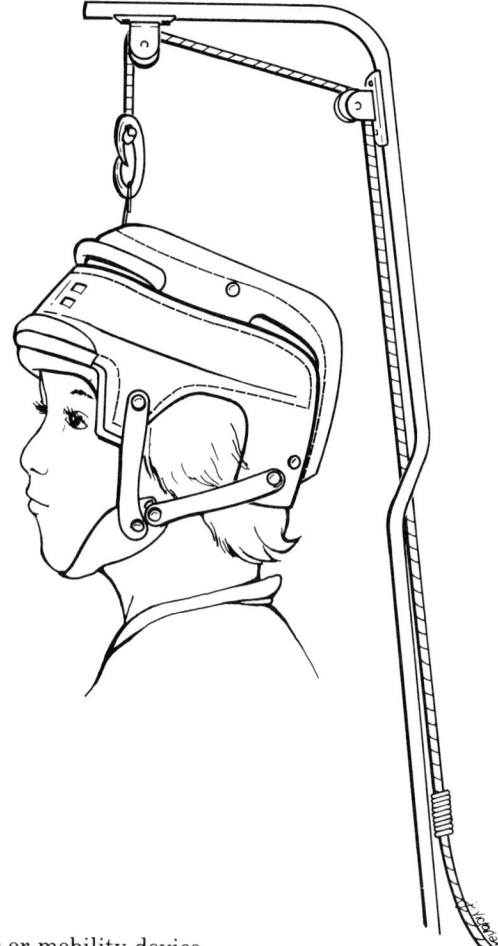

Fig. 22-3. Helmet and head holder. Can be attached to chair or mobility device.

Mobility

Ambulation includes rolling over, "commando crawl," reciprocal crawl, bunny-hopping, knee-walking, walking with support and walking alone (see Chapter 5). When assessment indicates that this area of development will be delayed or absent, assistive devices should be considered.

Assistive devices can be handled by the child alone, if capable, or can be pushed by the caretaker. Examples of these are a caster cart (with handle) (Fig. 22-4); a wheelchair with an orthopedic seat insert (if required for trunk support) (Fig. 22-5); and an electric wheelchair with an orthopedic seat insert (when required). Electric wheelchairs usually are not appropriate for the SMH child, unless it is demonstrated that the child understands where he or she needs to go.

When a mobility device is recommended, the following points need to be considered (1) Where will it be used? (2) How will it be transported? (3) How will the child be transferred in and out of it? (4) Can the child assist with the transfer and/or how many other personnel will be required to assist? (This of course, depends on the child's size and capability.) (5) Where will the device be kept—at home or school, or both? (6) What will be the durability, ease of repair, and ease of transport, both with and without the child?

376 Jean G. Kohn

Fig. 22-4. Caster cart—a mini-wheelchair. Detachable handle converts it to a stroller.

Feeding

The learning of independent feeding begins with the ability to swallow at first liquids, then solids—and continues with subsequent coordination of hand-to-mouth and spoon-to-mouth movements. These steps are easily mastered by normally developing children. Where mental capability is low, however, these same tasks will need much practice and encouragement, and, sometimes, the use of behavior management techniques. Assistive devices for children with neuromuscular impairment will also be necessary for the multiply handicapped. Examples of assistive feeding

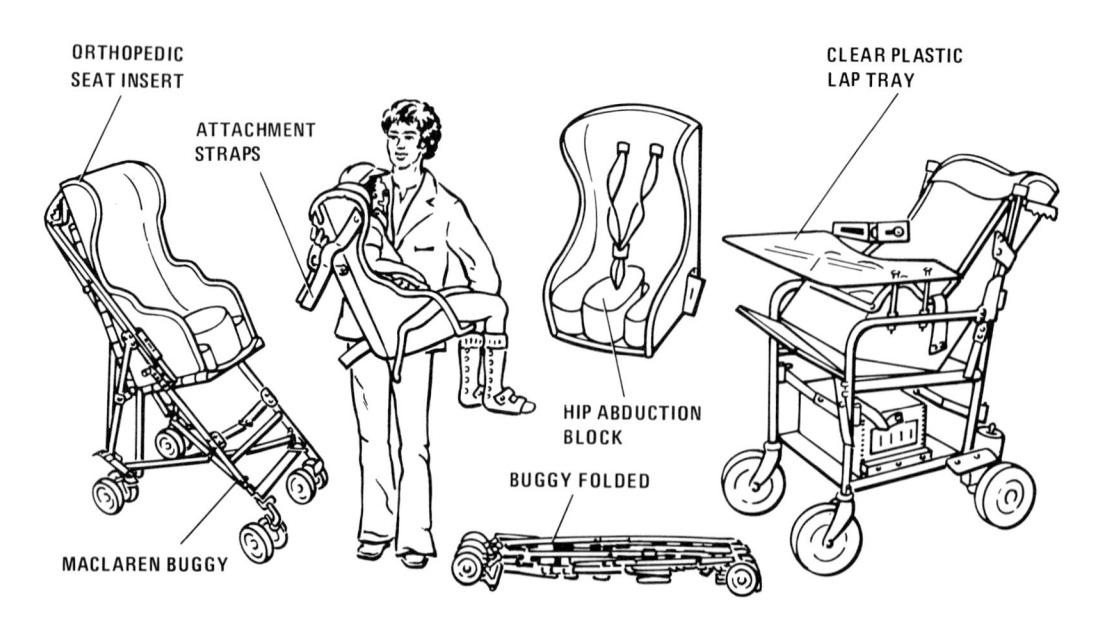

Fig. 22-5. Mobility and seating system. Countered seat insert can be placed in an electric wheelchair.

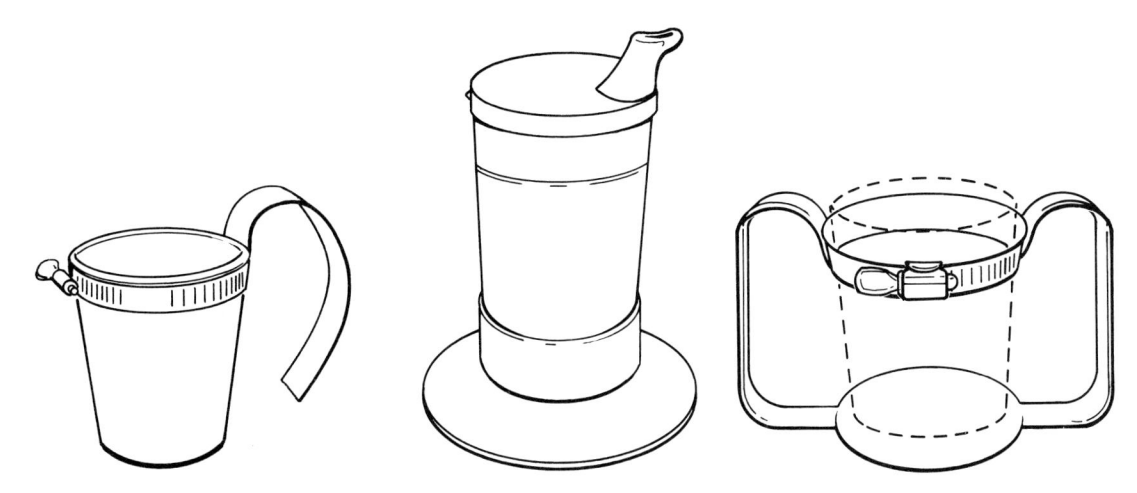

Fig. 22-6. Adaptive eating utensils.

equipment are the Toronto Feeder* and a variety of special adaptive utensils, such as spoons with large handles, turned angles, etc. Non-tipping cups and cups with straws also are available in most infant supply stores, or can be improvised (Fig. 22-6).[5]

Food consistency and quality must also be considered in feeding handicapped children. Some children have small appetites, some regurgitate easily, and some require semisolid foods or special diets. Advice from a nutritionist is invaluable in the management of severely involved children whose nutritional requirements are difficult to meet because of physical incapacity or unusual dietary requirements.

Control of Bowel and Bladder Function

Control may be delayed because of: (1) lack of understanding, (2) failure to develop sphincter control, or (3) inability to get to a toilet or to remain in a proper sitting position. Once again, it should be emphasized that assessment is the key to an effective plan aimed at teaching control. If the physical capability is present and the problem is lack of understanding, behavior management techniques—including rewards, regular programming, and the development of a habit pattern—may achieve the desired result.

Where the problem is a neurologically based lack of sphincter control, as in myelomeningocele, however, advice as to proper management should be sought from a physician or specialized nurse. A rather detailed managment schedule is often used in such children to attain regularity of bowel movements and some reflex control of the bladder. If no control of the bladder can be established, urinary collection systems can be used or urinary diversion surgery may be performed to permit the flow of urine into a collection device. In all such cases, medical consultation and supervision by trained nurses is required.[16]

Where the problem is inability to get to the toilet or inability to maintain proper position, assistive devices are often helpful. An example would be the Memphis potty seat† and a child's safety commode. (Fig. 22-7 and Fig. 22-8).

*Physico-Medical Systems Corporation, Montreal, Quebec, Canada.
†Everest & Jennings, Inc., Los Angeles, Calif.

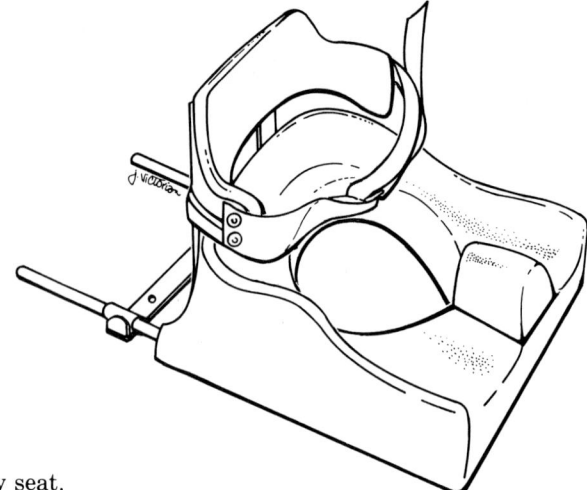

Fig. 22-7. Memphis potty seat.

In training the child in bladder and bowel control, as in other tasks, it is helpful to have a baseline (the child's present performance level), a goal (or goals), a set of methods, and reassessment to measure achievement within a reasonable time after the start of training.

Communication

Communication begins with the infant's cry of hunger or pain, normally proceeding through receptive and expressive stages to speech and language of a fairly complex nature by age 3 years. Severely multiply disabled children are often slow in both receptive and expressive speech,

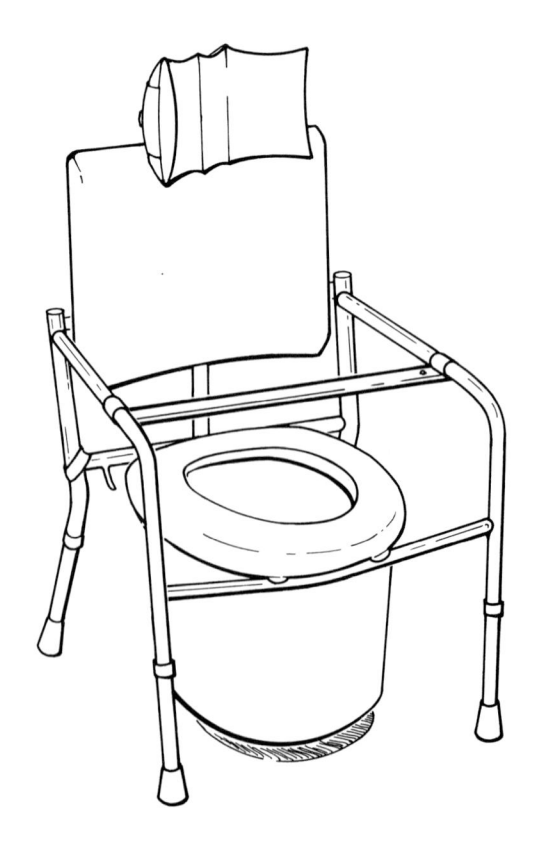

Fig. 22-8. Safety commode.

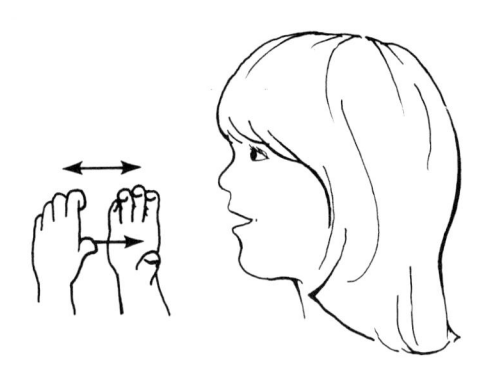

Fig. 22-9. Sign language.

however, and their "inner language," or comprehension may never exceed that of a normal 2-year-old—i.e., the naming of objects, the recognition of familiar places and people, and simple requests.

According to Piaget, the normal child passes the stage of sensory motor intelligence and enters the symbolic and preconceptual stage at about 18 months of age. If the child with severe and multiple disabilities is able to form mental images for recall and for the linking of objects with their uses, then communication devices of various kinds should be available to reinforce and extend this knowledge.[16]

Assuming there is adequate hearing, communication may be delayed due to: (1) problems with processing language, such as in mental retardation, aphasia, autism, and (2) the physical inability to speak, called *dysarthria* (Chapter 8). Where the problem is physical, communication devices of varying levels of complexity can substitute for spoken language. Sign language with simple signs has been used with some children (Fig. 22-9). Pointing devices with pictures are also useful and are especially versatile because the pictures can be of favorite people, animals, or toys and can be changed or added to as the child's capability increases.

The use of signs and pictures is helpful in children with processing problems as well, helping to motivate them to begin naming objects verbally and reinforcing their oral language. "On–off" switches can be used to motivate a child to indicate "yes–no" answers: they can be attached initially to attractive toys, and then switched to language indicators once

Fig. 22-10. Zygo nonverbal communicator (Zygo Industries, Portland, Ore.). Can be manually controlled or automatic to scan possible messages of 3 to 10 seconds. Displays (16 areas) are interchangeable plastic sheets.

the child has mastered the principle involved (Fig. 22-10). More complicated devices with lights, electrical pointers, and magnetic boards can also be tried if the child appears capable. In general, however, children who can operate such devices should be reassessed in class placement, since this ability indicates a more advanced capacity for processing of language.

Social Skills

To the extent that children can be trained to behave in a socially acceptable manner, they become more easily assimilated into classrooms and playgrounds with normal children. Parents who can take a child with them to a restaurant without embarrassment over behavior are appreciative of training at school. Knowing how to take turns in a game, knowing how to say or indicate "please" or "thank you," and control of crying and the throwing of objects are all legitimate goals for children able to comprehend them. Social courtesies may be acquired by a slow, laborious process in some multiply handicapped children.

The school day is usually structured around the learning of some of these skills—by repetition, demonstration, behavior management, rewards, reminders, and exclusion from the group, if necessary, as a last resort. The use of operant techniques for modifying the behavior of the severely and profoundly retarded has been discussed elsewhere,[17] and is considered beyond the scope of this chapter.

General Physical Management

Overcoming a child's lowered level of awareness and lack of interaction with the environment may require special efforts by the classroom personnel.[7] Motor, intellectual, and sensory training are intricately interwoven in the physical handling and care of these children. Pearson and Williams state:[18]

> Any child, with or without residual handicap, has a multitude of needs which require the personal contact of another individual . . . intellectual and emotional development are greatly affected by the kind of sensory and motor experiences provided. The child who is physically handicapped and cannot explore his environment may be just as impoverished as the deprived child left in his crib all day . . . the need to provide optimum sensory stimulation for the normal child is well recognized. In the handicapped child it becomes not only more critical, but often requires specifically directed kinds of stimulation to compensate for sensory, motor or intellectual deficits or to circumvent abnormal reactions to normal sensory stimuli [p. 10].

Physical or occupational therapists can be extremely helpful in evaluation and consultation regarding specific handling, positioning, and support activities and devices for these children.[19] For example, the therapist might recommend positioning the child in an upright frame for support (Fig. 22-11), might instruct the teacher in the proper position for carrying a child with limited head and trunk support, or might suggest the use of a large "bean bag" chair to stimulate interaction among children in the class.

Transportation is a special problem for multiply handicapped children. Safety and comfort are of prime importance. Therapists can be help-

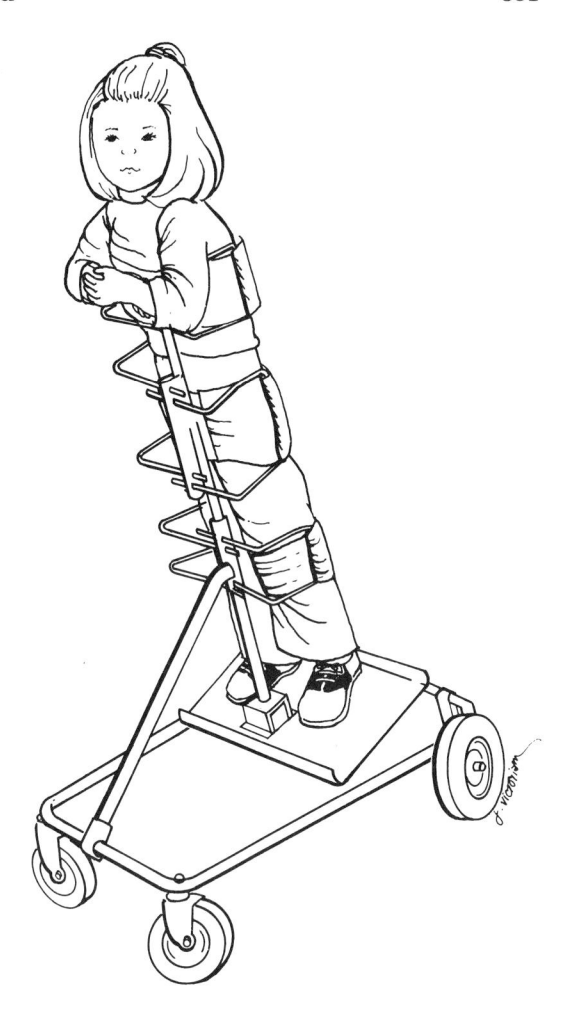

Fig. 22-11. Mulholland prone stander (L. Mulholland Corporation, Ventura, Calif.).

ful in recommending seat restraints and the best positions for transport situations. They may also suggest special equipment to accommodate children in wheelchairs, non-sitters, children with an apparatus, such as braces or a cast, and the children who are subject to seizures and thus require head protection (Figs. 22-12 and 22-13).

Reevaluation

The process of reevaluation requires successful interaction among the teacher and other school professionals, the medical and nursing personnel, and the child's parents. Each person involved in the child's management should be encouraged to utilize his or her area of expertise, without "building fences" to keep other workers out. An understanding of the role of the family in fulfilling the child's emotional and support needs is of prime importance. Families are the single *ongoing* influence in the child's development: they provide the child's primary emotional support, and they must always be included in plans for management of the child both at school and at home.

If it is realized that the goals for these children are, of necessity, different from the educational goals for other children, and if the child's education is focused on activities of daily living, self-help skills, and con-

Fig. 22-12. Bus adapted to take on wheelchair-bound child.

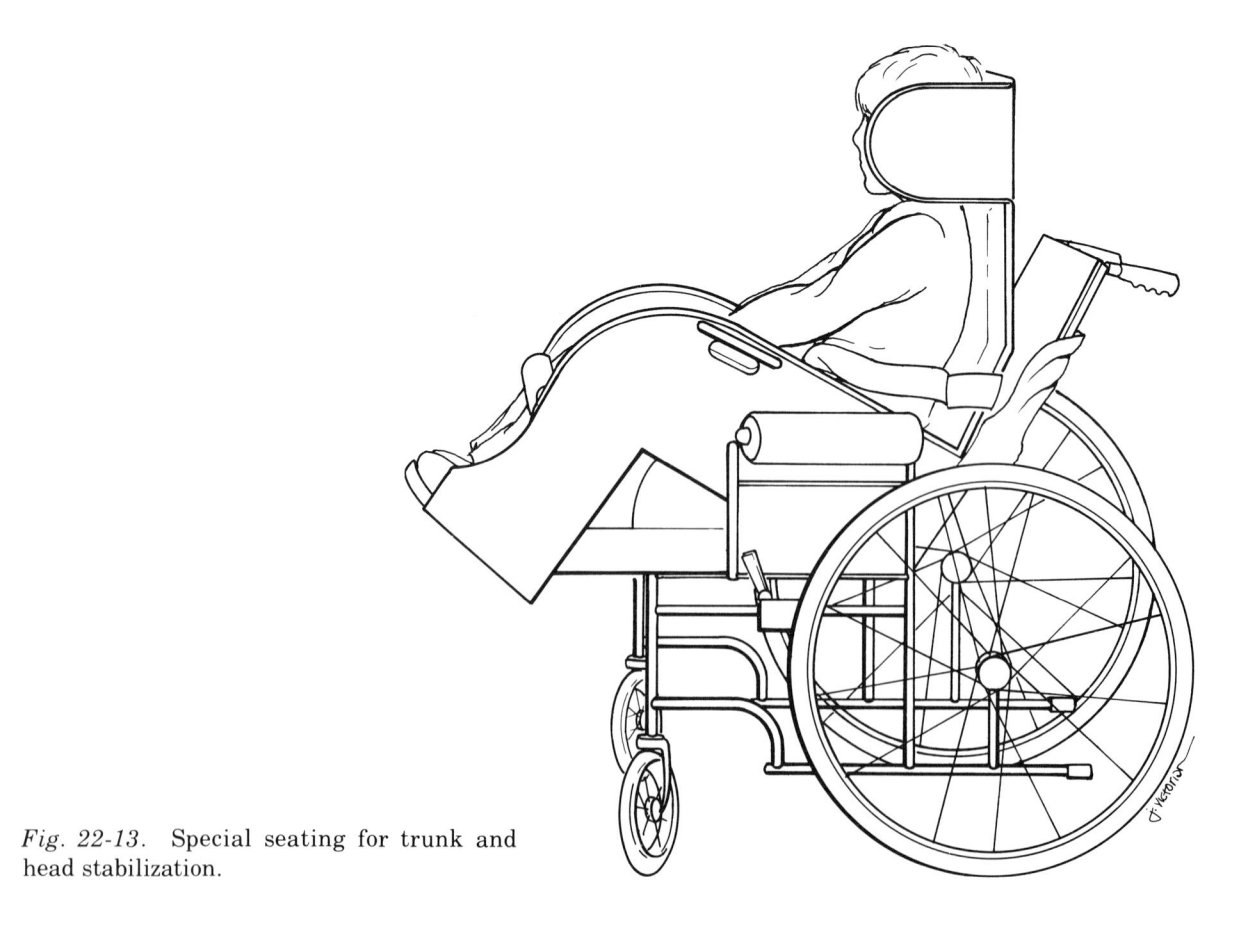

Fig. 22-13. Special seating for trunk and head stabilization.

trol of motor and body functions, then successful achievement will be recognized and will be satisfying to all concerned.

Flexibility in program placement will allow the child to transfer easily into other specialized programs from which he or she seems likely to benefit. Participation in regular school activities, to the degree allowed by disabilities, is helpful both to the handicapped child and to the regular school children who thereby broaden their knowledge and acceptance. Children with severe motor disabilities must be very carefully reappraised at regular intervals for evidence of cognitive function which would permit and benefit from more complicated communication and learning activities. Children with severe mental retardation who acquire basic self-help and motor skills may be able to transfer into classes for the trainable retarded.

CONCLUSION

Severely and multiply disabled children who were once excluded from public school classes are now being served in such classes in substantial numbers. This chapter has discussed some of the challenges that the management of these children presents to teachers. It is increasingly clear that school and community resources can be mobilized to provide support services for and to promote an understanding of these children and young adults. These efforts should result in an improved quality of life for the children and their families.

REFERENCES

1. Grossman, H. J. (ed.), *Manual on Terminology and Classification in Mental Retardation.* Washington D.C., American Association on Mental Deficiency, 1973.
2. Sontag, E., Burke, P. J., and York, R., Education and training of the mentally retarded, reprinted in Anderson, R. M., and Greer, J. C., *Educating the Severely and Profoundly Retarded.* Baltimore, University Park Press, 1976.
3. Bigge, J. L., and O'Donnell, P. A., *Teaching Individuals with Physical and Multiple Disabilities.* Columbus, Oh., Charles E. Merrill, 1976.
4. Farmer, T. W., *Pediatric Neurology.* New York, Harper & Row, 1964.
5. Dekaban, A., *Neurology of Infancy.* Baltimore, Williams & Wilkins, 1959.
6. Drillien, C., and Drummond, M. B. (eds.), *Neurodevelopmental Problems in Early Childhood: Assessment and Management.* Philadelphia, J. B. Lippincott Company, 1977.
7. Haslam, R. H. A., and Valletutti, P. J., *Medical Problems in the Classroom: The Teacher's Role in Diagnosis and Management.* Baltimore, University Park Press, 1975.
8. Gross, L., Bailey, E. *Enterstomal Therapy: Developing Institutional and Community Programs.* Wakefield, Mass., Nursing Resources, Inc., 1979.
9. Steele, S. (ed.), *Nursing Care of the Child with Long Term Illness.* New York, Appleton-Century-Crofts, 1977.
10. Christopherson, V. A., Coulter, P. P., and Wolanin, M. O., *Rehabilitation Nursing—Perspectives and Applications.* New York, McGraw-Hill Book Company, 1974.
11. Bryan, E., Warden, M. G., and Berg, B., Medical considerations for the multiply-handicapped children in the public schools. *The Journal of School Health* 48:84, 1978.
12. Bryan, E., Harlin, V., and Phillips, Z., The school physician in special education programs. *The Journal of School Health* 47:486, 1977.
13. Coley, I. L., *Pediatric Assessment of Self-Care Activities.* St. Louis, C. V. Mosby, 1978.
14. Finnie, N. R., *Handling the Young Cerebral Palsied Child at Home.* New York, E. P. Sutton, 1975.

15. Forrest, D., Management of Bladder and Bowel in Spina Bifida, in Borcklehurst, G. (ed.) *Spina Bifida for the Clinician*. Philadelphia, J. B. Lippincott, 1976.
16. Woodward, H., The application of Piaget's theory to research in mental deficiency, in Ellis, N. R. (ed.), *Handbook of Mental Deficiency*. New York, McGraw-Hill, 1963.
17. Nawas, N. H., and Braun, S. H., The use of operant techniques for modifying the behavior of the severely and profoundly retarded, part II. *The Techniques of Mental Retardation* 9:18–24, 1970.
18. Pearson, P. H., and Williams, C. E. (eds.), *Physical Therapy Services in the Developmental Disabilities*. Springfield, Ill., Charles C. Thomas, 1972.
19. Robinault, I. P., *Functional Aids for the Multiply Handicapped*. New York, United Cerebral Palsy Association, 1973.

BIBLIOGRAPHY

American Public Health Association (APHA) Guides, *Services for Children:*
    a. *Cerebral Palsy*
    b. *Communicative Disorders*
    c. *Emotional Disturbances*
    d. *Handicapped Children*
    e. *Vision and Eye Problems*
    f. *Cleft Lip and Cleft Palate*
    g. *Dentofacial Handicaps*
    h. *Heart Disease and Rheumatic Fever*
    i. *Orthopaedic Handicaps*
    j. *Epilepsy*
Available from the APHA, Washington, D.C.

Anderson, R. M., and Greer, J. G., *Educating the Severely and Profoundly Retarded*. Baltimore, University Park Press, 1976.

Barnard, K. E., and Powell, M. D., *Teaching the Mentally Retarded Child*. Chicago, C. V. Mosby, 1972.

Bruck, L. (ed.), *Access, the Guide to a Better Life for Disabled Americans*. New York, Random House, 1978.

Calhoun, M. L., and Hawisher, M., *Teaching and Learning Strategies for Physically Handicapped Students*. Baltimore, University Park Press, 1978.

Connor, F. P., Williamson, G. G., and Siep, J. M. (eds.), *Program Guide for Infants and Toddlers with Neuromotor and Other Developmental Disabilities*. New York, Teachers College Press, Columbia University, 1978.

Galka, G., Fraser, B. A., and Hensinger, R. N., *Gross Motor Management of Severely Multiply Impaired Students,* vols. 1 and 2. Baltimore, University Park Press, 1980.

Hale, G. (ed.), *The Source Book for the Disabled*. New York, Paddington Press Ltd., 1979.

Menolascino, F. J., and Pearson, P. H. (eds.), *Beyond the Limits—Innovations in Services for the Severely and Profoundly Retarded*. New York, Bernie Straul Publication Company, Inc., 1974.

Motloch, W. M., Seating and positioning for the physically impaired. *Orthotics and Prosthetics* 31(2):11–21, 1977.

Smith, D. W., *Recognizable Patterns of Human Malformation*. Philadelphia, W. B. Saunders, 1970.

Teaching Exceptional Children. Journal of the Council for Exceptional Children, 1920 Association Drive, Reston, Virginia, 22091. Special issue, *Progress by Partners in Step,* Spring 1978.

Thompson, J., Jr., and O'Quinn, A. N., *Developmental Disabilities: Etiologies, Manifestations, Diagnoses, and Treatments*. New York, Oxford University Press, 1979.

Ulrich, S., *Elizabeth: The Story of A Blind Child up to 5 Years of Age*. Ann Arbor, University of Michigan Press, 1972.

23

Muscular Dystrophy– Duchenne Type

EUGENE E. BLECK, M.D.

DEFINITION   Muscular dystrophy as discussed in this chapter is a progressive, diffuse weakness of all muscle groups, which is characterized by a degeneration of muscle cells and their replacement by fat and fibrous tissue. The type of muscular dystrophy described here is that which was first delineated by Duchenne in 1968. The commonly accepted diagnostic terms for this disease are: (1) muscular dystrophy—Duchenne type; (2) progressive muscular dystrophy; and (3) pseudohypertrophic muscular dystrophy.

Two other types of muscular dystrophy, which are not discussed here, are: limb-girdle muscular dystrophy, which does not occur in childhood; and facioscapulohumeral muscular dystrophy, a rare form that affects the facial and shoulder musculature and does not usually occur until the second decade of life. Other muscle-weakening diseases and their characteristics are listed in Table 23-1. Figure 23-1 depicts the major parts of the central and peripheral nervous systems involved in the various diseases.

Table 23-1. Classification of Muscle-weakening Diseases.

Diagnosis	Inheritance	CPK (Muscle enzyme) level in blood	EMG (Electromyograph)	Nerve Conduction	Muscle Biopsy (Microscopic characteristics)	Other
I. The Muscular Dystrophies						
A. Duchenne's (Pseudohypertrophic) 1. Early onset 2. Late onset—Becker's	Sex-linked	Markedly elevated	Myopathic pattern	Normal	Myopathic pattern	Heart involvement; intellectual involvement (30%)
B. Facioscapulohumeral (FSH)	Autosomal dominant	Normal to elevated	Myopathic pattern	Normal	Myopathic pattern	Usually no heart involvement or intellectual impairment
C. Limb-girdle	Autosomal recessive; rarely, autosomal dominant	Elevated	Myopathic pattern	Normal	Myopathic pattern	Usually no heart involvement or intellectual impairment
D. Others (Ocular, Distal, etc.)						
II. Spinal Muscular Atrophy (Werdnig-Hoffman, Kugelberg-Welander)	Autosomal recessive; rarely, autosomal dominant	Normal to slightly elevated	Neuropathic pattern	Normal	Neuropathic pattern	No heart involvement or intellectual impairment

III.	Hereditary Motor and Sensory Neuropathies				
A.	Type I Charcot-Marie-Tooth	Autosomal dominant (usually)	Normal	Neuropathic pattern	Markedly decreased	Neuropathic pattern	
B.	Type II	Autosomal dominant	Normal	Neuropathic pattern	Decreased to normal	Neuropathic pattern	
C.	Type III	Autosomal recessive	Normal	Neuropathic pattern	Decreased	Neuropathic pattern	
D.	Type IV	Autosomal recessive	Normal	Neuropathic pattern		Neuropathic pattern	High serum phytanic acid levels, eye changes, etc.
E.	Type V	Autosomal dominant	Normal	Neuropathic pattern	Normal to decreased	Neuropathic pattern	Spastic paraplegia
IV.	The Myopathies: Central Core, Nemaline, Minicore, Mitochondrial, Myotubular, etc.	Often familial	Often normal	Often normal or mildly myopathic	Usually normal	Myopathic changes on histo-chemical and electron microscopic studies	
V.	Poliomyelitis	Not inherited		Neuropathic pattern	Normal	Neuropathic pattern	Viral infection; history of acute disease
VI.	Guillain-Barré	Not inherited	Normal	Neuropathic pattern	Slow in acute phase	Neuropathic pattern	Possibly post-infectious
VII.	Polymyositis	Not inherited	Increased or normal	Myopathic pattern	Normal	Myopathic etc.	Treated with cortisone
VIII.	The Myotonic Diseases	Usually autosomal dominant	Usually normal	Diagnostic	Normal	Variable—normal to myopathic	Presence of myotonia
IX.	Myasthenia Gravis	Variable		Diagnostic			Treated with anticholinesterase compounds

From Irene Gilgoff, M.D., Orthopedic Hospital, Los Angeles, Calif., personal communication. Adapted and reproduced with permission.

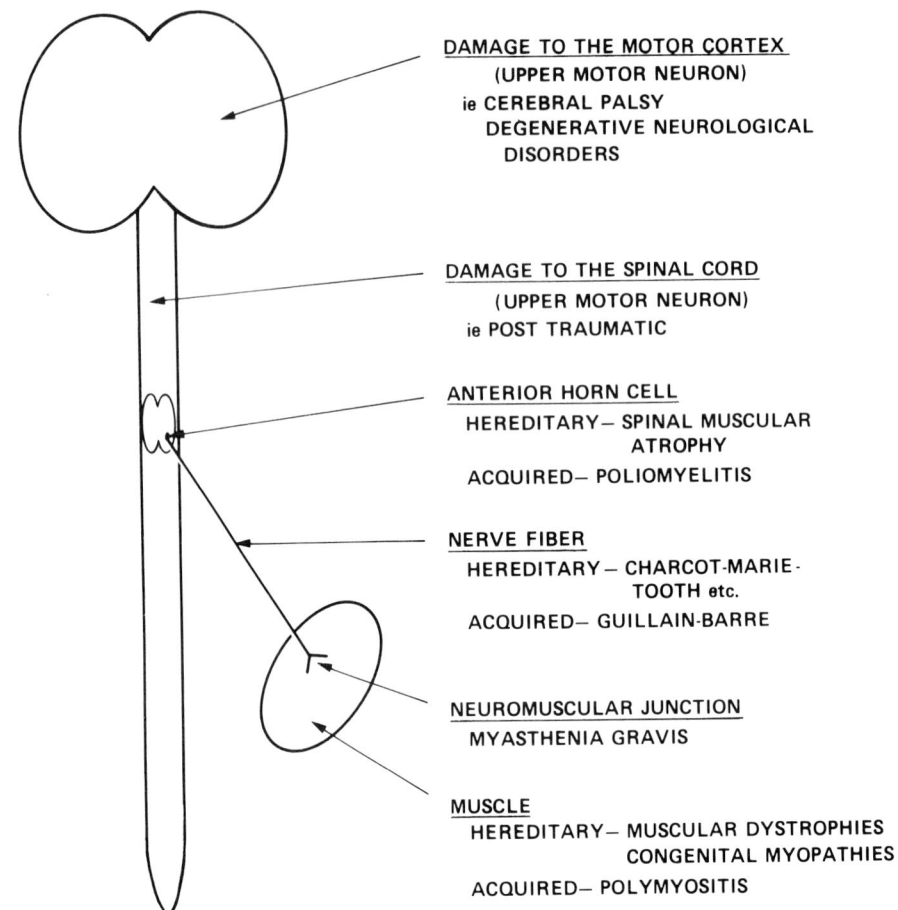

Fig. 23-1. Schematic drawing of the different parts of the nervous and muscular system that are involved in various muscle weakening diseases (Redrawn from Irene Gilgoff, M.D., Orthopaedic Hospital, Los Angeles, Calif., personal communication. With permission).

DAMAGE TO THE MOTOR CORTEX
(UPPER MOTOR NEURON)
ie CEREBRAL PALSY
DEGENERATIVE NEUROLOGICAL DISORDERS

DAMAGE TO THE SPINAL CORD
(UPPER MOTOR NEURON)
ie POST TRAUMATIC

ANTERIOR HORN CELL
HEREDITARY— SPINAL MUSCULAR ATROPHY
ACQUIRED— POLIOMYELITIS

NERVE FIBER
HEREDITARY— CHARCOT-MARIE-TOOTH etc.
ACQUIRED— GUILLAIN-BARRE

NEUROMUSCULAR JUNCTION
MYASTHENIA GRAVIS

MUSCLE
HEREDITARY— MUSCULAR DYSTROPHIES
CONGENITAL MYOPATHIES
ACQUIRED— POLYMYOSITIS

CAUSE (ETIOLOGY)

The cause of muscular dystrophy—Duchenne type is unknown. The disease mainly affects boys, and a clear-cut inheritance pattern can be demonstrated in family pedigrees. The inherited form is most often due to a gene carried by the mother and transmitted to her sons; the gene is carried on the female sex chromosome (X) and the disease is a sex-linked recessive trait. A few girls are afflicted; in these cases, the disease is transmitted by a gene located on a nonsex chromosome, called *autosome*, and is termed an autosomal recessive trait. There are some cases in which no family history is found. These sporadic cases are thought to be due to a spontaneous change in a gene, i.e., a *mutation*.

SIGNS, SYMPTOMS, AND CLINICAL COURSE

Early Symptoms

Parents who are keen observers of their children may notice that, when their boy is about 3-years-old, he seems awkward and clumsy, and that he runs "funny." Such parental observations are often dismissed as nothing to be concerned about, sometimes with a recommendation that special shoes be purchased for "flat feet." Tiptoeing is another early sign; it is due to early weakness in the muscles that pull the foot up (dorsiflexors of the ankle—mainly the anterior tibial muscle). Sometimes children are thought to have poor posture, with a protruding abdomen and a

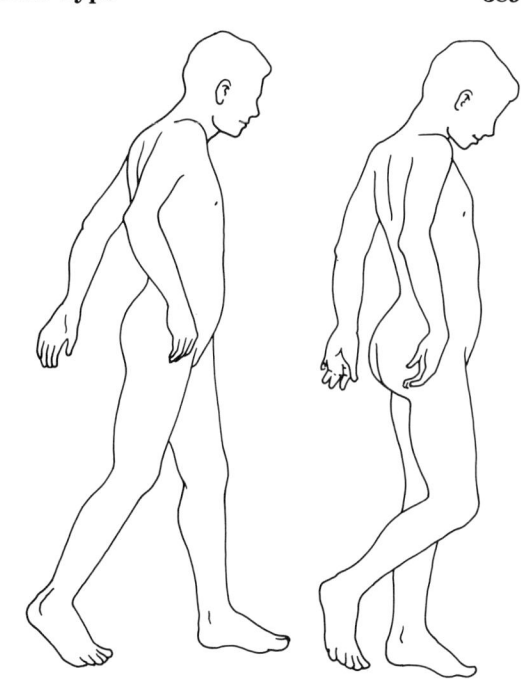

Fig. 23-2. Typical posture and gait of a child with progressive muscular dystrophy. Note that the shoulders are thrown backward and the lower back is swayed.

sway back (lordosis); the poor posture is due to early weakness of the muscles of the abdominal wall (Fig. 23-2).

Of special pertinence to teachers is that, when undiagnosed muscular dystrophy children enter kindergarten or first grade, their awkwardness, frequent falling, and the like, are apt to be immediately labeled with such now fashionable and extensively used terms as, *learning disability, educational handicap,* or *minimal cerebral dysfunction.* Batteries of psychometric tests are administered, and, often, an EEG is required for admission to a special class for educationally handicapped children. (The EEG may show some abnormalities, of course, but such changes are also known to occur in about 20 percent of the "normal" population.) The parents are then counseled by the psychologist and psychiatrist to accept the child's special educational needs, his behavior, and his slowness. Eventually, the muscle weakness will become so evident that the diagnosis of muscular dystrophy is, at last, made. It is then obvious that what has transpired over the past 3 to 4 years since the parent's mother first *knew* that something was wrong has consumed needless and excessive professional time and has been, in fact, inappropriate counseling. No wonder parents may be hostile in such instances.

Late Signs

Muscle patterns. The weakness usually develops in the body's muscles in a set order as follows: dorsiflexors of the foot, front thigh muscles (quadriceps), outside hip muscles (abductors of the hip), hip extension muscles (gluteus maximus), abdominal muscles, and the shoulder and elbow muscles. The hand, face, and neck muscles are affected only later (Fig. 23-3). The reverse progression occurs in the facioscapulohumeral type of muscular dystrophy: the face and shoulder muscles weaken first, and the lower-limb muscles are the last involved.

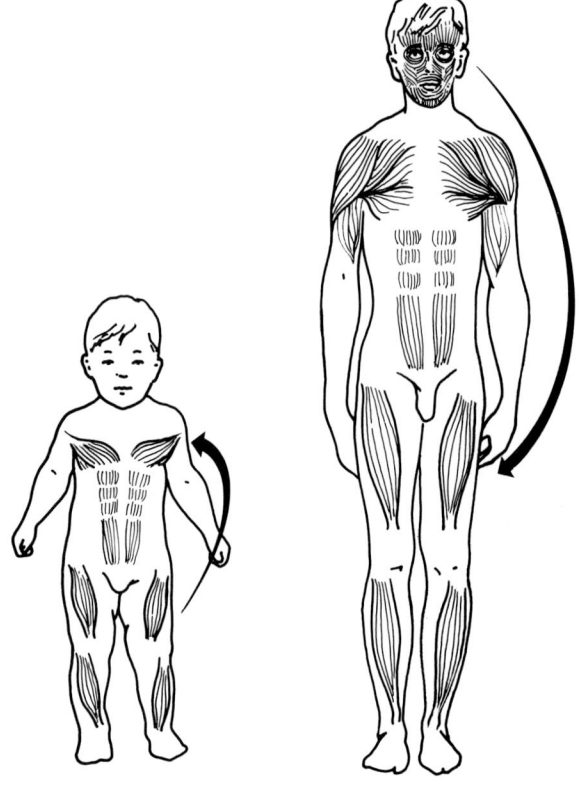

Fig. 23-3. (A) Typical progression of Duchenne-type muscular dystrophy—from the lower to the upper limbs. (B) The usual progression of weakness in the facioscapulohumeral type of muscular dystrophy—from the face to the shoulder girdle and, finally, the lower limbs.

Gower's sign. The classical sign of muscular dystrophy is that, when the child gets up from sitting on the floor, he "walks up" his lower limbs with his hands (Fig. 23-4).

Pseudohypertrophy. Another sign is an unusual, apparent enlargement of the muscles, called *pseudohypertrophy* (false enlargement). The "enlargement" is, in fact, due to replacement of muscle with fat. Calf enlargement is the most common form (Fig. 23-4).

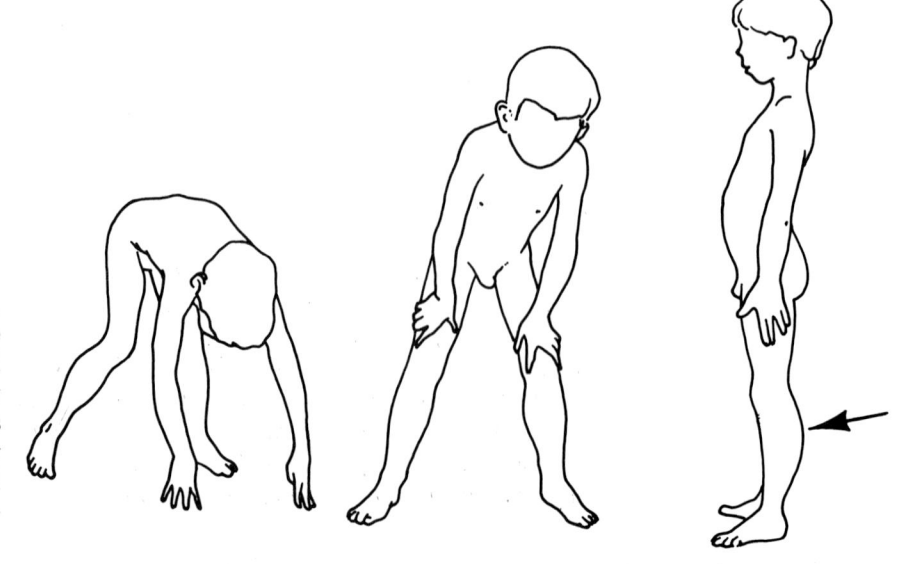

Fig. 23-4. Gower's sign. Due to weakness of the thigh muscles, the child gets up from the floor by "walking up" his thighs with his hands. The arrow points to the enlarged calves (pseudohypertrophy).

Muscular Dystrophy—Duchenne Type

Obesity and Atrophy. Because of restricted activity and, probably, compensatory overeating, these children are often very fat. A few children may be quite the reverse, however (atrophic type).

Skeletal deformities. The muscle weakness usually affects only one of two opposing muscle-groups; hence, the pull of the other muscle group is left unopposed, and a shortening (contracture) of the unopposed muscles occurs. As a result, the joints are usually pulled into their bent position (joint contracture). The most common such lower-limb deformity is contracture of the ankle, in which the foot points downward (equinus) and inward (varus). Knee and hip contractures are the next most frequent lower-limb deformities.

Because of trunk-muscle weakness, severe curvature of the spine (scoliosis) can also develop.

By the time the child is in the wheelchair, the muscles in the back of the neck (posterior cervical musculature) contract, limiting forward flexion (bending) of the neck.

In the upper limb, because of weakness of the elbow extensors (mainly the triceps muscle, which straightens the elbow), contracture in the bent position (flexion) occurs. An additional, usual, contracture is one in which the forearm is turned so that the palm faces downward (pronation).

Mental subnormality. Mental subnormality, manifested by slowness in learning and demonstrated by psychometric testing, is present in about 70 percent of children with Duchenne-type muscular dystrophy.[1-3] The IQ of these children is usually in the 80s.

LONG-TERM OUTLOOK (PROGNOSIS)

In Duchenne-type muscular dystrophy, the course is steadily downhill. Most children are in wheelchairs by the age of 10 years. The usual cause of death, which usually occurs in the late teens, is heart failure (the heart muscle eventually becomes weak, too) or overwhelming lung infection due to weakness of the muscles involved in breathing.

If the disease does not progress, then the diagnosis obviously is not

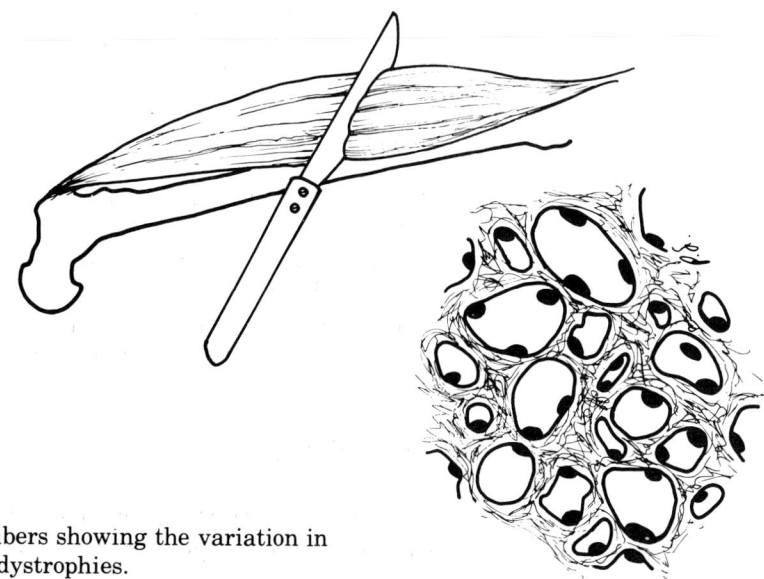

Fig. 23-5. A cross section of muscle fibers showing the variation in size and shape of the muscle fibers in dystrophies.

progressive muscular dystrophy—Duchenne type. Some other muscle disease (e.g., limb-girdle muscular dystrophy, nemaline myopathy, or central-core disease), may be present instead.

DIAGNOSIS

The diagnosis is based upon:

1. The signs and symptoms.
2. An elevation of a muscle enzyme, creatine phosphokinase (CPK), in the blood. (*Note:* Elevated CPK's are also found in most, but not all, female carriers.)
3. Electromyography (EMG). The electrical activity of muscle is recorded by placing needles through the skin and into the muscle. The electrical activity produced by muscle contraction is then recorded on a cathode-ray oscilloscope. An electrical wave form suggestive of muscular dystrophy can be found. It is not diagnostic, however, only indicating a diseased muscle.
4. Muscle biopsy. A small piece of the suspected weak muscle is removed surgically. The muscle tissue is appropriately processed so that its microscopic appearance can be examined for confirmation of the diagnosis (Fig. 23-5).

TREATMENT

Diet and Drugs

No effective treatment for Duchenne-type muscular dystrophy exists. Almost all vitamins (including C and E) have been tried, with negative results. Special diets, including extra amino acids (glycine), also have failed. Hormones, and even digitalis, have been tried and proved ineffective.

Physical Therapy

We have found that keeping the joints fixed with sandbags or other equipment in the position opposite the tendency toward contracture (and to do this with groups of muscular dystrophy children) is more effective than individual exercise or stretching. Group games directed at maintaining the child's range of motion and breathing capacity (e.g., blowing and shouting) also appear more rewarding than isolated, passive "exercises."

Some joint contractures should not be treated because the contracture serves to compensate for deficient muscles. A good example is contracture of the elbow joint in the bent position (flexion). A flexed elbow is more useful than a straight, stiff elbow. The shortened range of motion due to the flexion contracture allows greater function from the weakened elbow flexors. Similarly, it is better to have the hand face downward (pronation), as few activities are accomplished with the palm up.

Braces (Orthotics)

Selective application of long-leg aluminum or short-leg plastic orthoses is helpful in preventing contracture. Most children, by the time they are in wheelchairs, have discarded the braces as a nuisance. Plastic jackets are a help in holding the spine straight if scoliosis is developing.

Surgery

Surgical treatment is helpful, at times, in correcting early deformities of the lower limb, with the intent of keeping the child erect and walking longer. The heel cord (Achilles' tendon) can be lengthened, for example, to free up a foot that is fixed in the tiptoe position (equinus). Some authorities recommend cutting and lengthening the tight muscles and fibrous bands around the hip and knee (tenotomy, myotomy, fasciotomy) to correct extreme contractures of these joints. Surgery obviously must be timed and individualized.[4]

Mobility Aids and Adaptive Equipment

1. *Wheelchairs.* Ordinary portable wheelchairs suffice at first; however, motorized wheelchairs should not be withheld because of false reasoning that the child must use his arms to keep strong. In propelling the wheelchair, the energy requirements are so great that fatigue is debilitating. In the face of a progressive disease, we should at least make life tolerable, increase the child's mobility, and enlarge his horizons. Very good electric wheelchairs with a variety of hand controls are available. We have had softball games for muscular dystrophy children in electric wheelchairs. A large restraining canvas strap across the abdomen and chest is a great help to muscular dystrophy children, allowing them to lean forward and freeing their arms for action.
2. *Autovans.* The automobile vans now available permit great mobility for children in electric wheelchairs. With a ramp for the chair, family outings become facile and pleasurable.
3. *Lifts.* Because of obesity and the eventual inability of the child to move or help himself, mechanical lifts (e.g., Hoyer hydraulic lift) are valuable aids for parents in bathing and toileting the children.
4. *Clothing.* Loose-fitting shirts and, certainly, large, old-fashioned trousers are necessary for almost helpless, wheelchair-bound children.
5. *Toileting.* For boys, a male urinal is the easiest way to void. Bowel movements can usually be timed to occur once a day, either before or after school. Constipation can be a real problem. Plenty of fluids during the day and bowel softeners (e.g., Colace or Doxinate) at bedtime usually suffice.
6. *Bed.* As the child becomes more disabled and unable to turn himself, electric hospital beds offer a good deal of comfort and freedom. Some parents have found that a water bed keeps their child comfortable during the night.

EDUCATIONAL IMPLICATIONS

Because the prognosis seems so hopeless, professionals concerned with the care of the child may be disheartened. To sustain a positive attitude, one may, first, maintain hope that perhaps a cure will be found during that child's lifetime, and, second, hold to the principle that the shortened life-span of the child can be a life filled with enjoyment and creativity, not merely a "life of treatment."

As the children age, fatigue becomes more common. A rest period may be necessary.

The teacher in the classroom will, of course, keep in mind the modest intellectual retardation commonly reported in such children. Psychometric testing should be done.

SUMMARY

This chapter has described the second largest population of handicapped children in California's orthopedically handicapped schools.

Muscular dystrophy—Duchenne type, is progressive. Consequently, the children whom one teaches will show a changing disability to which numerous adjustments will be required.

REFERENCES

1. Allen, J. D., and Rodgin, D. W., Mental retardation in association with progressive muscular dystrophy. *American Journal of Diseases of Children* 100:208, 1960.
2. Worder, N. K., and Vignos, P. J., Jr., Intellectual functions in childhood progressive muscular dystrophy. *Pediatrics* 29:968, 1962.
3. Zellweger, H., and Hanson, J. W., Psychometric studies in muscular dystrophy type 3A (Duchenne). *Developmental Medicine and Child Neurology* 9:576–581, 1967.
4. Hsu, J. D., Management of foot deformity in Duchenne's pseudohypertorophic muscular dystrophy. *Orthopedic Clinics of North America* 7:979–984, 1976.
5. Hsu, J. D., Surgical correction of foot deformity in the SMA patient. *Orthopedic Review* 8:101–104, 1979.
6. Hsu, J. D., Extremity fractures in children with neuromuscular disease. *Johns Hopkins Medical Journal* 145:89–93, 1979.
7. Roy, L., and Gibson, D. A., Pseudohypertrophic muscular dystrophy and its surgical management. Review of 30 patients. *Canadian Journal of Surgery* 13:13–21, 1970.
8. Sakai, D., Hsu, J. D., Bonnett, C., and Brown, J. C., Stabilization of the collapsing spine in Duchenne muscular dystrophy. *Clinical Orthopedics* 128:256–260, 1977.
9. Siegel, I. M., The management of muscular dystrophy: A clinical review. *Muscle and Nerve* 1:453–460, 1978.
10. Spencer, G. E., Jr., Orthopaedic considerations in the management of muscular dystrophy. *Current Practice in Orthopedic Surgery* 5:279–293, 1973.

BIBLIOGRAPHY

Dubowitz, V., *The Floppy Infant*. Philadelphia, J. B. Lippincott, 1980.

Harris, S. E., and Cherry, D. B., Childhood progressive muscular dystrophy and the role of physical therapy. *Physical Therapy* 54:4–12, 1974.

Swinyard, C. A., Deaver, B. G., and Greenspan, L., *Progressive Muscular Dystrophy Diagnosis and Problems of Rehabilitation*. New York, Professional Education Division of the Muscular Dystrophy Associations of America, 1958.

Walton, J. N., *Disorders of Voluntary Muscle*. Boston, Little, Brown, 1964.

24

Temporary Orthopedic Disabilities in Children

DONALD A. NAGEL, M.D.

LEGG-PERTHES DISEASE

This condition still carries the names of the physicians who first described it in the early 1900s—Legg and Perthes, and, in some texts, Calve as well (Legg-Calve-Perthes disease). Each man, using the then newly developed technique of x-ray examination, described a condition in which the growth center (epiphysis) at the hip end of the thigh bone (femur) had been partially or completely destroyed (Fig. 24-1). Such x-ray changes are seen in children between the ages of 4 and 8 years and occur more frequently in boys than in girls. Affected children usually are brought by parents to the physician because they walk with a limp and complain of pain in the knee or thigh, and, occasionally, the hip joint. Similar complaints on the part of the child and similar x-ray findings can be produced by rare metabolic disease (e.g., hypothyroidism), by blood diseases (e.g., sickle cell disease), by lowgrade infection in the hip joint (e.g., that caused by tuberculosis), by injury, and by complications resulting from treatment of other conditions with medicines such as cortisone. The condition common to all of these causes is a loss of blood supply to the growth center at the hip end of the thigh bone. When metabolic and blood diseases, infection, and injury have been eliminated as causes, the condition is diagnosed as Legg-Perthes disease, a category that may, in fact, represent a large group of diseases for which the primary cause is unknown.

The natural history of growth center repair is one of resorption of dead bone and the laying down of new bone; this takes place over a period of 2 to 3 years. Generally speaking, the younger the child when the process starts, the faster will be the regeneration of the growth center

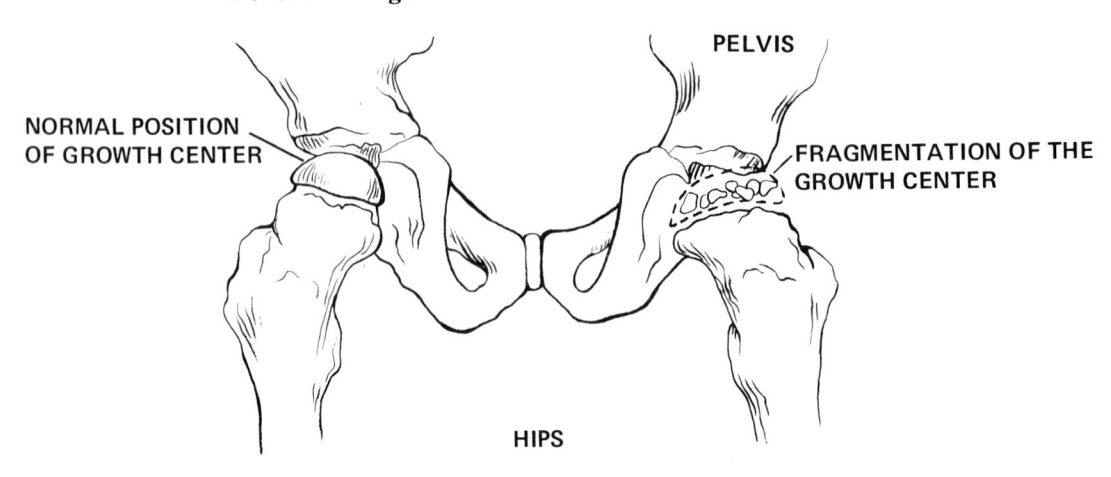

Fig. 24-1. Legg-Perthes disease. Destruction of the growth center may be partial or complete (as illustrated here) before the reparative process begins.

and the better the outcome. Repair is also more rapid and complete in cases in which only a portion of the growth center is involved. The aim of treatment is to protect the hip joint while the repair process is ongoing, as the involved growth center is soft and pliable during this process. It has been claimed that if such treatment is not carried out, then the femoral head will become flattened and irregular *(coxa plana)*, producing an incongruous joint that will lead to early degenerative arthritis of the hip. Many treatment programs have been advised in the past, each producing variable results. The programs can be grouped into three basic categories:

1. Recumbency Treatment

Many children receive this form of treatment, which requires absolute bedrest. Initially, traction may be applied to the involved leg. Some children are fitted with a brace that holds their legs wide apart, while others are placed in casts. Children in such a recumbency program who are not casted are usually advised to exercise their legs in a swimming pool or in another manner each day.

2. Ambulatory Treatment

Because recumbency treatment tends to take a child out of the mainstream of life for 2 to 3 years, some orthopedic surgeons have instead advised immobilization of the involved leg with either a sling, which keeps it flexed, or a special brace, which is thought to keep the forces of weight-bearing off the hip joint while the child ambulates with crutches. Special casts and braces have been devised for holding the child's leg in wide abduction, and these allow the children to walk, although with a rather unusual gait.

3. Operative Treatment

Operative treatment has also been advised in some cases of this disease. Treatment consists of either (a) drilling or bone-grafting the involved growth center for the purpose of speeding the repair process or (b) changing the angle of the thigh bone or of the cup portion of the hip joint so that, as the head of the thigh bone regenerates, it will do so better because the mold of the cup portion (acetabulum) of the hip joint is more horizontally placed.

No matter what the form of treatment, the period of involvement for children with complete destruction of the growth center is, on the average, 2 years—a considerable portion of their life span at this age. During this time they may be isolated from their friends, wear a cast or a brace, or have an operation. They will need emotional support, and, in many situations, special educational efforts as well. Special physical education programs also have to be devised—i.e., swimming, but no active sports.

SLIPPED CAPITAL FEMORAL EPIPHYSIS

Slippage of the growth center at the hip end of the thigh bone (the proximal femoral epiphysis) occurs in some adolescent children during the period of rapid growth between the ages of 11 and 16 (Fig. 24-2). It is usually seen earlier in girls than in boys, since girls mature earlier skeletally. The condition is found more frequently in boys, perhaps because boys have traditionally engaged in more vigorous sports and therefore have stressed this area more.

Several explanations have been given for occurrence of this condition. During adolescence, the junction between the growth center and the rest of the thigh bone changes from a horizontal to a more vertical plane, which makes slippage easier. In addition, it has been noted experimentally that, under the influence of increased levels of growth hormone, this junction between the growth center and the remainder of the thigh bone weakens. Normally, the level of growth hormone increases in prepuberty, followed during adolescence by an increase in the level of sex hormones, bringing about fusion of the growth center with the remainder of the bone. It has been noted clinically that the adolescents in whom slippage occurs tend to be sexually immature and either rather obese or extremely tall, suggesting that a disruption in hormone levels may, indeed, be involved.

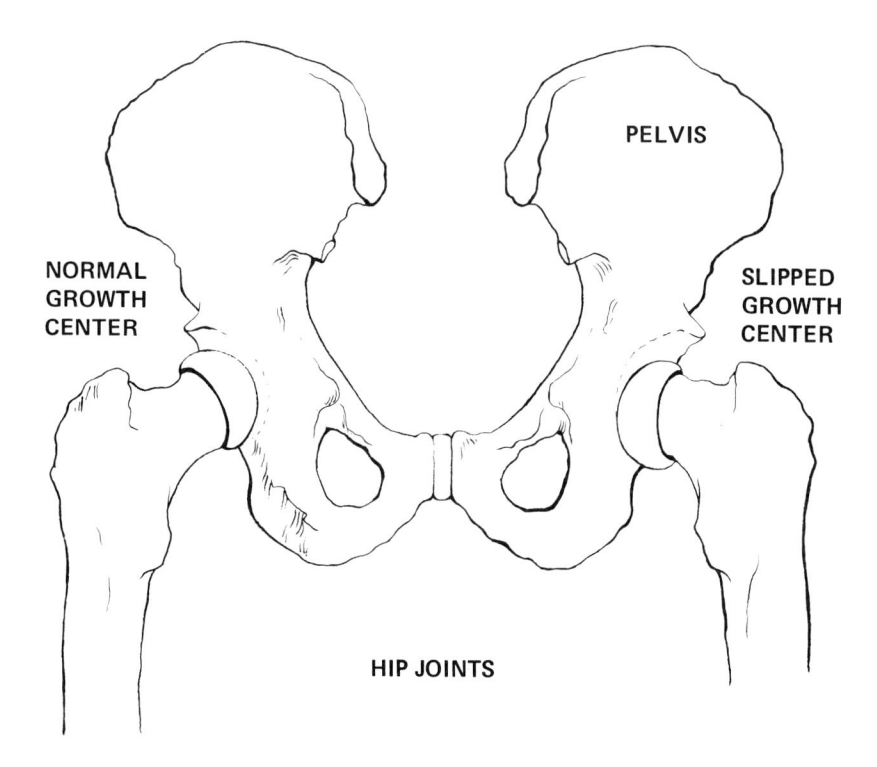

Fig. 24-2. Slipped epiphysis. The growth center usually slips inferiorly and posteriorly.

Although the problem is in the hip, the child may complain of pains in the thigh and knee and may limp for several months prior to the establishment of a diagnosis. If the condition goes undiagnosed and the child's hip is not protected during the slipping process, the growth center may slip off completely. The slip may be gradual at first and then become major following a slight fall, or it may be completely traumatic, following rather severe trauma to the hip. In the latter case, many physicians feel that a reduction of the slip can be carried out, and the growth center fixed to the remainder of the thigh bone by either pins or bone grafts to keep it in its normal position. If the growth center has not slipped more than a third off the thigh bone, it can be fixed in position with pins or bone grafts and thereby prevented from slipping further; a good hip joint can then be expected. If, however, the slippage is greater, the contact of the thigh bone with the pelvis will be such that early degenerative arthritic changes will develop. For this reason, orthopedic surgeons advise an operation to restore the relationship of the growth center to the cup portion of the hip (acetabulum) to a more normal configuration. Such an operation requires cutting across the thigh bone, restoring the relationship of the growth center to the thigh bone, and then holding this in place with metal pins, bone grafts, or a cast. Three or 4 months are required for the cut bone to heal and for the growth center to become solidly fixed to the involved bone. Following such surgery, the blood supply to the growth center may occasionally be interrupted and the growth center will die. Also occasionally, the smooth, glistening surface at the end of the growth center (cartilage) may undergo changes which produce stiffness of the hip joint.

The other hip must be watched closely in the patient who has a slipped capital femoral epiphysis, as approximately 20 percent of the patients will have a slip of the growth center of the opposite side. The slip on the second side, just as the first, can be mild to severe. In either situation, operative intervention is almost always necessary, and the child will be away from school for a protracted period of time. Upon return to school, he will usually not be able to engage in active sports for at least a year, but he may be encouraged to swim or take part in other specific, upper-extremity exercises.

OSGOOD-SCHLATTER'S DISEASE

This syndrome, independently described by Osgood and Schlatter in the early 1900s, consists of pain and swelling just below the knee (Fig. 24-3). It is most prevalent in adolescent boys between the ages of 11 and 15. If physical examination reveals tenderness and swelling in this area, and if x-rays show no other cause (such as a tumor), the diagnosis is confirmed. It is agreed that disease results from trauma, which may produce major changes either in a single, severe episode or in many episodes of lesser severity. The cause of the condition is described as a tearing away of the connective tissue surrounding the bone (periosteum) at the point where the tendon from the kneecap (patella) attaches to the anterior (forward) proximal portion of the leg bone (tibia). At least in some cases, this is due to inflammation of the tendon rather than to any problem with the underlying bone. Thus, in some cases, x-rays will show an irregularity of the bone at the insertion of the tendon; in others, small pieces of new bone are noted to be forming in the tendon itself; and, in still others, only soft-tissue swelling is seen.

The treatment of this disease depends partly on the severity of the problem and, partly on the treating physician's opinion as to its underly-

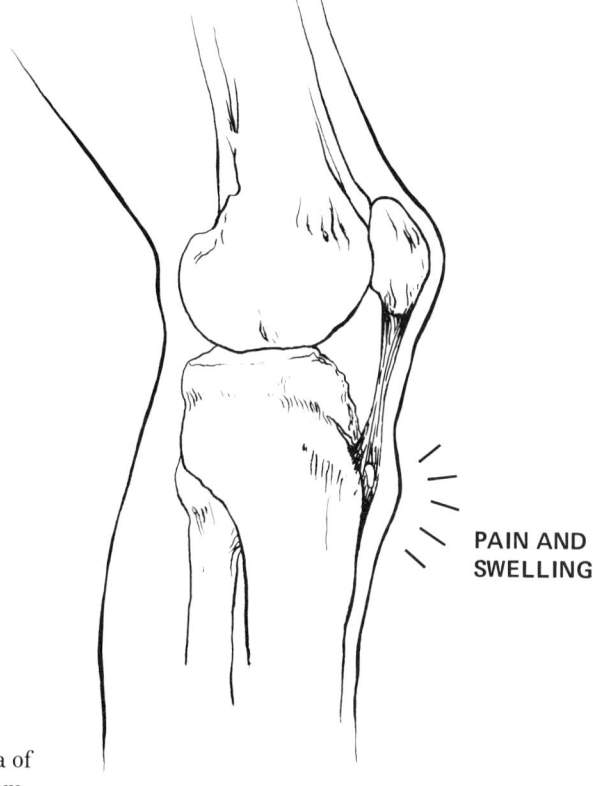

Fig. 24-3. Osgood-Schlatter's disease. Pain in the area of the insertion of the tendon from the kneecap is the complaint of people with this condition.

ing cause. Less severe cases are frequently treated only by limiting those activities that require major use of the muscles that act through the kneecap (patellar) tendon: running, jumping, active sports, climbing, bicycle riding, and even, in some cases, walking long distances.

Some physicians feel that the condition is caused by abnormal alignment of the leg and have prescribed heel wedges for the shoes. If the symptoms are more severe, and if the treating physician feels that the x-ray shows a tearing up or a lifting up of the periosteum at the attachment of the tendon, the extremity may be immobilized for a period of 6 weeks in a cast that limits knee motion. This is followed by cast removal and limitation of activities for a period of from 3 to 6 months. If the physician feels that tendonitis is present, he or she may elect to inject the area with an anti-inflammatory drug. In some few cases it is felt that the pieces of bone forming inside the tendon are the cause of irritation and pain, and surgery to remove these is performed.

Generally, this condition is self-limiting and the symptoms subside at about the age of 15 to 18 years. Cases have been reported, however, in young adults who vigorously engage in athletics. Obviously, a mild case will not interfere with the student's educational activities, but a more severe case will markedly affect the student's physical activities and will require special education, in some cases for a prolonged period of time.

OSTEOCHONDRITIS DISSECANS

Osteochondritis means "inflammation of bone and cartilage," and *dissecans* mean "cutting out from." At least the second of these Latin terms is pertinent, for the end result of this condition is in some cases a

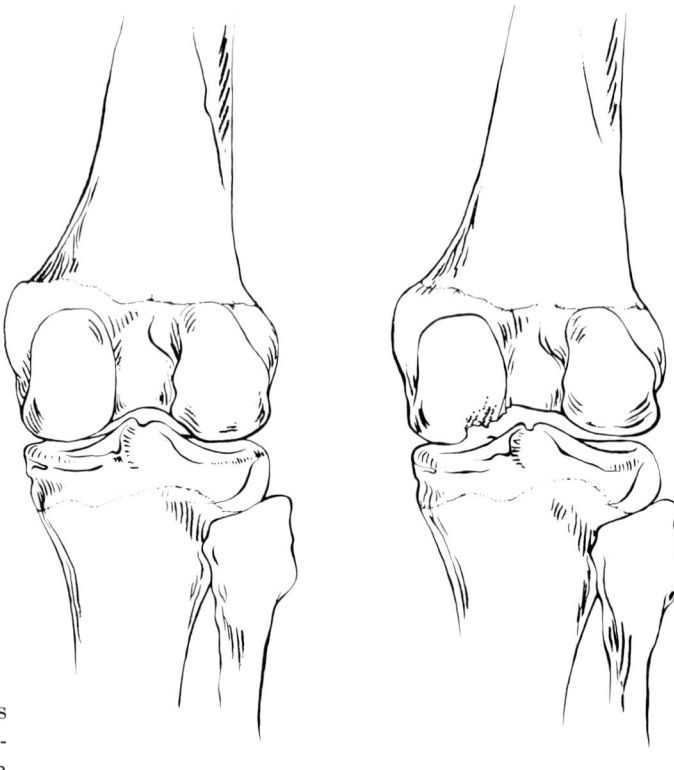

Fig. 24-4. Osteochondritis dissecans. This condition is most frequently found on the lateral aspect of the medial condyle of the thigh bone (femur).

NORMAL KNEE   **ABNORMAL KNEE**

breaking away of bone and cartilage from the joint surface, with the resulting formation of a loose body in the joint.

The diagnosis is made after a patient complains of pain in the joint and of occasional locking or giving way. Physical examination reveals no other cause, and x-rays show a characteristic irregularity of the bone just below the joint surface (Fig. 24-4). The knee joint is the most frequently noted site of this condition, but other joints, such as the elbow, ankle, and hip, have also been involved.

It is probable that several pathological conditions have been lumped together under this heading. They vary with the age of the patient and can be categorized as follows:

1. In children up to the age of 10, the formation of abnormal centers of ossification in the growth center of the bone gives rise to x-ray changes which have been called osteochondritis dissecans. Many of these lesions will heal spontaneously and are thought to be due to some developmental abnormality which, in many cases, may be hereditary.
2. In the adolescent, trauma producing a loss of blood supply to the bone just below the joint surface is thought to be the basic pathological condition for osteochondritis dissecans. Bone resorption occurs, and, without the underlying bony support, the overlying articular cartilage may break and become partially or completely dislodged into the joint space.
3. In the adult, a fracture through the articular cartilage and small portion of the underlying bone can produce x-ray findings identical to those noted above, as well as loose bodies within the joint.

Treatment depends upon the underlying condition and upon the extent of the lesion. If the child is young, and if the fragment of bone and cartilage is not separated, simple immobilization of the joint involved frequently results in healing of this lesion in 3 to 6 months. It has been stated that, after 16 years of age, these lesions seldom heal without some type of operative procedure. If the fragment has not completely detached itself, then drilling the bone and placing the articular cartilage back into its proper position is an acceptable form of treatment. If the fragment has already separated and is a small piece, however, then the loose body should be removed surgically from the joint and discarded. The underlying bone is drilled to stimulate the reparative process. If the fragment is a large piece of the weight-bearing portion of the joint, many surgeons are now replacing the articular cartilage and holding it in place with either a screw or pin after the underlying bone has been stimulated to produce healing. After the surgical procedure has been carried out and there is healing of bone, cartilage, and soft tissue, it is important that the musculature about the involved joint be redeveloped before the patient is allowed full use of the extremity.

The end result may be a perfectly normal joint. In some joints, however, there will be the formation of several loose bodies and, in some patients, the process may go on bilaterally, producing severe degenerative arthritis at an early age. Once the joints become irregular, it is important to pursue activities which spare these joints unnecessary trauma. Physical education will have to be restricted in these cases.

CHONDROMALACIA PATELLA

Chondromalacia (kon"-dro-ma-lay'-she-ah) *patella* literally means softening of the cartilage of the kneecap (Fig. 24-5). This is a frequent cause of pain and discomfort in the knee of the adolescent child and is diagnosed when pressure from the examining physician's hand on the kneecap produces a grating sensation as the kneecap rubs against the distal end of the thigh bone. Such an examination should reproduce the pain of which the patient complains. The diagnosis may be difficult to make and may require, in addition to x-ray studies, the insertion of a tube into the joint so that the cartilage may be seen directly (arthroscopy).

There are several causes for this condition. A direct blow to the kneecap can produce it. Almost any inflammatory disease process of the knee can likewise produce it, as the enzymes within the white blood cells in the fluid of the knee joint will cause a breakdown and softening of the cartilage on the underside of the kneecap. Improper tracking of the kneecap in the groove at the distal end of the thigh bone may likewise produce this condition over a long period of time.

Treatment consists of correcting the underlying condition that has caused the problem and increasing the nourishment to the cartilage so that it will heal itself. The articular cartilage of the kneecap is nourished by the fluid within the knee joint, not by blood vessels coming from the bone or soft tissues. To increase the nourishment to the cartilage, movement of the knee joint without undue pressure on the underside of the kneecap is advocated. Initial treatment includes straight leg-raising exercises and isometric tightening of the muscles attached to the kneecap. Later on, exercises such as bicycling are encouraged, progressing to resistive exercises of the muscles attached to the kneecap (quadriceps). Inflammatory conditions of the knee are of course treated by specific medicines and, occasionally, by surgery specific for the disease process.

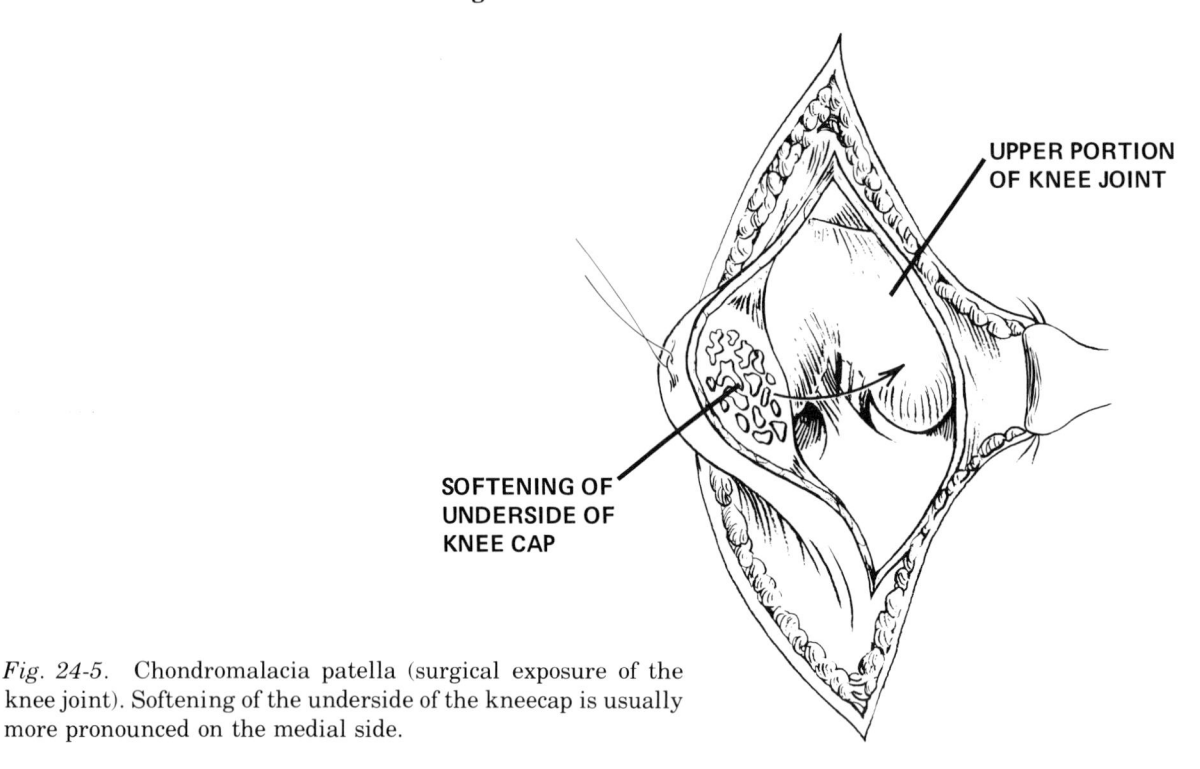

Fig. 24-5. Chondromalacia patella (surgical exposure of the knee joint). Softening of the underside of the kneecap is usually more pronounced on the medial side.

Aspirin in heavy doses is a nonspecific antiinflammatory drug and is used frequently for this condition. Occasionally, surgery to redirect the tracking of the patella in its groove at the knee joint is necessary. Such surgery usually requires a 6-week period of cast immobilization and exercises following this immobilization to strengthen the knee joint. Occasionally, none of these treatments solves the problem, and the underside of the kneecap is operated on or the entire kneecap is removed.

Schooling will be interrupted to varying degrees depending on the treatment undertaken for this condition. Special physical educational programs are helpful.

TORN CARTILAGES

Trauma to the knee joint is very common in young people, particularly those engaged in various athletic endeavors. Severe trauma can produce fractures of the bones or a separation of the growth plate from the end of the bone. It also can damage the ligaments about the knee joint and may cause injury to the wedge-shaped structures, called *cartilages* (menisci), between the articulating surfaces of the knee joint. Inadequate control of the musculature of the knee joint, such as might occur in a child with poliomyelitis or in a child who engages in vigorous sports without adequate training, will predispose the joint to injury. It is generally agreed that the mechanism of tears of the cartilages is one of rotation while the knee joint is partially flexed and then forcefully extended. The cartilage on the medial side of the knee joint is the more commonly injured (Fig. 24-6), and the basic rotational type of injury producing this tear is that encountered by a baseball player who places his right foot on the base and then rotates to the left and pushes off the base. Such a movement can produce a tear of the medial cartilage. The patient with a torn cartilage will complain of pain in the knee joint which is usually localized along the joint line, occasional giving way of the knee joint, and, some-

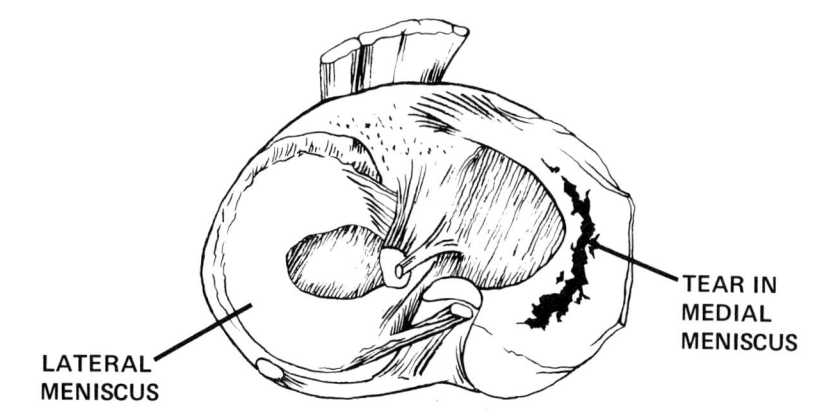

Fig. 24-6. Torn cartilage (lower portion of left knee joint seen on end). A tear in the middle of the cartilage will not heal, as there is no blood supply to this area.

times, locking of the knee joint so that it cannot be fully extended. This may or may not be associated with an effusion into the knee joint.

A torn cartilage may heal if the tear occurs in the portion of the cartilage located next to the joint capsule. The tear will probably never heal if it is in the substance of the cartilage, as this cartilage has no blood supply to bring about healing. Where there is some question about the diagnosis and the type of treatment to be undertaken, many physicians are now ordering special x-ray studies wherein a dye is injected into the knee joint before the x-rays are taken (arthrogram) or are looking at the joint through an arthroscope. The treating physician may choose to immobilize the patient's knee in a plaster cast or splint for a period of several weeks to allow a tear at the periphery of the menisci to heal if, indeed, it is torn at the periphery. If a longitudinal tear at a more central portion of the cartilage is the problem, then surgical removal of this cartilage is indicated. Following surgery, the patient needs to participate in an active rehabilitation program to strengthen the muscles about the knee. The knee should be as strong as the normal one before the child is allowed to return to competitive sports.

BIBLIOGRAPHY

Crenshaw, A. H., (ed.), Derangements of menisci, traumatic affections of joints, in *Campbell's Operative Orthopaedics*, vol. 1. St. Louis, C. V. Mosby, 1971, p. 907.

Outerbridge, R. E., The etiology of chondromalacia patellae, *Journal of Bone and Joint Surgery,* 43B:52, 1961.

Ponseti, I. V., and Cotton, R. L., Legg-Calve-Perthes disease: Pathogenesis and evolution. *Journal of Bone and Joint Surgery.* 43A:261, 1961.

Smillie, I. S., *Osteochondritis Dissecans.* London, E. and S. Livingstone, 1960.

Southwick, W. O., Osteotomy through the lesser trochanter for slipped capital femoral epiphysis. *Journal of Bone and Joint Surgery.* 49A:807–835, 1967.

Tachdjian, M. O., Osgood-Schlatter disease, in Tachdjian, M. O., *Pediatric Orthopaedics.* Philadelphia, W. B. Saunders, 1972, pp. 410–412.

25

Osteogenesis Imperfecta

EUGENE E. BLECK, M.D.

DEFINITION

Osteogenesis imperfecta (OI), (Os"-tee-oh-gen'-e-sis im"-per-fect'-ah) means imperfect bone formation. The common term is brittle bone disease, and, because the whites of the eyes almost always have a blue tint, some call it brittle bones and blue sclera.

CAUSES

The basic cause is unknown, but the condition is clearly inherited as a dominant trait in most children. Cases also appear without any clearcut history, apparently due to a spontaneous change in the genes (mutation). Males and females are equally affected, and no racial predominance is evident. OI has been described in Europeans, Jews, Japanese, Chinese, American Blacks, Indians, Egyptians, and Russians.

BASIC DEFECT

The basic defect appears to be in the protein matrix (collagen fibers) of the bone. In OI, the collagen fibers are in a feltlike mesh, rather than in the normal, linear arrangement. In many ways, the bone in OI is much like that observed in the developing fetus—i.e., it is immature. Because the protein matrix is deficient, the total amount of bone salts (calcium and phosphorus) is reduced, even though there is no basic defect and in calcification mechanism. The bones, then, are weak in structure, and the collagen of all tissues is immature, resulting in greater elasticity of the tissues, such as the joint ligaments and skin. The white of the eye (sclera), which also is collagen, becomes thin, the underlying layer of the eyeball (choroid) showing through as a blue discoloration.

SIGNS AND SYMPTOMS

Two types of OI are recognized: OI congenita (onset at birth) and OI tarda (late onset). In *OI congenita* the baby is born with short, deformed limbs, numerous broken bones, and a very soft skull. Some of these infants die at birth and others will survive only a short time. By contrast, in *OI tarda* the condition becomes evident only later in life and is usually mild; at times, the blue whites of the eyes may be the only sign.

The effects of the basic defect in OI congenita on various organ systems are as follows:

Bones and joints. The skull bones are soft at first. As the child grows, the forehead broadens and the temples bulge. The face is triangular. The facial appearance is so characteristic that relatives who have had the condition may be recognized by their photographs (Fig. 25-1).

All the limbs are small (micromelia) and are bowed in various contortions due to repetitive fractures and healing in the deformed position. Outward bowing of the thigh bones (femur) and forward bowing of the leg bones (tibia—saber shins) are the usual deformity. X-rays show crooked bones that have thin outer shells (cortices) and decreased whiteness or density (osteoporosis) (Fig. 25-2).

The chest is like a beehive: barrel-shaped with forward protrusion of the breast bone. The spine is rounded backward and often curved (scoliosis). The teeth are usually in poor condition: easily broken, prone to cavities, and often discolored.

The joints are excessively mobile. The thumb can be bent back to almost touch the forearm (so-called "double-jointedness" is, in reality, excessive mobility or laxity of the joints).

Eye. Blue sclera have been mentioned. Because of the great variability in severity of the disease, not all cases have definite, robin's-egg-blue sclera. An opacity at the periphery of the cornea is very frequent.

Skin. Because of the basic protein defect (collagen), it is not surprising that the skin is thin (atrophic) and sometimes appears translucent.

Ear. Deafness due to a bone defect of the inner-ear ossicles is common and, clinically, is no different than that seen in adult otosclerosis. Constant ringing of the ears (tinnitus) and dizziness (vertigo) are sometimes present.

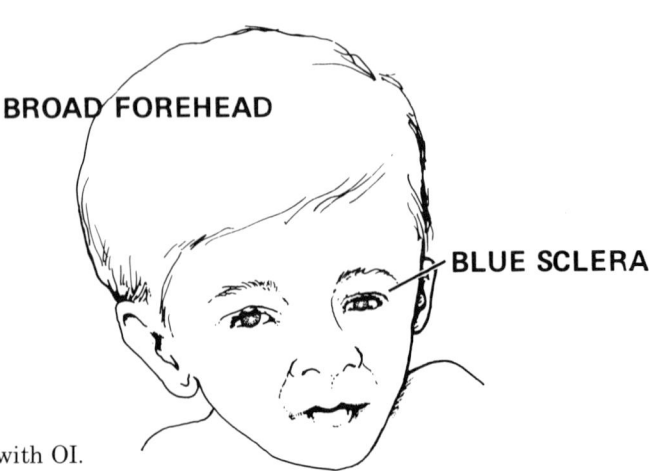

Fig. 25-1. Typical facial appearance of a child with OI.

Fig. 25-2. Drawing of a child with OI. Note the curved limb bones and gross deformities. The chest is frequently barrel-shaped.

PROGNOSIS

The child with OI congenita becomes the adult with OI. As long as there is no cure for the condition, a disease-oriented approach will fail. We therefore prefer a function-oriented approach, designed to achieve the goals of mobility and maximum self-care.

TREATMENT

No known food or chemical has been found to alter the disease favorably. Magnesium oxide taken orally has had a recent extensive trial. This chemical has changed some of the blood chemistry having to do with calcification (serum pyrophosphates) and has alleviated constipation and excessive sweating in children who had these complaints. Whether the fracture rate has been reduced by the chemical is an unanswered question, however.

In order to break the cycle of fracture–immobilization–osteoporosis–refracture (Fig. 25-3), we have used stressing the bone by weight-bearing to overcome osteoporosis and to maintain the strength of the bone structure. In this scheme, surgery to correct bone deformities is an established procedure. (Fig. 25-4). The entire shaft of the bone is removed, cut into pieces, and then threaded onto a steel rod that is inserted between the ends of the long bones.

After the bone heals, plastic braces (orthoses) are used to protect the bones from refracture and to allow earlier weight bearing. In the lower limb, these braces can protect the knee, ankle, foot (KAFO, or knee-ankle-foot orthosis), and, in some cases, the hip as well (HKAFO, or hip-knee-ankle-foot orthosis).

Weight bearing can be instituted utilizing walkers which provide external support for the child (e.g., Stanford weight-relieving walker). Eventually, the child may be able to use crutches. Rarely, however, do

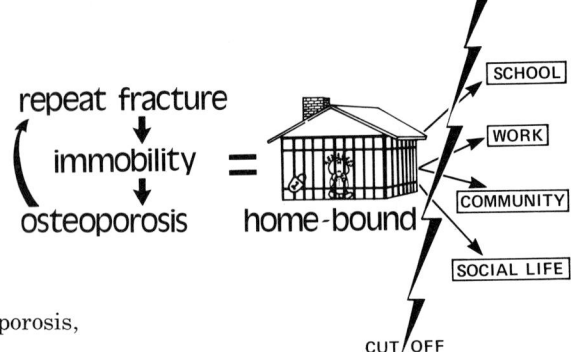

Fig. 25-3. Vicious cycle of fracture, immobility, osteoporosis, and repeat fracture keeps the child home-bound.

such children and adults become sufficiently functional in walking to do more than get around the house (household walker).

The management scheme is graphically depicted in Figure 25-5. In this scheme, which begins in infancy, compensatory equipment is used to permit the child a level of functioning and mobility consistent with the developmental level expected for his age. As the child matures, mobility in the community becomes essential for complete social integration. Powered wheelchairs permit effective neighborhood mobility, but, for total community participation, special motor vans with appropriate ramps and hand controls for driving are the most practical solution. (Fig. 25-6).

EDUCATIONAL IMPLICATIONS

OI children have normal intelligence. They are usually highly verbal, learn easily, and are a joy to the teacher. Certainly, given the appropriate mobility equipment and the ability to transfer out of their wheelchairs for toileting, integration into regular school should be no problem.

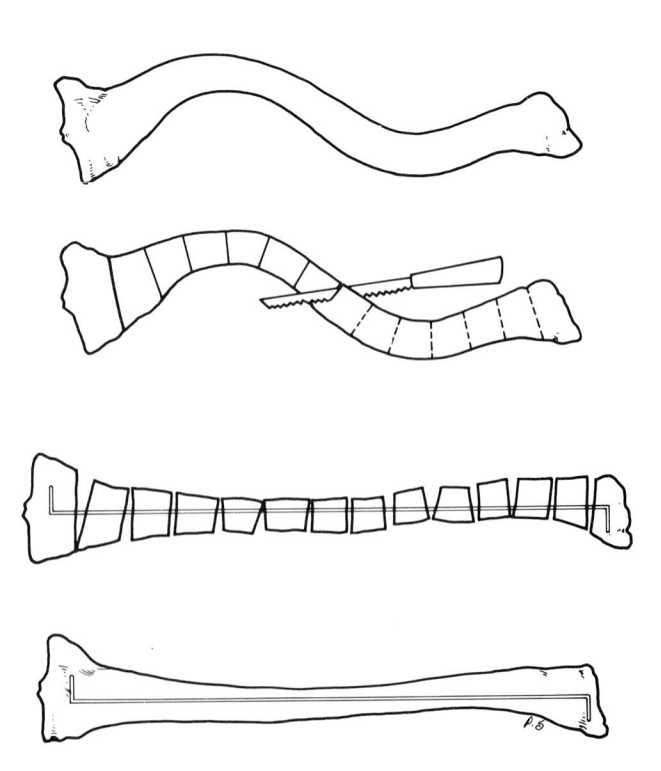

Fig. 25-4. Surgical method of straightening the crooked bones in OI. The shaft of the bone is removed and cut into pieces; the pieces are then rethreaded onto a rod inside the bony canal. Bone healing occurs and a reasonably straight bone results.

Osteogenesis Imperfecta

NORMAL MILESTONES WITHOUT AIDS

MILESTONES ACHIEVED WITH AIDS

Fig. 25-5. Graphic depiction of normal developmental milestones (*top*) and equipment that may be used to compensate for the lack of such milestones in the child with OI congenita (*bottom*). This is a program designed to match the normal child's motor development. (Adapted from Wallace Motloch, C.O., Rehabilitation Engineering Center, Children's Hospital at Stanford, Palo Alto, Calif.)

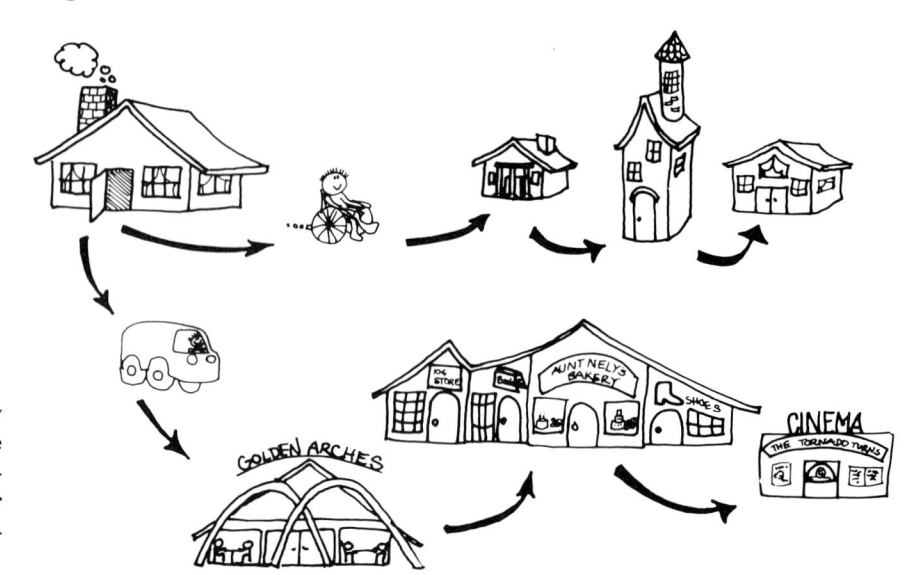

Fig. 25-6. For mobility in the neighborhood the wheelchair is quite satisfactory, but for the larger community a van is essential.

Hearing disorders are not common until the child ages. Conductive hearing loss may not occur until over the age of 20 years. Increased perspiration is a common symptom of OI. It is necessary that this be recognized and that the child avoid being exposed in the classroom to temperatures above 68–72°F. Constipation can be a persistent problem for the child, but possibly a boon for the teacher, as there is no need for a long toilet break.

The long-term goal should be toward academic achievement and toward more sedentary, intellectually demanding occupations. Physical education is out of the question. Skill in social games (chess or bridge, for example) ought to be encouraged. Musical talent might be ascertained and developed with instruments such as the violin, harmonica, or perhaps the banjo, ukulele, or concertina. Such measures help prepare the child for adult life and help him develop acceptable, and desirable, relationships with normal children, adolescents, and adults.

As the child grows older, the condition frequently stabilizes. Fewer fractures occur, and the need for a sheltered school situation diminishes (particularly once the long bones have been rodded). At this juncture, attendance at a regular school program with normal children should be encouraged.

BIBLIOGRAPHY

McKusick, V. A., *Heritable Disorders of Connective Tissue*. St. Louis, C. V. Mosby, 1966.

Tachdjian, M. O., *Pediatric Orthopaedics*. Philadelphia, W. B. Saunders, 1973.

READING MATERIALS AVAILABLE FROM OIF*

General Materials and Reprints from *Breakthrough*

Baxter, G., *A Study of Academic Achievement and Educational Experience of Children with Osteogenesis Imperfecta.*

Breakthrough. Quarterly publication and means of official communication with OIF membership. Back issues are available.

*Osteogenesis Imperfecta Foundation, Inc., (OIF), Gemma Geisman, Executive Director, 632 Center Street, Van Wert, Ohio 45891

Dubowski, F. M., *Care of an Osteogenesis Imperfecta Baby and Child* (Manual).
Gardner, D., *Auto Hand Controls*. Information on hand controls for cars and instructions for a booster seat.
Gardner, R., The heart of school adjustment. Reprinted from *Breakthrough* 1(2), 1970.
I Have Osteogenesis Imperfecta but CAN.... (Brochure). Summaries telling of the happy and productive lives led by sixteen adult OI congenita persons.
Kasper, R., Home tutoring: An educational barrier. Reprinted from *Breakthrough* 5(1), 1975.
Klapperich, C., A positive approach to controlling OI. Reprinted from *Breakthrough* 4(2), 1974. Article on genetics involved in OI.
Millar, E. A., An explanation of "rodding" surgery. Reprinted from *Breakthrough* 4(2), 1974.
Ott, J. E., Questions frequently asked about OI, Parts 1 and 2. Reprinted from *Breakthrough* 2(2,3), 1971.
Parents want to know. Reprinted from *Breakthrough* 1(2), 1970. An article dealing with various forms of education for a handicapped individual.
Parker, J., Get behind the wheel. Reprinted from *Breakthrough* 3(2), 1973. An article by an OI congenita patient on driving.
Shriners' Hospitals, *Questions Frequently Asked about OI*. Questions and answers concerning treatment provided by Shriners and how a child can qualify for treatment. For parents only, on request.

Speeches Delivered to OIF Chapters

Bleck, E. E., *Mobility Management of Osteogenesis Imperfecta*. Transcript of an address to the Arkansas chapter, December 1976.
Castells, S., *The Administration of Calcitonin to Infants and Young OI Children*. Delivered to the New York chapter, June 1975.
Levin, L. S., *The Teeth in OI*. Delivered to the Philadelphia chapter, February, 1977.
Solomons, C. C., *Recent Research and Implications for Treatment of Osteogenesis Imperfecta*. Delivered to Arkansas chapter, October 1975.

Magazine and News Articles

Care corner. Reprinted from *Even Break*, September 1977. (Magazine published by the Australian Osteogenesis Imperfecta Foundation.) This article provides practical suggestions for caring for an OI patient.
Geisman, G., Epilogue to a dream. Reprinted from *Redbook Magazine*, March 1970. This article is about the first OI clinic and the parents whose communication soom led to the organization of the OIF, Inc.
Geisman, G., A miracle for Mike. Reprinted from *The Annals of Good St. Anne de Beaupre* February 1967, pp. 59–60. This article concerns a mother's struggle and final acceptance of OI in her child.
Geisman, G., My prison of dreams. Reprinted from *Redbook Magazine*, March 1968. This article is about the frustrations and emotional reactions of a mother as she copes with the daily problems of having a child with OI.
Geisman, G., Osteogenesis Imperfecta Foundation. Reprinted from *The Exceptional Parent*, January/February 1974, pp. 22–23. This article provides information concerning OI and the OIF, Inc.
Geisman, G., We had a breakable baby. Reprinted from *Ladies Home Companion*, February 1964. This is an article concerning the problems and fears of parents in coping with an OI baby.

How to distinguish between child abuse and OI. Reprinted from *Even Break*, September 1977.

Kenihan, K., Must fractured bones mean broken hearts. Reprinted from *Even Break*, September 1977. This article takes a realistic look at some of the problems encountered by OI parents.

Newsletter article reprints on OI persons and OIF, Inc.

26

Traumatic Paraplegia and Quadriplegia

DONALD A. NAGEL, M.D.

The word *paraplegia,* according to *Dorland's Medical Dictionary* means "paralysis of the legs and lower part of the body, both motion and sensation being affected." *Quadriplegia* means paralysis of all four limbs. These conditions, broadly speaking, could be caused by congenital abnormalities, infections, tumors, or chemicals, as well as by injury (trauma). Traumatic paraplegia and quadriplegia are the subject of this chapter.

There are many causes of traumatic paraplegia and quadriplegia. Birth injuries can produce it; accidents about the home or school, which would include falls from a height, can produce it; and bullet wounds, sports injuries, and injuries from motor vehicle accidents can produce it. Of all of these, motor vehicle accidents are perhaps the most frequent cause. As younger people are increasing their exposure with high-speed bicycles, motor-driven bicycles, motorcycles, and sports cars, it is anticipated that the number of children who have traumatic paraplegia and quadriplegia will increase.

From ancient times this injury has been noted as one of the most devastating. It is frequently associated with fractures of the bones of the spinal column—but not always; the spinal cord can also be damaged by dislocation of one bone upon the other, without any signs of fracture (Fig. 26-1); and there also are many fractures of the back (spine) that do not damage the spinal cord. The paralysis is caused by an interruption of the nerves and pathways going from the brain to the involved limbs. These pathways are located in the spinal cord, which passes through the bones (vertebrae) that comprise the spinal column (Fig. 26-2). The function of

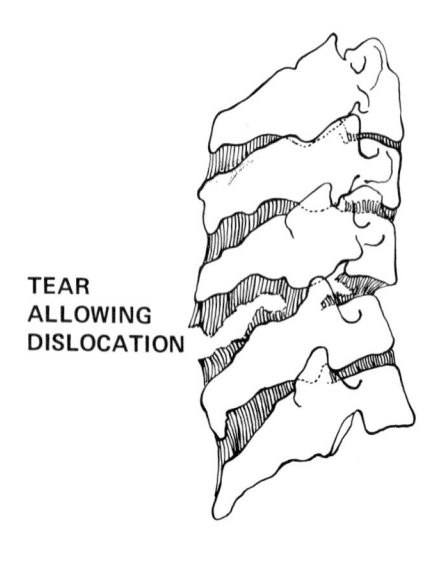

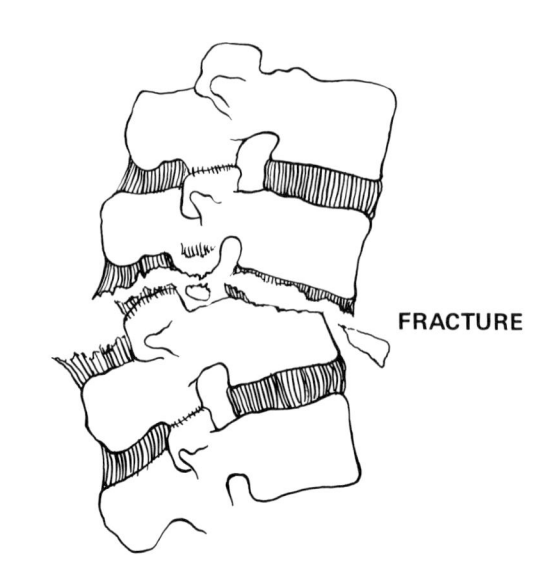

Fig. 26-1. Injuries to the spinal column. Dislocation and fracture dislocation of the spinal column may or may not cause serious injury to the spinal cord.

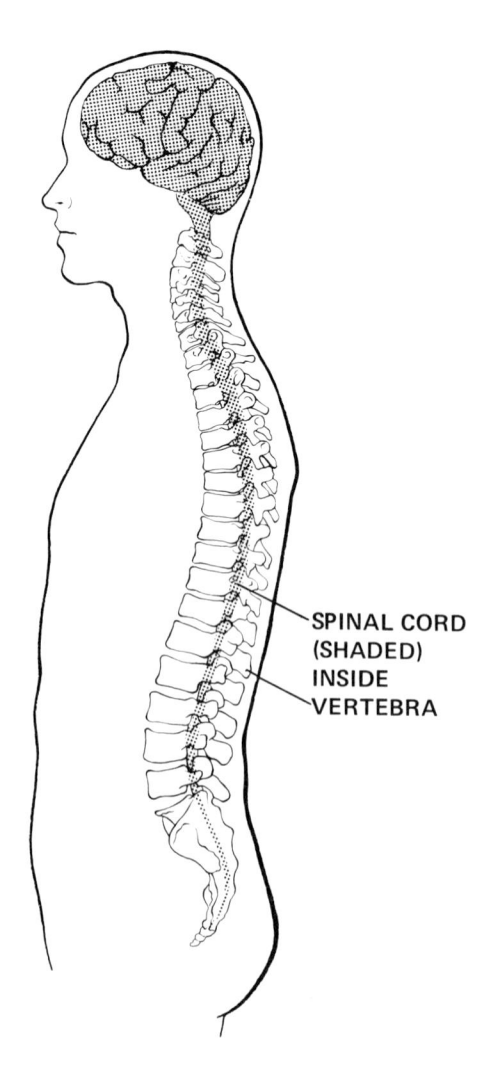

Fig. 26-2. Normal spinal column and spinal cord. The spinal column is composed of 7 cervical, 12 thoracic, 5 lumbar, and 5 fused sacral vertebrae through which the spinal cord and its branches pass.

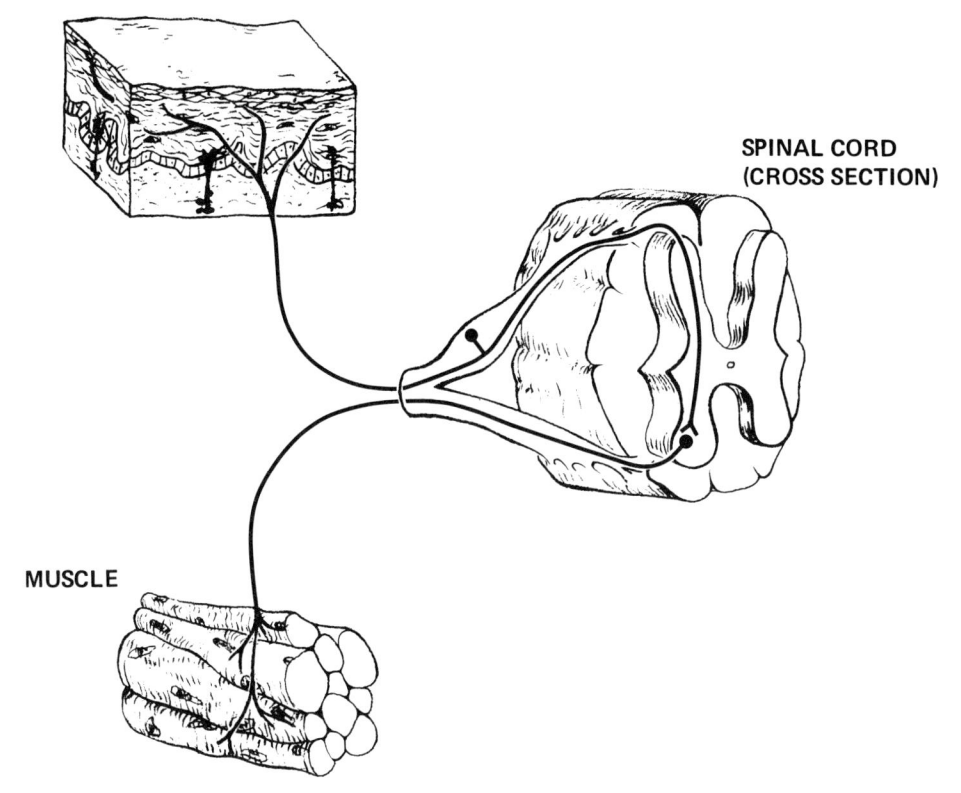

Fig. 26-3. Nerve pathway. Sensory nerves bring impulses into the cord, where they can be transmitted to the brain, and motor nerves carry impulses from the cord (and brain) to various muscles.

these pathways may be disturbed because of pressure exerted on the spinal cord by bony fragments or, in rare instances, soft tissue from the cushions (discs) between the vertebrae. If the pressure can be removed quickly enough and the blood supply to this area restored, then occasionally the nerves will begin to function again. Spinal cord pathways that have been completely torn apart by the injury will not regrow with our present repair techniques, however, and the resulting paralysis will be permanent. Research is ongoing in this area, and hopefully the future will hold discoveries that will allow us to repair these injuries successfully. Nerves located *outside* the spinal cord, which either bring impulses from the skin or carry impulses to muscles from the spinal cord, can be successfully repaired (Fig. 26-3).

ACUTE CARE

The handling of the patient with an injured spinal cord immediately following the injury can, in some cases, make the difference between an incomplete injury, which may recover, and a complete injury, which will not. Injured athletes or persons injured in a motor vehicle accident who are conscious but complain of being unable to move their limbs very well, or note an electric type of pain shooting into their limbs, should *not* be moved until they can be moved by people who have been trained to take care of such injuries. Such patients should be moved on a board that has attachments to fasten the head and body so that the head will not rotate in the process of moving. These patients must not be allowed to sit or to have their heads elevated to take a drink, and they must not be allowed to walk, even though they desire to. If transportation cannot be arranged quickly, patients who have little or no sensation and no motion in their extremities should be protected from shock.

Once these patients have reached a hospital, they should be placed in the hands of a physician knowledgeable in the care of such injuries. The patient's injured spine should be protected during the process of obtaining x-rays. Treatment will be based on the history, physical examination, and the x-ray findings. In injuries to the neck, tongs are usually placed into the skull so that traction can be applied to bring about a reduction or a realignment of the fractured bones. Injuries to the spine at the chest and at the abdominal level are usually cared for in special beds. Rubber tubes (catheters) are inserted into the bladder to allow drainage of urine, and care is given to see that the patient continues to have bowel movements. Of special importance is frequent turning so that the skin does not break down. There is some disagreement as to whether or not operations should be done on patients who have complete paralysis and loss of all nervous functions below the level of the injury. There is uniform agreement, however, that if the patient has some neurologic function, and if this diminishes during observation, the patient should have an operation. The operation usually consists of a decompression of the spinal cord, and may, in addition, be accompanied by a spine fusion. Depending upon the type of spine fusion, the patient will have to be immobilized in some type of device while the fusion becomes firm. This will take 6 weeks or longer.

REHABILITATION

Rehabilitation should begin shortly after injury. Perhaps the most important aspect of this is the patient's morale. Generally speaking, patients who develop traumatic paraplegia and quadriplegia have been active individuals. They should be encouraged to continue in their active approach to life. The seriousness of their injuries should not be ignored, but the fact that the personality of the individual and his or her mind are more important than any physical loss should be stressed. Patients should be encouraged to set goals for themselves, such as self-care and locomotion. If they can be treated in a spinal cord injury unit, where the personnel are geared to handling the problems of this type of patient and where the patients can see other people with problems as serious as theirs who are making progress towards their goals, then they will be encouraged.

Patients who are quadriplegic will have to set lower goals for themselves than patients who have the use of their arms. Nevertheless, such patients should be able to feed themselves with the assistance of various special devices, and locomotion should be possible, at least with a motorized wheelchair.

Paraplegic patients, in addition to being able to feed themselves, should learn to take care of their bladder and bowel functions. Many paraplegic patients develop some control of their bladder without the insertion of a tube. This involves the use of their hands on their abdomen to push out the urine. Male paraplegic patients will require the use of a urinal, and females generally use pads with special types of pants. The bowels are usually easier to regulate than the bladder; this is accomplished by means of suppositories or enemas. Even when the level of the spinal cord injury is high, paraplegic patients should at least be instructed in the use of crutches for ambulation. They may later choose to use the wheelchair as their primary means of locomotion, but if they have

Traumatic Paraplegia and Quadriplegia

the option of using crutches in particularly difficult situations, they will be better able to cope with their environment. Paraplegic patients will be taught a swing-to or a swing-through type of crutch walking and will be fitted with long-leg braces.

A major step in patients' rehabilitation occurs when they leave the hospital to return home; yet another occurs when they return to school. Patients must be accepted in each of these situations as individuals, and at times this will be quite awkward for patients, as well as family, teachers, and friends. They must be encouraged to take the positive approach—to seek out new friends and experiences and to develop their minds to the fullest so that they can become self-supporting in the future. Literature is available for these young people (some is listed at the end of this chapter), and, in many areas, associations of patients who are paraplegic and quadriplegic have been formed. There are, in fact, international wheelchair olympic games (Fig. 26-4), and young athletes might be encouraged to join organizations that participate in such activities.

There are problems to be faced and adjustments for family and teachers to make. Specifically, patients will need more time than the average for self-care and for attention to their bladder, bowels, and skin. They will probably need a special bed, wheelchair, and braces. Other assistant devices will be necessary. Patients should be encouraged to care for themselves as much as is physically possible and should not allow themselves to become dependent and depressed. They should seek guidance in vocational planning and training so that the employment that they plan for is obtainable for them. They should remain in close contact with the physician, who understands their problems completely. Urinalysis should be performed at least monthly, and x-rays should be taken yearly to evaluate the possibility of kidney-stone formation. In contradis-

Fig. 26-4. Wheelchair games. Games are important to some paraplegic patients.

tinction to adults, younger patients may develop deformities in the spine and in the extremities if they have asymmetrical muscle pull. Many patients with quadriplegia and paraplegia develop pain and muscle spasm. Various new medications are becoming available almost monthly. If these do not solve the problem, then neurosurgical consultation should be obtained to evaluate the possibilities of removal of scar from around the traumatized area or of other neurosurgical procedures to eliminate the pain.

One of the most important decisions that patients will make is what vocation to pursue. Patients who can become self-supporting are well on the way to an independent, fruitful life. It is recommended that each individual work closely with a vocational counselor and read the *Handbook for Paraplegics and Quadriplegics*. The following is quoted from the Handbook with the author's permission:

> Among some of the jobs or businesses that paraplegics and quadriplegics have successfully had are as follows: switchboard operator, secretary, salesman, teacher, watch repairer, jewelry designer and repairer, woodworkers, artist, bookstore operator, accountant, office manager, lawyer, doctor, physical therapist, architect, publicity man, actors, disk jockey, book reviewers, copy readers, writers, mail order businesses, stationery and greeting-card store, gift store, magazine agency, florist, weaving, hydroponic farming, statistician, IBM operator, Comptometer operator, plastics manufacturer, electrical assemblers, radio and TV repair, wheelchair repair, civil service, sewing machine operator, embroidery, leathercraft, photography, bookbinding, hobby shop, philatelist, real estate, phone solicitation, answering service, addressing envelopes, advertising, taxidermist, research worker, clipping service, designers, draftsman, and many others. These jobs and businesses are not conjecture, in each case at least one paraplegic or quadriplegic has worked or is working in the classification. If anything about them should impress you, it should be the variety of employment.

Setting realistic vocational goals and then setting about their achievement with determination should make living a successful adventure.

BIBLIOGRAPHY

Department of Health, Education and Welfare, *What You Should Know About Paraplegia*. Publication No. SRS-RSA-119-70. Washington, D. C., Government Printing Office, 1970.

Department of Health, Education and Welfare, *Spinal Cord Injury—Hope Through Research*. PH Service Publication No. 1747. Bethesda, Md., National Institute of Neurological Diseases and Stroke, National Institutes of Health, 1968.

Frost, A., *Handbook for Paraplegics and Quadriplegics*. Chicago, National Paraplegia Foundation, 1964.

National Paraplegia Foundation, *How to Get Help If You Are Paralyzed*. Chicago, National Paraplegia Foundation.

Norton, P. L., and Foley, J. J., Paraplegia in children. *Journal of Bone and Joint Surgery* 41A:1291, 1959.

27

Poliomyelitis

EUGENE E. BLECK, M.D.

DEFINITION

Poliomyelitis is a viral infection of the motor cells in the spinal cord (anterior horn cells, Fig. 27-1). The virus enters by way of the intestinal tract, travels through the bloodstream (hematogenous spread), and settles in the motor cells of the spinal cord. The effect is to knock out the function of these cells that control muscular contraction, and a lack of movement results (flaccid paralysis). If the infection has caused only a swelling of the cells and their supporting tissues (glial cells), then recovery follows. If the cells themselves are destroyed by the virus, however, no recovery takes place and the paralysis is permanent. About 18 months should elapse before a judgement is made as to the permanence of the paralysis.

SIGNS, SYMPTOMS, AND CLINICAL COURSE

Present at the onset are fever, painful muscle spasm, and inability to move an involved muscle, or an entire limb. The acute process then subsides, leaving the residual paralysis.

The pattern of paralysis varies a great deal because the damage to the spinal cord motor cells can be very spotty. Some muscles are completely out, whereas others are only weakened. Muscle-strength testing has been standardized, and a good muscle test by a physical therapist can give a mental picture of the child's disability.

Children who are in schools for the orthopedically handicapped will, for the most part, have moderate to severe residual paralysis of the lower limb and, at times, the trunk. They may need to walk with crutches or

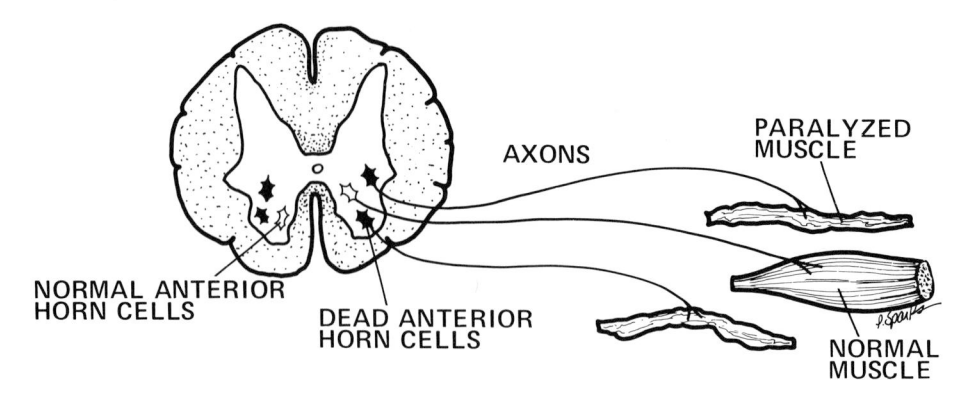

Fig. 27-1. Cross section of the spinal cord. The normal neurons (*anterior horn cells*), which send impulses from the brain to the muscles, are depicted in white. The dead anterior horn cells, which have been destroyed by the poliomyelitis virus, are black. Each nerve cell has an axon to the muscle; when the nerve cell dies, the muscle fiber dies also.

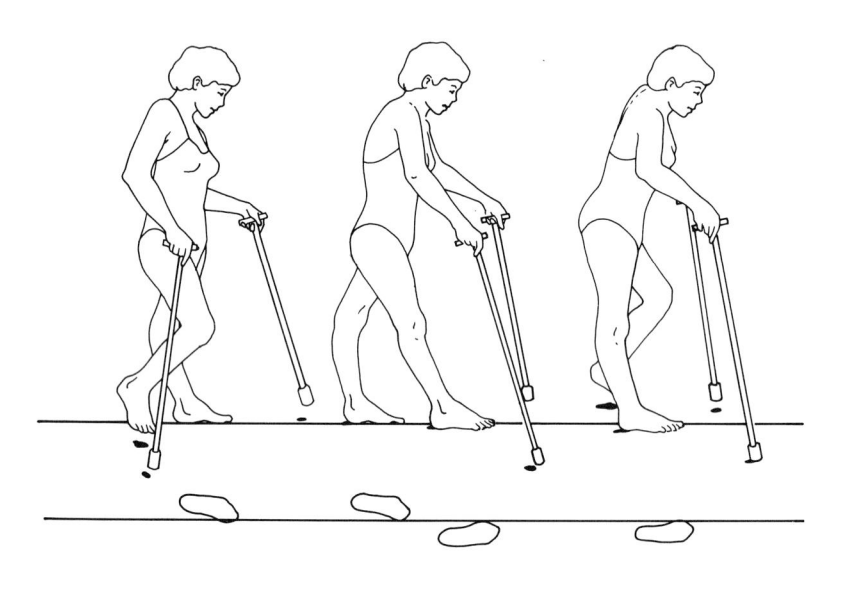

Fig. 27-2. The typical gait of a child with a flaccid paralysis of the lower limbs due to poliomyelitis. Walking sticks or crutches are necessary to support the lower limbs and trunk if the hip muscles are weakened. (Redrawn from Ducroquret, R., Ducroquret, J., and Ducroquret, P., *Walking and Limping,* Philadelphia, Lippincott, 1968.)

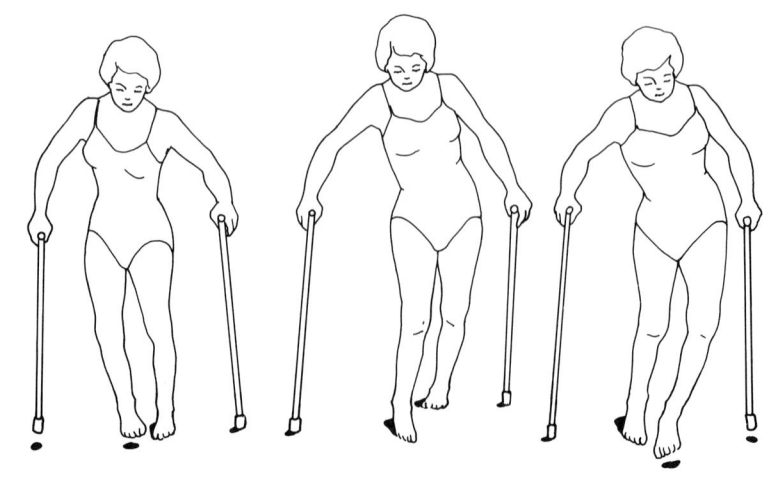

Poliomyelitis

canes (Fig. 27-2) and will have a limp or joint deformities, depending upon the location and inequality of the muscle weakness.

Spinal curvature (paralytic scoliosis) can be severe, particularly with trunk paralysis. Such children may be wheelchair users except for transfers in and out of the chair. The intellect, bladder, bowels, and sensation are unaffected by the virus. Consequently, the handicap is confined to only the neuromuscular system.

INCIDENCE

Due to widespread use of the polio vaccines, this type of paralysis is infrequent in children in handicapped children's schools. A few sporadic cases occur. Those who have only a single involved limb, although handicapped, can usually fit into a regular school program—with appropriate allowances made for physical education requirements.

TREATMENT

Treatment at the time of the acute phase is bed rest, passive movement of the paralyzed limbs, hot pack for the muscles in spasm, and splinting of the limbs to prevent deformity.

After the acute phase has passed, the therapist gives muscle reeducation and active and resistive exercise to the weakened muscles. Braces are used to support weakened joints, especially the knee and ankle. The therapist also teaches crutch walking or wheelchair use, if necessary, and how to manage transfers to and from the chair.

As the child grows, deformities of the feet, knees, and hips may develop. Orthopedic surgery to prevent or correct these deformities by tendon transfer or bone operations may be performed.

Spinal curvature due to poliomyelitis often does not respond to

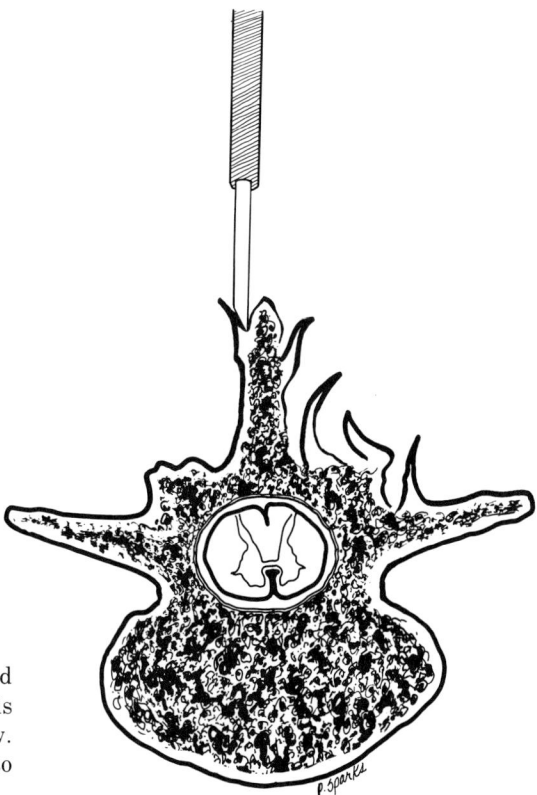

Fig. 27-3. Cross section of a vertebral body showing method of spinal fusion. The hard, outer portion of the bone (cortex) is chiseled away to expose the spongy, bleeding bone below. This induces new bone formation and allows one vertebra to fuse to the other.

braces. Plaster casts and operative correction are usual. Whatever method of correction is chosen (e.g., halo traction and Harrington instrumentation), spinal fusion is always included. By spinal fusion we mean that the bones on the back of the spine (spinous processes, lamina, and joints) are stripped bare, the hard surface of the bone (cortex) is removed to expose spongy bone, and then bone chips and additional bone grafts are put into this "bed" of raw bone (Fig. 27-3). New bone then forms into a solid mass. The entire fusion will not be completely solid for about 9 months. During this period, the child may have to remain in bed from 3 to 6 months and will most certainly be in a plaster body cast for 6 to 9 months. At times, the halo traction on the head is kept on with a cast so that the child can resume sitting rather early after spine fusion. A new method of spinal fixation devised by Edwardo Luque, M.D., of Mexico City—segmental spinal instrumentation—appears to allow earlier sitting and mobilization while fusion occurs and often eliminates the use of a plaster body cast.

EDUCATIONAL IMPLICATIONS

Inasmuch as the intellect is spared and the IQ distribution among these children will be the same as the bell curve for the general population, learning as such should present no problem.

If the child has total or partial upper-limb paralysis, however, compensatory methods and adaptive equipment for doing his paper work and for studying may be necessary, (e.g., electric typewriters and their adaptations, cassette tape recorders for long oral reports, or thicker pen or pencil handles to compensate for a weak pinch).

The child with partial or complete lower-limb paralysis should have playground activities adjusted to his handicap. Each child should be judged separately, according to the extent of paralysis and weakness and his actual level of function. Children who have extensive lower-limb paralysis, and who are really more functional sitting, ought to learn social games, such as chess or bridge, and might be encouraged to learn a musical instrument. Such children should be directed toward a vocation that will not require physical agility or stamina. Their prospects for independence in adult life are excellent compared with children who have cerebral palsy or myelomeningocele. President Franklin D. Roosevelt is an example of a severely handicapped adult who, without a doubt, achieved the most distinguished position of service in our country. Roosevelt had complete paralysis of both lower limbs, wore long-leg braces, walked little, spent much time in his wheelchair, and had a hand-controlled Ford convertible that he loved to drive on the red, dusty roads surrounding his country White House at Warm Springs, Georgia. The average citizen was completely unaware that their President had a handicap of this severity. It is obvious that his compensation for it was optimum and an example for all.

BIBLIOGRAPHY

Crenshaw, A. H., *Campbells Operative Orthopedics*. St. Louis, C. V. Mosby, 1963.
Tachdjian, M. O. *Pediatric Orthopedics*. Philadelphia, W. B. Saunders, 1972.

28

Juvenile Rheumatoid Arthritis

JOHN J. MILLER, III, M.D., PH.D.

Juvenile rheumatoid arthritis is a term used in the United States to refer to a group of diseases characterized by chronic arthritis of unknown cause. In England, *juvenile chronic polyarthritis* is the preferred term. Estimates of the number of children with these diseases in the United States vary from 30,000 to 250,000. It may occur in infants as young as 6 weeks of age. The most favored current hypothesis regarding cause is that the inflammation of joints results from an immunologic attack against normal body materials. In this type of disease, often referred to as *auto-immune,* we can identify abnormal antibodies—proteins circulating in the blood which usually destroy bacteria, viruses, and other foreign materials but which, in this instance, are directed against the body's own components. We do not know what causes these abnormal antibodies to appear. They are certainly not related to peculiarities of climate, diet, or patterns of living, as is often thought by patients or parents. They may be the result of an acute or chronic infection which is too subtle for us to detect. Occasionally, these diseases occur in several members of one family, but this is unusual. They are not considered inherited in the usual sense.

There are important differences between rheumatoid arthritis in adults and in children. The most important is that 60–70 percent of children will be free of active disease after a period of 10 years, whereas only 20 percent of adults have permanent remissions. The length of time that any given child will remain ill is unpredictable and will vary from months to years. All therapy must be performed with the assumption that a permanent remission will occur. Even when the disease simmers on into adulthood, the patients appear to function more productively than those who have onset of their disease as adults. With good care, less than 20 percent of children should be left with real functional limitations. The diseases in children have a much more variable presentation than rheumatoid arthritis in adults, and diagnosis is often difficult and delayed. The abnormal antibody most characteristic of adult rheumatoid arthritis, "rheumatoid factor," is not usually found in children. Children frequently have rash and fever, which adults do not have. Serious systemic effects on heart and lungs, not uncommon in adults, are only rarely seen in children.

THE THREE TYPES OF JUVENILE RHEUMATOID ARTHRITIS

Systemic

This type of juvenile rheumatoid arthritis probably affects 20 percent of patients or fewer. These children have high, "spiking" fevers once or twice a day, visibly enlarged lymph nodes, large spleens, a rapidly changing flat pink rash, and generalized malaise and fatigue. Laboratory tests show them to be anemic and to have high white blood cell counts and sedimentation rates, nonspecific indications of severe inflammation. When their temperature is high, up to 105' or 106°F, they look very ill indeed, but when their temperature falls a few hours later, down to 97° or 96°F, they look quite well. The arthritis seems a minor part of their illness, and, indeed, may not even appear for months after the onset of other symptoms. These children usually have to be admitted to hospital at first to rule out serious infections or cancer. The diagnosis is only established by the passage of time, unless someone with experience can identify the characteristic rash and fever patterns and the eventual appearance of arthritis. Attacks may last for months, disappear, and then reappear months or years later. The long-term outlook for these children is good, but about half will go on to develop polyarticular arthritis.

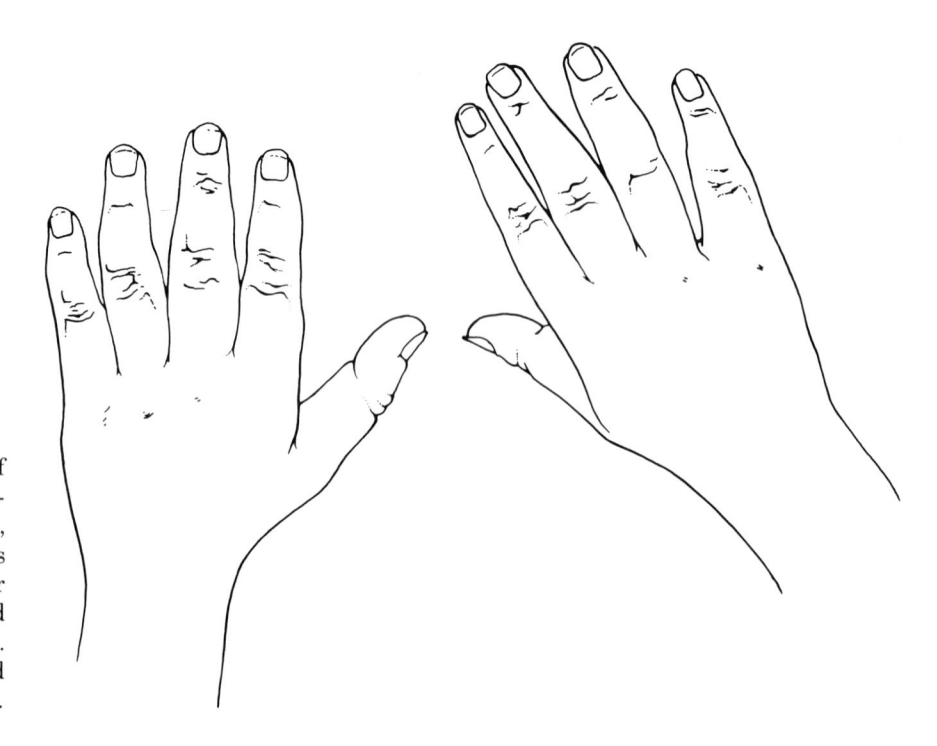

Fig. 28-1. The fingers of children with arthritis become fusiform in shape, with fat central portions around the swollen near (proximal) joint and pointed toward the tips. The joint farthest toward the tip is rarely involved.

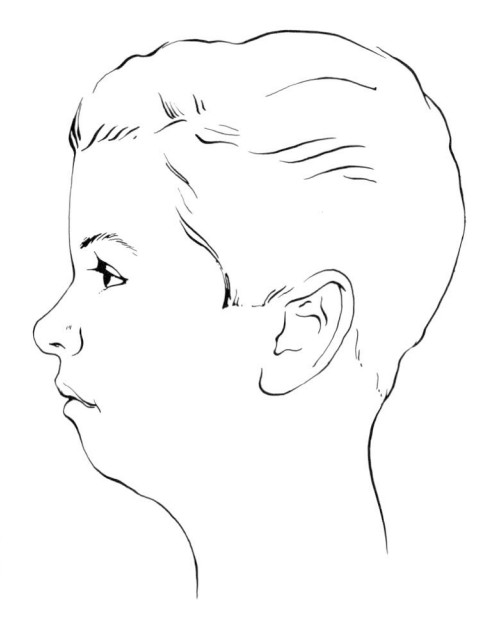

Fig. 28-2. A receding chin is the hallmark of the child with arthritis of the neck and/or the joints of the jaw. Not shown—the angle of the jawbone is reduced or nearly absent.

Polyarticular

There is no clear-cut distinction between the polyarticular and the systemic varieties, as most of these children also have fever, rash, anemia, etc. They all have severely involved joints, however—five or more by definition. The child, the parents, and the physicians are all concerned by the joints rather than by the systemic symptoms. The inflamed joints take characteristic patterns. Most frequently involved are the knees, ankles, and wrists, followed by the neck, fingers, elbows, and shoulders (Fig. 28-1). About one-fourth of the children will have hip involvement, but

Fig. 28-3. Characteristic posture of children with acute polyarticular arthritis. The joints of the arms and legs are flexed for maximum comfort. The neck is held rigidly, usually with slight flexion, and sometimes at a slight angle. Without physical therapy, the children can become fixed in this position.

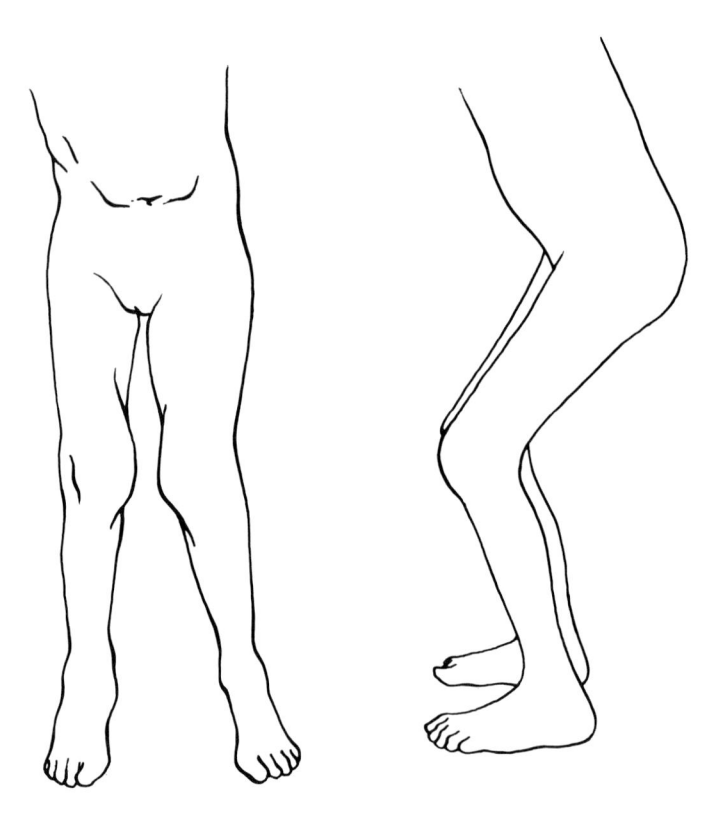

Fig. 28-4. Flexion contractures and "knock-knees" are common. Even if only the knees are involved with arthritis, contractures will occur at the hips. The child will keep the knee flexed to prevent pain, then be unable to straighten it, and have to flex at the hip to compensate. For reasons which are not so well known, many of the children with arthritis in their knees develop "knock-knees" (genu varus) which may require surgery to straighten.

this usually appears late in the course of the disease. Slightly more than 10 percent will have involvement of the jaw, which not only produces pain but also interferes with growth of the jaw bone (mandible) and results in a receding chin (Fig. 28-2).

These children are miserable. They sit as still as possible, with all joints in a flexed position, since this is most comfortable (Fig. 28-3). If they have been ill for any time, they are frequently small for their age because the disease interferes with growth and sexual maturation. The joints lose their range of motion, then develop contractures (tightening of the surrounding soft tissues so that the joints cannot be straightened) (Fig. 28-4), and, finally, subluxations (dislocation of the bone on the far side of the joint) (Fig. 28-5). Although these changes are usually preventable with adequate therapy, they happen frequently.

Fig. 28-5. This shows the "x-ray view" of a knee which has been allowed to develop a contracture and then a subluxation. The joint is bent by the contracture, but the bones of the lower leg (tibia and fibula) have also been dislocated backwards in relation to the bone of thigh (femur). Surgery will be required to obtain an alignment needed for walking.

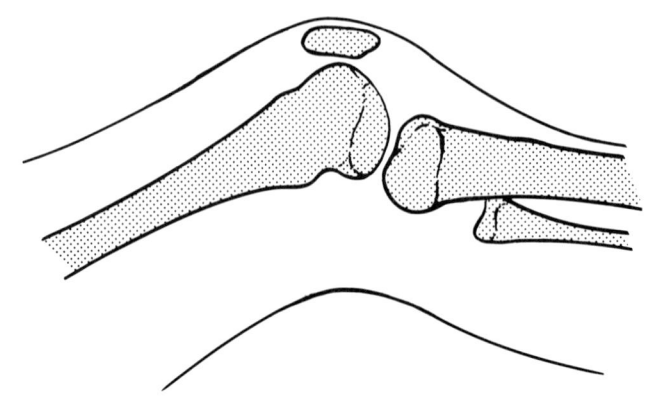

Pauciarticular

Children with four or fewer painful or swollen joints within the first 6 months of the disease may have one of several separate types of arthritis, but they all share some features. Together, these types are the most common form of juvenile rheumatoid arthritis, amounting to 50 or 60 percent of children with chronic arthritis. These patients usually do not have any systemic signs or symptoms such as fever or rash. They do not feel or look ill except for the joints involved. These children usually have little permanent damage, even when the arthritis lasts for a long time. However, some develop polyarticular disease after months or years.

The subgroups of pauciarticular arthritis are not completely defined, but we do know of two which can be distinguished by the presence of certain inherited antigens on the surfaces of cells. These antigens are similar to the ABO blood-group antigens, but are far more complex. One such antigen, HLA-B27, is associated with pauciarticular arthritis in children (usually boys around 10 years of age at onset) and with a back disease called ankylosing spondylitis in adults. We now believe that a large proportion of these children will develop back disease as they grow older. Another antigen, currently called TMo, is also associated with persistent disease which may spread to become polyarticular. Since these are new tests, most children with pauciarticular arthritis have not had their cells tested, and their prognosis should still be assumed to be good.

The most serious problem these children encounter is an inflammation of the iris and the muscle which controls the lens of the eye, called *iridocyclitis* or *anterior uveitis*. This problem occurs independently of the arthritis and may lead to blindness. The initial symptoms are often mild, and these children need be seen regularly by ophthalmologists so that the first signs can be discovered as early as possible. Treatment is usually easy and successful if early, but less certain if the eye disease is discovered late. The children most likely to get this complication are girls whose disease started before age 4, but it can occur in any type of juvenile rheumatoid arthritis.

COMPLICATIONS

Severe acute complications are not usual in juvenile rheumatoid arthritis. Inflammation without serious repercussions has been reported in the brain, lungs, kidneys, and hearts of some patients. The presence of inflammation and fluid around the heart (pericarditis) occurs commonly, but the only problem which appears life-threatening is the rare instance when the heart muscle is inflamed. Patients who have been ill for long periods without adequate treatment or control of their arthritis, may develop amyloidosis, a process in which there is deposition of large amounts of proteinaceous material in many organs, some of which are no longer able to function. This problem, a fatal one, is fortunately becoming extremely rare.

The major problem which involves all the children is the degree to which permanent joint changes occur. Any inflammation within a joint must be expected to cause some damage to cartilage—the smooth, soft, glistening surface which allows free movement of joints—and to cause scarring and tightening of the surrounding soft tissue. The degree to which these processes are allowed to go untreated or uncontrolled will determine the amount of permanent change or crippling of the joint. There are only a few children who do not appear to respond to medical and physical therapy and who become steadily worse despite good treatment. Since some damage to cartilage is inevitable, we assume that most patients will have an early onset of osteoarthritis, the "wear and tear" arthritis of old age.

Some of the more severe complications seen are actually results of therapy. Cortisone and drugs related to cortisone should be given to children only when their life or eyesight is threatened, but, unfortunately, they are given more frequently and their side effects are often obvious. The child stops growing and becomes obese with a characteristic "moon face." The child's bones become brittle, and the children become less resistant to severe infection. Ironically, although their joints are more comfortable, cartilage damage proceeds unabated. Some drugs used in adults, phenylbutazone and indomethacin, are too toxic to use in children. Gold salts, which are used, must be monitored very carefully to avoid damage to bone marrow, kidneys, and liver.

TREATMENT

There are no cures for rheumatoid arthritis, only ways to control its inflammation and the secondary effects until a natural remission occurs. Inflammation is controlled by medicine and by providing rest for the joint and for the child as a whole. The effects of the inflammation, i.e., loss of motion, contractures, and subluxations, are treated by appropriately designed exercises and, in some cases, by surgery.

The best medicine for treating the inflammation is aspirin. This is often difficult to explain to parents who think of this very easily obtained, widely used drug as only a mild pain killer. Although the mechanisms are still not entirely known, aspirin and related salicylate drugs happen to have a very specific effect on inflammation within joints. It is thought that salicylates interfere with the production of potent inflammatory substances called prostaglandins. Other drugs useful for decreasing pain are not effective in reducing inflammation and cannot be used as substitutes for salicylates. It is very important that the dose of aspirin be large enough. The amount prescribed often scares parents, usually about 1½ tables per day for every 10 pounts of weight. This is divided into four or more doses taken at regular intervals during the day. The dose should be adjusted by frequent tests of the actual amount of salicylates in the blood.

At the present time, a large number of drugs are being developed and sold which have similar effects on arthritis. These are called *nonsteroidal anti-inflammatory drugs,* or *NSAIDs*. Each drug company has its own, but all are similar except that a few need be taken only once or twice a day. Only one has been approved by the FDA for use in children, but others will be soon. These are no better than aspirin for the arthritis, but do have less effect on the stomach and may be easier to take. They are far more expensive.

The only other medicine which is widely used in children is "gold," actually a soluble preparation of sodium, gold, and a sulphur-containing sugar. This is given by injection, and is more toxic than aspirin, so it is only used after aspirin or a NSAID has been used for months without improvement.

Rest is very important. Children used to be put to bed completely, but this leads to many psychological and physical problems. During the most acute stages of the disease children should not be allowed to bear weight on inflamed joints and may need a wheelchair or crutches. Splints are often used to provide rest for individual joints. All children need rest, with longer sleep hours at night and lying down periods during the day.

Even when the arthritis appears in complete remission, patients should avoid fatigue—often a problem for the teenager aspiring to athletic prowess or late night parties.

Paradoxically, exercise of affected joints and maintenance of muscle are also an essential part of treatment. During acute stages, the inflamed joints must be moved once or twice a day through the greatest possible range of motion the patient can tolerate. Ideally, this will be done by a trained physical therapist, but a home exercise program to be done by the patient with help from parents is also needed. As the joint inflammation decreases, the exercise must become more vigorous, but a balance must always be maintained between obtaining maximum movement and strength and avoiding excessive stress on the joint. Exercise in warm water and, eventually, swimming are particularly useful because the buoyancy protects joints from weight bearing while the resistance to movement increases strength. Eventually, when the arthritis is inactive, and if joints are not too badly damaged, an exercise program emphasizing strength will be designed to provide stabilization of the joints by good musculature. Even at this time, however, children must avoid severe twisting or jarring, which tend to exacerbate or restart inflammation. For this reason most children with rheumatoid arthritis should have specially designed physical education programs.

Surgery is occasionally used to remove diseased tissue from joints, with the aim of reducing pain and damage to cartilage. This type of operation may be necessary to save tendons, which can be involved in the same process as joints. Many patients can benefit from corrective or reconstructive surgery for damaged joints once the disease is quiescent and growth has stopped. Total hip replacement is now performed in some teenagers and provides great relief of pain.

CLASSROOM PROBLEMS

There are several problems which appear to affect most of these children and which will be evident in their school behavior. They are almost always depressed and often angry. They are usually inhibited, shy, and introverted, so that their emotions are not generally released, but, on occasion, their anger is wildly and unacceptably acted out. It is important for them to have some person with whom or situation in which they can ventilate their feelings. Medical personnel, despite frequent contacts, only rarely can serve this purpose because they are seen as controlling power figures. Physical therapists, occupational therapists, and teachers must be willing to help the child cope with fear, pain, and depression.

Patients with juvenile rheumatoid arthritis are often quite changeable. Following a comfortable night and early morning, a child might be quite active and happy. If, as frequently happens, he has a night of pain, he will be fatigued, irritable, and unreachable. This type of variation must be understood and accepted. Older children often complain that no one seems to believe or understand that they have pain, a complaint often traceable to demands for more consistent behavior by a parent, teacher, or therapist. This is often exacerbated by the fact that affected joints may not be visible, and surrounding peers and others do not see and appreciate the amount of disease present.

One of the characteristics of these diseases is the phenomenon of "gelling." This leads to "morning stiffness," and inability to move joints freely for minutes or hours after awakening. It also occurs with prolonged sitting or maintenance of any given position. The child's day must be planned to allow fairly frequent movement from one seat, room, or activity to another. It is also important to allow adequate time for the stiff child to get from one place to another. The time allotted other children between classes may not be enough for the juvenile arthritic.

Most children taking aspirin will have a high-tone hearing loss. This may interfere with speech reception. Teachers are often the first to notice this problem. The deafness disappears when aspirin treatment is stopped. However, such children should have audiology testing to be sure some other process is not also involved. Similarly, teachers may be the first to detect vision problems in those children with insidious onset of iridocyclitis (see above), and these children should be seen by an ophthalmologist as soon as possible. In brief, the teacher must be part of the diagnostic and therapeutic team caring for the arthritic child.

BIBLIOGRAPHY

Brewer, E. J., Jr., *Juvenile Rheumatoid Arthritis*. Philadelphia, W. B. Saunders, 1970.

Calabro, J. J., and Wykert, J., *The Truth About Arthritis Care*. New York, David McKay, 1971.

Coley, I. L., The child with juvenile rheumatoid arthritis. *American Journal of Occupational Therapy* 26:325–329, 1972.

Jeremy, R., Schaller, J., Arkless, R., Wedgwood, R. J., and Healey, L. A., Juvenile rheumatoid arthritis persisting into adulthood. *American Journal of Medicine* 45:419–434, 1968.

Miller, J. J. III (ed.), *Juvenile Rheumatoid Arthritis*. Littleton, PSG Publishing Co., 1978.

Schaller, J., and Wedgwood, R. J., Juvenile rheumatoid arthritis: A review. *Pediatrics* 50:940–953, 1972.

29

Rubella Syndrome

EUGENE E. BLECK, M.D.

Rubella is another name for German Measles. If rubella infection occurs during the first months of pregnancy, a definite risk to the fetus exists, as has been recognized for many years. (The risk to the fetus in the first 4 months of pregnancy has been estimated to be between 10 and 66 percent.[3])

Rubella vaccine may eliminate the diverse and serious consequences of the rubella syndrome in children born of mothers infected during pregnancy. Sporadic cases may appear, however, and children whose mothers had received the live virus attenuated (weakened) from the wild rubella virus strains occasionally have been born with congenital malformations.[3] The newer vaccine, RA27/3, which is now part of routine pediatric immunizations, apparently carries little, if any, risk of such complications.[1] Immunity from vaccination seems to be durable thus far. However, many years need to pass before we can be certain that the immunity will persist through the child-bearing years in previously immunized girls. Sporadic epidemics can still occur, and a child with the rubella syndrome may occasionally be found in the classroom.

SIGNS AND SYMPTOMS

Children born with congenital rubella have a cluster of physical abnormalities. In one study of 243 children (aged 2½ to 5 years),[2] the incidence of each of these was as follows:

1. Cardiac defects, (the most common of which was pulmonary artery narrowing, or stenosis)—32.5 percent
2. Neurological defects, or spastic paralysis of limbs—32.5 percent
3. Hearing loss—72.8 percent
4. Visual problems—32.9 percent

No defects were found in 20.6 percent of the children studied; 29.6 percent had one defect; 19.3 percent had two defects; and 11.1 percent had four defects. The most prevalent single defect was hearing loss.[2]

BEHAVIOR DISORDERS

In the same study of 243 children, 49 percent had no psychiatric or neurotic behavior disorder.[2] Reactive behavior disorders due to stresses related to parental handling or environmental problems occurred in 15 percent. A few children (3.3 percent) had signs of mild cerebral damage, e.g., perseveration. Mental retardation was definite in 37 percent, and 7.4 percent were diagnosed as autistic (stereotyped actions, echolatic language, other specified language deviations, odd repetitive actions, and unusually strong attachments to objects).

In a second study, which reexamined 210 of the original 243 children at ages 8 to 9 years, the incidence of reactive behavior disorders increased slightly to 18.8 percent, as did the incidence of mild cerebral damage (from 3.3 to 12.4 percent). That a developmental change occurred is evidenced by an increase in neurotic behavior disorders from 0 to 2.4 percent. These data indicate that it is often difficult to diagnose impulsive and repetitive language and behavior problems until they persist and are identified at school age.

Mental retardation in the same group at the age of 8 to 9 years decreased to 25 percent. This decrease may represent a general trend to increased mental competence despite hearing losses. It is also possible that, in some patients, the chronic rubella viral infection was overcome by the body's immune mechanism, which, in turn, alleviated the brain dysfunction.

The fate of autistic children could not be evaluated accurately due to an inability to examine the autistic children at follow-up. Two who had been originally diagnosed as autistic had recovered by the age of 8 to 9 years.

EDUCATIONAL IMPLICATIONS

The above description of the physical defects and behavior disorders found in these children, although brief, may be sufficient to give the teacher an indication of what might be occurring in a particular child. As Chess et al. have observed,[2] "Reevaluation of defects and mental abilities at each new age period is essential for flexibility in management to conform to the changing status of the child" [p. 703].

Because behavior problems are so prevalent, the teacher must take into account the family situation—social, emotional, and economic. Medical advice is essential, however. In addition, the pediatrician is in the best position to follow and to reevaluate the whole child—his physical defects and behaviors—in order to counsel the parent as to the best course of management. In this condition, complexity and stress to parents resulting from conflicting opinions are the rule.

REFERENCES

1. Balfour, H. H., Groth, K. E., and Edelman, C. K., RA27/3 rubella vaccine. *American Journal Diseases of Children* 134:350–353, 1980.
2. Chess, S., Fernandez, P., and Korn, S., Behavioral consequences of congenital rubella. *The Journal of Pediatrics* 93:699–703, 1978.
3. Modlin, J. F., Herrmann, K., Brandling-Bennett, A. D., Eddins, D. L., and Hayden, G. F., Risk of congenital abnormality after inadvertent rubella vaccination of pregnant women. *New England Journal of Medicine* 294:972–974, 1976.

30

Scoliosis

LAWRENCE A. RINSKY, M.D.

DEFINITIONS

Scoliosis refers to sideways (lateral) deviation of the spine. As such, it is an anatomic and descriptive term rather than a specific disease entity. The normal spine has several curvatures in a front to back (antero–posterior) direction, but no curvature in the lateral direction (Fig. 30-1). The term for a curvature which is concave posteriorly is *lordosis* (e.g., the curvature at the small of the back). The curvature which is convex posteriorly is *kyphosis*. There is normally a mild kyphosis of the thoracic spine and lordosis of the lumbar spine, but *any* scoliosis is abnormal. Combined deformities are frequently present (e.g., *kyphoscoliosis*).

CLASSIFICATION

Scoliosis is associated with many causes. Thus, it is often a result or sign of other, more specific, disease entities. Traditionally, scoliosis is divided into structural and nonstructural scoliosis.

Nonstructural Scoliosis

In nonstructural scoliosis, the curvature is always secondary to a known cause and is usually of a minor degree. The curvature generally resolves when the underlying cause is corrected or when the child bends. Examples are scoliosis due to leg-length discrepancy or painful states, such as a herniated lumbar disc. Treatment is directed to the underlying

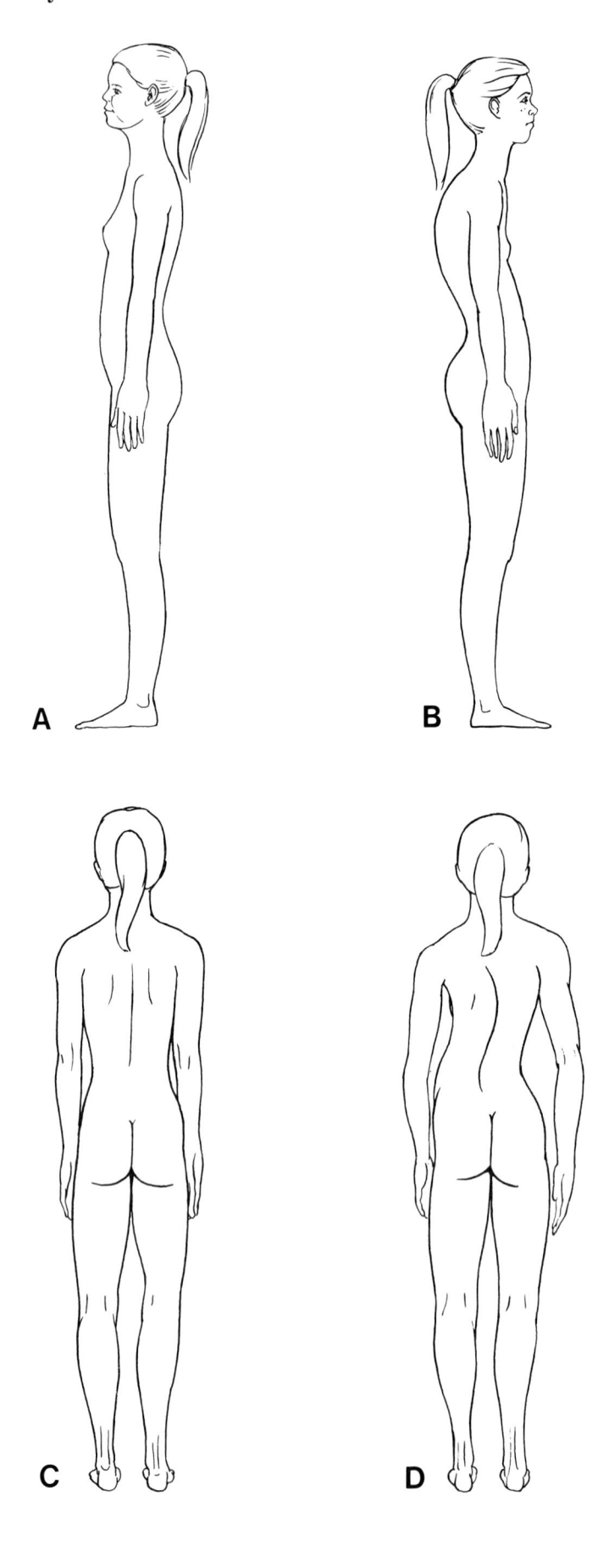

Fig. 30-1. (A) and (C) Normal spine. (B) Increased kyphosis (round back). (D) Scoliosis—any degree of scoliosis is abnormal.

Scoliosis

Table 30-1. Causes of Structural Scoliosis

1. Idiopathic	6. Radiation to the spine
2. Neuromuscular	7. Dwarfing syndromes
3. Congenital	8. Infections of the spine
4. Neurofibromatosis (Von Recklinghausen's disease)	9. Tumors
	10. Metabolic syndromes
5. Trauma (spine fractures)	

causes and not at the scoliosis per se. Only rarely would nonstructural scoliosis become a fixed deformity.

Structural Scoliosis

Structural scoliosis may be secondary to a variety of known causes (Table 30-1). In clinical practice, however, the underlying cause is most commonly unknown (idiopathic). A structural scoliosis does not resolve with treatment of the underlying cause nor with simple bending.

Idiopathic Scoliosis

Idiopathic scoliosis is by far the most common form and is usually seen in adolescent girls. Ordinarily these children are otherwise completely healthy. Progression of idopathic scoliosis does not always occur but is likely if the curvature is not treated. Only careful follow-up with x-rays will determine whether a curve is progressive or not. In some communities screening programs of adolescents have effected earlier diagnosis and, thereby, more effective treatment.

Neuromuscular Scoliosis

The second most common type of scoliosis is that caused by paralytic conditions; that is, by loss or impairment of motor function due to a nerve or muscle problem. In this type of scoliosis there may be an asymmetric paralysis of the torso musculature, or the whole spine may "sag" because of a generalized weakness. Poliomyelitis used to be the most common cause of paralytic scoliosis in this country but is rarely seen today, except in immigrant children from areas of Southeast Asia, Latin America, and so forth. Most commonly, paralytic scoliosis is now due to cerebral palsy, traumatic paraplegia, myelomeningocele, degenerative neurologic conditions, or muscular dystrophies.

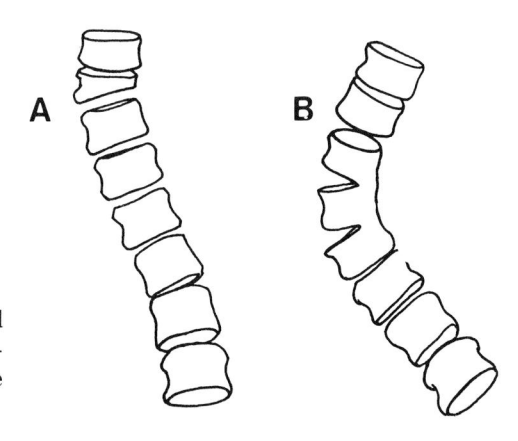

Fig. 30-2. (A) The second vertebra is only partially formed (hemivertebra). (B) The third, fourth and fifth vertebrae remained fused (attached) on one side. They can grow only on the unfused side.

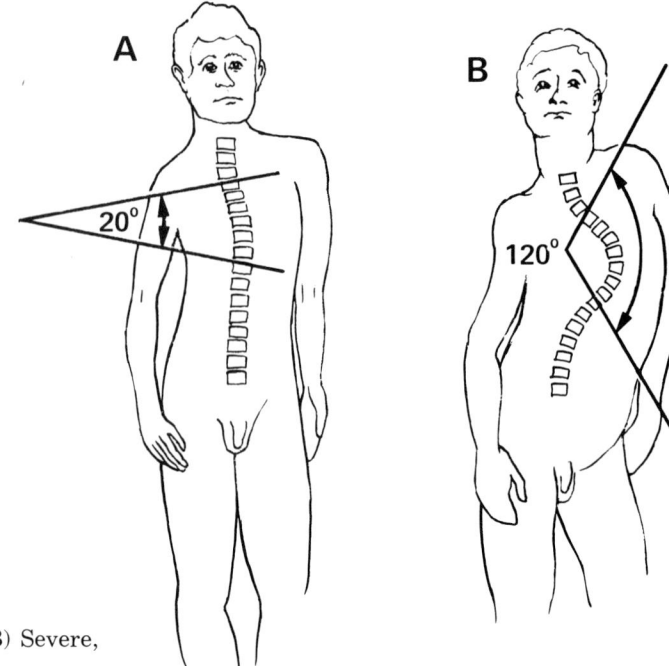

Fig 30-3. (A) Mild, 20-degree curvature. (B) Severe, 120-degree curvature.

Congenital Scoliosis

In congenital scoliosis, there is asymmetric growth of the spine because of improper formation or segmentation of the vertebrae (Fig. 30-2). If only one-half of a vertebra forms (hemivertebra), or if two adjacent vertebrae are fused on one side (unilateral bar), the longitudinal growth of the spine will be uneven. Because these developmental anomalies of the spine occur early in utero (about the 6th week of fetal development), other malformations frequently coexist and need to be watched for in cases of congenital scoliosis. Most commonly seen are genitourinary abnormalities.

Other Causes

There are many other, much less frequent conditions which will give rise to structural scoliosis; these are included in Table 30-1. In all of these cases of secondary scoliosis, the spine deformity requires treatment and may potentially become much more important to the patient than the underlying etiology.

CURVE LOCATION AND DESCRIPTION

Scoliotic curvatures are defined by a technique which measures the degrees of an angle which subtends the arc (portion of a circle) of the scoliotic curvature (Fig. 30-3). Curves are also described by the vertebra at the center or apex of the curve. The curvature is defined as either right or left according to the side of the convexity. The right thoracic curve is by far the most common curve type. Many patients have two, or even three, curves (e.g., right thoracic and left thoracolumbar).

INCIDENCE

Each type of scoliosis has a different incidence rate. Because of the introduction of school screening projects, the best statistics on scoliosis are on the incidence of the idiopathic type. Unfortunately, universal

Scoliosis

agreement does not exist as to what extent of curvature (i.e., the minimum number of degrees) constitutes scoliosis. For example, up to 7 to 8 percent of all children have an insignificant idiopathic curvature of 5 degrees or under. The vast majority of these do not progress, and some may even spontaneously resolve. When only clinically significant curves are considered (over 25 degrees), however, the incidence drops to less than 0.2 percent. For minimal curves, the incidence is evenly split between boys and girls. Many more girls than boys have progressive or significant curves, however.

In neuromuscular conditions such as cerebral palsy, the tendency for scoliosis roughly parallels the severity of the underlying illness. For example, in patients with mild spastic cerebral palsy, the incidence of scoliosis is about the same as in the general population. On the other hand, institutionalized patients with cerebral palsy have an incidence of scoliosis of over 33 percent. In certain other conditions, such as traumatic quadriplegia in young children, a scoliosis develops almost universally.

SIGNS AND SYMPTOMS

Parents of children with scoliosis often wonder how it has become so advanced before being noticed. There are several reasons for this common phenomenon. First, scoliosis usually develops *insidiously;* the rate of increase is rarely greater than one degree per month. Second, the most common types of scoliosis do not cause pain or discomfort in children and adolescents. Although adults may well have pain associated with their scoliosis, a child with deviation of the spine who experiences pain should be suspected of having a tumor or infection. Additionally, idiopathic scoliosis first becomes evident during early adolescence (age 10 to 12). Parents are not as likely to notice changes in the child's anatomy at that age since, by then, the child is dressing himself or herself and is becoming more modest. Finally, in scoliosis, there is a rotation of the vertebrae in a

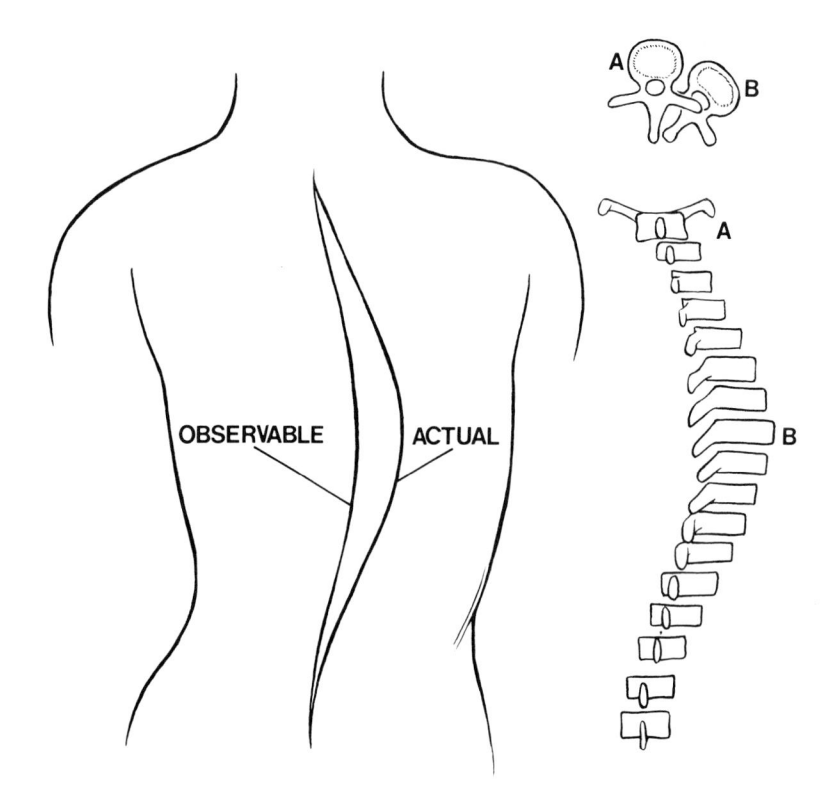

Fig. 30-4. The observed curvature *always* appears less severe than the actual curvature because of rotation of the vertebrae.

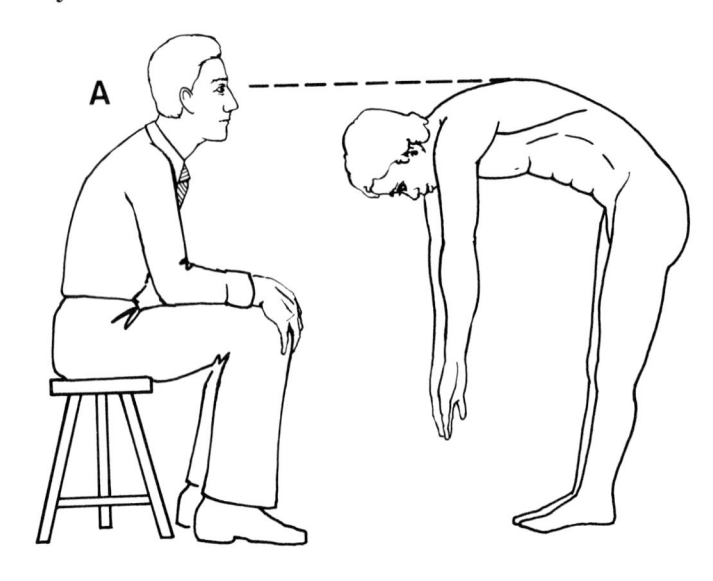

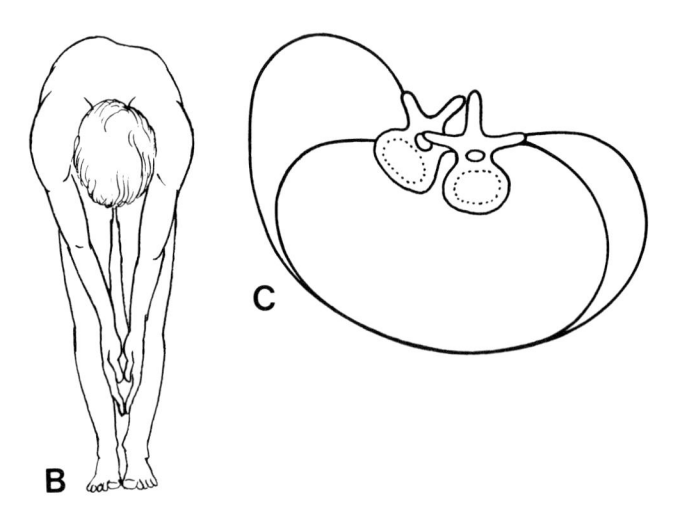

Fig. 30-5. (A) The correct way to screen for scoliosis. (B) The rib hump can be seen as higher on the child's right side. (C) The cause of the rib hump deformity is a vertebral rotation that carries the ribs backwards on one side and forward on the other.

direction such that the line of bony prominences of a patient's spine (spinous processes) *always* visually appears less than the true degree of curvature, which can only be measured by x-ray (Fig. 30-4).

In fact, looking at a child from the back is not a sensitive way of picking up scoliosis unless the condition is already somewhat advanced. A far better screening method is to gaze at the horizon of the back with the child bent 90 degrees at the hips. Because of the rotational element, the ribs protrude in a "hump" on the convex side of the curvature (Fig. 30-5). Other asymmetries first noted in patients include uneven heights of the shoulders and differing contours of the normal flanks. The breasts may appear unequal in size because of differences in the underlying rib cage. Because there are strong hereditary tendencies in scoliosis, one should be especially alert to signs of the condition in siblings of children known to have scoliosis.

Looking at a child's back as described above takes one minute and is known as scoliosis screening. The physical education class at school is a convenient place for screening, which should probably be done yearly. Since the technique of exam is so simple, however, anyone can screen for scoliosis, including the parent, or Little League coach.

COMPLICATIONS AND DISABILITIES

The presence of moderate-to-severe scoliosis (greater than 50 degrees) involving the thoracic spine will give rise to a significant chest-cage deformity. This restricts the efficiency of the heart and lungs. When very severe, the scoliosis will lead to heart failure (cor pulmonale) and early death. On the other hand, the presence of a mild degree of curvature at skeletal maturity (less than 30 degrees) will probably have no significant effect on life span, lung function, quality of life, or even appearance.

The incidence of back pain is probably increased in adults with scoliosis, although there is some disagreement among several long-term follow-up studies. Those adults with back pain and scoliosis tend to have a very difficult problem for which the usual treatments are not very effective.

In rare cases—especially in severe kyphoscoliosis—deformities of the spine will lead to lower-extremity paralysis (paraplegia). This catastrophe is caused by excessive tension on the spinal cord.

In patients with neuromuscular scoliosis who are confined to a wheelchair, scoliosis can rob patients of the ability to sit upright without using their hands. This occurs when the pelvis becomes oblique to the long axis of the torso (Fig. 30-6). Eventually, pressure sores occur because of uneven weight-bearing on the buttocks.

Psychologically, the scoliosis may give rise to problems of self-image

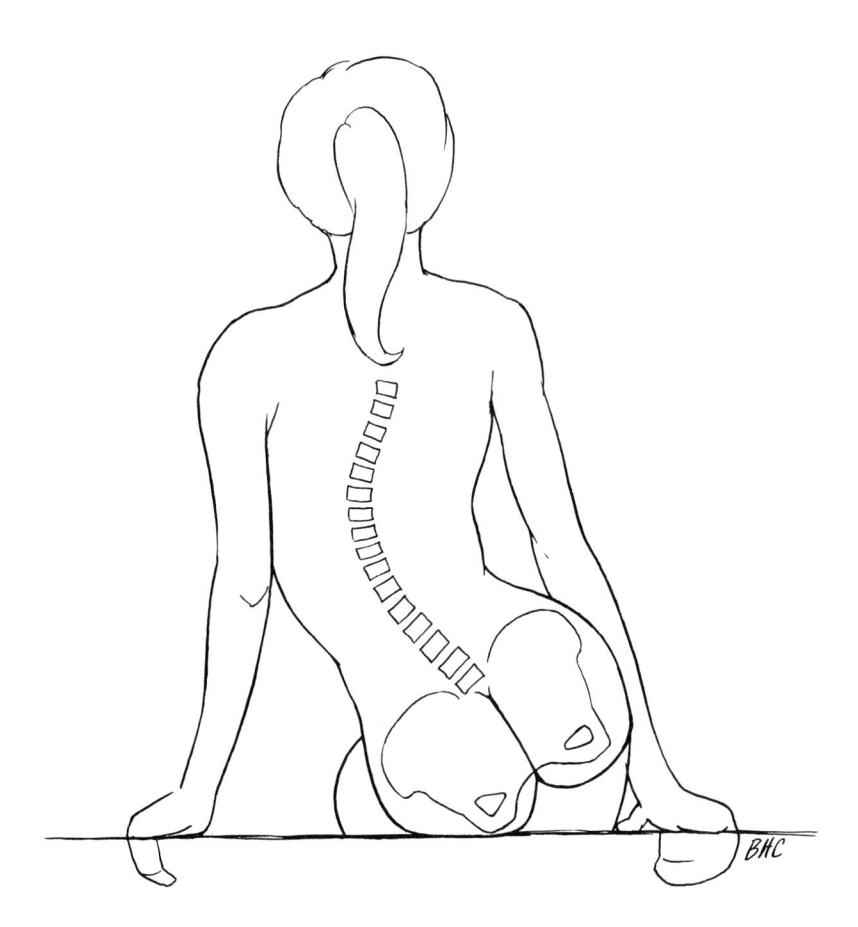

Fig. 30-6. Pelvic obliquity. The patient must use hands or restraints to keep from falling over.

("hump back") or even guilt ("Why me?"). Partly for these reasons, perhaps, patients with severe scoliosis are much less likely to marry.

Finally, although it used to be thought that scoliosis did not increase after skeletal maturity (at approximately 15 years in girls, 17 years in boys), it is now recognized that some patients will have progression of their curvatures by as much as 20 to 30 degrees during adult life. Since there is no way to predict which curves will remain stable, patients should be followed well into adulthood.

TREATMENT

In general, the child with a mild deformity (less than 20 degrees) will be followed with periodic observation and x-rays to determine whether the curve is progressive or not. Although an exercise program to keep the spine supple is usually prescribed, it is unlikely that exercises alone will have any effect on a curvature. It is far more important that the child engage in a normal life-style, without the fear that any specific activities per se might increase the curvature. Only in certain cases in which the progression of scoliosis is universal (e.g., high myelomeningocele) would one start treatment with a lesser degree of curvature.

The child with a moderate curvature (20 to 45 degrees) is usually treated with a brace (orthosis), depending on the underlying cause and the child's age and cooperativeness. The Milwaukee brace is the most commonly used bracing system and is probably the most versatile (Fig. 30-7). It consists of a molded pelvic portion of plastic, front and back metal uprights, and a ring around the neck. Pressure pads are affixed to the uprights so as to apply corrective forces. There is some passive corrective force, but the Milwaukee brace works because of the dynamic effect

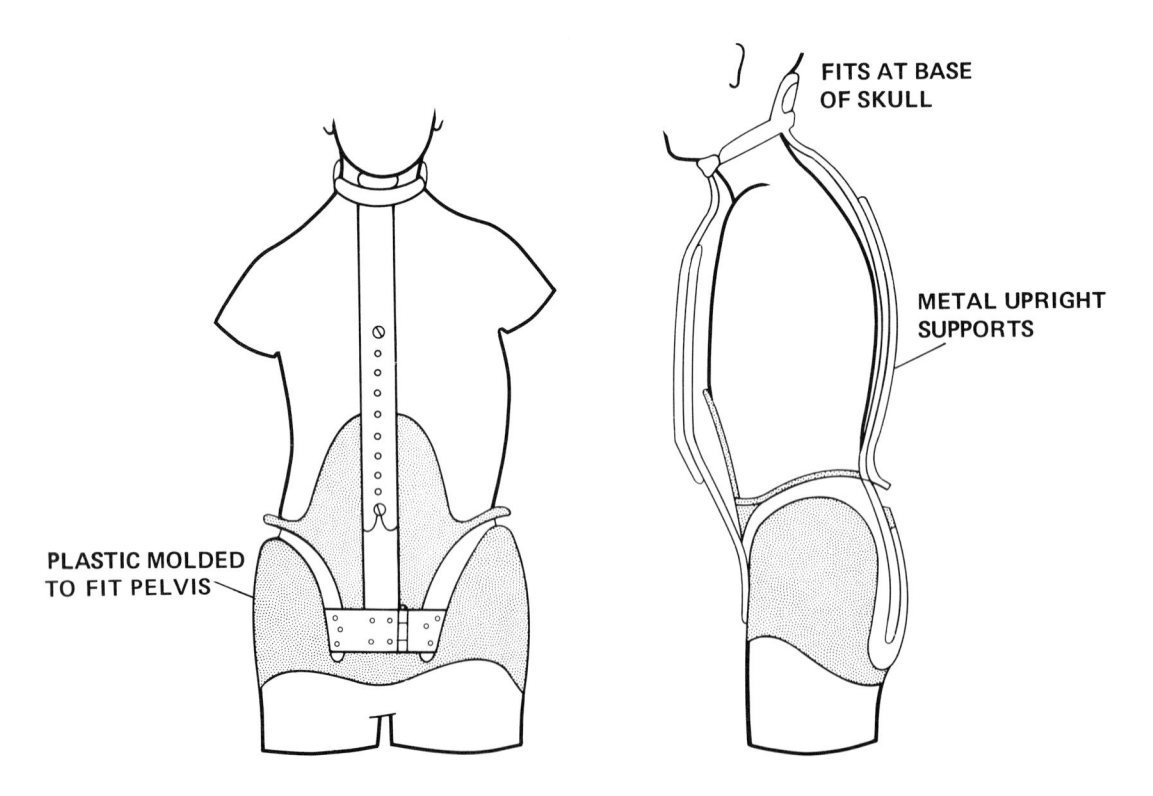

Fig. 30-7. The Milwaukee brace.

Scoliosis

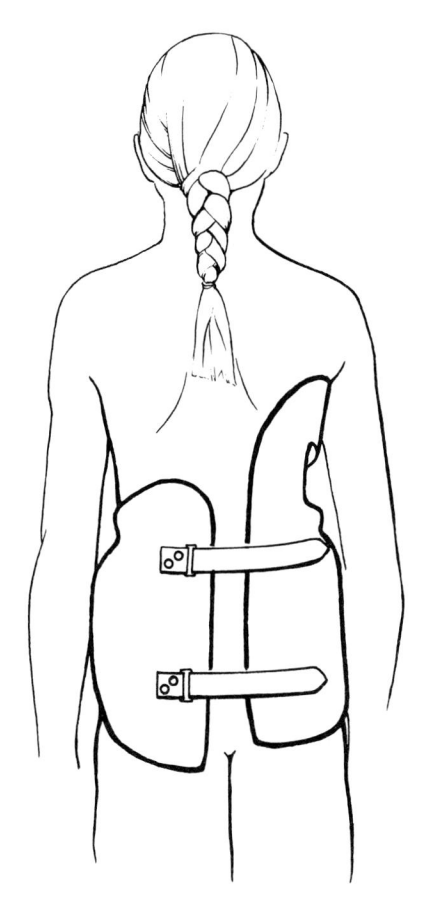

Fig. 30-8. The TLSO, or "Boston brace," is completely hidden under clothes.

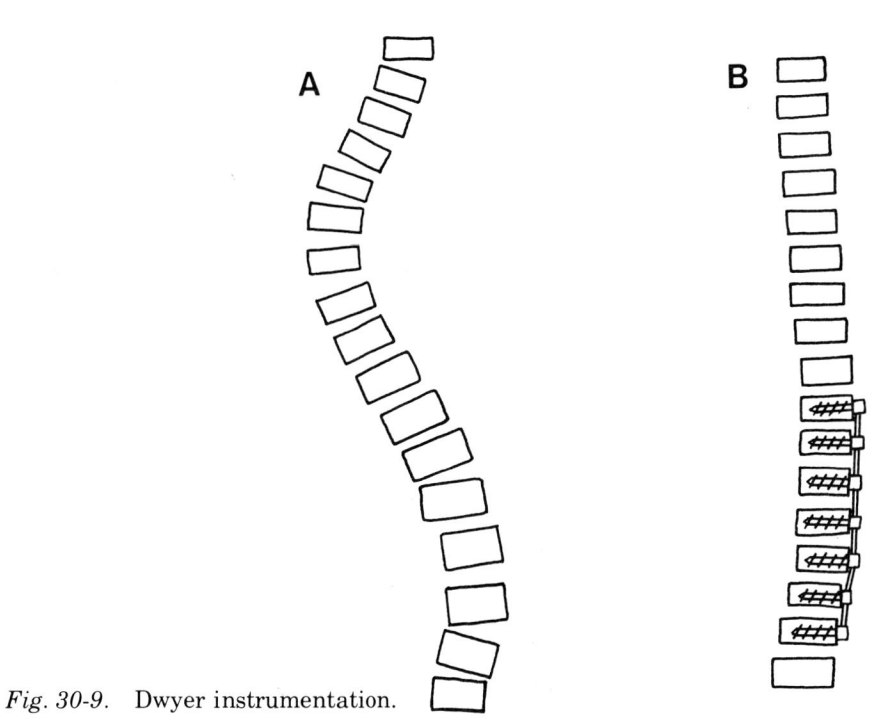

Fig. 30-9. Dwyer instrumentation.

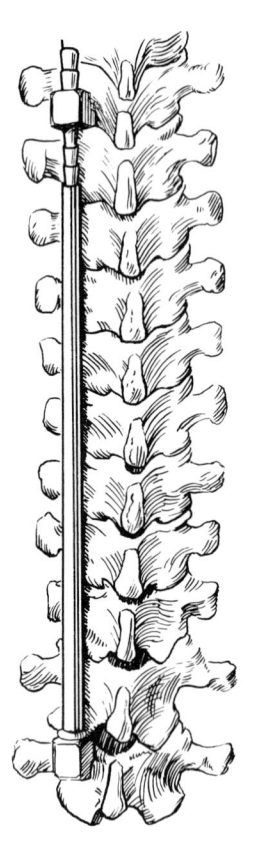

Fig. 30-10. The Harrington rod in place.

(i.e., the patient must stand as straight as possible to be comfortable in the brace). Because of the throat ring, the brace cannot be hidden completely and is noticeable by the patient's peers.

In an effort to improve patient acceptance, several similar types of plastic body jackets have been developed that extend no higher than the armpits (axilla). These orthoses simply squeeze the spine straighter and thus do not have true dynamic effect. Because of their improved cosmesis, however, they are preferred in the treatment of curvatures in the lower half of the spine (Fig. 30-8). This type of brace is known as a TLSO (thoracolumbosacral orthos).

In most cases of brace treatment, the orthosis must be worn full time (22 to 23 hours per day) until the child reaches skeletal maturity. The brace may be removed at any time for bathing or sports but should be worn to school and, usually, during sleep. The vast majority of children adapt surprisingly well and successfully wear the brace for 2 to 4 years until skeletal maturity is reached. When conscientiously worn, the brace will prevent progression of most, but not all, curves.

In more severe curves (greater than 50 degrees), surgery may be recommended, depending on the child's age, underlying cause, and results of previous brace treatment. Surgery usually means fusion (joining together) of the individual vertebrae of one segment of the spine. Nowadays, surgery usually also entails the implantation of a metal device adjacent to the spine to aid in achieving correction. Bone graft is added from the patient's pelvis. The fusion ordinarily takes about one year to become solid. The patient wears a cast or brace for 6 to 12 months but is usually able to be up walking within a week or two after the operation. In the most severe cases, surgery is performed in stages, with intervening periods of traction; this permits a greater degree of correction. Despite recent innovations in spine surgery, it is yet rarely possible to straighten the spine completely. In the severe cases, the spine is approached first from the front, and a fusion of the vertebral bodies is performed. The metal fixation device consists of screws and a cable known as the Dwyer instrumentation (Fig. 30-9). The most commonly performed spine surgery is directly from the back using the Harrington instruments (Fig. 30-10). The fusion does result in some stiffening in the area of the curvature. However, the patients maintain an adequate, if not surprising, degree of motion following spine fusion. A new type of metal spinal implant known as the Luque rod allows fusion without the need for a body cast or brace.

SUMMARY AND EDUCATIONAL SIGNIFICANCE

Scoliosis may be secondary to a variety of known causes or may be idiopathic in origin. Treatment of a minimal curvature consists mainly of periodic observation to determine whether the curve is progressive. A more moderate degree of deformity is treated with a brace, which is usually effective in arresting progression of the deformity. When scoliosis progresses despite brace treatment or is diagnosed late, surgery is often indicated to prevent respiratory compromise and pain, as well as to improve appearance.

The vast majority of patients with idiopathic scoliosis should participate in the usual activities for their age. Scoliosis is not an excuse to exempt out of physical education class. Patients wearing a Milwaukee brace are frequently very self-conscious at first and will need an extra measure of understanding and acceptance in the classroom. Patients with secondary scoliosis may be attending orthopedically handicapped classes or other special education classes. Their scoliosis needs to be treated so that it will not become more of a disability than their underlying problem. In cases in which surgery becomes necessary, between 6 weeks to 3 months of regular classes will be missed; there is no reason, however, why the patient cannot continue their classwork with a home tutor.

BIBLIOGRAPHY

Moe, J. H., Winter, R. B., Bradford, D. S., and Lonstein, J. E., *Scoliosis and Other Spinal Deformities*. Philadelphia, W. B. Saunders, 1978.

Tachdjian, M. O., *Pediatric Orthopaedics*. Philadelphia, W. B. Saunders, 1972.

Nachemson, A., A Long-term Follow-up Study of Non-treated Scoliosis. *Acta Orthopaedica Scandinavica* 39:466–476, 1968.

Collis, D. K., and Ponsetti, I. V., Long-term Follow-up of Patients with Idiopathic Scoliosis Not Treated Surgically. *Journal of Bone Joint Surgery* 51A:425–445, 1969.

Kane, W. J., Scoliosis prevalence. *Clinical Orthopedics and Related Research* 126:43–46, 1977.

31

Sexual Development in Handicapped Children and Adolescents

IRIS F. LITT, M.D.

In the physically handicapped child, the development of sexuality is limited only to the extent that the underlying defect or injury interferes with the receipt of pleasurable bodily sensations, peer interaction, or the development of a healthy self-image. These limitations aside, the curiosity about sex, sexual feelings, and development of secondary sex characteristics are similar to that experienced by any developing youngster. The need for information and recognition of sexual development is at least as great as for any other child. Unfortunately, these needs are often unrecognized, or worse, denied by caring adults.

The components of sexual development are complex and encompass all of the physical, social, cognitive, and psychological processes which occur during childhood. While it is not possible to explore each of these in detail, emphasis will be placed on those ways in which being handicapped may interfere with their usual patterns.

PHYSICAL DEVELOPMENT

One aspect of sexual development which is physically based is that of gender identity. Chromosomally and hormonally determined, the individual's gender is apparent at birth on inspection of the external genitalia. In rare cases, however, it may be difficult to interpret the sex from the genitalia (ambiguous genitalia), and the incorrect sex may be assigned. The same hormonal determinants of prenatal genital development are though to affect the cortex of the brain in such a way as to cause the individual to feel "male" or "female," although this hypothesis is still controversial.

In the prepubertal period, increasing amounts of growth hormone and sex hormones begin to be secreted by the pituitary gland in association with each sleep cycle. These hormones are responsible for stimulating the physical changes of puberty—growth in height and development of secondary sex characteristics (breasts, genitalia, pubic hair, facial hair, body odor, acne, and voice change). The age at which a given individual will begin metamorphosis into a reproductively capable adult is quite variable. The average age of onset of menstruation (menarche) in the United States currently is 12.5 years, but the normal range for this event is 10 to 15½ years. The age at which a given individual will enter menarche is affected by (1) familial factors, such that there is a close correlation in age at menarche between mothers and their daughters; (2) body weight, in that obese girls tend to menstruate early and slim females, late; and (3) health status, in that girls with chronic illness such as diabetes, kidney disease, or colitis are late in their menarche. A relationship between certain handicapping conditions and menarche has been described but is not well understood. For example, blind or deaf girls, and those with spinal bifida, have been found to reach menarche earlier than controls. The implications of this trend toward earlier physical maturation in girls with these handicaps are far-reaching. It suggests the need for earlier preparation for menarche, both psychologically and hygienically, and also the need for earlier education about reproduction and pregnancy-prevention. Of interest, is the observation that, in the same study of development among meningomyelocoele patients, the males did not show advanced puberty.[2] The actual fact of delayed maturation in these boys, coupled with the belief found in more than one-third of the parents of meningomyelocoele children that their child will be incapable of reproduction, contributes to the tendency to infantalize.[2]

SOCIALIZATION

Deriving pleasure from one's own body is a lesson learned early in infancy. The random searching movements of the baby's hands cause pleasurable sensations, especially when the genitalia are touched. The response of parents who observe this process will, to a large extent, determine the youngster's attitude toward the giving and receiving of physical pleasure. Punishment of masturbatory activity may result in anxiety surrounding the genitalia. Little is known of the early genital experience of those with spinal deformities, but it is unlikely that the touching produces the same pleasurable sensations as are experienced by those with intact spinal cords. The capability for erection is present in healthy infants from the first weeks of life. Theoretically, this should be possible for those with meningomyelocoele, but no data are available on this point. Toilet training at 2 to 3 years of age in intact children provides another opportunity for socialization by parents. It is then that modesty and the control of body functions necessary for future sexuality are taught.[3] The spinal-injured child is denied this experience at the conventional time, because of the lack of capacity for bladder and bowel control. The next phase in normal sexual development is that of exploration of the genitals of playmates. By 5½ years of age, 98 percent of physically normal boys in one study knew the difference between their genitals and those of females.[4] The lack of opportunity for unsupervised peer contact in the young handicapped child may deprive him of this experience, as well. An even greater consequence of the lack of peer interaction has been described by Dorner:[5] the absence of access to the most important vehicle for gathering information about sex during adolescence—namely peers.

This lack of information about sex was found by Hayden in a study of adolescents (mean age 14½) with meningomyelocoele. She observed that three-fourths of the group studied had less than the average knowledge of sex, as compared to only one quarter of a healthy, age-matched control group.[2]

COGNITIVE DEVELOPMENT

The way children process information has been shown to undergo changes with advancing development. Adapting Piaget's approach to understanding cognitive development during childhood, Bernstein[6] has described a similar developmental progression in the way that children synthesize information about sex. Children, by the age of 3, are at the stage of *geography;* they believe that babies who now exist have always existed, which leaves where they have been as the only problem to be solved. By the next level, that of *manufacturing,* children believe that babies have not always existed, but must be built. The first two levels would correspond to Piaget's preoperational stage, in which children cannot categorize or solve problems by intuition. Level three, called *transitional* by Bernstein, occurs at about 7 years of age and falls between Piaget's stages of preoperational and concrete operational thinking. At this level, the explanation for where babies come from includes a poorly integrated mixture of physiology and technology. Children at this stage "talk about non-living and living things as if all possessed will and acted purposefully" [p. 33].[6] Level four, which is achieved after 8 years of age, is that of *concrete physiology*. At this stage, children know the physical facts of life, but cannot integrate the concept of simple genetics into it. By 11 to 12 years, level five, that of "preformation" is reached. Level-five children understand the necessity for the egg and sperm to join, but most feel that a baby exists preformed in one of the germ cells. By level six, the stage of *physical causality* (around 12 years of age), youngsters have integrated all the necessary information, including the genetic, moral, and social aspects.

Bernstein believes that the proper way to teach about sex is first to determine the youngster's level of understanding, by asking the question, "How do you get a baby?" One can then proceed by presenting material at the next developmental level.

When the youngster is judged to be at level one, for example, Bernstein suggests that level two information be communicated: "Only people can make other people. To make a baby person, you need two grown-up people, a woman and a man, to be the baby's mommy and daddy. The mommy and daddy make the baby from an egg in the mommy's body and a sperm from the daddy's body" [p. 35].[6]

For level two children who believe that babies are manufactured, she suggests saying: "That's an interesting way of looking at things. That's the way you'd make a doll . . . but making a real live baby is different. . . . Mommies and daddies have special things in their bodies that they use to make babies, mommies have tiny eggs and daddies, tiny sperms. When (these) join together they grow into a baby . . . inside the mommy's body" [p. 35].[6]

At level three, the task is to clear up misapprehensions and provide other physiological explanations. To the youngster who stated that a baby comes when mothers and fathers love each other, she would respond: "It's really important for a baby that mothers and fathers love each other and love the baby . . . but loving is a feeling and can't start the baby all by itself. A baby is a living creature and it starts growing from living material. When the mother and father make love, a sperm from the father goes through his penis into the mother's vagina. When the sperm (and the egg join, they) form one new thing which grows into a baby" [p. 35].[6]

At levels four and five, the children need to learn that the baby does not exist until the sperm and egg unite and that it inherits its physical characteristics from both parents. Bernstein suggests explaining genetic contribution in terms of coded information, stressing that neither sperm nor egg contains the entire code until they unite: "Together, they complete the message to develop into a baby that is the child of a particular set of parents" [p. 35].[6]

PSYCHOSOCIAL DEVELOPMENT

Erikson[7] has promulgated the theory that development proceeds through a series of life crises, each of which must be mastered before the next is experienced. These stages of crises have relevance to the development of sexuality and, for that reason, are included here. The most important of these is the stage of identity development, normally reached during adolescence. It is at this stage when the developing adolescent integrates all of the recent changes in physical appearance with all of the previous developmental stages and comes to terms with who he or she really is. Experimentation with drugs, sex, and even a variety of potential adult roles occurs in an effort to clarify identity. Adolescents with physical handicaps are limited in opportunities for experimentation in the service of identity-formation. In the Hayden study, adolescents with myelodysplasia had significantly lower self-esteem than the control group. Moreover, the boys in the group "had more concerns about sexual attitudes and mastery over the environment."[2] These same concerns are voiced by boys with urogenital anomalies, as was reported by Cogan et al.[8] They advise that early effort be directed at "developing sound compensatory modes designed to reinforce masculinity, mastery, and control" and "open discussion and exploration of fears" well before adolescence (p. 376).

The next crisis is that of development of intimacy. For individuals with physical handicaps this stage is perhaps of paramount importance. In the words of Rhodes, "loving relationships, expressed sexually, are important to all those who are handicapped in any way. The fact that a man or woman can feel nothing because of a nervous system disease, does not diminish delight in being able to give pleasure and comfort to the partner. The other senses and the mind make up for much physical loss" [p. 692].[9]

The major challenge we face is to convince parents, who often overprotect their handicapped children, who tend to their toilet needs and deny them even basic household chores, that sexuality is developing, with or without adult guidance and support. To permit the latter to happen by default, to allow our discomfort with sexuality to interfere with our ability to assist in the process, is to miss a unique opportunity to improve the functional adjustment of a handicapped adolescent.

REFERENCES

1. Tanner, J., *Growth at Adolescence,* 2nd Ed. Oxford, England, Oxford University Press, 1962.
2. Hayden, P. W., Davenport, S. L. H., and Campbell, M. M., Adolescents with myelodysplasia: Impact of physical disability on emotional maturation. *Pediatrics* 64:53–59, 1979.

3. Sears, R. R., Maccoby, E. E., and Levin, H., *Patterns of Child Rearing.* Evanston, Ill., Row, Peterson, and Co., 1957.
4. Kreitler, H., Kreitler, S., Children's concepts of sexuality and birth. *Child Development* 37:363–378, 1966.
5. Dorner, S., Sexual interest and activity in adolescents with spina bifida. *Journal Child Psychology and Psychiatry* 18:229–237, 1977.
6. Bernstein, A., How children learn about sex and birth. *Psychology Today* 6:31–34, 66, 1976.
7. Erikson, E. H., *Identity, Youth, and Crisis,* New York, W. W. Norton, 1968.
8. Cogin, S. F., Becker, R. D., and Hofmann, A. D. Adolescent males with urogenital anomalies, their body image and psychosexual development. *Journal of Youth and Adolescence* 4:359–373, 1975.
9. Rhodes, P., Psychosexual problems of chronic handicapping disease. *The Medical Journal of Australia* 2:688–692, 1976.

BIBLIOGRAPHY

Buscaglia, L., *The Disabled and Their Parents: A Counseling Challenge.* Thorofare, N.J., Charles B. Slack, 1975.

Gordon, S., *The Sexual Adolescent: Communicating With Teenagers About Sex.* Belmont, Calif., Auxbury Press, 1973.

Johnson, W., *Sex Education and Counseling of Special Groups: The Mentally and Physically Handicapped, Ill, and Elderly.* Springfield, Ill., Charles S. Thomas, 1975.

Wright, B., *Physical Disability–A Psychological Approach.* New York, Harper & Row, 1960.

32

Short Stature and Growth

WILLIAM A. HORTON, M.D.
DAVID L. RIMOIN, M.D., PH.D.

Man has a very long childhood compared to other members of the animal kingdom, and he requires many years to reach his adult form. The combination of quantitative and qualitative changes which occur during this period is known as growth. It is a smooth and continuous process in which all tissues participate, although there is considerable variation in timing and rate of growth in different tissues and regions of the body. Traditionally, the bony skeleton has been considered a good index of overall growth. It is a single tissue and is relatively easy to measure, i.e., in height, or stature. In fact, the term *growth* generally refers to skeletal growth unless otherwise stated. This chapter will briefly review the current concepts of normal skeletal growth and maturation, as well as disturbances of these processes.

NORMAL HUMAN GROWTH

Man's growth potential is determined primarily by genetic factors through the additive effects of many genes (polygenic inheritance); a child's growth characteristics closely resemble those of his parents.[4,26,31,37] Thus, at time of conception, a child's growth rate and final height are predetermined, and a genetic growth curve can be projected upon which environmental factors are subsequently superimposed. The general shape of this curve is common to all persons, as well as many other primates, and is characterized by rapid fetal growth, a prompt deceleration of growth following birth, a period of relatively slow but constant growth

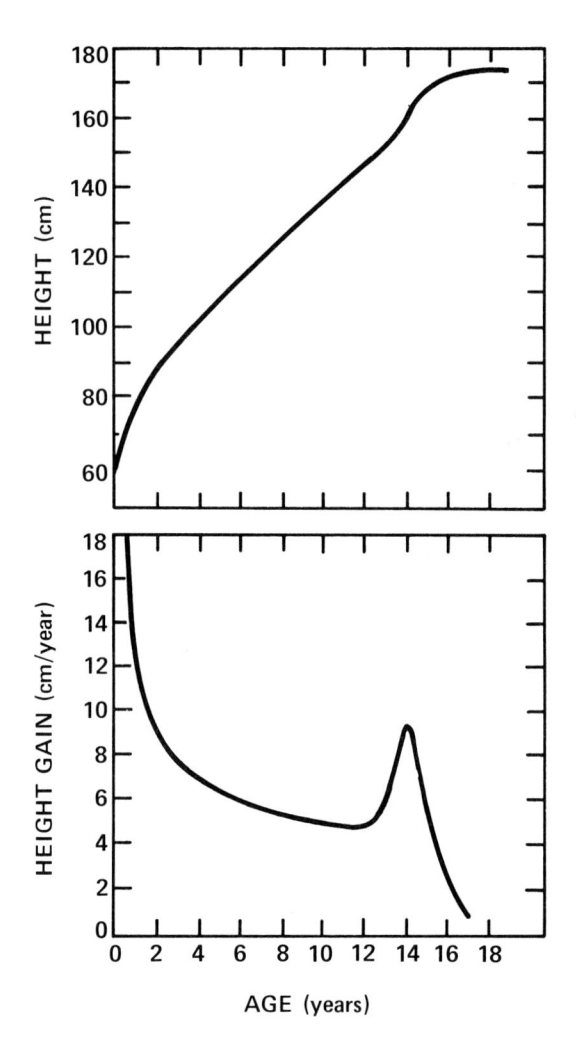

Fig. 32-1. Idealized growth curves: accumulated height (distance) above and height gain (velocity) below.

during childhood, and a growth spurt at puberty, after which all growth ceases (Fig. 32-1). There is a strong tendency for an individual to grow along his genetic curve; in fact, only a major long-term event that interferes with growth will permanently change it. For example, a child's growth rate will be temporarily suppressed by a major illness, but, after the illness, compensatory, or catch-up, growth usually returns him to his original growth level.

Life before birth (intrauterine) is characterized by very rapid growth, with the peak velocity occurring approximately 4 months after conception (gestation).[37] The decreasing growth rate during the last 5 months of pregnancy probably results from two factors: (1) a progressive decrease in the rate of cell division (mitosis) and (2) the constraint of the wall of the uterus on the unborn infant (fetus), which becomes more limiting as the end of pregnancy nears. Uterine constraint appears to be greater for the first pregnancy and is more evident with a pregnancy of multiple births.[37] A number of factors related to the mother (maternal) are recognized to affect fetal growth adversely, including small maternal size, malnutrition, and illness (such as high blood pressure or hypertension, kidney and heart disease, and toxemia of pregnancy) as well as the use of alcohol, cigarettes, and certain medicines (hydantoins, which are used to control seizures, and warfarin, a blood thinner).[35] On the other hand, maternal diabetes mellitus is associated with excessive fetal growth and large birth size.[20] In fact, birth length appears to be determined more by maternal factors than by the genetic makeup of the newborn.

Following birth, the growth rate continues to decrease. This is the period during which the infant makes adjustments for maternal factors that influenced birth length.[36] When growth retardation occurs because of the ingestion of growth-suppressing agents mentioned above, compensatory growth is usually not observed, and it appears that the growth potential for these children is permanently reduced.[36] Most catch-up or slow-down growth occurs during the first 6 months, so that by 1 year the infant is growing near his projected growth rate. By age 2 years, growth has slowed further and the child is clearly following his own genetically determined curve.[42]

Between the ages of 2 to 3 years, the rapid deceleration of growth rate levels off, giving way to a very slow decrease in velocity which lasts until the rapid growth period that accompanies puberty (pubertal growth spurt). The typical child will drop from a rate of approximately 6.5 cm/year at age 5 years to about 5 cm/year prior to puberty.[42] There are a few individuals, usually late-maturing boys, who have an additional drop in velocity just prior to puberty, while others may exhibit a slight increase in growth rate between the ages of 5 and 8 years, the so-called midgrowth spurt. In general, however, these are years of relatively slow, constant growth. A change in body proportions becomes evident during this period. At birth the trunk is proportionately longer than the limbs. From birth on, however, the limbs grow at a slightly greater rate than the trunk, so that, by approximately age 8 years, the two segments are equal and, thereafter, the limbs become proportionately longer.

Puberty is associated with the development of the sex glands (gonads) and secondary sexual characteristics, such as enlargement of the external sex organs (genitalia) in both sexes and of breasts in females. There is also an increase in muscle mass, a redistribution of fat, and a marked increase in the rate of skeletal maturation, accompanied by a marked acceleration in growth rate. Thereafter, growth ceases. The entire process usually lasts 2 to 5 years. The growth spurt is integrated into the scheme differently in the two sexes. In the female it occurs early, while in males it occurs later. Thus, although the average male enters puberty only 6 to 8 months later than the average female, his growth spurt occurs a full 2 years later.[42] The total height gained during this spurt averages 28 cm for males, which is only slightly more than the average of 25 cm for females.[44] Hence, the adult difference in height between the sexes appears to be primarily due to the longer growth period prior to puberty in the male (Fig. 32-2). The height gained during the growth spurt is independent of height attained prior to it, although there is a slight tendency for those individuals entering puberty early to have a greater spurt. In females, the first menstrual period (menarche) serves as a marker that growth is nearing an end (the average girl gains 6 cm in height after menarche), but there is no such marker in the male.[42]

There are a number of factors which may influence growth rate throughout the entire growth period. Many children show seasonal changes, most frequently growing faster in the spring than in the fall. Interestingly, blind children do not show this seasonal effect.[42] Long-lasting (chronic) diseases and prolonged malnutrition both reduce growth rate, but catch-up growth usually occurs following improved nutrition or resolution of the disease if it has not lasted too long. Certain drugs used to treat hyperkinetic children, such as methylphenidate (Ritalin), may suppress growth, but their effects on final adult height are not known.[29]

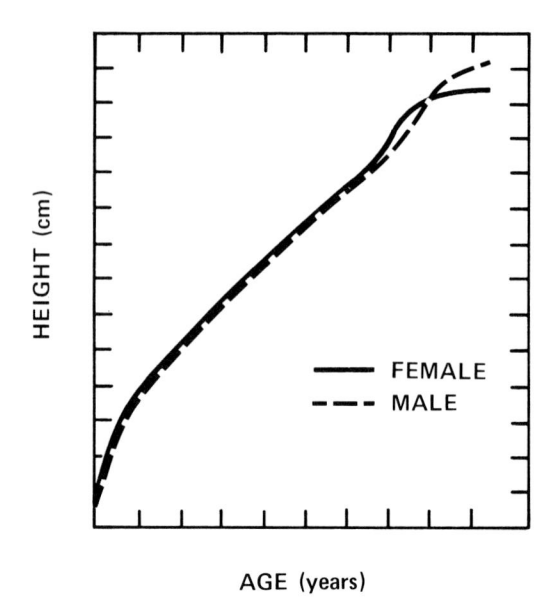

Fig. 32-2. Idealized distance curves comparing males and females.

Short-term (acute) illnesses, however, have little effect on growth in well nourished, otherwise healthy children.[37]

In addition to height, maturity, or the degree to which the skeleton has completed its total growth, is an important element of growth.[28] Skeletal maturity reflects the overall biologic maturation of an individual; it is complete following puberty. Girls generally mature faster than boys; however, the rate of maturation varies widely and appears to be genetically determined.[10,37] Some children may take 14 years to reach final adult height, whereas others may require 20 years. Thus, height at a particular age is determined not only by one's genetic growth potential (which determines final adult height), but also by the degree of skeletal maturation. For example, a "tall for age" children may be so either because they have average growth potential but are more mature than their peers or because they have the genetic potential to be tall and are of average maturity. Factors which affect skeletal growth, such as illness, malnutrition, etc., usually delay skeletal maturation.

MEASURES OF GROWTH

To determine if a child has normal growth, he must be compared to standard growth curves. Such curves have been developed both for absolute accumulated height, the so-called "distance curves," and for growth velocity.[18,40] They are based on either cross-sectional (different individuals are measured at different ages) or longitudinal (the same individuals measured at different ages) data. The cross-sectional curves are used to compare the height of an individual at a given time to the heights of other children in the general population. The longitudinal curves are used to follow a single child over a period of time. The differences between the two types of curves are most evident during the rapid growth which occurs during puberty. Cross-sectional curves tend to disguise and diffuse the pubertal growth spurt, since different children of the same age may be at different phases of puberty and thus have different growth rates. The growth curves generally used are divided into percentiles, with the 50th percentile representing an arithmetic mean (Fig. 32-3). Although the 95th and 5th percentiles are generally taken as the upper and lower limits of normal, it must be emphasized that, by definition, 5 percent of

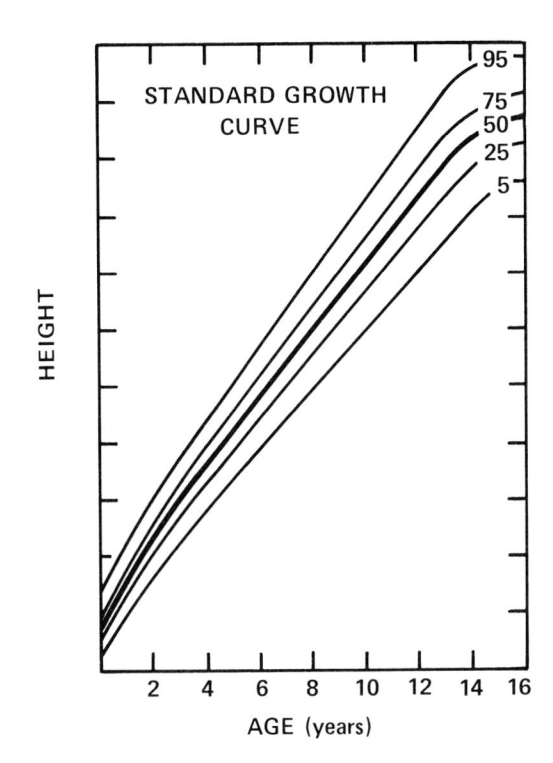

Fig. 32-3. Standard distance growth curve showing percentiles.

"normal children" lie beyond both of these percentiles. Because of the correlation between a child's height and his parents' stature, adjustments for parental height add to the accuracy of the assessment. Moreover, such adjustments tend to compensate for ethnic and racial differences in growth rates, final adult height, etc. For example, a child with short parents who falls at the 3rd percentile for height might be considered abnormally short; but, if his parents are short and their average height (midparental height) is considered, his corrected height may well be within the normal range. Growth curves allowing for parental height corrections have been developed by Tanner and his colleagues.[43]

There is a tendency for each child to follow along the same percentile of the growth curve after age 2 years.[40] At puberty, however, he may deviate from this percentile, depending upon the timing of his pubertal growth spurt (Fig. 32-4). Those maturing early will move up, while late developers will drop in percentiles. Growth-curve data are often used to calculate height age. The height age of a child is defined as the age at which his height would fall at the 50th percentile. Although this measurement is widely used to correlate the height of an individual with his degree of skeletal maturation, it is somewhat inaccurate because it assumes that all individuals grow at the same rate (50th percentile).

Growth velocity curves are based on increments in height measured over intervals of time, usually a year. The tendency for an individual to follow along a given percentile on the distance curves throughout childhood and adolescence is not found in the case of the growth velocity curves.[40] On the contrary, there is a tendency for each person to oscillate above and below the mean while averaging near it (Fig. 32-5). Consistent growth above or below the mean velocity would result in abnormally tall or short stature.[26] For example, a child growing consistently along the 3rd percentile velocity curve would reach an adult height of less than 4 ft. This episodic nature of growth velocity reflects seasonal differences, per-

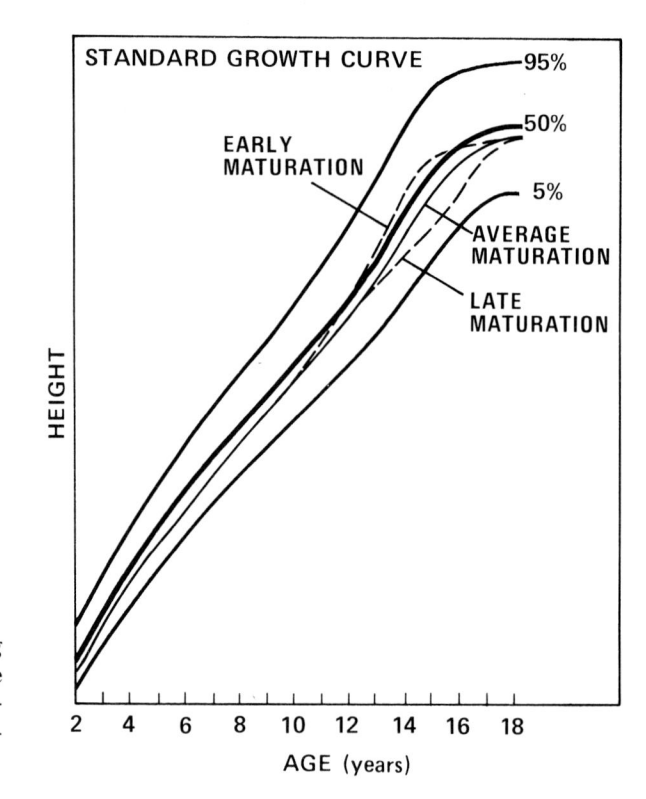

Fig. 32-4. Standard distance growth curve showing child growing at approximately the 40th percentile and maturing at the average rate. Deviations resulting from early and late maturation are also illustrated.

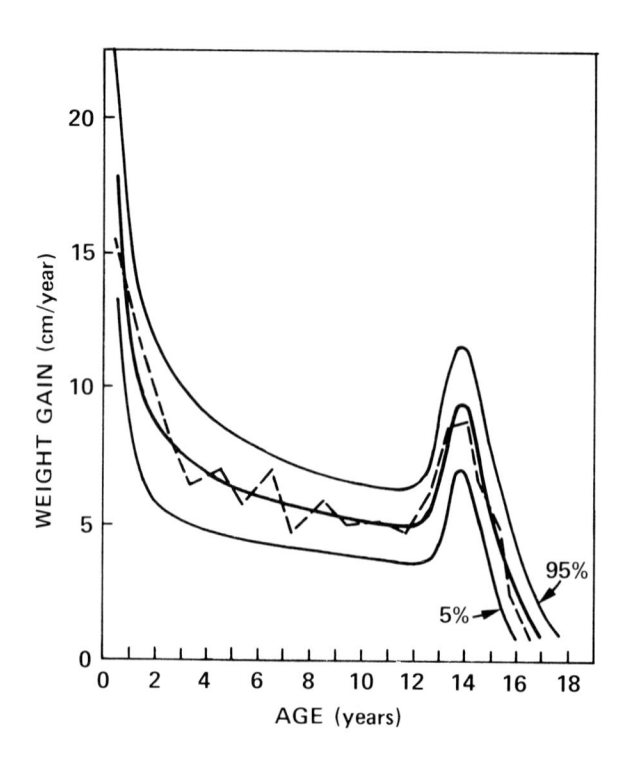

Fig. 32-5. Standard height gain (velocity) curve. The growth of a typical child is plotted.

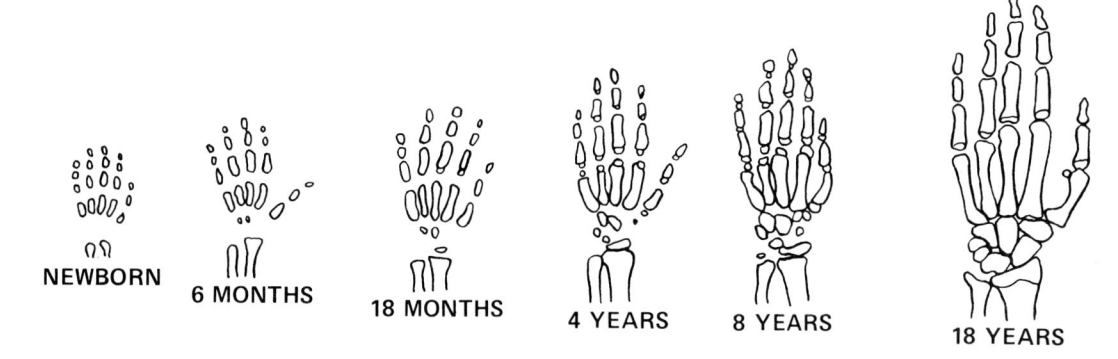

Fig. 32-6. Drawing of a developing hand as seen by x-ray. Note the increasing complexity and number of bones in addition to the increasing size of the individual bones.

iods of catch-up growth following short-term illnesses, measuring errors, etc.

A variety of standards have been developed to assess maturity.[2,41] Skeletal maturity serves as a good index of overall biologic maturation and correlates well with other parameters, such as dental maturity and onset of puberty. Skeletal maturity is based on the rate at which the sites of bone growth (epiphyses) become calcified, as viewed by x-ray. Although a number of areas of the body have been used to evaluate this process, the hand and wrist provide a large number of growing bones to examine and are the most convenient for general use (Fig. 32-6). A hand x-ray of the child is compared to a set of standard hand x-rays at different ages; that age standard which most clearly resembles the child's x-ray is given as the bone age.[11] Different standards must be used for boys and girls because of differences in the rate of maturation. In certain diseases, such as a severe deficiency of thyroid hormone (cretinism) or disorders in which the growing portion of the bones develop abnormally (epiphyseal dysplasias), this method of assessing skeletal maturation is inaccurate, since the calcification process can be markedly altered.

Because of the change in body proportions, measurements of body segments provide another index of maturity. The upper/lower segment (U/L) ratio, is an easily obtained and useful measurement (Fig. 32-7). The lower segment is measured from the point where the pubic bones come together in the pubic area (the symphysis pubis) to the floor at the inside of the heel. The upper segment is obtained by subtracting the lower segment from the total height. Standard U/L ratio curves have been published for both Caucasian and Black Americans.[17] For example, Caucasian infants have an U/L ratio of approximately 1.7, which reaches 1.0 at approximately 7 to 10 years and then falls to an average of 0.95 in adults. Blacks, on the other hand, have relatively longer limbs and reach an U/L ratio of approximately 0.85 as adults.

A number of methods have been employed to predict a child's adult height. Traditionally, the calculation is made simply from height, chronologic age, and degree of skeletal maturity.[2] Recently, methods have been devised in which factors such as parental height and weight are also taken into account.[41] Although none of these methods is totally accurate because of the inability to predict the amount of height that will be gained during the pubertal growth spurt, they provide a general range of expected adult height and are of great assistance in reassuring normal, slow-maturing children that they will eventually be of normal stature.

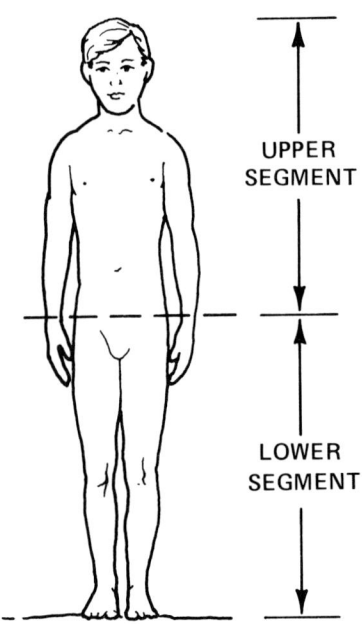

Fig. 32-7. Determination of body proportion.

PHYSIOLOGY OF GROWTH

Growth is the product of a continuous interaction between the hormonal (endocrine) and skeletal systems (Fig. 32-8). Nearly all of the body's hormones influence growth.[3,5,7,26] For example, hormones from the pituitary (growth hormone), thyroid (thyroxin), pancreas (insulin), and adrenal (corticosteroids) glands affect growth rate, whereas those from the parathyroid gland (parathormone), the active forms of vitamin D, and, possibly, a second hormone from the thyroid gland (calcitonin) modulate skeletal maturation. In addition, hormones from the sex and adrenal glands (gonadal and adrenal steroids) are of primary importance in skeletal maturation and the pubertal growth spurt. Another pituitary hormone, prolactin, which is mainly involved in stimulating breast development, also has slight growth promoting action on a skeleton.

The key factor in this growth regulatory scheme is human growth hormone (hGH). This small protein (peptide) hormone is made by specific cells (somatotrophs) in the anterior pituitary gland, which is located at the base of the brain. Centers in the adjacent brain area (hypothalamus) control the actual release of hGH. Although hGH has many direct effects on the body, such as regulating the way in which sugar (carbohydrate) and fats (lipid) are utilized, its effects on skeletal growth are indirect, acting through a second hormone, termed *somatomedin* (SMD), which is made in the liver.[19,47] SMD may actually consist of many distinct substances which are referred to collectively as SMD activity at this time. The level of SMD activity in the blood remains relatively constant compared to the level of hGH, which shows episodic swings; the former thus provides a constant stimulus for growth. Indeed, SMD appears to be the final, common pathway through which a variety of factors influence growth.[5,7] For example, despite elevated levels of hGH, SMD activity is low in severe malnutrition (kwashiorkor); both hormones return to normal following improved nutrition. Excessive adrenal hormones (glucocorticoids), either produced by the individual himself or taken as medication, suppress SMD generation. Likewise, reduced SMD activity is associated with the administration of female hormones (estrogens). On the other hand, there is evidence that the pancreatic hormone insulin

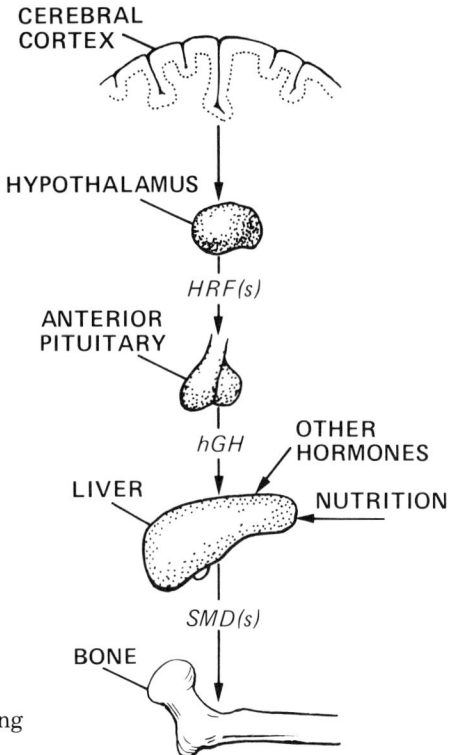

Fig. 32-8. Endocrine growth scheme (HRF, hypothalmic releasing factor).

may promote SMD production in the liver and that thyroid hormone may modulate its effects on the skeleton to some extent.[6]

Skeletal maturation appears to be primarily under the control of hormones from the thyroid, adrenal, and sex (gonad) glands. An excess of any one of these will accelerate bone maturation, whereas a deficiency will cause a delay. At puberty, both the sex hormones and growth hormone participate in producing the pubertal growth spurt. It has been estimated that each contributes equally to the rapid growth, although the halt in growth which follows this spurt is due primarily to the sex hormones.[1,45]

The skeleton responds to the stimuli described above by producing bone (ossification) by two distinct processes.[26,33] In the first, termed *endochondral ossification*, the precursor for the bone is formed as cartilage. The development and subsequent growth of those bones results from the transformation of this cartilage into true bone. Endochondral ossification is largely responsible for the elongation of individual bones and is thus the major process contributing to increase in height or "growth." In the second type, *membranous ossification*, the bone is formed directly from the membrane which surrounds the bone (periosteum); there is no cartilage intermediary. The process occurs primarily in the bones of the head which cover the brain (calvarium), the collar bone (clavicle), and parts of the jaw, spine, and pelvic bones. In addition, the widening of limb bones results from this process. Thus an increase in length of a bone is due to endochondral ossification, whereas an increase is its width is due to membranous ossification.

Endochondral ossification commences at 7 weeks of fetal life, when very primitive tissue forms cartilage in areas destined to become bone. Within 2 weeks, blood vessels penetrate into the center of the bone to be, and the ossification process then begins. The transformation spreads rap-

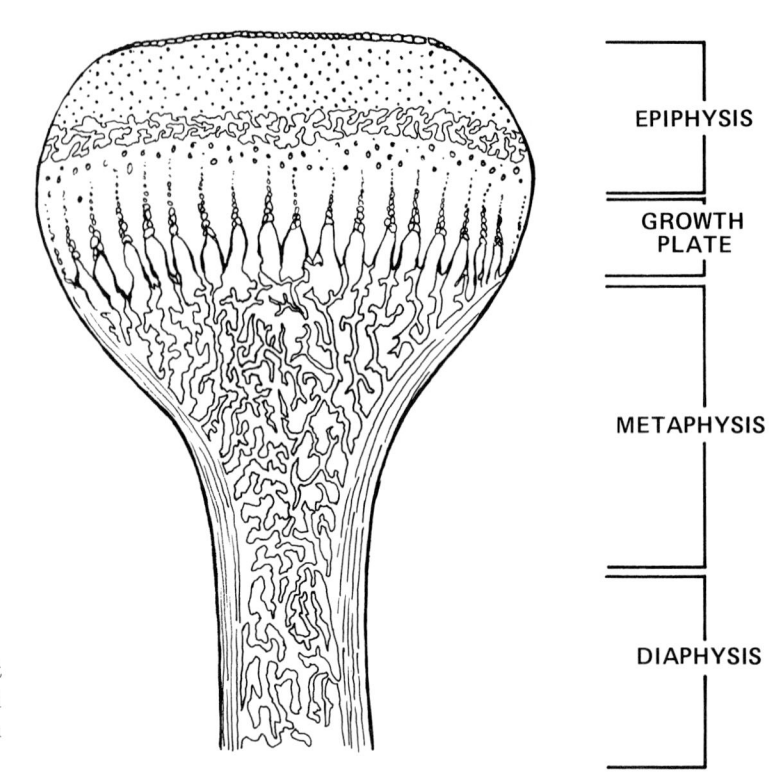

Fig. 32-9. Illustration of different portions of a growing bone. All growth occurs within the growth plate.

idly, and, by three months, most of the precursor has been converted to true bone.[26] Cartilage is retained only at the ends of the bones, where it continues to grow and be converted into bone. This site, which is similar in all bones, is termed the endochondral growth plate (Fig. 32-9). It can be seen under the microscope as a very orderly process consisting of distinct zones of cartilage cells which synchronously proliferate, mature, degenerate, and finally, die, as the cartilage is replaced by bone.[22,26,33] Several of the hormones mentioned previously, especially SMD, are thought to regulate this process.[7,9,12,26,48] After puberty, the growth plate disappears and all remaining cartilage is replaced by bone and skeletal growth ceases.

GROWTH FAILURE

There are many causes of short stature. This is because the sequential nature of growth makes it susceptible to a multitude of conditions and events which interfere with the normal process. Numerous classifications of short stature have been proposed. The following discussion groups short stature primarily on the basis of cause (etiology). Each of the major types of growth failure will be reviewed briefly.

Familial Short Stature

Because of the wide variation in normal height, both within and among populations, many individuals who are normal for their genetic background may consider themselves abnormally short. If an individual who has no evidence of disease falls above the fifth percentile on charts allowing for parental height adjustment, he can be said to be normal for his genetic constitution, and the diagnosis of familial short stature can be made.[26] Familial short stature is probably the most common cause of short stature in children who are referred to a physician for evaluation.

Constitutional Growth Delay

The second most common cause of referral is known as constitutional delay of growth, or constitutional slow maturation.[37] Such children have no disease, but are small for their age and have skeletal maturation that is commensurately delayed. These persons can be expected to undergo puberty at a relatively late age, but they have a normal pubertal growth spurt and reach the normal adult range for stature. Constitutional growth delay, therefore, represents the lower end of the normal curve depicting the rate of skeletal and pubertal development; these children are simply programmed to take longer than average to become adults. Slow maturation is observed more frequently in boys; a similar history is often found in other family members.[42] In the absence of severe psychological problems related to short stature and delayed puberty, treatment is not needed.

Psychosocial Dwarfism (Emotional Deprivation Syndrome)

In certain children, severe emotional disturbance results in marked growth retardation. A history of emotional deprivation is often difficult to obtain, and these children often have siblings of normal stature. A transient abnormality of the pituitary gland may be demonstrated in some, but not all, patients.[7] Bone maturation is usually markedly delayed. The only way to establish the diagnosis is to remove the child from his environment and to observe the striking catch-up growth which then occurs. The disorder presumably results from pituitary suppression by higher brain centers.

Malnutrition

Long term (chronic) malnutrition retards growth. In severe protein deficiency (kwashiorkor), elevated hGH and low SMD levels are consistently found; these levels return to normal after improvement of nutrition.[7] Somatomedin generation is apparently impaired. In addition, circulating levels of the nutrients needed for growth are reduced.

Chronic Diseases

Many chronic diseases are associated with diminished growth. Decreased somatomedin concentrations have been found in chronic kidney disease[32] and chronic liver disease[49] and have been associated with an excess of adrenal hormones (corticosteroids),[47] whether produced by the patients' own gland or administered. In addition, many chronic diseases result in a state of protein breakdown which impairs growth. Moreover, poor absorption of nutrients may be found in gastrointestinal disorders, such as regional ileitis.[14] After cure or control of the disease, there is usually catch-up growth; the final adult stature depends on the duration and severity of the disease.

Intrauterine Growth Retardation

When growth deficiency begins before birth, it is termed *intrauterine growth retardation*. In most cases, the cause (etiology) is obscure. Many of these children, however, have recognized syndromes, some of which are genetic, while others probably have other causes.[26] The genetic syndromes include the Bloom syndrome, Seckel syndrome, Donahue syndrome, Dubowitz syndrome, progeria, Hallermann-Streiff syndrome, Russell-Silver dwarfism, Cornelia De Lange syndrome, and Williams syndrome. In addition, there are a variety of events which occur prior to birth which may severely reduce growth.[35] These include intrauterine infections associated with rubella virus, cytomegalic inclusion disease virus, syphilis, and toxoplasmosis. The maternal consumption of certain drugs such as hydantoins, warfarin, and ethanol (teratogens) is also known to interfere with fetal development.

Chromosomal Anomalies

The genetic material in humans is organized into structures termed *chromosomes*. Abnormalities in the chromosomes are associated with growth retardation, which is usually evident at birth.[23] Many of the abnormalities are not compatible with survival beyond infancy, but those that are, such as Down's syndrome (due to an extra number 21 chromosome—Trisomy 21) and the Turner syndrome (due to the absence of one of the two X chromosomes in females) are characterized by continued slow growth into adulthood and, often, a lack of the pubertal growth spurt. Certain syndromes due to an excess of sex chromosomes (an extra X in the XXY syndrome and an extra Y in the XYY syndrome), are associated with tall stature, however.

Endocrine Disturbances

The hormonal (endocrine) system is responsible for many disturbances that can impair growth. In general, such patients show normal proportions between their trunk and limbs (proportional short stature) (Fig. 32-10). The prototype of these conditions is hGH deficiency. It can result from many causes,[23,25] the most common of which are birth trauma, a tumor arising near the pituitary gland (craniopharyngioma), and x-ray therapy for cancer in the pituitary area. Abnormal embryologic development of the central nervous system can be associated with hGH deficiency, as in isolated absence of the pituitary gland. More generalized syndromes are found in which there is a near complete lack of brain development (anencephaly). There is also a group of syndromes in which the structures which lie along a line drawn between the front and back of the brain (midline structures) fail to develop properly. In its mildest form, this latter defect may exist as simple cleft lip and palate associated with insufficiency of the pituitary gland.[30]

A deficiency in hGH may occur together with a deficiency of one or more other pituitary hormones, such as those which stimulate the sex glands (gonadotropins), thyroid (thyrotropin) and adrenal glands (adrenocorticotropin) to make their respective hormones. The general syndrome is termed *multitropic pituitary hormone deficiency* or, formerly, *panhypopituitarism* and usually occurs without a genetic basis, although

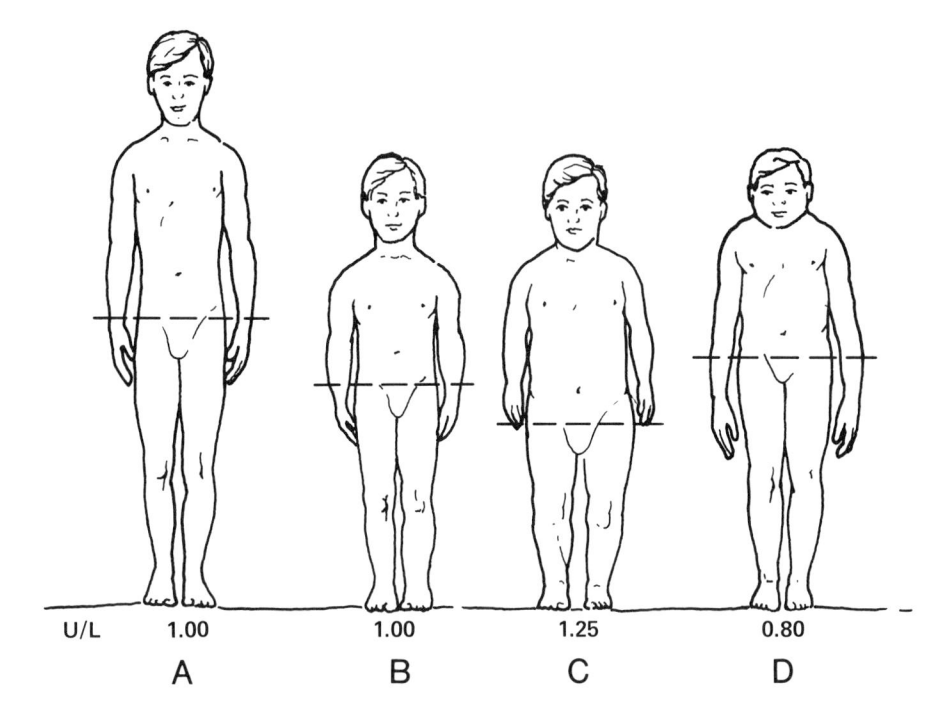

Fig. 32-10. Four children aged approximately 10 years. (A) Normal. (B) Proportionate dwarfism. (C) Disproportionate short limb dwarfism. (D) Disproportionate short trunk dwarfism. Upper segment to lower segment (U/L) ratio is given for each child.

genetic forms have been described.[25] The clinical features depend upon which of these hormones are deficient.[23] Deficiency of hGH results in proportional dwarfism, increased fatty tissue under the skin, a high-pitched voice, and wrinkled skin. During infancy, low blood sugar (hypoglycemia) may occur. Gonadotropin deficiency produces poorly developed sex organs (genitalia) and a lack of secondary sex characteristics. When thyrotropin deficiency occurs, it is usually mild and does not often lead to severe thyroid deficiency. Low levels of adrenocorticotropin hormone may contribute to low blood sugar (hypoglycemia) in infancy and childhood.

An hGH deficiency may also occur as an isolated defect with otherwise normal pituitary function. Such persons have proportionate dwarfism, with normal sexual development. Several distinct forms have been identified which differ slightly in their clinical and laboratory features, as well as by the mode of inheritance.

Although these hormonal deficiencies were originally thought to represent pituitary disturbances, it now seems likely that many of them are due to abnormalities of the brain area adjacent to the pituitary gland (hypothalamus) which regulates its function.[25]

There is a form of proportionate short stature which resembles dwarfism due to pituitary insufficiency that is associated with normal or high levels of hGH.[15] It is called Laron dwarfism, and these children have diminished somatomedin activity, indicating that the basic defect lies in SMD generation.

The Skeletal Dysplasias

The skeletal dysplasias are a large group of disorders in which dwarfism results from failure of the skeleton to respond to the normal hormonal growth stimuli. They thus represent defects of endochondral ossification and are also known as the chondrodystrophies. In general, they are characterized by abnormalities in the size and shape of the limbs, trunk, and, often, the skull, which result in a disproportionality between the trunk and limbs (Fig. 32-10).[24] Until 1960, most disproportionate dwarfs were considered to have one of two types of dwarfism: achondroplasia (those with predominantly short limbs) or the Morquio syndrome (those with a short truck). It is now apparent, however, that there are well over 75 distinct disorders. Each has its own specific set of clinical and x-ray features and a specific pattern of inheritance. Moreover, when bone specimens (biopsies) are examined under the microscope, many have characteristic features (histopathologic features).[24,34,39] In addition, a large number of the disorders have associated abnormalities of other tissues, such as stiff or loose joints, nearsightedness, clubfoot, or hernias, which aid in making a diagnosis.

Except for all of the conditions being termed *dysplasias* (Greek—abnormally formed), the naming of the conditions is terribly confusing. In some cases, the name is based on the part of skeleton that is most affected by x-ray (epiphyseal dysplasias). For others, a Greek term describing the x-ray appearance of the bone—e.g., diastrophic (twisted) dysplasia—or the course of the disease—e.g. thanatophoric (death seeking) dwarfism—has been used. Still other syndromes have been named after the individual who initially described or characterized them—e.g., the Kniest dysplasia or Ellis van Crevald syndrome—while, in yet other cases, the type of inheritance has been used in the designation—e.g., X-linked spondyloepiphyseal dysplasia. In an attempt to develop a uniform nomenclature of these syndromes, an international conference was held in 1977. The classification resulting from the meeting provides a framework within which the disorders can now be organized.[27]

CLINICAL EVALUATION OF SHORT STATURE

Once an abnormality in stature is established by the use of the appropriate growth curves, with adjustment for ethnic background and parental height, the general category of disease must be identified: skeletal, endocrine, nutritional, chromosomal, or intrauterine growth retardation. In general, patients with disproportionate short stature have skeletal dysplasias, while those with relatively normal body proportions have endocrine, nutritional, or other nonskeletal defects. There are exceptions to these rules, such as severe thyroid deficiency which can lead to disproportionate short stature, and several of the skeletal dysplasias which may result in normal body proportions. Disproportionality may not be readily apparent on casual physical examination. Thus measurements such as the upper/lower segment ratio must be obtained before the possibility of a mild skeletal dysplasia, such as hypochondroplasia can be excluded. In those patients with normal body proportions and no evidence of body deformity, a nonskeletal form of short stature should be considered. A history of small birth length suggests one of the forms of intrauterine growth retardation or a chromosomal abnormality, whereas a proportionate child whose birth length was normal is more likely to have an endocrine, nutritional, emotional, or some other form of chronic disease. A complete history and physical examination will often help rule out these diseases. In those patients with intrauterine growth retardation, a careful search for other abnormal physical features may result in the diagnosis of a specific syndrome. Chromosomal studies may help in some situations.

Proportionate short stature with onset after birth and without other manifestations of chronic disease suggests an endocrine, emotional, or nutritional disorder. The measurement of bone maturation (bone age) is frequently useful in determining the relationship between skeletal development and height. When the former is far behind the latter, multitropic pituitary hormone deficiency or severe hypothyroidism is suggested. When skeletal maturation is appropriate for the person's height, constitutional delay, psychosocial dwarfism, and isolated growth hormone deficiency should be considered. Patients with constitutional delay, however, are usually not as severely growth retarded as those with hypopituitarism. In those patients with significant proportionate short stature with onset after birth, endocrine laboratory evaluation is essential. The measurement of the somatomedin level in the blood may be a useful screening test; however, more definitive tests of pituitary function are needed if a low level is found.

If disproportionate dwarfism is found, a careful medical history and physical examination comprise the first step in attempting to make diagnosis. Are the limbs relatively short compared to the trunk (short limb dwarfism), or is the trunk primarily affected (short trunk dwarfism)? Are all of the segments of the limbs equally shortened, or does the shortening primarily affect one? Is the disease limited to the skeleton, or are there extraskeletal abnormalities such as loose joints or nearsightedness? Are there other family members with dwarfism, and, if so, what is the inheritance pattern? The answers to these questions may be sufficient to allow an accurate diagnosis or, at least, to limit those diagnoses to be considered (differential diagnosis) to a relatively small number.

The next step in the evaluation of the disproportionately short patient is to obtain x-rays of the entire skeleton. They alone will often be sufficient to make specific diagnosis, since the classification of the skeletal dysplasias has been based primarily on x-rays. Attention should be paid to the specific parts of the skeleton that are involved (spine, limbs, pelvis, or skull) and to the part of each bone which is most abnormal. Since the skeletal x-ray features of many of these diseases change with age, it is usually beneficial to review x-rays that have been taken at different ages, when possible. In some disorders the abnormalities observed following puberty are nonspecific, so that the accurate diagnosis of an adult disproportionate dwarf may be impossible unless films taken prior to puberty are available.

In some instances, examination of skeletal tissue under the microscope, or even under the electron microscope, may be helpful in making a diagnosis. In many of the chondrodystrophies, specific alterations have been identified, although, in others, no specific changes are seen.

Thus, in most cases, the evaluation of short stature requires extensive testing. Although definitive therapy to promote growth is currently available only in the disorders due to hormonal abnormalities and the acquired nutritional, emotional, and chronic disease states, once the bases of the remaining forms of short stature are identified, specific forms of treatment or prevention may evolve. Furthermore, diagnosis of the precise form of short stature can have great importance in advising children and their parents of the expected future course of their condition, in taking action to prevent or minimize anticipated problems and for providing an accurate assessment of the likelihood that the condition will recur in a family (genetic counseling).

REFERENCES

1. Aynsley-Green, A., Zachman, M., and Prader, A., Interrelation of the therapeutic effects of growth hormone and testosterone on growth in hypopituitarism. *Journal of Pediatrics* 89:992, 1976.

2. Bayley, N., and Pinneau, S. R., Tables for predicting adult height from skeletal age revised for use with the Greulich-Pyle hand standards. *Journal of Pediatrics* 40:423, 1952.
3. Brazel, J. A., and Blizzard, R. M., The influence of the endocrine glands upon growth and development, in Williams, R. H. (ed.), *Textbook of Endocrinology*. Philadelphia, W. B. Saunders, 1974, p 1030.
4. Carter, C. O., and Marshall, W. A., The genetics of adult stature, in Falkner, F., and Tanner, J. M. (eds.), *Human Growth*, vol. 1. New York, Plenum Press, 1979, pp. 299–305.
5. Daughaday, W. H., Herrington, A. C., and Phillips, L. S., The regulation of growth by endocrines. *Annual Review of Physiology* 37:211, 1975.
6. Daughaday, W. H., Phillips, L. S., and Mueller, M. C., The effects of insulin and growth hormone on the release of somatomedin by isolated rat liver. *Endocrinology* 98:1214, 1976.
7. Daughaday, W. H., Hormonal regulation of growth by somatomedin and other tissue growth factors. *Clinics in Endocrinology and Metabolism* 6:117, 1977.
8. D'Ercole, A. J., Underwood, L. E., and Van Wyk, J. J., Serum somatomedin-C in hypopituitarism and in other disorders of growth. *Journal of Pediatrics* 90:375, 1977.
9. Garabedian, M., Bailly du Bois, M., Corvol, M. T., et al., Vitamin D and cartilage, I. In vitro metabolism of 25-hydroxycholecalciferol by cartilage. *Endocrinology* 102:1262, 1978.
10. Garn, S. M., and Bailey, S. M., Genetics of maturational process, in Falkner, F., and Tanner, J. M. (eds.), *Human Growth*, vol. 1. New York, Plenum Press, 1979, pp. 307–330.
11. Greulich, W. W., and Pyle, S. I., *Radiographic Atlas of Skeletal Development of the Hand and Wrist*. Stanford, Stanford University Press, 1959.
12. Hall, K., Takano, D., Frykland, L., et al., Somatomedins. *Advances in Metabolic Disorders* 7:19, 1975.
13. Hintz, R. L., Suskind, R., Amatayakul K., et al., Plasma somatomedin and growth hormone values in children with protein-calorie malnutrition. *Journal of Pediatrics* 92:151, 1978.
14. Kelts, D. G., Grand, R. J., Shen, G., et al., Nutritional basis of growth failure in children and adolescents with Crohn's disease. *Gastroenterology* 76:720–727, 1979.
15. Laron, Z., Syndrome of familial dwarfism and high plasma immunoreactive growth hormone. *Israel Journal of Medical Science* 10:1247, 1974.
16. Marshall, W. A., Puberty, in Falkner, F., and Tanner, J. M. (eds), *Human Growth*, vol. 2. New York, Plenum Press, 1974, pp. 141–181.
17. McKusick, V. A., *Heritable Disorders of Connective Tissue*. St. Louis, C. V. Mosby, 1972.
18. National Center for Health Statistics, NCHS growth charts. *Vital and Health Statistics* 25 (suppl. 3):76, 1976.
19. Nero, Z., and Laron, Z., Growth factors. *American Journal of Diseases of Children* 133:419–428, 1979.
20. North, A. F., Jr., Mazumdar, S., and Lagrillo, V. M., Birth weight, gestational age and perinatal deaths in 5,471 infants of diabetic mothers. *Journal of Pediatrics* 90:444, 1977.
21. Powell, G. F., Brazel, J. A., Raiti, S., et al., Emotional deprivation and growth retardation simulating idiopathic hypopituitarism. II. Endocrinologic evaluation of patients. *New England Journal of Medicine* 276:1279, 1967.
22. Reide, U. N., Experimental aspects of growth plate disorders. *Current Topics in Pathology* 59:181, 1974.
23. Rimoin, D. L., and Schimke, R. N., *Genetic Disorders of the Endocrine Glands*. St. Louis, C. V. Mosby, 1971.
24. Rimoin, D. L., The chondrodystrophies. *Advances in Human Genetics* 5:1, 1975.

25. Rimoin, D. L., Hereditary forms of growth hormone deficiency and resistance. *Birth Defects Original Article Series* 12:15, 1976.
26. Rimoin, D. L., and Horton, W. A., Medical progress: Short stature, Part I. *Journal of Pediatrics* 92:523, 1978.
27. Rimoin, D. L., International nomenclature of constitutional diseases of bone with biography. *Birth Defects Original Article Series* 15:1–29, 1979.
28. Roche, A. F., Bone growth and maturation, in Falkner, F., and Tanner, J. M. (eds.), *Human Growth*, vol. 2. Postnatal Growth. New York, Plenum Press, 1979, pp. 317–355.
29. Roche, A. F., Lipman, R. S., Overall, J. E., et al., The effects of stimulant medication on the growth of hyperkinetic children. *Pediatrics* 63:847–850, 1979.
30. Rudman, D., David, T., Priest, J. H., et al., Prevalence of growth hormone deficiency in children with cleft lip or palate. *Journal of Pediatrics* 93:378, 1978.
31. Ryman, N., Linsten, J., Leikrans, S., et al., A genetic analysis of the normal body-height growth and dental development in man. *Annals of Human Genetics* 39:163, 1975.
32. Saenger, P., Wiedemann, G., Schwartz, E., et al., Somatomedin and growth after renal transplantation. *Pediatric Research* 8:163, 1974.
33. Serafini-Fracassini, A., and Smith, J. W., *The Structure and Biochemistry of Cartilage*. Edinburgh, Churchill-Livingstone, 1974, p. 138.
34. Sillence, D. O., Horton, W. A., and Rimoin, D. L., Morphologic studies in the skeletal dysplasias. *American Journal of Pathology*, 96:811–870, 1979.
35. Smith, D. W., Prenatal growth deficiency. *Birth Defects Original Article Series* 12:31, 1976.
36. Smith, D. W., Truog, W., Rogers, J. E., et al., Shifting linear growth during infancy, illustration of genetic factors in growth from fetal life through infancy. *Journal of Pediatrics* 89:225, 1976.
37. Smith, D. W., *Growth and Its Disorders: Major Problems in Clinical Pediatrics*. Philadelphia, W. B. Saunders, 1977.
38. Spranger, J. W., Langer, L. O., and Wiedemann, H. R., *Bone dysplasias: An Atlas of Constitutional Disorders of Skeletal Development*. Philadelphia, W. B. Saunders, 1974.
39. Stanescu, V., Stanescu, R., and Maroteaux, P., Etude morphologique et biochemique du cartilage de croissance dans les osteochrondrodysplasias. *Archives Francaises de Pediatrie* 34 (suppl. 3):1, 1977.
40. Tanner, J. M., Whitehouse, R. H., and Takaishi, M., Standards from birth to maturity for height, weight, height velocity, and weight velocity: British Children, 1965, Parts I and II. *Archives of Disease in Childhood* 41:454, 613, 1966.
41. Tanner, J. M., Whitehouse, R. H., Marshall, W., et al: Assessment of skeletal maturity and prediction of adult height. New York, Academic Press, 1975.
42. Tanner, J. M., Physical growth and development, in Forfor, J. O., and Arneil, G. C. (eds.) *Textbook of Pediatrics*. Edinburgh, Livingstone, 1973, pp. 224–291.
43. Tanner, J. M., Charts for the diagnosis of short stature and low growth velocity, allowance for height of parents, and prediction of adult height. *Birth Defects Original Article Series* 12:1, 1976.
44. Tanner, J. M., Whitehouse, R. H., Marubini, E., et al., The adolescent growth spurt of boys and girls of the Hardpenden growth study. *Annals of Human Biology* 3:109, 1976.
45. Tanner, J. M., Whitehouse, R. H., Hughes. P. C. R., et al., Relative importance of growth hormone and sex steroids for the growth at puberty of trunk length, limb length, and muscle width in growth hormone deficiency children. *Journal of Pediatrics* 89:1000, 1976.
46. Vale, W., Brazeau, P., Rivier, C., et al., Somatostatin. *Recent Progress in Hormone Research* 31:365, 1975.

47. Van Wyk, J. J., and Underwood, L. E., Relation between growth hormone and somatomedin. *Annual Review of Medicine* 26:427, 1975.
48. Wong, P. Y. K., Majeska, R. J., and Wuthier, R. E., Biosynthesis and metabolism of prostaglandins in chick epiphyseal cartilage. *Prostaglandins* 14:839, 1977.
49. Wu, A., Grant, D. B., Hambley, J., et al., Reduced serum somatomedin activity in patients with chronic liver disease. *Clinical Science and Molecular Medicine* 47:359, 1974.

33

Sickle Cell Disease

F. RALPH BERBERICH, M.D.

HISTORY AND DEMOGRAPHY

Sickle cell anemia was first described at the turn of the century by Herrick, who observed the crescent-shaped red blood cells, from which the disease derives its name, in the blood of an anemic Black West Indian student. Since that time, a wealth of information has accrued defining this disease—from its molecular origins to its protean clinical manifestations. Modalities of therapy have lagged behind our understanding of the disease process, however, and remain far from satisfactory.

In the United States, sickle cell disease has been identified with the Black population, but it is by no means unique to this group. Its distribution is extensive and crosses both racial and continental lines (Fig. 33-1). The disease, which results from an inherited genetic defect, is most prevalent in areas of the world where malaria is common. It has been found that normal people carrying the sickle cell gene are relatively resistant to the malaria parasite. The distribution of sickle cell disease illustrates the principle of Darwinian selection, since the survival of a child carrying the sickle gene in a malaria ridden area is relatively more likely. In areas of the West Coast of Africa, thought to be the ancestral homeland of most American Blacks, about 30 percent of the populace has the sickle cell gene. About 10 percent of the American Blacks carry the sickle cell gene. These people are physically normal, and, under usual circumstances have no symptoms of sickle cell disease. Approximately 1 in 1000 Black newborn infants will have sickle cell anemia, having inherited two defective sickle cell genes.

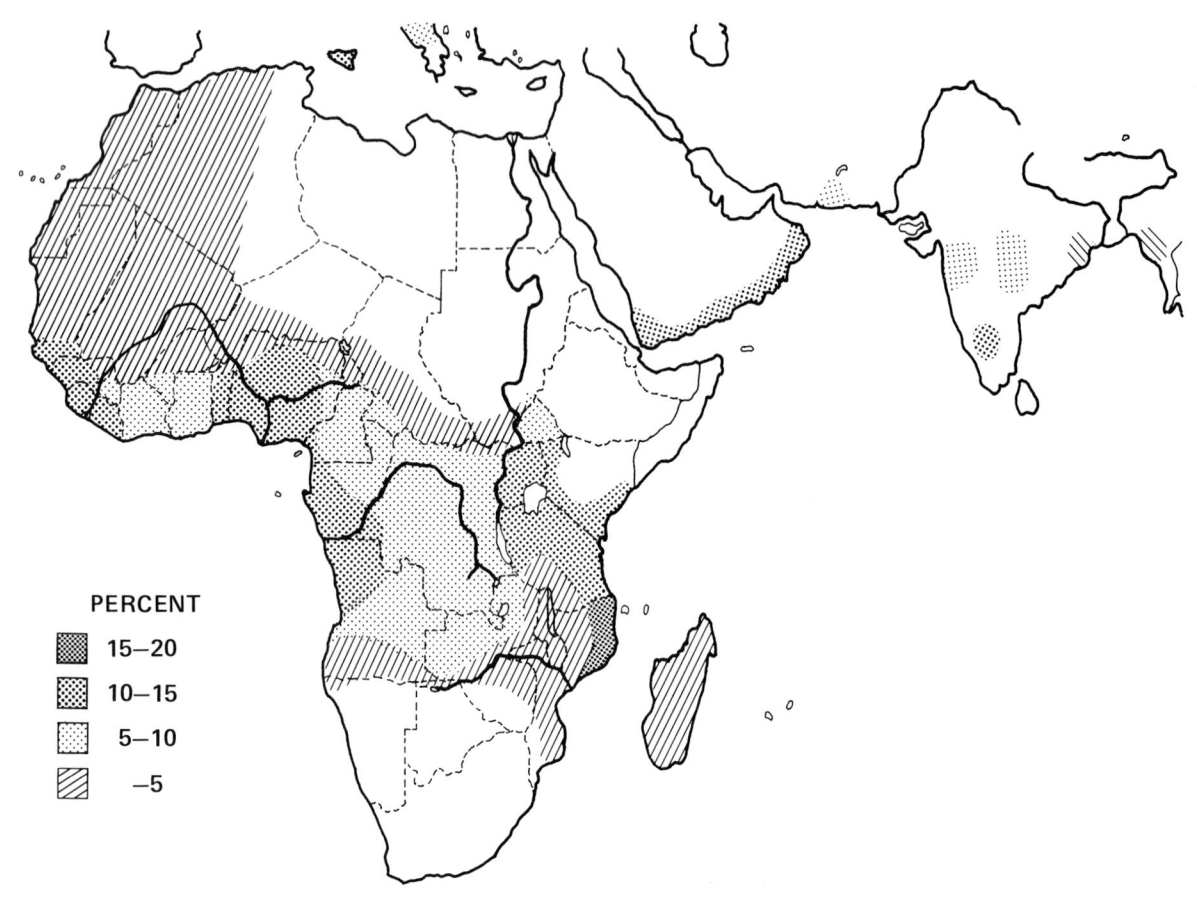

Fig. 33-1. Distribution of sickle cell gene in Africa and Asia.

PHYSIOLOGY AND DISEASE EVOLUTION

The red cell is the blood constituent responsible for the transport of oxygen to the tissues. Its biconcave shape, flexibility, and chemical composition are all designed to perform this function with maximum efficiency, so that the greatest amount of oxygen can be extracted from respired air (Fig. 33-2). In this way, all tissues, even those most remote from the major blood vessels, receive sufficient oxygen to carry out normal metabolism.

The molecule within the red cell that carries the oxygen and comprises over 90 percent of the cell's composition is called *hemoglobin*. Its complex structure includes an iron-containing pigment, called *heme,* and a carrier protein, called *globin*. The iron in heme binds oxygen in a reversible reaction, which permits its later release to tissues. Four heme molecules are bound to two pairs of globin chains to form hemoglobin. These two pairs of globin chains are designated as either α or non-α. In adults, the predominant non-α chain is the β chain. Normal adult hemoglobin (HbA), therefore, contains two α and two β globin chains (Fig. 33-3). Prior to birth, the primary non-α chain is termed the γ chain, which gives rise to fetal hemoglobin (HbF).

A number of paired β globin chains are schematically illustrated in Figure 33-4. As shown, a variety of hemoglobins are possible, each of which is determined by a unique protein composition and each of which may be inherited from generation to generation. The initial alterations that produce the genetic changes responsible for the evolution of these different hemoglobin molecules are termed *mutations*; these alterations

Fig. 33-2. An illustration showing normal red blood cells (*left*) and sickle cells (*right*).

Fig. 33-3. Schematic representation of the structure of hemoglobin: Iron-containing pigment (heme) is shown in dark grey. Carrier proteins (α and β globins) are shown in light grey and white. Reprinted, by permission, from the *New England Journal of Medicine* 299(14):754, 1978.

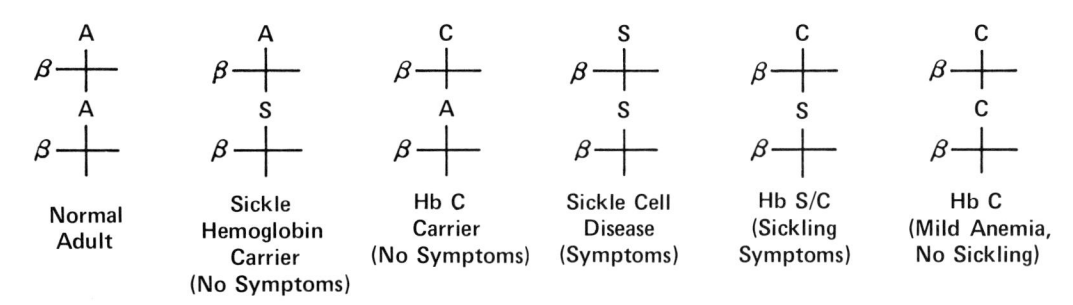

Fig. 33-4. Schematic representation of paired β globin chains, showing possible combinations of 3 variants (A, normal; S, sickle; and C) and symptoms resulting from each combination. As long as at least one normal β chain is present, no symptoms are observed. When both chains are abnormal, the symptoms observed are determined by the chemical properties of the abnormal globin chains.

occur in the basic genetic material that dictates protein structure. In the case of the sickle cell defect, a change in only one protein building block (amino acid) among the 146 that comprise the β globin chain results in the production of the sickle hemoglobin molecule (HbS). The clinical consequence of a hemoglobin alteration depends on the particular chemical properties of the modified hemoglobin and on whether both or only one of the paired β globin chains differs from normal. If one globin chain is normal, then a defect in the other may not be noticeable. If both chains are abnormal, then the interaction between them may further or retard the deleterious effects of either. Most abnormal non-sickle hemoglobin chains found in combination with sickle cell globin bring out the sickling defect. Some, however, such as α, γ hemoglobin, actually protect against sickling.

The ramifications of the molecular alteration which results in sickle hemoglobin become evident when HbS-containing red cells are exposed to an oxygen-deficient environment (hypoxia). Once the concentration of HbS is at a certain level in a hypoxic environment, it gels to form an insoluble structure called a tactoid. HbS in tactoid formation causes the red cell to become rigid and assume the sickle shape (Fig. 33-2). For a time, this sickling process is reversible, but, eventually, a cell may become irreversibly rigid, distorted in shape, and permanently damaged.

The fate of the sickled cell determines the symptoms and complications of sickle cell disease. Within the circulation, sickled red cells increase the viscosity of the blood and block its flow through smaller blood vessels. The tissue beyond such a blockage becomes oxygen deprived, which gives rise to further sickling of red cells and causes pain. An event leading to oxygen lack that causes tissue injury (infarction) can occur in any organ. An infarct in a vital organ, such as the brain, can cause irreparable damage.

A second consequence of sickling is anemia, which results from the premature destruction of red cells. The spleen is the organ normally responsible for the removal of old red cells from the blood, and its function may be likened to that of a fine-meshed filter. Red cells must squeeze through a narrow space as they circulate through the spleen in order to leave that organ. About 5 percent of the total blood volume is filtered through the spleen at any single moment. If the spleen is removed or injured, the liver takes on a similar function. Old, rigid red blood cells are thus removed from the circulation, but, in addition, any abnormal cell will also be trapped within the spleen. The area where filtration takes place is relatively devoid of oxygen, which encourages sickling, red cell rigidity, and the removal of additional sickled cells. This form of red cell destruction is termed *hemolysis,* and leads to profound anemia.

Anemia reduces the oxygen-carrying capacity of the blood, which causes pallor, weakness, limited exercise tolerance and forces the heart to work harder in order to supply oxygen to the tissues. Chronic anemia can lead to growth retardation, delayed sexual maturation, and other developmental problems. The organ of red cell production, the bone marrow, is stimulated to expand as it attempts to increase production of red blood cells. Certain alterations of bone growth therefore occur, which give the sickler recognizable physical characteristics, such as a prominent forehead, high cheekbones, and long, thin arms and legs.

As sickle cells are eliminated by the spleen, the chemical products of their breakdown are metabolized by the liver. When these exceed the liver's ability to process them, a yellow pigment, called *bilirubin,* may become elevated in the blood. This can produce a recognizable yellowing

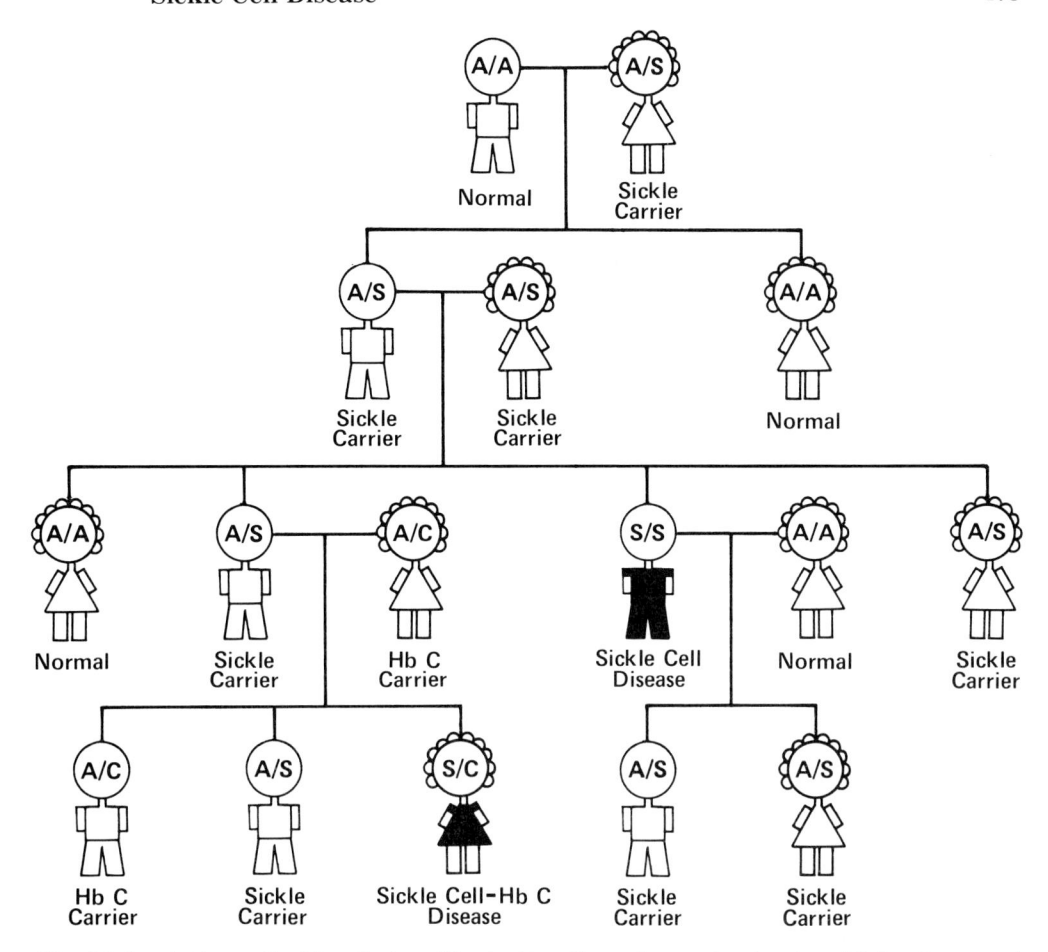

Fig. 33-5. A theoretical family tree illustrating the autosomal codominant inheritance pattern in sickle cell disease. Also presented is the offspring pattern of a mating between carriers of the sickle gene and the gene for another abnormal hemoglobin, HbC. All carriers show no disease manifestations because they also produce the normal hemoglobin, HbA.

of the skin and the whites of the eyes, termed *jaundice*. The liver and spleen may also enlarge, giving the child a potbellied appearance.

GENETICS

Sickle cell disease is a genetically transmitted disorder. Its pattern of inheritance is one wherein an affected child is born to two apparently normal parents. There may be no history of sickle cell disease in preceding generations. The term for this particular mode of inheritance is *autosomal codominance*. Two genes of equal dominance are inherited, one from each parent, and, together, determine the hemoglobin composition. The individuals who transmit the disease but have no symptoms, are carriers of a single sickle gene (sickle cell trait). Only one of their two β globin chains is abnormal. A child born to two carriers has a 25-percent chance of receiving an abnormal sickle gene from both parents and thus of having sickle cell disease. The same 25-percent chance applies to each offspring born to carrier parents. In Figure 33-5, the transmission of the sickle cell gene is illustrated. Included also is a theoretical mating in which the offspring inherits the sickle gene from one parent and a different hemoglobin abnormality from the other. This child is expected to have sickling problems because he produces no normal HbA.

It is now possible to screen populations for the presence of sickle cell trait or other abnormal hemoglobin carrier states. Individuals planning to have children who are at risk for the sickle cell gene, may wish to have this testing performed. In some communities, mass screening programs have been undertaken. The social and political implications of genetic screening programs are beyond the scope of this chapter. It is also possible to screen newborn children at risk for sickle cell disease. There is potential benefit in the early detection of the infant with sickle cell disease, since such children are prone to life-threatening infections, and since parents of such a child may desire early genetic counseling.

CLINICAL MANIFESTATIONS

During early childhood the major manifestations of sickle cell disease are age related and include profound anemia, pain crisis due to sickling, severe infections, and disorders of growth and development. The severity of these symptoms may vary widely.

Newborn infants generally do not exhibit symptoms, since the predominant hemoglobin at birth is HbF, and little HbS is produced. Normal adult or abnormal sickle cell hemoglobin levels are attained at 3 to 6 months of age, and symptoms may be anticipated at this time.

Anemia

Anemia becomes prominent. Children may be noticeably pale. Although the bone marrow attempts to replace the red blood cells destroyed in the spleen, the number produced does not equal the number lost. If the rate of red cell destruction accelerates beyond the liver's capacity to metabolize the by-products, jaundice may also occur. A sudden increase in pallor or jaundice can indicate a dangerous acceleration of the anemic process.

Hand-Foot Syndrome

The first manifestation of sickle cell disease in the preschool-aged child may be the *hand-foot syndrome,* in which sudden pain and swelling arise in the limbs. Another sign that sometimes leads to the diagnosis is unexpected, overwhelming bacterial infection.

Pain Crisis (Sickling)

A more typical sign of sickle cell disease is the pain crisis, which may affect virtually any area of the body. A variety of initiating events, such as oxygen deprivation, altered blood flow, infection, dehydration, or stress, can lead to sickling of red blood cells and the occlusion of small blood vessels. The loss of oxygen and nutrients leads to pain (ischemia) and can result in tissue death if the circulation is not restored (infarct). There is no specific treatment for such a crisis, and therapy is directed at pain control and a reversal of conditions that may have initiated the sickling. Because of the severity of the pain and its duration of several days, narcotic medication may be prescribed. The potential for addiction in adolescents and young adults with sickle cell disease is a challenging therapeutic problem.

Several important sickling target areas are described below. The spleen is especially prone to infarcts because of its filtration function. Recurrent splenic infarction leads to the gradual shrinkage and scarring of this organ in childhood. Infarction of the spleen is often accompanied by severe left-sided abdominal pain. The loss of splenic function contributes to these children's susceptibility to certain infections. Some protection may be provided by specific immunizations against organisms to which sicklers are particularly vulnerable.

Sickling in bones causes pain, which may be confused with infection (osteomyelitis). Some bones, such as the hip (femur), are especially vulnerable to tissue death following sickling because of an inherently poor blood supply (asceptic necrosis). Patients with bone pain, therefore, require prompt attention and early initiation of treatment.

If sickling occurs in the brain, the result may be comparable to that of a stroke. Children with severe headache, unexplained abnormal behavior, sleepiness, or a relative weakness of one side of their body may be experiencing a sickling event in the brain. Immediate treatment is mandatory. One approach to this problem is the rapid exchange of normal blood for sickle blood in such a patient.

Sickling in the lung may mimic pneumonia and may cause cough, fever, and shortness of breath. When the intestines are involved, the pain may be so severe that appendicitis is suspected and surgery is performed. If sickling occurs in the liver, right-sided abdominal pain and jaundice may result. The abdomen may enlarge and the patient may become nauseated, confused, or lethargic. The heart may be involved, but damage due to sickling usually does not become apparent until adulthood. The heart is stressed primarily because of the anemia. Failure to maintain adequate blood flow to meet the demands of the tissues is termed cardiac failure. Cough, liver enlargement, and swelling of the ankles, especially when all three occur together, may indicate the presence of cardiac failure requiring prompt medical attention.

Sickling in the kidney can result in urinary bleeding, which is characteristically painless. Reduced kidney function may arise with recurrent episodes. Other, indirect, effects of anemia and recurrent sickling may be the appearance of gallstones in childhood, growth retardation, and delayed skeletal maturation.

Aplastic Crisis

Another potential complication is the so-called aplastic crisis, which occurs when there is a sudden diminution of red cell production by the bone marrow. An aplastic crisis may be precipitated by viral infections and should be suspected if there is sudden weakness or profound pallor. This complication is especially dangerous, since the blood count is low to begin with and may fall precipitously in the absence of continuing brisk red cell production.

TREATMENT

Prevention of red cell sickling remains an unaccomplished goal. Various agents that prevent sickling in test tube situations have not proved useful or practical in human beings. Therapy, therefore, emphasizes the judicious avoidance of those situations which precipitate sickling. Since these may include emotional stress, physical exercise, medical illness, fever, injury, dehydration, altitude change, or any event which diminishes the availability of oxygen to tissues, the task is difficult and inherently frustrating. Overprotection can also be deleterious and stifling to normal development.

Once a sickling event has been triggered and symptoms develop, early treatment is warranted. This may include hospitalization, pain medication, intravenous fluids, and, on occasion, oxygen. In certain situations, blood must be given, sometimes by exchange transfusion—in which larger volumes can be replaced by blood from a normal adult. Where sickling crises are very frequent, dangerous in location, or prompted by chronic conditions, regular (prophylactic) blood transfusions are often given. Prophylactic or exchange transfusions dilute the sickle hemoglobin with normal hemoglobin. They thereby reduce the likelihood of sickling and also ameliorate the anemia. Unfortunately, frequent blood transfusions carry the hazard of transfusion reactions, and overload the body with excess iron, which subsequently remains deposited in the tissues. Once deposited, iron is difficult to remove, requiring daily infusions with iron-binding drugs (chelators). For this reason, transfusion is reserved for situations wherein it is judged absolutely necessary.

EDUCATIONAL IMPLICATIONS

The crises and complications of sickle cell disease are capricious. The sickler faces uncertainty, episodes of recurrent pain, and debilitation. Sickling may interfere with personal goals, impede development, and frustrate progress.

The teacher may anticipate school absences due to crises, and these may increase in frequency with the stresses of adolescent years. They usually last several days or longer. Students with sickle cell disease may, therefore, require additional support to maintain grades and keep up with their peers. This is a pressing responsibility, since education and the acquisition of skills can foster vital self-reliance and independence in adulthood. The sickler should also be encouraged to develop normally with his peers. He should acquire a sense of his own limitations and learn to avoid those situations that regularly and specifically precipitate sickle crises. The universal stresses involved in becoming a productive member of society can obviously not be escaped, and the sickler should be taught to accommodate to these and live with them. These experiences may be accompanied by understandable frustration and hostility. Manipulative behavior may also occur, and parents and medical personnel should be alert to this possibility so that proper psychosocial intervention can be initiated early.

BIBLIOGRAPHY

Brown, E., Dowdy, H., Rosner, F., et al., The effectiveness of sickle cell education in New York City public elementary schools. *Journal of the National Medical Association* 70:571–574, 1978.

Honig, G. R., Sickling syndromes in children. *Advances in Pediatrics* 23:271–313, 1976.

Lehmann, H., Huntsman, R. S., Casey, R., et al., Sickle cell disease and related disorders, in Williams, W.J., Beutler, E., Erslev, A. J., et al. (eds.), *Hematology,* 2nd ed. New York, McGraw-Hill Book Company, 1977, pp. 495–524.

34

Spinal Muscular Atrophy of Childhood

JUDITH KOEHLER, M.D.

Spinal muscular atrophy (SMA) results from a progressive degeneration of the motor nerve cells of the anterior portion of the spinal cord and of the brain stem. The specific cause for this degeneration is at this time still unknown.

SMA of childhood has traditionally been divided into (1) Werdnig-Hoffman disease, which affects young infants and has a rapidly progressive course that usually ends in death before school age, and (2) Kugelberg-Welander disease, which develops at an older age and has a more benign course compatible with long life.[1-3] It must be emphasized, however, that this type of subdivision is highly artificial and can be misleading, as has been pointed out in several recent reviews.[4-10] It is more correct, as well as fairer to the patient and family, to say that SMA has a variable course ranging anywhere from a chronic, minimally disabling weakness to a rapidly downhill progression ending in complete incapacitation and early death. Obviously, the less severely involved patients will be seen in a regular school and the more severely involved in special schools for the handicapped, while those who die at an early age will not come to the attention of teachers.

SIGNS AND SYMPTOMS

The most characteristic features are progressive weakness and wasting of proximal muscles, symptoms that in many cases may mimic other primary muscle diseases (Fig. 34-1). Weakness affecting the hip muscles may cause delay or difficulty in sitting or walking, or, at a later age, frequent falling, unsteadiness of gait, and difficulty in climbing stairs. Shoulder muscle weakness will cause symptoms such as weakness and

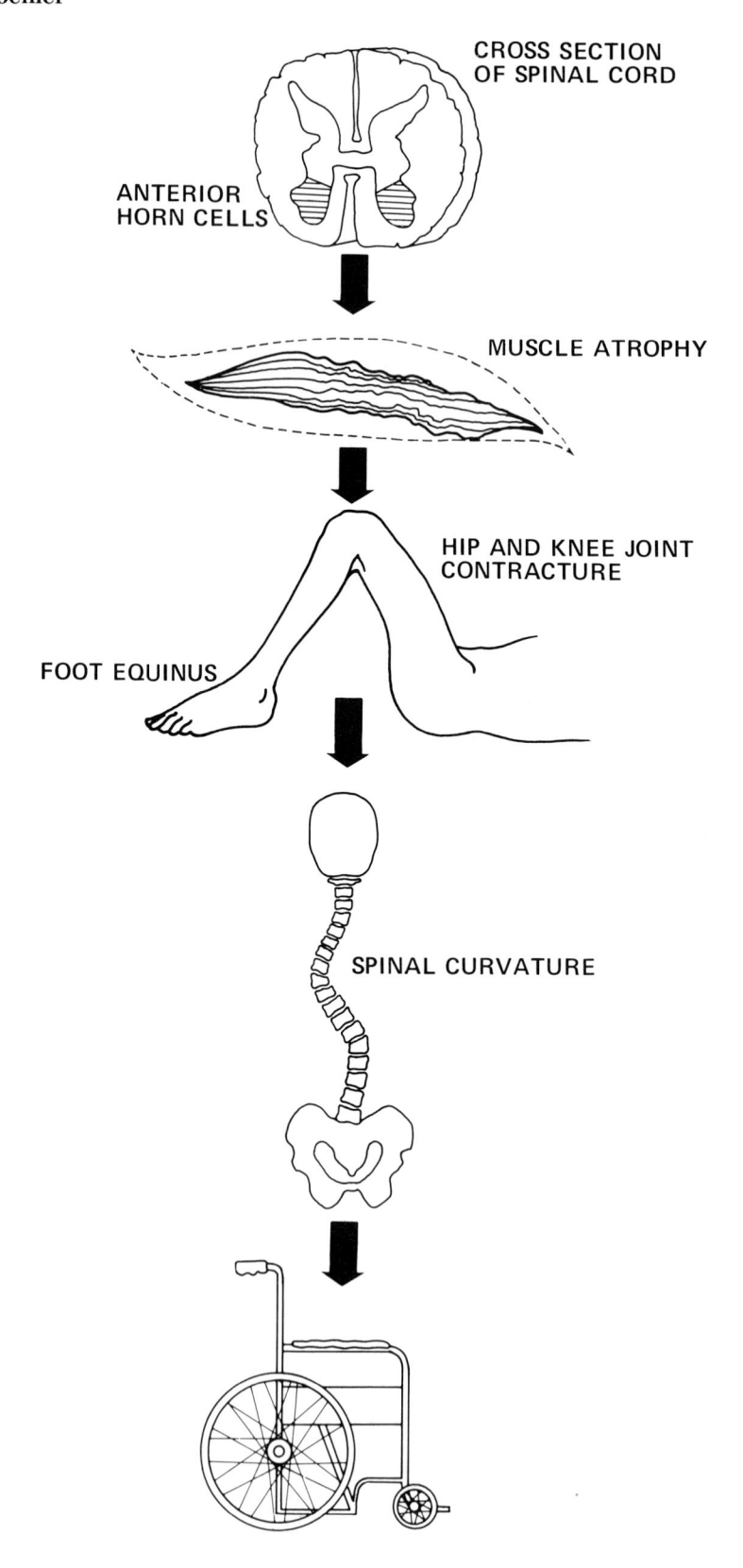

Fig. 34-1. Spinal muscular atrophy. Graphic representation of the effects of disease of the anterior horn cells of the spinal cord, with resultant muscular atrophy, joint contractures, spinal curvature, and, finally, disability leading to a wheelchair existence.

fatigue in raising the arms and difficulty in lifting objects, combing hair, climbing ropes, or doing chin-ups. Back-muscle weakness and paraspinal weakness may cause back pain or spinal curvature. Occasionally, the distribution of weakness may affect distal as well as proximal muscles; in these cases, weakness of the feet, ankles, hands, and wrists may be prominent. Such a child may have difficulty writing. A particular form of SMA that affects mostly the shoulder (scapular) muscles and the muscles of the outside of the leg and foot (peroneal muscles) has been termed *scapuloperoneal muscular atrophy*. Involvement of the lower cranial nerves can result in difficulty in swallowing and aspiration, a poor cough reflex, and slurred speech. Diaphragmatic and chest-muscle weakness may result in respiratory insufficiency.

The distribution of weakness may be such that it is impossible to differentiate SMA clinically from various other types of muscular dystrophy. If such symptoms are noticed in a school child, they should be brought to the attention of a physician for proper diagnosis.

SMA may be differentiated from other similar diseases in that signs of spastic muscles (as seen in cerebral palsy), imbalance (ataxia), sensory loss, seizures, and mental impairment are notably absent. Orthopedic deformities are commonly seen in the benign forms of SMA. Usually, wasting (atrophy) and loss of muscle strength are followed by tightening of the muscles and secondary joint contractures. The primary disease process, then, may be compounded by disuse atrophy. As the muscle shrinks and is not used, loss of bone substance also occurs, leading to susceptibility to fracture and, sometimes, to growth arrest. A special form of contracture may result when the fetus is involved early in utero; this is termed *arthrogryposis multiplex congenita,* of neurogenic origin, and is evident at birth. Heart disease, particularly with respect to distribution of the electrical conduction system of the heart (conduction blocks) and irregular heartbeats (arrhythmias), or slow heartbeat (bradycardia), has been reported.[6,11] Rarely, however, does this play a significant role in the symptomatology of SMA.

As pointed out by Munsat et al.,[8] factors such as the patient's age at onset and sex, the distribution of weakness, and whether the disease is sporadic or inherited are not good prognostic indicators of the disease course and ultimate outcome. Other workers, however, have reported that the disease, particularly its older-onset form, may occur somewhat more frequently and follows a slightly more severe course in males.[9] It must be emphasized that even in the face of what seems a progressive downhill course, clinical stabilization may occur at any time. Clinical arrest for a period of 2 years is a good prognostic sign, after which plateauing of the deficit or perhaps even clinical improvement may occur.

INHERITANCE

While sporadic cases of SMA do occur, hereditary factors play a definite role in many families with SMA.[12] The usual mode of inheritance is in an autosomal recessive pattern. This means that a double dose of defective genetic material is needed for expression of the disease, or, in other words, that both parents must carry a defective gene. The chances are 25 percent (or 1 in 4) that such a couple will have another similarly affected child, 25 percent that they will have a perfectly normal child, and 50 percent that they will have a clinically normal child who is, nonetheless, a carrier of the defective gene.*

---

*See also the appendix to the chapter on Down's Syndrome for a more detailed discussion of these inheritance patterns.

The second most common mode of inheritance, particularly in older-onset SMA, is autosomal dominant. In this case, a strong family history is present; affected siblings and parents are the rule. A couple in which one parent is affected has a 50 percent chance of having an affected child.

Less commonly, sex-linked recessive inheritance has been implicated. Unfortunately, our present level of knowledge does not yet enable us to make the diagnosis in utero in a family with already one affected child.

SPECIFIC THERAPY

Specific therapy involves full cooperation of neurologic, orthopedic, and rehabilitation services. Treatment is directed particularly toward prevention of secondary joint and bone complications and vigorous therapy of these conditions if they do occur. Daily progressive range of motion of all joints should be carried out, and mild to moderate exercises also should be performed daily. Lightweight braces to lend knee, ankle, or spine stability may be necessary as progression occurs; surgical correction of spinal curvature (scoliosis) may also be required. Special devices, such as a long-handled spoon with special grips to enable the patient to carry out activities of daily living, are readily available from occupational therapists. Again, it cannot be emphasized sufficiently that exercise and therapy are necessary even in the face of what seems a downhill course. It is hoped that a child can be maintained until clinical stabilization occurs. Clinical arrest and stabilization for a period of 2 years is a good prognostic sign. A fixed level of neurologic and orthopedic deficit and, in some patients, slight clinical improvement may then occur.

Respiratory infection, aspiration of secretions or food resulting in secondary pneumonias, and pulmonary disease may also be problems. For the same reasons outlined above, vigorous therapy is indicated in all patients.

EDUCATIONAL IMPLICATIONS

It should be emphasized that these children have normal intellectual capacities and that most will ultimately have to make their living utilizing these capacities rather than their motor strengths. Some children may be minimally involved and therefore able to take part in normal classroom activities. The more severely involved will require special schooling. These students may need longer time to finish an assignment. If they are unable to write with a pencil, they may be able to use an electric typewriter or a dictating machine. With diminished motor skills, the emphasis must be on nonmotor skills. The best teachers will recognize the frustration of the physically handicapped child at not being able to demonstrate what he understands, and will provide the encouragement needed.

Because these patients possess normal intellectual capacities, most, even those with significant neurologic and orthopedic handicaps, are able to live useful and functional lives. Realistic job goals and vocational training are indicated for the clinically stable patient.

REFERENCES

1. Liversedge, L. A., The central neuronal muscular atrophies and other dysfunctions of the anterior horn cells, in Walton, J. N. (ed.), *Disorders of Voluntary Muscle,* 2nd ed. Boston, Little, Brown, 1969, pp. 653–669.
2. Tizard, J. P. M., Neuromuscular disorders in infancy, in Walton, J. N. (ed.), *Disorders of Voluntary Muscle,* 2nd ed. Boston, Little, Brown, 1969, pp. 579–605.
3. Swaiman, K. F., and Wright, F. S., *Neuromuscular Diseases of Infancy and Childhood.* Springfield, Ill., Charles C. Thomas, 1970, pp. 58–89.

4. Byers, R. K., and Banker, B. Q., Infantile muscular atrophy. *Archives of Neurology* 5:140–164, 1961.
5. Dubowitz, V., Infantile muscular atrophy: A prospective study with particular reference to a slowly progressive variety. *Brain* 87:707–718, 1964.
6. Gardner-Medwin, D., Hudgson, P., and Walton, J. N., Benign spinal muscular atrophy arising in childhood and adolescence, *Journal of Neurological Science* 5:121–158, 1967.
7. Hausmanowa-Petrusewicz, I. et al., Infantile and juvenile spinal muscular atrophy. *Journal of Neurological Science* 6:269–287, 1968.
8. Munsat, T. L., Woods, R., Fowler, W., and Pearson, C. M., Neurogenic muscular atrophy of infancy with prolonged survival, *Brain* 92:9–24, 1969.
9. Namba, T., Aberfeld, D. C., and Grob, D., Chronic proximal spinal muscular atrophy, *Journal of Neurological Science* 11:401–423, 1970.
10. Van Wijngaarden, G. K. and Bethlen, J., Benign infantile spinal muscular atrophy, *Brain* 96:163–170, 1973.
11. Mawatari, S., and Katayama, K., Scapuloperoneal muscular atrophy with cardiopathy, *Archives of Neurology* 28:55–59, 1973.
12. Zellweger, H., Schneider, H., and Schuldt, D. R., A new genetic variant of spinal muscular atrophy, *Neurology* 19:865–869, 1969.

BIBLIOGRAPHY Hausmanowa-Petrusewicz, I., *Spinal Muscular Atrophy: Infantile and Juvenile Type*. Springfield, Va., U.S. Department of Commerce, National Technical Information Service.

35

Visual Disorders

A. RALPH ROSENTHAL, M.D.

The eye is a sensory organ in which light rays pass through a transparent media and are focused by these media upon the retina. In the retina, electrical impulses are then formed which are transmitted to the occipital cortex of the brain, via the optic nerve and higher visual pathways, to produce the final visual impression. The purpose of this chapter is to discuss the anatomy of the eye and the basic mechanisms of vision and to provide a brief description of conditions which lead to severe visual impairment in children. Included will be remarks on methods of therapy and a final section which briefly summarizes the aids available for the visually handicapped child.

ANATOMY AND PHYSIOLOGY

The eyeball (Fig. 35-1) is roughly spherical in configuration and consists of three concentric tunics, or layers: (1) the external, fibrous layer, which is composed of the cornea and the sclera, (2) the middle, vascular layer—the uveal tract—the components of which are the iris, the ciliary body, and the choroid, and (3) the inner, nervous layer, or retina. Within these layers, the internal structures which aid in the refraction of light are located. From front to back there is, first, the aqueous humor, next, the crystalline lens, and, finally, the vitreous body. All three are normally transparent, thus allowing light to hit the retina. The globe and its associated structures are contained within the body cavity called the *orbit*.

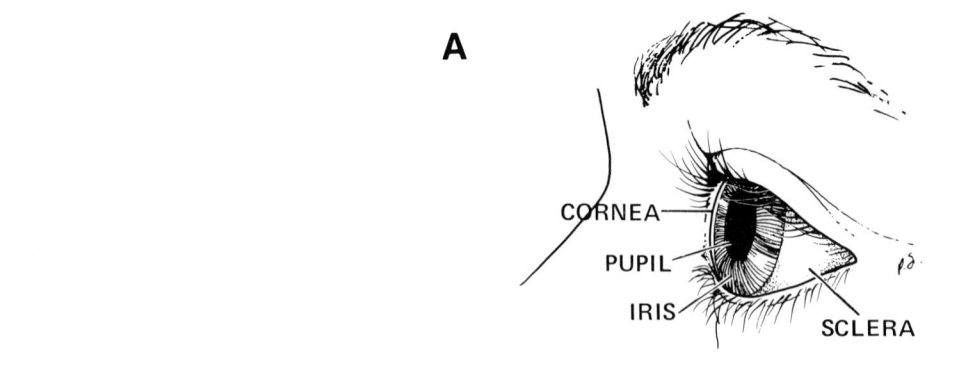

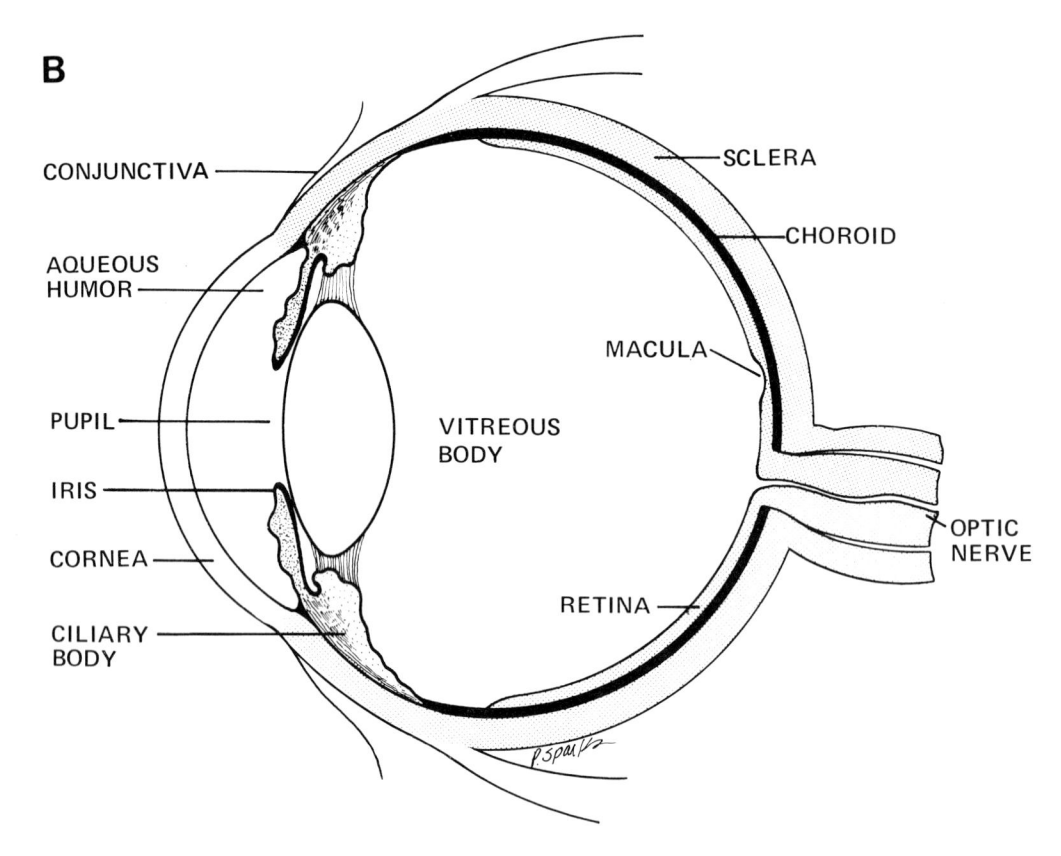

Fig. 35-1. (A) Surface anatomy of the eye. (B) Internal structures of the eye.

Fibrous Layer: Sclera and Cornea

The sclera, or the white of the eye, is opaque and forms the posterior five-sixths of the eye's outer layer. It functions as the protective coat of the eye, being composed of collagen fibers that give the globe its semirigidity.

The anterior one-sixth of the fibrous layer is the cornea. Clear and transparent, with a brilliant shiny surface, it acts as "the window of the eye." The greatest refraction of light rays occurs at the front surface of the cornea.

Uveal Tract: Ciliary Body, Iris, and Choroid

The uveal tract (Greek *uva,* grape) is pigmented and highly vascular and consists of three segments: the iris, the ciliary body, and the choroid.

The iris is the most anterior structure. At its center is an opening, the pupil, through which light passes to reach the retina. The iris acts like the diaphragm of a camera, regulating the size of this opening in response to the amount of light present: thus, with decreasing light, the pupil enlarges (dilates), while, with increasing light, the pupil becomes smaller (constricts). The iris thereby regulates the amount of light reaching the retina.

The ciliary body is directly continuous with the iris. Its major functions are production of the aqueous humor (by the ciliary processes) and regulation of accommodation of the lens, i.e., the changing of the curvature of the lens in response to the forward (lens becomes more convex) and backward (lens becomes less convex) movement of objects.

The third segment is the choroid, the most vascular part of the uveal tract. This is the posterior portion of the uveal tract and its function is to nourish the layers of the retina adjacent to it.

Neural Layer: The Retina

The retina is a transparent, light-sensitive membrane that converts light rays into nerve impulses and then transmits these impulses to the higher centers of the brain by way of the optic nerve. This photochemical conversion occurs within the photoreceptors—the rods and cones. The rods are sensitive to light at low intensities (night vision). The cones respond to the higher intensities (daylight vision). Color vision is primarily dependent on the functional integrity of the cones. Most of the cones are concentrated in the area of the retina known as the *macula,* the center of which, the *fovea,* is responsible for the most distinct vision. Hence, damage to the macula and fovea can severely reduce central vision.

The optic nerve is located at the posterior pole of the globe and is composed of nerve fibers that arise from the retina. The nerve is the path by which impulses reach the brain. Visual perception, or the integration of these various impulses into a complete image, actually occurs in the occipital cortex of the brain.

Internal Structures

The aqueous humor is a fluid having the consistency of water which fills the anterior chamber of the eye. It is responsible for the pressure within the eye. The aqueous is continuously being produced by the ciliary processes and exits from the eye through the structures of the anterior chamber angle—the angle between the iris and the cornea. Abnormalities of the chamber angle are frequently associated with the development of increased pressure within the eye (glaucoma).

The lens is a biconvex transparent structure which lies behind the iris and in front of the vitreous body. Its main function is to aid in the focusing of light rays on the retina. It can change its shape (accommodation) when objects move closer (it becomes more convex) or when objects move further away (it becomes less convex). Any clouding of the lens is called a *cataract.*

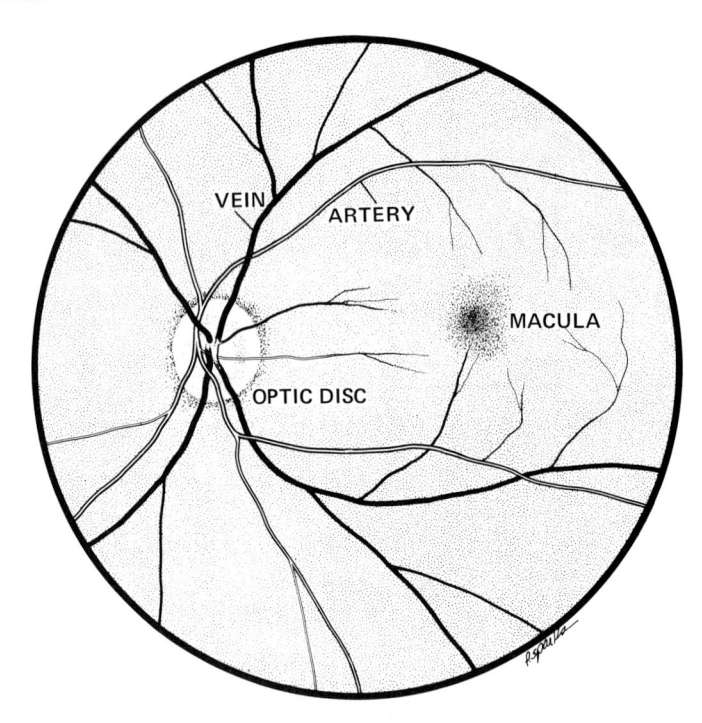

Fig. 35-2. The normal human fundus.

The vitreous body is a jellylike structure that is thick and viscous and occupies the posterior part of the eyeball. It occupies two-thirds of the volume of the globe and is attached to the retina. Diseases of the vitreous body may lead to retinal detachment.

Since the cornea, aqueous humor, lens, and vitreous body are transparent, the physician has the unique opportunity to view the back of the eye—i.e., the retina and the entrance of the optic nerve into the eye. Figure 35-2 shows what an individual would see in the fundus of a normal eye. Note the optic nerve head (disk), the macula (responsible for distinct central vision), and the retinal vasculature (arteries and veins).

Extraocular Muscles

The globe is moved by six extraocular muscles (Fig. 35-3). The medial rectus moves the eye horizontally toward the nose (adduction). The lateral rectus moves the eye horizontally away from the nose (abduction). The superior rectus primarily elevates the eye (supraduction), the inferior rectus depresses the eye (infraduction). The superior and inferior oblique muscles are responsible for torsional movements. The extraocular muscles are not normally visible, as they are covered by the lining of the globe—the conjunctiva.

A final muscle located within the upper lid—the levator palpebrae superioris—serves to elevate the lid. If this muscle is weak or absent, the lip droops, a condition called *ptosis.*

STRABISMUS

Single binocular vision or fusion exists when the images of a particular object are projected onto the maculae of both the right and left retina and are subsequently fused into a single visual perception in the brain. The presence of fusion is dependent upon (1) the visual axes of the two

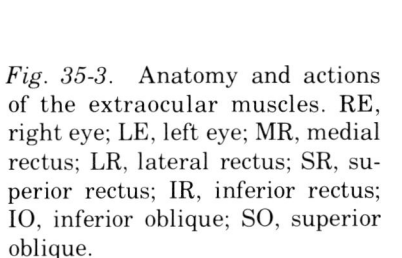

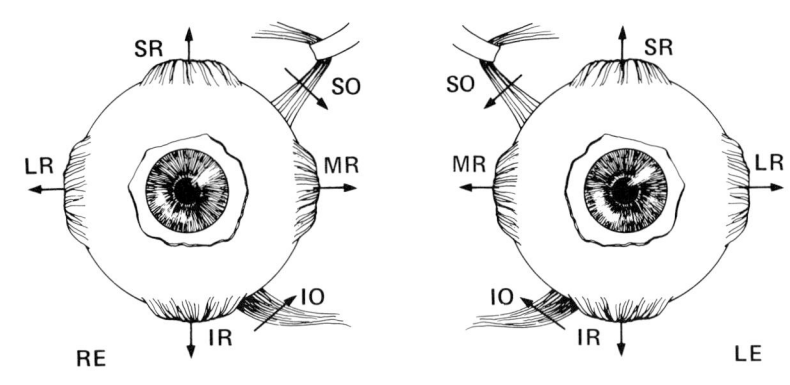

Fig. 35-3. Anatomy and actions of the extraocular muscles. RE, right eye; LE, left eye; MR, medial rectus; LR, lateral rectus; SR, superior rectus; IR, inferior rectus; IO, inferior oblique; SO, superior oblique.

Fig. 35-4. Strabismus. (A) Esotropia (eye turns in). (B) Exotropia (eye turns out).

eyes being straight and (2) the coordinated movements of the extraocular muscles of both eyes. If the visual axes are not straight, the condition *strabismus* or *squint* exists. If one eye turns in, it is called an esotropia (Fig. 35-4A). If one eye turns out, exotropia is present (Fig. 35-4B). The presence of a deviation of one eye in the young child will actually cause double vision. Since this is annoying, the brain, through a mechanism not really understood, will suppress or ignore one image, thus avoiding the double vision. It is this constant habit of actively suppressing the image in the deviated eye that eventually leads to loss of vision, or amblyopia, commonly referred to as a "lazy eye."

Strabismus is present in 1 to 2 percent of all children. Its incidence is particularly high in children with cerebral palsy and other neurological diseases. It is also frequently seen in hyperactive children. When therapy is instituted early enough, amblyopia can be reversed by patching the good eye. Treatment is usually successful if implemented before age 5 or 6; after this age it often fails. This observation underscores the necessity for preschool testing of vision in all children, and particularly those who have strabismus.

REFRACTIVE ERROR

Vision (visual acuity) is measured using a letter chart (Snellen chart), which patients are asked to read from a distance of 20 ft. If patients can read letters that subtend an angle of 5'* at 20 ft., then they have 20/20, or normal, vision. If, however, they can read only those letters that subtend an angle of 50', then vision is recorded as 20/200. (The 20/20 letters are 9 mm high and 9 mm wide; the 20/200 letters are 10 times as large.) A correctable form of visual impairment (reduction of vision to less than 20/20) occurs when, because of a refractive error, light rays do not focus on the retina. Corrective spectacles are then required to bring the vision to 20/20.

The three common refractive errors are:

1. Myopia, also known as near-sightedness, or long eyeball. (Light rays focus in front of the retina.)
2. Hyperopia, also known as far-sightedness, or short eyeball. (Light rays focus behind retina).
3. Astigmatism, a condition in which refraction in different meridians of the eye is not the same, e.g., the curvature of the cornea is like that of a kitchen spoon in which one meridian has a certain curvature while that at right angles has a different curvature. (Some light rays focused in front and some behind the retina.)

Hyperopia and a low degree of astigmatism can be compensated for by the accommodative mechanism of the eye. The eye has no compensory mechanism to handle myopia, however; thus, glasses are almost always required for myopic children. Refractive errors requiring glasses are common in handicapped and mentally retarded children. Noteworthy is the high degree of myopia prevalent in children who were born prematurely.

RETINAL DEGENERATIVE DISEASES

Degenerative diseases that affect the retina in children are often hereditary. They can be divided into two groups: those that affect the macula (the central degenerations) and those that affect the periphery of the retina (peripheral degenerations).

Central retinal degenerations cause a decrease in central vision, often reducing vision, even after correction, to the level of 20/200 (normal, as mentioned previously, is 20/20). The periphery is not usually affected; hence the child maintains good peripheral vision. There is a variable course in visual deterioration, and profound visual loss may not be seen until the individual is in his, or her, late twenties. Macular degeneration is frequently seen in deaf-mutes, in children with myotonic dystrophy (a form of muscular dystrophy), and in individuals afflicted with hereditary spinal cord degenerations. Lenses with high magnification (reading aids) are invaluable in permitting the child to read. Distance telescopic aids may be used intermittently in the classroom for viewing the blackboard.

Many types of peripheral retinal degenerations exist. The most common and well known is *retinis pigmentosa*. This condition will, therefore, be used as the prototype to describe the clinical features. The child will initially complain of defective night vision, or difficulty seeing in the dark *(nyctalopia)*. This is followed by loss of peripheral vision. Eventually, central vision is lost. Examination of the retina reveals peripheral clumping of pigment, narrowing of the arteries, and pallor of the optic nerve head (Fig. 35-5). Eventual blindness may result at various ages, de-

---

*5' means 5 minutes of arc; 50', 50 minutes of arc.

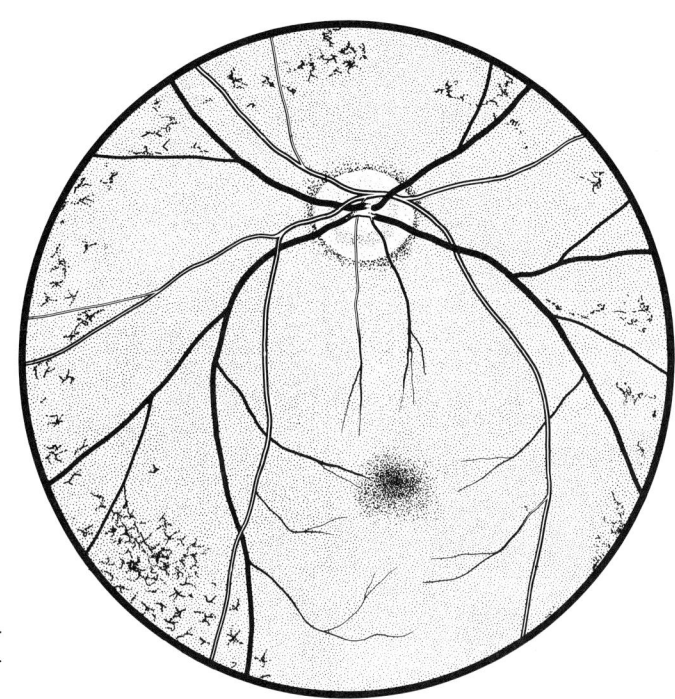

Fig. 35-5. Retinitis pigmentosa. Note narrowed vessels and pigment deposits in the retina.

pending on the hereditary pattern of the condition. Some patients with retinitis pigmentosa, however, retain some useful vision throughout life. Retinitis pigmentosa is frequently associated with other degenerative diseases of the central nervous system.

GLAUCOMA

Two forms of glaucoma occur in children, congenital and infantile. Both types are rare but both can result in blindness.

Congenital glaucoma usually occurs within the first year of life; usually the child is born with the disease, although it may not be detected until 6 months to 1 year of age. The child most often presents with photophobia (avoidance of light) and excessive tearing and clouding of the cornea. All the symptoms are secondary to increased pressure within the eye and damage to the cornea. Because the cornea is distensible in the first 2 to 3 years of life, the child will develop enlarged corneas (megalocornea) (Fig. 35-6). Surgery may alleviate the condition, but, often, eyedrops are also required to control the pressure—thus leading to the problem of chronic eye drop administration.

Infantile glaucoma, also a rare condition, develops between the ages of 6 and 13. Its onset is insidious in nature, and the disease usually is not discovered and diagnosed until after profound damage has already occurred. Treatment is in the form of eyedrops and pills used to lower the pressure. Surgery may have to be performed. These cases are often associated with anomalies in the anterior chamber angle. Since blindness is the inevitable result of untreated glaucoma, early diagnosis and treatment are mandatory.

Glaucoma may also result secondary to other ocular disease processes, and these will be discussed under other headings (Genetic diseases, Infectious diseases, Neurological diseases, and Retrolental fibroplasia.)

Fig. 35-6. Congenital glaucoma. Note enlarged cornea of left eye.

CATARACTS

A cataract is any opacification, or clouding, of the crystalline lens. Often these opacities will progress to the point where they grossly interfere with vision (Fig. 35-7). When the diminution of visual acuity hinders the child's ability to work and play, the cataract must be surgically removed. After the operation, the child is required to wear thick corrective lenses (aphakic lenses). Perceptual problems then result—increased magnification, reduced peripheral vision, and problems with depth perception. The latter difficulty occurs when one eye does not see as well as the other. Contact lenses may be used in selective cases, thus reducing some of the problems associated with cataract glasses.

Fifty percent of cases of congenital cataract are associated with other ocular anomalies, such as small eyes (microphthalmos), involuntary movements or fluttering of the eyes (nystagmus), amblyopia, and strabismus. If such other ocular abnormalities exist, the chance of perfect vision after surgical correction is markedly reduced. A retardation in intellectual development may occasionally be caused by a lack of distinct vision, and some children may improve mentally after vision has been restored, although this is not universally true.

The major causes of bilateral cataracts in children are as follows:

1. Metabolic—juvenile diabetes mellitus, infantile tetany (low blood calcium in newborn period), and galactosemia undiagnosed at birth (inability to normally metabolize the sugar, galactose) are the most important causes of metabolic cataracts. Diabetic cataracts occur between ages 3 and 25. Galactosemia and neonatal tetany cataracts occur shortly after birth.
2. Maternal infection with German measles (rubella) during the first trimester is associated with cataracts in 75 percent of cases. These children are also born with heart defects, deafness, and/or mental retardation. The cataracts are usually discovered at birth and should be surgically removed before 6 months of age if they are advanced. Congenital glaucoma and cloudy corneas also may result from maternal rubella infection.

Fig. 35-7. Unilateral cataract, left eye.

3. Mongolism—approximately 60 percent of children with Down's syndrome show cataract formation between ages 8 and 17.
4. Children with allergic dermatitis may also have a rapid development of cataracts. The skin condition usually precedes the cataracts by 10 years.
5. Children who receive large doses of systemic or topical steroids may develop cataracts.
6. Familial hereditary cataracts—lens opacities occur in many members of the family and are passed down from one generation to the next (autosomal dominant), or may occur without any antecedent history (autosomal recessive). Sex-linked pedigrees have also been reported.

A common cause of unilateral cataract in children is trauma (Fig. 35-7). Blunt or penetrating injury to an eye often leads to the development of a cataract, either shortly after the injury or later on in life.

GENETIC DISEASES

Several hereditary conditions exist which affect the eye either exclusively or in association with other organ systems. Many are discussed in other sections (e.g., Retinal degenerative diseases, Cataracts, Glaucoma, Neurological diseases). Five further conditions are discussed to show the variability of the ocular involvement in hereditary diseases.

1. *Marfan's syndrome* is an autosomal dominant condition in which the affected individual has long spindly fingers (arachnodactyly), hyperextensibility of the joints, pigeon breast, heart lesions, and large blood vessels. Almost invariably, the crystalline lens is subluxated or dislocated. This causes poor vision which can be corrected with corrective glasses, often of high power. Other associated findings are anterior chamber angle anomalies, high myopia, and retinal detachment.
2. *Albinism* is an autosomal recessive condition in which skin and hair pigments are absent. The affected individual also lacks pigment within the uveal tract, resulting in the "pink eye" of the albino. These patients invariably have poor vision (around 20/200), involuntary oscillations of the eyes (nystagmus), and an-

noyance with bright light. They usually require dark glasses for the latter symptom. No cure is known.

3. *Aniridia* is an exclusively ocular disease which consists of mild to severe partial absence of the iris, nystagmus, cataract, glaucoma, and decreased vision. It is usually inherited as an autosomal dominant trait. In its recessive form, aniridia has been associated with the development of a malignant tumor of the kidney (Wilm's tumor).

4. *Mucopolysaccharidoses* is a group of systemic disorders, of which Hurler's syndrome or gargoylism is the best known. The ocular involvement includes progressive corneal clouding and retinal degeneration.

5. *Dwarfism* of various types may be associated with ocular abnormalities such as cataract, glaucoma, and retinal detachment.

INFECTIOUS DISEASES

Infectious agents may affect the eye, causing severe visual impairment. This may occur prior to birth from an infection in the pregnant mother, giving rise to congenitally defective vision. The ocular manifestations may be (1) Large scars in the choroid and retina, as in congenital toxoplasmosis (a parasitic infection) or congenital cytomegalic inclusion disease (a viral infection). Both conditions may be associated with mental retardation. (2) Cataracts, congenital glaucoma, or corneal clouding, as occur with maternal rubella (German measles). The eye findings may be associated with deafness, mental retardation, and heart defects. (3) Scarring and degeneration of the choroid and retina along with deep scarring of cornea as in congenital syphilis. Also seen are dental, skeletal, and nasal deformities.

Infectious agents may also damage a child directly immediately after birth, leading to severe visual loss. The most serious offender is gonococcal infection of the cornea in the newborn (ophthalmia neonatorum). This is a bacterial veneral infection passed on to the child during its passage through the birth canal. If untreated, it may lead to severe corneal scarring, perforation, and blindness. The prevalence of this infection and its serious consequences have led to nationwide laws requiring penicillin or silver nitrate application to the eyes immediately after birth in order to prevent the development of this infection.

The most common cause of blindness in the world (though rare in the United States) is trachoma. This is a viral infection of the eye which leads to corneal and lid scarring. The infection responds to treatment with sulfa drugs, and dangerous sequellae can be prevented. It is seen in the American Indian population in the Southwestern United States.

NEUROLOGICAL DISEASES (NEURO-OPHTHALMOLOGY)

Since the retina and optic nerve are in close connection with the brain, diseases of the central nervous system will often affect the eye. A common problem is inflammation of the optic nerve (optic neuritis). It may be caused by (1) invasion of pathogenic organisms (viruses), (2) a hereditary degeneration of the nerve (Leber's optic atrophy), or (3) loss of the myelin coverings of the nerve (multiple sclerosis). Optic neuritis is usually unilateral but can be bilateral. Severe visual deterioration with no recovery is most common in viral infections and hereditary degenerations. In multiple sclerosis, the vision usually returns to normal or near normal. After a bout of optic neuritis, some paleness (pallor) of the optic nerve head is seen on examination of the back of the eye.

Visual Disorders

A rarer, but extremely interesting, group of hereditary diseases affect the brain, the skin, and the eye. These are called the *phakomatoses* (Greek, mother spot). A brief description of each follows.

1. *Neurofibromatoses.* Tumors of the skin, eyelids, iris, and peripheral and cranial nerves (particularly the optic nerve) are frequent manifestations.
2. *Tuberous sclerosis.* A facial rash of the cheeks, epilepsy, mental retardation, and retinal tumors are the most common findings.
3. *Angiomatosis retinae and cerebellae* (Von Hippel Lindau's disease). Vascular tumors of the retina and brain are present.
4. *Encephalotrigeminal angiomatosis* (Sturge-Weber syndrome). A large, red birthmark on one side of face (port wine nevus), congenital glaucoma on the same side, convulsions, mental retardation, and vascular tumors of the choroid are seen in this syndrome.

Extraocular muscle abnormalities are frequently observed by the neuro-ophthalmologist. One may see paralysis of one of the nerves to the extraocular muscles, which may be associated with peculiar positioning of the head (head turn or head tilt). This is very common in superior oblique palsy. Weakness of the extraocular muscles caused by muscular disease (myasthenia gravis) results in a droopy lid (ptosis) and/or double vision. A very common extraocular muscle movement abnormality is nystagmus—a constant oscillation of the eyes ("dancing eyes"). This is frequently seen in patients who have been born with defective vision—e.g., albinism, congenital cataracts, retrolental fibroplasis. It is also seen as a hereditarily transmitted disorder not associated with other ocular abnormalities (congenital nystagmus). In the latter situation, vision is reduced due to the constant movement of the eyes and the inability to fixate accurately and constantly on objects. No known therapy is currently available.

One final neuro-ophthalmological condition should be mentioned. This is a condition in which a child is blind due to severe insult to the visual cortex in the brain; it may follow partial drowning or a prolonged period of shock caused by an accident or severe blood loss. The ocular structures are normal. It is appropriately labelled *cortical blindness.*

INFLAMMATORY DISEASES

Inflammation of the anterior uveal tract (anterior uveitis, iritis, cyclitis) in children is frequently seen in children with juvenile rheumatoid arthritis (Still's disease). The inflammation is chronic, indolent, and unrelenting. Complications such as cataract and glaucoma may develop.

A second form of anterior uveitis may be observed in children. Usually no other associated diseases are present. The uveitis is acute and resolves with therapy. Complications are rare.

Posterior uveal inflammations (chorioretinitis) are commonly seen in children. Some have been discussed under congenital infections. However, one may see the onset of posterior uveitis long after birth and unassociated with maternal infestation. The most commonly observed are (1) parasitic infection (toxoplasmosis), acquired after birth probably from cat feces; (2) fungal infection of the macula (histoplasmosis), thought to be passed through chicken fecal matter and quite common in the Midwestern United States, (3) inflammation due to a worm (nematode endophthalmitis) transmitted from canine fecal material.

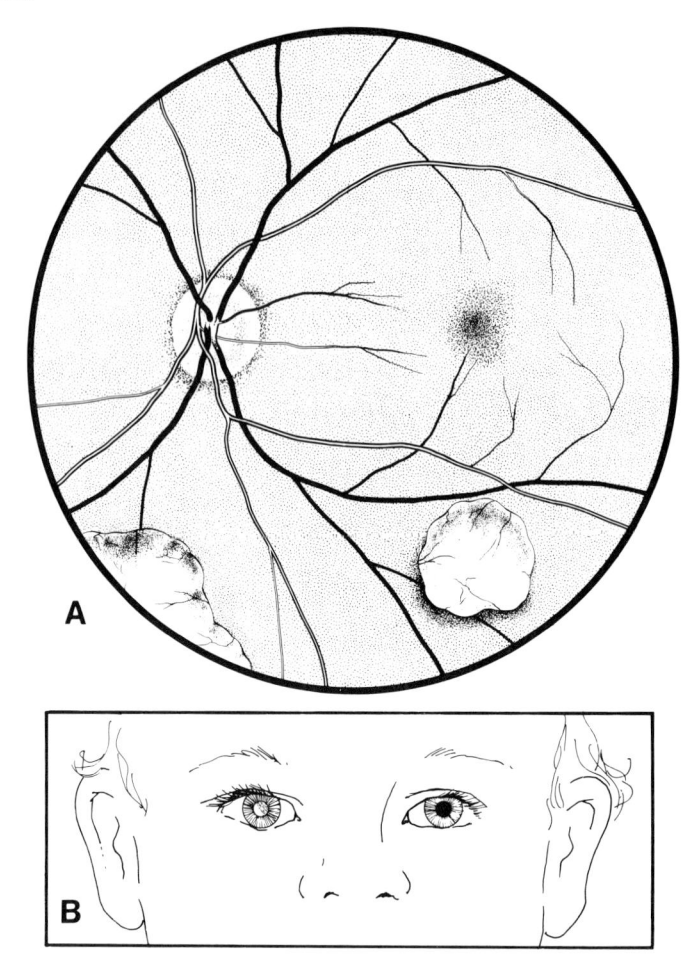

Fig. 35-8. Retinoblastoma, right eye. (A) Funduscopic appearance. (B) External appearance. Note white spot (reflex) in pupillary opening of the right eye.

TUMORS

The two most serious tumors involving the eye and orbit are retinoblastoma and rhabdomyosarcoma.

Retinoblastoma is the most common malignant tumor arising in the eyes of children. It is usually not detected until the first or second year of life, at which time strabismus is often the presenting complaint. Diagnosis is made by seeing a white spot (reflex) in the pupillary zone and retinal tumors in the back of the eye (Fig. 35-8). It is dominantly inherited in 5 percent of cases, while 95 percent develop in families with no history (spontaneous mutations). Death results from direct extension into the brain and from distant metastases. One-third of the cases are unilateral, two-thirds bilateral. Treatment consists of radiation therapy to the affected eye, or eyes. Removal of a severely affected eye is often recommended. A 90- to 95-percent cure rate is obtained if involvement at first examination is not extensive.

Rhabdomysarcoma is a very rare, rapidly growing tumor which grows in the orbit and pushes the eye out of the orbit (proptosis). It is treated with irradiation and chemotherapy. Its cure rate is approximately 50 to 60 percent.

More recently, children with leukemia are developing invasion of the optic nerve and surrounding retina. This leads to a decrease in vision in the affected eye. Occasionally, it is observed bilaterally. Treatment by irradiation of the posterior portion of the eye has been effective.

TOXICOLOGICAL DISEASES

Retrolental fibroplasia is a condition observed in some premature infants. Infants of low birth weight (below 4 pounds) are particularly vulnerable. The condition is generally bilateral, and 20 percent of patients who develop it are permanently blinded. The cause of this dread disease is generally agreed to be the high concentrations of oxygen used to treat the respiratory difficulties which often develop in premature infants. The use of the oxygen predisposes to new vessel formation in the periphery of the retina, with subsequent hemorrhages, connective tissue formation, retinal detachment, and the formation of a thick membrane behind the lens (thus the name retrolental fibroplasia).

Chronic lead intoxication due to the continued ingestion of lead-containing paint can lead to permanent loss of vision.

Prolonged use of chloroquine, a drug utilized in the treatment of rheumatoid arthritis, lupus erythematosis, and other severe autoallergic diseases, may result in severe retinal degeneration, with loss of central vision and pigmentary changes in the macula.

Corticosteroid therapy (either systemic or in eyedrop form), when used over a very long period of time, may cause cataracts and/or glaucoma.

Lye (caustic soda, or NaOH) has a very serious effect if splashed into the eye. Corneal scarring, opacification, and even perforation can result. If the lye burn is severe, blindness results.

READING AIDS

Ordinary spectacles may be used to correct vision in children who have minimal visual impairment. Profound reduction in central vision will usually require special corrective devices, however. Low-vision, or reading, aids have been developed to compensate for visual disabilities that ordinary spectacles do not help. These devices work by increasing the size of the retinal image (magnification). Aids currently available include: high-power reading additions, high-power stand magnifiers, projection magnifiers, television reading aids, fixed-focus low-power stand magnifiers, hand magnifiers, and telescopic magnifiers.

Low-vision centers with specialists trained in prescribing reading aids should be consulted when the child cannot be helped by simple spectacle correction. Each patient should have the opportunity to sample a variety of aids in order to determine which best suits their individual needs. Changes in reading habits, such as reading with one eye only, holding the book at a shorter distance, or seeing only a few words at a time, are often required to enable the child to read with reasonable speed, accuracy, and comfort. Reevaluation at regular intervals is mandatory because of changing needs.

Glossary*

abduction. A movement away from the axis (midline) of the body.
acetabulum. The large cup-shaped cavity on the lateral surface of the hip bone into which the head of the femur fits.
Acetest tablets. Proprietary tablets used for measuring the amount of acetone in the urine.
acetone. A colorless liquid, dimethyl ketone ($CH_3CO \cdot CH_3$), excreted in small quantities in normal urine but in larger amounts in diabetic urine.
adduction. A movement toward the axis (midline) of the body.
aerosols. A liquid substance (such as a disinfectant or insecticide) sealed in a container under pressure with an inert gas (such as Freon or other fluorocarbons).
albinism. Congenital absence of pigment in the skin, hair, choroid coat, and iris; either localized or general.
allergen. A substance that produces an allergy.
allergic rhinitis. Inflammation caused by allergens of the mucous membrane of the nose, as in hay fever.

*References: *American Heritage Dictionary of the English Language* (Boston, Houghton Mifflin, 1969); *Blakiston's Illustrated Pocket Medical Dictionary*, 2nd ed. (New York, McGraw-Hill, 1960); *Dorland's Illustrated Medical Dictionary*, 24th ed. (Philadelphia, W. B. Saunders, 1965); *Random House Dictionary of the English Language* (New York, Random House, 1966); *Webster's Third New International Dictionary* (Springfield, Mass., Merriam, 1966).

allergy. An excessive sensitivity to certain otherwise harmless substances coming in contact with the body.

amblyopia. Congenital or acquired dimness of vision not due to organic disease or lesions of the eye.

ambulation. The act of walking about or moving. (Ambulatory, *adj.*)

amelia. Absence of a limb or limbs.

amphiarthrosis. A joint or articulation where there is little motion because of fibrocartilage between the two surfaces.

amputation, acquired. Removal of a limb or appendage through surgery or accident.

amputation, congenital. The failure of a limb or appendage to develop in a fetus *(in utero)*. Also, the absence of a whole or a part of a limb at birth.

amyloidosis. The accumulation of a starchlike formation (probably a glycoprotein) in various body tissues or organs; also called *tissue proteinosis*.

anemia. Insufficiency of red blood cells (erythrocytes), in either quality or quantity, resulting in easy fatigability, pallor, and decreased exercise tolerance.

angiocardiography. X-ray photographs of the heart and thoracic vessels after intravenous injection of radiopaque material such as diodrast. (Greek *angio,* vessel + *kardia,* heart + *graphein,* to write.)

angiomatosis retinae. Multiple angiomas (tumors whose cells tend to form blood vessels) of the retina; also known as *Lindau-von Hippel disease.*

aniridia. Absence or defective structure of the iris.

anterior. In front of, or toward the "face" side of body.

antigen. Any substance that stimulates the production of or reacts with antibodies. Usually a high molecular weight protein or protein-polysaccharide.

aorta. The main trunk of the arterial system, arising from the left ventricle and distributing arterial blood to all parts of the body.

aortic stenosis. Narrowing of the cross-sectional diameter of the aorta.

aphasia. Loss or impairment of the ability to use words as symbols or ideas due to lesions in the cortex and associated nerve pathways in the brain.

aplastic crisis. Inability to form new tissue; suppression or failure of an organ to develop.

arrhythmia. Absence of rhythm, especially in reference to the heartbeat.

arthrogryposis. A congenital disease manifested by stiff and curved joints (Greek *arthro,* joint + *gryposis,* a crooking).

arthrogryposis multiplex congenita. Generalized lack of musculature or muscle development from birth, with contraction or crooking of the joints.

articular. Pertaining to a joint; put together with joints.

articulation. (a) The place of union or juncture between two bones; (b) the enunciation of words and sentences.

arytenoid cartilages. Cartilages shaped like a jug or pitcher, located in the voice box (larynx).

asphyxia. Deprivation of oxygen resulting in suffocation and ending in coma. Distinguished from *anoxia,* which means *inadequate supply* of oxygen.

astereognosis. Inability to recognize objects by feel and touch.

asthma. A disease due to spasmodic contraction of the bronchi because of allergies or other irritations, resulting in wheezing, coughing, and paroxysmal panting.

astigmatism. A defect of the eye in which rays or objects are not sharply focused but spread diffusely over the retina.

asymmetrical. Lack of symmetry, i.e., lack of similarity between corresponding parts or organs on opposite sides of the body that are normally alike.

ataxia. Defective muscular coordination, sometimes due to lesions in the cerebellum, pons, or medulla oblongata.

atelectasis. Imperfect or incomplete expansion of the lungs at birth, or collapse of the lungs due to occlusion or external compression.

athetosis. A disorder chiefly of childhood marked by slow, sinuous, and continual change of position of the fingers, toes, hands, and other parts of the body, usually due to brain lesion.

atonia. Poor or insufficient muscle tone.

atrophy. A wasting away or reduction in size of a cell or organ.

autosomal inheritance. Transmission of a trait in which the responsible gene is located on an autosome. *Dominant* if only one dose of the gene is required for the trait to be expressed; *recessive* if the trait is expressed only when two doses of the gene—one inherited from each parent—are present.

autosome. An ordinary chromosome as distinguished from a sex chromosome.

axon. The central core or conducting part of a nerve fiber.

Babinski sign. An abnormal reflex action marked by extension of the big toe and extension of the other toes in response to scratching of the sole of the foot; indicates a disturbance in the motor neurons of the brain.

benign. Mild. In reference to a tumor, one that is slow-growing and localized, without invasion of adjacent tissues and with no tendency to spread.

bilaterally. Pertaining to or affecting both sides of the body.

bilirubin. Orange-red bile pigment; occurs in the bile as sodium bilirubinate and is sometimes found in the urine, blood, or tissues of persons with jaundice.

bone marrow. The soft tissue inside long bones; it is highly vascularized and is the site where blood cells are formed.

bradycardia. Slowness of the heartbeat or pulse rate, usually less than 60 beats/min.

brainstem. The base of the brain which connects the upper end of the spinal cord with the cerebral hemispheres.

bruxism. The grinding of teeth.

capsule. A membranous sac enclosing a body part or organ.

cartilage. The "gristle" attached to bones to provide a slippery articulating surface; the temporary skeleton of the embryo.

cataract. Partial or complete opacity of the crystalline lens of the eye.

catch-up growth. The accelerated growth which occurs after a period of reduced growth, often following an insult which suppresses growth.

catheter. A hollow tube for withdrawing fluids from body cavities, especially one inserted into the bladder through the urethra to withdraw urine.

Glossary

cephalocaudal direction. In the direction of the long axis of the body from the head to the tail.

cerebellar cerebral palsy. Cerebral palsy affecting the cerebellum; equivalent to ataxia.

cerebellum. The "little brain," or inferior part of the brain lying below the cerebrum and above the pons and medulla; concerned with the coordination of movements.

cerebral hemispheres. The two halves of the cerebrum, the part of the brain that controls motion, the interpretating of sensations, and mental activity. The cerebrum is the main portion of the brain occupying the upper portion of the cranium.

cerebral palsy. A disorder of movement and coordination caused by cerebral defect or injury; it is nonprogressive and occurs in infancy and childhood.

cerebrum. *See* cerebral hemispheres.

chemotherapy. The use of chemical agents in the treatment or control of disease.

chloroquine. A compound used in the treatment of malaria and of certain forms of cardiac arrhythmias.

chondromalacia patella. Abnormal softness of the cartilage of the kneecap.

chorea. A nervous disorder characterized by irregular or involuntary jerky movements of the muscles of the extremities and the face.

chorioretinitis. Inflammation of the choroid—the thin, vascular membrane of the eye that lies between the retina and sclera.

chromosomes. Small rod-shaped or v-shaped bodies which appear in the nucleus of a cell during cell division and which contain the genes, or hereditary factors. Humans normally have 46 chromosomes: 22 pairs of autosomes and 2 sex chromosomes.

Clinitest tablets. Proprietary name for tablets used to determine glucose content of the urine.

coarctation. A narrowing or compression of the walls of a vessel, reducing the flow or volume, as in coarctation of the aorta.

cochlea. The organ of hearing, part of the inner ear, shaped in a spiral tube resembling a snail shell.

collagen. The gelatinous "glue" composing the white fibers of connective tissue, supportive of skin, tendon, bone, and cartilage.

congenital. Existing from birth.

cornea. The transparent fibrous sheath covering the iris and pupil in the eye through which light passes.

corticosteroid therapy. Treatment of hormonal disorders with natural or synthetic compounds like those found in the adrenal cortex. (Cortex + *steroid*, meaning solid, in reference to chemical structure.)

coxa plana. Flattening of the head of the femur at the hip joint.

cyanotic congenital heart disease. Heart disease due to a birth defect causing poor oxygenation of blood which results in a bluish discoloration of the skin and mucous membranes.

cyclitis. Inflammation of the eyelids, sclera, and cornea.

cystic fibrosis. A hereditary disease of children involving defective production of enzymes in the pancreas, with disturbances throughout the body and usually with pulmonary involvement.

degenerative. A change in tissue from a higher to a lower or less functional form.

dermatomyositis. Inflammation of the skin, tissue, and underlying muscle. (Greek *derma*, skin + *mys*, muscle.)

diabetes mellitus. A metabolic disorder of the islets of Langerhans of the pancreas in which there is faulty production of insulin leading to high blood sugar levels, weight loss, and coma.

diarthroidal joint. A freely movable joint.

differentiation. The process of developmental change from an immature to a mature form, especially in a cell, in the course of which a specific shape and function are assumed.

digitalis. The dried leaf of the plant *Digitalis purpurea* ("purple fingers" or "foxglove"), used as a heart stimulant.

dorsal. Pertaining to or situated on the back. Also termed *posterior*.

double-blind. Describing a type of study or evaluation (of drugs or medicines) in which neither the patient nor the physician knows whether the patient is receiving the drug in question or a harmless placebo.

Down's syndrome. Mongolism. (Named after the English physician, J. L. H. Down.)

Duchenne muscular dystrophy. A type of muscular dystrophy characterized by progressive weakness of the limbs and trunk.

ductus arteriosus. A fetal blood vessel connecting the pulmonary artery directly to the aorta. Also called *Botallo's duct*. See patent ductus arteriosus.

dwarfism. Underdevelopment of part or all of the body, due to malfunction of the endocrine glands or to disease, congenital organ defects, and the like.

dysarthria. Imperfect articulation or speech; stammering.

dyslexia. Impaired ability to read due to brain lesion.

dysplasia. Abnormal development or growth.

dystrophy. Defective or faulty musculature. (Greek *dys-*, bad + *trephein*, to nourish.) See muscular dystrophy.

ecchymosis. Passage of blood into the surrounding tissues, as from a blow or rupture; seen as purple or brown discoloration of the skin.

echoencephalography. Examination and measurement of the internal structures of the skull by means of ultrasound equipment.

eclectic. Selecting what appears to be the best of certain doctrines, theories, or methods.

eczema. An inflammatory skin condition marked by scaly, crusted, or hardened lesions, accompanied by general redness of the area.

effusion. Escape of a fluid into a tissue.

electrocardiogram. A graphic tracing of the electric current produced by contraction of the heart muscle; used to detect irregularities in the heartbeat (abbreviated EKG or ECG).

electromyographic examination. Recording of the changes in muscle electrical potential by means of electrodes and an oscilloscope; used to determine if the muscle is contracting properly, as in neuromuscular disorders (abbreviated EMG).

embolus. A blood clot, cell mass, or air bubble that dislodges from one blood vessel and travels through the bloodstream to another, smaller vessel.

emphysema. A swelling of the lungs due to the presence of trapped air or to dilatation of the pulmonary alveoli or sacs, usually as the result of chronic inflammation.

encephalitis. Inflammation of the brain. Also called *sleeping sickness*.

encephalopathies. Various degenerative diseases of the brain characterized by demyelination or loss of the myelin sheath.

encephalotrigeminal angiomatosis. A neurological term meaning the malformation of multiple blood vessels in the nucleus of the fifth cranial nerve in the brain (trigeminal nerve).

endocarditis. Inflammation of the endocardium or endothelial membrane lining the inside of the heart.

endosteum. The tissue lining of the medullary cavity of a bone.

enzyme. An organic compound, frequently a protein, capable of accelerating or producing by catalytic action some change in a substrate, for which it is often specific.

epilepsy. A central nervous system disorder marked by transient periods of unconsciousness or psychic disturbance, twitching, delirium, or convulsive movements.

epiphysis. The end portion of long bone. It contains cartilage as well as bone and is the site at which bone growth occurs.

erythrocyte. A red blood cell which transports oxygen in the blood.

etiology. The total knowledge concerning the cause of a disease.

extraocular muscles. Muscles situated outside the eye serving to move the eyeball.

Factor VII, Factor IX. Factors I through XII are *coagulation factors* or substances in the blood essential for stopping the flow of blood from an opening in a blood vessel. The twelve factors are present in fixed amounts in normal blood, and any change may lead to clotting problems.

fatty acids. Any of a group of aliphatic acids (acids containing carbon atoms linked in open chains), such as palmitic, stearic, or oleic acid, present in vegetable and animal fats and oils. In combination with glycerol they are the principal component of body fat.

femur. The thigh bone.

fibroplasia. The growth of fibrous tissue in the healing of a wound.

flaccid paralysis. An abnormal condition in which the muscle function is weak or absent, with the absence of normal reflexes.

Friedreich's ataxia. A hereditary disease of childhood or youth involving hardening of the dorsal and lateral columns of the spinal cord; accompanied by paralysis of the lower extremities, speech impairment, and swaying movements. (First described by Nikolas Friedreich, 1825–1882.)

fusion. Abnormal coherence of adjacent parts or bodies.

galactose. A simple sugar obtained from the breakdown of lactose or milk sugar, a form of which is found in the fatty acids in brain cells and also in the blood in the disorder *galactosemia,* in which the body is unable to metabolize galactose.

gamma globulin. A form of protein found in the blood serum, which functions in the formation of the body's protective antibodies.

German measles. A milder form of measles in which the skin eruption lasts only a few days and does not scale off as in the more severe form of measles known as *rubeola.* German measles (rubella) is accompanied by sore throat and fever and is associated with enlargement of the lymph nodes.

glaucoma. A disease of the eye characterized by intraocular pressure, hardening of the globe or eyeball, decreased vision, and threat of blindness.

glial cells. Specialized nerve cells which support and nourish adjacent neurons.

glucocorticosteroids. Natural or synthetic compounds that increase carbohydrate metabolism and raise the concentration of liver glycogen and blood sugar.

glucose. More correctly, D-glucose or dextrose, a sugar resulting from the incomplete decomposition of starch. It is a constituent of the blood and is a major source of energy in the body.

glucose tolerance test. A laboratory test for diabetes which determines the patient's ability to metabolize a large measured quantity of glucose in food.

Gower's sign. A classical sign of muscular dystrophy, indicating weakness of the thigh muscles.

grand mal. A complete epileptic seizure, including sudden loss of consciousness, convulsion, spasm, incontinence, and frothing at the mouth.

growth curves. Growth standards based on normal growth during childhood and adolescence. The distribution of the growth parameter is determined as percentiles at each age; connection of the same percentiles across ages gives the curves.

hemimelia. An abnormal development in the fetus which results in absence of all or part of an arm or leg at birth.

hemiplegia. Paralysis of one side of the body.

hemoglobin. The oxygen-carrying pigment contained in red blood cells, or erythrocytes.

hemophilia. A serious hereditary disorder in which the blood fails to clot and in which deep tissue bleeding occurs following injury or bruising.

histoplasmosis. A severe fungal infection of the body accompanied by septic fever, enlarged spleen, involvement of the lymph nodes, anemia, and other complications.

homozygous. Having an identical pair of genes for any given hereditary characteristic.

hormone. A chemical substance secreted into the blood by the endocrine glands, or by other secreting cells, which produces a specific effect at another site.

hydrocephalus. An abnormal condition in which excessive amounts of cerebrospinal fluid accumulate in or around the brain; accompanied by enlargement of the head, prominence of the forehead, atrophy of the brain, and convulsions. (Greek *hydro,* water + *cephale,* head.)

hyperglycemia. Abnormally high blood sugar.

hyperhemolytic crisis. An excessive destruction of the red blood cells and resultant escape of hemoglobin, as in sickle cell disease.

hyperopia. A form of farsightedness, due to shortness of the eyeball from front to back.

hypertension. Abnormally high blood pressure.

hypertrophy. Enlargement of a body organ or part.

hypoglycemia. Abnormally low blood sugar.

hypoxia. Insufficient oxygen in the lungs and blood.

idiopathic. Of unknown causation, as a disease.

ileum. The lower portion of the small intestine.

ileus. A paralysis of intestinal movement.

immobilize. To render incapable of being moved.

immunity. Quality or state of being immune; possessing resistance against a particular disease, especially by inhibiting growth of a pathogenic organism or by counteracting the effects of its byproducts.

inflammation. The reaction of tissues to injury, manifested by pain, heat, redness, or swelling.

insulin. A hormone produced by the pancreas which is essential to the metabolism of glucose (sugar) and other carbohydrates; absent or insufficient in patients with diabetes mellitus.

iridocyclitis. Inflammation of the iris and of the ciliary body.

iris. The circular pigmented membrane around the pupil; contains muscles that dilate or contract the pupil opening.

isometric. Of equal dimensions. In exercise, contraction of the muscle without movement of adjacent joints.

jaundice. A disorder in which bile pigment is deposited in the skin and mucous membranes, giving a yellow appearance (French *jaune,* yellow.)

joint. A place of union between two or more bones. *See also* articulation.

ketoacidosis. The accumulation of excessive ketone bodies in the body, as in diabetes mellitus.

ketone bodies. Any of three compounds—acetoacetic acid, beta-hydroxybutyric acid, or acetone—that are intermediates in the metabolism of fatty acids; found in abnormal quantities in the blood and urine of patients with diabetes and other pathological conditions.

Landau reflex. An infantile automatic posture. When the baby is held face down (prone) with the examiner's hand on the chest, the head and trunk extend; when the head is flexed, the trunk and lower limbs flex.*

lateral. Pertaining to the side.

lazy eye. A form of strabismus or squint which appears when the patient is tired or has been using his eyes for prolonged periods.

Legg-Perthes or **Legg-Calve-Perthes disease.** A degenerative disease of the ball of the hip bone or femur. Also known as *osteochondritis deformans juvenilis,* coxa plana.

leukemia. A form of cancer in which there is a malignant proliferation of abnormal cells in the bone marrow, interfering with the production of normal components of the blood; the leukemic cells may spread into the blood and other body tissues.

leukopenia. A condition in which the number of leukocytes circulating in the blood is abnormally low.

longitudinal. Pertaining to the long axis of the body.

lordosis. An abnormally increased forward curvature of the lower spine (swayback).

lumbar. Pertaining to the loins, or to the lower back in the area of the kidneys.

lumbar puncture. The insertion of a needle through the back and into the spinal canal, permitting withdrawal of the spinal fluid (the water-like fluid that bathes the brain and spinal cord); also used to inject drugs into the spinal fluid.

---

*Paine, R. S., and Oppé, T. E., *Neurological Examination of Children.* Clinics in Developmental Medicine. London, William Heinemann, 1966.

lupus erythematosis. A patchy red skin rash, "the disease of the red wolf," covering the nose, cheeks, and other parts of the body; accompanied by fever and joint pain in the more severe cases.

lymph node. Small organ along the course of the lymphatic vessels which functions in removing foreign substances from the lymph (a pale fluid resembling plasma and containing white blood cells that is channeled via the lymphatic vessels into the bloodstream).

lymphoma. A tumor composed of lymph node tissue.

macula. A discolored spot on the skin, not elevated about the surrounding area (plural, *maculae*). Freckles are a form of maculae.

malaria. A parasitic disease caused by *Plasmodium* protozoa and transmitted by mosquitoes; marked by chills and fever occurring at regular intervals; becomes chronic with occasional relapses. (Italian, "bad air.")

malignant. Dangerous to life. In reference to a tumor, one that is rapidly growing, with a tendency to spread and to return after surgical removal.

Marfan's syndrome. A hereditary disorder of connective tissue involving abnormalities of body structure, especially the chest and palate, with dislocation of the lenses of the eyes and various forms of cardiovascular lesions involving the aorta and the interatrial septum.

medial. Pertaining to the middle.

medulla. The central portion of an organ as distinguished from its outer layer or cortex. Sometimes used to refer to the medulla oblongata—the part of the brainstem where the spinal cord fuses with the brain itself.

megalocornea. An abnormal development of the cornea of the eye, beginning at birth and reaching a diameter of up to ⅝ inch.

meninges. The three membranes enveloping the brain and spinal cord; namely, the dura mater, the pia mater, and the arachnoid.

meningocele. A protrusion of the meninges through a defect in the skull or spinal column.

menisci. Crescent-shaped disks of fibrocartilage attached to the surface of the tibia and present in some synovial joints.

metabolic. Pertaining to body metabolism or the sum of all physical and chemical processes by which living, organized substance is produced and maintained or is broken down to provide energy for use by the organism.

metastasis. The transfer of disease from one organ to another not directly connected with it, due to the transfer of microorganisms or viruses or, in the spreading of tumors, to the transfer of malignant cells.

mongolism. A nonhereditary congenital defect marked by chromosomal abnormality, mental retardation, and some degree of physical deformity. Also called *Down's syndrome*.

monogenic inheritance. Transmission of a trait in which a single gene is involved.

Moro reflex. The "embracing" reflex of an infant lying on its back on a table when the table is struck.

mucopolysaccharidosis. Abnormal production of mucopolysaccharides or glycoproteins, the chief constituents of mucus.

mucoviscidosis. Cystic fibrosis of the pancreas, so called because of the abnormal secretion of viscous mucus caused by the disease.

muscular dystrophy. A hereditary disease marked by progressive shrinking and wasting of skeletal muscle, with no apparent lesion of the spinal cord; symptoms usually manifest themselves in early childhood or adolescence. There is no known cause.

myasthenia gravis. A muscle disease characterized by rapid fatigue of muscles, especially of the face, hips, throat, and neck.

myelin. The fatlike sheath around certain nerve fibers.

myelination. The process of supplying or accumulating myelin during the development or repair of nerves. Also called *myelinization*.

myeloma. A tumor composed of cells of the type normally found in bone marrow.

myelomeningocele. Protrusion of the spinal cord and its covering through an opening in the bony spinal canal. *See also* meningocele.

myofilament. A filament in a muscle fiber rubbing parallel with the long axis of the fiber and presumably containing the contractile elements. Also called *myofibril*.

myopia. Nearsightedness, the result of the eyeball being too long from front to back. *See also* hyperopia.

necrosis. Death of tissue, usually as individual cells or groups of cells.

neonate. A newborn infant.

neoplasia. Tumor formation, or the unrestrained, abnormal, and persistent proliferation of cells.

neural plate or tube. A midline stretch of thickened ectoderm just forward of the primitive streak in the developing embryo.*

neuroblast. An embryonic cell that develops into a nerve cell or neuron.

neurofibromatosis. A hereditary disorder involving the development of neurofibromas or tumors of the peripheral nerves, numbering into the hundreds, and distributed over the entire body, accompanied by other changes in the nervous system, muscles, nones, and skin. Also known as *neuroma, neuromatosis,* or *von Recklinghausen's disease.*

neuro-ophthalmology. Study of the portions of the nervous system related to the eye.

nyctalopia. Night blindness, or imperfect vision at night, with good vision only on bright days.

nystagmus. Involuntary rhythmic jerking of the eyes when turned sharply to right or left.

ontogenic progression. Development of the individual from fertilized egg to adult, as distinguished from phylogenetic progression, or development of the race *(phylum)* to which the individual belongs.

ophthalmia neonatorum. Conjunctivitis or irritation of the eye in the unborn, caused by gonorrhea transmitted at birth.

optic nerve. Either of a pair of cranial nerves conducting impulses from the retina to the brain.

orthopedic surgery. Surgery concerned with the straightening, preservation, and restoration of the musculoskeletal system. (Greek *ortho*, straight or normal + *paidos*, child.)

orthotics. The science or practice of straightening a deformed part with mechanical devices; e.g., braces.

ossification. The process of bone formation, or the change from cartilage to bone.

*Arey, L. B., *Developmental Anatomy.* Philadelphia, W. B. Saunders, 1940.

osteoblast. A cell arising from a connective tissue cell or fibroblast, which eventually matures into a bone cell.

osteochondritis dissecans. A condition of a joint, usually the knee, marked by partial detachment of a fragment of cartilage and underlying bone from the joint surface (*dissecans,* cutting away).

osteoclast. A multinuclear cell associated with the absorption and removal of a bone.

osteogenesis imperfecta. A defect of bone formation characterized by bone fragility, and sometimes deafness, which results in multiple fractures even before birth and during infancy.

otitis media. Inflammation of the middle ear.

palliation. Relief, but not necessarily a cure, of a condition.

parachute reaction. Infantile reflex in which when an infant is suddenly lowered in a prone position (supported face down and horizontal), his or her hands automatically reach toward the floor.

parahemophilia. A hemophilic-like disorder due to the congenital absence of blood coagulation Factor X.

paraplegia. Paralysis of the legs and lower part of the body caused by spinal injury, ataxia, brain lesions, and other factors.

Parkinson's disease. A progressive disease of later life involving tremor, masklike appearance, awkward gait, slowing of voluntary movements, and weakening of muscles. Also called *paralysis agitans* and *shaking palsy.*

patella. The kneecap.

patent ductus arteriosus. An abnormal condition in which the shunt connecting the pulmonary artery directly to the aorta (thus permitting blood to bypass the pulmonary circulation before the lungs are inflated following birth) remains open, causing progressive strain on the heart and requiring surgical correction.

pathological. Caused by or involving disease; said of structural and functional changes in tissues and body organs which are abnormal or injurious to health.

pathology. The study of the nature of diseases and of the structural and functional changes they produce, based on the examining of diseased tissues.

pauciarticular rheumatoid arthritis. Rheumatoid arthritis affecting only a few joints.

periosteum. A specialized connective tissue covering all bones of the body, consisting of dense connective tissue and loose collagenous bundles and fibers.

periphery. The outward part or surface of an object or organ.

peritoneum. The membranous lining of the abdomen wall, surrounding the viscera or abdominal organs and forming a closed sac—except in the female, where it is continuous with the mucous membrane of the uterine tubes.

petit mal. A mild convulsive disorder related to epilepsy; characterized by sudden brief blackouts of consciousness, followed by immediate recovery. (French, *little illness.*)

phakomatoses. A hereditary disorder involving the formation of tumors or lenslike masses, as in neurofibromatosis.

phocomelia. A developmental abnormality in infants in which the hands or feet are attached directly to the trunk and the normal connective arm or leg bones are missing.

phylogenetic progression. See *ontogenetic progression.*

pinna. The external ear, including the earlobe. (Latin, *wing.*)
placebo. An inactive substance in pill or liquid form, formerly given to please or soothe a patient (Latin, *I will please*), but now used in controlled studies to test the effect of various medicines or drugs.
plasma. The fluid portion of the blood in which the blood cells are suspended. *Serum* is plasma with the fibrinogen or clotting agent absent as a result of blood clotting.
platelet. Small, colorless, circular or oval discs in the blood which function in blood clotting.
plexus. A network of lymphatic vessels, nerves, or veins.
pneumoencephalogram. An x-ray film of the head after injection of air or gas into the subarachnoid space, permitting visualization of the cortex and ventricles.
poliomyelitis. An acute viral disease originating in the gastrointestinal tract and invading the nerve cells in the spinal cord or brainstem, resulting in paralysis or muscular atrophy. A mild form of the disease may involve only fever, sore throat, stiff neck, and headache.
polyarticular rheumatoid arthritis. Rheumatoid arthritis affecting all or most of the joints of the body.
polydipsia. Excessive thirst over a long period.
polygenic inheritance. The transmission of a trait due to the effect of several genes.
polyphagia. Excessive or voracious eating or craving for food.
polyuria. Passage of large volumes of urine.
porencephaly. The presence of cysts or cavities in the brain cortex.
prognosis. A forecast as to the recovery or outcome of an attack of disease, based on the current knowledge of the disease and its natural history.
protein. One of a group of complex organic nitrogenous compounds, essentially combinations of amino acids and their derivatives, which form the principal constituent of the cell protoplasm and are thus essential to life.
proximal. Nearest to the point of reference; opposed to *distal*, meaning farthest from the point of reference.
pseudohypertrophy. Increase in size without true hypertrophy of muscles. *See* hypertrophy.
ptosis. Drooping of the upper eyelid due to paralysis of the third nerve.
pubertal growth spurt. An acceleration in growth which occurs during puberty.
pulmonary. Pertaining to the lungs. (Latin *pulmo*, Greek *pneumon*, lung.)
pulmonary thrombosis. Lodging of a blood clot or thrombus in the lungs.
pulmonic stenosis. Narrowing or blocking of the pulmonary artery.
pyramidal cerebral palsy. Cerebral palsy due to lesions of the cerebral cortex and its motor tracts (pyramid of longitudinal fibers). Extra pyramidal refers to lesions outside of the cortex and its tracts, e.g., in the basal ganglia.

quadriceps muscle. The group of four large muscles in the front of the thigh that acts to straighten the leg at the knee joint.
quadriplegia. Paralysis of both arms and both legs; a.k.a. *tetraplegia.*

radiation therapy. A technique for killing cancerous cells by directing high-energy emissions at a tumor; the energy from the radiation disrupts the cellular components, causing cell death or destroying the cells' ability to reproduce.

recumbency. The position or act of lying down or being prostrate.

relapse. The return of a condition after apparent recovery from it.

remission. Abatement or lessening of intensity in a disease, or the period during which such abatement occurs.

resorption. Act of absorbing or swallowing up, referring to the loss of substance through physiologic or pathologic means.

reticulocytes. A young (immature) red blood cell or erythrocyte showing a network or reticulum when stained with cresyl blue.

retina. The light-receptive layer of the eye, continuous with the optic nerve, on which light rays are focused by the crystalline lens.

retinitis pigmentosa. A hereditary disorder involving hardening and atrophy of the retina with pigmentation; accompanied by contraction of the field of vision plus defective vision in bright light.

retinoblastoma. A tumor of the retina.

retrolental fibroplasia. An abnormal condition of the eye marked by the presence of opaque tissue behind the lens; leads to detachment of the retina and interrupted growth of the eye in premature infants; often due to excessive use of oxygen during premature care.

rhabdomyosarcoma. A malignant tumor of the striated muscles. (Greek *rhabdo,* rod-shaped + *mys,* muscle + sarcoma, a malignancy of connective tissue.)

rheumatoid arthritis. A chronic disease characterized by inflammation of the joints, usually accompanied by marked deformities, inflammatory changes in the synovial membranes and joints, and wasting away of the bones.

Rh factor: An agglutinogen, first found in the red blood cells of the rhesus monkey, which induces antibody formation in Rh-negative blood (blood in which this factor is absent). The resultant antigen–antibody reaction causes what is termed a *transfusion reaction;* about 15 percent of individuals are Rh-negative and thus might have transfusion reactions from Rh-positive blood.

rhinitis. Inflammation of the nose or its mucous membrane. (Greek *rhis,* nose.)

righting reactions. Automatic or involuntary attempts in an infant or young child to regain its original position when forcibly moved or restrained.

rubella. *See* German measles.

saggital. An anatomical term referring to the front-to-back plane of the body.

sarcoma. A tumor made up of a substance like the embryonic connective tissue, composed of closely packed cells in a homogeneous substance, and often highly malignant.

scapuloperoneal muscular atrophy. Muscular dystrophy involving the shoulder and the fibula or outer side of the leg.

sclera. The tough, white supporting tunic or outer coating of the eyeball; anteriorly it forms a transparent, rounded bulge—the cornea—through which light passes.

scoliosis. A lateral or side-to-side curvature of the spine in the shape of an elongated letter S. (Greek *skolios,* twisted.)

sensorineural loss. Loss of sensation through the sensory nerves.

sex-linked inheritance. Inheritance of a trait in which the responsible gene is located on the X (female sex) chromosome. *Dominant* if only one gene need be present for the trait to be expressed; *recessive* if the trait is expressed only when no other form of the gene is present.

sickle cell. A shrunken, fragile red blood cell shaped like a sickle.

sickle cell anemia. A hereditary form of anemia, occurring mainly among blacks, characterized by sickle cells and an abnormal type of hemoglobin; accompanied by acute abdominal pains, ulceration of the legs, and bone pain.

sickling phenomenon. The tendency toward development of sickle cells in the blood.

spasticity. The state of increase of tension in a muscle.

spica. A type of plaster cast that includes both an extremity and the trunk of the body.

spina bifida. A congenital cleft in the bony encasement of the spinal cord, with meningeal protrusion. If the meninges do not protrude, it is called *spina bifida occulta*.

spinal cord. That part of the central nervous system contained within the vertebral column.

spinal muscular atrophy. A disease of unknown cause affecting the motor cells of the spinal cord and causing atrophy of the muscles controlling movement of the head, neck, thorax, and vertebral column.

Still's disease. Chronic polyarthritis of childhood, with enlargement of spleen and lymph nodes and irregular fever. (After George Frederick Still.)

strabismus. Failure of the eyes to converge properly on an image, leading to squint, crosseye, or walleye.

Sturge-Weber syndrome. A disorder involving new vascular growths along the trigeminal nerve and the pia mater of the brain, as well as glaucoma of the eye nearest the affected trigeminal nerve.

synarthrosis. Articulation in which the bony elements are united by continuous intervening fibrous tissue.

syndrome. A group of symptoms which occur together and are thought to be due to a single cause.

synovitis. Inflammation of a synovial membrane, affecting joint cavities, bursae, and tendon sheaths. *See also* synovium.

synovium. The synovial membrane that secretes a clear fluid resembling the white of an egg, found in various joint sacs or bursae and in tendon sheaths, which facilitates or lubricates the motion between tendon and bone, or bone and socket.

syphilis. A contagious venereal disease due to the microorganism *Treponema pallidum*, transmitted by direct contact and from the placenta to the fetus of an infected mother.

tachycardia. Extreme rapidity of the heartbeat, usually above 100/min. *See also* bradycardia.

tetralogy of Fallot. A four-way combination of congenital heart defects, all of which can occur simultaneously, including pulmonary stenosis, defects in the dividing wall between left and right ventricles, abnormal position of the aorta so that it receives blood from both right and left ventricles, and excessive growth of right ventricle.

thrombocytopenia. A condition in which the level of platelets in the blood is abnormally low, resulting in easy bruisability and excessive bleeding.

thrombosis. The development of a clot (Greek *thrombos*) or plug in a blood vessel formed by coagulation of the blood and remaining at the point where it can block blood flow.

thymus gland. A glandlike body located near the trachea which gradually diminishes in size with maturity and is believed to play a significant part in the body's immunity to disease.

tibia. The inner and larger bone of the leg below the knee; the shinbone.

tinnitus. A ringing, hissing, or roaring sound in the ear or ears. (Latin, *ringing*.)

toxoplasmosis. A severe disease of the nervous system caused by the *Toxoplasma* genus of sporozoan protozoa.

trachoma. A virus disease of the cornea and conjunctiva of the eye, producing fear of light, pain, and weeping reaction, accompanied by redness and swelling.

traction. The act of pulling; a remedial procedure in the setting or straightening of bones.

trauma. A wound or injury.

tremor. Involuntary trembling or quivering in one or more parts of the body, usually in the extremities. An *intention tremor* is not evident when the part is at rest but begins as soon as the part is put into action.

tuberous sclerosis. A hereditary disease involving progressive mental deterioration and epileptic convulsions, caused by tumors on the surface of the lateral ventricles and sclerotic patches on the surface of the brain. Other tumors may be present in the eye, the viscera, and the kidney and heart muscles. Also called *Bourneville's disease* or *epiloia*.

uveal tract. The vascular or vessel-laden tunic covering the eyeball, comprising the choroid, ciliary body, and iris.

uveitis anterior. Inflammation of the cornea involving the front part of the uvea.

vaccine. Killed, or markedly weakened (attenuated), organisms given in solution to stimulate the body to produce antibodies against that organism; used to confer immunity to specific diseases.

Valsalva maneuver. Increase of intrapulmonic pressure by forcible exhalation against the closed glottis or vocal apparatus of the larynx.

valvulotomy. Incision of a valve, such as a valve of the heart. Also called *valvotomy*.

vascular. Full of blood vessels, as vascular tissue or organs.

vaso-occlusion. Blocking of a blood vessel.

ventricle. A small cavity, such as those of the brain or lower chambers of the heart.

Von Hippel-Lindau's disease. *See* angiomatosis retinae. Also known as Lindau-von Hippel's disease.

X-linked inheritance. *See* sex-linked inheritance.

Index

Aarane (disodium cromoglycate; Intal), 41
Abdominal injuries in hemophilia, 328
Abduction in motor development, 337
Above-elbow amputees, 24
Accidents. *See* Injury and trauma
Acetest tablets, 273
Acetone, 270, 273, 274
Achilles tendon in cerebral palsy, 61
Achondroplasia, 464
Achondroplastic dwarfism, 290
Acquired amputations, 17, 20
Acquired cardiovascular disorders, 313
Acquired cerebral palsy, 59
Acquired heart disease, 322–323
Actin, 10
Acute lymphocytic leukemia (ALL), 54
Adapted Driver Education Program, 299
Adapted sports, literature on, 248–249
Adaptive equipment, for muscular dystrophy patients, 393. *See also specific types of adaptive equipment; for example:* Mobility aids
Adduction in motor control, 336
Adenoids and adenoidectomy, asthma and, 34–35, 41
ADL (activities of daily living), 88, 90–93
Adolescents, counseling handicapped, 191–192

Adrenaline-like drugs for asthma, 41, 42
Adult hemoglobin (HbA), 473
Adult-onset diabetes, 272
Adults, disgorging foreign body from choking, 303, 304
Aerosol medications
    for asthma, 38, 40, 41
    for cystic fibrosis, 261, 262
Afferent fibers, 8
Airway obstruction (choking), 301–304
Akinetic (astatic; inhibition) epilepsy, 175
Albinism, 491–493
Alcohol
    for cerebral palsy, 101, 102
    effects of, on intrauterine growth, 452
    during pregnancy, congenital heart disease and, 314
Alert reflexes, 335
ALL (acute lymphocytic leukemia), 54
Allergic conjunctivitis, 33
Allergic eczema, 33, 36
Allergic rhinitis, 33, 34, 36, 37
Allergic triad (dermal respiratory syndrome), 37
Allergies. *See also* Asthma
    cataracts and, 491
    literature on, 218
Allergy tension fatigue syndrome, 37

Ambivalence, as parental response to handicap diagnosis, 195
Amblyopia, 487
Ambulation. *See also* Mobility aids
  with Legg-Perthes disease, 396
  with SMH, 375–376
Amniocentesis, 327
Amphiarthroses, 14
Amputations, 17–26
  defined, 17–18
  educational implications of, 24–25
  functional considerations on, 23–24
  prosthetics for, 20, 22–24
  treatment of, 18–22
Amyloidosis in rheumatoid arthritis, 427
Anatomy, 1–16
  of bones, 12–13
  of ear, 135
  of eye, 483–486
  of joints, 13–15
  of muscle, 10–11
  of nervous system, 2–10
  terminology related to, 1
Anemia. *See also* Sickle cell anemia
  Cooley's, literature on, 219
  hemolytic, 68
Anger, as parental response to handicap diagnosis, 195–196
Angiography for congenital heart disease, 314, 315, 320
Angiomatosis, encephalotrigeminal, 495
Angiomatosis retinae and cerebellae (Von Hippel Lindau's disease), 494
Aniridia, 492
Anoxia, 68–70, 366, 369
Anterior uveitis (iridocyclitis), 427, 493
Antibiotics
  for congenital heart disease, 316, 317, 319
  for cystic fibrosis, 260, 262
Antibodies
  in asthma, 33, 39, 40
  development of, and factor replacement therapy for hemophilia, 329
Anticonvulsants, 177–179, 311
Aorta, 315, 319–322
  coarctation of, 321–322
  stenosis of, 309, 320–321, 431
  transposition of, 319–320
Apert's syndrome, 290
Aphasia, 134, 136, 138, 139, 379
Aplastic crisis in sickle cell anemia, 475
Aqueous humor of eye, 485, 486
Architectural accessibility for the handicapped, literature on, 234–236
Armless drivers, 299
Arteriography for cancer, 46
Arthritis. *See also* Juvenile rheumatoid arthritis
  dermatomyositis and, 266
  and rheumatic fever, 322
  rheumatoid, 288
  septic, 15

Arthrogryposis multiplex congenita (multiple congenital contractures), 27–30, 479
Articulation. *See* Joints
Articulation disorders (speech), 140–141
Arts and crafts for the handicapped, literature on, 236–237
Asphyxia, cerebral palsy and fetal, 68, 69
Aspirin
  for chondromalacia patella, 402
  for juvenile rheumatoid arthritis, 428, 430
Assisting devices and equipment, literature on, 237. *See also specific types of assisting devices*
Astatic (akinetic; inhibition) epilepsy, 175
Asterognosis in cerebral palsy, 71
Asthma, 31–42, 259, 260
  causes of, 32–35
  causes of wheezing other than, 37
  course, prognosis and mortality with, 38
  educational implications of, 41–42
  emotional factors in, 35
  history of, 31–32
  incidence of, 32
  literature on, 218
  pressurized aerosols for, 38, 40, 41
  symptoms of, 35–36
  treatment of, 39–40
  types of, 36–37
Astigmatism, 488
Astrocyte cells of brain, 4
Asymmetrical tonic neck reflex, 76–77, 337
Ataxia. *See* Cerebral palsy; Friedreich's ataxia
Atelectasis, 257
Athetosis, 64–65, 101, 172, 367
Atonic cerebral palsy, 66
Atrial balloon septostomy, 320
Atrial septal defect, 317–318
Atrophy, muscle, in muscular dystrophy, 391
Atypical petit mal (petit mal variant; Lennox-Gastaut syndrome), 175
Auditory (VIIIth cranial) nerve, 135
Auditory problems. *See* Hearing loss and disorders
Augmentative Communication System, 146–154
  Blissymbolics in. *See* Blissymbolics
  teacher's role in, 152
Augmentative speech aids, 159
Autism, 379, **432**
Autoimmune disorders. *See specific autoimmune disorders; for example:* Dermatomyositis
Autocans. *See* Vans
Automobiles. *See* Physically handicapped drivers
Automotive systems for physically handicapped drivers, 293–294
Autonomic epilepsy, 176
Autosomal inheritance, 288–290, 473
Autosomes, 288, 388
Axial rotation in infancy, 338
Axons (nerve fibers), 2, 5, 10

Babinski sign, 309
Back pain, scoliosis and, 439

Index

Bacterial endocarditis, congenital heart disease and, 316–319, 321–323
Bacterial infections. *See* Infections
Barbiturates
   for cerebral palsy, 102
   for convulsive disorders, 178
Basal ganglia, 2
   and extrapyramidal damage in cerebral palsy, 67
Basic motor-maturity evaluation in cerebral palsy, 82, 84–85
Becker's muscular dystrophy, 386
Beds for children with muscular dystrophy, 393
Behavior modification for stuttering, 141
Behavioral disorders associated with rubella, 432
Belly of muscle, 10
Below-elbow amputees, 18, 24
Bereavement. *See* Grief
Beta cell of pancreas, 270
Bilirubin, 472
Biopsies
   for cancer, 46, 52
   muscle, for muscular dystrophy, 392
Birth defects, literature on, 218–219, 227. *See also specific birth defects*
Birth injury
   cerebral palsy and, 68–70
   SMH and, 366, 369
   traumatic paraplegia and, 413
Bladder
   paralysis of, in myelomeningocele, 349
   of SMH children, 377–378
   in traumatic paraplegia, 416
Blast cells, 53–54
Bleeding. *See* Hemophilia
Blephoritis, 281
Blindness, 159, 367
   color, 290
   cortical, 493
   due to glaucoma, 489
   and iridocyclitis, 427
   literature on, 225
Blood clotting. *See* Clots; Coagulation
Blissymbolics, 145–152
   and functions of language
   history of, 147
   symbols of, 147–148
   and use of blissymbols, 151–152
Blood examination for cerebral palsy, 75
Blood transfusions for sickle cell anemia, 476
Blood vessels. *See also* Aorta; Pulmonary artery; Vena cava
   collateral, 321
   transposition of great, 319–320
Bloom syndrome, 462
Blue babies (tetralogy of Fallot), 318–319
Bobath neurodevelopmental therapy for cerebral palsy, 82–83
Bone marrow
   in leukemia, 53–54
   testing, for cancer, 46, 47

Bones, 12–13. *See also* Fractures; Temporary Orthopedic disabilities, *specific bones; specific diseases affecting bones; and entries beginning with elements:* oss; osteo
   deformities of, in meningocele, 347
   necrosis of, 12
   in sickle cell anemia, 472, 475
   surgery for tumors of, 17
Bowel
   paralysis of, in myelomeningocele, 349, 357–358
   of SMH children, 377–378
   in traumatic paraplegia, 416
Brachial plexus, 8, 9
Bradykinin, 33
Braces. *See* Orthotics
Brain. *See also* Electroencephalogram; *and entries beginning with terms:* cerebellar, cerebral *and element:* enceph
   abcesses of, severe and multiple handicaps due to, 366
   development, organization and function of, 5–8
   malignant tumors of, 45
   ossification of bones covering, 459
   scan of, for cerebral palsy, 75
   sickling occurring in, 475
   structure of, 2–4
Brainstem, 2, 3
Bridging reflex, 339
Bronchitis, 37, 38, 260, 383
Bronchus
   of asthmatics, 31, 32
   in cystic fibrosis, 258
Bruises, care of, in hemophilia, 327
Bruxism (teeth grinding) in cerebral palsy, 70

Camera lens spectacles, 298
Cancer, 43–58
   defined, 43–45
   and dermatomyositis, 265
   diagnostic tests for, 45–48
   epidemiology of, 43
   leukemia as. *See* Leukemia
   malignant tumors as, 44, 52–53
   most frequently encountered types of, 44–45
   psychological implications of, 55–56
   treatment of, 48–54
Capital femoral epiphysis
   in Down's syndrome, 286, 288
   slipped, 397–398
Carbamazepine for convulsive disorders, 179
Cardiac catheterization, 314–315, 320
Cardiac drugs for Friedreich's ataxia, 311
Cardiopulmonary resuscitation (CPR), 305–307
Cardiovascular disorders, acquired, 313. *See also* Heart disease
Carditis, rheumatic fever and, 323
Cars. *See* Physically handicapped drivers
Cartilages
   rheumatoid arthritis and damage to, 427–428
   torn, 402–403
CAT (computerized axial tomography), 47, 75, 76

Cat-cry (cri du chat) syndrome, 291
Cataracts, 485, 490–493
Catheterization, cardiac, 314–315, 320
Caustic soda (lye), 495
CB radios for physically handicapped drivers, 297
Central-core disease, 392
Central hearing loss, 136
Central-to-peripheral direction of maturation, 333
Cephalocaudal direction of maturation, 333
Cerebellar ataxia (Friedreich's ataxia), 212, 309–312, 371
Cerebellar cerebral palsy, 67–68
Cerebellum, 2, 4
Cerebral anoxia, 69
Cerebral arteriography for cerebral palsy, 75
Cerebral cortex, 2, 6
Cerebral hemorrhages, cerebral palsy and, 69, 70
Cerebral infections, cerebral palsy and, 69, 70
Cerebral tumors, cerebral palsy and, 69
Cerebral palsy, 7, 59–132, 366
    classification of types of, 60–66
    counseling adolescents with, 191
    defined, 59
    devices for communication in, 100, 159
    diagnosis of, 74–76
    drugs for, 101–102
    educational implications of, 105
    epilepsy and, 71, 172
    etiology of, 68–70
    functional development assessment of children with, 105–125
    handicaps associated with, 70–74
    incidence of, 59–60
    literature on, 219, 225, 226
    long-term outlook for, 102–104
    mental retardation in, 72, 79, 103, 104
    with microcephaly, 69, 366, 367, 369
    neuroanatomical classification of, 66–68
    occupational therapy for, 88–93
    physical therapy for, 80–88
    policy statement on therapy prescription for, 128–131
    prescriptive therapy for, 89
    prognosis with, 76–80
    rehabilitation for, 89, 93–101, 159
    Rh factor in, 60, 68, 70, 71
    scoliosis and, 435, 437
    surgery for, 89, 94
Cerebrum, 2
Chemotherapy, 494
    for cancer, 50–55
Chorea
    in cerebral palsy, 64
    rheumatic fever and, 323
Chair restraints for physically handicapped drivers, 296
Childhood (developmental) aphasia, 138, 139
Chloroquinine, 495
Choking (airway obstruction), 301–304
Chondodystrophies (skeletal dysplasias), 463–465

Chondromalacia patella, 401–402
Choroid, 483–485, 492
Christmas disease (hemophilia B), 327
Chromosome disorders, 290–291
Chromosomes, growth failure and anomalies of, 462, 464. See also X chromosome; Y chromosome
Chronic diseases, growth failure and, 453, 461, 464. See also specific chronic diseases
Chronic lead poisoning, 495
Chronic polyarthritis. See Juvenile rheumatoid arthritis
Chronic sorrow in parents of handicapped children, 197
Ciliary body of the eye, 483, 485
Classic hemophilia (hemophilia A), 327
Classroom survival signs, examples of, 155–158
Cleft lip or palate
    literature on, 219, 226
    and speech disorders, 139, 140
Clinitest tablets, 273
Clinodactyly, 281
Clonic (jerking) phase of grand mal, 173
Clonus in cerebral palsy, 61
Clothing for children with muscular dystrophy, 393
Clots, cerebral, cerebral palsy and, 69
Coagulation, 12
    disorders of. See Hemophilia
    in fracture healing, 13
    physiology of, 327
Coarctation of aorta, 321–322
Coccyx, 8
Cochlea (inner ear), 135
Cognitive development, 447–448
Colace, 357, 393
Collagen fibers in osteogenesis imperfecta, 405
Collateral blood vessels, 321
Color blindness, 290
Coma, diabetic, 271, 274
Communication. See also Augmentative Communication System; Language; Nonoral communication
    devices for, in cerebral palsy, 100, 159
    disorders of, 133–135. See also Hearing loss and disorders; Language disorders; Speech disorders
    literature on, 223–224
    with SMH children, 378–380
Community colleges with adaptive physical education classes, 238
Community resources
    created by parents, 251–252
    literature on recreational, 238–239
    for recreation and leisure, 229–233
Compact cars, modified, for physically handicapped drivers, 296
Computerized axial tomography (CAT), 47, 75, 76
Conductive hearing loss, 136
Congenital amputation, 17, 20

Index

Congenital cataracts, 493
Congenital cerebral palsy, 59
Congenital contractures, multiple, 27–30, 479
Congenital cytomegalic inclusion disease, 492
Congenital glaucoma, 489–490, 492, 493
Congenital heart disease, 28, 313–324
    aortic stenosis as, 309, 320–321, 431
    atrial septal defect as, 317–318
    coarctation of aorta as, 321–322
    Down's syndrome and, 283
    great vessels transposition as, 319–320
    literature on, 219
    murmurs as, 317–318, 323–324
    patent ductus arteriosus as, 315–316
    tetralogy of Fallot as, 318–319
    valvular pulmonic stenosis as, 322
    ventricular septal defect as, 316–317
Congenital hypothyroidism, 370
Congenital limb deficiency, 17, 20
Congenital nystagmus, 493
Congenital scoliosis, 435, 436
Conjunctiva, 486
Conjunctivitis, allergic, 33
Consumer organizations, 240–241
Constitutional growth delay, 461
Contractures, multiple congenital, 27–30, 479. *See also* Cerebral palsy
Convulsive disorders (epilepsy; seizures), 171–180, 367, 493
    cerebral palsy and, 71
    classification and types of, 172–176
    defined, 171
    as emergencies, 307–308
    etiology of, 172
    Friedreich's ataxia and, 311
    incidence of, 172
    literature on, 220, 226
    patient evaluation in, 176–177
    treatment of, 177
Cooley's anemia, literature on, 219
Corena, 484, 486, 492
Cornelia de Lange syndrome, 462
Cortical blindness, 367, 493
Cortical deafness, 367
Corticosteroids, 395
    for asthma, 41
    for rheumatoid arthritis, 428
    and visual disorders, 495
Cough medicine for asthma, 40
Counseling, 182–192. *See also* Parental counseling
    leisure, literature on, 241–242
    literature on, 223–224
CPK (creatine phosphokinase) in muscular dystrophy, 392
CPR (cardiopulmonary resuscitation), 305–307
Crawling, control of, 339–340
Creatine phosphokinase (CPK) in muscular dystrophy, 392
Creeping position, 340
Cri du chat (cat-cry) syndrome, 291

Crossed extension kicking in motor development, 338
Croup, 37
Cruising in motor development, 341
Cryptogenic seizures, 172
Cuts, care of, in hemophilia, 327
Cyanotic heart disease, 314. *See also* Great vessels; Tetralogy of Fallot
Cystic fibrosis, 37, 255–263
    body organ changes in, 256–258
    diagnosis of, 260
    educational implications of, 262–263
    etiology of, 256
    frequency of, 255
    literature on, 219
    mode of inheritance of, 256
    physical appearance with, 260, 261
    prognosis with, 262
    symptoms of, 258–259
    treatment of, 260, 262
    wheezing in, 37
Cystitis, myelomeningocele and, 349
Cytomegalic inclusion disease, 68, 462, 492
Cytomegalovirus infections, 366, 369

Dancing eye. *See* Nystagmus
Dantrolene sodium for cerebral palsy, 102
Deafness. *See* Hearing loss and disorders
Deaver therapy for cerebral palsy, 83
Deep tendon reflex in Friedreich's ataxia, 309
Dendrites, development of, 6
Denial, as parental response to handicap diagnosis, 194–195
Dental abnormalities and disorders
    in cerebral palsy, 70–71
    in Down's syndrome, 283
    in hemophilia, 327
Deoxyribonucleic acid (DNA), 288
Depression, counseling for parental, 186–187
Dermal respiratory syndrome, 36
Dermatoglyphics in Down's syndrome, 281
Dermatomyositis, 265–268
    educational implications of, 268
    onset and course of, 266, 267
    treatment of, 266, 268
Development. *See also* Cognitive development; Motor development; Normal infant motor development; Physical development; Psychosocial development; Sexual development
    defined, 333
    and developmental activities for SMH children, 374–383
    functional assessment of, in cerebral palsy, 105–125
    lag in, in cerebral palsy, 73
    literature on, 226
    severe and multiple handicaps due to disorders of, 369
Developmental (childhood) aphasia, 134, 138, 139

Developmental approach to counseling. *See* Counseling
Dextroamphetamine for cerebral palsy, 102
Diabetes mellitus (DM). *See also* Juvenile diabetes mellitus; Maternal diabetes mellitus
   adult-onset, 272
   literature on, 219–220, 226
   menstruation and, 446
Diabetic coma (ketoacidosis), 271, 274
Diarthroses, 14
Diastrophic dwarfism, 290
Diastrophic dysplasia, 464
Diazepam (Valium)
   for cerebral palsy, 101
   for convulsive disorders, 179
Diet. *See also* Vitamins
   and cystic fibrosis, 260
   diabetic, 275–276
   growth and, 453, 454
   for muscular dystrophy, 392
   role of, in management of paralysis associated with myelomeningocele, 358
Digitalis
   for congenital heart disease, 315
   for muscular dystrophy, 392
Diphenylhydantoin (Dilantin) for convulsive disorders, 178
Diplegia, spastic, 60, 62, 66, 68
Disodium cromoglycate (Aarane; Intal), 41
DM. *See* Diabetes mellitus
DNA (deoxyribonucleic acid), 288
Dominant trait, defined, 288
Donahue syndrome, 462
Down's syndrome (Mongolism), 279–288, 367
   cataracts and, 490
   clinical features of, 281–283
   and congenital heart disease, 314
   genetic factors in, 279–280, 291
   and growth failure, 462
   management of, 284–288
   sensory-integration therapy for, 85–86
   SMH in, 366, 368
   x-ray features of, 283–284
Doxinate, 357, 395
Driver education for physically handicapped drivers, 299–300
Drivers. *See* Physically handicapped drivers
Drooling in cerebral palsy, 70
Drugs. *See* Chemotherapy; *and specific drugs*
Dubowitz syndrome, 462
Ducolax, 358
Dwarfism
   achondroplastic and diastrophic, 290
   Laron, 463
   psychosexual, 461, 465
   Russell-Silver, 462
   thanatophoric, 464
   visual problems and, 492
Dysarthria, 140, 379

Dysplasia
   Kniest and epiphyseal, 464
   skeletal, 463–465
   X-linked spondyloepiphyseal, 464

Ear. *See also* Hearing loss and disorders
   anatomy of, 135
   in Down's syndrome, 281
Eardrum (tympanic membrane), 135
Early infancy, sequence of gross motor control in, 337–338
Early sitting, control of, 339
Early walking, control of, 340–341
Echocardiography for congenital heart disease, 314
Eclectic physical therapy for cerebral palsy, 87
Eczema, allergic, 33, 36
Education
   driver, for physically handicapped drivers, 299–300
   literature on, 226
Education for All Handicapped Children Act (Public Law 94-142; 1975), 25, 89, 105, 299
Educational implications
   of amputations, 24–25
   of arthrogryposis, 30
   of asthma, 41–42
   of cancer, 56–57
   of cerebral palsy, 105
   of cystic fibrosis, 262–263
   of dermatomyositis, 268
   of DM, 276–277
   of Friedreich's ataxia, 311–312
   of heart disease, 324
   of hemophilia, 329–330
   of juvenile rheumatoid arthritis, 429–430
   of meningocele, 358–362
   of muscular dystrophy, 393–394
   of poliomyelitis, 422
   of rubella, 432
   of scoliosis, 442–443
   of severe and multiple handicaps. *See* Severely and multiply handicapped children
   of sickle cell anemia, 476
   of SMA, 480
   of speech and hearing disorders, 139
EEG, *see* Electroencephalography
Efferent fibers, 8
VIIIth cranial nerve (auditory nerve), 135
Electrocardiography (EKG), 309
   for congenital heart disease, 314, 318
   for Friedreich's ataxia, 309, 311
   for heart murmurs, 323
Electroencephalography (EEG), 4, 389
   for cerebral palsy, 75
   for convulsive disorders, 177
Electromyography (EMG), 12
   for cerebral palsy, 75–76
   for muscular dystrophy, 392
Ellis van Crevald syndrome, 464

Index

Embryology of meningocele, 345–347
Emergencies, 301–308
   airway obstruction as, 301–304
   convulsions as, 307–308
   CPR as, 305–308
   fainting as, 308, 318
EMG. *See* Electromyography
Emotional deprivation (psychosocial) dwarfism, 461, 465
Emotional factors in asthma, 35
Emphysema, 38
Encephalitis, 367
   cerebral palsy and, 69
   and convulsive disorders, 172
   severe and multiple handicaps due to, 366, 371
Encephalotrigeminal angiomatosis (Sturge-Weber syndrome), 493
Endocarditis, bacterial, congenital heart disease and, 316–319, 321–323
Endochondral ossification, 459–460
Endocrine disorders, growth failure and, 462–463. *See also specific endocrine disorders*
Endolymphatic fluid, 135
Endosteum, 13
Endophthalmitis, nematode, 493
Epilepsy. *See* Convulsive disorders
Epimysium of muscle, 10
Epineurium, 10
Epiphysis, 12, 464. *See also* Capital femoral epiphysis
Equilibrium reactions, 335–336, 340–341
Erythroblastosis fetalis, 68
Escheria coli (*E. coli*) infections at birth, severe and multiple handicaps and, 366
Esotropia, 71, 487
Ethanol, 462. *See also* Alcohol
Ethics, literature on, 226
Ethosuximide (Zarontin) for convulsive disorders, 179
Eustachian tubes, 135
Exercise
   for asthma, 39
   for chondromalacia patella, 401–402
   for diabetics, 275–276
   for juvenile rheumatoid arthritis, 428, 429
   for scoliosis, 440
Exotropia, 71, 487
Extensor thrust in cerebral palsy, 77, 78
Extraocular muscles, 486, 487
Extrapyramidal damage in cerebral palsy, 67
Eye, anatomy and physiology of, 483–486. *See also* Visual disorders
Eyeglasses, 488
Eyelids, drooping, 488, 493

FA. *See* Friedreich's ataxia
Facial features in Down's syndrome, 281
Facioscapulohumeral (FSH) muscular dystrophy, 385, 386
Factors VIII and IX in hemophilia, 327–329
Fainting (syncope), 308, 318
Familial short stature, 460–461
Farsightedness (hyperopia), 71, 488
Fatty acids, 270
Fay-Doman therapy for cerebral palsy, 83
Feeding
   devices for, in cerebral palsy, 100
   independent, by SMH children, 376–377
   by traumatic paraplegics, 416
Feet
   amputation of, 21
   in Down's syndrome, 281–282, 284–285
   in Friedreich's ataxia, 309
   in meningocele, 347, 348
Femoral epiphysis. *See* Capital femoral epiphysis
Fetal anoxia and asphyxia, cerebral palsy and, 68, 69
Fetal hemoglobin (HbF), 470, 474
Fibroplasia, retrolental, 493, 495
Fibrous layer of the eye, 484
Financial assistance, literature on, 241
Fine motor development in cerebral palsy, 105, 106, 111–116
Flaccid paralysis, meningocele and, 347
Flailing muscles in cerebral palsy, 64–65
Flexed position of newborns, 336
Focal fits (March epilepsy; Jacksonian epilepsy), 173–175
Food allergies, 33
Foreign body, choking due to ingestion of, 302–304
Forme fruste of Friedreich's ataxia, 311
Fovea of the eye, 485
Fractionated radiotherapy, 49
Fracture-immobilization-osteoporosis-refracture cycle in osteogenesis imperfecta, 407, 408
Fractures, healing of, 12–13. *See also* Osteogenesis imperfecta
Friedreich's ataxia (FA; cerebellar ataxia; spinocerebellar ataxia), 212, 309–312, 371
FSH (facioscapulohumeral) muscular dystrophy, 385, 386
Fundus of the eye, 486

Galactosemia, cataracts and, 490
Gamma globulin for asthma, 41
Gargoylism (Hurler's syndrome), 492
Gastrointestinal disorders
   cystic fibrosis and, 259, 260
   dermatomyositis and, 265, 266
Gastrointestinal (GI) series, 46
Gene, defined, 288
Gene-level disorders, 290
Genetic diseases. *See also specific genetic diseases*
   severe and multiple handicaps and, 366, 368
   visual disorders due to, 491–492
Genetics. *See also* X chromosome; Y chromosome; *and entries beginning with terms:* congenital; familial

Index

Genetics (*continued*)
  of arthrogryposis, 27
  and autosomal inheritance, 288–290, 473
  of cancer, 44
  of cataracts, 491
  of cerebral palsy, 68
  and chromosome disorders, 290–291
  of congenital heart disease, 314
  of convulsive disorders, 172
  of cystic fibrosis, 256
  of DM, 272
  dominant and recessive traits in, 288
  of Down's syndrome, 279–280, 291
  of Friedreich's ataxia, 311
  and gene-level disorders, 290
  of growth failure, 462–464
  of hemophilia, 326–327
  of muscular dystrophy, 388
  and sex-linked inheritance, 288–289
  of sickle cell anemia, 473–474
  of SMA, 479–480
German measles. *See* Rubella
Glaucoma, 485, 489–490, 493
Globin, 470
β Globin chains in sickle cell anemia, 470–472
Glucocorticoids in dermatomyositis, 266, 268
Glucose
  in DM, 269. *See also* Diabetes mellitus; Juvenile diabetes mellitus
  in Friedreich's ataxia, 311
Gold salts, 428
Gonadotropin, 463
Gonococcal infections (ophthalmia neonatorum), 492
Gower's sign in muscular dystrophy, 390
Grand mal, 173
Great vessels, transposition of, 319–320. *See also* Aorta; Pulmonary artery; Vena cava
Grief
  counseling for parental, 183–184
  as parental reaction to diagnosis of handicap, 197
Gross motor development, 335–343
  in cerebral palsy, 105–111
  chart on, 341–343
  and development of primitive reflexes, 335–336
  sequence of, 336–341
Growth, 451–468
  defined, 451
  diabetes and, 274
  failure of. *See* Short stature
  fractures and, 13
  measures of, 454–457
  normal, 451–454
  of partially absent limbs, 22
  physiology of, 458–460
Guillain-Barré syndrome, 387

Hallerman-Streiff syndrome, 462
Halo tractions for poliomyelitis, 422

Hand-foot syndrome, 474
Hands
  amputation of, 22–23
  in Down's syndrome, 281, 288
Handwriting in Friedreich's ataxia, 309
Harrington instrumentation for poliomyelitis, 422
HbA (adult hemoglobin), 473
HbF (fetal hemoglobin), 470, 474
HbS (sickle hemoglobin molecule), 472, 474, 475
Head control
  in motor development, 337–338
  of SMH children, 374–375
Head injuries
  cerebral palsy and, 69
  in hemophilia, 327–328
  severe and multiple handicaps due to, 367, 370
Hearing loss and disorders, 135–136, 159
  in cerebral palsy, 71
  cortical deafness, 367
  drivers with, 298
  and hearing mechanisms, 135
  literature on, 220, 225
  osteogenesis imperfecta and, 406, 410
  rubella and, 431, 492
  temporary, aspirin and, 430
  types of, 136
Heart disease. *See also* Congenital heart disease
  acquired, 322–323
  and dermatomyositis, 265
  diagnosis of, 314–315
  educational implications of, 324
  etiology of, 313
  Friedreich's ataxia and, 309
  maternal, effects of, on intrauterine growth, 452
  SMA and, 479
Heart failure. *See also* Congenital heart disease
  with muscular dystrophy, 391
  scoliosis and, 439
  sickle cell anemia and, 475
Heart massage for CPR, 305, 306, 308
Hemiplegia, spastic, 60, 61, 63, 73, 79, 102
Hemoglobin, 470–474
Hemoglobin A (adult hemoglobin; HbA), 473
Hemoglobin F (fetal hemoglobin; HbF), 474
Hemolysis, 472
Hemolytic anemia, 68
Hemophilia, 288, 290, 325–331
  clinical manifestations, treatment, and prognosis, 327–329
  educational implications of, 329–330
  genetics of, 326–327
  history of, 325–326
  and physiology of coagulation, 327
Hemophilia A (factor VIII deficiency; classic hemophilia), 327
Hemophilia B (Christmas disease; factor IX deficiency), 327
Hemorrhages, cerebral, cerebral palsy and, 69, 70
Hepatitis, 329
Heredity. *See* Genetics

Index

Herpes simplex virus infections, 366, 369
Herpes zoster virus infections, 68
hGH (human growth hormone), 458, 461–463
Hip and hip joint. *See also* Capital femoral epiphysis
   in arthrogryposis, 28–29
   in Down's syndrome, 284–286
   in Legg-Perthes disease, 395–396
Histamine, 33
Histoplasmosis, 493
HLA-B27 (antigen), 427
Hopping in motor development, 340
Hormones. *See also specific hormones*
   defined, 470
   for muscular dystrophy, 392
Human growth hormone (hGH), 458, 461–463
Humpback. *See* Kyphosis
Hurler's syndrome (gargoylism), 492
Hydantoins, 178, 452, 462
Hydrocephalus, 76, 349–351, 358, 368
Hydronephrosis, myelomeningocele and, 349
Hyperbilirubinemia, 68
Hyperkinetic children, 453
Hyperopia (farsightedness), 71, 488
Hypertension, 322, 323, 453
Hypoglycemia, 172, 176, 274, 276, 463
Hypothyroidism, 370, 395, 465
Hypoxia
   and congenital heart disease, 320
   sickle cell anemia and, 472
   and tetralogy of Fallot, 318

Idiopathic scoliosis, 435, 436
Idiopathic seizures, 172
IEP (Individual Education Plan), 373–374
Inadequacy, parental feelings of, 196–197
Independent walking by infants, 341
Individual Education Plan (IEP), 373–374
Indomethacin for juvenile rheumatoid arthritis, 428
Induction phase of therapy for leukemia, 54
Infant motor development. *See* Motor development; Normal infant motor development
Infantile spasms (West syndrome; Salaam seizures; jactitation; massive myoclonia; jackknife seizures), 176
Infants. *See also* Development; Neonatal tetany; Normal infant motor development
   with cerebral palsy, therapy programs for, 87–88
   counseling for handicapped, 189–190
   disgorging foreign body from choking, 303–304
Infarcts, sickle cell anemia and, 472
Infections. *See also specific types of infections and infectious diseases*
   cerebral, 68–70
   choking due to, 302
   cytomegalovirus, 366, 369
   diabetes and, 276
   Down's syndrome and, 283

   E. coli, 366
   gonococcal, 492
   herpes simplex virus, 366, 369
   herpes zoster virus, 68
   and Legg-Perthes disease, 395
   severe and multiple handicaps due to, 366, 369
   visual disorders due to, 492
Inferior vena cava, 315
Inflammatory diseases, visual disorders due to, 493
Information sources. *See* Literature
Inhalants, allergies to, 33–34, 37, 39
Inheritance. *See* Genetics
Inhibition (akinetic; astatic) epilepsy, 175
Injury and trauma. *See also* Abdominal injuries; Birth injuries; Head injuries
   amputations due to, 17
   cataracts and, 491
   and chondromalacia patella, 401
   and cortical blindness, 493
   and Legg-Perthes disease, 395
   in osteochondritis dessicans, 400
   severe and multiple handicaps due to, 366, 371
   sickle cell anemia and, 475
   spinal. *See* Traumatic paraplegia and quadriplegia
   torn cartilages and, 402
Inner ear (cochlea), 135
Insertion of muscle, 10
Insulin, production of, in DM, 269. *See also* Diabetes mellitus; Juvenile diabetes mellitus
   secretion of, in Friedreich's ataxia, 311
   for treatment of DM, 272–274
Insulin reaction (hypoglycemia), 172, 176, 274, 276, 463
Intal (Aarane; disodium cromoglycate), 41
Intellectual function, prognosis for, in cerebral palsy, 80. *See also* Mental retardation
Internal eye structures, 485–486
International Classification of Epilepsy, 174
International resources for recreation and leisure, 229–233
Interventricular foramen of brain, 3
Intrauterine growth retardation, 451–453, 462, 464
Intravenous pyelogram (IVP), 46
Iridocyclitis (anterior uveitis), 427, 493
Iris of the eye, 485
IVP (intravenous pyelogram), 46

Jackknife seizures (infantile spasms), 176
Jacksonian epilepsy (focal fits), 173–175
Jactitation (infantile spasms), 176
Jaundice, 473, 474
Jerking (cloning) phase of grand mal, 173
Joints (articulation), 13–15. *See also specific joints and entries beginning with element:* arthr
   effects of osteogenesis imperfecta on, 406
   hemophilia and bleeding in, 328

Journals, information, 242–243
Juvenile diabetes mellitus (DM), 269–277
  adjustment problems with, 276
  cataracts in, 490
  diet and exercise for, 275–276
  educational implications of, 276–277
  genetics of, 272
  infections and, 276
  insulin for. See Insulin
  metabolism in, 270–272
  testing urine in, 273–274
Juvenile rheumatoid arthritis (juvenile chronic polyarthritis; Still's disease), 15, 423–430
  complications of, 427–428
  Down's syndrome and, 288
  educational implications of, 429–430
  literature on, 221
  pauciarticular, 427
  polyarticular, 425–426
  systemic, 424
  treatment of, 428–429
  visual disorders and, 493

Kabat and Knott therapy for cerebral palsy, 83
Kernicterus, 68
Ketoacidosis (diabetic coma), 271, 274
Ketone bodies, 270, 273, 274
Kicking extension, 338
Kidney disease
  literature on, 221
  maternal, effects of, on intrauterine growth, 452
  menstruation and, 446
Kidney function
  dermatomyositis and, 265
  in glucose metabolism, 271
  sickle cell anemia and, 475
Klinefelter's syndrome, 291
Knee-chest position, 318
Knee-flexion gait patterns in cerebral palsy, 89
Knee and knee joint, 14–15
  in arthrogryposis, 29
  in chondromalacia patella, 401–402
  in Down's syndrome, 284, 286
  in Osgood-Schlatter's disease, 398–399
  in osteochondritis dessicans, 400
  in rheumatoid arthritis, 426
  torn cartilages of, 402–403
Kniest dysplasia, 464
Kugelberg-Welander muscular dystrophy, 386, 477
Kwashiorkor, 461
Kyphoscoliosis. See Scoliosis
Kyphosis (humpback)
  in Friedreich's ataxia, 309
  in meningocele, 347

Labyrinthine righting reactions, 335–337
Lamina, 8
Laminography (tomography), 46
Landau reflex, 338

Language
  Blissymbolics and functions of, 148–151
  cerebral palsy and language development, 105, 106, 116–120
  sign, 155–158
Language disorders, 134, 137–139. See also Speech disorders
  language mechanisms and, 137
  types of, 138–139
Laron dwarfism, 463
Lead poisoning
  cerebral palsy and, 69
  chronic, 495
Learning disabilities
  associated with cerebral palsy, 86–87
  and language disorders, 138
Leber's optic atrophy, 492
Legg-Perthes disease (Legg-Calve-Perthes disease), 395–397
Lennox-Gastaut syndrome (atypical petit mal), 175
Lens of the eye, 485, 486
Lente insulin, 272, 273, 276
Lesh-Nyhan syndrome, 290, 366, 368
Leukemia, 44–45, 53–55
  Down's syndrome and, 283
  visual disorders and, 494
Life expectancy with cerebral palsy, 80
Life-support services for SMH children, 372–373
Lifts for children with muscular dystrophy, 393
Limb deficiency (congenital amputation), 17, 20
Limb-girdle muscular dystrophy, 385, 386, 392
Lips. See Cleft lip or palate
Literature
  on osteogenesis imperfecta, 410–412
  for parents and professionals, 217–228
  on recreation and leisure, 234–239, 241–242, 244–251
Liver
  in cystic fibrosis, 257
  hepatitis, 329
  sickle cell anemia and, 472–473, 475
Lordosis (swayback)
  lumbar, in cerebral palsy, 89
  meningocele and, 347
  and muscular dystrophy, 389
Low blood sugar (hypoglycemia), 172, 176, 274, 276, 463
Low vision, drivers with, 298
Lowerlimbs
  flaccid paralysis of, in meningocele, 347
  loss of, 20–22, 24
Lumbar lordosis in cerebral palsy, 89
Lumbar plexus, 8, 9
Lumbar puncture (spinal tap), 46, 47, 177
Lungs. See also Respiratory infections; and entries beginning with term: pulmonary
  in cystic fibrosis, 257–261
  sickling in, 475
Lye (caustic soda), 495

Index

Lymphangiogram for cancer, 46
Lymphomas, 45

Macula of the eye, 485, 486
Magazines, 242–243
    on OI, 411–412
    for parents and professionals, 223
Magnesium oxide for OI, 407
Malaria, sickle cell anemia and, 469
Malignant tumors, 44, 52–53. *See also specific types of malignant tumors*
Malnutrition, growth and, 453, 461, 464. *See also Diet*
Malocclusion, speech disorders and, 139, 140
March epilepsy (focal fits), 173–175
Marfan's syndrome, 491
Mass adjustments of vocal cords, phonation and, 139
Mass primitive reflexes, 337
Massive myoclonia (infantile spasms), 176
Maternal diabetes mellitus (DM)
    cerebral palsy and, 68
    effects of, on intrauterine growth, 452–453
Maternal factors
    affecting intrauterine growth, 452–453
    in cataracts, 490
    in cerebral palsy, 68
    in congenital heart disease, 314
Maturation, concepts of, 333. *See also Normal infant motor development*
Membranous ossification, 459
Meningitis, 351
    and cerebral palsy, 69
    convulsive disorders and, 172
    severe and multiple handicaps and, 366, 371
Meningocele and myelomeningocele, 345–362
    defined, 345
    disabilities associated with, 347–351
    educational implications of, 358–362
    embriology and causes of deformities in, 345–347
    with hydrocephalus, 368
    incidence of, 345
    long-term outlook for, 358
    predictable activity in, 355
    scoliosis and, 435
    severe and multiple handicaps due to, 366
    sexual development and, 446
    treatment of, 351–358
Menstruation, 12, 446
Mental retardation, 379, 492. *See also Severely and multiply handicapped children*
    cerebral palsy and, 72, 79, 102–104
    Down's syndrome and, 283, 284. *See also Down's syndrome*
    evaluating, 193
    Friedreich's ataxia and, 311
    hydrocephalus and, 350
    literature on, 225–227

    and muscular dystrophy, 391
    phakomatoses and, 493
    profound, defined, 363
    rubella and, 432
Mephobarbital for convulsive disorders, 178
Metabolic disorders
    cataracts and, 490
    convulsive disorders and, 172
    maternal, cerebral palsy and, 68
Metabolism, 269–272
    in DM, 270–272
    normal, 269–270
Metharbital for convulsive disorders, 178
Methotrexate for dermatomyositis, 268
Methyphenidate (Ritalin), 453
Microcephaly, cerebral palsy and, 69, 366, 367, 369
Microprocessors, use of, in cerebral palsy rehabilitation, 100
Mixed cerebral palsy, 66
Mixed hearing loss, 136
Mixed-type epilepsy, 176
Mobility aids
    for cerebral palsy victims, 98–101
    for muscular dystrophy victims, 393
    for osteogenesis imperfecta, 407–408
    for paraplegics, 416–417
    for poliomyelitis victims, 419–421
    for severely and multiply handicapped children, 375, 380–382
Mongolism. *See Down's syndrome*
Moon face, 428
Moro reflex (startle reflex), 77, 282, 339, 375
Morquio syndrome, 464
Mosaic Down's syndrome, 279–280
Motor development. *See also Gross motor development; Normal infant motor development*
    basic motor-maturity evaluation in cerebral palsy, 82, 84–85
    in cerebral palsy, 72–74, 105, 106, 111–116
Motor neuropathies, 387
Mouth, bleeding from, in hemophilia, 327. *See also Cleft lip or palate; Oral disorders*
Mouth-to-mouth ventilation for CPR, 305–306
MS (multiple sclerosis), 140, 492
Mucopolysaccharidoses, 492
Mucoviscidosis. *See Cystic fibrosis*
Multiple congenital contractures (arthrogryposis multiplex congenita), 27–30, 479
Multiple sclerosis (MS), 140, 492
Multitropic pituitary hormone deficiency (panhypopituitarism), 462, 465
Murmurs, 317–318, 323–324
Muscle-weakening diseases, classification of, 386–387. *See also Muscular dystrophy—Duchenne type*
Muscles, 10–12. *See also Dermatomyositis; and entries beginning with term: muscular, and element: myo*

Muscles (*continued*)
  atrophy of. *See* Spinal muscular atrophy
  extraocular, 486
  in Friedreich's ataxia, 309
  hemophilia and bleeding in, 328
  tone of, in Down's syndrome, 282
Muscular dystrophy—Duchenne type (progressive muscular dystrophy; pseudohypertrophic muscular dystrophy), 371, 385–394
  diagnosing, 392
  educational implications of, 393–394
  etiology of, 388
  literature on, 221
  prognosis with, 391–392
  scoliosis and, 435
  symptoms and course of, 388–391
  treatment of, 392–393
Mutations, 388, 370, 372
Myasthenia gravis, 387, 493
Myelin, 7, 10
Myelination, 7
Myelodysplasia, 448
Myelomeningocele. *See* Meningocele
Myoclonic epilepsy, 175, 176
Myofilament, 10
Myopathic arthrogryposis, 28
Myopathies, 387, 392
Myopia (nearsightedness), 71, 488
Myosin, 10
Myotonis diseases, 387
Myotonic dystrophy, 488

Narcotics for sickle cell anemia, 474
National resources for recreation and leisure, 229–233
Nearsightedness (myopia), 71, 488
Neck extension, 377
Neck reflexes, 76–78
  righting, 77, 78, 337
  tonic, 76–77, 335, 337
Negative supportive phase of motor development, 338
Nematode endophthalmitis, 493
Neonatal tetany, cataracts and, 490
Neonates. *See* Infants
Nerve fibers (axons), 2, 5, 10
Nerves, 8–10
Nervous system, 2–10. *See also* Brain; Spinal cord; Spine
Neural layer of the eye, 485
Neuritis, optic, 492
Neuroblast of brain, 4
Neuroblastoma, 45
Neurofibromatoses, 366, 368, 493
Neurological disorders, visual disorders due to, 492–493. *See also specific neurological disorders*
Neurology, literature on, 221
Neuromuscular scoliosis, 435, 439

Neurons, 2, 4, 5, 7, 8
Neuropathic arthrogryposis, 28
Neuropathies, sensory, 387
Neurosurgery for meningocele, 351
Newborns. *See* Infants
Newsletters, 242–243
Nonoral communication, 145. *See also* Augmentative Communication System
  systems and devices for, 159–169
Nonsteroidal anti-inflammatory drugs (NSAIDs), 428
Nonstructural scoliosis, 433–435
Nontension athetosis, 64
Normal growth, 451–454
Normal infant motor development, 333–344
  definitions of terms, 333
  gross motor development in. *See* Gross motor development
  primitive reflexes and, 334–336
  progression of reflexes and voluntary controlled movements in, 333–334
Nosebleed in hemophilia, 328
NPH insulin, 272–274, 276
NSAIDs (nonsteroidal anti-inflammatory drugs), 428
Nutrition, *See* Diet
Nyctalopia, 488
Nystagmus (dancing eye), 493
  albinism and, 491
  in cerebral palsy, 86
  in Friedreich's ataxia, 311

Obesity
  diabetes and, 272
  menstruation and, 446
  in muscular dystrophy, 391
  aa side effect of cortisone, 428
Occupational therapy
  for cerebral palsy, 88–93
  for Friedreich's ataxia, 311
  for myelomeningocele, 354
OI. *See* Osteogenesis imperfecta
Oligodendroglial cells of brain, 4
Ontogenetic progression of development, 334
Ophthalmia neonatorum (gonococcal infections) 492
Optic nerve, 486, 492, 494
Optic neuritis, 492
Optical righting reactions, 336, 337
Oral disorders. *See also* Cleft lip or palate; Mouth
  in cerebral palsy, 70–71
  malocclusion, 139, 140
Orientation reflexes, 335
Origin of muscle, 10
Orthopedic disabilities. *See* Temporary orthopedic disabilities
Orthopedic surgery for meningocele, 354
Orthotics (braces)
  for cerebral palsy, 95, 98
  for Legg-Perthes disease, 396

Index

for muscular dystrophy, 392–393
for OI, 407
for paralysis due to myelomeningocele, 351–354
for poliomyelitis, 421, 422
for scoliosis, 440–442
for SMA, 480
Osgood-Schlatter's disease, 398–399
Ossicles of ear, 135
Ossification, membranous and endochondral, 459–460
Osteoblasts, 12–13
Osteoclasts, 13
Osteochondritis dessicans, 399–401
Osteogenesis imperfecta (OI), 405–412
　educational implications of, 408–410
　etiology and basic defect in, 405
　literature on, 410–412
　prognosis with, 407
　treatment of, 407–408
Osteogenesis imperfecta (OI) congenita, 406, 407
Osteogenesis imperfecta (OI) tarda, 406, 407
Osteoporosis, osteogenesis imperfecta and, 407
Ostomy, literature on, 221
Otitis media, conductive hearing loss and, 136
Outdoor recreation and camping, literature on, 244
Oxazolidines for convulsive disorders, 179

Pain
　pain crisis in sickling, 474–475
　scoliosis and back, 439
Palate. See Cleft lip or palate
Pancreas, in cystic fibrosis, 255–257, 259, 260. See also Diabetes mellitus; Juvenile diabetes mellitus
Panhypopituitarism (multitropic pituitary hormone deficiency), 462, 465
Parachute reaction, 77–79, 339
Paralysis. See also Diplegia; Hemiplegia; Paraplegia; Quadriplegia; Traumatic paraplegia and quadriplegia
　Down's syndrome and, 286
　myelomeningocele and, 347, 349, 351–354
　spastic, rubella and, 431
Paraplegia. See also Traumatic paraplegia and quadriplegia
　defined, 413
　scoliosis and, 439
　spastic, 60–62, 68
　and transportation for paraplegics, 294
Parental counseling, 183–188
　for building competence, 185–186
　to deal with parental depression, 186–187
　to help parents focus on child's abilities, 184–185
　on interaction with other parents, 187–188
　and parental grief, 183–184
　teacher's role in, 194–201
Parents of handicapped children, 202–210
　example of community resource program created by, 251–252
　literature for, 217–228

Parking by physically handicapped drivers, 297
Parkinson's disease, 66, 140
Patent ductus arteriosus, 315–316
Pauciarticular juvenile rheumatoid arthritis, 427
Pediatricians, and management of myelomeningocele, 357–358
Penicillin
　for gonococcal infections, 492
　for rheumatic fever, 323
Perceptual disorders in cerebral palsy, 72–74
Pericarditis, rheumatoid arthritis and, 427
Perinatal causes of cerebral palsy, 68–69
Perineurium, 10
Periosteum, 12
Peripheral nerves, 8
Personal-social development. See Psychosocial development
Perspiration, salt content of, in cystic fibrosis, 259, 260
Petit mal triad, 175
Phakomatoses, 493
Phelps therapy for cerebral palsy, 83
Phenobarbital
　for cerebral palsy, 102
　for convulsive disorders, 178
Phenylbutazone for rheumatoid arthritis, 428
Phenylketonuria (PKU), 176, 290, 366, 368
Phocomelia, 18
Phonation disorders, 139–140
Phylogenetic progression of reflexes, 334
Physical activities, literature on, 248–249. See also Exercise
Physical education
　community colleges with classes in, 238
　literature on, 127–128
Physical development, 445–446
Physical handicaps. See also Physically disabled drivers; and specific physical handicaps
　literature on, 225
　resource information on recreation and leisure for individuals with, 234–242
Physical therapy. See also Exercise; Occupational therapy
　for cerebral palsy, 80–88
　for dermatomyositis, 268
　for muscular dystrophy, 392
　for myelomeningocele, 354
　for poliomyelitis, 421
　for SMA, 480
　for SMH children, 380–381
Physically disabled drivers, 293–300
　armless, 299
　with auditory and visual problems, 298
　automotive systems for, 293–294
　chair restraints for, 296
　driver education for, 299–300
　handling of problems outside the car by, 297
　mechanical controls for, 294–295
　modified compact cars for, 296

Physically disabled drivers (*continued*)
   servo controls for, 295
   vans and large sedans for, 295–296
Physiologic flexor hypertonus, 336
Pink eye, 491
Pinna of ear, 135
PKU (Phenylketonuria), 176, 290, 366, 368
Plexus, 8, 9
Pneumoencephalogram for cerebral palsy, 75
Pneumonia, 260
   and dermatomyositis, 266
   and Down's syndrome, 283
   and ventricular septal defect, 316
   wheezing in, 37
Poliomyelitis, 419–422
   educational implications of, 422
   incidence of, 421
   scoliosis and, 435
   symptoms and clinical course of, 419–421
   treatment of, 421–422
Poliomyositis, 387
Pollution, asthma and, 34
Polyarthritis. *See* Juvenile rheumatoid arthritis
Polyarticular juvenile rheumatoid arthritis, 425–426
Polydactyly, 281, 288
Positive supporting reactions in motor development, 338
Posterior uveitis, 493
Postnatal causes of cerebral palsy, 69–70
Postural reflexes, 335
Prader-Willi syndrome, literature on, 227
Pregnancy, 227, 366. *See also* Intrauterine growth retardation; Toxemia of pregnancy; *and entries beginning with terms:* fetal, maternal
Prematurity, 68, 70, 104, 366
Prenatal causes of cerebral palsy, 68. *See also* Pregnancy
Preschool handicapped children, counseling, 190
Preschool programs of physical therapy for cerebral palsy, 87–88
Primidone for convulsive disorders, 178
Primitive reflexes, 334–337
Primitive standing reflex, 337
Primitive walking reflex, 337
Professionals, literature for, 217–228
Progeria, 462
Progressive muscular dystrophy. *See* Muscular dystrophy—Duchenne type
Prosthetics, 20, 22–24
Pseudohypertrophic muscular dystrophy. *See* Muscular dystrophy—Duchenne type
Psychological effects
   of cancer, 55–56
   of scoliosis, 440
Psychosocial development
   cerebral palsy and, 105, 106, 120–125
   sexual and, 448
Psychosocial dwarfism (emotional deprivation syndrome), 461, 465
Psychosocial needs of amputees, 19
Ptosis (drooping eyelids), 488, 493
Public Law 94-142 (P.L. 94-142; Education for All Handicapped Children Act; 1975), 25, 89, 105, 299
Pulmonary artery, 315
   transposition of, 319–320
Pulmonary stenosis, Friedreich's ataxia and, 309, 311
Pupil of the eye, 484, 485
Pyelonephritis, myelomeningocele and, 349
Pyramidal damage in cerebral palsy, 67

Quadriplegia, 65. *See also* Traumatic paraplegia and quadriplegia
   defined, 413
   devices for nonoral communication in, 159
   spastic, 60, 61, 63, 79, 102

Radionuclide scanning for cancer, 47, 48
Radiation therapy, 49–53, 494
Rashes. *See* Skin rashes
Reading aids, 495
Recessive trait, 288
Recreation and leisure
   community, state, national and international resources for, 229–233
   general resource information on, 234–253
   journals, magazines and newsletters on, 242–243
   literature on, 227–228
   outdoor, literature on, 244
Recumbency treatment for Legg-Perthes disease, 396
Reflexes, progression of, 333–334. *See also specific reflexes*
Refractive error, 488
Regular insulin, 272, 273
Rehabilitation. *See also* Exercise; Occupational therapy; Physical therapy
   for cerebral palsy, 89, 93–101, 159
   literature on, 228
   for torn cartilages, 403
   for traumatic paraplegia, 416–418
Rejection, as parental response to handicap diagnosis, 195
Relapses in leukemia, 54, 55
Remission phase of leukemia, 54
Respiratory infections. *See also specific respiratory infections*
   asthma and, 35, 40
   SMA and, 480
   wheezing and, 37
Retina, 483–486, 492, 494
   degenerative diseases of, 488–489
Retinis pigmentosa, 489–490
Retinoblastoma, 494
Retrolental fibroplasia, 493, 495
Rh incompatibility, cerebral palsy and, 60, 68, 70, 71

Index

Rhabdomyosarcoma, 494
Rheumatic fever, 322–323
Rheumatoid arthritis. See Juvenile rheumatoid arthritis
Rheumatoid factor, 424
Rhinitis, allergic, 33, 34, 36, 37
Righting reactions, 335–337
   labyrinthine, 335–337
   neck, 77, 78, 337
   optical, 336, 337
Rigidity in cerebral palsy, 65, 306
Ritalin (methyphenidate), 453
Rolfing for cerebral palsy, 87
Rolling movements in early infancy, 338–339
Rood therapy for cerebral palsy, 83
Rotation, axial, in infancy, 338
Rubella (German measles), 367, 431–432
   cataracts and, 490
   cerebral palsy and, 68
   and intrauterine growth retardation, 562
   maternal, congenital heart disease and, 314
   severe and multiple handicaps due to, 366, 369
   visual disorders and, 431, 492
Rubella vaccine, 431
Russell-Silver dwarfism, 462

Salaam seizures (infantile spasms), 176
Salt content of perspiration in cystic fibrosis, 259, 260
San Fillipo syndrome, 290
Sarcomeres, 10
Scapuloperoneal muscular dystrophy, 479
School-age handicapped children, counseling, 190–191
Sclera of the eye, 483, 484
Scoliosis (spinal curvature), 433–443
   curve location and description, 436
   defined, 433
   disabilities due to, 439–440
   in Down's syndrome, 286
   educational implications of, 442–443
   in Friedreich's ataxia, 309
   incidence of, 436–437
   meningocele and, 347
   nonstructural, 433–435
   poliomyelitis and, 421–422
   SMA and, 479, 480
   structural, 435–436
   symptoms of, 437–439
   treatment of, 440–442
Scrapes, care of, in hemophilia, 327
Seating devices for cerebral palsy victims, 98–100. See also Wheelchairs
Seckel syndrome, 462
Sedatives for asthma, 40
Seizures. See Convulsive disorders
Sensorineural hearing loss, 136
Sensory deficits
   in cerebral palsy, 71
   in meningocele, 347

Sensory-integration method of therapy for cerebral palsy, 83, 85–86
Sensory neuropathies, 387
Septic arthritis, 15
Septostomy, atrial balloon, 320
Serotonin, 33
Severely and multiply handicapped children (SMH children), 363–384
   developmental activities for, 374–383
   estimated number of, 364
   evaluation of, 365–367
   features associated with disorders found in, 368–372
   functional assessment of, 373
   life-support services for, 372–373
Sex chromosomes, 288. See also X chromosome; Y chromosome
Sex-linked recessive inheritance, disorders associated with, 290. See also specific disorders; for example: Hemophilia
Sexual development, 445–449
   cognitive and, 447–448
   physical and, 445–446
   psychosocial and, 448
   socialization and, 446–447
Short stature (growth failure), 460–465
   evaluation of, 464–465
   sickle cell anemia and, 472, 475
Sickle cell anemia, 290, 469–476
   educational implications of, 476
   evolution and physiology of, 470–473
   genetics of, 473–474
   history and demography of, 469, 470
   and Legg-Perthes disease, 395
   literature on, 221
   manifestations of, 474–475
   treatment of, 475–476
Sickle cell trait, 473
Sickle hemoglobin molecule (HbS), 472
Sight. See Eye; Visual disorders
Sign language, 155–158
Silver nitrate, 492
Sinusitis
   asthma and, 34, 35
   Down's syndrome and, 283
Sitting balance of SMH children, 374
Skeletal deformities. See also specific skeletal deformities; for example: Scoliosis
   in Friedreich's ataxia, 309
   in muscular dystrophy, 391
Skeletal dysplasias (chondodystrophies), 463–465
Skeleton. See Bones; Growth; and entries beginning with term: skeletal
Skin disorders
   in dermatomyositis, 265, 266, 268
   osteogenesis imperfecta and, 406
   rheumatic fever and, 322
Skin rashes
   in rheumatoid arthritis, 424, 427
   tuberous sclerosis and, 493

Index

Skull x-rays
   for cerebral palsy, 74
   for convulsive disorders, 177
Slipped capital femoral epiphysis, 397–398
SMA (spinal muscular atrophy), 386, 477–481
SMD (somatomedin), 458–461, 463, 465
SMH children. *See* Severely and multiply handicapped children
Smoking
   effects of, on intrauterine growth, 452
   during pregnancy, congenital heart disease and, 314
Socialization, 416–447
Society
   the handicapped and, 212–216
   literature on the handicapped and, 227
Somatomedin (SMD), 458–461, 463, 465
Spastic diplegia, 60, 62, 66, 68
Spastic hemiplegia, 60, 61, 63, 73, 79, 102
Spastic quadriplegia, 61–63, 68, 366, 369
Spasticity, 367
   in cerebral palsy, 61–63, 67
   convulsive disorders and, 172
Speech
   with nonoral communication devices, 163–164
   speech aids, 159
   speech development in cerebral palsy, 79–80
Speech disorders, 139–141
   articulation, 140–141
   in cerebral palsy, 71, 110
   in Friedreich's ataxia, 309
   in hydrocephalus, 350
   literature on, 221
   in phonation, 139–140
   stuttering as, 141
Speech therapy, 140, 141
Spina bifida occulta, 345, 446. *See also* Meningocele and myelomeningocele
   literature on, 228
Spinal cord, 8, 9. *See also* Scoliosis
   axons of, 2, 5, 10
   pathways of, in traumatic paraplegia, 413–415. *See also* Traumatic paraplegia and quadriplegia
   in poliomyelitis, 419, 420
Spinal extension, 336, 377
Spinal fusion
   for poliomyelitis, 422
   for scoliosis, 442
Spinal muscular atrophy (SMA), 386, 477–481
Spinal tap (lumbar puncture), 46, 47, 177
Spine
   curvature of. *See* Kyphosis; Scoliosis
   injuries to, in hemophilia, 327–328
Spinocerebellar (Friedreich's) ataxia, 212, 309–312, 371
Spleen function, sickle cell anemia and, 472–473
Sports, literature on adapted, 248–249
Sprains, 15
Squint (strabismus), 281, 486–487

Standing in infancy, 340
Startle (Moro) reflex, 77, 282, 339, 375
State resources for recreation and leisure, 229–233
Stature. *See* Growth
Steroids, cataracts due to, 491. *See also specific steroid drugs*
Stiff (tonic) phase of grand mal, 173
Still's disease. *See* Juvenile rheumatoid arthritis
Strabismus (squint), 281, 486–487
Strain of joint ligament, 15
Sturge-Weber syndrome (encephalotrigeminal angiomatosis), 493
Stuttering, 141
Subarachnoid space, 3
Substitutive speech aids, 159
Succinimides for convulsive disorders, 178
Sulfa drugs, 492
Superior vena cava, 315
Supportive reactions, 335–336, 338, 340
Supravalvular aortic stenosis, 320
Surgery
   amputation by, 17, 19
   for aortic stenosis, 321
   for arthrogryposis, 28–30
   for atrial septal defect, 318
   for cancer, 48–49, 52, 53
   for cerebral palsy, 79, 89, 94
   for chondromalacia patella, 401–402
   for coarctation of aorta, 322
   for deformities associated with poliomyelitis, 421, 422
   for knee and foot problems associated with Down's syndrome, 285, 286
   for glaucoma, 489
   for great vessels transposition, 320
   for juvenile rheumatoid arthritis, 428, 429
   for Legg-Perthes disease, 396–397
   for muscular dystrophy, 393
   for myelomeningocele, 351, 354
   for osteochondritis dessicans, 401
   for patent ductus arteriosus, 316
   for problems associated with SMA, 480
   for rheumatic fever, 323
   for scoliosis, 442
   for slipped capital femoral epiphysis, 398
   for speech disorders, 140
   for tetralogy of Fallot, 318–319
   for torn cartilages, 403
   for valvular pulmonic stenosis, 322
   for ventricular septal defect, 317
Swallowing difficulties in cerebral palsy, 70
Swayback. *See* Lordosis
Swimming and aquatics, literature on, 237–238
Synarthroses, 13–14
Syncope (fainting), 308, 318
Syndrome, defined, 311*n*
Synovitis, 15
Syphilis, 462, 492
Systemic juvenile rheumatoid arthritis, 424

Index

Tay-Sachs disease, 367
Teachers, 152. *See also* Education; Educational implications
  role of, in parental counseling, 194–201
Teeth grinding (bruxism) in cerebral palsy, 70
Temporary orthopedic disabilities, 395–403
  chondromalacia patella as, 401–402
  Legg-Perthes disease as, 395–397
  Osgood-Schlatter's disease as, 398–399
  osteochondritis dessicans as, 399–401
  slipped capital femoral epiphysis as, 397–398
  torn cartilages as, 402–403
Tension athetosis, 65, 366, 369
Tetany, cataracts and neonatal, 490
Tetralogy of Fallot (blue baby), 318–319
Thalamus, 2
Thalidomide, 17
Thanatophoric dwarfism, 464
Theophylline for asthma, 40–42
Thymus gland, asthma and, 35
Thyrotropin, 463
TM$_0$ (antigen), 427
Toileting for children with muscular dystrophy, 393
Tomography, 46
  computerized axial, 47, 75, 76
Tongue, bleeding of, in hemophilia, 327
Tonic labyrinthine reflex, 335
Tonic neck reflex, 76–77, 335, 337
Tonic (stiff) phase of grand mal, 173
Tonsils and tonsillectomy, asthma and, 34–35, 41
Torn cartilages, 402–403
Toxemia of pregnancy
  cerebral palsy and, 68
  effects of, on intrauterine growth, 452
Toxicological diseases, visual disorders due to, 495
Toxoplasmosis, 68, 366, 369, 462, 492, 493
Trachoma, 492
Training. *See* Rehabilitation
Transfusions for sickle cell anemia, 476
Trauma. *See* Injury and trauma
Traumatic paraplegia and quadriplegia, 413–418
  acute care for, 415–416
  rehabilitation for, 416–418
  scoliosis and, 435, 437
Travel, literature on, 246–248
Tremor in cerebral palsy, 66
Trimethadione for convulsive disorders, 179
Trisomy 13, 366
Trisomy 18, 366
Trisomy 21. *See* Down's syndrome
Trunk, flaccid paralysis of, in meningocele, 347
Tuberous sclerosis, 176, 366, 368, 493
Tumors
  bone, surgery for, 17
  cerebral, cerebral palsy and, 69
  malignant, 44, 52–53. *See also* specific types of malignant tumors
  visual disorders due to, 494
Turner's syndrome, 291

Tympanic membrane (eardrum), 135
Typical petit mal spell, 175

Ultrasonography for cancer, 47
Universal distress signal, 301
Upper limbs
  driving without, 299
  loss of, 20–24
  prognosis for use of, in cerebral palsy, 80
Urine
  blood in, in hemophilia, 328
  examination of, in cerebral palsy, 75
  in meningocele, 355–357
  testing, in diabetes, 273–274
Uveal tract of the eye, 483, 485
Uveitis
  anterior, 427, 493
  posterior, 493

Valium. *See* Diazepam
Valproic acid for convulsive disorders, 179
Valvular aortic stenosis, 320
Valvular pulmonic stenosis, 322
Vans
  for children with muscular dystrophy, 393
  for physically handicapped drivers, 295–296
Vascular malformations, convulsive disorders and, 172. *See also specific vascular malformations*
Vena cava, 315
Ventricles of brain, 2, 3, 6
Ventricular septal defect, 316–317
Vertebrae, 8. *See also* Spinal cord
  in scoliosis, 435–437
  in traumatic paraplegia, 414, 415
Visual disorders, 483–495. *See also* Blindness; Nystagmus; Uveitis
  albinism and, 493
  amblyopia as, 487
  astigmatism, 488
  cataracts as, 485, 490–493
  cerebral palsy and, 71–74
  Down's syndrome and, 281
  drivers with, 298
  due to genetic diseases, 491–492
  due to infectious diseases, 492
  due to inflammatory diseases, 493
  due to neurological diseases, 492–493
  due to toxicological diseases, 495
  due to tumors, 494
  exotropia, 71, 487
  eye anatomy and physiology and, 483–486
  with Friedreich's ataxia, 311
  glaucoma as, 485, 489–490, 493
  hyperopia as, 71, 488
  iridocyclitis as, 427, 493
  literature on, 222
  myopia as, 71, 488
  osteogenesis imperfecta and, 405, 406
  reading aids for individuals with, 495
  refractive error as, 488

Visual disorders (*continued*)
    retinal degenerative diseases as, 488–489
    rheumatoid arthritis and, 428
    rubella and, 431, 492
    strabismus as, 281, 486–487
Vitamins
    for cystic fibrosis, 260
    for muscular dystrophy, 392
Vitreous body of the eye, 483, 484, 486
Vocal cords, phonation and mass adjustments of, 139
Vocational training. *See* Occupational therapy
Voice therapy, 140
Voluntary controlled movements, 333–334
Von Hippel Lindau's disease (angiomatosis retinae and cerebellae), 494

Walking
    aids for. *See* Mobility aids
    in infancy, 340–341
    prognosis for, with cerebral palsy, 76–77
Walking reflex, 333–334, 337
Warfarin, 453, 462
Werdnig-Hoffman muscular dystrophy, 386, 477
West syndrome (infantile spasm), 176

Wheelchairs
    for children with muscular dystrophy, 393
    literature on, 248–249
Wheezing. *See* Asthma
Whooping cough, 37
Williams syndrome, 462
Wilms' tumors, 45, 492

X chromosome, 288, 291, 326, 388, 462
X-linked spondyloepiphyseal dysplasia, 464
X-rays. *See also* Radiation therapy; Skull x-rays; *and specific diagnostic methods using x-rays*
    for cancer, 46–47
    congenital heart disease and, 314, 318
    for Down's syndrome, 283–284
    for growth failure, 465
    for heart murmurs, 323
    for Legg-Perthes disease, 395
    for scoliosis, 435
    for skeletal dysplasias, 464
    for torn cartilages, 403
    for traumatic paraplegia, 416

Y chromosome, 288, 291, 462

Zarontin (ethosuximide) for convulsive disorders, 179